# Currents of Thought in American Social Psychology

# Currents of Thought in American Social Psychology

GARY COLLIER
HENRY L. MINTON
GRAHAM REYNOLDS

New York   Oxford
OXFORD UNIVERSITY PRESS
1991

Oxford University Press

Oxford   New York   Toronto
Delhi   Bombay   Calcutta   Madras   Karachi
Petaling Jaya   Singapore   Hong Kong   Tokyo
Nairobi   Dar es Salaam   Cape Town
Melbourne   Auckland

and associated companies in
Berlin   Ibadan

Published by Oxford University Press, Inc.,
200 Madison Avenue, New York, New York 10016

Oxford is a registered trademark of Oxford University Press

Library of Congress Cataloging-in-Publication Data
Collier, Gary.
Currents of thought in American social psychology
/ Gary Collier, Henry L. Minton, Graham Reynolds.
p.   cm.   Includes bibliographical references and index.
ISBN 0-19-506129-2
1. Social psychology—United States—History.
I. Minton, Henry L.
II. Reynolds, Graham.   III. Title.
HM251.C654 1991 302—dc20 90-26340

9 8 7 6 5 4 3 2 1

Printed in the United States of America
on acid-free paper

*Dedicated to our fathers and sons*
*James, Tristan, and Gerrit Michael Collier*
*Irving and Gregory Minton*
*Philip and Paul Reynolds*

# Preface

This project began in 1981 as an attempt to say something about interpersonal relations. This seemed to be a badly neglected area within American social psychology and one that seemed important if American social psychology was to break away from its exclusive focus on individual psychological processes. As we began to review the literature, we discovered that the area of interpersonal relationships had not been neglected at all. It had been treated, and treated quite well, by such eminent thinkers as Emile Durkheim, Harry Stack Sullivan, and George Herbert Mead. Moreover, these thinkers could be placed within broader intellectual traditions, such as European social theory, psychoanalysis, and American pragmatism. This led us to believe that the concept of interpersonal relations could be treated historically by tracing the roots of these ideas to major thinkers in the nineteenth century.

During the second stage of the project, we envisioned a historical critique based on four major areas—evolutionary theory, psychoanalysis, European social theory, and phenomenology. Each section was to begin with an extended discussion of the thoughts and ideas of the founders of each theory and a briefer discussion of those who developed these ideas within a social-psychological perspective. Finally, we wanted to trace the development of these ideas within American social psychology in order to discover when they

appeared and when they were abandoned or how they continue to shape contemporary thinking, either directly or indirectly. The various currents of thought soon swelled well beyond the original four, and the current work covers eleven more or less distinct intellectual traditions.

As we began to review this literature, we became more and more sympathetic to some of the changes that had taken place in American social psychology and more critical of others. Many of the former topics, such as personality and social development, had evolved into distinct areas of psychology. Other topics had been abandoned because they could not be studied experimentally. The central question now became: *Why, out of all the possible topics that could legitimately be considered part of social psychology, had American social psychologists selected the ones they did?*

This question led us to conceive of our project as a historical analysis of the development of American social psychology. Our aim is to provide an understanding of how the discipline has been shaped by internal developments, such as theory, concepts, professionalization, and research procedures, as well as external social forces—that is, the political, economic, ideological, cultural, and intellectual facets of American society. Biographical factors have also played a role, and in those cases where theorical traditions have been influenced by the personal lives of the theorists, biographical information is included.

Realizing the potential scope of the project and the finite limits of the human mind, we decided to write a book that was relatively brief yet broad enough to cover all the necessary material. The current text is not an "introduction" to social psychology. Several hundred introductory texts have already been written, and more are published each year. Nor is it an extended discussion of social-psychological theories written by people who describe it from an internal perspective (e.g., Karpf, 1932; Sahakian, 1982). What we have attempted to do is to trace the development of various theoretical traditions within American social psychology and show that they have been shaped by developments taking place within the broader social context. By placing social psychology within the larger social context, this book seeks to achieve a comprehensive understanding of social psychology as a social-scientific discipline.

Many of the ideas contained in this book were developed while the first author was a visiting researcher at the Laboratoire de Psychologie Sociale of the University of Paris (VII), and we would like to thank members of the group who became involved in the project, Erika Apfelbaum and Ian Lubek in particular. We would also like to thank Serge Moscovici and Geneviève Paicheler of the Ecole des Hautes Etudes en Sciences Sociales, who read parts of the manuscript and made several comments and suggestions. Other people who have seen parts of the manuscript include Ella DiCarlo, Richard Keshen, Gregory McGuire, and Robert Russell. Funds were made possible through a series of internally administered grants provided by the Social Science and Humanities Research Council of Canada.

The book was written by a collaborative team that includes a more traditionally trained social psychologist, a historian of psychology, and an intellectual historian. It was written primarily for social psychologists, social scientists, intellectual historians, and those concerned with the history and philosophy of science, but the style of the book is sufficiently simple that it may appeal to a much more general audience. We believe that it would be an excellent supplement to more standard texts in courses on social psychology, intellectual history, and theories and systems of psychology. The scope of the book, together with a commitment to keep it as brief as possible, prohibits a thorough and more systematic exploration of all of the ideas introduced. Those wishing more information on particular topics should consult the original texts.

*Nova Scotia*                                                              G. C.
*December 1990*

# Contents

## Part IV Social Psychology in the Postmodern Era (1970–1990)

# Currents of Thought in American Social Psychology

# 1

# Introduction

Many of the problems of social psychology are based on definition. Social psychology has been defined so broadly that it includes virtually all of psychology and the social sciences as well. John Dewey (1917), for example, in an address before the American Psychological Association in 1917 distinguished two types of psychological processes—physiological and social. Physiological processes include elementary drives and sensations, whereas the greater part of our mental life, our beliefs, our ideas, and our desires, were seen as socially derived.

Katz and Schanck (1938) went even further. They suggested that social psychology consists of three relatively distinct areas: (1) social stimulation; (2) people's experience of and reaction to social stimulation; and (3) the long-term effects of the social environment on the individual. The first area includes most of society's institutions and values, other people (either present or implied), and their by-products. It would subsume the subject matter of all the social sciences, the natural sciences (since accumulated wisdom is a social product), the arts, and the humanities. The second area focuses more narrowly on the individual's immediate response to these sources of stimulation, while the last constitutes what has more or less become two disciplines, abnormal psychology and personality, including cross-cultural differences in personality.

Perhaps the most general definition was provided by Insko and Schopler (1972), who defined social psychology as "that discipline which people who call themselves social psychologists are interested in studying" (p. xiv). But even this definition is too narrow, because it ignores the contributions of people who would not consider themselves social psychologists. Curtis (1960) has suggested that there are four types of social psychology—psychological, sociological, anthropological, and psychoanalytic—each with its own problems and areas of interests. Contemporary social psychology also borrows from other psychological subdisciplines, such as learning theory and cognitive psychology.

The purpose of citing these definitions is not to expand the scope of social psychology beyond its legitimate limits. Social stimuli and our reaction to them do constitute a major part of our day-to-day life and play a significant role in shaping personality, but they are no more fundamental to psychology than such processes as perception and memory. Rather, these definitions suggest that what has constituted the field of social psychology is so potentially broad that some selection has always been necessary—that is, social psychologists have always focused on certain areas and ignored others.

Previous histories of American social psychology such as Karpf (1932) and Sahakian (1982) have traced the ideas and trends *within* the discipline. Although valuable to students and teachers as resource guides, these accounts are limited to providing an exclusively internal history of the discipline. In contrast, this book provides a history that examines individuals and trends within the discipline together with the external social and intellectual developments that have helped shape social psychology in America.

## ANALYSIS OF SOCIAL PSYCHOLOGY TEXTBOOKS

We began our study with an analysis of social psychology textbooks. Thomas Kuhn (1962, 1970) has argued that textbooks popularize a discipline and introduce it to new generations of practitioners. They must be rewritten each time the language, problems, or methods change or when a discipline undergoes what Kuhn called a "paradigm shift." Textbooks typically contain very little history, and the history they do present is frequently misleading because great authors from previous periods are described as if they were part of the current tradition. Through selection, distortion, and omission the readers are led to believe that they are part of a long tradition that has always focused on those problems of current interest. The tendency to "rewrite history" is augmented within social psychology by a tendency to stress current research. Findley and Cooper (1981), for example, compared chapters in nine widely used social psychology textbooks and calculated that fully half of the articles cited were published within the previous six years.

While any single textbook is therefore of only limited use in understanding the overall history of a discipline, it does provide a source of information about what was considered important and unimportant during a particular period. When two or more disciplines are attempting to explain the same phenomenon from different perspectives, then textbooks can be used to decipher differences in theoretical orientation. By summarizing the most recent literature, textbooks also provide an indication of the type of research actually conducted at a given time. In short, textbooks provide a way for readers to understand the history of a discipline by transporting themselves back in time so that they can reexperience the discipline from the perspective of the person who is learning it for the first time.

It should be noted, however, that Kuhn's description of the structure of a scientific revolution was developed in order to account for changes taking place in the physical sciences, and it is only partially applicable to developments within behavioral and social sciences. In physics, for example, facts that are either consistent or inconsistent with a given theory accumulate, and when there is sufficient evidence and consensus a paradigm shift may occur that represents a complete transformation of scientific thinking. Once a new paradigm has been established, there are no reversions to previous paradigms. Thus, no post-Copernican scientist would revert to the assumptions and methods of Ptolemy or Aristotle in calculating the position and movements of the stars.

Transformations within the social sciences are rarely so complete. Competing theories exist side by side and form schools of thought. Topics of interest may be abandoned by one generation and "rediscovered" by a later one. Actual research is more sensitive to changing social pressures and reflects not merely the preoccupations of professionals but the public at large. While there is some question about whether social psychology has undergone a paradigm shift in Kuhn's sense, it has undergone shifts in interest that reveal themselves in the literature cited. Each generation of textbooks stresses current interests while previously popular areas and authors are either downplayed or ignored.

In order to trace the history of these ideas, we decided to briefly review all of the social psychology textbooks published before 1990. Gordon Allport (1954a) compiled a list of 52 textbooks published before 1952, and his list was updated by Gibson and Higbee (1979), who provided a total of 105 references. A subsequent search of *Psychological Abstracts* and *Books in Print* identified 29 additional texts published in the late 1970s and 1980s. Since we were interested in contrasting the psychological and sociological approaches to American social psychology, eight of these were eliminated. One text was written by a medical doctor (Myerson, 1934), and a second was written by a British philosopher (Sprott, 1952), and these were not included. Also excluded were six textbooks coauthored by psychologists and sociologists (LaPiere & Farnsworth, 1936; Secord & Backman, 1964; Newcomb, Turner, & Converse, 1965; Dewey & Humber; 1966; Kaluger & Unkovic, 1969; Secord, Backman, & Slavitt, 1976). A total of 89 psychological and 40 sociological textbooks were reviewed in all (see Appendix A). The utter preposterousness of obtaining and "briefly reviewing" over a hundred introductory textbooks seems funny only in retrospect.

Three aspects of social psychology textbooks were of primary importance in the present study: (1) the topics covered; (2) descriptions of research methods; and (3) the authors most frequently cited. Once trends were identified, we attempted to trace their histories both backward to discover their historical roots, and forward to discover remnants within contemporary social psychology. The order of the chapters represents the emergence of dominant trends within social psychology, whereas the discussion of these trends focuses primarily on individual authors.

Just as one can tell a great deal about individual authors by looking at their sources, one can also tell a great deal about a period by looking at those authors generally cited. A disadvantage of this approach is that it tends to obscure individual differences and overestimate the consensus within a discipline. A second problem is the typical time lag between preparation and publication. Bonner (1953), for example, stated that he began his book twenty years before it was published and modified it because of events during and after World War II. Despite these changes, his book retains many of the characteristics of texts published during the depression. It is problem-centered and highly critical of economic institutions. Garvey and Griffith (1971) have found a five-year interval between the conception and publication of a typical research project, and a similar period could be expected for social psychology textbooks.

**Table 1.1.** The Ten People Most Frequently Cited by Psychological and Sociological Textbook Authors During Six Major Periods. Authors Cited Frequently by Both Groups in the Same Period are in Italics. Brackets Indicate Ties in Rank.

| | 1908–1929 | 1930–1942 | 1948–1953 | 1960s | 1970s | 1980s |
|---|---|---|---|---|---|---|
| People cited most frequently by psychological authors | | | | | | |
| 1. | W. McDougall | F. Allport | G. Allport | *T. Newcomb* | *L. Festinger* | L. Festinger |
| 2. | W. James | T. Newcomb | *G. Murphy* | L. Festinger | H. Kelley | E. Walster |
| 3. | F. Allport | G. Allport | K. Lewin | H. Kelley | E. Aronson | *H. Kelley* |
| 4. | C. Darwin | G. Murphy | H. Cantril | *M. Sherif* | S. Schachter | E. Jones |
| 5. | J. Baldwin | *W. McDougall* | T. Newcomb | S. Schachter | L. Berkowitz | E. Berschied |
| 6. | G. Allport | S. Freud | *M. Sherif* | C. Hovland | E. Jones | S. Schachter |
| 7. | S. Freud | L. Murphy | F. Allport | S. Asch | J. Carlsmith | J. Darley |
| 8. | G. LeBon | D. Katz | J. Dollard | M. Deutsch | C. Hovland | S. Milgram |
| 9. | J. Watson | M. Mead | *S. Freud* | K. Lewin | I. Janis | L. Berkowitz |
| 10. | *G. Tarde* | E. Thorndike | O. Klineberg | *G. Allport* | S. Asch | B. Latané |
| | J. Cattell | | | | *S. Freud* | |
| People cited most frequently by sociological authors | | | | | | |
| 1. | E. Ross | *F. Allport* | *G. Murphy* | S. Freud | G. Mead | E. Goffman |
| 2. | C. Cooley | W. Thomas | *T. Newcomb* | G. Mead | E. Goffman | G. Mead |
| 3. | W. McDougall | L. Bernard | G. Mead | C. Cooley | *S. Freud* | R. Turner |
| 4. | J. Dewey | E. Faris | J. Dewey | *M. Sherif* | H. Blumer | P. Berger |
| 5. | J. Williams | *W. McDougall* | *M. Sherif* | H. Sullivan | C. Cooley | H. Blumer |
| 6. | C. Ellwood | E. Burges | E. Faris | A. Strauss | *L. Festinger* | G. Stone |
| 7. | T. Veblen | R. Park | K. Young | *G. Lindzey* | *A. Strauss* | A. Strauss |
| 8. | G. Tarde | C. Cooley | *S. Freud* | *T. Newcomb* | T. Newcomb | G. Simmel |
| 9. | *F. Allport* | K. Young | W. Thomas | *W. Thomas* | M. Sherif | *H. Kelley* |
| 10. | F. Giddings | J. Dewey | E. Boring | *G. Allport* | T. Shibutani | A. Schultz |

What is somewhat surprising is that gaps occur in publications, and these gaps can be used to mark transitions. No text was published between 1942 and 1948, and a second gap occurred between 1953 and 1960. Using these gaps, along with more natural divisions, we were able to divide social psychology textbooks into six periods based on the date of publication: (1) the first two decades (1908–1929); (2) the depression (1930–1942); (3) the postwar period (1948–1953); (4) the 1960s; (5) the 1970s; and (6) the 1980s. Table 1.1 gives the ten most cited individuals during each period for both psychological and sociological textbook authors based on an exhaustive review of all social psychology textbooks published before 1990.

This table will be referred to repeatedly throughout the text, but some general points should be discussed first. Perhaps the most striking feature is the almost total absence of overlap in the literature cited by sociologists and psychologists. Except for the postwar period (1948–1953), the overlap consists of two or three authors during each period and only one during the 1980s.

This table, since it does not include figures,[1] cannot show the full extent of this lack of overlap, so some examples may prove useful. During the first decades, the sociologist Edward Ross was cited 99 times by sociological authors but only four times by psychologists. Charles Cooley was cited 63 times by sociologists but only twice by psychologists. The citations for John Dewey were 44 and 2 during this same period. In striking contrast, six of the authors most cited by psychologists during the 1960s— Leon Festinger, Harold Kelley, Kurt Lewin, Solomon Asch, Stanley Schachter, and Morton Deutsch—were never mentioned by sociological authors. This in itself should dispel the persistent myth that social psychology stands between two disciplines and draws equally from each. *Since its inception, American social psychology has existed not as one but as two separate disciplines, each with its own literature and interests.*

A second point that should be noted is the general decline in sociological textbooks and an increase in psychological texts. The

number of authors in each group was as follows:

| Period | Psychologists | Sociologists |
|---|---|---|
| 1908–1929 | 7 | 8 |
| 1930–1942 | 9 | 7 |
| 1948–1953 | 10 | 3 |
| 1960s | 12 | 3 |
| 1970s | 30 | 8 |
| 1980s | 21 | 11 |

This shows that, *although social psychology began largely as a branch of sociology, it has become increasingly dominated by psychological texts.* While there appears to be a slight reversal of this trend in the 1980s, what these figures do not show is the large number of psychological texts brought out in later editions (16 versus 2 by sociologists). When these are added to the new texts introduced in the 1980s, the ratio of psychological to sociological textbooks remains about the same—that is, about three to one. These figures also suggest why a total frequency count of citations would be misleading. The disproportionate number of psychological writers during the postwar period would simply obscure the sociological trends.

This trend has also been noted by Liska (1977) in an article entitled "The dissipation of sociological social psychology." He argues that social psychology has shifted from a multidisciplinary enterprise to one increasingly dominated by psychology. Not only has psychological social psychology expanded enormously in the past few decades, but sociological social psychology has contracted. Although sociological authors keep abreast of developments within psychological social psychology, psychologists rarely cite sociological authors or journals. While many adhere to the ideal of a multidisciplinary approach, this ideal is being constantly eroded by the fact that social psychology is becoming a psychological subdiscipline.

A final point is that a citation count does not distinguish between positive and negative references. Perlman (1979) noted that citation rates are highly correlated with opinion polls of eminence, based on scholars' ratings of one another for overall importance. The present ranking corresponds well with Lewicki's (1982) survey of the Society of Experimental Social Psychology, where leading social psychologists ranked the persons who had the most influence on them. But some authors are cited because they aroused opposition.

William McDougall (1908), for example, was cited frequently by sociological authors during the first two periods, but these references were almost uniformly critical, because sociologists strongly opposed the tendency to explain social behavior through social instincts. Similarly Floyd Allport (1924) was frequently cited by sociologists during the 1930s because they objected to his strong emphasis on the individual. Both McDougall and Allport, however, forced sociologists to make major revisions in their own theories. One could argue that these authors were influential *because* they were controversial, and therfore it makes little difference whether a citation is supportive or critical.

It should be stressed that textbook analysis is merely a starting point. It is a very crude way to identify major authors and research traditions during a particular period. Once these have been identified, they can be placed within the context of more broad-based intellectual traditions. These ideas did not suddenly pop up, dominate, and then disappear. They often had a long period of development before they became popular. Those who developed these ideas most fully were often not recognized and seldom cited.

In attempting to trace the history of an idea, one must be wary of citing sources in which a topic is casually mentioned and then dropped. It is one thing to have a sudden insight into a problem and another to develop this insight in a painstaking and meticulous manner. One can, for example, find forerunners of Freud's concept of the unconscious in the writings of Leibniz, or in Dostoevski for that matter. But their unconscious is merely a lack of awareness and does not include Freud's concept of the dynamically repressed. Freud explored the depths of the unconscious, used it to explain phenomena that were previously incomprehensible, and shook our faith in the power of human reason. Anyone who addresses these issues today knowingly or unknowingly follows in Freud's footsteps (see Chapter 6).

It is not always easy to trace the history of an idea. Social psychology, as mentioned previously, did not develop in a social vaccum. Ideas have been shaped by both internal and external sources. Promising lines of research have been prematurely abandoned and rediscovered later. This is illustrated by the concepts of imitation and suggestion, which were popular at the turn of the century and have been revitalized and given scientific credibility by Neil Miller and John Dollard (1941) and Albert Bandura (1971) under the name of social-learning theory. Similarly, the detailed yet impressionistic descriptions of crowd behavior inspired work on social facilitation and inhibition and their subsequent explanation through physiological arousal (Zajonc, 1965). Thus, progress does occur in social psychology, but it is easy for researchers to lose contact with previous insights, because they often undergo name changes so profound as to obscure their origins. "Social instincts" (McDougall, 1908), for example, became "human proponent reflexes" (Allport, 1924), then "native impulses" (Ellwood, 1925), and later "dependable motives" (Klineberg, 1940). Ethology and sociobiology may be regarded as recent attempts to deal with the same theme. A history of these ideas may prove useful, because it can lead researchers back to previous sources that contain a great many valuable insights.

The focus on broad-based intellectual traditions forced a chronological division somewhat different from that in Table 1.1. American social psychology has undergone four major periods of development. The first represents the formative period, which began at the turn of the century and is characterized by the development of two distinct social-psychological approaches—one sociological, the other psychological. Disciplinary differences were temporarily obscured during the depression and World War II as pressing social problems forced social psychologists to view social behavior within a broader social context. Differences between disciplines became even more pronounced in the postwar period, as both disciplines underwent increased professionalization. The social and political unrest of the 1960s inspired a new phase of self-criticism and critical reappraisal among both psychological and sociological social psychologists, and the impact of this reassessment is still being felt today.

## TWO SOCIAL PSYCHOLOGIES

A brief look at Table 1.1 shows that social psychology began as two separate disciplines—one psychological, the other sociological. Social psychologists in these two areas have differed significantly in their theories, interests, and research methods. Moreover, these disciplines have developed in slightly different ways, in response to both internal and external conditions. If we focus on the most recent publications—those of the 1980s—the most striking feature is the complete lack of overlap of the authors most frequently cited. The purpose of this book is to trace the history of these developments. Contemporary psychological and sociological approaches will be discussed in more detail in Chapters 10 and 11, but it may be useful to describe them here in very general terms.

Comtemporary psychological social psychology is probably most distinguished by its methodology. Psychologists use experimental procedures to study cognitive processes, often using some form of deception. A recent examination of studies published in the *Journal of Personality and Social Psychology* and the *Journal of Experimental Social Psychology* during the 1970s found that over 80 percent were based on experiments (Higbee, Millard, & Folkman, 1982). A sample of the literature in the same journals between 1959 and 1979 showed that almost two-thirds used some form of deception, in which subjects were either not fully informed or were intentionally misled about the purpose of the study. The use of deception in social-psychological experiments has opened up a number of content areas, and some topics—such as conformity, altruism, and aggression—are

represented by virtually no studies in which deception is not used.

A second characteristic of the contemporary psychological approach is the absence of any real theoretical integration. Topics within social psychology texbooks are often loosely organized by content areas rather than theory. Psychological social psychologists have shown a preference for middle-level theories, such as cognitive consistency, social comparison, and attribution models, and there has been an abundance of atheoretical research. If we look at the content areas that have received full-chapter treatment in recent texts, there is a striking sameness among the topics covered. Certain subjects, such as attitude development and change, altruism, aggression, person perception, group dynamics, and interpersonal attraction, are covered in practically every textbook published during the 1970s and 1980s. What is less obvious, however, is that even though the same topics are covered, the same literature is seldom cited. Findley and Cooper (1981) compared the overlap in citations in pairs of chapters from nine widely used social psychology texts and found a range from 7% (for conformity) to 25% (for aggression). Other areas, such as altruism (9%), interpersonal attraction (10%), and attitude change (15%), fell in between. Even when writers discuss the same topics, they seldom cite the same studies. It is not clear by what criteria sources are selected, except personal affinity or perhaps random selection (see Perlman, 1979).

If we turn from topics to individuals, the authors most frequently cited by psychologists are usually active researchers who have made one or more theoretical contributions. Leon Festinger's theories of social comparison and cognitive dissonance have put him at the top of the lists throughout the 1960s, 1970s, and 1980s. Ellen Berscheid and Elaine Walster (née Hatfield) are frequently cited because of their work on equity theory and interpersonal attraction. The presence of Edward Jones and Harold Kelley among the top ten reflects the current importance of attribution theory, while Bibb Lantané and John Darley are mentioned most frequently for their systematic work on altruism and bystander intervention. Others, such as Leonard Berkowitz, Stanley Milgram, and Stanley Schachter, have made multiple contributions but are most closely associated with the areas of aggression, obedience, and emotions, respectively. There is a reasonably good correspondence between content areas and the people most frequently cited, but the presence of so many theorists among the top ten suggests a desperate search for theoretical integration. Problems associated with the fragmentation of social-psychological knowledge and lack of theoretical integration are discussed in more detail in Chapter 12.

A third trend in psychological social psychology is a growing emphasis on applied areas. Every textbook published during the 1980s devotes at least one chapter to applied areas, and many have incorporated the terms "applied" or "applications" in their title. This contrasts sharply with those published during the 1960s and 1970s when applied areas were not stressed and applied researchers were treated as something of an underclass among those committed to controlled experiments. This new trend reflects a growing concern for social relevance, plus a desire to test experimental findings in more realistic settings. If we look at chapters devoted to applied areas, the most important topics appear to be environmental psychology, racial prejudice, social psychology and the law, sexual discrimination, and organizational behavior (in that order). The emergence of applied areas, which is a topic within Chapter 12, has the potential for reducing much of the friction among disciplines. Anyone wishing to understand the origins of sexual discrimination, for example, must have at least a passing knowledge of biology, sociology, and history.

If we turn from psychological to sociological textbooks, we get a very different picture. The contemporary sociological approach is based primarily on the theory of symbolic interaction introduced by George Herbert Mead (1934) and developed by people such as Herbert Blumer, Erving Goffman, and Anselm Strauss. Mead's position is somewhat akin to Festinger's in terms of citations. He was one of the people most frequently cited by sociological textbook authors in all four post–World War II periods. His contribution is also shown by the topics covered within chapters. While there is more diversity among sociological textbooks, key areas include social roles and socialization, the self, language, interaction, and collective behavior—all central to symbolic interaction. While psychologists concentrate primarily on individual processes, such as attitudes, person perception, and cognition, sociologists are more likely to take dyads or groups as their basic unit of analysis.

Sociological social psychologists are also more variable in their research methods. While experiments appear to play an increasingly important role, sociologists employ a variety of alternative strategies, including interviews, surveys, and participant observation. Higbee, Millard, and Folkman (1982) found that over 60 percent of the studies published in the two major sociological social psychology journals during the 1970s, the *Journal of Social Psychology* and *Social Psychology Quarterly,* were based on experiments—a 50 percent increase over the previous decade. This move toward experimental procedures may decrease some of the aversion felt by psychological social psychologists, who regard experiments as the instrument of choice.

A unique feature of the sociological approach is a tendency to start with the broader social context and use it to help explain individual behavior. Individual differences are attributed to differences in reference groups and culture. Differences occur not just in attitudes but in perception and the *way* people think. Language and other symbolic processes, which provide a powerful tool for dealing with people and situations, are stressed because they allow people to coordinate activities and work toward common goals. This tendency to start with society means that sociologists avoid two of the most serious problems of the psychological approach—the tendency to view social psychological processes as timeless and universal and the failure to deal with interaction. These problems will also be discussed in more detail in Chapters 12 and 13.

The two social psychologies, while poles

apart today, have both made significant contributions to our knowledge of social behavior and interaction. The psychological approach has produced a hard body of experimental data, while sociologists have focused on areas typically avoided by psychologists. The development of these two disciplines is (in our opinion) a fascinating story, full of false starts and premature terminations. Social psychologists have been among the most critical of their own discipline, but we are convinced that there is nothing fundamentally wrong with social psychology that cannot be corrected through a more thorough understanding of its own history.

## PRESCIENTIFIC SOCIAL THOUGHT

Although this work is concerned with the history of American social psychology and not with a history of social theory in general, a brief review of some of the forerunners of American social psychology may help to put the discipline in perspective. Social theory, in contrast to social science, has a very long tradition. Throughout history people have been interested in the nature of society and have developed theories to explain it.

Plato (427–347 B.C.), for example, developed a theory that stressed the values of social interaction within a stratified community. He wrote the *Republic* in order to defend traditional Athenian civilization against the excesses of demoncracy. The book presents a model of an ideal society based on Plato's conception of human nature and individual differences. The body, according to Plato, was divided into three regions—the head, the heart, and the stomach—that were the seat of three psychological processes—thought, volition, and appetite. Society consisted of three corresponding classes—philosophers, warriors, and workers—and in the ideal society all individuals were placed in their appropriate class. Although Plato defended this hierar-

chical social order against the leveling tendency of democracy, he did advocate an open society in which gifted children from the warrior or working classes could become part of the ruling elite and less gifted children of philosophers could also find their appropriate place.

Aristotle (384–322 B.C.) expressed similar views in his *Politics*. He regarded man as a social animal and gregarious by nature. Human society existed before the individual, and a particular person's ability to fulfill his or her potential could only be realized within a social context. Fulfilling one's potential meant finding one's proper place within the existing social order, while outside of society the individual ceased to exist as a human being. Aristotle, like Plato, regarded social stratification as absolutely essential. For both, an aristocracy ruled by an intellectual elite and supported by a working or slave class was the only reasonable form of government.

Much later, in seventeeth-century England, the British philosopher Thomas Hobbes (1588–1679) developed quite a different theory in his book *Leviathan*. Hobbes viewed man as naturally selfish and aggressive. Because people placed their own preservation and interests above those of others, they came into inevitable conflict with others pursuing their own selfish interests. To resolve this conflict, individuals formed a community through a social contract. But since selfish drives were still strong within individuals, Hobbes advocated an absolute monarchly as the best form of control.

One could cite other examples, but what these three writers have in common is that they postulated theories of human nature based on existing social conditions and then used these theories to justify existing forms of government. The political philosophy of Plato and Aristotle reflected the classical ideas of the Athenian city-state, whereas Hobbes wrote his *Leviathan* largely as a response to the anarchy and violence he witnessed during the English civil war. The problem in each case is that the writers lacked a point of comparison from which to view their societies. They took their institutions for granted and tried to derive models of society from them. Modern social theory began to develop once writers gained a critical perspective. The first source of this critical perspective was a new concept of history.

Maurice Mandelbaum (1971) has pointed out that our tendency to see things historically is so firmly ingrained in our culture that it is difficult to realize that this tendency itself has a history, and not a very long one. In the early eighteenth century the Italian philosopher Giambattista Vico (1668–1744) introduced the notion that the laws and customs of society are influenced by historical conditions. He advocated a new science that would study the way in which these laws and customs and the language of social groups are developed within a historical context. History, as we know it, hardly existed before this time. What did exist were chronicles of political events, descriptions of battles, and glorified accounts of the coronations and marriages of kings and queens—mere description without interpretation. During the eighteenth-century Enlightenment, two developments gave rise to the modern historical method.

The first is the notion of progress. People began to believe that they could shape their own destiny through science and technology, and they began to look at the past as a record of successive human accomplishment. The second was a gradual expansion of what was considered historically significant. History before the Enlightenment was primarily political history, but during the Enlightenment people became interested in other areas of history. History was expanded to include intellectual history, and later the history of art, culture, and social life. It then became possible to see different aspects of society as interconnected.

A widespread interest in history is one of the distinct features of the nineteenth century. The use of historical methods to study society is very pronounced in the writings of Karl Marx, for example, who compared nineteenth-century industrial society to pre-industrial societies. Marx showed that not only institutions but modes of thought were shaped by social conditions. Not only were

the Middle Ages different from the modern world, but medieval people actually perceived their world differently than did their nineteenth century counterparts.

But the use of the historical approach by itself does not make a work scientific. Auguste Comte (1790–1857), who coined the term "sociology" and is widely regarded as the discipline's founder, attempted to place a historical perspective within his comprehensive analysis of the nature of human knowledge. In his early writings he developed the idea that knowledge passes through three stages: the theological, the metaphysical, and the scientific. Theological explanations are based on a belief in supernatural beings and appeal to authority, while metaphysical explanations use abstract concepts that are integrated into elaborate systems through reasoning. The scientific or positivist stage is based on systematic observation, comparison, and experiment.

In his later writings Comte added a fourth stage, which he labeled "la morale." In this final stage the historical context stemmed from an interdependence between an individual and society. His moral science was also a "religious construction" in which knowledge was based on a subjective synthesis of feelings and sentiments. As Samelson (1974) has pointed out, Comte's advocacy of a science based on historical context, spirituality, and subjectivity has generally been ignored in the twentieth-century interpretations of his work. Instead, his "positivist" conception of an empirical science has generally been cited as the origin of modern social science in general and social psychology in particular. The concept of this "origin myth" will be discussed in more detail in Chapter 5 when we examine the rise of experimental social psychology.

The theories of Plato, Aristotle, and Hobbes, although containing many astute observations of the political and social institutions of their day, were essentially metaphysical accounts of human nature and society. The scientific study of society did not begin until the nineteenth century, when the development of the comparative and historical perspectives allowed for the discovery and examination of underlying social structures. Social psychology emerged later, largely as an attempt to provide a sociological explanation for individual behavior.

The disciplines of history, sociology, and social psychology developed in a lockstep manner. The development of a historical perspective was necessary before one's own institutions could be perceived and studied objectively, and a description of society was necessary before one could study its impact on the individual. The development of a historical perspective encouraged social thinkers to base social theory on direct observation and comprehensive analysis rather than on deduction and formal reasoning. Struck by the rapid and profound changes affecting all aspects of society by the end of the ninteenth century, social theorists became increasingly suspicious of abstract theories not based on comparative or empirical evidence. The abandonment of metaphysical speculation marks the transition from prescientific to scientific social theory.

## TRADITIONS OF SOCIAL THEORY DURING THE NINETEENTH CENTURY

By the end of the nineteenth century, distinct traditions of social thought had developed in Britain, France, Germany, and the United States. These will be covered in more detail later when the movements that they helped generate are discussed. But it may be useful to compare and contrast these traditions briefly before going on to specific currents of thought.

British social theory was based on Charles Darwin's theory of evolution. Darwin provided in his own work a concrete example of the power of empirical procedures and helped establish empirical methods within the British social sciences. The most immediate application of evolutionary theory to society, however, was based not on empirical evidence but on the speculative writings of Herbert Spencer (1820–1903).

Spencer had developed a theory of social evolution independent of Darwin, but he later used Darwin's theory to support his own. Spencer believed that societies evolved through a process of natural selection. Each individual pursued his or her own self-interest, and the resulting competition led to the elimination of the weak and helpless and the preservation of the strong. Spencer enjoyed considerable popularity in both Britain and the United States because his theory was used to justify the accumulation of wealth within a free-market system with as little government intervention as possible.

The concept of natural selection also helped produce a cult of individual differences and gave rise to a eugenics movement. The most forceful spokesman for this movement was Darwin's cousin, Sir Francis Galton (1822–1911), who used empirical methods in an attempt to identify superior and defective individuals for the purpose of selective breeding. A third trend was an attempt to use evolutionary theory to derive a list of basic social instincts, which could then be used to explain social behavior through biological drives. William McDougall (1908) provided one of the more sophisticated versions of social instinct theory, but the concept of social instincts eventually came under attack because of its seemingly endless proliferation of specific instincts, and because for many it provided a static view of human nature and gave additional support to conservative economic and political policies.

The French influence can be divided into three general areas. Auguste Comte provided a general framework in which research could be carried out. He not only advocated a scientific approach to the study of society but provided a hierarchy of sciences with "la morale" at the top and sociology, biology (including psychology), chemistry, physics, astronomy, and mathematics below. The sciences became more and more exact as one moved down the hierarchy and more complex as one moved up. The more complex sciences rested on more basic ones, but they possessed laws of their own and were therefore not reducible to the more basic sciences. Comte planned to write a treatise on social psychology *(Le Système de Morale Positive)* but died before he could do so. Comte advocated a scientific approach (albeit selectively interpreted in modern renditions), but he never used it and is therefore more properly regarded as a system builder who provided a framework within which sociology and social psychology could be studied (Karpf, 1932).

Emile Durkheim (1858–1912) was one of the first social theorists to actually use quantitative procedures to study social phenomena. In his classic work on suicide, Durkheim (1897/1964) used multivariate procedures to study social factors in what seemed to be a purely private act. He opposed the then existing psychological explanations based on introspection and physiology and argued that, since the biological equipment and psychological structure of people were fundamentally the same, they were irrelevant for explaining the variability of social behavior. Perhaps because his position was so opposed to the psychology of his time, his impact on American social psychology has been somewhat limited and indirect.

The French writers who had the greatest impact on American social psychology were Gabriel Tarde (1843–1904) and Gustave Le Bon (1841–1931). They were both influenced very much by the concept of hypnosis and used it to explain the erratic behavior of crowds. Tarde and Le Bon were frequently cited by both psychological and sociological textbook authors during the first two decades, and Gordon Allport (1968) described Le Bon's work *The Crowd* as "perhaps the most important book ever written in social psychology" (p. 35).

The German tradition began with Johann Gottfried Herder (1744–1803), who developed a historical approach to the study of society. Though developed independently, his perspective was very similar to Vico's earlier proposal for a historical science. Herder emphasized the role of the cultural community or *Volk* in shaping the personality of the individual. Like Vico, he stressed the significance of language in the acculturation process. G. W. F. Hegel (1770–1831) developed a more comprehensive system that focused on both the socialization of the individual and the evolution of society. Hegel's ideas were especially influential in Europe and America during the nineteenth century. Karl Marx (1818–1883) used Hegel's dialectics to formulate a theory of consciousness based on social conditions, and the concept of socialization was incorporated and developed by Sigmund Freud (1856–1939).

In fact, one of Freud's great contributions was his ability to fuse the French tradition, with its emphasis on the irrational, and the German tradition, with its emphasis on the social development of character. Freud, who was thoroughly Germanic in both taste and disposition, developed an interest in hyponosis early in his career and studied under Jean-Martin Charcot in Paris and Hippolyte Bernheim at Nancy. This seems to be an instance of cross-fertilization leading to a theory that was more encompassing than either of its sources.

Wilhelm Wundt (1832–1920), who is commonly regarded as the founder of experimental psychology, was also the first German writer to present a comprehensive treatment of social psychology. Indicative of Herder's influence, he called his social psychology *Volkerpsychologie* (Danziger, 1983). His interest in the field began around 1860, and his ten-volume treatise on the subject appeared between 1900 and 1920. Wundt viewed social psychology and experimental psychology as complementary. While experimental psychology was limited to the study of consciousness, social psychology examined the social aspects of mental processes as expressed in objective products, such as language, customs, and myth, and used comparative and historical analysis rather than introspection. Wundt therefore advocated a comprehensive psychology based partly on the natural sciences (experimental psychology) and partly on social sciences (social psychology).

Wundt's work on social psychology was influential in the development of the social sciences at the turn of the century, especially cultural anthropology, sociology, and linguistics (Farr, 1983). Durkheim, for example, used Wundt's distinction between experimental and social psychology as the basis for his claim that sociology could not be explained in psychological terms.

Wundt's influence can also be seen in the work of George Herbert Mead, who spent a year studying with Wundt at Leipzig. However, aside from Mead, Wundt's *Volkerpsychologie* was largely ignored by American social psychologists.

It is clear that the traditions developed in Britain, France, and Germany were shaped in part by economic and social conditions. Britain was undergoing a period of rapid industrial expansion, which helped foster the doctrines of social evolution, laissez-faire, and an overly rationalistic utilitarian philosophy. France was in social and political turmoil, and its social thinkers responded by describing social behavior as irrational, erratic, and driven by unconscious forces. Germany was a fragmented collection of nation-states, hardly a nation at all, and its authors responded by trying to piece together a national character that could unify its various peoples and distinguish them from the rest of the world.

America, like Britain, was undergoing a period of rapid industrial expansion, and for a while it adopted a social and economic philosophy similar to that developed in Britain. In fact, Spencer's social Darwinism was even more popular in America than in Britain. But the problems of unrestrained capitalism—poverty, unemployment, and unhealthy working and living conditions—soon gave rise to a new social philosophy that interpreted evolutionary theory in a different way. This new movement, known as progressive or reform Darwinism, saw intelligence as a product of evolution that could be used to modify social conditions. Society was no longer perceived as evolving according to fixed laws. People were now regarded as responsible for their own evolution. These two opposing positions can be seen most clearly in two of the founders of American sociology—William Graham Sumner and Lester Ward.

William Graham Sumner (1840–1910) adopted a position similar to Spencer's. He believed that the laws of natural selection, where the population exceeded the food supply, operated with absolute certainty in both advanced societies and nature. By interfering with such laws one would only weaken society as a whole. The wealth of a nation could be used to encourage individual initiative, or it could be spread evenly at a universally low level. The justification for existing social institutions was that they had evolved and come into existence. While imperfect, they were nevertheless better than what had come before. For Sumner, the mind was entirely a product of the social environment, and people should adapt to these conditions and abandon any attempt to remodel the world.

Lester Ward (1841–1913), in contrast, made a sharp distinction between natural and social evolution. According to Ward, social evolution occurs when people began to understand the laws of society and use them for their own benefit. Two important prerequisites were a free and open educational system and support for scientific research. For Ward, sociology was a means for facilitating social change, and the knowledge gained through the study of society could be used for both eradicating social evils and planning the future society. Ward felt that the initial emphasis should be on overcoming social problems, such as inflated prices, monopolies, and unhealthy working conditions, but eventually this new scientific understanding could be used in a more positive way to restructure all aspects of society.

Closely related to "reform Darwinism" was the philosophical movement of American pragmatism, as developed by Charles Peirce (1893–1914), William James (1842–1910), John Dewey (1859–1952), and George Herbert Mead (1863–1931). Pragmatists contend that thought emerges during the course of concrete activity, in an attempt to solve problems and make decisions more rationally. Since language is the primary vehicle of thought, each generation can build on a foundation established by the previous generation. Pragmatism was not a sociological movement, at least not initially. It was a philosophy, a psychology, and ultimately a moral position about the nature of man in society. It drew heavily from British evolutionary theory, but it was diametrically opposed to the doctrine of laissez faire. By the start of World War I, the progressive doctrines of pragmatism and social reform had replaced social Darwinsim as the most dominant tradition within social thought.

Each of the three European traditions of social theory helped shape American social psychology. But they focused on different aspects of social behavior. McDougall (1908) was very much a product of the British evolutionary tradition and helped develop a theory of social instincts that dominated the psychological approach during the first two decades. The early sociological authors drew heavily from the French tradition of Tarde and Le Bon, while the German emphasis on socialization and personality permeated social psychology during the 1930s. Each of these European traditions underwent considerable modification before being applied to social phenomena in America, and these transformations will be discussed within each chapter. Other important European movements include Marx's socioeconomic theory, the Gestalt approach, and the field theory of Kurt Lewin. American pragmatism has had the most belated effect, but George Herbert Mead and symbolic interaction are currently the most important influences on sociological social psychologists. These traditions will be described more fully in the following chapters within the context of the movements they helped generate.

# NOTES

1. We have not included figures in this table because we do not feel that textbook analysis is a precise methodology. Two fundamental problems are identifying textbooks and identifying citations. We used a list provided by Gibson and Higbee (1979). They included two texts by Charles Ellwood, *An Introduction to Social Psychology* (1917) and *The Psychology of Human Society* (1925), as examples of introductory texts, but they did not list his *Sociology in Its Psychological Aspects* (1912), from which these later texts were derived. Other texts included in their list, such as Kaluger and Unkovic (1969), Wrench (1969), and Wallace (1971), are introductory psychological texts written from a social psychological perspective. This is not intended as a criticism of Gibson and Higbee, who did an admirable job in collecting as much information as possible. We are simply pointing out that there are probably both additional texts and possible deletions that might alter a frequency count.

The second problem is identifying a citation. Someone treated at length within a text may be mentioned only once in the index, e.g., 349–361. In these twelve pages, the author may be referred to sporadically along with many others. Is this one citation or twelve? Some older texts do not even have indexes, and one is forced to look through and count citations page by page. We adopted the convention of including each reference, such as the above, as a single citation, but we are aware that different results might have been obtained if a different method had been used.

Finally, we have noted that the rank of an author may move up or down with the addition of a single text. This is particularly true for those at the lower ranks. Thus, we can say with relative certainty that McDougall and Ross were the two most frequently cited individuals during the first two decades and that their influence has steadily diminished. We can also say that Leon Festinger and George Herbert Mead are the most cited authors among contemporary psychological and sociological authors. But we cannot say that Morton Deutsch was more influential than Kurt Lewin during the 1960s because he was cited 84 times whereas Lewin was cited only 83.

# PART I

# THE ORIGINS OF SOCIAL PSYCHOLOGY IN AMERICA (1870–1930)

# 2

# Social Psychology as Social Instincts

While publications before 1908 dealt with social-psychological topics, the origin of American social psychology is commonly associated with the publication of two introductory textbooks in 1908—Edward Ross's *Social Psychology: An Outline and a Source Book,* and William McDougall's *Introduction to Social Psychology.* These books are radically different in their scope and subject matter, and each represents a very different approach to the discipline. Ross's book reflects the sociological perspective and stresses the influence of imitation and invention. According to Ross (1908), social psychology is the branch of knowledge that deals with the psychic interplay between man and his social environment. It attempts to describe those uniformities in feeling, beliefs, or volition—and hence action—that are due to the interaction of human beings, i.e., to *social* causes. Ross summarized a substantial body of literature and attempted to lay the foundations for a discipline that he regarded as a subbranch of sociology.

McDougall's approach, in contrast, reflects the British evolutionary tradition and stresses the importance of innate biological factors. Human behavior, according to McDougall, was the consequence of instincts that provided the "native basis of the mind." The main task for social psychology was to show how, given the native propensities and capacities of the individual human mind, all the complex mental life of societies is shaped by them.

While McDougall's text is commonly regarded as one of the first two textbooks of American social psychology, his book is neither American nor, despite its title, particularly concerned with social psychology. McDougall was born in Lancashire, England, and graduated from the University of Manchester at age 17. He studied physiology at Cambridge and obtained a medical degree at London in 1898. He wrote *Introduction to Social Psychology* in 1908 while at Oxford.

The content of *Introduction to Social Psychology* was devoted almost entirely to McDougall's theory of social instincts. One critic complained that McDougall "seems to do a great deal of packing in preparation for a journey on which he never starts" (McDougall, 1936, p. xvi). McDougall later recognized this and suggested that a better title would have been "propaedeutic" or "an indispensable preliminary to social psychology." His later work *The Group Mind* (1920) attempted to deal more specifically with social-psychological issues.

Despite its limitations, McDougall's *Introduction to Social Psychology* remains a landmark in social-psychological thought. Because it stressed social instincts just before the attack on instinct theory, it was the first *and the last* social-psychological textbook of its kind. By 1936, it had gone through 23 editions and had sold 62,000 copies in the English editions alone. In the preface to the 1936 edition, McDougall stated that public opinion seemed to suggest that this was the best of his books, and he was convinced that the public was right. Ross and McDougall's textbooks serve to highlight two of the major intellectual traditions that contended for dominance during the formative period of American social psychology. This chapter will trace the origin and development of social instinct theory in the context of British and American evolutionary thought. The following chapter will focus on the development of the sociological approach to American social psychology.

## DARWIN AND THE BRITISH EVOLUTIONARY TRADITION

Charles Darwin (1809–1882) was born in Shrewsbury, England, the fifth of six children. His father was a wealthy physician and his mother was the daughter of Josiah Wedgwood, who founded the Wedgwood pottery firm. His paternal grandfather was Erasmus Darwin, a distinguished naturalist and a forerunner of evolutionary theory. In short, Darwin was raised in a moderately wealthy rural environment where the leisurely pursuit of intellectual interests was encouraged and had had a long history. Although he was expected to choose a profession, he was never forced to earn a living.

Darwin studied medicine at Edinburgh and theology at Cambridge, but his major interest at both places was the study of nature. In 1831, he was offered an unpaid position as naturalist aboard the HMS *Beagle* and spent five years touring the world. When he embarked on this voyage, he was a firm believer in the fixed nature of species, but during his tour he was repeatedly exposed to natural variations due to climate and geography, which he recorded in minute detail and published after his return. But it was not until 1838, according to his own account (1887–1898), after reading Malthus's (1798) essay on population, that he grasped the full implications of his theory of natural selection.

He wrote a draft of his ideas in 1844, which he circulated among friends; by 1858, he had written ten or eleven chapters. He continued to publish accounts of his voyage, which established his reputation as a naturalist, but he seemed to have had no intention of publishing his ideas on evolution during his life. In the same year, however, he received a brief manuscript written by Alfred Russel Wallace, a young naturalist who had independently arrived at the same theory. This forced Darwin to prepare a summary of his theory to be published jointly with Wallace's paper. *Origin of Species* appeared the next year, 1859.

The theory of evolution has become so firmly entrenched in our manner of thinking that this book seems quite unremarkable in retrospect. In it, Darwin begins with a description of variations in domestic animals and argues that human beings have simply sped up the process of evolution by breeding these animals selectively. He then discusses the laws of variation and finishes with a description of instincts. In each section, he amasses so much evidence that the reader is simply overwhelmed with details. But Darwin was gifted not only as a theorist but as a careful observer and recorder of details, and this is what gave the book scientfic credibility during his own life.

The idea of evolution is quite simple. Each generation produces more offspring than can possibly survive, and those that do survive are those most adapted to their environment. This overproduction can be seen most clearly in certain species of insects and fish, which may produce in some cases more than a million eggs, of which only one or two grow into adults. Differences among individuals may be small—a slight streamlining of the body or a resistance to an insecticide—but they accumulate over generations. Different environments place different demands on individuals and produce natural variations. While body features are the most visible result, animals also inherit instincts for the same reason—because they increase the chance of individual or species survival.

Darwin's influence on our understanding of ourselves is immeasurable. The publication of *Origin of Species* in 1859 was a monumental achievement that established a naturalistic explanation for the development of all life forms. Through the twin mechanisms of random variation and natural selection, he built a convincing case that explained how some species survived while others became extinct. Darwin based his theory on more than twenty years of observation and evidence drawn from such diverse fields as geology, comparative anatomy, and studies of domestic animals.

Although Darwin initially made no direct attempt to apply evolutionary theory to human beings, the implications were almost immediately apparent. Human beings were now regarded as a part of nature and subject to the same natural forces that shaped all forms of life. In 1871, Darwin wrote *The Descent of Man,* which provided a natural history of human development. He drew a great deal of his evidence from comparative anatomy in order to show the evolutionary kinship between humans and primates. Not only were people "descended from some less highly organized form," but they shared such features as the sense of pleasure and pain, instincts for self-preservation, sexual attraction, and the emotions of love, fear, and curiosity. These similarities suggested that the differences between people and animals were differences of degree and not of kind.

Darwin's comparative analysis had important implications for the study of the mind. Although he preferred to remain a biologist rather than becoming a psychologist, he eagerly pursued psychological issues in private. As a forerunner of comparative psychology, Darwin argued that the instincts and mental faculties of human beings were common to other species as well. Nor was this a one-way comparison. Darwin believed that human consciousness had evolved and that it was reasonable to assume that some animals possessed the rudiments of conscious processes as well. He argued that the mind was a function of the brain and that both were shaped by the mechanisms of variation and natural selection. Fortuitous changes in the structures of the brain could produce functional changes in mental activity that became habitual and produced further structural changes.

Darwin also helped to provide a naturalistic basis for social psychology through his work on social instincts and moral development. For Darwin, the foundation of the moral sense lay in the social instincts, including sympathy, and these instincts were derived, as in the case of lower animals, through natural selection. In speculating about moral development, Darwin stressed the role of the Lamarckian principles of inheritance of acquired characteristics, particularly those resulting from prolonged practice. He felt that after a period of prolonged practice it was not improbable that virtuous tendencies may be inherited.

The influence of Darwin's psychological speculations were ultimately limited because of his tendency to fall back on the more dated Lamarckian concept of evolution. Stated briefly, the Lamarckian theory held that behaviors acquired during an animal's lifetime through strenuous and prolonged effort could modify the body and this trait would then be passed on to the next generation. A common example is the stretching of the giraffe's neck in order to reach leaves higher up on trees. This theory, though generally discredited by the turn of the century, was widely held during the nineteenth century. Charles Darwin, Herbert Spencer, William McDougall, Gustave Le Bon, Carl Jung, and even Sigmund Freud all based their theories to some extent on Lamarck's concept of evolution and had those aspects of their theories called into question when Lemarck's theory was abandoned.

Although Darwin did not develop a systematic theory of social evolution, it is fair to assume from his brief statements on the subject that he did not endorse an individualistic creed based on the "struggle and survival of the fittest." The so-called social Darwinism that is often associated with rugged individualism and a laissez-faire ideology was largely a product of Herbert Spencer's work and the social and economic environment of the late Victorian industrial society. For this reason, much of what has come to be known as social Darwinism should be more correctly labeled "Spencerianism."

### Herbert Spencer (1820–1903)

Spencer developed his own theory of social evolution independent of Darwin, and most of the major components of his theory were worked out before the publication of Darwin's *Origin of Species*. After *Origin of Species* appeared, Spencer used Darwin's theory as well as Lamarck to support his own view of social progress. Spencer developed his evolutionary perspective not as a naturalist but as a speculative social theorist. For Spencer (1873/1961), "the study of sociology [was] the study of Evolution in its most complex form" (p. 385).

Spencer felt that history had shown a gradual evolution in the forms of society as they adapted to natural conditions and social pressures from within. These changes could be formulated as "natural laws" of social evolution, which operated at least in part independently of the wills and actions of individuals. Because society was evolving on its own accord, Spencer felt that individuals should occupy themselves with personal matters and leave social evolution to go its own way. Spencer derived from evolutionary laws a strongly individualistic interpretation of human relations. The state was completely subordinate to individuals and merely helped them secure greater individual freedom. The best form of government was as little government as possible. He provided support for the laissez-faire and hedonistic doctrines of his day by grounding both in evolutionary theory.

Spencer softened his views with a theory of empathy, which he saw as playing a strong role in the family. For Spencer, the family was the basic social unit, where children survived not only because they were strong but because they were cared for and protected by sympathetic parents. Spencer believed, however, that sympathy should be limited to the family and not allowed to interfere with the more general law of evolution, where rewards go to the strong. People should not be coddled. Spencer was vehemently opposed to any concept of a welfare state, including free public education.

Underlying virtually all of Spencer's major writings was an ongoing effort to explain evolution in terms of what he regarded as a single unifying law of progress that linked all forms of evolutionary development, individual and social (Peel, 1971). Unlike some of his American followers, such as William Graham Sumner, who

transformed his theory into a conservative endorsement of existing economic conditions, Spencer was inspired with a mood of "aggressive optimism" about the future of industrialized society. Evolution in all its forms demonstrated a universal process of advancement from simple to complex. Spencer's support for laissez-faire economic policies was not an endorsement of the status quo. Nature did not operate according to blind undirected forces but functioned in a purposeful and moral manner, and advancements within industrialized societies were part of this progression.

For Spencer, the natural history of each race was recapitulated in the development of the individual and was analogous to the evolution from a savage to a civilized state. Morality and the development of social virtues were based on the modification of human instincts, which transformed the individual from a primitive egocentric savage into a civilized cooperative adult. With adulthood came consciousness, which allowed the individual to make reasoned choices in response to changing circumstances. Through the interaction of experience, instinct, and consciousness the individual progressively adapted and changed. Since society was basically an aggregate of individuals, the process of adaptation and the continual modification of each individual helped move society toward a more advanced form (Spencer, 1870, 1873/1961). For Spencer, laissez faire and individualism were essentially natural and therefore beneficial, but they were not ends in themselves. They were the means whereby, through struggle and adaptation, society would reach a more advanced state. The final product would be a fully evolved interdependent society in which individual desires and needs would be in harmony with the interests of society as a whole (Peel, 1971).

Spencer's combination of sociology and Lamarckian evolutionary theory produced what today seems a strange blend of social and biological determinism. Cultural differences were considered to be, at least in part, the result of genetically inherited acquired characteristics. Adaptations that individuals made to their social environment were passed on genetically and then submitted to the laws of natural selection. Thus, social evolution occurred because maladaptive individuals, the poor and unemployed, were eliminated from the gene pool, and successful individuals passed their acquired characteristics on to new generations. Although these laws seem harsh at times, Spencer envisioned a time when people would be fully evolved and completely adapted to their environment. Thus, Spencer arrived at not only a social theory but a biological and economic theory as well, all based at least to some extent on the now-discredited theory of Lamarckian evolution.

Spencer's attempt to establish a social science on the basis of a single underlying principle was wide-ranging and ambitious. He was one of the last of a generation of nineteenth-century thinkers and system builders who believed that scientific advancement was the key that unlocked the secrets that governed the universe. His approach was necessarily speculative and theoretical and lacked the solid empirical foundation that characterized the work of Darwin and other scientists associated with the British Association for the Advancement of Science. For this reason, in part, Spencer's ideas did not receive wide support among the British scientific community and might have been forgotten were it not for his enormous popularity in the United States.

## Sir Francis Galton (1822–1911)

While Spencer's writings lacked credibility within the British scientific community, they nevertheless helped extend the range of evolutionary theory and prepare the way for other evolutionary thinkers, such as Darwin's cousin, Sir Francis Galton. Galton inherited a substantial fortune at the age of twenty-two, which enabled him to devote his entire adult life to the pursuit of personal interests. Galton was one of the universal men characteristic of the nineteenth century but rare today. Explorer, statistician, and psychologist, today Galton is best known for his work on individual differences and the appplication of statistical procedures to heredity. But Galton also helped foster an alternative strategy for social progress—eugenics—that was quite popular at the turn of the century.

Galton's theory differed from Spencer's in several ways. He was justifiably dubious about the inheritance of acquired characteristics and based his theory exclusively on natural selection, which he considered to act with "unimpassioned, merciless severity" on both physical and mental characteristics. Second, he attempted to provide proof for his speculations through observations, questionnaires, and experiments. No person expressed the nineteenth century's fascination with measurement and empirical procedures more than Galton. Measurement was Galton's god. He attempted to quantify boredom, carried out a statistical inquiry into the efficacy of prayer, and constructed a "beauty map" for the British Isles (Gould, 1981).

Galton's most important psychological work, however, was in the field of heredity. He read Darwin's *Origin of Species* soon after it was published and became one of Darwin's strongest supporters. One of Galton's most fundamental contributions to evolutionary theory is the notion that mental ability is inherited in the same way as physical characteristics. He was struck by the observation that eminence seemed to run in families, including his own. He examined the family trees of various samples of eminent men and found that the proportion of eminent men with eminent relatives was much greater than that of eminent men in the general population. Furthermore, these proportions were higher in close relationships than in distant ones—for example, higher among fathers and sons than among uncles and nephews. The notion that mental ability was inherited was novel during Galton's time and surprised even Darwin, who attributed individual differences to degrees of effort.

Galton's belief in the inheritance of mental abilities led to the idea that the human race could be improved through a program of selective breeding, to which he gave the name "eugenics." This was simply the application to human beings of principles long used by animal breeders. Convinced of the predominance of nature over nurture, Galton believed that social improvement could only come about by identifying individuals with superior traits and gradually eliminating defective individuals from the gene pool. Some of Galton's sharpest criticisms were directed against organized religion and reflected the general antagonism felt by supporters of Darwin in England. Galton hoped to replace traditional religious beliefs with a new "religion" based on evolutionary principles and eugenics. This new religion dominated Galton's thinking during the latter part of his life, and he frequently wrote and spoke on the subject.

While much of Galton's work on eugenics tends to focus on positive aspects of finding gifted individuals and encouraging them to mate, he also discussed the larger issue of racial differences in intelligence. Galton felt that different environments placed different pressures on the various races and had led to the genetic inheritance of different characteristics. The harsh northern conditions and bellicose nature of the "white" race had more frequently eliminated individuals of lower intelligence, whereas the less harsh conditions of blacks had allowed the retention of such people. The result was a large number of "half-witted men" among the black population. This thoroughly racist position was used as "proof" that nature was more important than nurture.

Galton's subsequent attempts to develop tests of intelligence were primarily aimed at placing eugenics on a scientific footing. He set up an anthropometric laboratory at the International Exposition of 1884, where for three pence visitors could have their sensory acuity and reaction time measured. Individual tests measured keenness of vision and hearing, color perception, highest audible frequency of pitch, strength of pull and squeeze, and force of blow. These tests reflected the assumption that intelligence consisted of elementary sensations. Thus, the most intelligent people would have the fastest reaction time and most acute senses. This belief was reinforced by the fact that severely retarded individuals tend to be defective in sensory discrimination. These attempts to measure intelligence were ultimately a failure because intelligence is not

highly correlated with sensory acuity, but they were one of the first attempts to create an easily administered test for intelligence. By the end of the health exhibition, almost ten thousand people had been tested. After the exposition, the lab was transferred to a London museum, where it was maintained for six years.

Galton also encouraged a number of schools to keep systematic records of their students and initiated twin studies by soliciting information about twins. While he recognized the role of the environment, he stressed biological factors. Galton felt that any person with sufficient intelligence and a desire to work could overcome environmental obstacles and become a success. This assumption overlooked—and indeed justified—the great advantages enjoyed by members of the upper class, including Galton himself.

The charge that he neglected environmental factors stimulated him to conduct a second study of inherited ability. He sent lengthy questionnaires to 200 fellows of the British Royal Society gathering information about their backgrounds. The result was published in the book *English Men of Science: Their Nature and Nurture* (1874/1970). While the bulk of his analysis supported his view that scientific eminence was inherited, he found that a disproportionate number of British scientists were Scottish and attributed this to their superior educational system. By framing the question in terms of nature and nurture, Galton helped establish the framework for the debate that dominated much of the social-scientific literature at the turn of the century.

Galton's stress on individual differences and eugenics reflects the social, political, and economic priorities of late Victorian British society (Buss, 1976). The development of modern capitalism created a need for a more diversified labor force, specialized according to level of ability. The capitalist economy was also becoming increasingly dependent on measuring and quantifying its material products. A quantifiable science of individual differences was merely an extension of a successful model from the material world to the human level. Finally, Galton's genetic interpretation of individual differences was consistent with the prevailing political climate of liberalism and democratic individualism. As Buss (1976) states, "Given the belief that each individual did indeed have the freedom and opportunity to fulfill his potential, it naturally followed that the existent hierarchical class structure reflected innate differences in mental ability" (p. 54).

## EVOLUTIONARY THEORY IN AMERICA

The reception and development of evolutionary theory occurred differently in America. In contrast to England's increasingly secular and empirical tradition, Americans were more conservative and much slower to relinquish their traditional views about science and religion. This factor, together with the social conditions of the post–Civil War period, gave a unique flavor to all forms of American evolutionary theory. The impact of British evolutionary theory on America can best be understood as a succession of waves representing the ideas of key evolutionary thinkers—first Darwin and Spencer, and then men like Galton and McDougall, who applied evolutionary theory to genetics and social instinct theory.

### Progressive Darwinism

Although the full impact of evolutionary theory was delayed in America because of the Civil War, Darwin's *Origin of Species* was introduced to America through a penetrating and sympathetic review by the Harvard biologist Asa Gray (1860/1876). As a result, Gray became Darwin's chief spokesman in America, and his defense helped insure that evolutionary theory would receive an honest and fair hearing. In England, Darwinism was supported by unyielding agnostics, such as Sir Francis Galton and T. H. Huxley, and the lines of battle were clearly drawn between the supporters of evolution and the defenders of traditional religion. Although many intellectuals

sought some kind of middle ground, there was a growing minority of educated thinkers who were willing to abandon religion in favor of a faith based solely on the methods and principles of science.

This conflict was most dramatically demonstrated during the debate between Thomas Huxley and Samuel Wilberforce, the Bishop of Oxford, in 1860. When the bishop asked if Huxley claimed his descent from monkeys on his grandmother's or his grandfather's side of the family, Huxley replied that he would rather have a monkey as an ancestor than be connected with a person who would use his intellect to obscure the truth. For Darwinians like Huxley there was no real dispute between evolutionary theory and religion. Darwin was simply right and the defenders of traditional Christianity were wrong.

The reception of Darwinism was much more complex in America. Many American universities originated as divinity schools, and no serious-minded American thinker could have adopted a straightforwardly agnostic position like that of Darwin's bulldog Huxley. Asa Gray steadfastly defended a position that accepted Darwin's theories of variation and natural selection but saw in them examples of an ultimate design. Behind nature's chaos and carnage were principles that allowed one to understand nature in terms of universal laws of progress. Beneath the shimmer of bloodshed and death was a reign of order.

A belief in Providence or design in nature reflected the dominant view among American scientists at the time. Such a view helped reconcile traditional Christian views with the American assumption of constant progress and change. From the time of the first English settlements, Americans had believed that they had a special relationship to God and that the destiny of their country was an expression of this relationship. In the nineteenth century, this original Puritan vision gave way to a more secular theory of manifest destiny in which Americans felt that it was their right and duty to spread their civilization to the frontiers of America and beyond. Implicit in this vision was a belief in progress and the idea that America was the only nation in history that began with perfection and sought to improve (Hofstadter, 1955).

For many Americans the idea of evolution seemed to provide scientific proof for their belief in progress, but this combination of religion and evolutionary theory also helped prevent the spread of "pure" Darwinism in America. The number of Americans who could accept Darwinism as a scientific theory without viewing it as an example of ultimate design was small. Pure Darwinism appealed to only more rigorous intellects, such as Chauncey Wright, John Dewey, and William James. As a result, the impact of progressive Darwinism waxed and waned. The prevailing climate seemed, in the short run, to insure the success not of Darwin's but of Spencer's version of evolutionary theory. Progressive Darwinsim was gradually absorbed into the American intellectual tradition and provided a strong basis for social reform. These developments, however, which will be described in more detail in Chapters 3 and 4, were delayed substantially by the success of Spencer in America.

## "Social Spencerianism"

In contrast to his modest influence in England, Herbert Spencer enjoyed an enormous popularity in the United States after the Civil War. In fact, as Perry Miller (1954) has pointed out, the bulk of American "thought" during this period, measured solely in terms of the weight of printed paper, was not thought at all but merely a recapitulation of Spencer. Spencer was one of the forerunners of modern social theory and helped to stimulate the development of American sociology through his impact on William Graham Sumner and Lester Ward, who used Spencer's theory to develop opposing models for social change. At the popular level, Spencer's theory of social evolution had a broad-based appeal that far exceeded that of Darwin's.

Spencer's popularity in the United States stems from the compatibility between his concept of social evolution and the climate of opinion in America at the time. His philosophy stressed individualism, laissez faire,

and evolution in accordance with universal laws of progress. These were essential American beliefs, and it was reassuring to have them reinforced by such a profound prophet of science. More important perhaps was the fact that Spencer's speculations coincided with a period of unprecedented growth in America. By placing the process of industrialization within the framework of natural law, Spencer made sense of the awesome and bewildering array of forces shaping American society after the Civil War. Such "laws" as supply and demand, survival of the fittest, and elimination of the weak were seen as so pervasive that American businessmen could conduct business as usual and let nature take its course. Above all, no "artificial" interference by the state should be tolerated, since such interference only subverts the iron laws of nature. In short, American society according to Spencer should continue just as it was and no one should interfere or complain.

Spencer's chief spokesperson in the United States, William Graham Sumner (1841-1910), placed even more emphasis on individualism and social determinism. Sumner's stress on rugged individualism was so strong that he alienated even the business community. He opposed protectionism and imperialism and had as much contempt for corrupt businessmen as for social reform. He argued that the mind was entirely molded by social circumstances. The abstractions and "universal truths" by which people pretend to live, such as "honor," "justice," and "common sense," are a product of social conditions and should not be used to guide social reform. Sumner's ideal was the agrarian America of the founding fathers, which became increasingly out of line with industrial developments at the turn of the century. He lost hope in America near the end of his life and predicted that the next generation would experience war and social chaos. With him died the last major supporter of "social Spencerianism" in America.

Herbert Spencer's influence has diminished considerably over the years, and his stature as a social theorist has long since been overshadowed by more prominent thinkers of his day. This fact was dramatically displayed to the third author when he was a graduate student in London. While visiting the monumental tomb of Karl Marx in Highgate cemetery, he stepped back onto an overgrown ivy-covered marble slab in order to photograph Marx's larger-than-life-size bust. Looking down, he discovered that he was in fact standing on the neglected grave of Herbert Spencer.

## Eugenics and Race Psychology

The popularity of "social Spencerianism" set the stage for another wave of British evolutionary thought in America. This third wave represents the ideas of Sir Francis Galton. By the time Galton died in 1911, the eugenics movement had become quite strong in the United States. A Eugenics Record Office had been set up on Long Island by Charles Davenport, with financial support from John D. Rockefeller and others, in order to determine "America's most effective blood lines." Courses in eugenics were being given at major colleges and universities throughout the country, and eugenics was seen by many people as a biological panacea for all social problems.

The success of the eugenics movement in America was due in part to social and economic conditions at the turn of the century. Industrialization had brought with it a rising tide of immigration. This peaked between 1906 and 1915, when roughly a million immigrants came each year. Moreover, the sources of immigration had changed from northern to southern and eastern Europe. Whereas previous immigrants had come from England, Ireland, Germany, and Scandinavia, the new immigrants were Poles, Italians, Russians, and Jews. These immigrants flocked to urban centers for social support and jobs. By 1910, almost one in seven people in the United States was foreign-born, and major cities were bursting at the seams.

The new immigrants were mostly peasants, and their unusual customs and languages made easy assimilation difficult. The disruption brought on by urbanization caused them to seem strange to the native

population. A belief in genetic differences along national and racial lines had wide support under such conditions. This belief was given scientific respectability by the rise of intelligence testing in the United States. The American tests were based on the scales developed by Alfred Binet in France, beginning in 1905, but the Americans ignored Binet's environmental perspective. Instead, they chose to follow Galton's genetic explanation of mental differences (Minton, 1988b). Thus, when H. H. Goddard (1917) gave intelligence tests to selected immigrant samples at Ellis Island, he argued that their low test scores reflected native differences in human ability and concluded that 83 percent of Jews, 80 percent of Hungarians, 79 percent of Italians, and 87 percent of Russians were feeble-minded. Such results were cited by Goddard and other leaders of the mental testing movement in the early 1920s in their attempt to influence the passage of legislation restricting immigration, but the psychological data had relatively little impact on the subsequent quotas for immigrant populations. The biological arguments of eugenicists, such as Charles Davenport, had already swayed congressional opinion (Samelson, 1985b).

Whereas the eugenics movement in Britain focused on identifying and promoting selective breeding among people with superior ability, the eugenics movement in the United States was part of a widespread attempt to keep the nation "racially pure" by restricting immigration. Other expressions of racism appeared in such widely read books as Madison Grant's *The Passing of the Great Race* (1916) and Lothrop Stoddard's *The Rising Tide of Color* (1920). Opposition to immigration reached its peak just after World War I and culminated in the emergency Immigration Act of 1921, which placed severe restricitons and differential quotas on foreign immigration. In 1924, new quotas were established that virtually eliminated immigration from southern and eastern Europe. This "racial nationalism" within the United States was matched by an equally bellicose foreign policy, which led to the annexation of Hawaii in 1893, the Venezuelan boundary dispute of 1899, and the Spanish-American War in

1898. In both Britain and the United States, there was a growing tendency to identify race and nationality and to use the supposed inferiority of other groups as an excuse for military intervention.

During the early 1920s, psychologists continued to present data supporting innate racial differences in intelligence. Whites were judged to be superior to blacks, and within the former group, northern Europeans surpassed those from other parts of Europe. The term "race psychology" was used to refer to a new specialization in which psychology was applied to the study of racial differences (Samelson, 1978). There was some ambiguity, however, about the relationship between race psychology and social psychology. The early social-psychological textbooks did not include much material on intelligence, race, or mental testing. Yet, the authors of the first two texts, Edward Ross and William McDougall, wrote other works on racial differences. As early as 1912, Ross had written several articles about the racial inferiority of immigrants from southeastern Europe. In 1921, McDougall published a book called *Is America Safe for Democracy?* in which he supported eugenics and restrictive immigration based on his belief in innate racial and social-class differences.

The eugenics movement and race psychology maintained a certain degree of scientific respectability throughout the 1920s, but the positions came under increasing attack. Some critics like Franz Boas and Otto Klineberg began to question the "fairness" of intelligence tests when given to non-English-speaking populations. By 1930 many psychologists no longer accepted the hypothesis of innate racial differences in intelligence. Samelson (1978) points to two factors that contributed to this dramatic reversal in psychological opinion. First, the passage of the restrictive immigration legislation in 1924 defused the interest in immigration issues. There was now a rising concern for racial tolerance between native and foreign elements already in the country, and social psychologists began to focus on the study of race relations. Another factor was the increasing number of psychologists and social scientists with minority backgrounds, especially Jews, but also a small number of blacks. These social scientists, because of their personal experience, were particularly sensitive to the ways in which research findings could be distorted at the expense of minority groups. In the 1930s the movement away from innate explanations for racial differences was further accelerated by the impact of the depression and the rise of fascism in Europe.

The popularity of the eugenics movement represented a brief triumph of biological explanations for social conditions, in which social problems were attributed to genetic weaknesses within immigrant groups and racial minorities. Similar arguments were used to justify concentration camps in Nazi Germany. In fact, the eugenics movement in Germany was merely the flip side of Galton's program for identifying and breeding people with superior ability. If superior people could be encouraged to breed, then inferior ones could be discouraged. The first concentration camps in Germany contained people with genetic defects. The real tragedy of the eugenics movement was that the quotas set in the United States in 1924 were maintained throughout the 1930s, and millions of Jewish refugees seeking to emigrate were denied admission. As Stephen Gould (1981) has pointed out, we may never know how many died as a result, but it demonstrates that ideas kill just as effectively as bullets.

The extreme biological determinism of eugenics, along with its racist connotations, drew heavy opposition from more progressive social thinkers. Given the social conditions in the 1930s, any dispassionate debate of the nature-nurture issue was impossible. The eugenics movement helped discredit any form of biological explanation for social behavior, and this was a major setback for all forms of evolutionary theory. Environmentalists were in no mood for a compromise and developed equally extreme positions in which biological factors were downplayed or ignored (see Freeman, 1983). This led to the development of behaviorism, on the one hand, and cultural anthropology, on the other. These movements will be discussed in Chapters 5 and 6.

## WILLIAM MCDOUGALL AND
## SOCIAL-INSTINCT THEORY

If the eugenics movement is considered the third wave of British evolutionary thinking in America, then McDougall's social-instinct theory can be regarded as the fourth. McDougall was not the first to develop a theory of social instincts. Such formulations were common at the turn of the century. His version is simply the most sophisticated, since it shifted the emphasis from reflexive behavior to some kind of driving force responsible for behavior. Unlike previous evolutionary theories, social-instinct theory did not undergo a modification in the hands of American interpreters. William McDougall brought his theory with him when he moved from Oxford to Harvard in 1921.

As mentioned previously, William McDougall (1871–1938) was born and trained in Britain and was very much a part of the British evolutionary tradition. He was a person of wide background and interests. In addition to his formal training at Manchester, Cambridge, and London, he traveled to the Torres Straits, where he carried out psychological observations of natives. He later studied color vision under George Müller at Göttingen and published a book on physiological psychology in 1905, which was highly regarded at the time. His later writings include a text on general psychology (1923) and one on abnormal psychology (1926), but his most influential work by far was *Introduction to Social Psychology* (1908).

Although this latter work deals with imitation, suggestion, the development of sentiments, and purposeful behavior, it is noted primarily for its theory of instincts, which was considered the foundation on which the other processes rest. In a characteristically eloquent passage, McDougall (1936) states:

> directly or indirectly instincts are the prime movers of all human activity ... and supply the driving power by which all mental activities are sustained.... Take away these instinctive dispositions with their powerful impulses, and the or-

ganism would become incapable of activity of any kind; it would lie inert and motionless like a wonderful clockwork whose mainspring had been removed or a steam-engine whose fires had been drawn. (p. 38)

McDougall developed his theory of instincts partly as a reaction to what he considered faulty theorizing in the social sciences. Because these sciences predated psychology and evolutionary theory, they were based on concepts of human nature that were often inadequate and out of date. He was particularly critical of the doctrine of rational hedonism, according to which people sought as much pleasure as possible through enlightened self-interest. This account was the foundation for both laissez-faire economic theory and utilitarian morality, but McDougall regarded it as too superficial because it ignored unconscious processes and the effects of suggestion. He felt that the concept of instinct in the social sciences was often used as "a cloak for ignorance" to explain behaviors that were not well understood.

For McDougall, instincts consisted of three components: (1) the cognitive or perceptual, which is a tendency to perceive or pay attention to certain objects; (2) the emotional; and (3) the behavioral, a tendency to react in a given way. In some animals this stimulus-response chain is more or less rigidly built in through evolution. In human beings, however, previous experience determines both the stimuli to which we pay attention and our response to them, so that the emotion is the only invariant feature.

Because each instinct is accompanied by a distinct emotion, emotions can be used to identify instincts. McDougall listed seven instincts with clearly defined emotions: (1) flight (fear); (2) repulsion (disgust); (3) curiosity (wonder); (4) pugnacity (anger); (5) self-abasement (negative self-feelings); (6) self-assertion (positive self-feelings); and (7) the parental instinct (tender feelings). He added four others—reproduction, gregariousness, acquisition, and construction—which lacked clearly defined corresponding emotions. McDougall felt that joy, sorrow, and surprise were not primary emotions but were experienced along with primary drives and added to their emotional tone. Pleasure and pain did not motivate behavior but simply indicated whether the behavior was successful or unsuccessful in fulfilling an instinctive drive.

The modifiability of instincts can be seen most clearly in fear. Fear is a natural reaction to anything perceived as dangerous, but animals can learn to fear things to which they were previously indifferent, and they can become indifferent to objects that previously frightened them. Loud noises, for example, seem to instinctively produce fear in many animals, but deer that graze close to train tracks eventually show little fear. Flight is a natural reaction to fear, but we may learn to respond to frightening objects by hiding our emotions or dealing with them in a rational way. Thus, the instinct of flight can be modified both in terms of the stimulus that provokes it and our response, but the emotional experience of fear remains more or less the same.

Disgust also appears to be an innate reaction, and the objects with which it is associated have a tendency to generalize. In infants, disgust is directed most frequently at foul odors and tastes. Facial expressions associated with disgust have been found even in newborns when a bitter substance is placed on the tongue. In adulthood, people, foods, and even scenes from motion pictures can elicit disgust, and what people find disgusting varies enormously with experience.

McDougall considered his social instincts as a tentative list subject to future verification. Subsequent psychological research has provided additional evidence for some drives but not for others. The location of the reticular activating system within the brain, for example, and experiments in which monkeys manipulate toys and objects without ulterior motives (e.g., Harlow, 1953) have generally confirmed that curiosity is an innate drive. Moreover, this drive would have considerable advantage from an evolutionary point of view, because curious animals would explore their environment and discover escape routes and resources before being placed in danger. There is now considerable ethological evidence that dominance and submission play a major role in social interaction. Dominance displays help to establish pecking orders in social animals and give dominant individuals first choice of foods and mates. Submissive displays tend to inhibit attacks by more dominant individuals and are found in both animals and human beings.

McDougall postulated a parental instinct rather than the more widely accepted maternal instinct. Nature seems to preserve species in one of two ways—through a large overproduction of offspring, as in insects and fish, or through a maternal instinct, which is more characteristic of birds and mammals. The parental instinct is particularly strong in higher primates because of the prolonged period of infancy. McDougall felt that the parental instinct was one of the strongest biological drives and that males inherited it as well, although in a weaker form, through cross-transmission of sexual characteristics. This process can be seen in the physical development of many species and is responsible for horns and antlers on females in certain species of sheep and deer and, one might add, nipples on males. McDougall believed that the parental instinct was present in all species in which family life is the norm, and in human beings, it generalizes into indignation for mistreatment of any helpless creature.

McDougall originally dealt only briefly with the reproductive instinct, but in 1914 he added an additional chapter on the sex instinct to the eighth edition, partly to deal with the growing interest in psychoanalysis. Although McDougall listed this as an example of an instinct without an emotion, the emotion is obviously lust. One can only speculate that a general squeamishness on his part or the part of his audience prevented him from mentioning it.

Several of McDougall's instincts seem more suspect. Because acquisition appeared widespread in both humans and animals, McDougall postulated an instinct to account for it. One could argue, however, that the need to acquire is often in the service of other more basic drives (e.g., Klineberg, 1940). Acquisition in animals is a means by which food is conserved and consumed later. Among people, acquisition appears to be at least in part a means for gaining power and prestige. McDougall's final instinct, the need to construct, also appears to be derivative. People must construct shelters for warmth and protection, but the play of children and the meaningful work of adults seem to stem from a more general need to keep active. Experiments with monkeys have shown that it is not just the desire to see a novel stimulus but the desire to manipulate them that is biologically built in. This drive, like curiosity, is capable of a very high degree of refinement in humans and can lead to the pursuit of intellectual and artistic activities.

McDougall pointed out that the strength of these drives varies from individual to individual and may even be absent in some. He states, for example, that "there are certainly among the celibates of our population a certain number of persons who know of sexual desire only by hearsay and who regard it as a strange madness from which they are fortunately free" (1936, p. 235). There are men, and even some women, who lack the parental instinct and some who lack pugnacity. These differences help produce differences among people in both the type and strength of motivation.

It is interesting to note that, although McDougall is often seen as having given the death blow to instinct theory because of his endless proliferation of instincts, his list is quite small. Modern facial expression studies have generally confirmed many of the specific emotions on his list (e.g., Izard, 1971). There are distinct facial expressions for fear, disgust, curiosity, and anger that appear either at birth or shortly after. While there are no facial expressions for self-abasement and self-assertion, there are body movements associated with dominance and submission present not only in human beings but in many animals as well. McDougall recognized the danger of generating too many instincts and even warned against it: "Lightly to postulate an indefinite number and variety of human instincts is a cheap and easy way to solve psychological problems, and is an error hardly less serious and less common than the opposite error of ignoring all instincts" (1936, p. 75).

McDougall's theory of social instincts

was not the only version to appear in Britain (van Ginneken, 1988). In fact, in 1908 when McDougall's textbook first appeared, two other publications on social instincts occurred as well. One, *Herd Instinct and its Bearing on the Psychology of Civilized Man,* was written by Wilfred Trotter (1872–1939), who was a surgeon at London University College Hospital. He argued that, because individuals fear solitude, they naturally come under the influence of the herd or crowd. Such individuals become susceptible to leaders and seek recognition that they are members of the herd. It is likely that, through his brother-in-law, Ernest Jones (Freud's biographer), Trotter helped shape Freud's notion of the primal horde and the prehistoric source of the superego. The second book, *Human Nature in Politics,* was written by Graham Wallas (1859–1932), who was an activist in the British socialist movement. Wallas discussed the role of irrational forces in politics and argued for the the need to educate both the politicians and the public so that they could become aware of the unconscious psychological processes that shaped their lives.

Theories of social instincts appeared to have a special appeal to Edwardian British society. Van Ginneken (1988) notes that, in the first decade of the twentieth century, Britian's economic dominance was challenged by both Germany and the United States, and the fate of the Empire was starting to be undermined by unrest in Ireland and South Africa. Competitive individualism and laissez-faire capitalism, which had pervaded Victorian society, were giving way to a call for collective solidarity and social reform. People were now attracted to the Darwinian concept of social instincts rather than the emphasis on the struggle for life and the survival of the fittest.

Social instinct theory became influential in America as well. Both Edward L. Thorndike's *The Original Nature of Man* (1913) and Robert S. Woodworth's *Dynamic Psychology* (1918) exemplified this trend. In his address to the American Psychological Association, John Dewey (1917) announced that the science of social psychology must be founded on the doctrine of instincts. The same decade was marked by the spread of

Freudian ideas, with its strong emphasis on the sexual drive. But all was not well among instinct theorists.

## THE ASSAULT ON INSTINCT THEORY

In 1919, Knight Dunlap published the first of a series of critical articles. He felt that the basic tendency to develop a social psychology on the basis of instincts led to as many different social psychologies as there were classifications, and cited McDougall, Trotter, and Freud as examples. He also argued that grouping activities into "instincts" was useful as a matter of convenience, but it became dangerous once it began to suggest that the responses were biologically fixed, as with writers who postulated a "pugnacious instinct" and then inferred that war was inevitable.

Kuo (1921) went further and argued that each discipline tended to generate its own list of instincts. Social psychologists listed instincts that were socially significant, while economists and theologians discovered quite different ones. I uther L. Bernard (1924) collected 5684 terms from approximately 500 writers and showed that these could be grouped into 22 classes. Some terms, such as sex, self-assertion, and gregariousness, appeared more often than others, but even here there was wide disagreement.

The concept of instinct was so confused during this period that both McDougall (1908) and Bernard (1924) provided extensive summaries of its misuse before providing very different definitions of their own. It was not unusual to find writers talking about "the instinct to liberate Christian subjects," "the instinct to mummify corpses" or "the instinct for engaging the groceryman in conversation while a companion makes off with the bananas." Bernard (1924) defined instinct as "a specific response to a specific stimulus" (p. 126) and then went on to argue that behaviors of this type seldom occur in humans. He tried to show that many of McDougall's instincts were not universal but culturally acquired.

John Dewey (1922), who was an early advocate of instinct theory, also changed positions. He argued that it was difficult to identify instincts because the same behavior can have many different motives, and the same motive can be expressed in many different ways. Going to war, for example, can be motivated by hostility or may stem from such needs as curiosity, adventure, or companionship.

But instinct theorists countered with arguments of their own. Edward C. Tolman (1923) argued that valid criticisms of instinct theory rest on two objections—nonvariability and arbitrary grouping. He felt that animal studies refuted a purely reflex theory of instincts because nothing like a built-in reflex pattern existed anywhere in nature. Even such behaviors as nest building in birds do not occur in a precise and invariable form but show considerable variability due to interruption and learning. He argued, however, even if all behaviors were acquired or modified through stimulus-response association, this does not preclude the possiblity of instincts. Instincts are simply those associations that *must* be acquired or those that are acquired *more easily.*

Tolman felt that the large number and arbitrary grouping of instincts were due primarily to the excesses of sociologists and economists, and this did not prevent the possibility of a "truly psychological grouping." In a rhetorical article, "Can instincts be given up in psychology?" (1922), he concluded, "let us confess our own faith that *instincts cannot be given up in psychology,* but rather that they must be retained, and retained under some such conception as that of the driving adjustment" (p. 152).

And Tolman was right, at least in the short run. Even Dunlap, who had delivered the first blast against instinct theory, included in his book *Elements of Scientific Psychology* (1922) a list of nine "fundamental desires." These included ailment, excretion, rest, activity, shelter, conformity, dominance, parental protection, and sexual gratification. Floyd H. Allport (1924) also rejected the notion of inherited behavior in human beings, but was led to postulate "human proponent reflexes" such as starting and withdrawal, rejection, pugnacity, hunger, and sex. Emory Bogardus (1924) devoted seven chapters of his text to "human nature," while Charles Ellwood used the terms "native impulses" and "instinctive tendencies."

By the late 1930s, the issue of instincts was by no means resolved. Otto Klineberg (1940) devoted almost a third of his textbook to the question of human nature. He argued that instincts, or what he called "dependable motives," could be identified by using three criteria: (1) cross-species; (2) physiological; and (3) cross-cultural. Sex, maternal behavior, and self-preservation were both physiologically based and universal but were modified by social factors and might not even appear in individual cases. Aggression, flight, and self-assertion had physiological correlates, were widespread in both animals and humans, but were not universal and were often enhanced by cultural conditions such as scarcity and competition. Gregariousness had no known physiological correlates but was common in animals and universal in humans. Acquisitiveness was without physiological correlates, often served more fundamental drives among animals, and showed very wide cultural differences up to and including communal ownership.

Although instinct theory did not disappear as a result of criticism, it was severely shaken and never regained the central role that it had with McDougall. Despite assurances by its supporters (e.g., McDougall, 1908; Tolman, 1922, 1923) that instincts were tendencies and not rigidly built-in behavior, critics continued to argue against instinct theory because of its implied rigidity. To a great extent advocates and critics were talking at cross-purposes—one group defending a notion of instinctive *tendencies* subject to considerable cultural variation, and the other arguing that instinctive *reflexes* did not exist.

The attack on instinct theory seems to have occurred not just for scientific reasons, but because it implied for many people a fixed concept of human nature with little variability—two ideas in opposition to the American ideals of progress and individuality. As previously mentioned, McDougall

had unfortunately published a book in 1921 called *Is America Safe for Democracy?* which linked his thinking to the eugenics movement. However, this association is entirely unnecessary. Both eugenics and social-instinct theory do focus on biological factors, but it is easy to hold the position that human beings are biological creatures subject to the laws of natural selection and have acquired certain biological drives as a result of evolution, without postulating that drives or abilities vary from race to race. Indeed, the universality of traits and characteristics is often used as proof of their genetic base (e.g., Darwin, 1872; Klineberg, 1940). As Gould (1981) has pointed out in his book *The Mismeasure of Man,* "Hereditarianism becomes an instrument of assigning groups to inferiority only when combined with a belief in ranking and differential worth (p. 307)." In fact, what is astounding about McDougall's earlier book, *Introduction to Social Psychology,* is its almost total lack of racist comments given the racist climate of his time.

By linking social-instinct theory to the increasingly unpopular eugenics movement, McDougall virtually insured the demise of biological explanations for social behavior. McDougall (1930) later attributed the hostile reception he received in the United States largely to the publication of his book *Is America Safe for Democracy?,* but this was simply one of a series of strategic blunders. It was simply the tragedy of this brilliant man's career that he was constantly boarding the boat, so to speak, just as everyone else was abandoning ship. He introduced his notion of social instincts just before instinct theory came under attack. His book *The Group Mind* (1920) appeared just before Floyd Allport's (1924) devastating critique destroyed the concept for all practical purposes. And he spent his final years at Duke University carrying out work on Lamarckian genetics and psychic research. Jones (1987) has shown that the image of McDougall conveyed by *The New York Times* before 1906 and 1940 was significantly more negative and satirical than two other psychologists (Joseph Jastraw and Edward L. Thorndike) who were cited a similar number of times. By the 1960s, references to social instincts had all but disappeared from social psychology textbooks, suggesting a trend that has become all too familiar within American social psychology. If one cannot discredit a concept, one can at least ignore it, and in time it will disappear.

The most serious criticism of social-instinct theories, however, is that they cannot account for the diversity of human social behavior. The more sophisticated theories, such as McDougall's (1908), recongized that instincts provide the "spark" for social behavior but that these needs can be fulfilled in a number of different ways. Even such basic drives as eating and drinking undergo considerable cultural modification. If instincts can manifest themselves in many different ways, then one must be able to explain not just why they occur but why they take one particular form rather than another. An adequate explanation requires an understanding of the larger social context—and the search for this understanding led to a shift away from biological explanations to those based on sociology.

# 3

# Psychosociology

If William McDougall's (1908) textbook on social psychology is regarded as British, then it is relatively easy to defend the position that American social psychology developed as a subdiscipline of sociology. Indeed, during the first three decades of the twentieth century, sociology and social psychology were so closely associated that the two disciplines were almost identical. Eight of the eleven textbooks published between 1908 and 1928 were written by sociologists, and two others (Gualt, 1923; Dunlap, 1925) were written by psychologists from a perspective so similar as to be indistinguishable. The only exception was the text written by Floyd H. Allport (1924), which will be discussed in Chapter 5.

The reason that sociologists got off to a quicker start than psychologists is because there was already a substantial body of sociological literature on social-psychological topics by the time the first textbook was written. In fact, the first American textbook on social psychology, written by Edward Ross in 1908, was merely a summary and a synthesis of the existing literature. The authors that Ross cited were not aware that they were creating a new discipline. Writers such as Charles Horton Cooley, Emile Durkheim, and Gabriel Tarde simply discussed social-psychological topics within the context of more general sociological issues. By 1908, this literature had grown sufficiently large that Ross decided to bring it together in a text called *Social Psychology: An Outline and a Source Book.*

This is not to downplay the contribution of Ross. By synthesizing the literature, Ross virtually created the discipline of social psychology as a distinct subject area. The contrast between Ross's book and McDougall's is so striking that many people have noted that they have little in common except the title. While McDougall focused primarily on social instincts, Ross stressed social factors acquired through imitation and suggestion and drew heavily from French writers, such as Tarde and Le Bon, as well as contemporary American sociologists. The synthesis of French and American traditions and their juxtaposition to the British position based on evolutionary theory helped fuel the debate about the relative contribution of nature and nurture and shaped American social psychology for the next two decades.

Ross did not see social psychology as a distinct discipline. He defined it as "one narrow tract in the province of sociology" (Ross, 1908, p. vii). The author of the second American textbook on social psychology, Charles Ellwood (1917), shared this opinion and felt that "social psychology" was just another term for "psychological sociology" or what he called "psycho-sociology." While there was general agreement that sociology and social psychology belonged together, the common origin and overlapping content of the two areas makes it difficult to determine whether social psychology evolved as a branch of sociology or sociology might be better seen as a specialty within social psychology. Because of the strong association between sociology and social psychology at the turn of the century, it might be useful to begin with a brief discussion of the origin of sociology in America.

## THE INSTITUTIONALIZATION OF AMERICAN SOCIOLOGY

Although the work of Comte, Spencer, Sumner, and Ward provided a theoretical base for sociology in America, the actual development of sociology, especially academic sociology, was more a result of the peculiar circumstances of the post–Civil War period. Much of the inspiration for establishing academic sociology stemmed from the reform spirit associated with the social-science movement that began during Reconstruction in America. This movement was dominated by Protestant middle-class reformers who sought remedies for social problems brought on by a rapidly industrializing urban society. Academic sociology in America gradually advanced from a broad-based movement of social reform to a more narrowly defined discipline that gradually won acceptance at American universities.

In 1878, an assembly of Bible teachers formed the Chautauqua Library and Scientific Circle, which sought to educate its members on the social problems of the day. The circle was organized along the lines of a seminar or study group, which lasted four years and ended with a certificate. This was part of a larger assembly called the Chautauqua Movement. At a time when universities were closed to so-called radicals, Chautauqua provided a save haven for notable social critics. For a brief period, Chautauqua became a community of inquiry that brought together leading educators across America, including Charles Eliot, the president of Harvard University, Herbert Adams, the president of Johns Hopkins, and William Harper, the future president of the University of Chicago. In 1893, the Chautauqua Movement formed the American Institute of Christian Sociology, which had as its object "the application of the moral traditions and principles of Christianity to the social and economic difficul-

ties of the present time" (Obershall, 1972, p. 201).

The postwar period also brought an unprecedented growth in higher education. From 1870 to 1920, the college student population rose from 52,000 to almost 600,000, the number of faculty increased from 5,553 to 48,615, and the number of institutions doubled. This growth was accompanied by a demand for greater specialization and professionalization. The typical college teacher during the 1870s was a jack of all trades who taught everything from land surveying to moral philosophy. In order to establish more rigorous standards, American universities increasingly adopted the German model of graduate education, which stressed research and a doctoral dissertation within an area of specialization. The first graduate program was established at Johns Hopkins University in 1876 using the German model, and this was soon followed by other institutions throughout America.

The American Social Science Association was instrumental in promoting the social sciences during this period (Haskell, 1977). Founded after the Civil War along the lines of the British Association for the Advancement of Science, the American Social Science Association was a loose coalition of amateur social inquirers made up of academics, clergy, philanthropists, and social theorists. Although its members bore little resemblance to modern social scientists, the association helped develop modern sociology by sponsoring a number of more specialized scientific and reform organizations, such as the National Prison Association, the Civil Service Reform Association, and the National Conference of Charities and Corrections (later known as the National Conference of Social Work). The latter organization established a standing committee on the instruction of sociology in institutes of higher learning. Professionalization eventually transformed the broad movement for social reform into a number of discrete disciplines, including sociology, economics, and political science.

The alliance between sociology and social reform continued well into the twentieth century, although the emphasis shifted from

Christian reform to more secular forms of social reform characteristic of the progressive era. During this period, sociology was problem-oriented and lacked a central theoretical or methodological core. While this proved to be a major obstacle in the long run, in the short run, it gave sociology a broad appeal. Given the wide concern for social reform during the progressive period, more and more socially conscious individuals turned to sociology as a way of understanding and addressing the issues of the day.

The vast majority of early American academic sociologists received their training in economics. Seventy-one of the 115 founders of the American Sociological Society were also members of the American Economic Association, including all of the major figures at the turn of the century (Oberschall, 1972). But by 1891, sociology had progressed sufficiently as an independent discipline that the first chair in sociology was established at Columbia, and F. H. Giddings, a journalist, was recruited for the position. Giddings had no advanced degrees but was an active member of the American Economic Association and had taught sociology at Bryn Mawr. Under his direction (or perhaps in spite of it), Columbia became one of the two most important centers for sociology in America.

The real center for sociological research during this period, however, was to be the University of Chicago. Albion Small, a historian and promoter of sociology, had been brought to the University of Chicago in 1892 in order to set up a first-rate department of sociology. Small was a great entrepreneur for sociology, established the *American Journal of Sociology,* and surrounded himself with some of the best social thinkers of the time—W. I. Thomas, Robert Park, and George Herbert Mead. The *American Journal of Sociology* was a blend of scholarly papers, Chicago Ph.D. dissertations, and popular articles written for a progressive audience, and it helped establish the reputation of the University of Chicago as *the* center for sociological research. Unlike Small, Giddings surrounded himself with second-rate thinkers for the most part who were no threat to his authority, and his dog-

matism, prejudice, and conceit almost insured that Columbia's sociology department remained less advanced. Although Columbia established the first chair in sociology, the Chicago School dominated American sociology throughout the 1920s and 1930s (see Chapter 4).

The early association between sociology and social reform created a number of difficulties for those trying to establish sociology as an academic discipline. Academic supporters such as Albion Small had to walk a thin line. Small recognized the importance of maintaining Christian values but felt that an overly close association between sociology and social reform would weaken the new discipline's academic credibility. As Small (1905) noted, "Sociology made its entry into the competing universities without any intellectual or scientific program or content, in completely opportunistic fashion, in order to cater to students', reformers', philanthropists', and social workers' demand for vocational training before professional schools of social work were established" (p. 2). Sociologists began with the conviction that there was something to study, then set out to find it. If there was any single unifying theme among early sociologists, it was the conviction that sociology was a distinct discipline with a unique area of focus and a growing consensus that the proper basis for understanding human behavior was to be found not in the biological processes occurring within the individual but in the social institutions of contemporary culture.

## FRENCH SOCIAL THEORY

The lack of a strong theoretical base forced American sociologists to borrow from more established European theories. British evolutionary theory played a major role in early explanations of social behavior but gradually gave way to more sociologically oriented theories derived mainly from France. While there were some similarities between France and the United States due to the fact that each was undergoing a similar urban industrial transformation,

French social theory was unique for two reasons (Apfelbaum & McGuire, 1985).

First, France had gone through a series of social upheavals that were far more severe than those occurring in the United States. French social theory was in many ways a reaction to the social and political unrest that occurred between the French Revolution of 1789 and the Third Republic, established in 1870. Seven governments had come and gone during this period, including two republics, two empires, and three monarchies. These governments had produced fourteen separate constitutions. Many people still living at the turn of the century had seen the barricades go up in Paris, King Louis-Phillipe abdicate, and the Second Republic proclaimed. They had also seen this republic converted into the Second Empire and then swept into oblivion by the Paris Commune (Merton, 1960). The constant social unrest and the perceived decline of France as an international power convinced many that the French Revolution had robbed France of its superior members and had produced a series of evolutionary regressions. A number of writers, collectively known as the decadent movement, contrasted France at the turn of the century with the ancien régime and argued that France was a nation in the midst of political and moral decay (McGuire, 1987).

A second condition that was uniquely French was a long history of interest in and research on hypnosis. Tarde and Le Bon were part of a long French tradition which began with Franz Anton Mesmer (1734–1815). Mesmer was trained in Vienna but practiced in Paris. He postulated a theory of universal "animal magnetism," which pervaded the entire animal world but was unevenly distributed. Some individuals, such as himself, had unusually high concentrations and could therefore heal others who were deficient and prone to illness. This theory is partly responsible for the misconception that hypnosis involves some sort of mysterious power possessed by the hypnotist. Mesmer gained wealth and an extensive popular following from his séances with "animal magnetism" before being forced to stop his practice.

The first scientific study of hypnosis was carried out not in France but in England. James Braid (1843/1899) performed controlled experiments on hypnotic suggestion, noted that it corresponded with a restricted field of consciousness, and invented the term "hypnotism" to describe the process. But the concept of hypnosis returned to France, where it was adopted by both the Nancy school (Bernheim, 1844) and their opponents at the Salpêtrière Hospital in Paris (Charcot, 1878). Jean-Martin Charcot felt that the ability to be hypnotized was a sign of hysteria and was limited to a small group of individuals who were biologically predisposed, while Hippolyte Bernheim and his associates treated it as a phychological phenomenon and saw it as relatively universal. There is little evidence, however, that either Tarde or Le Bon made a clear distinction between the two competing schools, and they seemed to refer to aspects of each indiscriminately depending on their purpose. From Charcot, they had a direct link between suggestibility and psychopathology. From Bernheim, they were able to extend the notions of suggestibility and hypnosis to various forms of crowd behavior and view them as widespread and quite common. The concept of hypnosis simply served as a powerful metaphor that could be easily understood by the nonscientific community and used to discredit the various socialist and trade-union movements that were quite common in Paris at the time (Apfelbaum & McGuire, 1985).

Le Bon equated crowd behavior with individual behavior under the effects of hypnosis and felt that many actions that seem deliberate and conscious appear so only because their cause is unknown. He used the idea of unconscious suggestibility to explain crowd behavior, while Tarde based his theory of social behavior on the closely related concept of imitation, which he considered a form of social sleepwalking ("somnambulisme social"). The concept of hypnosis gave the notion of crowd psychology scientific respectability because of the tremendous amount of experimental and clinical work being conducted at the time. The immense importance of the social stimulus in shaping behavior through imitation and suggestion was made apparent by these authors, and it is commonly agreed that social psychology was founded on their ideas (Murphy & Murphy, 1931).

The three themes that dominated social psychology during its first decades were imitation, suggestion, and the more general concept of "group mind." Tarde and Le Bon covered the first two and were frequently cited by American authors at the turn of the century. France's leading sociologist, Emile Durkheim, was rarely cited but seems important because he developed one of the most sophisticated models for what became collectively known as the group-mind concept. Durkheim was also an adversary of Tarde, and their debate forced Tarde to take a more extreme individualistic position, which ultimately won acceptance in the United States. Tarde's individualism was more compatible with the general social climate in America, which stressed individual initiative and laissez-faire economics. While crowd psychology seems to focus on the behavior of groups, the use of hypnosis as a metaphor restricts it to processes occurring within the individual, and this contrasts sharply with the more collective perspective developed by Durkheim.

## Gustave Le Bon (1841–1931)

Le Bon was born in Nogent-le-Rotrou in Normandy and became a provincial physician who gave up medicine in order to popularize science. He continued a long tradition of amatuer scholars and pamphleteers, which included Mesmer and Saint-Simon. Le Bon's political conservatism alienated him from the more progressive thinkers of the period, and the universities remained closed to him, but he was successful enough to live from his writing and rub shoulders with the rich and famous.

Le Bon's book *The Crowd* is generally credited as being the first extensive treatise on crowd psychology. In fact, because it became so influential, Gordon Allport (1954a, 1968) claimed that it was perhaps the most important book ever written in social psychology. Le Bon included many of the topics that would later form the core of social

psychology. In this small book, which is less than two hundred pages in a recent paperback translation, Le Bon covers not only crowd behavior but conformity, the leveling of taste, popular culture, self-alienation, leadership, and the role of the unconscious in social behavior.

There are, however, questions about the originality of Le Bon's ideas. When the book first appeared in 1895, Scipio Sighele, and Italian lawyer and criminologist, accused Le Bon of plagiarism (van Ginneken, 1985). Sighele, who had published a book on crowd behavior in 1891, charged Le Bon with pirating large sections of his own work. Le Bon, without any acknowledgment, also seems to have borrowed many ideas from Tarde, as well as from another French physician, Herni Fournial, who also wrote on crowd behavior.

While Le Bon's credibility as an original thinker appears to be dubious, he can be justly recognized as playing a major role in creating interest in social psychology. *La Psychologie des Foules* went through 45 editions and was translated into 16 different languages. Le Bon's writing simultaneously fascinates and offends. By focusing on temporary groups (mobs), Le Bon was able to identify psychological principles that he considered characteristic of groups in general—loss of individuality, rigid conformity, and leadership. By dealing with so many issues, Le Bon was able to cover each to only a limited extent, but his impact was almost as strong on his critics as on those who supported his position. Sigmund Freud's most important work on social psychology, *Group Psychology and the Analysis of the Ego* (1921/1955), begins with a critique of Le Bon, who seems to have inspired Freud to extend his theory to explicitiy include collective behavior (see Chapter 6).

In general, the French and Italian treatises on crowd psychology during the 1890s reflected an increasing concern with the impact of mob events (van Ginneken, 1989). A century before, the French Revolution had dramatically demonstrated how political change could be sparked by mass protest. Throughout the nineteenth century there were episodic periods of social and political upheaval, and the 1890s were a time of particular anxiety over the threat of mob violence. Le Bon was just one of many writers who were reacting to events during this period, and their reading of events during and after the French Revolution. Before the 1890s, crowds were seen as historical aberrations of little importance, and their behavior was attributed to a kind of insanity.

Le Bon pointed out that individual and collective madness were different. The former involves insufficient incorporation of the individual within a group, whereas individuals are overincorporated in crowds. One of the central assumptions of Le Bon's work is that, when individuals gather, certain psychological processes not present in the individual emerge. There is a degeneration to a collective (or racial) unconscious, which according to Le Bon was especially volatile in Latin (as opposed to Anglo-Saxon) types. Particular individuals lose their identity and come to show a common character. No personal interest, not even self-preservation, can make itself felt.

Le Bon distinguished between remote and immediate causes for crowd behavior. Remote factors are common cultural conditions that prepare the way for immediate causes. Le Bon speculated, for example, that a general dissatisfaction with society was necessary before a group of individuals would attack a particular official who is seen as responsible for these conditions. A strong leader can mobilize a crowd, but only if they are prepared to accept his ideas in advance. When the structure of civilization is rotten, it is the masses who bring it down. In groups, foolish, ignorant, and envious individuals lose their sense of impotence. While crowds are capable of useful destructive acts, such as destroying a degenerate society, Le Bon believed that they were totally incapable of the intelligent behavior necessary for rebuilding a new one.

Le Bon had an equally pessimistic view of leadership. He felt that when people gathered, they instinctively placed themselves under the authority of a leader. Leaders were described as "morbidly nervous, excitable, half-deranged persons who are bordering on madness" (Le Bon, 1895/1977, p. 118). Leaders rise spontaneously within crowds and share their obsession. They are

men of action rather than thinkers, who use emotional appeal, repetition, and emotional contagion to move their audience. Leaders may occasionally be educated and intelligent, but Le Bon felt that these qualities did more harm than good, because they make leaders indecisive and blunt the intensity of their convictions.

Le Bon distinguished leadership based on charisma and prestige. In stable societies, rank, title, and other signs of prestige are used to give leaders formal authority. Charismatic leaders emerge during unstable times when people gather in crowds. Although each leader and situation is unique, they share certain characteristics. Charismatic leaders tend to be physically imposing, have a precise and commanding way of speaking, make decisions without hesitation, and have a gift for phrases and theatrical settings. Once in a position of power, they maintain their distance and surround themselves with a cloak of mystery. This mystery causes followers to place them on a pedestal and exaggerate their strength.

Although charismatic leaders are catapulted to power during unstable times, they are at a comparative disadvantage because they have little to fall back on when their charisma fails. Their ultimate success depends on their ability to charm crowds. For these reasons, charismatic leaders often adopt symbols of formal authority when they come to power. They have themselves crowned or promoted to important military positions. Le Bon's charismatic leader is not the same and is in many ways the exact opposite of Machiavelli's prince. Unlike the cold, dispassionate manipulator, charismatic leaders sincerely believe what they say and are often victims of fixed ideas.

Individuals in crowds are often indifferent to contradictions and may hold several conflicting ideas at the same time. This makes them susceptible to rapid changes in policy—believing the exact opposite of what they seemed to believe the previous day. To capture their imagination, half-measures are useless. What is needed is exaggerated arguments and spectacular examples. Crowds often swing from pole to pole without touching intermediate positions. This makes charismatic leaders vulnerable. The same people who idealize them one moment may turn on them when the climate changes (see Moscovici, 1981/1985, for a more detailed discussion).

A speculative work of this scope typically contains both insight and errors, and this is certainly true with Le Bon. *The Crowd* is racist, sexist, and thoroughly conservative in tone. Racism and sexism were widespread at the turn of the century, but Le Bon's work stands out even in this particular climate. Women and primitive individuals were treated as "inferior forms of evolution." His central assumption, as Freud (1921/1955) pointed out, is based on the dubious notion that each race possesses memories and modes of thought acquired during the course of evolution.

A further problem with LeBon's work is the questionable assumption that mob behavior is characteristic of group behavior in general. The heightened suggestibility, rigid conformity, and irrationality characteristic of mobs is due to intense emotional arousal and does not appear common among groups gathered for more benign reasons. Le Bon suggested that *all* individuals, no matter how intelligent, would degenerate to a common level of behavior in crowds, but studies of lynch mobs in the United States found that active participants were drawn from the lowest elements of society (Miller & Dollard, 1941).

It is somewhat ironic that, although the central assumption behind Le Bon's work is false, many of the processes explained by it do occur. Emotional contagion, feelings of invincibility, emotional vacillation, anonymity, and loss of personal responsibility are aspects of crowd behavior that have been well documtented and repeatedly confirmed in experimental studies of small groups. Le Bon wanted to go beyond the visible facts in order to probe the hidden causes behind behavior, but he was most accurate in his description of overt behavior and almost completely wrong in his speculations about unconscious processes. Perhaps his greatest contribution was the simple suggestion that there *were* explanations below the surface.

It is easy to look back and find faults in Le Bon's work, but what is remarkable is the number of insights. His identification of feelings of invincibility, anonymity, and oversimplified thinking seems a remarkable precursor of Irving Janis's (1968) work on "group think." His isolation of heightened emotionality and diminished intellectual capacity helped inspire work on social facilitation and inhibition, while his assessment of leaders in mob situations seems as true today as ever.

## Gabriel Tarde (1843–1904)

While Le Bon was a marginal social theorist and a popularizer of ideas, Tarde was a much more systematic thinker who had a far greater impact on American social psychology. Tarde was the chief statistician for the Ministry of Justice and a professor of modern philosophy at the Collège de France. He was chosen for the latter post by a vote of 18 to 7 over Henri Bergson, one of the most celebrated philosophers of the day. Tarde's many years in court convinced him that criminal behavior was based more on social factors than on native endowment. The criminal was usually a person brought up among criminals, while the noncriminal was raised in a more favorable environment.

Tarde was a strong supporter of statistical procedures and an early advocate of attitude measurement. He used frequency counts to show how ideas spread within populations and postulated fundamental laws of imitation. Tarde wrote numerous books on criminology, philosophy, archeology, history, and literature, but his contribution to social psychology was based primarily on his concepts of imitation and invention. Tarde had originally intended to write a single book with two parts, *Social Psychology and Social Logic,* dealing with both ideas, but he was forced by his publisher to release them separately because their length and potential cost were becoming prohibitive for a single volume. *Les Lois de L'imitation (The Laws of Imitation)* was published in 1890 and was an instant success.[1] The second volume, dealing with invention, *La Logique Sociale,* appeared in 1895 but sold only 2500 copies and was never translated, although it was read and cited by American social thinkers at the time. According to Tarde, all social behavior is based on either imitation or invention. Invention is much rarer and occurs as a result of previous imitation. Inventions are then passed on through imitation according to general laws.

Tarde extended Le Bon's ideas to people not in face-to-face contact—publics—and formulated a number of laws to show how ideas spread within the general population. Imitation begins with internal states, such as beliefs and desires within individuals. Groups develop common attitudes and feelings before they express them publicly. Literature, fine art, customs, religion, and even language itself merely reflect changes that have already taken place within individuals. These outward displays give individuals confidence that their private feelings are widely shared and help establish new traditions that are transmitted from generation to generation. As further change occurs, formal modes of expression can become mere rituals, devoid of meaning.

Tarde also felt that imitation is based on prestige. Trends are initiated by people with status and copied by those who are socially inferior. Tarde regarded this as a general tendency rather than an absolute law. Socially inferior groups may be copied if they possess useful behaviors. The Egyptians, for example, adopted the Asians' use of horses even though their own culture was more advanced. But the tendency to adopt behaviors of superior groups is so pervasive that it occurs even when it is counterproductive. The Japanese, for example, possessed the rudiments of syllabic writing before contact with the more socially advanced Chinese but adopted the more cumbersome Chinese style of writing despite its many disadvantages. The basis of superiority varies. In primitive societies, strength and courage played a major role. Inherited status became more important as societies progressed. Wealth was a major source of prestige at the time that Tarde wrote, but Tarde, like many of the thinkers of this period, envisioned a time when status might be based on intelligence and education. He felt that

in certain areas, such as science and industry, ideas spread because they are true or useful but in other areas prestige was a major factor.

Imitation also proceeds according to the law of geometric progression. The spread of ideas within a population usually starts slowly, builds rapidly, and then levels off. Tarde used statistical data to show these changes over time and predicted that these could be used to plot a growth rate for fashions, fads, and rumors. With time, ideas that were once new and original become widely accepted or even commonplace, but they can also lose some of their original meaning.

Finally, ideas can combine or compete like waves. Two similar ideas can join like two waves flowing in the same direction and increase their strength. Two dissimilar ideas clash like competing waves. Tarde felt that a clash of ideas tends to occur between *two* opposing camps for the same reason that battles involve two opposing armies. Each side gathers allies during the height of tension and attempts to reconcile differences after the tension is over. Intellectual movements progress by replacing the opposition. Or one side may displace another and then reinterpret its findings within a new theoretical perspective.

For Tarde, social change occurs only through imitation and invention, but he did not regard either as a particularly rational form of social behavior. Imitation was seen as a kind of hypnotic sleepwalking in which individuals act out the behaviors of previous models with little attention or forethought. Invention is an individual act based on combining two or more ideas previously acquired through imitation. Tarde's description of inventors was similar to Le Bon's account of charismatic leaders—"the inventor and initiator is, given his strangeness and monomania, his solitary and unshakeable faith in himself and his ideas, of whatever kind he may be, a kind of madman" (Tarde, 1985, cited in Moscovici, 1981/1985, p. 174).

As society progresses, conversation and crowd behavior give way to one-way communication. Instead of meeting and discussing issues, isolated individuals now receive the same message through the mass media. Opinions generated through group discussion are associated with specific people and places, but in mass society opinions become anonymous and take on a life of their own. Power becomes concentrated in the hands of fewer and fewer individuals who control the means of communication and can reach millions of people at the same time. Charisma gives way to acting ability. The rhythm of life was quite simple for Tarde. First there are individual inventions, followed by wave after wave of imitation (again see Moscovici, 1981/1985, for a more detailed discussion).

## Emile Durkheim (1858–1917)

Durkheim is often regarded as one of the principal founders of modern sociology, since he not only advocated but actually used empirical procedures to study social behavior. Durkheim's sociology rests on his four major books: *The Division of Labor in Society* (1893/1964), *The Rules of Sociological Method* (1895/1964), *Suicide* (1897/1964) and *Elementary Forms of Religious Life* (1912/1965). Although these works seem to deal with different topics, there are a number of underlying themes that run through all of them. Central to each of these is the general concept of *conscience collective*. This can be translated as either "collective conscience" or "collective consciousness," and, in fact, the concept of *conscience collective* takes on both connotations because it is both a set of obligations (conscience) and the basis for experience (consciousness) (see Giddens, 1971).

Underlying Durkheim's idea of the *conscience collective* is the notion that social phenomena, such as religion, customs, and fashions, are "social facts"—that is, things with objective characteristics that exist outside the individual. Social facts have three characteristics: they are external, general, and constrain behavior. Social facts are not subjective in the sense of being purely private but are cultural objects. They exist outside the presocial individual and are expe-

rienced by group members in more or less the same way. They provide guidelines or the actual means by which social behavior takes place.

The best example of a social fact is probably language. When a child is born, the language that it will ultimately speak is already being used, and the language will continue to exist long after the person is dead. Language is, on the one hand, a set of rules and vocabulary acquired in an imperfect form by each individual, but it is also a general system of rules and vocabulary that can be analyzed and described by linguists. The same is true for a religion. Church members adopt beliefs and practices that were in existence long before they were born, and they are free to modify these beliefs only to a limited extent. Although social facts constrain behavior by setting limits for what is appropriate and inappropriate, conformity rarely rests on force. We speak to our friends in a language they understand, we pay our bill when leaving a restaurant, and we drive on the right side of the road because we have come to accept these norms without question.

One of the most important social facts is the division of labor in modern society. This division hardly existed in primitive societies, where group members do more or less the same thing. A seemingly peculiar consequence is that, while people within a primitive society are more similar, they are mutually interchangeable and, therefore, less dependent on each other. As societies become more complex, there is a necessary division of labor as people begin to specialize in particular occupations. Since people derive their self-concept in part through their occupation, separate individuals and the concept of individuality begin to develop. Individuals in a modern society are mutually dependent and need each other in a way that primitive people did not. Durkheim's treatment of the division of labor in modern society is discussed more fully in Chapter 8.

Durkheim applied his concept of social facts in his study *Suicide* (1897). By systematically ignoring psychological explanations, he was able to show how the highly individual act of suicide varied with social conditions. He returned to the study of primitive culture in his last book, *Elementary Forms of Religious Experience* (1912), where he argued that the sacredness of religious objects lies not in the objects themselves but in their meaning as symbols for a particular group. Animals, birds, and other objects come to represent characteristics of the group in general. This kind of totemism is not entirely absent in modern societies. The American eagle, Russian bear, and Canadian beaver epitomize for each nation certain aspects of their respective cultures (and it is fortunate for Americans that Benjamin Franklin was unsuccessful in his efforts to make the turkey the national symbol).

The objective character of social facts makes the systematic study of society (that is, sociology) possible but it has psychological implications as well. Society exists prior to each individual and helps to mold his or her character. For Durkheim, individuals are "carriers" of society, in the sense that they internalize existing social customs and norms. Our modern concept of society as made up of separate individuals, each pursuing his or her own narrow self-interest, is itself a social product and a relatively recent one at that. The fact that we share this vision with others in our society is due to our common upbringing. The important step that Durkheim took was to recognize that the *conscience collective,* because it was a social product, varied with different cultures and could change.

There is nothing inconsistent or contradictory in Le Bon's notion of "emotional contagion," Tarde's "imitation" or Durkheim's *conscience collective.* In fact, one could argue that they mutually complement one another and provide a more balanced picture of social influence in different social contexts. Durkheim, however, went well beyond the simple ideas of imitation and suggestion in his treatment of the division of labor in industrialized societies. Imitation and suggestion imply conformity, whereby individuals become more and more alike, whereas a division of labor leads to increased specialization and individual differences.

Tarde and Durkheim represent two extremes in social psychology, and there was a running debate between them at the turn of the century. Durkheim started from humble origins and rose to the pinnacle of academic success—a chair at the Sorbonne. Tarde had taken the equally prestigious chair in modern philosophy away from France's leading philosopher, Henri Bergson, and gave gripping public lectures at the institution across the street—the Collège de France. The Collège de France had been set up in 1530 by François I in order to create an alternative to the overly scholastic and intolerant attitude of the Sorbonne, and the two institutions remained rivals up to the 1960s, when the entire university system in France was restructured.

But the conflict between Tarde and Durkheim was more than a clash of personalities or institutional rivalry. It was a struggle for the heart and soul of French social theory. Durkheim was widely seen as France's leading sociologist, whereas Tarde was more widely regarded as a criminologist, statistician, and philosopher. Durkheim preached an extreme collectivism, whereas Tarde reduced social processes to actions occurring within individuals. Lubek (1981) has pointed out that this contest represented a paradigm clash, but in this clash the two contestants were very unevenly matched.

Durkheim was not only widely regarded as France's leading social theorist; he was also editor of the leading sociological journal, *L'Année Sociologique,* which was the first journal devoted to sociology and served as an organ for the spread of his ideas. He had many gifted students and supporters who continued his tradition, and his ideas were more in tune with the cooperative/collectivist spirit in France at the time. Tarde, on the other hand, was a marginal figure, despite his reputation. His chair at the Collège de France did not provide graduate students who could promote his work. His sons established a journal, *La Revue de Psychologie Sociale,* to continue his ideas after his death, but it lasted only one year (1907–1908). The debate with Durkheim forced him to take a more extreme individualistic position, and this, along with the fact that Tarde was moderately religious, branded his approach as elitist and out of step with the social changes occurring in France at the time. What appeared to be a potentially fruitful collaboration with France's leading psychologist, Alfred Binet, was cut short by Tarde's death in 1904.[2] Ironically, the ideological difference that favored Durkheim in France made Tarde more acceptable in the United States.

## THE AMERICANIZATION OF FRENCH SOCIAL THEORY

French social theory helped fill a void in American social thinking at a time when original theory was noticeably absent. Given the similarity of conditions, it is not surprising that American sociologists drew heavily from French social theory. Tarde's *Les Lois de L'imitation* (1893) was translated into English a year after its publication, with a preface by James Mark Baldwin. A translation of *Les Lois Sociales* (1893) appeared in 1903, with an introduction by F. H. Giddings. Le Bon's *Psychologie des Foules* (1895) was also translated almost immediately into English under the title *The Crowd* (1899). While French social theory helped Americans understand changes occurring in their own society, conditions were significantly different that French ideas were considerably modified when brought to America (see Paicheler, 1988).

In France, urban industrialization was based on a movement of French people from rural to urban areas. Imitation and invention were used to describe general forms of social behavior that applied to everyone. Invention was a more sophisticated process but was not significantly different. Similarly, Le Bon's description of crowd behavior assumed that it applied to all individuals no matter how sophisticated or intelligent. Individuals in crowds simply degenerated to a low level of social behavior where they were irresponsible, suggestible, and incapable of rational thought.

Urban industrialization in America was accompanied by a massive flow of immigrants from southern and eastern Europe, whose customs and traditions were noticeably different form those already in America. The concepts of imitation and invention were extended to account for different types of people. The vast majority of people were seen as being socialized through simple imitation, whereas invention was reserved for a small minority of gifted individuals whose intelligence and education allowed them to strike out in new and different directions. Invention was seen as the key to social progress but one limited to an intellectual elite.

While the French favored collective solutions to social problems, Americans continued to stress individual initiative. This was true not only for conservative thinkers but for progressive thinkers as well. Progress was attributed to the individual effort of certain gifted people who recognized the need and strived for social change. Thus, paradoxically, many social thinkers who advocated social reform simultaneously held the position that the vast majority of people were incapable of critical thought. This form of elitism was not based exclusively on a belief in differences in native endowment. It represented a belief that, while the majority of people simply accepted attitudes and opinions already prevalent in society, progress *could* occur through education (Purcell, 1973). The three men most responsible for importing French ideas to America were James Mark Baldwin, F. H. Giddings, and Edward Ross. Ross and Giddings were both sociologists and will be discussed here, whereas Baldwin, who was a psychologist, will be considered in the next chapter. Each differed in his treatment of French social theory, but each shared the assumption that imitation and invention were the bases for social behavior.

### Edward Ross (1866–1951)

Edward Ross was raised in the Midwest and sought to retain the traditional values of individualism and public morality while encouraging social progress at the same time. He felt that the virtues of the past could survive if supernatural religions were abandoned and rational solutions to social problems were applied in a sophisticated manner. Ross received a Ph.D. in economics from Johns Hopkins University and was a protégé of Lester Ward, whom he regarded as a father figure. He later became a member of the Ward family by marrying Ward's niece. He taught briefly at Stanford University, but his populist-progressive views drew opposition from California conservatives. Mrs. Leland Stanford, wife of the founder of Stanford University, repeatedly asked the president of the university for Ross's resignation, and in 1900 the president complied. His dismissal became a cause célèbre among academics at the time, and Ross gained considerable notoriety by his firm stand. He had no difficulty obtaining a new position at the University of Nebraska, and in 1906 moved to the University of Wisconsin, where he became chair of the department and remained until his retirement. At the time, Wisconsin was the most progressive state in the nation and a center for populist-progressive ideas.

Ross wrote the first American textbook on social psychology in 1908, but this work drew heavily from a previous work, *Social Control* (1901), which had been published serially in the *American Journal of Sociology* between 1896 and 1899. Ross (1908) defined "social psychology" as "one narrow tract in the province of sociology" (p. vii). It included two main subdivisions: social ascendancy, the dominance of society over the individual through fashions, fads, customs, and conventions, and individual ascendancy, which was based on leadership, invention, and the role of great men. Ross felt that no two individuals had the same genetic endowment. Because of this, one would expect to find a great deal of diversity among people. But the shaping of individuals through imitation and suggestion triumphs over hereditary differences, producing individuals who were more or less alike. Ross substituted the term "mob mind" for "group mind" in order to stress its negative connotation. He speculated about social conditions that would produce "rugged individualism" and prevent social ascendancy. These included a superior education, knowledge of the classics, physical

fitness, avoidance of sensational press, country living, and a united family.

It is not hard to recognize the influence of Tarde on Ross. Ross quotes Tarde extensively and openly acknowledged his debt to him. Ross's distinction between social and individual ascendancy is an almost perfect parallel of Tarde's distinction between imitation and invention. But in Ross's hand the distinction became a trait difference— the molding of the ordinary person by his or her social environment and the molding of the social environment by the extraordinary individual. Ross also used Tarde's distinction between custom and convention. Customs are made up of ideas and values borrowed from previous times, whereas conventions are derived from contemporaries through imitation. Imitation can be based on reason, fashion, or prestige. Rational imitation considers the merits and utility of a particular behavior rather than its source. Ross felt that social progress occurs when outdated customs are replaced by conventions more appropriate for a particular age.

Ross was a persistent social reformer and used the sale of his books to finance his travels to trouble spots around the world. He went to China in 1910, South America in 1913–1914, Russia during the revoluation, Mexico in 1922 and 1928, Angola and Mozambique in 1924, and to India, Indonesia, and the South Pacific. He interviewed Trotsky in 1917 and was caught up in the fighting while traveling through Siberia. As a result of his contact with other cultures, he eventually softened his views about the natural superiority of Anglo-Saxons and began to stress the importance of social factors in accounting for racial differences (Ross, 1936).

### F. H. Giddings (1855–1931)

As mentioned previously, F. H. Giddings was given the first chair in sociology in America when a position was established at Columbia University in 1891. Giddings was familiar with Tarde's work, corresponded with him, and defended his ideas, but it would be misleading to call Giddings a follower of Tarde. Giddings was a great synthesizer rather than an original thinker, and he drew openly from a wide range of European and American sources. By bringing together such diverse sources as Aristotle, Adam Smith, Comte, Spencer, and Galton, he helped to differentiate sociology as an academic discipline. He also drew heavily from psychological sources such as Wilhelm Wundt, Edward Bradford Titchener, and William James, which gave his sociology a distinct psychological character. He used the ideas of others as building blocks for his own unique version of sociology, and among these Tarde's concepts of imitation and invention played a fundamental role.

Giddings' most important contribution to sociology was his concept of *consciousness of kind.* This was a like-mindedness brought on through imitation and exposure to a common culture. Human groups differed from animals in that they saw themselves as belonging together, sharing common attitudes and values, and differing from other groups in their beliefs and ideas. For Giddings, a society was a group of like-minded individuals who knew and enjoyed their common perspective and were, therefore, able to work together toward common goals. Giddings felt that a psychology that focused exclusively on the individual was entirely inadequate for understanding the individual mind. Individualistic psychologies took consciousness for granted, ignored its social origins, and could not account for the varieties of conscious experiences that occurred among different groups. For Giddings, consciousness and even self-awareness developed gradually through a process of socialization.

Giddings differentiated three types of social activity that played a part in socialization—impulsive, traditional, and rational activity. *Impulsive social behavior* was based on spontaneous emotional contagion and was characteristic of crowds, mobs, and individuals in panic situations. It also included ideas and beliefs acquired through unconscious suggestion. These were blind responses not guided by deliberation and reason. *Traditional social behavior* was also based on imitation but occurred through accepting traditional values rather than

emotional contagion. Giddings believed that most of society's ideals and values were perpetuated through uncritical imitation. Like Karl Marx, he felt that ideas developed through practical activity and the most fundamental were those based on economic activity.

*Rational social behavior,* like Tarde's concept of "invention," was much more rare. Rational social behavior was based on critical reflection and knowledge and occurred only when a previously accepted belief was questioned. People doubt the accuracy of a previous belief, look for new information, and come to some deliberate decision. Giddings felt that social progress occurred because previous beliefs were reexamined from time to time and that communication and free expression of ideas were essential. He also believed that some people were more gifted at this process than others and supported an elitist position based on social class. For Giddings, social class reflected not merely a division of wealth but a division of talent. He believed that the dominant social class did most of the original thinking, and therefore provided the leading edge for social change.

Consciousness of kind is responsible not only for similarities but differences among people as well. Giddings felt that racial and ethnic groups could be ranked on a scale of creative genius, with blond-haired Aryans at the top. He also believed that there were instincts for conquest and aggression that led to conflict whenever civilized nations met savage ones or young and growing nations met old ones in a state of decay. He was anti-Semitic, anti-German, and anti-bolshevik and gave long diatribes against his pet hates during his lectures at Columbia (Oberschall, 1972).

Giddings' greatest contribution to social psychology was his attempt to reconcile the apparent inconsistency between the individual and society. The social mind had no metaphysical reality as something hovering above individuals. It was simply "a like-responsiveness of like minds to the same stimulus" (Giddings, 1898, p. 353). It was acquired through imitation by members within the same group or culture. For Giddings there was no inconsistency between

Durkheim's "social facts" and Tarde's focus on the individual. Individuals internalized social facts through imitation.

Giddings helped bring together a wide range of literature that became the subject matter for sociology, wrote introductory texts, and provided a critical summation of previous ideas. But he also helped perpetrate a sociological point of view that was racist, anti-Semitic, and elitist, treating class differences as differences in native endowment. His conservative philosophy repeatedly brought him into conflict with those advocating progressive reform. Although Giddings stressed scientific and quantitative procedures, he did not carry out a single study of any significance. His lack of students weakened his influence, and Giddings like many others during this period quickly faded into oblivion.

### Other Textbook Authors

The influence of Giddings and Ross on social psychology was based largely on their ability to reinterpret and synthesize Tarde's views within an American context. Ross and McDougall, whose book appeared the same year, helped popularize social psychology as a distinct area of study. Ross was the most frequently cited author among sociological textbook writers throughout the first two decades, and most social psychology textbooks published during this period incorporated substantial aspects of his work. The most important sociological textbooks after Ross were probably those of Ellwood (1917, 1925), Bogardus (1924), and Bernard (1926). Each of these authors drew from the work on imitation but added additional elements of his own. In a way, their books rest on each other and provide a progressively more sophisticated version of social psychology.

Charles Ellwood (1873–1946) met Ross while he was a visiting lecturer at Cornell and decided to switch from the study of law to sociology and economics. He studied under W. I. Thomas, John Dewey, and George Herbert Mead at the University of Chicago. His first and probably most important work was *Sociology in its Psycho-*

*logical Aspects* (1912), from which he derived his two subsequent social psychology textbooks. *Introduction to Social Psychology* (1917) was merely a revised and simplified version of his original work.

The central theme in both these books was that sociology is a synthetic discipline that derives higher-order generalizations from more basic sciences, such as biology and psychology. Ellwood felt that there was no reason for sociologists to discover facts independently if they had already been uncovered by other disciplines. "The chief and most fruitful method in modern sociology has been to take truths discovered in other sciences and carry them over and apply them to explanations of social life" (Ellwood, 1917, p. 12). These books were not meant as a comprehensive review of sociological theory but focused only on those topics that rested immediately on psychology.

Ellwood (1917) recognized the role of instincts in social behavior but concluded that learning plays a far greater role. Instincts are modified through learning and there are numerous differences across cultures. The family is the primary socializer, and socialization occurs primarily through imitation. Ellwood thought that the intellect could function either as a master or a slave of the instincts. Ellwood also rejected models that portrayed people as passive, hedonistic, or egotistical. People are drawn together in groups, and these groups can function as individuals. They can make plans and work collectively toward common goals. There is also a form of "group egotism," which makes a group self-centered and insensitive to the needs of other groups.

Ellwood later came to regard this psychological approach as inadequate because it did not recognize the influence of culture and tradition in shaping mental development. His later work, *Psychology of Human Society* (1925), attempted to address this deficiency by covering a much wider range of subjects. It begins with a discussion of instincts, emotions, and intellect and then introduces sociological topics, such as social unity, continuity, and change. Fay Karpf (1932) pointed out that the scope of this book was both a strength and a weakness.

Ellwood's treatment was broad, comprehensive, and dealt with social issues from a variety of different perspectives, but his coverage of individual issues was both simplistic and superficial.

Emory Bogardus (1882–1973), like Ellwood, received his Ph.D. from the University of Chicago. His first textbook, *Introduction to Social Psychology* (1918) is quite short, with only one hundred pages of actual text, but his later book, *Fundamentals of Social Psychology* (1925) is far more comprehensive. Bogardus began from a position similar to Ellwood, holding that social behavior is based on more basic biological and psychological principles, but his book is even broader in scope than Ellwood's because it includes additional material on personality. In fact, Bogardus (1925) defines social psychology as the "the study of personalities in groups" (p. 13). He saw personality as developing through social interaction, according to laws of accommodation and assimilation.

Luther L. Bernard (1881–1951) was a student of Ellwood at the University of Missouri and received his Ph.D. from the University of Chicago in 1910. His work *Instinct* (1924) was based on 15 years of research and established his reputation as a careful and meticulous scholar. His social psychology text was published two years later and is by far the most comprehensive textbook published during this period (652 pages in all). It begins with a discussion of the psychological foundations of social behavior (i.e., biology, instincts, and learning theory), moves on to a treatment of personality, and ends with a discusison of collective behavior. Bernard regarded all previous texts as partial treatments and sought to remedy the situation by bringing together research on instinct theory, psychology, and sociology. For him, social psychology rested on *both* psychology and sociology, and he attempted to cover each. He was far more critical of instinct theory than any of the previous authors, and his chapter on the misuse of the concept of instincts (Chapter 9) is one of the best in his book.

The scope of his book is probably responsible for its popularity during the 1930s, but it is also an indication of a discipline reaching the point of saturation. As social psychology evolved, it seems almost inevitable in retrospect that some of its particular topics, such as social development and personality, would become disciplines of their own. Bernard's text is an early indication of this trend. The study of social development and personality continued to be important areas of research and theory throughout the 1930s and early 1940s, but even by the late 1920s social psychology was already bulging at the seams, and a separate treatment of these areas was simply a matter of time.

## THE LEGACY OF THE FRENCH CONNECTION

The phrase "French social theory" should not be taken to represent a unified field of knowledge. The common thread that linked Durkheim, Tarde, and, to a lesser extent, Le Bon was a shift in emphasis from biological to social explanations for behavior. French social theory offered an alternative to the British tradition based on evolution, genetics, and social instincts. Within this broad framework, however, there were considerable differences among individual writers. Tarde focused on individual psychological factors and general trends within the population leading to uniformity of beliefs and attitudes through socialization. Durkheim emphasized a division of labor within modern industrial societies and stressed specialization, individual differences, and mutual cooperation. R. E. L. Faris (1967) has argued that Ross was aware of these differences and deliberately neglected Durkheim through "a sort of doctrinaire blindness" (p. 8). It seems more likely, however, that Tarde's doctrine was simply more in keeping with the American emphasis on personal responsibility as the basis for social change. Tarde was more influential among other American social thinkers as well, and they each showed a corresponding neglect of Durkheim.

In any case, the Americanization of French social theory involved a radical transformation of its content—a transfor-

mation involving the occasional reintro-
duction of genetic factors into what was
otherwise a pure social theory. Imitation
and suggestion were treated as unconscious,
irrational processes by the French, but they
were used to explain the socialization of the
unthinking masses in the United States.
Most individuals were considered more or
less passive recipients of ideas, whereas critical thinking was reserved for a small minority of intellectual elite. Membership in
the elite was based on a combination of education and genetic endowment.

Although Giddings and Ross drew heavily on French social theory, each placed his
own stamp on it and deserves to be regarded
as an innovator rather than an imitator.
They, together with Charles Horton Cooley
(1864–1929), who will be discussed in the
next chapter, have the dual distinction of
being America's first generation of sociologists *and* social psychologists. Each focused
primarily on the interaction between individuals and society and regarded the self as
a social product. Cooley's "looking-glass
self," Giddings' "consciousness of kind"
and Ross's application of imitation to social
behavior were all attempts to explain the social origins of individual self-awareness.

As part of the same generation, each witnessed the urban-industrial transformation
and arrived at a common social-psychological perspective. They were acutely aware
that America was undergoing a radical
change as it moved from a small-town rural
society to a much more complex urban industrial society. The prospects of social
change were in many ways unsettling, because it meant a loss of the close-knit relationships and values associated with small
communities. But urbanization also
brought previously separate groups closer
together, loosened the ties of old dogmas
and customs, and increased personal autonomy. Each of these writers shared an ambivalence toward modernization and attempted to carry over old-world values to
the new urban environments (see Quandt,
1973).

Part of this ambivalence was based on a
distrust of the urban population. Social
problems were attributed, at least in part, to
a lack of understanding. While technology

had advanced at a rapid pace, a comprehension of technological change had not kept
pace. Industrialization had created a temporary vacuum that fostered isolation, conspicuous consumption, and greed. Since
problems stemmed from a lack of understanding, education was offered as the solution, but few felt that education would
transform the thinking of the majority of
people in America. The only hope for the
future was the small minority of intellectual
elite who could transcend the shackles of
traditional society and offer creative solutions for social change.

The conflict between old and new values
heightened the awareness of the positive aspects of small communities. Each writer incorporated his own idealized version of the
small town into his sociological descriptions
of modern society, and in so doing, he
sought to construct America's future society
with materials from the past. Unlike their
European counterparts, who traced the beginning of modern society to the primitive
tribe, America's first generation of social
thinkers contrasted urban and rural communities and their descriptions contained
all the idealized virtues of small-town life,
including individualism, self-reliance, and
the face-to-face intimacy of small primary
groups.

This focus on individual understanding
and primary groups led to a corresponding
neglect of larger social and economic institutions. While European thinkers, such as
Durkheim and Marx, stressed the primacy
of these institutions, the first generation of
American sociologists focused primarily on
individuals and small groups. This gave a
distinctly psychological tint to their sociological theories and makes it difficult to
draw a clear distinction between sociology
and social psychology. The systematic study
of social institutions in modern society was
left to a second generation of sociologists,
which centered around W. I. Thomas and
Robert Park at the University of Chicago
(see Chapter 4).

One of the most striking aspects of this
approach in retrospect is the problem of
conceptual clarity. Concepts like imitation,
suggestion, and group mind were used in a
very general sense to describe all types of so-

cial influence. Tarde used the concept of imitation to cover both the incorporation of ideas within an individual and the spread of ideas within the population. Discussions of fashions, fads, and rumors were quite common in social psychology texts written during this period and reflect the tendency to move back and forth from the individual to the group level. From a sociological perspective, the difference is not important, because individuals merely incorporate ideas already existing within the group. But there was also considerable discussion about *how* individuals developed attitudes and on this point there was some disagreement. Some, such as Tarde, treated imitation as a form of mindless activity, whereas others, such as Ross, differentiated rational imitation from imitation based on fashion and prestige. It is quite clear in retrosepct that the concept of imitation was being used very broadly to cover a number of distinct psychological and sociological processes.

The concept of suggestion was equally ambiguous. It was derived from the discovery of hypnotic suggestion that was being extensively researched in France. The concept was used to describe both the actor who calls up an idea and the recipient who is the target of the message. Ross defined suggestion very broadly to include all immediate external stimulation. Stimuli from within were impulses, whereas those from without were suggestions. He treated suggestion and imitation as cause and effect. Ideas and images were taken in through suggestion and later acted out. This distinction parallels the distinction between learning and performance made by Bandura (1971) in his social-learning theory.

Ross also discussed the concept of suggestibility and contrasted it with "will power"—the capacity to withstand, ignore, or throw off suggestions. He believed that suggestibility varies with the prestige of the speaker, the number of times the message is repeated, the size of the reference group, and characteristics of the recipient, such as age, sex, race, and temperament. This treatment is very close to that of Hovland, Janis, and Kelley (1953). They found that *persuasion* varies with the credibility of the communicator, the organization of the arguments (including repetition), group membership, and personality.

The most ambiguous concept of all was the general notion of *group mind*. The different uses of this concept will be discussed in more detail in Chapter 5, but for now it is sufficient to say that the group-mind concept was used metaphorically to describe the product of the socialization process. It implied some sort of collective agreement about norms and values that allowed separate individuals to share a common perspective, interact, and communicate. This concept was not a unique product of French social theory. Durkheim presented one of the more sophisticated versions of this concept, but it was also widely discussed in England, Germany, and the United States. The group-mind concept reflected a growing awareness that consciousness was socially rather than biologically derived, but the ambiguity of the concept made it vulnerable to attack by Floyd Allport in 1924.

The concepts of imitation, suggestion, and group mind were not only ambiguous; they were also not distinct. Imitation and suggestions were often used interchangeably. Le Bon's treatment of crowd behavior involved all three concepts. The ambiguity of the concepts made it difficult to carry out systematic research, and therefore psychologists, with the notable exception of Binet (1900), tended to stress processes occurring within the individual and largely neglected the work of sociologists. Thus, social psychology proceeded along two parallel tracks with little overlap in content areas.

Despite the ambiguity of these terms, the concepts of imitation, suggestion, and group mind were instrumental in shifting the focus from biological to sociological explanations for behavior. Although biological factors were recognized by sociologists, society rather than native endowment was now seen as the primary source of social behavior. Virtually all social theories in the post–Civil War period described society as an aggregate of individuals, but by 1920 this relationship had been completely reversed. The ordinary American probably still maintained the illusion of autonomy, but intellectuals agreed that the individual was a social product (Wilson, 1968). The concepts of imitation, suggestion, and group mind formed the distinct core for most of the sociological social psychology textbooks written during the first two decades. Ross's (1908) text provided the foundation, and his ideas were incorporated along with extended discussions of new areas in the texts that followed. Ellwood (1917) coined the term "psycho-sociology" to describe this approach, and most agreed with Ross (1908) when he characterized social psychology as "one narrow tract in the province of sociology" (p.vii).

Crowd psychology also had a more direct effect on people's lives. Both Adolf Hitler and Benito Mussolini read Le Bon and incorporated many of his ideas. Le Bon's influence on fascist dictators is often used as an excuse for dismissing his ideas, but their use of Le Bon violates one of his central assumptions. Le Bon felt that leaders rise spontaneously within crowds and share their point of view. Hitler and Mussolini were both high Machiavellians who manipulated crowds and the mass media in order to deliberately *change* public opinion. Many of their techniques are similar to those used in advertising and were systematically explored by attitude researchers during and after World War II (see Chapters 8 and 10). Besides, democratic leaders, such as Theodore Roosevelt and Charles de Gaulle, were also strongly influenced by Tarde and Le Bon, even though their overall effect was not as strong. As Serge Moscovici (1981/1985) points out, while most social sciences were made *by* history, crowd psychology and economics are the only two disciplines that have radically changed the course of human events.

## NOTES

1. Chapters 1, 3, 4, and 5 had been published previously in *Revue Philosophique,* beginning in 1882.

2. Alfred Binet (1857–1911) occupied a position somewhat similar to Durkheim's—director of the psychological laboratory at the Sorbonne and founder and editor of the journal *L'Année Psychologique.* Binet had studied law but went on to specialize in natural science and obtained a doctorate after working at the Salpêtrière Hospital. Binet is known in America primarily for his work on intelligence testing, but he was also a highly sophisticated social theorist who was well aware of social variables in intelligence. Binet wrote a book, *La suggetibilité* (1890), and also carried out some early social psychological experiments. His influence on experimental social psychology in America will be considered in Chapter 5.

# 4

# Social Psychology as Social Interaction

Although British and French social theories were major influences in the development of social psychology in America, these perspectives were considerably modified to fit the new milieu when they crossed the Atlantic. However, there were also currents of thought that were inherently rooted in the American experience. Unlike Europe, where the individual's place in the social order was more a product of birth than opportunity, people in America were assumed to be active agents with unlimited physical and social potential striving to establish their identity and master their environment.

Within such a cultural landscape, patterns of American social thought focused on the nature of the self and its relation to society. By the end of the nineteenth century, the new philosophical movement of pragmatism appeared. One of its aims was to provide an account of how the self developed within a social context. Other social thinkers also examined the social origins of the self, and these works on self and society provided the foundation for a social psychology that focused on social interaction rather than on social instincts or imitation and suggestion. The individual was portrayed as an active agent who was both an object and a source of social influence.

While the interactionist approach to social psychology was basically a product of American thought, it also drew from various European sources. This combination of theories will be considered as we look at each of the theorists. Unlike the social-instinct or psychosocialogical writers discussed in Chapters 2 and 3, social interactionists were not particularly concerned with disciplinary issues, such as the debate about whether social psychology was a branch of psychology or sociology. In fact, the pragmatists were more interested in developing a general system of philosophy that could be applied to all the social sciences. But by 1930, social interaction had become closely associated with the sociological approach, displacing French social theory as the principal influence.

We will begin our discussion of social interaction with two major theorists who were not affiliated with any particular school of thought—James Mark Baldwin and Charles Horton Cooley. This will be followed by a brief treatment of two of the founders of American pragmatism, Chares S. Peirce and William James. We will then consider the contributions of John Dewey and George Herbert Mead, the two pragmatist thinkers who were especially influential in the development of social psychology. Their influence is shown in the Chicago School of sociology, which is the final topic of this chapter.

## SOCIAL INTERACTION THEORIES AT THE TURN OF THE CENTURY

At the turn of the century both psychology and sociology were young, budding disciplines with only a handful of people working in each area. The division between disciplines was not clearly drawn, and those working in one area frequently made major contributions to the other. F. H. Giddings (1899) pointed out that "Any new contribution to either Psychology or Sociology is likely to be found also a contribution to the other, and we may look in the near future for a number of books of which it will be difficult to say whether they are primarily works on Psychology or Sociology" (p. 16). This overlap can be seen most clearly in the case of James Mark Baldwin and Charles Horton Cooley. Baldwin, a psychologist, and Cooley, a sociologist, started from different perspectives but developed social interaction theories that were very similar. Baldwin, whose career began earlier, also had some influence on Cooley.

### James Mark Baldwin (1861–1934)

James Mark Baldwin was born in Columbia, South Carolina, and was attracted to psychology because of an early interest in religion. In the 1880s as a student at Princeton he studied with James McCosh, a philosopher who became an adherent of Wilhelm Wundt's new experimental psychology. After completing his studies at Princeton, he spent a year abroad, which included a period at Wundt's laboratory in Leipzig. Baldwin occasionally dabbled in laboratory work and set up the first psychological laboratory in Canada while at the University of Toronto, but he became increasingly dissatisfied with it and turned more and more to social psychology.

Baldwin approached social psychology through developmental psychology, and his initial writings bore the influence of Gabriel Tarde. As with Baldwin's career in general, his relationship to Tarde is shrouded in controversy. In 1891, he published an article on suggestion in infancy in the journal *Science*. This article made no mention of Tarde's (1890) book, which had appeared the previous year. Meanwhile, Baldwin secured the translation rights for Tarde's work and delayed its publication. He also wrote Tarde in 1898 and suggested that the principle of imitation be called the "Tarde-Baldwin principle," the order indicating the priority.

But in 1902 G. Totsi, an Italian medical student, sparked a scandal by accusing Baldwin of plagiarism. He presented in a letter to *Science* lines from Baldwin's *Social and Ethical Interpretations* beside those from Tarde's *Les Lois de L'imitation* and concluded that Baldwin had merely translated Tarde's ideas in "bad English" and presented them as his own. The controversy over plagiarism was never fully resolved, and it plagued Baldwin throughout his life. Nevertheless, Baldwin's treatment of imitation and invention represents a radical shift in emphasis, and Baldwin extended his analysis to include an account of how the self develops through social interaction.

Baldwin drew heavily from evolutionary theory, and he was primarily responsible for extending Darwin's ideas to the area of mental development. For Baldwin, the mind of a child is distinguished from that of other animals primarily by its enormous capacity to learn through imitation. Unlike lower animals, which are born with the instinctive ability to deal with their environment, human beings acquire their capacity by watching other people and imitating their behavior. The ability to learn by imitation and invention was for Baldwin the key to understanding human social behavior.

Baldwin (1895, 1897) described three stages of child development—the projective, the subjective, and the ejective. Initially, children passively receive impressions from the outside world and are unable to distinguish people from impersonal objects. The behavior of other people begins to attract their attention, and they gradually begin to recognize differences in people's responses to them. Parents are particularly important and become models for imitation.

Repeated attempts to imitate, along with occasional failures, force children to recognize their parents as distinct individuals different from themselves. The child becomes self-conscious for the first time, and the subjective individual is formed. Self-consciousness is a distinctly human characteristic not found in other animals, which gives people the capacity to come up with creative solutions to new problems and provides us with an evolutionary edge. Baldwin's inclusion of self-consciousness is drawn from James's (1890) conception of the self. However, while James only implicitly assumes a social genesis of self-development, Baldwin explicitly describes how this process unfolds (Scheibe, 1985).

During the final stage, children use their new subjective awareness to understand the behavior of new people in their environment. They "eject" their own feeling and motives onto others and begin to make attributions about the causes behind behavior. For Baldwin, self-awareness and the awareness of others develop together. There is no opposition between self and society. The self is merely one participant within social encounters.

Baldwin considered imitation a much more active process than Tarde. Children are not passive recipients of information. They are drawn to certain individuals and uninterested in others. Children think and imagine in their own way—assimilating and transforming information so that they could not repeat it precisely even if they wished. Ideas are incorporated within a pre-existing perspective, and these transformations form the bases for each child's unique character. For Baldwin, the unique person was not a "socialized individual" but a "society individualized."

Differences were, nevertheless, sufficiently small to cause concern. Baldwin shared a deep distrust of mass democratic society. He felt that most people tend to be conservative and unoriginal—near-perfect copies of their social group. Occasionally society produces an exceptional individual who can rise above the bonds of traditional society by making an original contribution. Invention, in Baldwin's view, was the key to constructive social change. Human beings are able to transcend the restraints of biological evolution by experimenting with new ideas. Ideas that are socially useful survive and eventually become part of the culture.

Baldwin had a considerable impact on psychology at the time. He helped establish two of the leading psychological journals, the *Psychological Bulletin* and the *Psychological Review*. He was also co-founder and president of the American Psychological Association. When James McKeen Cattell (1929) asked prominent psychologists to rank their colleagues in order of eminence in 1903, Baldwin ranked fifth behind William James, Cattell himself, Hugo Münsterberg, and G. Stanley Hall, but ahead of such notables as E. B. Titchener and John Dewey (Mueller, 1976). But in 1908 his career was rocked by a second scandal when he was caught in a brothel. Although he claimed that he was there for scientific purposes, he was dismissed from his position at Johns Hopkins University and spent the rest of his career abroad, first in Mexico and then in France. His most lasting contribution is based on the fact that his work helped inspire more systematic research on moral and mental development by Jean Piaget. As developmental psychology began to emerge as a distinct subdiscipline within psychology, Baldwin's influence on social psychology began to diminish, and today he is rarely cited.

### Charles Horton Cooley (1864–1929)

Although American sociology lacked a firm theoretical base at the turn of the century, one notable exception was the work of Charles Horton Cooley (1864–1929). While most social thinkers writing during this period quickly sank into oblivion, Cooley has had a lasting impact on both sociology and sociological social psychology (see Table 1.2). Unlike the sociologists considered in Chapter 3, he was not strongly influenced by French social theory. Instead, he drew on James's and Baldwin's concepts of self and society.

Cooley was born in Ann Arbor, Michigan, and lived there virtually all of his life. His father was a Michigan Supreme Court justice and the first dean of the University of Michigan Law School. Cooley began teaching economics at the University of Michigan in 1890, while still a graduate student, and received his Ph.D. in sociology and economics in 1894. Throughout his life, Cooley was shy and unassuming, more prone to reading than to socializing. Former students described his lectures as intellectually competent but uninspiring. At a time when other sociologists, such as Small, Ross, and Giddings, were struggling to establish major centers for sociology, Cooley worked inconspicuously as an independent scholar, avoided administration duties, and had no sizable following at his own university. His impact on sociology rests almost exclusively on three major books, *Human Nature and Social Order* (1902), *Social Organizations* (1909), and *The Social Process* (1918).

Cooley's contribution to social psychology is based on three aspects of his work: (1) his general social theory; (2) his concept of the social or "looking-glass" self; and (3) his distinction between primary and secondary groups. For Cooley, society was not an aggregate of individuals but an organic whole in which individuals constantly interacted. All aspects of life—economic, religious, and cultural—were seen as intimately connected, so that an adequate understanding of social behavior depends on taking each of them into account. Cooley criticized the tendency to portray individuals and society as antagonistic. For Cooley (1902), "a separate individual is an abstraction unknown to experience and so likewise is society when regarded as something apart from the individual" (p. 1). He felt that certain groups or subgroups may oppose the existing social order but that the antithesis of individual and society was false and misleading whenever it was used as a general explanation for social behavior.

The interrelationship between individual and society can be seen quite clearly in Cooley's concept of the "looking-glass" self. For Cooley, self-awareness occurs through interaction with other people. Children gradually learn to see themselves as others see them. They imagine how they appear to other people and what others think of them. At times, this heightened sense of self-awareness can be painfully acute, but sensitivity to the opinions of others is commonplace and out of such sensitivity the self-concept gradually develops. For Cooley (1902), the social self contained three elements—a mental image of how we appear to others, a sense of their judgment of us,

and some sort of feeling such as pride or mortification.

To Cooley, an independent individual, such as the "I" in Descartes' "I think therefore I am," was not possible. Descartes took this as an unquestionable truth and the starting point for his philosophy. For Cooley, as with Baldwin, self-awareness and consciousness itself are formed through interaction with others. Self-consciousness and awareness of others develop together, since it is not possible to imagine oneself without reference to others or to think of a group of which one is a member without including oneself. As Cooley (1909) pointed out, "self and society are twin-born, we know one as immediately as we know the other, and the notion of a separate and independent ego is an illusion" (p. 5).

The self-concept or looking-glass self develops through interaction in what Cooley called "primary groups." Primary groups are small face-to-face groups, such as the family, the neighborhood, or a child's play group, where intimate association and mutual cooperation are the norm. They usually arise spontaneously and last a relatively long time. The relationship between members is more intense in primary groups than in secondary groups, and individuals react to one another as complete personalities. Primary groups are distinguished from secondary groups by the fact that members refer to themselves as "we." Secondary groups include such things as businesses, churches, political parties, and professional organizations. These are usually deliberately formed for some particular purpose. They include an extended membership not based on face-to-face contact, in which members interact primarily through a limited number of roles. Within primary groups, there is a "certain fusion of individualities in a common whole, so that one's very self, for many purposes at least, is the common life and purpose of the group" (Cooley, 1909, p. 23).

Primary groups are primary in several senses. They are the child's *first* source of social contact. They provide people with companionship, affection, and a sense of self-worth. Primary groups are instrumental in the development of a self-concept, since individuals interact with one another as complete personalities rather than as representatives of a specialized role. Finally, primary groups are agents of socialization, in which people acquire attitudes and social norms. They are responsible for "bringing" individuals into society and give them an opportunity to express and compare attitudes and revise them from time to time.

The unity within primary groups is not based exclusively on harmony and love. Some primary groups, such as the family, have differentiated social roles based on age and sex. Competition and self-assertion occur along with sympathy and love. Primary groups bear the mark of the larger society in which they occur. At the time that Cooley was writing, for example, the German family and school contained elements of German militarism that made them quite different from those existing in France or the United States. But similarities among different groups of people are based on primary groups as well. Cooley felt that what passed for "human nature" did not depend on biology but was based on a common core of experience derived from similarities in primary groups around the world. Foreign religions and governments may seem alien and strange, but we can relate immediately to small groups such as families and friends.

Cooley's approach to sociology stands in sharp contrast to the individualism of Spencer and his American supporters. It is somewhat paradoxical that such a bold attack on entrenched social and economic views could be initiated by a man who was otherwise quiet and unassuming. American universities during the 1890s were generally run by conservative administrators who had few qualms about imposing their views on faculty. At a time when there were few safeguards protecting academic freedom, progressive academics who openly advocated social reform found themselves in conflict with university authorities, and in a few cases, such as that of Ross, they were actually dismissed. Cooley (1930) later wrote that he did not know that sociology was seen as a "radical subject" but, if it was, it

was probably to his advantage that he came from a conservative background and did not attract the attention of the administration.

Much of Cooley's work is social commentary rather than social theory. His description of the primary group was both a reflection of the way things were and an idealized account of the way he thought things should be. It was a description of relationships in small-town America before the urban industrial transformation. The stark realities of urban life brought a shift in emphasis from primary to secondary groups, but Cooley and many others of his generation remained optimistic that primary forms of cooperation and intimate association could be carried over to the city from the small town. They favored the creation of new social structures, such as urban neighborhoods, community centers, professional associations, service clubs, and neighborhood schools, which would preserve the intimacy and moral integrity of small-town America and prevent the social disintegration associated with urban life.

Cooley has had a profound influence on American sociology. By working quietly as an independent scholar, he helped provide sociology with the solid content that gave it respectability as an academic area. His conception of human nature and the social self offered a sociological alternative to the biological views of his time. For Cooley, human nature was not something built into the individual; it was acquired during the course of socialization. Aspects of Cooley's theory were later incorporated by George Herbert Mead. Although Mead was critical of some of this work, he nevertheless profited a great deal from Cooley's influence.

## EARLY PRAGMATISM—SETTING THE FOUNDATION

The psychological and philosophical movement known as pragmatism was part of a broad rejection of European speculative thinking during the nineteenth century, and an appeal to science as the ultimate arbitrator of all theoretical disputes. In general, American social thinkers were more concerned with practical questions than their European counterparts. This focus reflected the dramatic social changes that were taking place in American society at the end of the nineteenth century, such as industrialization, urbanization, and the absorption of new waves of immigration from southern and eastern Europe.

Pragmatism drew from British evolutionary theory and attempted to explain consciousness, knowledge, and the "function" of behavior in terms of their evolutionary significance. For pragmatists, consciousness occurs during the course of concrete activity when there is a decision to be made or a problem to be solved. Pragmatism was both a method for understanding and a theory of truth, but it took a slightly different form with each of its principal supporters. Pragmatism was introduced by Charles S. Peirce, popularized by William James, and later applied to social problems by John Dewey and George Herbert Mead.

### Charles S. Peirce (1839–1914)

Peirce was born in Cambridge, Massachusetts, in 1839. His father was a professor of mathematics at Harvard University, and Peirce received his B.A. (1859), M.A. (1862), and Sc.B. in chemistry (1863) from the same institution. Peirce was first and foremost a scientist, and in his formulation of pragmatism, he attempted to lay a solid foundation for a new philosophy on which others could build. He felt that many of the problems associated with philosophy were either meaningless gibberish or unsolvable in their current form. When these were identified and eliminated, what remained was a set of problems that could be tested empirically. For Peirce, correct thinking was a serious undertaking, and he had no intention of coddling his readers. He introduced his concept of pragmatism in 1878 in a paper called "How to make our ideas clear" and developed it in a series of articles published in *Popular Science Monthly* and

*The Monist.* Peirce was interested primarily in problems with concrete solutions, but in order to identify these problems he had to deal with abstract issues, such as the meaning of reality and the nature of truth and error.

For Peirce, reality is characterized by three features. First, it is independent of our thinking. Reality helps shape our thoughts, but it is not affected by what we happen to think. Since our thoughts do not change reality, it appears the same to others and forms a common ground for conceptions and thought. Finally, if studied sufficiently, it leads to a common opinion. Reality is independent of the vagaries of you and me, and it is that at which information and reasoning should eventually arrive.

If reality is independent of our thoughts, the second question is: How do we come to know it? Peirce, like subsequent phenomenological thinkers, began by distinguishing two types of awareness—the raw or prereflective experience and our knowledge of this experience. The raw experience occurs before thought. It is this experience that is potentially shared by everyone and remains the same no matter what we think. Thought occurs when we describe this experience in general terms using language. Thinking draws our attention to specific features at the expense of others and increases the logical connection between ideas.

For Peirce, the concepts we use in thought are based on universal, abstract features. Our attention is aroused when the same characteristic is encountered repeatedly. Experiences are compared with previous ones in order to understand their general nature and the present is connected to the past by a series of infinitesimal steps. Peirce (1868/1972) called this the "train of thought," and it was later called the "stream of thought" or "stream of consciousness" by William James (1890). The fundamental law of the mind—a process Peirce called "synechism"—was that ideas spread continuously, affecting other related ideas, and lead to generalizations. These general features are described by words, but words refer to specific characteristics of concrete objects that recur in different situations.

The most important contribution of pragmatism is the assertion that thought is *practical*. Pragmatism is difficult to understand because we are accustomed to think of consciousness as a passive spectator, taking in but not actively involved. This is the type of disinterested awareness often described by philosophers, and it has been taken as a prototype for consciousness in general. We assume that consciousness correctly mirrors reality and provides us with an accurate picture of the outside world. For pragmatists, consciousness occurs during the course of practical activity, when habitual forms of activity are no longer appropriate. We must plan a new course of action and carry it out. The planning of the activity and its deliberate completion constitute the entire experience and the meaning of the action.

Consciousness also occurs during doubt. Doubt arises from indecision or exposure to other people with different ideas. It produces an uneasiness from which we struggle to escape. For Peirce, doubt always has an external source, resulting in surprise, and it is as impossible to create genuine doubt as it is to surprise oneself. The irritation of doubt causes a struggle to remove the uncertainty by creating a new belief, and doubt ceases as soon as the new belief is formed. Belief is an enduring and largely unconscious habit of the mind. A person who holds a belief is perfectly satisfied until he or she encounters a new uncertainty. The past is a source of information, but the ultimate test of a belief is its correspondence with current reality.

If beliefs are based on agreement with reality, then a final question is: How can they be wrong? Peirce suggested several reasons why our conception of reality may be wrong. First, our search for certainty may not proceed far enough. When doubt is removed we are entirely satisfied and cling tenaciously to our new beliefs. Belief produces a calm, reassured state of mind that we do not wish to change, but it is not necessarily true. What we believe today may be thoroughly discredited tomorrow. The dread of doubt causes people to cling to beliefs even when faced with conflicting evidence. Peirce called this the "method of tenacity," but pointed out that it is opposed to the social impulse, which often brings people into contact with other people who think differently.

To avoid this, it is possible to use the "method of authority," which fixed beliefs in the community. Those in authority enforce the beliefs of their group far more severely than their own individual beliefs. Because doubt threatens the solidarity of the group sympathy and fellowship produce a ruthless authority, as shown by the Inquisition and a general intolerance for differing opinions in all ages. The method of authority governs the thinking of the vast majority of people, but it is never entirely effective. A small number of people begin to see that people in other cultures and times held different opinions, and doubt causes them to reexamine their own views.

Beliefs may also be incorrect because people do not think logically. Peirce felt that the ability to think logically is the last faculty to develop, and it may never develop in some people. It is not a natural gift but an art acquired by experimenting with good and bad forms of reasoning. In his article "How to make our ideas clear," Peirce (1868/1972) maintained that a single unclear idea may lead a philosopher astray for a lifetime, and that whole nations may be led astray when they base their values on abstract ideals divorced from concrete experience. Unclear thinking about abstract concepts is likely to lead one into a metaphysical tangle the only resolution of which is to return to the world of concrete reality as the ultimate source of verification.

A final source of error is due to an element of chance in the universe itself. The notion of absolute chance or *tychism* is another of Peirce's central concepts. He felt that evolution depended on chance variations and that chance added an element of uncertainty to what would otherwise be a dead, mechanical universe. Chance was a product of the mind—that is, people have free will and behave unpredictably—but, for Peirce, it was also a characteristic of the physical universe. He felt that a belief in the absolute certainty of scientific laws was a metaphysical "presupposition" that could never be proved. For this reason, scientific statements would always remain probabilistic.

Peirce applied his pragmatic method to understanding some specific phenomena. One of the more important is knowledge of one's self. In a remarkably early paper on the topic, Peirce (1868/1972) concluded that self-knowledge is only an inference derived from contact with other people. When a child hears a sound, he thinks of the object producing it and not himself. The body is discovered through manipulating objects. Children also learn that what others say is often a better source of evidence than their own perception, and they begin to doubt appearances when others disagree. The disagreement leads to the concept that appearances are occasionally *private*. The notion of private, however, does not mean divorced from reality. Even feelings, which are one of the most private events, are directed toward specific objects. They seem private because they are less widely shared and they recur with some consistency— what interests one person may bore another person to death. Peirce felt the disorder of "split personality" showed that self-awareness is based on some kind of coordination of ideas. The split personality has two different sets of memories and therefore two different identities.

For Peirce, the individual was only the instrument of thought. He felt that there should be something like personal consciousness, or esprit de corps, in people who were intimate and intensely sympathetic. While he recognized natural selection, he favored a Lamarckian explanation for the evolution of ideas. The mind was reaching out, actively groping for solutions to concrete problems, acquiring habits that were then passed on to the next generation. The force behind this was called "agapism," a kind of all-encompassing love. Peirce rejected the utilitarian values derived from free enterprise and felt that the great attention paid to economic questions during the nineteenth century exaggerated the beneficial effects of greed. He belittled attempts to portray the "Wall Street sharp" as a good angel who takes money from careless people who do not guard it properly and wrecks

feeble enterprises that do not deserve to stay in business.

For Peirce, science was the product of a community of inquirers and truth was based on their collective opinion. The method of science rested on agreement with external reality. People may start with different views, but if they base their beliefs on facts, their ideas will tend to converge. No ratio is great enough to express the proportion of known to unknown, but any concrete question can be addressed and ultimately resolved if explored in sufficient detail. Science is a collective enterprise, and each new achievement is based on what has come before.

It may seem strange that the person who is usually given credit for originating pragmatism should so categorically deny that discoveries are made by single individuals, but Peirce's ideas are the result of a unique individual and a product of his time. His views were, in many ways, typical of his generation. He, like many others who had reached maturity in the post–Civil War period, reflected the trends in higher education that were generated by the demands of a rapidly expanding urban-industrial society. Unlike his father's generation, who had been taught according to a traditional curriculum that contained a strong mix of piety and moral philosophy, the younger generation received a more secular education that emphasized empirical and historical procedures. They were largely trained specialists, many with Ph.D.s from German universities, and they chose to concentrate mainly on the natural and social sciences. Despite the shift in emphasis, much of the old curriculum continued to be taught in some form or other, and there was still a strong allegiance to older ethical values among the new breed of specialists. Many of these espoused a strong sense of social conscience and were often critical of the crude naturalism and individualism they felt characteristic of the Gilded Age.

Peirce's philosophy shared many features of the social thinkers of his age, especially Baldwin, Ross, and G. Stanley Hall (Wilson, 1968). Indeed, Peirce is regarded as a radical spokesperson for the ideal of the community and an uncompromising critic of individualism and social evolution. He argued that, outside the community and apart from interaction with other people, the individual as a separate entity could exist only in "error and ignorance."

Peirce's personal life stands in sharp contrast to these lofty ideals. Early in his career, he held various lecturing positions and in 1879 obtained a teaching position in philosophy at Johns Hopkins. However, in 1884, for reasons never explained, he was dismissed from Johns Hopkins and never held an academic position again. He also worked for many years as a surveyor for the federal government, but his government career ended abruptly in 1891. Although he was regarded as brilliant by his friends and associates, he became increasingly alienated from his own generation of scholars and lived out the end of his life in poverty, writing about philosophy but unable to publish.

The fact that Peirce was seen as an outsider to the academic community severely limited his initial impact. His ideas were embedded in extended discussions of logic, mathematics, and molecular physics. This and his propensity to use neologisms—such as tychism, syncchism, and agapism—made his ideas difficult, and he was virtually unknown outside a small circle of friends until William James introduced him as the originator of pragmatism in 1898. Peirce laid the foundation, but it was James who built on this foundation and produced the doctrine that became known at the turn of the century.

## William James (1843–1910)

Peirce was only three years older than James, but he had graduated from Harvard in 1859 and began lecturing before James even began his career. The elder Henry James (father of William) devoted his life to the education of his children, and the family had moved from New York to London, Geneva, Paris, Boulogne-sur-mer, Newport, and Dresden before settling in Cambridge, Massachusetts, in 1866. William James received a medical degree from Harvard in

1869 and taught there from 1872 until his death. Although James and Peirce remained close friends, the differences between them were striking. James was sociable and outgoing—a man of the world—while Peirce was touchy, ill at ease in public, and found it increasingly difficult to associate with others in later life. Peirce was trained in science and expected accuracy and precision in thought, whereas James was equally at home in literature, psychology, or religion. Peirce was one of James's many correspondents, whereas James was one of Peirce's few and served as both friend and public. James tried hard to find lectures for Peirce at Harvard but was unable to find a full-time position.

James acknowledged his debt to Peirce in his *Principles of Psychology* (1890) and later dedicated his book *The Will To Believe* (1897) to him. Their ideas were sufficiently different, however, that it is unclear whether James got his ideas from Peirce or merely used Peirce to support ideas he already had. James's biographer Ralph Perry (1935) has pointed out that it is an open question whether one can "derive" from a philosopher ideas he never had, and that it is perhaps more accurate to say that "the modern movement known as pragmatism is largely the result of James's misunderstanding of Peirce" (p. 181). Although James gave Peirce full credit for originating pragmatism, it was James's version that became popular, and the brunt of the criticisms fell on him.

James began his career at Harvard by teaching anatomy, then psychology, and finally philosophy. James crossed the line between philosophy and psychology so many times that the distinction became obliterated (Perry, 1935). James later chose the term "radical empiricism" to distinguish his position from British empiricism, which he regarded as a form of analytic philosophy, but the method of radical empiricism underlies all of James's work, from *Principles of Psychology* to his later work on mysticism and religion (Wilde, 1969). Radical empiricism is the study of immediate experience. Its aim is to avoid theoretical constructs and recover the world as it is experienced—not in retrospect but during the act itself. Because radical empiricism underlies all of James's work, the best introduction is his first and perhaps most important work, *Principles of Psychology* (1890).

James's *Principles of Psychology* does not include a single chapter on social psychology, but it does include a description of several closely related phenomena, such as social instincts and the self. For James, psychology was the "science of mental life," focusing on the description and explanation of conscious states. Its subject matter includes feelings, thoughts, perception, and the acquisition of habits. His account of these processes is not based on speculation or even a summary of then-current research. It is an actual description of these processes as he experienced them, with occasional extrapolations from animal research.

Behavior in lower animals is determined largely by instincts, which James defines as a tendency to behave in a particular way without foresight or previous experience. These instincts are the product of evolution and operate in such a way as to be right *most of the time.* As James says, there are more worms unattached to fishhooks than impaled upon them, so nature says to her fishy children, bite every worm and take your chance. Humans possess all the impulses of lower animals and more, but they are more likely to be held in check through foresight and modified by habit.

From a physiological point of view, habit is nothing but a new pathway formed in the brain. A pathway once traversed is traversed more easily a second time. Habits simplify our movements, make them more accurate, and diminish fatigue. Previous ends become means toward new ends, and one builds up a repertoire of habitual responses that allows one to function smoothly with a minimum of effort in most situations. Habit creates a "second nature" uniquely adapted to specific environmental conditions. Habit preserves not only what is good but what is bad, and it is therefore important to establish good habits early and make a concerted effort to eliminate bad ones. Without habits, no progress could occur, and each act

would have to be performed with the same difficulty as the first time.

Purposeful activity occurs when a habitual response is no longer appropriate. The person hesitates before an object to which he or she has previously acted habitually. James described this in terms of a reflex arc with three components: (1) perception; (2) conceptual understanding; and (3) behavior. This process would be purely automatic were it not for the fact that the central component directs activities at both ends. Although James used this threefold distinction for the purpose of analysis, the three processes normally occur together. Thought determines both the stimulus to which we attend and the way in which we respond.

One of the most remarkable facts of life is that we notice so few of the many sensations that impinge on our senses at any given time. Consciousness is primarily a "selecting agent" that focuses on certain objects at the expense of others. Our attention is focused on things that help us or resist us in our struggle with life. In human beings, where indecision occurs frequently, attention is agonizingly intense. It is vastly expanded by language, which allows us to explore the meaning of new situations and imagine solutions that have never been previously imagined. Discrimination, analysis, and comparison make things clear, but nothing will be clarified unless it is sharply focused.

The second step in this sequence is reasoning or conceptual understanding. Reasoning always has a purpose. It breaks up the total phenomenon and uses language to highlight abstract similarities among concrete objects not previously associated. Language can never fully describe concrete experience, so our conceptual understanding is much less detailed than the raw experience. Abstract thinking slurs over individual differences and treats particular objects as if they are more or less the same. This simplification, on the other hand, is handled with much less effort than the original data. James was concerned primarily with concrete thinking and regarded speculative thinking as a derivative. Concrete thinking is not shut up within the head of an individual—it is stretched out toward objects in the outside world.

Thinking occurs within a stream that James called the "stream of thought" or "stream of consciousness." Thought is not a thing but a system of relationships. The stream of consciousness is constantly changing. Each thought contains the residue of the previous thoughts and foreknowledge of things to come. The mind is always thinking, but much is immediately forgotten. The only gaps occur during injury or sleep, and here the person reaches back to connect the stream with thoughts occurring before the break. No object is ever experienced in precisely the same way on two different occasions. The experience is always different because the later experience is embedded within a different stream of associations and contains the memory of the previous encounter.

For James, self-consciousness also occurs within the stream of thought. Thinking and feeling are active processes directed by the individual. As James (1890) states, "The universal conscious fact is not 'feelings and thoughts exist,' but 'I think' and 'I feel'" (p. 226). James distinguishes between the self as a source of experience (the "I") and the empirical self (the "me"), which is what we can observe about ourselves. The "I" can become aware of the various constituents of the empirical self, including (1) the material self, which is the knowledge of possessions (including one's own body); (2) the social self, which is the awareness of the roles we play; and (3) the spiritual self, which includes beliefs about morality and the meaning of life. Underlying all of these components is a sense of personal unity and continuity that serves as a central source of motivation for people's active engagement with the social environment (see Scheibe, 1985, for a more detailed discussion).

A complete cycle of activity terminates in behavior. Deliberate activity need not be well thought out in advance, however. All that is required for most activities is a vague notion of the end state. Some activities, such as dressing or going to bed, are so habitual that they are carried out automatically. Deliberation may last for weeks,

months, or even years, occurring at intervals during the course of other activities. For James, free will was based on both the fact that people choose the stimulus to which they attend and that they plan a deliberate course of action—not always, not invariably, but with enough frequency that it can be recognized as a psychological fact. Deliberation makes good evolutionary sense for a species in an unpredictable environment. Such hesitation would be a hindrance rather than an advantage if the new response were not somehow better than the previous one.

James's *Principles of Psychology* contained the seeds for his later version of pragmatism. According to James, each individual has a stock of old opinions derived through habit and contact with other people. These are used to make sense of the world until they are contradicted by new opinions or the evidence at hand. Consciousness increases during uncertainty. The person must invent new beliefs and test them during the course of activity. Often people must behave before all the evidence is collected, and in these cases the success of their behavior confirms the truth of their beliefs. James uses the example of a lone mountaineer who must leap to a ledge to escape a difficult situation. The success of the leap confirms the belief that the jump was possible.

Truth is based on agreement between a belief and some particular reality. Facts themselves are not true; they simply *are*. Many people think of truth as something that is timeless and universal and exists in itself whether or not people know it. The common-sense notion is that truth exists in advance and is discovered. But for James, truth is dependent on both a thinking individual and an external reality. Truth does not exist until a belief has been formulated and confirmed. A belief is a way of conceiving and organizing reality, and there is nothing inconsistent in the fact that a number of seemingly competing beliefs may all be true at the same time. A Beethoven string quartet, for example, may be accurately described as a scraping of horses' tails on cats' bowels, but such a description in no way precludes an entirely different formulation. By theorizing we invent and develop new systems of beliefs, but these are not known to be true until they have been verified.

James's version of pragmatism differs from that of Peirce in several ways. Peirce stressed the abstract, universal character of concepts used to organize experience, whereas James focused on the particularity and variety of individual experiences. For James, no two experiences, even when they focus on the same external object, are precisely the same. James's early training was in art, and he brought the painter's eye to every analysis of concrete experience. It is often said that James's brother, Henry James, wrote novels as if they were psychological textbooks, whereas William wrote psychological textbooks as if they were novels. All of William James's work is filled with vivid descriptions and personal details.

Somewhat related is James's strong emphasis on the individual. Peirce's pragmatism is to a great extent a social theory. Beliefs become doubtful when they are contradicted by the beliefs held by others. Science is a community of inquirers building on one another's research and seeking agreement. Truth is correspondence between an assertion and the consensus of a number of qualified observers. Two individuals may begin with different perspectives, but if they stick to the facts they will ultimately reach an agreement. These social aspects of Peirce's version of pragmatism are not well developed, but they are implicit in his formulation.

James's treatment is much more individualistic. For James, no two experiences even by the same person are precisely the same, so it is preposterous to assume that two different individuals can "share" the same experience. Each individual brings to each situation a unique collection of experiences and memories. In a series of lectures that later became the foundation for his book *Pragmatism* (1907), James chose the term "individualistic philosophy" to characterize his position. James (1902/1958) even defined religion as *"the feeling, acts, and experiences of individual men in their solitude, so far as they apprehend themselves to stand in relation to whatever they may consider divine"* (p. 42, italics in original). This is in striking contrast to Durkheim's view of religion as the shared beliefs that hold a community together. For James, organized religion was a derivative and a pale shadow of this original private vision.

While James is technically correct in stating that no two people ever experience the same event in *precisely* the same way, by stressing particulars he missed the social implications of pragmatism. Although they are never precisely the same, experiences can be very similar because they focus on the same situation. Similarity can be increased through communication. In fact, if we focus on the concepts rather than the raw experience, we can say that two individuals have precisely the same conceptual understanding whenever they use the same words to describe the same situation. The stress on the uniqueness of each person's experience is probably one of the reasons James did not discuss social psychology in his *Principles of Psychology*. James grappled with the problem of how two minds could be said to have the same object and ultimately wrote a paper on the topic, which was published posthumously in his *Essays in Radical Empiricism* (1912). It is somewhat ironic that the withdrawn scholar, Charles Peirce, should stress the social nature of knowledge, while the gregarious and outgoing William James should focus on the individual. James's emphasis on the individual was based partly on his wide circle of friends and his deep respect for individual differences.

A final difference was that James took pragmatism into areas never envisioned by Peirce. Pragmatism, for Peirce, was basically a theory about the nature of scientific beliefs. Scientific beliefs can be confirmed or disconfirmed using objective criteria. James applied pragmatism to ethics, morality, and religious experience, and in doing so he invented new criteria for their confirmation. For James, religious beliefs were "true" if they brought positive benefits to the individual in the form of improved health and character. This considerably weakened the claim that pragmatism was a scientific procedure and opened the way for the criticism that pragmatism endorses anything that "feels good."

James's *Will to Believe* (1897) was dedicated to Peirce, but it was over this volume that Peirce split with James. He likened the "will to believe" without sufficient evidence to his own "principle of tenacity" and felt that encouraging such action would do more harm than good. In 1905–1906, Peirce introduced the term "pragmaticism" to distinguish his version from that of James: "So then, the writer, finding his bantling 'pragmatism' so promoted, feels that it is time to kiss his child goodbye and relinquish it to its higher destiny; while to serve the purpose of expressing the original definition, he begs to announce the birth of the word 'pragmaticism,'" which is ugly enough to be safe from kidnappers" (Peirce, 1905–1906/1972, p. 255).

Peirce may have been a sounder thinker, but James was a more popular writer and a more lovable man. James's humanity and understanding stemmed from several sources. He had the sufferer's sensitivity for the suffering of others. He experienced depression and hypochondria throughout most of his life. A ten-hour hike in the Adirondacks produced an irreparable valvular lesion in 1898. The following summer he was lost in the same mountains for thirteen hours and thereafter entered a period of invalidism. Much of his subsequent writing, including his work on pragmatism, ethics, and religion, was done in bed during two or three hours of work per day. James's own suffering caused him to invariably side with the underdog. James was concretely humane and tolerated individual differences not just in principle but in practice. He sympathized with socialism but disliked its depreciation of the individual (Perry, 1935).

James's pragmatism was the most popular philosophy in American history, but it ultimately had a limited impact. James attributed the success of pragmatism to its timeliness, with its strong faith in science and its distrust of speculative reasoning. James's professional colleagues accused him of being a "popular philosopher" because he wrote in a popular style and was widely read. Scientists accused him of bowing to superstition, while theologians accused him of making all truth relative.

Gordon Allport (1943) has pointed out that James's radical empiricism could have served as the basis for an American school of phenomenology, but it did not. Among psychologists, his radical empiricism came into conflict with two emerging schools of thought—behaviorism and psychoanalysis. James did not live to see Watson's (1913) behaviorist manifesto, but he deplored any attempt to overlook consciousness or treat it as an epiphenomenon. He recognized the importance of psychoanalysis, but the recognition came too late. When Freud gave his lectures at Clark University in 1909, James, though fatally ill, came to hear him. At the close of the lecture, James came up to pay his respects and said, "the future of psychology belongs to your work" (Jones, 1957). No finer example of baton-passing exists anywhere in the history of psychology.

Ironically, James's pragmatism, which bears the strong imprint of American culture, may have had more influence in Europe than in America. Edmund Husserl, the founder of phenomenology, read James's *Principles of Psychology* very closely and incorporated many of his ideas. The French social theorist Georges Sorel discovered in James's pragmatism what he believed was the key for understanding social behavior. France's foremost philosopher during this period, Henri Bergson, and James were close friends and carried on a cult of mutual admiration, while Max Weber drew from James in his own study of religion. As H. Stuart Hughes (1958) has pointed out, no American thinker before or since has enjoyed more success on the Continent.

Nevertheless, it was James's younger colleagues and fellow pragmatists John Dewey and George Herbert Mead who ultimately had the greatest impact on American social psychology. James had a limited influence because he discussed social psychology so infrequently. However, his conception of the self laid the foundation for the social-psychological approaches of Dewey and Mead, as well as Baldwin and Cooley.

## PRAGMATISM AS A SOCIAL-PSYCHOLOGICAL PERSPECTIVE

In contrast with James's strong emphasis on the individual, John Dewey and George Herbert Mead, like Baldwin and Cooley, placed a much greater emphasis on the interaction between people and the individual and society. In fact, for Dewey and Mead, there was no individual outside the social context. In this sense they were closer to Peirce's version of pragmatism as a social theory in which truth arises from a community of observers. On the other hand, they were closer to James because of their interest in psychological processes. What distinguishes Dewey and Mead from both James and Peirce was their concern for how society could best meet the psychological needs of the individual. Social reform was an inherent part of their pragmatist position.

### John Dewey (1859–1952)

John Dewey was born in Burlington, Vermont, and attended graduate school at Johns Hopkins from 1882 to 1884 when Charles S. Peirce, G. Stanley Hall, and G. S. Morris made up the department of philosophy. Peirce had already developed the outline for the pragmatist position that Dewey would adopt twenty years later, but he had little influence on Dewey during this period. Hall had been a student of both Wilhelm Wundt and William James and was an active researcher and a strong advocate of the experimental method (see Ross, 1972). His appointment in the philosophy department was as a lecturer in psychology and pedagogy. In 1884, he was made a full professor and given the first chair in psychology in America. Although James established a psychological laboratory for demonstration purposes in 1875, Hall set up the first American laboratory devoted to experimental research in 1884.

Hall instilled in Dewey a great respect for experimentation, but the strongest influence on Dewey was G. S. Morris, a Hegelian who represented a new current of thought in America (see White, 1943). As Perry Miller (1954) has pointed out, one of the greatest changes in American intellectual history occurred shortly after the Civil War. The conservative Scottish "common sense" philosophy that had dominated American universities in the prewar period disappeared virtually without a trace and was replaced by Hegel's German idealism. Hegel's idealism, like evolutionary theory, was a philosophy of progress and one more in keeping with the spirit of the time. Whereas evolutionary theory stressed biological development, idealism was more concerned with the underlying processes of change, particularly in relation to the evolution of thought and society.

For G. W. F. Hegel (1770–1831), thought was a product of the social context and needed to be seen within a historical perspective in order to be understood. The concepts that we use to understand ourselves and the world are derived through social contact and change as conditions change. These concepts are generally taken for granted, but they can become the object of attention through a dialectical process of self-reflection. This involves a threefold process whereby existing concepts are first questioned, then these concepts are contrasted with their opposites, and then new concepts are formed based on a reconciliation of the two opposing views. Knowledge constantly improves, approaching the certainty of an absolute understanding (*Weltgeist*).

In his *Phenomenology of Mind* (1807/1967), for example, Hegel explains that perception can be conceived at one level as entirely objective, since it focuses on objects in the outside world. Many people simply assume that their perception accurately reflects events in the outside world. This common-sense assumption can be questioned, however, and perception can be conceived as completely subjective, since it involves processes occurring within the mind of each individual. The apparent discrepancy can be reconciled at a higher level by seeing perception as an interaction between the person and the outside world. Moreover, this reconciliation is a closer approximation to the truth than either of the one-sided formulations. What is true of perception is true of all psychological processes, from simple sensations to conceptual understanding. The dialectical process is not limited to understanding mental processes. It can be applied to history, law, theology, and science. Progress occurs through the process of imagining and resolving conflicting ideas.

Hegel (1821/1967) attempted to develop a systematic social theory, but this must be seen within his particular social context in order to be understood. Germany at the end of the eighteenth century consisted of over 300 independent and semiautonomous states. At a time when England was a rising industrial power and was developing modern forms of parliamentary government, Germany was still a feudal society. Germany needed a strong central government, and this was provided by Friedrich Wilhelm III, who ruled Prussia from 1797 to 1840.

Hegel totally rejected the economic and political institutions of England as a model for Germany. He felt that a society based exclusively on the accumulation of wealth produced isolated, self-centered individuals who treated each other as means to their own ends. The state with its powerful bureaucracy and civil servants was the only force sufficiently strong to regulate the economy so that the benefits could be shared by all. Hegel therefore juxtaposed what he called "civil society," based on "universal egotism," to the state. The state was based on "universal altruism" and embodied absolute reason through the knowledge possessed by its civil servants.

For Hegel, reason evolves as individuals come to understand their society. An individual who has obtained complete understanding would be completely aware of how his or her mind has been shaped by social circumstances and able to use this knowledge for constructive social change. Complete understanding is referred to as "absolute mind," and Hegel felt that each individual shared a part of this total understanding. Understanding is often motivated by human suffering, and social change is guided by the attempt to reduce this suffering. Hegel believed that intellectual breakthroughs are irreversible because they provide a new way of understanding reality not known by the previous generation. Thus, social and intellectual evolution occur simultaneously, each fueling the other, progressing toward a hypothetical end-state based on complete understanding.

The mind of an individual was seen as merely a finite expression of this larger absolute mind. The community approaches this absolute more closely than any single individual, and the state represents the highest degree of intellectual development. It was, therefore, the duty of individuals to subject themselves to the state. Mead (1936) has pointed out that this conception reflects the bureaucratic structure of Hegel's Prussian society, where knowledge was to a great extent a collective enterprise and individuals worked within a framework where the "total picture" was more all-encompassing than the perspective of any single person.

Hegel had a strong impact on both Dewey and Mead. Indeed, Dewey's brand of pragmatism can perhaps best be described as Hegelianism *without the absolute.* The notion of an absolute mind of which individuals were merely an expression gave Dewey's initial position a social emphasis that was missing in that of James. Dewey later abandoned the notion that knowledge was progressing toward some hypothetical end-state in favor of a development based on evolutionary theory, but he retained the idea that thought is historically conditioned by social circumstances, that categories of thought are publicly shared, that thought originates in order to deal with concrete social problems (such as human suffering), and that understanding holds the key to constructive social change.

After Dewey obtained his Ph.D. in 1884, he was appointed as an instructor at the University of Michigan, teaching philosophy and psychology. While at Michigan he published a textbook on psychology (Dewey, 1887) which preceded James's (1890) *Principles of Psychology* by three years. Dewey's text, however, was not as popular because it lacked James's eloquence. In 1891 George Herbert Mead began teaching at Michigan in the same department, and Dewey and Mead developed a close personal and intellectual relationship. In 1894 Dewey accepted an invitation to become the head of the department of philosophy at the University of Chicago, which was then only two years old, on the condition that Mead be given an appointment in the same department. Dewey was also appointed as head of the department of pedagogy, and he used this connection to start a model elementary school, known as the "Laboratory School." In 1904 Dewey left Chicago because of a disagreement with the president of the university about the Laboratory School (Rucker, 1969), and he spent the rest of his academic career at Columbia University, where he concentrated on philosophy and education.

The Chicago years were especially significant in shaping Dewey's version of pragmatism. Because of the close ties between the university and the city, theory and practice were reciprocally related, and Dewey used the urban environment as a source and testing ground for his ideas. Dewey also profited from the presence of Mead. Although each man wrote independently, they had a significant influence on each other throughout their careers, and the common core of their thinking has become known as the Chicago School of pragmatism.

There are three major features that characterize Dewey's pragmatism—functionalism, intersubjectivity, and humanism. Dewey's functionalism is derived from Darwin. Like Peirce and James, he felt that thought begins with uncertainty. Daily events contain a mixture of the known and the unknown, and the need for security compels each person to use knowledge that is certain in order to explain the irregular and confused. One of the things that distinguishes Dewey is his complete acceptance and use of evolutionary theory in an attempt to explain these processes. Between 1900 and 1910, Dewey stressed that pragmatism was the Darwinian method applied to philosophy. Every distinct organ and process was considered an instrument of adaptation. In order for life to persist, behavior must be continually adapted to the environment. Thought is the instrument of adaptation in human beings, and like other instruments it is used to reshape the natural world.

Underlying this conception is the notion of constant change. "Every existence is an event" (Dewey, 1925, p. 61). Even the mountains appear and disappear like clouds. Time is relatively indifferent to change in solid substances—a million years is like a day—but whatever depends on a large number of variables is in an unstable equilibrium and changes rapidly. Events are ongoing and unfinished and therefore possess the possibility of being managed and steered toward specific ends. We live in an unfinished world—"a world in the making"—and the uniqueness of each experience means that all knowledge is provisional and consciously retested. A world that is transient *must* be a world of discord but a world filled with possibilities as well.

When a situation is doubtful, the person must pause and consider possible courses of action. Ideas formerly accepted as facts are now viewed with suspicion. The individual forms hypotheses by imagining new courses of action and their probable consequences, but these hypotheses are merely predictions until they are actually tested and confirmed during the course of practical activity. The hypotheses form the expected content of the action to be performed but certainty reside in the finished product. Purposeful activity consists of checking a habitual or direct course of action, imagining alternatives, and then carrying these out and examining the results. Language makes it possible both to critically examine the ongoing behavior and to imagine alternative courses of action, but language merely describes specific characteristics of concrete objects. Thought does not reside *within* the individual but within the interaction. Dewey felt that it was misleading to consider thought or consciousness a thing. It is better described as an adjective or an adverb because it gives a certain quality to the interaction—a quality that would be missing if behavior was carried out in an unthinking way.

Thought begins with concrete activity—both in its evolutionary development and in the human infant—but it is not limited to such activity. Thought once developed can be applied to *any* sort of problem, real or imagined. It can be used to examine abstract concepts derived from experience or during the course of socialization. Thinking about abstract concepts is merely a case of selective attention. Dewey adopted the term "experimentalism" and later "instrumentalism" to distinguish his psychology from the rationalistic psychology based on "armchair" speculation.

Dewey's most influential presentation of a functionalist psychology is contained in his article on the reflex arc (Dewey, 1896). He criticized the tendency in psychology to reduce action into distinct elements such as sensation, thought, and movement. Instead, he argued that these elements are phases of a coordinated system of action. For example, in a game of tennis, seeing an approaching ball serves as a sensory stimulus that coordinates our movements of running and swinging (Cook, 1977). These movements in turn serve as stimuli for the way we look at and see the ball. According to Dewey, the coordination involved in action is an organic circuit rather than a reflex arc connecting discrete units. Moreover, all action is functionally related to the individual's adaptation to the environment.

Dewey's emphasis on social factors is based on his assumption that both the individual and the environment are essential, and interaction is the key to understanding human consciousness. Each individual is born into a world with traditions and institutions already intact. A vast network of customs, manners, conventions, language, and traditional ideas lies ready for each newborn child and forms the solid content of each person's "subjective" mind. Thus, there is a process of *intersubjectivity* whereby the thought of each individual evolves within a social network. Interaction is facilitated by communication, where thought is expressed in speech. Language functions as a link in cooperative activity as people make their intentions known. Communication does not express an "inner world" of ideas. It is more akin to thinking out loud. One person can complete the thoughts of the other, and the statements often surprise the speaker as much as the person being addressed.

The social origins of knowledge can hinder thinking as well. Many incorrect beliefs are acquired during the course of socialization. Everyday experience is saturated with the prejudices and misconceptions of previous generations. Ordinary people are creatures of habit, and critical skills are acquired only through a discipline that is antithetical to human nature. The routine of custom tends to deaden even scientific thinking, so the major breakthroughs are often initiated by people who are only marginally associated with a particular discipline. The dead weight of tradition can be escaped only by subjecting *all* beliefs to an empirical test and retaining only those that prove useful.

For Dewey, knowledge is produced by individuals but it is not an individual possession. The modern idea of the mind as personal or even private is based on two commonplace phenomena—daydreaming and creative thought. Creative thought means discovering what no one has known before, but these discoveries rest on a solid basis of social knowledge and scientific tradition. It simply means envisioning possibilities not previously imagined. That the mind can be involved in daydreams is not surprising. The mind when awake must have some content. It cannot remain literally vacant for long. If it is not involved in concrete activity or some form of speculative thinking, it often fabricates little stories to amuse itself that it seldom divulges to other people. But the contents of our fantasies are the stuff of our waking life—the world as we would like it to be. The mind that appears in an individual is not an individual mind, since each person brings to each situation a set of conventions and beliefs acquired through social contact. According to Dewey (1925), "It is not exact nor relevant to say 'I experience' or 'I think.' 'It' experiences or is experienced, 'it' thinks or is thought, is a juster phrase (p. 190)."

Dewey's thinking about social psychology began to crystallize in connection with his interests in education, logic, and ethics (Karpf, 1932). His first treatment of the subject appeared in his article, "The need for social psychology" (Dewey, 1917), which was based on an address given on the twenty-fifth anniversary of the American Psychological Association. He noted that all psychological phenomena are either physiological or social. Since only elementary sensations and "appetite" constitute the physiological, "all that is left of our mental life, our beliefs, ideas and desires, falls within the scope of social psychology" (Dewey, 1917, p. 267). Thus for Dewey, psychology was primarily social psychology.

In prescribing the direction that social psychology should take, Dewey was critical of both the imitation and instinct schools because of their monistic conceptions, which reduced complex phenomena to one simple explanation. He accepted the notion of native instincts but argued that the task of social psychology was twofold. It must account for both how endowment operates within the social context and how control of the environment is achieved through the operation of instincts. With the increasing attack on the concept of instinct, Dewey later shifted his emphasis from instinct to habit as the basic unit in social psychology. In his book on social psychology, *Human Nature and Conduct* (Dewey, 1922), he defined habit as a disposition or attitude, implying will and intention, which both shapes and is shaped by social conditions.

Dewey's perspective of humanism is reflected in his concern with ethics. For Dewey, ethical decisions are to be evaluated by their consequences. Some actions are good because they expand, invigorate, or harmonize the individual with the environment. Others are bad because they narrow the individual, obscure reality, or diminish a person's power over the situation. Dewey categorically rejected any attempt to base ethics on timeless, universal principles. Each situation is unique and must be evaluated in terms of its own unique consequences. A changing world—a world still in the making—requires constant readaptation.

Dewey was especially interested in promoting a humanistic model of science. He believed that scientific procedures should be used to examine ethical and moral questions. However, he felt that although modern science was highly developed in a technological sense, it was extremely underdeveloped when applied to social problems. For Dewey (1948), the problem was one of neglect:

When "sociological" theory withdraws from consideration of basic interests, concerns, the actively moving aims, of a human culture on the ground that "values" are involved and that inquiry as "scientific" has nothing to do with values, the inevitable consequence is that inquiry in the human area is confined to what is superficial and comparatively trivial, no matter what its parade of technical skills. (p. xxvi)

Social theory then exists as an idle luxury rather than a concrete guide to constructive social change.

When Dewey was at the University of Chicago in the 1890s, he began to put his ideas about science into practice. The city itself was a focal point for social reform during the Progressive Era, and one of the mandates of the new university was to become a resource for dealing with social problems within the community. Dewey spearheaded efforts among philosophers and psychologists to become involved in community projects by applying scientific procedures to social problems. In these endeavors he worked especially closely with Mead (Joas, 1985).

Both men were associated with Hull House, the settlement house founded and directed by Jane Addams. Like other American settlement houses, Hull House was located in a slum district of the city and served the needs of the local community. This consisted largely of recent immigrants, working women, and former farm workers who had been attracted to Chicago by the new job opportunities. Hull House was a prototype of the settlement-house movement and was therefore committed to the goal of educating its clientele so that they could become active participants within the various social institutions that affected their lives. The settlement houses were engaged in a process of giving power to disadvantaged groups so that they could function within mainstream society and become part of a bona fide participatory democracy.

For Dewey, the principle of participatory democracy embodied his blueprint for a humanistic science. Scientific thinking, which is based on empirical verification, was to contribute to constructive social change.

The justification for such intervention rests on the ethical desirability of creating social conditions that enable individuals to function as active agents within their environment. Thus, social institutions, such as settlement houses, which are committed to social reform serve as experimental laboratories for testing the effectiveness of intervention programs.

Dewey's major social laboratory at Chicago was The Laboratory School. According to Dewey, the goal of education was to maximize an individual's potential to function as an active agent within society. Thus, schools should prepare children to become adults who are capable of actively participating in democratic institutions. To accomplish this, he instituted a program of educational reform that made the children's own activities and their informal group life the focus of the school experience. The educational process was to involve children in an ongoing interaction with their environment, thereby developing their intellectual, practical, and social skills. Dewey's work at the Laboratory School formed the foundation for his later work in "progressive education."

As a result of his early textbook on psychology, Dewey's writings began to attract the attention of James in 1887, and the two began a correspondence that extended over eighteen years. Initially, Dewey expressed the opinion that he was merely rendering back James's thought in a more logical form (letter to James in Perry, 1936, p. 509), but eventually James was deriving as much if not more from the relationship than Dewey. James saw Dewey as more radical and self-consistent than himself, since his own work included areas that were irrelevant if not alien to pragmatism (Perry, 1935). Dewey did not have Peirce's demonic drive or James's literary genius, but he had the patience and thoroughness that they both conspicuously lacked, plus a career that lasted almost seventy years. As Gordon Allport (1943) pointed out, "so whole-hearted is [Dewey's] conversion to the functional position that he accuses James of faint-heartedness (p. 107)." Dewey not only overtook James but surpassed him.

## George Herbert Mead (1863–1931)

George Herbert Mead was born in South Hadley, Massachusetts, but his family moved to Oberlin, Ohio, when he was seven years old. His father was a Congregational minister who taught homiletics (writing and presenting sermons) at Oberlin Theological Seminary. His mother was a well-read, cultured woman who taught briefly at Oberlin College after her husband died and later became President of Mount Holyoke College. Mead entered Oberlin in 1879 at the age of 16. Although the curriculum was limited, Oberlin was a center for social and political activity. It had been founded in 1833 on a major path of the Underground Railway, was one of the first colleges to admit blacks, and in 1841 was the first coeducational institution to grant degrees to women.

While at Oberlin, Mead became close friends with Henry Castle, who came from a powerful and wealthy landowning family in Hawaii. After graduating in 1883, Mead taught grade school for a brief period, worked on a survey crew for three years, and then joined Castle at Harvard in 1887 for graduate study in philosophy. The two were roommates until Mead began tutoring William James's children and moved into his home. Despite their proximity at Harvard, Mead took no courses from James, and there is no evidence that they were close friends. Mead's mentor at Harvard was the neo-Hegelian Josiah Royce.

After receiving his master's degree in 1888, Mead decided to specialize in experimental psychology rather than philosophy because he felt that scientific research would give him more freedom to develop his ideas (Joas, 1985). Henry Castle had gone to Europe to pursue more advanced studies, and Mead joined him and spent the winter semester of 1888–89 at the University of Leipzig. It was here that Wilhelm Wundt had established the first laboratory for experimental psychology. Mead enrolled in one of Wundt's classes in philosophy and was thus exposed to Wundt's epistemological orientation in general as well as his ideas about social psychology. After one semester in Leipzig, Mead transferred to the University of Berlin, where he spent the next two years. Among his teachers were Hermann Ebbinghaus, an experimental psychologist, and Wilhelm Dilthey, a philosopher and psychologist. These two held very different positions. Dilthey advocated a psychology based on the interpretive methods of the humanistic sciences, whereas Ebbinghaus saw psychology as a natural science and advocated empirical research. Mead later developed a position that straddled this controversy and incorporated both extremes. His objective was to study the interpretive accomplishments of the human "soul" with the methods of natural science (Joas, 1985).

For his doctoral dissertation, under Dilthey's supervision, Mead chose to study the role of vision and touch in spatial perception. However, in 1891 he left Berlin with his new bride, Helen Castle (Henry's sister) to accept a position as instructor of psychology in the Department of Philosophy at the University of Michigan. He never completed his dissertation. At Michigan, Mead became a close friend of John Dewey, who was in the same department. The two developed a partnership and to a great extent a division of labor that lasted for the rest of Mead's life. While Dewey contributed range and breadth, Mead concentrated on a few basic issues and gave depth and precision to their ideas (Morris, 1962). According to David L. Miller (1973), Dewey was "the one person he respected and admired above all others. There is not a word of criticism of Dewey in Mead's work, and where Dewey is not altogether clear, Mead suggests that he must have meant 'thus and so'" (p. xx). Mead and Dewey's close friendship makes it difficult to separate their ideas. Dewey (1931) described Mead as "the most original mind in philosophy in America of the last generation" (p. 310) and confessed that it was difficult to imagine what his own position would have been without him. Lewis and Smith (1980) contend that the social aspects of Dewey's theory were taken directly from Mead and are tangential to his central thesis that thought occurs during a process of adjustment. They concede, however, that the question of who influenced whom is difficult if not impossible to resolve. Dewey was given the opportunity

to set up the Department of Philosophy (which also included psychology) at the University of Chicago in 1894 and agreed on the condition that he could bring Mead with him. Dewey moved to Columbia in 1904, and Mead remained at Chicago until 1931. That year he accepted an appointment at Columbia but died before he could begin the new position.

Although Mead never obtained his Ph.D., this did not prevent his rapid promotion. He became an Associate Professor in 1902 and was promoted to Full Professor in 1907. Mead became something of an institution at Chicago. He was a large, handsome man who often jogged down the Midway and rode to lecture halls on a bicycle. He was mild-mannered, soft-spoken, and seldom looked at his students while he lectured. Mead was friendly with the professors in the Department of Sociology but taught in the Department of Philosophy (psychology became a separate department in 1905).

His close relationship with the sociology department produced a steady stream of students taking his courses, especially the one on social psychology. He began teaching this course in 1900 and worked out his ideas throughout the remainder of this life. Lewis and Smith (1980) have collected data on the impact of Mead's course and found that 43 percent of all Ph.D.s in sociology during this period took at least one of Mead's courses, typically social psychology, and another 28% of all graduate students sat in or audited his courses. Mead was also widely discussed among students, and his ideas were passed on by such people as Herbert Blumer and Ellsworth Faris. Mead's students included many of the most influential people in American sociology, including the later editors of both major journals.

A brief treatment of Mead's ideas is difficult for several reasons. First, Mead never published an overview of his work, and the articles published during his life are too difficult and obscure to serve as an introduction (see Mead, 1964). Miscellaneous writings and lecture notes were gathered after his death and published in four separate volumes (Mead, 1932, 1934, 1936, 1938), but there is no evidence that Mead would have published any of them in the form in which they appeared. Many of Mead's most important concepts, such as the self, phases of the act, and the play and game stages of development were introduced quite early, but the simultaneous publication of all Mead's writings on a given topic in the edited volumes makes it difficult to see the development of his ideas. Old treatments are presented along with refinements made much later. Helen Swick Perry (1982), the biographer of the American psychoanalytic theorist, Harry Stack Sullivan, has suggested that Mead resembles Sullivan in this respect. Neither published any books while they were alive and both seemed to have been constantly reworking their ideas, possibly too intensively and rapidly to pause for publication (Strauss, 1956). According to Dewey (1932), the real tragedy of Mead's untimely death was that "there is every reason to think that he was beginning to get a command of his ideas which made communication to others easier and more effective" (p. xi).

As in the case of Dewey, Mead wrote on a wide variety of philosophical and social issues. His interests included such diverse topics as social reform, education, the history of philosophy, and the theoretical foundations of physics. However, the core of Mead's pragmatism, like Dewey's, can be characterized by the three themes of functionalism, intersubjectivity, and humanism.

Mead's functionalism is an outgrowth of Dewey's critique of the reflex arc concept in psychology (Cook, 1977). As mentioned, Dewey's 1896 article attacked the atomistic model of behavior that was becoming increasingly popular at the time among physiologically oriented psychologists. In place of the division between sensory stimulus and motor response, Dewey saw behavior as a coordinated system of acts with sensory and motor functions and stressed that behavior must be understood as an adaptation to the environment. Dewey's essay served as a launching pad for the functionalist school of psychology at Chicago, which was guided by Mead and James Rowland Angell after Dewey's departure. From a series of articles beginning in 1900 through the publication

of his lectures given in 1927 (Mead, 1934), Mead extended Dewey's functionalism to include social dimensions of behavior.

By the 1920s, Mead chose the term "social behaviorism" to characterize his position. There were two reasons for the choice (Cook, 1977). First, he began to feel that many psychologists who described themselves as functionalists no longer upheld Dewey's nondualistic position. He also felt that "behaviorism" more accurately reflected the emphasis that he and Dewey placed on overt behavior. However, he clearly distinguished their model from the version developed by John B. Watson.

For Mead, behaviorism is a psychological approach that focuses on overt behavior. Behavior, however, is linked with internal states of consciousness, such as attitudes, intentions, and social meaning. While the study of behavior is the primary subject of psychology, psychologists must also consider the relationship between thought and behavior. Mead was critical of both introspectionists and Watsonian behaviorists because he felt that they both fell into the dualistic trap. Introspectionists studied consciousness and excluded behavior, whereas the Watsonians studied behavior but excluded consciousness. Mead's approach includes behavior, consciousness, and their interaction. Unfortunately, Mead's interpretation of behaviorism was quickly overshadowed by Watson's so that by the 1920s "behaviorism" became virtually synonymous with Watson's approach. Watson's impact on social psychology will be discussed in the next chapter.

The term "social behaviorism" was chosen in order to convey the message that thought and action had to be understood within a social context. Mead criticized Watson's approach not only because it neglected inner experience but also because it neglected the social dimensions of human behavior. In building Dewey's functionalism, Mead sought to explain how thoughts and actions are influenced by social factors. Although Mead, like Dewey, never used the term "intersubjectivity," this concept best reflects how Mead viewed the interaction between the individual and society (Joas, 1985). The thoughts and actions of an individual evolve within a social network of language, customs, conventions, and beliefs. The communication of thoughts as expressed in speech is especially significant in shaping human development, and each person functions within a network of interpersonal relations.

Mead's social psychology is thus based on a conception of an individual as part of a social group. There can be no individual without social relations. Society exists prior to the individual, and each person is born into a world with cultural patterns and social institutions already intact. In Mead's (1934) words:

> We attempt, that is, to explain the conduct of the individual in terms of the organized conduct of the social group, rather than to account for the organized conduct of the social group in terms of the conduct of the separate individuals belonging to it. For social psychology, the whole (society) is prior to the part (the individual), not the part to the whole; and the part is explained in terms of the whole, not the whole in terms of the part or parts. (p. 7)

Mead's approach to social psychology initially drew from Wundt and Darwin (Farr, 1983, 1987b). The first two volumes of Wundt's multivolume *Völkerpsychologie* were published in 1904 and dealt with the development of human speech. Wundt extended some of the ideas that Darwin (1872) had introduced in his book *The Expression of Emotions in Man and Animals.* While Darwin described innate facial and bodily expressions associated with emotions, Wundt focused on human gestures and placed them within a social context.

Mead was especially interested in the relationship between gestures and language. He contrasted the "conversation of gestures" that occurs during a dog or cat fight and expresses emotions more or less automatically, with human gestures, which acquire meaning through social interaction and serve as the basis for language development. Because language as a means of communication shapes consciousness, Mead was able to show that consciousness is derived from human interaction. This position enabled him to bridge the gap between Wundt's experimental and social psychology. Wundt's belief that language was a product of consciousness (rather than the other way around) obscured the connection between consciousness and the social context and led him to develop two separate disciplines—experimental and social psychology—that were equally important yet disconnected. For Mead, gestures and language as forms of social behavior served as the social origins of consciousness itself.

The concept of self is a key component in Mead's approach. According to Mead, self-awareness occurs as an aspect of consciousness and is derived through exchange with other people. Mead, like James, differentiated two aspects of the self—the "I" and the "me." The "I" serves as the source of people's ability to create and transform their environment, whereas the "me" represents their objective self-awareness. Mead's views about the self were also influenced by Cooley's concept of the "looking-glass self," but Mead felt that Cooley had not gone far enough in explaining the self's social origins. For Cooley (1902), the self consisted of an "instinctive" feeling that "exists in a vague though vigorous form at the birth of each individual" (p. 137). By starting with the self rather than society, Cooley was stuck with the problem of how independent selves come to know each other, and his only recourse was the process of "sympathetic introspection." Mead also felt that Cooley's treatment provided an overly subjective theory of mental activity. For Cooley (1902), the "imaginations which people have of one another are the solid facts of society" (p. 121). Mead, on the other hand, felt that society existed prior to each individual, and he argued that self-awareness and self-conscious mental activity arose during the process of socialization. The ideas of independent selves and subjective mental activity were precisely the sort of problems that Mead sought to surmount. Mead's social-psychological perspective gave rise to the symbolic interaction movement in sociology which began in the 1930s at the University of Chicago, and these developments will be discussed in more detail in Chapter 11.

Mead, like Dewey, stressed the link between theory and practice. While functionalism and intersubjectivity provided the theoretical foundations for this thought, social problem solving was the testing ground for his ideas. Mead's humanism, like Dewey's, is rooted in his concern with the ethical implications of human behavior. While Mead was strongly influenced by Dewey, his concern with social and political reform predates his contact with Dewey. His exposure to Hegel and the notion of the self as a creative force are expressed in his earlier writings on ethics. Mead also developed an interest in socialism while he was in Germany and had been impressed with the German social-democratic labor movement. In America, he and his wife were active in the women's suffrage movement, and because they were independently wealthy, they donated money for social research.

According to Mead, ethics is not based on any universal or predetermined system of values (Joas, 1985). Ethical decisions involve a reflective process engaged in by actors when they attempt to solve moral problems. Because all relevant values must be considered, individuals cannot successfully deal with moral problems alone. They must communicate with other people who can judge the validity of each step in the decision. Solutions to moral problems are thus based on a process of cooperation and communication with other members of the community.

For Mead, moral development occurs within a social context and involves a process in which each individual is able to understand the needs and concerns of others and participate in communal decisions. Mead believed that the extent to which people can develop this potential depends on the type of society of which they are a part. For Mead, the ideal society is one in which people are free from domination. Only under such conditions can people fully engage in communal decisions and change outmoded social institutions. Joas (1985) has pointed out that Mead, like Dewey, did not explicitly deal with the social conditions that could enhance or impede progress toward a fully functioning democratic society. Within the optimistic progressive climate,

they believed that American political and social institutions could accommodate democratic processes.

Mead, like Dewey, also believed that science could significantly contribute to constructive social change. Mead (1936) argued that the problem-solving process inherent in the scientific method could be applied to social issues as well. Scientists through their training and work develop a "reflective intelligence" in which they systematically weigh alternative solutions to problems. Scientific theories and data, therefore, undergo a continual process of evaluative criticism and revision. The gathering of empirical data parallels the communal decision-making process of moral problem solving in which all relevant values are assessed and initial solutions are revised through a process of communicative exchange. According to Mead (1936), "The scientific method is that by means of which the individual can state his criticism, can bring forward the solution, and bring it to the test of the community" (p. 415).

Consistent with his view about the social relevance of science, Mead was involved with various community projects (see Deegan & Burger, 1978; Joas, 1985). With Dewey, he worked with Jane Addams at Hull House. He was also associated with Dewey's Laboratory School and other educational reforms. Other commitments included participation in strike-arbitration committees, the women's rights movement, and various groups concerned with the elimination of government corruption. After World War I, he focused on international relations and advocated the need for mutual cooperation and understanding, the rational resolution of conflicts, and the application of scientific procedures to world problems.

Both Mead and Dewey shared a pragmatist commitment to evolutionary social change (Mills, 1966; Roberts, 1977). In his analysis of the development of Western thought, Mead (1936) argued that a democratic society based on the ideals of the French Revolution requires gradual change. Overthrowing a constitutional government was unnecessary, since the democratic system itself incorporates the mechanisms necessary for constitutional change. Mead felt that it was important to maintain some conservative elements in the form of customs and tradition. Democratic systems were viable if the populace maintained aspects of tradition and became actively involved in political processes. Both Mead and Dewey felt that education was important in preparing youth to become socially responsible and politically active adults. In essence, education provided the training ground for developing socialized individuals who could participate rationally in community problem solving. Mead and Dewey also felt that community institutions, such as settlement houses, were necessary for socializing relatively powerless segments of society, such as women and immigrants, so that they could become a part of the political process.

Dewey and Mead's prescription for a psychology that was holistic rather than atomistic, social rather than individualistic, and humanistic rather than value-free had little impact on psychology. Within two decades of Dewey's 1896 functionalist manifesto (the reflex arc article), Watson's 1913 behaviorist manifesto helped make behaviorism a leading approach to American psychology. Watson did not really redirect American psychology. He simply articulated the direction in which the discipline had been moving—a positivist science in the mold of the Newtonian mechanistic world view (see Chapter 5). The pragmatist perspective of a psychology with a strong philosophical foundation, concerned with self-reflection as well as observable behavior, and oriented toward social reform fell out of fashion. During the social unrest of the 1930s and 1960s, some psychologists returned to Dewey and Mead's concern for social relevance (see Chapters 8 and 13), but their major impact was on the development of a sociological rather than a psychological approach to social psychology.

While each of the four originators of pragmatism chose a different term to distinguish his particular version of pragmatism—"pragmaticism," "radical empiricism," "instrumentalism," and "social behaviorism"—the differences should not mask the similarities. For each, thought is based on language and begins with uncertainty. The thinking individual plans a future course of action, carries it out, and then examines the consequences in order to verify the prediction. Thought arises during the course of concrete activity but can be applied to other areas as well. Correct thinking does not come naturally but requires a great amount of difficult work. The self is a social product and changes with changing social conditions. Our most deep-seated prejudices and beliefs are often the product of an unquestioned acceptance of traditional ideas, and constructive social change comes only through examining these carefully and retaining only those that deserve to be retained. All four were strong supporters of the experimental method and used it as a prototype for correct thinking in general. As Morton White (1943) has pointed out, nineteenth-century America, although unsuccessful in producing scientific thinkers of the first rank, did produce four of its loudest cheerleaders. The differences between these formulations are "in-house" variations, which may have been important to the originators but pale in comparison to the similarities.

## THE CHICAGO SCHOOL OF SOCIOLOGY

The origin of the Chicago School of sociology has already been discussed in Chapter 3. Charles Ellwood, Emory Bogardus, and Luther L. Bernard each received his Ph.D. at the University of Chicago. While they drew heavily from the French work on imitation, they were also influenced by the courses they took from Dewey and Mead (Rucker, 1969). For the faculty members who constituted the sociology department, the reduced teaching load and emphasis on research established by President Harper, along with the administrative skills of Albion Small, made the school possible. The school itself was based on a coordinated series of studies that focused on the disruptive effects of migration, urbanization, and industrialization.

The Chicago School included, among others, three interesting thinkers—W. I. Thomas, Robert Park, and Kimball Young. Thomas initiated the research tradition that helped shift sociology away from abstract social theory with his massive five-volume work, *The Polish Peasant in Europe and America* (Thomas & Znaniecki, 1918–1920). While the beginning of the Chicago School is usually associated with Robert Park and his associates, Park (1939) acknowledged that W. I. Thomas established the research tradition that he later extended. Park took over after Thomas left the University of Chicago in 1918. He was an outstanding teacher who coordinated the dissertations of a whole generation of graduate students, directing them toward problems associated with urban life in Chicago. Both Thomas and Park had their initial contacts with Dewey and Mead as students—Park with Dewey at Michigan and Thomas with both at Chicago.

Kimball Young was a student of Thomas and Mead who carried on the Chicago tradition in his subsequent work. Young, however, also studied with Lewis M. Terman, one of the leaders in the mental testing movement. He was thus exposed to both the social interaction perspective and the hereditarian approach and is therefore an interesting case study of someone caught between two conflicting world views. A subtheme running throughout this section is the relationship between these men and George Herbert Mead.

## W. I. Thomas (1863–1947)

W. I. Thomas was born in Virginia and raised in Tennessee. He received a Ph.D. from the University of Tennessee in 1886 and taught Greek, Latin, French, German, and English there from 1884 to 1888. During the 1888–1889 academic year he studied at the Universities of Göttingen and Berlin, where he was exposed to German folk psychology and the new field of ethnology. After his return to the United States he taught English at Oberlin College and took a year's leave of absence to complete a doctorate in sociology at the University of Chicago. After receiving his second Ph.D. in 1896, he was given an academic appointment at Chicago in the Department of Sociology. Before he started teaching, he traveled extensively throughout Europe, where he developed the idea that it would be interesting to compare European immigrants before and after immigration.

Although Thomas received his Ph.D. in sociology, he claimed that Franz Boas, the cultural anthropologist, had a greater influence on him than his teachers in sociology (Murray, 1988). He read widely in related areas, including biology, psychology, and philosophy. He was one of Mead's first students and took three courses from him—two on comparative psychology and one on psychological methods. Thomas began his career as a biological sociologist, with a Ph.D. on metabolism in men and women. His notion of four "wishes"—the desire for new experience, security, response, and recognition—attempts to explain social behavior by positing driving forces within the individual. However, during the first decade of the twentieth century, he began to stress the interaction between people and their social environment. This shift in emphasis appears to be based on his increasing involvement in various social reform activities, including the work of Jane Addams at Hull House (Deegan & Burger, 1981). He also became increasingly interested in the special problems of minority groups and began to study women, immigrants, and blacks.

Thomas received a grant for $50,000 in 1908 in order to carry out research on immigrant problems. He decided to study Polish people because of the large Polish population in Chicago. The choice proved to be a fortunate one, since Polish peasants had lived under conditions virtually unchanged for centuries. Their migration to the United States produced massive social disruption as they left what were essentially feudal conditions and moved into urban-industrial society. Thomas spent a considerable time in Europe between 1908 and 1913—approximately eight months a year. Florian Znaniecki (1882–1952), a Polish philosopher who headed the Bureau for the Protection of Immigrants in Warsaw, was brought in on the project in 1914. By 1918, they had amassed over 8,000 personal documents, including letters, newspaper articles, and government records, which formed the data base from which *The Polish Peasant* was derived.

Thomas and Znaniecki's (1918–1920) study traced the disruptive effects of urbanization, migration, and industrialization on the day-to-day lives of individuals in Poland and Chicago. It resembles Durkheim's (1893/1964, 1895/1964) research on suicide and the division of labor to a certain extent but with a much greater emphasis on the individual. They began by distinguishing social attitudes and social values. Social values, like Durkheim's "social facts," exist outside of the individual in the broader social context, whereas attitudes are the subjective social-psychological counterpart of social values. A person internalizes attitudes during the process of socialization and modifies them as social conditions change. While they persist they form the bases for a person's interpretation of the situation. The same "thing" has a different meaning for a philosopher and a child. Behavior is determined not by attitudes alone but by a combination of attitudes and situational factors.

The disruptive effects of immigration in the Polish peasant were due to the breakdown of traditional values based on the family and group solidarity and the development of new individualistic attitudes that stressed vanity, personal achievement, and self-indulgence. In Poland, the extended family was the basic social unit. The individual reacted to praise or blame directed toward the family as personal criticism, and the community refused to disassociate the individual and his or her family. The family and the community as a whole were held together by a unanimity of opinion, and shared attitudes were retained even when they were no longer useful, because they provided mutual solidarity for the group.

The demise of the family as a source of personal prestige is an inevitable consequence of urbanization. When individuals can no longer depend on the family for social recognition, they must rely on personal achievement or ostentatious displays of wealth. New values based on hedonism,

that is, pleasures such as food, drink, and tobacco that cannot be shared, and vanity based on "showing off" with fashionable clothes and jewelry develop. If individuals confront no opposition within the family, they merely adopt the new attitudes and lose interest in the family. If opposition occurs, they may break ties with the family by immigrating. If people meet opposition but retain traditional attitudes, they experience conflict and hostility and antisocial behavior may result.

But individuals cannot remain isolated for long. If they separate themselves from their family, they begin to associate with other people with similar hedonistic attitudes. Thomas found that the Polish peasant extended the principles of solidarity to strangers initially but often went to the opposite extreme when these were not reciprocated. Disorganization is complete once people begin to apply self-serving and dishonest behavior to their own social group. As long as antisocial behavior is limited to a few people, it is treated as abnormal, but it can become institutionalized if widespread. Criminal behavior is often based on new bonds of solidarity, with criminal elements, and the community begins to lose the uniformity of opinion that makes a common perspective and cooperative behavior possible. The original solidarity based on the extended family cannot be regained once lost, because the individual who has learned to operate on hedonistic principles cannot unlearn them and return to the primarily "we" attitude associated with the family.

The disruptive effects of urbanization depend not just on social conditions but on temperament as well. Thomas identified three personality types—the Philistine, the Bohemian, and the creative individual. Philistines completely accept the existing social norms. Their need for security is stronger than their desire for new experience. Bohemians, on the other hand, have a strong desire for new experience and reject prevailing social norms. They show a degree of adaptability unknown to the Philistine, but their adaptability is provisional and they may be unable to form a coherent personality because of their desire to avoid being controlled. The creative man reconciles the desire for security and the desire for new experience by redefining the situation and creating new social norms more appropriate for the changing social conditions. No individual is strictly one type or the other. Each person contains a mixture of Philistine and Bohemian elements, and the precise combination may change as the person matures. Young people often have a strong desire for new experience, but the need for security increases as they grow older. Temperament can be modified by social conditions, but it is also in part a "chemical matter," dependent on individual biochemistry.

Thomas also distinguished revolt and revolution. Revolt is an individual outburst against existing social conditions. Revolution is a premeditated attempt to change society and is guided toward specific social goals widely shared by the community. Revolutionary attitudes in the Polish peasant were often inspired by intellectuals from the noble class, who formalized attitudes already present but unexpressed. The Polish intelligentsia changed revolt into revolution by showing that the discontent experienced by individual peasants was due to general social conditions and that grievances were widely shared.

While Thomas, like the pragmatists, assumes that consciousness occurs when an individual confronts a specific problem, it would be a mistake to assume that most behavior occurs with a great deal of deliberation. Habit plays an important role, and consciousness occurs only when a new experience cannot be properly assimilated. Thomas (1966) stated that "the prepossessions of all of us are at a given moment deeper than we suspect, that society is in a hypnoidal state with lucid intervals" (p. 178). Nevertheless, behavior is always based on a person's interpretation of the situation. The prejudices and preconceptions that one brings to a situation determine one's response to it. Or as Thomas (1966) put it, "if men define those situations as real, they are real in their consequences" (p. 301, also in Thomas & Thomas, 1938). Individuals living in society have to fit into a preexisting social world, but their reaction to it is based on beliefs and attitudes as well as concrete social conditions.

*The Polish Peasant* was an ambitious project that tried to capture the total change occurring within an immigrant population as they were absorbed into American society, but it was originally envisioned as part of a larger project that would compare various immigrant groups. It used an open-ended methodology where techniques were improved as the study progressed. Thomas saw *The Polish Peasant* as a pioneering study that would be supplemented by later studies with better methods. The case study method was seen as providing the background and the social context within which more limited statistical studies could be understood.

It would be difficult to overestimate the impact of *The Polish Peasant*. Thomas helped develop the idea that more could be gained by inspecting social conditions than from reading other theories and helped move sociology from the armchair into the field. Many of the topics introduced in *The Polish Peasant*—the disruptive effects of urbanization and migration, leadership, education, cooperative institutions, and the mass media—dominated sociology for the next decade. Thomas's work was instrumental in establishing attitudes as the central concept within social psychology and was a direct forerunner of the culture and personality studies carried out during the 1930s and 1940s (see Chapter 6). He showed that maladjustment within immigrant groups was a result of social disruption rather than genetic weakness, and attitudes of social workers toward these groups changed radically as a consequence. *The Polish Peasant* was singled out by members of the American Sociological Society in 1938 as the most important sociological work ever written.

It is somewhat ironic that the first two volumes of *The Polish Peasant* appeared in 1918, the same year that Thomas was forced to leave the University of Chicago for alleged violations of the Mann Act and false hotel registration. Thomas taught briefly at

Harvard and the New School for Social Research, but without the institutional base provided by the University of Chicago and the intellectual support of those within and outside the Department of Sociology, he never regained his intellectual agenda. Thomas's work can perhaps be best understood as a transitional work between individual psychology and sociology. Thomas did not directly examine social institutions but relied on personal documents that described social changes as they were being experienced by those who were affected. Thomas's work was extended by his close friend Robert Park, who based his conclusions on direct observation of social institutions.

### Robert Park (1864–1944)

The Chicago School of sociology is most closely associated with the urban reseach directed by Robert Park and his associate, Ernest Burgess (1886–1966), during the 1920s. With the exception of W. I. Thomas, the prewar Department of Sociology at the University of Chicago had not been exceptional. Park joined the department in 1914 but taught part-time until the early 1920s. Between 1915 and 1925, the number of people in the department actually fell from eight to five and consisted of three sociologists, Park, Burgess, and Ellsworth Faris, and two anthropologists, Edward Sapir and Fay Cooper-Cole (Bulmer, 1984). The small size of the department encouraged close personal contact between students and teachers and an interdisciplinary approach.

Robert Park was born in Pennsylvania but grew up in a small town in Minnesota. He studied under John Dewey as an undergraduate and received a bachelor's degree from the University of Michigan in 1887. He worked as a reporter on a number of daily papers between 1887 and 1898 before returning to academic life at Harvard, where he took courses from Hugo Munsterberg, Josiah Royce, and William James, and received an M.A. in 1899. This was followed by a period of study in Germany, where he came into contact with Georg Simmel at the University of Berlin and received a Ph.D. from Heidelberg in 1904. He

was William James's assistant at Harvard for one year and then served as secretary and companion to the black civil-rights activist, Booker T. Washington, from 1905 to 1914.

Park thus alternated periods of academic life with periods of social involvement, serving as a newspaper reporter where he was often given special assignments to study urban problems in depth (Coser, 1977) and as an aide to someone trying to reduce the problem of racial prejudice. He was well-versed in pragmatism through his association with Dewey and James, but pragmatism formed only a relatively minor aspect of his intellectual development. His European training made him open to European ideas, and he had an extensive knowledge of both German and French social theory. His travels in both Europe and the United States caused him to look at the community as a social organism with a life of its own that was at least partially independent of the will and desires of the individuals contained within it.

Thomas met Park on a visit to the Tuskeegee Institute in 1914, when Park was fifty, and arranged for him to teach a summer course at the University of Chicago. They collaborated on a project eventually published as *Old World Traits Transplanted* (Park & Miller, 1921), published without Thomas's name, and remained close friends after Thomas was forced to leave the university in 1918. Ernest Burgess joined the department in 1919, and throughout the 1920s he shared an office with Park and collaborated in writing and supervising graduate students. Burgess had skills that Park lacked and often made methodological improvements on general projects suggested by Park. He was also able to obtain "seed money" for students whose dissertations required extensive field work, but Park remained the central figure in the development of the Chicago School. He shared the leadership with Thomas and Burgess, but neither Thomas nor Burgess could have created the Chicago School without him (see Bulmer, 1984).

Park's career as a sociologist was in many ways an extension of his career as a journalist. As a reporter, he was often given special assignments to study urban problems in depth, and he encouraged the same kind of extensive coverage in his students. He functioned somewhat like a city editor, assigning projects to individual students, coordinating projects, making suggestions, and helping rewrite the final version. Looking back, Park later described the sociologist as "a kind of super-reporter."

There were, nevertheless, several important differences. First, Park felt that sociologists should place a much greater emphasis on scientific accuracy. He and Burgess encouraged their students to use a number of different approaches—interviews, observations, a search of newspaper files and court records, and so on—to deal with the same topics. Discrepancies were checked and cross-checked to insure as much accuracy as possible. Since there were no deadlines, projects often took years to complete. Second, Park quickly realized that the detached, cynical perspective of reporters was not sufficient and encouraged his students to get to know their subjects from the inside out. Park and Burgess pioneered what later became known as "participant observation," which attempts to overcome the limitations of ethnocentrism by active involvement in the daily lives of those being investigated. The main criteria for success was that the study penetrate beneath the conventional mask worn by others and tap their true thoughts and feelings.

The conceptual framework for urban research was provided by Park (1915) in an article called "The City" and extended by Burgess (1925) in an essay called "The Growth of the City," which described urban development in terms of concentric zones. Both rejected the idea that society consists of independent individuals who create social institutions through voluntary association. The city is only partially planned and contains various features that direct and control the behavior of the individuals who live in it.

One of the most characteristic features of the city is a marked division of labor. Every vocation, even that of beggar, becomes a profession, and people respond to one another superficially as vocational types. This high degree of specialization creates a mu-

tual dependence far greater than that found in rural communities. All sorts of people meet and mingle who do not know or understand each other, and secondary institutions begin to replace primary institutions based on intimate face-to-face contact.

Under these conditions, status is determined largely by fashion and a knowledge of superficial styles and manners. The superficiality of day-to-day relations allows individuals to move freely from one group to another and encourages them to live in more than one social group at the same time. Not only do people play social roles or wear masks, but these masks become their true selves and an integral part of their personality. This gives the city an exciting quality that tends to break down old-world values, speed up social change, and draw young people from outlying areas. The removal of social restraints tends to promote vice, delinquency, and criminal behavior and creates subgroups who specialize in these activities.

Burgess (1925) described urban development in terms of a series of concentric zones. At the center of the city is a business district, consisting of banks, high-rise buildings, department stores, and the best hotels and restaurants. This is where transport routes converge, and property prices are so high that other activities are excluded. Encircling this is a zone of transition where property is held for future business expansion. This area, often known as "skid row," tends to become a slum and the center for homeless individuals. It is unplanned but occurs with remarkable similarity in city after city and persists in spite of public and official opposition. Outside of this is a working-class district made up of families who have escaped from the area of deterioration but want to live close to factories and facilities where they work. Beyond this is a residential zone made up of apartment buildings and exclusive middle-class homes. And finally there is a commuter zone consisting of suburbs and satellite cities within an hour's access of the central business district. Rates of crime and juvenile delinquency are highest in the central slum district and progressively decrease as one moves outward from the center of the city. Moreover, high

rates tend to persist through successive occupations by different ethnic groups. There
are numerous departures from Burgess's
zonal pattern based on waterways, street design, hills, and heavy industry, but the overall pattern is quite common. It is approxi-
mated most closely in Cleveland and
Chicago and hardly at all in Boston and
New York.

The reputation of the University of Chicago as the center for sociological research
rested on a series of urban studies published
in the 1920s and early 1930s under the supervision of Park and Burgess. Park and
Burgess regularly sent students into the city
as part of their course requirement. These
observations often grew into papers, dissertations, and occasionally books. The Sociological Series of the University of Chicago
Press published nearly two dozen books in
less than two decades, including *The Negro
in Chicago* (Johnson, 1922); *The Hobo* (Anderson, 1923); *Family Disorganization*
(Mowrer, 1927); *The Gang* (Thrasher,
1927); *The Ghetto* (Wirth, 1928); *The Gold
Coast and the Slum* (Zorbaugh, 1929); *The
Taxi-Dance Hall* (Cressy, 1932); and *Vice
in Chicago* (Reckless, 1933). Each one included an introduction by either Park or
Burgess explaining the work and its theoretical significance.

The Chicago School was based on a number of fortuitous circumstances—leadership, student participation, financial support, and the city itself. Many of the studies
could not have been conducted without financial support. Nel Anderson, for example, received $300 for his study of the hobo,
which allowed him to live among them during his period of participant observation.
Large block grants were given by the Local
Community Research Committee and the
Rockefeller Foundation and distributed to
individual students by Burgess (see Bulmer,
1984). The city provided a natural laboratory for urban research. When Max Weber
visited Chicago in 1904, he compared it to
a man whose skin had been peeled off and
insides exposed. Chicago was a raw and
open city, and this openness stimulated research.

The urban research at the University of
Chicago was so successful that if often appeared to be the exclusive focus and obscured other trends occurring at the same
time. Park himself had many other interests. He had completed his Ph.D. on crowd
behavior and kept this interest alive by frequently teaching a course on the subject.
Because of his early association with Booker
T. Washington, Park maintained a strong
interest in race relations and encouraged
Emory Bogardus to develop the social-dis-
tance scale, which was the first real attempt
to quantify individual attitudes (see Chapters 8 and 10). Park and Burgess (1921)
wrote the classic textbook *Introduction to
the Science of Sociology,* popularly known
as the "green bible" (Bulmer, 1984), which
helped standardize the discipline and introduce the European tradition of Simmel,
Durkheim, and Weber to America.

More important for our purposes were
developments within sociological social
psychology. Neither Park nor Burgess had
strong qualifications as a social psychologist
(R. Faris, 1967). Park was a personal friend
of George Herbert Mead and spoke highly
of him in public, but he does not appear to
have been greatly influenced by him (Coser,
1977). During Park's tenure at the University of Chicago, five doctoral dissertations
focusing on social psychology were carried
out. This pales in comparison to the number of studies on urban issues, but it does
suggest that social psychology was a significant subtheme within the Chicago School.
This emphasis became even stronger after
Park retired in the early 1930s and Faris became head of the department (see Chapter
11).

### Kimball Young (1893–1973)

Kimball Young was born in Utah. His
grandfather was the Mormon leader,
Brigham Young. After completing his undergraduate studies in 1915 at Brigham
Young University, he went to the University of Chicago to do graduate work in sociology. His mentor at Chicago was W. I.
Thomas, and he also studied with Mead.
After receiving his master's degree in 1918,
Young was involved in the World War I
army testing program, and when he decided

to further his graduate education in 1919, he chose to study psychology at Stanford University with Lewis M. Terman, one of the architects of the mental tests used during the war. Terman was eager to adapt the army intelligence tests for widespread use in the schools. While he was working on a revised version of these tests for the elementary grades, his students conducted preliminary studies in the schools with the army Alpha and Beta tests.

For his doctoral study, Young followed up his sociological interests by investigating racial and ethnic differences in intelligence among schoolchildren (Minton & O'Neil, 1988). He administered the army Alpha and Beta tests to elementary school children in San Jose, a city near Stanford with a high proportion of immigrants from such Latin countries as Italy, Portugal, Spain, and Mexico, and compared the intelligence of "American" and "Latin" schoolchildren. IIis results showed that Latin school children scored significantly lower than Americans, and he, like Terman, attributed these differences to differences in native ability. He used the results to support his recommendation that only those with average or above-average performance on intelligence tests be exposed to the traditional academic curriculum. For those with below-average performance, and this included most of the Latin children, vocational training should be the focus. As it turned out, the San Jose school system followed his recommendation.

Young's hereditarian position, however, was a revision of his own initial view. As a result of his earlier training in sociology, he had adopted Thomas's environmental views of race and culture and had become convinced that intellectual performance was largely determined by social conditions. When he first arrived at Stanford and took part in one of Terman's graduate seminars on mental measurement, he and Terman had engaged in an intellectual free-for-all over the question of biological inheritance of intelligence, but by the time he began work on his dissertation, he had made an about-face and adopted Terman's hereditarian position.

The contrasting environmental and he-

reditarian perspectives to which Young was exposed reflect two different paradigms or world views. Thomas subscribed to a social interactionist perspective, in which individuals are understood within their cultural context. Personality and individual differences are seen as a product of social interaction carried on within a particular culture with unique habits, thoughts, attitudes, and values. Terman's hereditarian position implies that differences in intellectual performance represent real differences in native ability that can be understood without reference to the social context. This position is consistent with the eugenic approach discussed in Chapter 2.

After Young completed his doctoral studies in 1921, he went on to forge a career as a social psychologist, first as a psychologist and then as a sociologist, and taught at several universities including the University of Wisconsin and Northwestern. By 1925, he had given up the biological explanation for racial differences and had become a strong advocate of the interactionist approach. The reasons for the transformation are not altogether clear. It may have been that his acceptance of the hereditarian position was a simple case of compliance that was no longer necessary once he had obtained an independent position. There was also a general shift away from hereditarian explanations during the 1920s. Finally, there is the possibility that Young experienced a growing sympathy for persecuted minorities within the United States because of his own association with a minority on the fringe of American society (i.e., the Mormons). Young (1925) defined social psychology as the study of "personality as affected by social and institutional stimuli and as in turn affecting these" (p. 202). He felt that the organism and the environment are inseparable and that the individual and society must be conceived as a single unit. In 1930, he expanded his interactionist perspective in a textbook on social psychology that later became the prototype for sociological social psychology textbooks written during the 1930s.

The Chicago School of sociology that Thomas, Park, and Young helped to create dominated American sociology between the wars and established a satellite system through its graduates that spread out to universities across the United States, but it was not an unqualified success. Its concentration on urban problems caused it to neglect national and international issues, such as the depression, social stratification, and growing world tension, which dominated American society during the 1930s (Ober-schall, 1972). Chicago was soon challenged by other institutions such as Columbia and Harvard, but in one sense it was an unqualified success. It helped to establish "symbolic interaction," which has become *the* sociological approach to social psychology. These developments will be discussed in more detail in Chapter 11.

# 5

# Social Psychology as Individual Psychology

The development of American social psychology during the first decades of the twentieth century paralleled the general historical and intellectual currents of the period. Social psychology can be seen as evolving in a pendulum manner, swinging from an emphasis on society and group to one on self and the individual. Although social psychology was relatively well established by 1924, Floyd H. Allport's text was the first written from a psychological perspective. Allport has to be seen as a monumental figure, coming at the end of an epoch and reshaping social psychology largely in his own image (Post, 1980). He was the first person to openly challenge the view that social psychology was a subbranch of sociology. He argued that, although social psychology had grown up largely as a product of the work of sociologists, "there is no psychology of groups which is not essentially and entirely a psychology of individuals." For this reason, "social psychology must not be placed in contradistinction to the psychology of the individual; *it is a part of the psychology of the individual*" (Allport, 1924, p. 4, italics in the original).[1]

The success of Allport's text was due in part to the circumstances and mood of America after World War I. The Progressive Era had generated a spirit of optimism and social reform that inspired social thinkers with communitarian ideals in which individuals were seen as a product of society and progress occurred through changing social institutions. World War I shattered the belief that civilization was moving inevitably forward and all but extinguished the op-

timism that inspired social thought and reform during the progressive period. Postwar labor strikes, anarchist bombings, and social unrest reinforced the uncertainty of modern industrial society and set in motion a number of defensive and conservative reactions that were characteristic of the 1920s. Anticommunism and a growing distrust of everything foreign gave rise to a strong nativist movement and eventually lead to legistation restricting immigration. The Ku Klux Klan gained wide support in the south, and its membership reached an estimated high of between three and eight million. The conservative climate also inspired various forms of religious fundamentalism, which were expressed in the temperance movement and in efforts to suppress the teaching of evolutionary theory, culminating in the famous Scopes trial of 1925.

Feelings of anxiety and uncertainty were also evident in major scientific and intellectual trends during this period. Einstein's theory of relativity shattered the Newtonian belief in absolute space and time. Heisenberg's uncertainty principle pointed out that the behavior of subatomic particles could not be measured precisely because measurement interfered with their movement. Common-sense assumptions about the nature of the physical universe were no longer valid, and it was becoming apparent that there were definite limits to what the human mind could study and understand. A Harvard mathematician writing at the time expressed the uncertainty of the period when he said "the physicist thus finds himself in a world from which the bottom has dropped clean out" (Tindall, 1927/1984, p. 1007).

Freud's discovery of the unconscious confirmed the existence of a dark and irrational side of the mind and dealt a serious blow to the traditional view that humans were fundamentally rational and capable of fully controlling their behavior. This aspect of Freudian psychology was brought to the public's attention in America through the dramatic Leopold and Loeb trial of 1924, which involved the senseless murder of a young boy by two classmates. The famous trial lawyer Clarence Darrow used Freudian theory to argue that the two youths were not responsible for their behavior because they had been driven by unconscious impulses (Nash, 1970).

Anthropologists such as Franz Boas, Ruth Benedict, and Margaret Mead revolutionized the concept of culture by providing evidence of vast differences in social customs and values. The notion of cultural relativism challenged the validity of traditional values. Society was no longer described as a product of rational planning but was seen as a set of entrenched institutions governed at least in part by hidden motives and irrational prejudices.

The culture of the roaring twenties was also characterized by tremendous advances in technology and mass consumption, the chief examples of which were the revolution in leisure pursuits such as the spread of neighborhood cinemas, the introduction of radio, and affordable mass-produced automobiles. In 1924 Henry Ford's Model T sold for $290, and by 1929 more than 23 million Americans owned cars. The technological advances of the 1920s ushered in a fast-paced, highly mobile urban culture that increasingly centered on private consumption and the pursuit of leisure.

The 1920s were distinctly individualistic at all levels. Americans were spellbound by a host of popular personalities such as movie stars, sports heroes, and pioneers of aviation like the legendary Charles Lindbergh. The literature of the period included a new school of popular biography that described in detail the personal lives of the nation's leading heroes. These accounts often lead to the sensational practice of "debunk-

ing" these heroes by revealing details of their improprieties and personal shortcomings (Mowry, 1965). Other best-selling books during this period included autobiographies such as *The Education of Henry Adams,* which stressed personal experiences and accomplishments. The decade also witnessed the increased popularity of pseudo-psychological self-help literature offering instructions and techniques on how to improve one's image through proper voice control, conversation, and public speaking. The new literature stressed aspects of personality that could be changed quickly in one's leisure time, and the goal was to develop traits and qualities that would help one succeed in business or in one's chosen profession.

These developments heightened the concern about mass democratic society. Faced with an emerging mass consumer society in which everyone seemed more and more alike, Americans sought new channels for personal expression that would at least give the appearance of individuality. Although the full impact of fascist and communist dictatorships was yet to be felt, there were disturbing indications that people were susceptible to political manipulation and prone to irrational behavior even when it went against their own self-interest. This concern about the mechanisms governing social behavior was a growing area of interest and a central focus of social psychology. Ross's book *Social Control* (1901) was reissued in the 1920s and sold even better than when it was first released.

Psychologists were also turning their attention to social psychology, but they were increasingly dissatisfied with vague, nonverifiable sociological theories. Floyd H. Allport (1919) delivered a paper before the American Psychological Association in which he strongly criticized social psychology for lagging behind psychology in general. He called the social psychology of the period "rationalistic" and "pre-experimental" and argued that existing textbooks still clung to pseudoscientific concepts, such as social instincts, "crowd consciousness," and "group mind." The lack of progress in applying behaviorism and experimental procedures was seen as a matter of urgent concern. For Allport, the war had shown that the behavior of soldiers must be studied not as part of crowd behavior but through the reactions and interactions of individuals. Industrial conflict was not due to conflict between groups or classes, motivated by an instinct of pugnacity, but to conflict between individuals. He argued that the true cause for social behavior must be sought by the scientific "scrutiny of individual cases in which direct and indirect social stimulation has produced definite responses" (Allport, 1919, p. 298).

Allport's attack on sociological social psychology should be seen as part of the process of professionalization that was occurring in all the academic disciplines during this period. In America, this process was intensified by the urban industrial transformation that created increasingly more specialized forms of knowledge. Professionalization was also an outcome of the rapid expansion of higher education and the growth of graduate schools throughout America. Over two hundred learned societies appeared during the 1870s and 1880s, and these were forerunners of such modern groups as the American Historical Association (1884), the American Economic Association (1885), the American Psychological Association (1892), and the American Sociological Society (1905). Such groups set standards, policed their members, and protected them to a certain extent from unjustified censorship or dismissal. This kind of protection was particularly important for social scientists because of their tendency to advocate social reform.

The emergence of a distinct psychological approach to social psychology was aided by the uncertainty and conservative climate of the times. In the struggle for academic status and funds, Allport's critique played a decisive role. The conservative climate favored psychological rather than sociological solutions to pressing social problems, but Allport's ultimate success rested on his ability to convince his generation and subsequent generations that psychology rather than sociology provided a more secure foundation for a scientifically respectable social psychology. Because Allport played such a key role in reshaping social psychol-

ogy, this chapter will be devoted exclusively to him and the trends that he helped develop.

## FLOYD H. ALLPORT

Floyd H. Allport (1890–1978) came to social psychology from a background radically different from that of his sociological counterparts. He was born in Milwaukee and received his Ph.D. in experimental psychology from Harvard in 1919. Allport studied under Hugo Münsterberg and Edwin Bissel Holt. Münsterberg was a German experimental psychologist who had been brought to Harvard by William James in order to direct the first psychological laboratory established in America. Holt was an eminent psychologist-philosopher who had an important influence on the development of the behaviorist movement founded by John B. Watson. Allport adopted the approaches of both his teachers and applied the methods and assumptions of behaviorism and experimentation to social psychology. His initial success can be seen from the fact that he is one of the most frequently cited authors throughout the 1920s, the 1930s, the 1940s, and into the 1950s, and his own textbook was one of the most popular texts in the field.

Allport taught briefly at Harvard and then moved to Syracuse University in 1924, where he set up the first doctoral program in social psychology in America. He remained at Syracuse until he retired in 1956. Although he published experimental studies in the early 1920s, his greatest influence was based on his textbook, *Social Psychology* (1924). The text begins with a general discussion of psychological processes, such as the physiological bases of human behavior, instincts, feelings and emotions, and personality and its measurement. It then goes on to discuss social behavior, using the distinction between social stimulus and response. Social stimuli include language, gestures, and various forms of emotional expression, while social responses include such reactions as social facilitation, behavior in crowds, development of attitudes, and social adjustment. In doing this, Allport brings together scattered pieces of experimental studies and supplements them with studies and speculations of his own. He also reinterprets much of the previous sociological material from a psychological perspective.

The importance of this work, however, rests not on the material itself but on Allport's treatment of this material. By downplaying social factors and stressing psychological factors within the individual, Allport helped create a distinctly different type of social psychology. He helped displace the old controversy based on the relative importance of nature and nurture with a new controversy based on the relative importance of individual psychological processes.

Allport focused on two trends within psychology—behaviorism and the experimental method—and used them to organize and integrate the material. He also mentioned "the Freudian concept of personality" as deserving treatment but failed to develop this line of thought. Behaviorism and the experimental method, along with his focus on the individual, represent the central themes within Allport's work. Although Allport's influence was somewhat delayed by events taking place during the Great Depression, the development of these themes by Allport and others helped to shape social psychology in its contemporary psychological form and distinguish it from the sociological approach.

While the concepts of behaviorism, experimentation, and a focus on the individual may seem closely related, they must be kept separate. A person may adopt any one of these three positions and reject the other two. Experimentation is a method for studying physical and psychological phenomena by systematically manipulating one set of variables (the independent variables) in order to assess their effect on a second set of variables (the dependent variables). In psychology this is usually done under highly controlled conditions so that other factors can be eliminated, and the variables are usually a stimulus and a response. The response can be either an overt behavior or a subject's report of his current attitude, evaluation, or probable response. Experimentation existed long before behav-

iorism emerged. It was used by introspectionists and is currently used by cognitive psychologists, who focus on mental processes rather than overt behavior.

Experiments can be conducted either on individuals or on groups. A group of individuals—for example, a simulated jury—can be subject to an experimental manipulation, such as variations in room temperature, in order to assess its effect on their decision. The experimental study of groups became a major focus of attention during World War II, and these developments will be discussed in Chapter 9.

Finally, the behavior of individuals can be studied through nonexperimental procedures, such as direct observation, role playing, or archival research. The use of "nonreactive" measures is currently being advocated by a number of contemporary researchers (e.g., Webb, Campbell, Schwartz, Sechrest, and Grove, 1981) because they typically involve situations that are more realistic and less artificial than controlled laboratory experiments (see Chapter 12). Allport advocated all three trends, but he was far more successful in helping to estabish experimentation and a focus on the individual within social psychology than he was in establishing behavorism as an approach to social psychology. Because they are distinct, the trends will be discussed separately.

## BEHAVIORISM

On February 24, 1913, John B. Watson (1878–1958) began a series of invited lectures on animal psychology at Columbia University. His first lecture, entitled "Psychology as the Behaviorist Views it," was published one month later in the *Psychological Review*. Watson's "behaviorist manifesto" started with the pronouncement, "Psychology as the behaviorist views it is a purely objective experimental branch of natural science. Its theoretical goal is the prediction and control of behavior. Introspection forms no essential part of its method" (Watson, 1913, p. 158).

Watson's edict, however, was greeted with only limited support and a good deal of resistance (Samelson, 1981). The response reflected the fact that Watson was not proclaiming anything that was especially new. The functionalist approach of Dewey and Mead had already been progressing toward an emphasis on behavior (Leahey, 1987; O'Donnell, 1985). The study of consciousness through the use of introspection was still seen as an essential part of psychology, but there was an increasing emphasis on the use of objective methods to study observable behavior. While still clinging to a definition of psychology as the study of consciousness, the functionalists were beginning to develop theories of perception and learning that made consciousness less essential, but they had not clearly worked out the objective experimental procedures necessary for studying behavior. Nor was Watson able to provide specific guidelines for his behaviorist manifesto until 1920 when he adopted the model of Pavlovian conditioning and reported it in his study of Little Albert. Thus, it is not surprising that there was considerable resistance to Watson's call for the elimination of introspection. Psychologists were unwilling to throw out the baby with the bath water.

Watson should be seen as a charismatic leader rather than the founder of behaviorism, because he articulated the direction in which psychology was already moving (Burnham, 1968a). Yet, as Samelson (1981) points out, he did propose something radically new. The *goal* of psychology was to be the "prediction and control of behavior." While the idea of control had been mentioned previously, it became fundamental in Watson's 1913 paper. Before Watson, the aim of psychology was generally cast in terms of pure science, but Watson's emphasis on control pointed to psychology as an applied science. Pragmatists, such as Dewey and Mead, had foreseen this applied thrust, but they focused on science as a humanistic enterprise in the service of participatory democracy. Watson's emphasis on social control was more compatible with the conservative climate of the 1920s, where prediction and control could be used to achieve efficient management and maintain the existing social order.

Indeed, during the 1920s all of the social sciences were being reshaped by entrepre-

neurial research enterprises concerned with the study of behavior and social control (Samelson, 1985a). The various philanthropic foundations, such as the Laura Spelman Rockefeller Memorial and the Carnegie Foundation, played a major role in this movement. Ironically, Watson himself had been cast out of the academic scene in 1920 when he was dismissed from Johns Hopkins University because of his scandalous affair with Rosalie Rayner, his graduate assistant, whom he subsequently married after divorcing his first wife. In that same year, Watson and Rayner (1920) published their influential article on Little Albert, which purportedly showed how human emotions could be learned through Pavlovian conditioning. In fact, after reviewing the original data, Harris (1979) concluded that the study produced uninterpretable results, and the study itself has never been replicated (Samelson, 1980). Despite such a shaky foundation, the story of Little Albert's conditioned fear was generally accepted by psychologists in the 1920s as the empirical basis of Watson's behaviorism. Only within the last 15 years has this "origin myth" been critically examined. During the 1920s, Watson and Rayner's original work provided the credibility for a scientific psychology concerned with social control.

After leaving Johns Hopkins and starting a new career as an advertising executive, Watson continued to write on behaviorism, and his various magazine articles and books appealed to a general audience. Drawing from the study of Little Albert, Watson offered popular advice on childrearing, women, family relationships, and work (Harris, 1984). For example, claiming to have shown how emotional behavior could be conditioned in children, he emphasized the importance of raising children who would become independent and self-controlled. Because displays of affection would make children emotionally dependent, he suggested that parents show as little affection as possible and shake hands with them rather than kiss them, a practice he and Rosalie Rayner carried out with their own two sons (Hannush, 1987). Watson's advice on child care was aimed at the middle-class parents who were the audience for his work. While personal freedom was appropriate at higher levels of the social order, he stressed the importance of social control for those with less status. Women were encouraged to adopt careers as wives and mothers, and the goal for members of the working class was to fit the worker to the job.

While behaviorism became the dominant approach during the 1920s, not all psychologists who identified themselves as behaviorists subscribed to Watson's particular version. George Herbert Mead's "social behaviorism," for example, emphasized the social context and had little in common with Watson's concepts (see Chapter 4). Most behaviorists, however, shared Watson's focus on behavior and his concern with social control, but even within this group there was a wide range of opinions.

Traditionally, a distinction has been drawn between methodological and philosophical forms of behaviorism (see Leahey, 1987). As a methodology, behaviorism advocates the study of overt behavior. It is undoubtedly this aspect that appealed to many psychologists during the 1920s and 1930s. It was assumed that by focusing only on overt behavior psychologists could discover a great deal about how people learn and what motivates them. It has been argued that overt behavior is easily quantifiable and relatively free from many of the problems based on verbal reports of experience. Moreover, the possibility of studying overt behavior in children and animals should lead to the discovery of simpler forms of general principles, unhampered by the influence of previous experience and culture. Nevertheless, methodological behaviorists have generally been willing to accept the existence of internal processes, such as drives and cognition, which are inferred from overt behavior. It is also widely recognized that internal states help determine overt behavior. The positions of Edward C. Tolman and Clark L. Hull, developed in the 1930s, are early examples of methodological behaviorism. Tolman believed that learning occurs through a cognitive integration of environmental stimuli, while Hull postulated several internal links between the stimulus and the response.

But behaviorism has a philosophical side as well. This is based on a tendency to treat consciousness as an epiphenomenon—something that occurs along with behavior but plays no causal role. The famous evolutionary theorist T. H. Huxley (1874/1896), for example, equated consciousness with the steam given off by a steam whistle, which accompanies the operation of a locomotive but does not affect its operation. But the counterargument from the evolutionary point of view is that, if consciousness serves no purpose in guiding behavior, why did it evolve in the first place? Why evolve such a complex psychological process, if it is only a useless appendage to mechanical behavior? This was the objection raised by pragmatists, such as William James and George Herbert Mead. The acceptance of consciousness as an epiphenomenon, however, supplies the philosophical justification for behaviorism. If consciousness or other internal states play no causal role in shaping behavior, then an adequate understanding of overt behavior is all that is necessary. This form of radical behaviorism characterized the approach of Watson and, more recently, B. F. Skinner.

In order to place Allport in this context, it is important to note the influence of his Harvard mentor, Edwin Bissel Holt (1873–1946). Holt was a philosophical behaviorist who developed a much more sophisticated version than Watson did. Along with his Harvard colleague Ralph Barton Perry (William James's biographer), Holt advanced a neorealist view of consciousness (Leahey, 1987). According to Holt, consciousness is not inside a person's head. The contents of consciousness are simply a set of specific responses to the objects in the environment that control a person's behavior. Holt provided the analogy of a flashlight's beam, which determines what we see. Consciousness thus has no causal qualities. In this sense Holt agreed with Watson, but Holt did not rule out the possibility of using verbal reports of conscious experience as descriptive data.

Holt's view of consciousness was an extension of James's concept of thought as a system of relationships—that is, a stream of consciousness. In contrast, Dewey and Mead advocated a functional theory of consciousness in which the mind played an active role in understanding and changing the world. Dewey criticized both Holt and Perry for holding a spectator theory in which consciousness is fully determined by the objects in the environment. Unlike the behaviorists, Dewey and Mead felt that consciousness was an active process that is both shaped by and influences behavior. Consciousness was also seen as a product of social interaction rather than a private response of an individual to physical changes in the environment.

In his textbook, Allport (1924) examined the two major themes of Watsonian behaviorism—the behavior-consciousness debate and the issue of social control. Consistent with Holt's view, Allport defined psychology as the scientific study of behavior and consciousness. He went on to clearly point out, however, that behavior was the more fundamental term because, unlike consciousness, it was an "explanatory principle." Social psychology as a subspecialty of psychology was concerned with social behavior, which consists of "the stimulations and reactions arising between an individual and the *social* portion of his environment; that is, between the individual and his fellows" (p. 3). For Allport, social behavior was essentially understood within the context of social influence.

Allport (1924) felt that, although "consciousness does not explain events" (p. 3), it was a necessary part of the study of behavior. According to Allport (1924), "Introspection on conscious states is both interesting in itself and necessary for a complete account. . . . The introspective account will aid in our interpretations and will supplement them upon the descriptive side" (p. 3). Allport's view of social psychology thus contains both social consciousness and social behavior. By social consciousness Allport meant the individual's awareness of social objects and social reactions. A specific example is a person's awareness of his or her attitude toward others or toward society at large. Allport (1924) also used the social self as an example when he said,

> Our consciousness of ourselves is largely a reflection of the consciousness which others have of us. This introspective phase of

the self has been aptly termed by professor Cooley as the "looking glass self." We shall refer to it . . . as the *social self.* (p. 325)

For Allport, social psychology was explanatory when it dealt with social behavior and descriptive when it dealt with social consciousness.

In the last chapter of his text, Allport focused on the relationship between social behavior and society. The central concept in this discussion was social control. According to Allport, social control is exercised through the conditioning of an individual's responses and inhibitions. A child, for example, is conditioned to inhibit forbidden behavior through the threatened loss of social approval by adults. Social institutions exercise a similar control through their system of rewards and punishments. In general, "society uses the fundamental responses of its members in order to control them" (p. 392).

Like Watson, Allport stressed the need for individuals to function independently within society, striking a balance between self-expression and concern for others. Social progress was to be based on the well-being of the individual. Yet, in a vein similar to Watson's elitist view of the social order, Allport cautioned that the working class must adjust to its "modest" economic and vocational status. Consistent with the conservative climate of the time, Allport felt that the wave of industrial unrest in the early twenties was a threat to social continuity and argued that business and industry should use their power in a way that would bring "contentment" to their workers.

In his later career, Allport (1955) moved away from his early behaviorist position and endorsed the postwar trend toward a more cognitive social psychology. He began to consider cognitions, motivations, and personality factors as explanations for behavior rather than mere descriptions or epiphenomena. He was also critical of his 1924 textbook because of its mechanistic approach and argued for reciprocal or circular notions of causality similar to those expressed by John Dewey (1896) in his paper on the reflex arc. These themes will be reconsidered in Chapters 9 and 10.

## EXPERIMENTATION

Modern sociology, as opposed to social theory, can almost be defined by the application of scientific and statistical procedures to social phenomena, but Allport advocated a more systematic application of these procedures, with a strong emphasis on experimentation. While sociological researchers emphasized observation and the careful recording of data, Allport stressed the subdivision of problems into component parts that could be studied separately. Both trends represented an attempt to base social psychology on objective data, but psychologists, such as Allport, were much more sympathetic to experimental procedures than their sociological counterparts.

Allport was far more successful in promoting the use of experimentation within social psychology than in getting social psychologists to adopt a behaviorist approach. His advocacy of the experimental method must be seen as part of a more general reaction against the use of rationalistic and deductive approaches to science, characteristic of the nineteenth century—what Morton White (1957) called "the revolt against formalism." Much of the social-scientific speculation at the turn of the century was based on deduction from given principles, such as those derived from evolutionary theory. It was quite clear that authors could arrive at radically different positions depending on which aspect of the general theory they chose to stress. Human beings could be portrayed as naturally egotistical and competitive because competition among individuals is one of the general characteristics of natural selection (e.g., Spencer, 1876); or they could be seen as cooperative and mutually dependent because group living aids survival (e.g., Cooley, 1902). The implications of evolutionary theory were so numerous and diverse that supporters could use it (like the Bible) to defend almost any position they chose.

Near the turn of the century, there was a general movement to cleanse science of its ethical and a priori assumptions by basing it on observation and quantification. As Purcell (1973) has pointed out, social scientists during this period may not have agreed on a definition of scientific objectivity, but most of them agreed that objectivity was their goal. The only way they could build a body of scientific knowledge was by dealing with observable, physical phenomena that could be restudied, remanipulated, or remeasured by anyone who wished to test the conclusions offered. The instrumentalism of John Dewey and the radical empiricism of William James can be seen as part of this movement. But while James and Dewey advocated observational methods similar to those used in biology, a more radical group, which included Floyd H. Allport and John B. Watson, stressed positivistic procedures more characteristic of the physical sciences, with a strong emphasis on experimentation. Their approach rested on the assumption that the basic reality is physical reality, and all *true* science must have as its object some definite empirically measurable element of physical reality. Studying these elements was the only way in which generalizations could be made and scientific theories tested.

Floyd Allport vehemently denounced the concepts of group mind and social instincts characteristic of earlier social psychology textbooks because he regarded them as vague, rationalistic, and nonexperimental. His work marks a turning point in American social psychology because he both advocated experimentation and brought together the results of previous experimental studies. Indeed, the stress on experimentation eventually became one of the major criteria distinguishing the psychological approach to social psychology from the sociological approach.

Murphy and Murphy (1931) pointed out that experimental social psychology was in existence long before social psychology was recognized as a distinct discipline. They traced the origins of experimental social psychology to James Braid's experiments on hypnotic suggestion between 1841 and 1860 in England. Braid, a medical doctor, introduced the term "hypnosis," but it received little attention and much abuse in his own country. The British Medical Association, for example, refused even to hear Braid's paper on the subject. While Braid used the term "suggestion," Haines and Vaughan (1979) have noted that his concept contained no connotation of interpersonal influence. During the period of his writing, suggestion merely referred to the process by which one idea suggests another.

Suggestion assumed its modern meaning as an interpersonal process in the 1880s when Hippolyte Bernheim began his work on hypnosis. By the turn of the century, Bernheim's work was extended to the experimental study of suggestion in normal subjects without recourse to hypnosis. The French psychologist Alfred Binet (1900) carried out extensive experimental research on suggestibility and published a book that summarized his research and that of others. Some of these studies anticipated the subsequent work by Solomon E. Asch on social conformity (see Chapter 9). Largely because of Binet, suggestion became social psychology's first experimental topic.

In America, Boris Sidis (1898) conducted extensive research on suggestion and Lewis M. Terman (1904) expanded Binet's work, but aside from these studies, suggestion did not become a popular area of experimental research. Rather, a series of miscellaneous social psychology topics were studied experimentally. According to Haines and Vaughan (1979), the earliest American study appears to have been published by Joseph Jastrow in 1894. Though not conceived as a social psychology experiment, it focused on how word associations are influenced by a "community of ideas." The concept of a "community of ideas" was a reflection of the then-fashionable notion of group mind. The following year, Josiah Royce (1895) published a more explicitly social-psychological experiment in which imitation was studied through introspection.

In a study that has become well known, Norman Triplett (1898) investigated the effects of competition on motor performance. He had been impressed by the well-established fact that cyclists attain higher speeds when paced or in competition. He designed an experiment in which children wound fishing reels either alone or in competition. Of 40 subjects, 20 improved during competition, 10 did worse, and 10 showed no difference. He also conducted studies using counting and jumping.

The Triplett study is important because it has been widely cited as the first experiment in social psychology. This "origin myth" can be traced to Gordon W. Allport's selective history of social psychology, first published in 1954. As Haines and Vaughan (1979) indicate, Gordon Allport (Floyd's brother) viewed Triplett's experiment as the introduction of the laboratory method to social psychology and Triplett as the founder of the area subsequently identified as "social facilitation." By selecting the Triplett study and ignoring others, Gordon Allport was able to make a convincing case for steady progress within modern experimental social psychology. Triplett's research neatly anticipates the investigation of the general area of social influence, which became a central topic within American social psychology. The earlier research on suggestion, on the other hand, would not have made a convincing origin myth because suggestion has often been an unfashionable topic.

Gordon Allport (1954a) was also responsible for creating the myth that Auguste Comte was the founder of a scientific social psychology (see Chapter 1). By reaching back into the mid-nineteenth century and selectively interpreting Comte's work, Allport presented a cumulative history of how modern social psychology evolved from a much earlier positivist conception of science. The Triplett experiment was a significant addition to this cumulative advance because it introduced modern experimental methods. As Samelson (1974) and Haines and Vaughan (1979) point out, such "whiggish" or celebratory history serves the purpose of justifying the current fashion and practice. By the 1950s, the experimental method had become entrenched as the dominant psychological approach to social psychology, and Allport's history provided a success story of consistent progress within an established tradition (Pychyl, 1988).

Floyd Allport played a central role in developing the experimental tradition in social psychology. In his book, he reviewed Triplett's study as well as a series of related experiments conducted in Germany by August Mayer (1903) and W. Moede (1920). He also reported his own experimental work in the area, which generally supported the earlier research. But he also found evidence of social inhibition. In one of his experiments, subjects read philosophical passages and then wrote rebuttals. Although subjects wrote longer arguments in groups, the quality of the arguments was greater when subjects worked alone.

Allport drew a distinction between coacting and face-to-face groups. Individuals in coacting groups are preoccupied with stimuli other than each other. Improvements in performance in coacting groups are based on a combination of social facilitation and rivalry. Individuals in face-to-face groups react mainly or entirely to each other and their behavior is influenced by conversation and interaction. The early experimental study of groups focused almost entirely on coacting groups. Allport noted this discrepancy and attempted to supplement it with speculations about behavior in face-to-face situations.

A second line of experimental research reviewed and extended by Allport was the recognition of facial expressions. Allport studied the accuracy of recognition, the effect of imitation and training, and the techniques that subjects used in judging facial expressions. He found that training had a limited effect and resulted in a regression toward the mean—that is, poor judges did better but good judges actually did worse after they were trained. He also included some studies on reaction to persuasive communication, based largely on verbal reports.

In short, although Allport advocated experimentation, his review of the literature was limited to some extent by the shortage of research at this time. It is significant that a full third of his book is devoted to general psychological topics, such as physiology, instincts, and learning. Many of the more frequently cited individuals were only indirectly concerned with social psychology. Allport, however, was also selective in reviewing the research relevant to social psychology. For example, while he included a brief section on suggestion (the contents of which were primarily descriptive and anecdotal), he made no mention of Binet's extensive experimental research in this area. Nor was there any mention of Terman's extension of Binet's work or Sidis's work on suggestion. It is not altogether clear why such an oversight occurred. He may have been unfamiliar with the research or he may have chosen to deliberately ignore it. One clue appears to be Gordon Allport's (1954a) attempt to recast specific concepts in behaviorist terms. In the case of suggestion, he defined it as "a process involving elementary behavior mechanisms in response to a social stimulus" (pp. 251–252). He may have thus chosen to ignore the French work because it did not fit his definition.

Aside from the influence of his textbook, Allport played a more direct role in promoting an experimental approach to social psychology. In 1921, he was asked by Morton Prince, the publisher and editor of the *Journal of Abnormal Psychology,* to become a coeditor (Pychyl & Cherry, 1989). Prince had decided to expand the journal to include the field of social psychology because the two areas were seen as closely related. Allport's address to the American Psychological Association calling for a behaviorist and experimental approach to social psychology had been published in the journal in 1919. The journal was retitled the *Journal of Abnormal Psychology and Social Psychology* (and later shortened to the *Journal of Abnormal and Social Psychology* in 1925). Throughout the 1920s, the journal featured a number of position papers by Allport and others who were similarly inclined advocating the use of experimental procedures. During the same period there was an increase in the number of experimental studies published in the journal.

The establishment of experimentation as the distinct psychological approach to social psychology was closely connected with the general turn toward behaviorism. Reflecting the behaviorist view of psychology as a natural science, Floyd Allport played a key role in proselytizing for an experimentally based social psychology. Furthermore, the behaviorist concern with social control reinforced trends that were already affecting the conception and practice of experimental procedures in America (Danzinger, 1979, 1985; Scheibe, 1988). Experimental participants became "subjects" rather than "observers." Anonymous groups of undergraduates and schoolchildren began to replace psychological collaborators as a source of data. These changes increased the authority of the experimenter and created a new kind of relationship in which the experimenter was in total control. Although behaviorist theory gave way to the cognitive perspective in social psychology by the late 1940s, the behaviorist model of experimentation was unchallenged until the mid-1960s (see Chapter 12).

## THE FOCUS ON THE INDIVIDUAL

Allport's book represents a turning point in American social psychology not only because it changed the way social psychologists approached their subject but because it changed the nature of the subject itself. Early social psychology textbooks approached social psychology through the study of groups—particularly small face-to-face groups—but Allport initiated a trend that stressed psychological processes occurring within the individual.

Allport (1924) did not identify his focus on the individual as one of his major areas of emphasis because he totally identified the focus on the individual with psychological approach. He described his purpose as "to adhere to the psychological (that is, the individual) viewpoint. For I believe that only *within the individual* can we find the behavior mechanisms and the consciousness which are fundamental in the interactions between individuals" (p. vi). This focus on the individual was not "simply a convenient way of conceiving facts," like behaviorism, or a way of gathering information, like experimentation. For Allport, the individual approach was *the* psychological approach, and social psychology was "the

study of the social behavior and the social consciousness of the individual" (p. 12).

Allport began his defense of his individualistic position by attacking the concept of "collective mind" or "group consciousness." This concept had become vulnerable because it was used to cover a whole range of phenomena that appear quite distinct. Allport identified three different usages of the group-mind concept and addressed each in turn, but it is possible to make numerous subdivisions within his three categories. The group-mind concept seems to have been used wherever some sort of common experience was implied.

Allport's distinction between coacting and face-to-face groups can be used to differentiate several forms of the group-mind concept. Probably the simplest form of the group experience is the co-perception that occurs when two people passively attend to a common stimulus—for example, two people at the beach watching a sunset or two people at home watching the same program on television. As long as they are absorbed in their perception, their experience will be similar. A second type of group experience that occurs in coacting groups is when individuals both perceive and respond to a common stimulus or situation. An example would be a group of people trying to escape from a burning building. Each individual works alone, but the reactions of all are similar because they are responding to the same emergency.

In face-to-face groups, behavior is based on actual interaction. Allport noted the lack of research on face-to-face groups, but subsequent studies have provided many examples of mutual influence in face-to-face groups. One example is the "cooperative thinking" that occurs when three people with different backgrounds (e.g., two social psychologists and an intellectual historian) share their ideas and build up an understanding that is more complex than that with which any of them began. Other examples would include norm fixing and norm sharing within reference groups (Sherif, 1936) or the negative example of "group think" (Janis, 1968). Group dynamics, in general, has studied the way in which people in small groups work together toward a common goal, and it has shown that, as long as a group's attention is focused on a common goal, their experiences are similar (see Chapters 7 and 9).

A slightly different formulation of the group-mind concept begins outside the group with the notion of a common culture (e.g., Durkheim). To the extent that individuals are exposed to a common language, common values, and common norms, their experiences and reactions are similar. This common exposure is responsible for the sameness of thought and action among various natural groups, such as members of an army, a political party, or a trade union, and for "public opinion" in general. The person becomes aware not only of separate elements within this *conscience collective* but of the relationships between elements, and this is responsible for the "permanent organization" within large groups—the mutual cooperation and respect for individual roles characteristic of larger institutions.

Finally, similarities in experience lead to similarities in personality, so that individuals carry within themselves a predisposition to perceive and characterize reality in a particular way. This "collective personality" has both a conscious and an unconscious side, with the latter making up the socially acquired hidden assumptions and processes behind experience.[2] For Giddings (1898), the social mind was what caused individuals to react in the same way to the same stimulus.

These various formulations of the group-mind concept converge, so that the most similar experience would occur among individuals with a common background and culture reacting to the same situation. What makes the concept of the group mind even more complicated is that actual contact is not necessary in order for people to "share" aspects of each other's experience. There are similarities in experience among people on the east and west coasts of America watching the same program on television. Repeated exposure to events of this type leads to similarities in personality among people who have never had direct contact with one another.

It can be argued, however, that while the experiences in all these cases are similar, they are never the *same*. Two people looking at a sunset bring different memories and associations with them. A group of people fleeing a burning building approach the exit from different angles and with different barriers between themselves and safety. Two thinkers attacking a common problem approach it from different perspectives, according to their own background and interests. And, when you get right down to it, two people's cultural experiences are never so similar as to produce identical personalities. An experience is never literally "shared" (G. Allport, 1985) but always resides within the individual, because only the individual thinks, perceives, and acts on reality.

Floyd Allport's fundamental argument was that there *is* no "group consciousness," because consciousness depends on a nervous system and this is possessed only by the individual. There is no counterpart to the brain within a crowd. A group is simply a number of distinct individuals, reacting to each other or a common situation according to fundamental psychological principles. Sociology, which he defined as the study of the group as a whole, therefore had to be derived from psychology. As he noted, "psychological data, such as innate reactions and habitual and emotional tendencies of individuals, are explanatory principles upon which sociology builds in interpreting the life of groups" (Allport, 1924, pp. 10–11).

Allport's attack on the group-mind concept marked the end of its use within social psychology, in much the same way that Dunlap's criticism of social instinct theory marked the beginning of the end for that theory as a dominant approach to social psychology. Explicit references to a "group mind" virtually disappeared during the 1930s. But Allport's success was more apparent than real. Twenty-four years later, Krech and Crutchfield (1948) wrote, "despite its burial at the hands of F. H. Allport and others, the group-mind concept still seems to lead a ghostly life in the thinking of many social psychologists" (p. 20).

The reason that the group-mind concept continued to lead a "ghostly" existence within social psychology is that Allport was only half right in his conception of conscious experience. In one sense, consciousness can only reside within an individual. But in another sense, consciousness is a reaction of an individual to the outside environment. Phenomenologists, such as Edmund Husserl (1913/1962), who systematically study and describe conscious experience, have repeatedly stressed that consciousness is always consciousness *of something.* Consciousness depends on a brain and a nervous system, but a brain by itself would be no more conscious than a rock since there would be nothing to be conscious of. Consciousness is a process rather than a thing—a process by which an individual becomes aware of the outside world. In logical terms, the brain and the nervous system are *necessary* conditions for conscious experience, that is, no consciousness can occur without them, but they are not *sufficient* conditions, since consciousness develops as a result of an interaction between an individual and an outside reality.

After people have become aware of their surroundings, they can recall former experiences or recombine them in new and different ways. These images and memories *are* purely private, but it would be misleading to see them as the basis for experience. They are made possible by previous experience with external objects. Because the objects of consciousness are often outside an individual (such as a sunset or a program on television), they are "public property," so to speak, and can be perceived by any number of individuals. Their objective features can be studied and analyzed, and people can come to some sort of mutual understanding about them through communication and social comparison.

This is true not only for physical objects but for social objects as well. As Durkheim, Dewey, and Mead have pointed out, norms and institutions have an existence outside the individual. They constrain the behavior of individuals and have a duration that both precedes and outlasts them. People must adapt themselves to their social environment in much the same manner that they adapt themselves to their physical environ-

ment. And their adaptation helps to shape their character.

There is also an important sense in which thoughts can be shared. A person's thoughts are usually based on language and therefore exist in a form that can be communicated (see Merleau-Ponty, 1945/1962). In fact, it is possible to see thinking as merely a form of "internal communication," in which people speak directly to themselves. Although thinking differs from overt communication in a number of fundamental ways (Vygotsky, 1934/1962), both rely on language, and thoughts can therefore be made public if the person chooses. The question of symbolic interaction will be discussed more fully in Chapter 11, but the point to be noted here is that people can "share" their thoughts and experiences, and this ability is the foundation for both social interaction and mutual understanding.

Allport's extreme individualistic position and his attack on the group-mind concept in all of its many forms laid the groundwork for the psychological approach to social psychology, but it is also one of the weakest aspects of his book. After making the distinction between coacting and face-to-face groups, Allport conceded that there were few experimental studies of face-to-face groups because the direct control of social stimuli is more difficult in face-to-face groups. To compensate for this neglect, Allport offers some speculations about social interaction in face-to-face groups. His treatment, however, is almost a caricature of his own individualistic position. For Allport (1924) conversation is a form of social control:

> There is a fairly universal readiness to communicate to others thoughts or feelings which we regard as significant. We are usually aware that the information will produce a sensation, create a laugh, impress the hearer with our importance, or otherwise control the reactions of our fellows. (p. 322)

Conversation is treated merely as a monologue designed to impress, control, or inform other people. It is a kind of combat between two individuals, each trying to impress the other with their own importance. Speakers talk *at* each other but never *with* each other. His treatment of social problems, such as social conflict and exploitation in business, is also limited by his tendency to treat social problems as problems occurring within the individual.

On the positive side, however, Allport did succeed in shifting the emphasis to processes occurring within the individual. When Neil Miller and John Dollard returned to the study of imitation in the late 1930s, their treatment was radically different than that of Tarde's. Tarde (1890/1903) had described the spread of ideas within a population, whereas Miller and Dollard (1941) focused on drives, the interpretation of stimulus, covert responses, and other cognitive processes occurring within the individual. The Gestalt tradition initiated by Kurt Lewin in the late 1930s intensified this emphasis on individual psychological processes and led ultimately to the development of cognitive social psychology. Cognitive social psychology is currently the most important approach among psychological social psychologists and will be discussed in Chapter 10.

For better or worse, Allport's stress on experimentation and his focus on the individual have had a profound effect on contemporary social psychology. His impact was not immediate, however. During the 1930s, the growing fields of anthropology and psychoanalysis focused attention on social aspects of personality development, and the Great Depression aroused an interest in the psychological study of social issues. These were two areas in which the experimental study of individuals in controlled laboratory situations were of limited use. During World War II, Kurt Lewin's pioneering research in group dynamics diverted attention away from the study of the individual toward the experimental study of groups. However, as the study of personality began

to evolve into a distinct area and interest in group dynamics began to diminish during the 1950s, the experimental study of individuals began to increase. The stress on precise measurement of individual behavior and the use of experimentation that Allport helped initiate became the dominant features of psychological social psychology by the 1960s.

Nor should Allport's personal influence be neglected. He set up and directed the first doctoral program in social psychology in America and helped train some outstanding social psychologists, such as Daniel Katz (1903–   ). The mutual influence exerted by Floyd Allport and his brother Gordon Allport is one of the rare instances of collaboration between siblings in the same general area. Few social psychologists adopted Allport's extreme position without modification, and he modified his position as he grew older. But by taking an extreme position, he helped shape the dominant trends in the psychological approach to social psychology. As his biographers concluded in the 1960s, the voice "crying in the wilderness" in 1924 has "proved to be the voice both of the leader and the prophet" (Katz & Kahn, 1966, p. 68).

## NOTES

1. This contrasts sharply with Durkheim (1897/1964), who claimed, "We see no objection to calling sociology a variety of psychology, if we carefully add that social psychology has its own laws which are not those of individual psychology" (p. 312). For Durkheim, there is no precise point at which the individual ends and society begins.

2. This unconscious side of a "collective personality" should not be confused with Carl Jung's (1953) more mystical concept of the "collective unconscious" based on archetypes and racial memories.

# PART II

# SOCIAL PSYCHOLOGY IN THE CONTEXT OF THE DEPRESSION AND WORLD WAR II (1930–1945)

# 6

# Socialization and Personality Development

Although experimental reseach continued to increase throughout the 1930s, the conflict between psychology and sociology was temporarily obscured by the brief entry of two new disciplines, psychoanalysis and cultural anthropology, and by a more general concentration on the psychological study of social problems brought on by the Great Depression. The stock market crash of 1929 and the depression marked a dramatic shift in cultural and intellectual trends and a pendulum swing away from the conservative focus on the individual that was characteristic of the 1920s. Social psychologists, like other social scientists, were profoundly aware of the impact of the environment during the depression and began once again to look for the causes of behavior within the broader social context. The development of social psychology during the 1930s reflected a blend of progressive ideals prevalent in America before World War I and new trends imported from Europe, such as Marxism and psychoanalysis.

The knowledge acquired previously, however, continued to motivate much of the research and provided an underlying continuity despite the radical shift in interests. Ironically, Floyd Allport's emphasis on the individual led to what Boring (1950) called "an invasion of 'general psychology' by 'social psychology'" (p. 748). Social psychologists began to examine how individual psychological processes, such as learning, perception, and memory, were shaped by social conditions, and they began to look at the long-term effects of the social environment on a person's character and personality. Kimball Young (1930), for example, in one of the first texts written during this period, stated that "social psychology is concerned with the personality as it operates in a world of other personalities" (p. vii). The 1930s were a time in which the study of personality and social psychology were inseparably fused, and the person most responsible for this shift was Sigmund Freud.

The study of personality did not begin in the 1930s. Floyd Allport (1924) had mentioned Freud's contribution to psychology as a field of progress that deserved special recognition and had devoted two chapters to personality and its measurement. Bernard (1926) and Ewer (1929) also dealt with the concept of personality and included additional material on abnormal psychology. By the time Gardner and Louise Murphy (1931) introduced the first text on experimental social psychology, roughly half of the book was devoted to socialization and personality development, and this increased coverage continued throughout the 1930s.

The close link between personality, social psychology, and abnormal psychology was also reflected in the 1920s by the appearance of the *Journal of Abnormal and Social Psychology*. Morton Prince, who like Freud had studied under Charcot in Paris, had published the journal since 1906 under the title *Journal of Abnormal Psychology* and had asked Freud to contribute an article to the first issue (Jones, 1957). Ernest Jones, Freud's close friend and biographer, served as "Assistant Editor for the British Isles," and the journal was one of the few outlets for the spread of psychoanalytic ideas in America. Between 1911 and 1912, Prince was threatened with prosecution by the Boston police for publishing "obscenities." In 1921 the journal was expanded to include social psychology and was subsequently divided in 1965 into the *Journal of Abnormal Psychology* and the *Journal of Personality and Social Psychology* because the number of articles simply exceeded the capacity of a single journal.

Freud's impact on American culture was manifested in two different waves (Burnham, 1978). The first wave coincided with progressive reform and the new thinking about the place of children and sexuality in American society. During this period, physicians, such as Prince, were the primary disseminators of Freud's ideas. The second wave accompanied the bureaucratic society that emerged in the 1930s and the post–World War II era. During these periods America had to help fulfill the needs of a large number of people undergoing the social disruption of the Great Depression and the war itself. Freud's influence on social psychology was especially notable during this second wave. During the 1930s, Freud was the sixth most cited author among psychology textbook authors (see Table 1.1). Among sociologists, Freud's influence seems to have been somewhat delayed. He was not frequently cited during the 1930s but moved into eighth place during the postwar period, was the most frequently cited person during the 1960s, ranked third during the 1970s, and was in eleventh place during the 1980s. Freud is one of the few people who has had a persistent impact on both psychological and sociological social psychology, although this impact has been considerably weakened in recent years.[1]

## SIGMUND FREUD

Sigmund Freud (1856–1939) wrote four books specifically devoted to social psychology, *Totem and Taboo* (1913/1955), *Group Psychology and the Analysis of the Ego* (1921/1955), *The Future of an Illusion* (1927/1961), and *Civilization and its Dis-*

*contents* (1930/1961), but it is a serious error to limit discussion to these four works. The truth is that Freud's theory is social in almost all of its aspects. The ego and the superego develop because of the child's growing need to deal with reality, and this reality is primarily social reality—that is, other people. Restrictions imposed by others help to shape the unconscious. The passage through or fixation at one of the psychosexual stages is determined by the reactions of the parents. The entire character, according to Freud, was based on a combination of genetic differences and the treatment by the parents during the first five years of life.

No one was more clearly aware of the close link between individual and social psychology than Freud himself. In *Group Psychology* (1921/1955), he wrote:

> The contrast between individual psychology and social or group psychology, which at a first glance may seem to be full of significance, loses a great deal of its sharpness when it is examined more closely. It is true that individual psychology is concerned with the individual man and explores the paths by which he seeks to find satisfaction for his instinctual impulses; but only rarely and under certain exceptional conditions is individual psychology in a position to disregard the relations of the individual to others. In the individual's mental life someone else is invariably involved, as a model, as an object, as a helper, as an opponent; and so from the very first individual psychology, in this extended but entirely justifiable sense of the words, is at the same time social psychology as well. (p. 1)

World War I and its aftermath had a profound effect on Freud's psychoanalytic theory (L. Hoffman, 1981). The impact of the war and the subsequent political events were significant influences in moving Freud away from his earlier focus on biological determinants and intrapsychic conflict. He began to place more stress on external social reality. This was reflected in several new aspects of Freud's theory, including the notion of an innate destructive drive, the treatment of the superego, and the mechanisms of social psychology. Because Freud's theory is so implicitly social in all its aspects, general features of his theory will be discussed first, before we turn to Freud's work on social psychology and culture.

## Freud's Concept of the Unconscious

Freud did not invent the concept of the unconscious. Whyte (1960) has provided a review of the concept of the unconscious before Freud and suggests that the term "unconscious" had been used in English for at least a century and a half before Freud began his work. The general concept seems to have passed through three historical periods. Before the 1700s, there seems to have been a vague recognition that behind conscious processes, such as thought and imagination, were other processes unavailable to awareness. During the 1700s, the unconscious was seen as a vital seat of passion and a source of inspiration for art and creative thought. During the 1800s, there was the growing recognition that the unconscious played a role in pathological behaviors, such as hysteria, epilepsy, and dreams.

By 1868, this literature had grown sufficiently large that Ernst von Hartmann (1842–1906) decided to bring it together in his massive work, *Philosophy of the Unconscious.* This work went through nine editions in German before 1882. It was translated into French in 1877 and into English in 1884. The English edition is 1,100 pages long and contains 26 subtopics plus an extensive review of the literature. By the 1870s, the concept of the unconscious was common, not only in science and literature but in conversations within polite society as well.

Virtually all of Freud's central concepts—the unconscious, infantile sexuality, the sexual origins of neurosis and, possibly, repression itself—can be found somewhere in the previous scientific literature (see Sulloway, 1979). But they were scattered like pieces of string on a table. What Freud accomplished was a grand synthesis that wove the separate pieces into a unified theory. By linking the concept of the unconscious with the notion of sexual repression, Freud showed that, far from being a small insignificant part of the mind, the unconscious contained most of a person's vital urges and the larger part of the personality. The contents of the unconscious are kept unconscious through various defense mechanisms, such as repression, projection, and rationalization, of which a person is also unaware. Although Freud's early formulation equated unconsciousness with repression, he later expressed the opinion that all mental processes begin unconsciously and some cross the barrier and become conscious.

This later formulation is a considerable advance, because it changes the question from how people can be unaware of certain things to how they become conscious in the first place. Freud's answer was that people become conscious through the use of language, by labeling and describing their experience. Most of a person's character is acquired before he or she has a good grasp of language. This is one of the reasons why people can remember very little from their early childhood.

In later life, we normally tend to think over and recall pleasant experiences but ignore the unpleasant ones if we can. A person going through a difficult relationship, for example, may look for and acknowledge signs of affection but screen out signs of rejection, and therefore be misled about the beloved's intent. This is why rejected lovers are often surprised when a relationship finally dissolves. For Freud, people become conscious only when they think about what they are going through. Unlabeled experiences simply slip from awareness. He developed his method of "free association,"[2] where patients describe anything and everything that comes to mind, so that patients could talk about aspects of their lives that they had previously refused to face.

Freud saw his description of the unconscious as one of three blows to humanity's inflated self-image. The first, delivered by Copernicus, removed man from the center of the universe. The second, delivered by Darwin, took away his special place in nature. The third, Freud's description of the unconscious, destroyed the belief that at the center of personality is a conscious ego or soul informed about all that is going on and capable of making rational decisions by freely selecting from properly weighed alternatives. Freud did not deny the concept of free will. He simply showed how rare and difficult it is to obtain. By teaching that the conscious mind is only a tiny and often misleading fragment of the mind as a whole, Freud changed our way of thinking about ourselves and each other.

## Freud's Theory of Personality

Freud did more than develop the concept of the unconscious. He also used his technique of free association to explore personality and provided the first comprehensive theory of its development and structure. For Freud, personality consisted of three basic components—the id, the ego, and the superego. The *id* is the original component and includes the basic instincts and biological drives. Freud's theory of instincts underwent several modifications during the course of his life. Freud (1915/1957) initially postulated two types of instincts: (1) the *ego instincts,* such as hunger and thirst, aimed at self-preservation; and (2) the *sex instinct,* broadly defined, aimed at the preservation of the species. Although ego instincts function similarly to the sex drive, they must be gratified if the person is to survive and they can therefore be denied only to a limited extent. Hungry people are often preoccupied with thoughts of food. They notice food cues and smells that others may ignore, and their dreams may be filled with food imagery. But ultimately they must eat, and therefore only rarely (as in the case of anorexia nervosa) is hunger associated with psychological problems.

Later Freud combined the ego and sexual instincts into a more general life instinct and postulated a "death instinct" as its counterpart. Freud's concept of the death instinct appeared in 1920, two years after the end of World War I. The protracted violence and destruction of the war suggested a need to elaborate on humanity's innate destructive tendencies (L. Hoffman, 1981). Since the death instinct cannot be fulfilled without self-destruction, it is often projected outwardly in the form of aggression. War itself is an extreme form of this projec-

tion. Aggression, for Freud, builds up in the individual and must be periodically released, either directly or vicariously. Later in life, Freud became very pessimistic about the possibility of reducing aggression in our society and felt that the best that one could do was direct it into more constructive forms.

Freud introduced his ideas on the death instinct as a tentative speculation in *Beyond the Pleasure Principle* (1920/1953) but later came to accept them completely. Fortunately (or unfortunately), the same cannot be said for other psychoanalysts. Ernest Jones (1957) stated that this was one aspect of Freud's theory on which he and Freud differed completely. He went on to say that of the 50 or so papers devoted to the topic in the first three decades after its introduction, only half supported it during the 1920s, a third during the 1930s, and none at all during the 1940s. William McDougall (1936), who was generally sympathetic with psychoanalysis, described the death instinct as "the most bizarre monster of all [Freud's] gallery of monsters" (p. 96).

The *superego* consists of the internalized values of society acquired through identification with one's parents. Since all parents are different, children develop values that are in many ways unique. The problem with the superego is that it is acquired early, before a person has the capacity to assess these values and make thoughtful choices. People, therefore, acquire a number of erroneous and often conflicting assumptions that they carry with them into adulthood. In a changing society the superego is also responsible for a kind of "cultural lag," in which adults relate to their society as if it were the society of their childhood. Freud felt that an important part of the superego was unconscious and that this repressed part was far harsher than the part consciously known.

In Freud's theory, an instinct is a drive rather than a built-in behavior. It can be displaced, postponed, or even suppressed. The sexual drive was of primary importance because its repression was a frequent problem for his patients. Repressed sexuality causes people to suffer because they must control their thoughts as well as their behavior, and the ignored sexual needs are often driven into the unconscious, where they can cause psychological problems. One of Freud's central theses is that society forces people to suppress basic human impulses, such as sex and aggression, so that they must find expression in indirect and often distorted ways. Initially, he believed that *every* neurosis could ultimately be linked to some form of sexual repression.

It is useful to see the *ego* as the mediator between the id and the superego—attempting to meet the demands of the id within the restraints imposed by the superego and by external society. The ego is the only rational aspect of personality, but it also contains unconscious defense mechanisms designed to protect the person from excessive anxiety. It is often recognized that the superego is socially acquired through identification, but what is seldom stressed is that the ego is a social product as well. It is formed and modified as people attempt to adapt to the demands superimposed by the superego and by other people. From a Freudian point of view, individuals are social not simply because they react to others but because they carry society within themselves in the form of the ego and the superego.

Socialization is never fully successful, however, and no one is ever fully assimilated into society. The id continually strives to assert itself, and when it cannot the frustration may lead to hostility and aggression or various types of antisocial behavior. If the person cannot act out the aggression, the hostility may be turned inward and take the form of masochism or neurotic symptoms.

### Psychosexual Stages

Freud believed that a person's personality is acquired very early in life during the passage through or fixation at one of the psychosexual stages. Each stage focuses on a particular zone or region of the body. The *oral stage* occurs during the first year and focuses on the mouth. Young infants suck not just for nourishment but for the sheer joy that sucking brings. Anything and everything that can be put into the mouth is put into the mouth, and the child explores the environmental orally. If the need for food is met dependably, the child will come to perceive the world and other people as dependable. If the child's needs are met erratically or in a way not associated with demands, it will come to perceive the world as undependable and unresponsive to its needs. The reason why this stage is so important is that it is the child's *first* form of social contact and it sets up expectations that the child carries over into other relationships.

The *anal stage* occurs during the second year and focuses on toilet training. Toilet training is the child's first experience with self-control. Strict toilet training, according to Freud, leads to excessive self-control and produces an orderly and compulsive personality. While toilet training may not seem central to personality development, strictness in toilet training often goes hand in hand with strictness in other areas, and toilet training may therefore serve as a general predictor for behavior. What makes this stage important is not the occurrence of a single traumatic event but numerous minute incidents that set up expectations and leave an impression. A child strictly brought up is simply different—more inhibited and self-controlled—than one raised in a more lenient manner.

The *phallic stage* is the most explicitly social and the one described most fully by Freud. Freud called this period the phallic stage because he believed that the child's concept of sex differences during this period was based on the presence or absence of a penis rather than a recognition of two different reproductive systems. Children at this stage discover and then become obsessed with sex differences. They want to know whether the people and even the animals that they know are male or female. They assign sex to stuffed animals and even cartoon figures. What is more, they discover that most people are paired up—mom and dad, grandfather and grandmother, Minnie and Mickey Mouse—and they select a mate for themselves from the limited choice available. It is not surprising that in many cases little boys and girls "fall in love" with the parent of the opposite sex and talk openly of marriage. The inaccessibility of this choice causes them to suppress and abandon it, but people often select mates later in life who resemble the parent of the opposite sex to some extent. This stage is also characterized in most cases by an identification with the same-sex parent and the subsequent acquisition of sex roles and differences.

The phallic stage is followed by a latency period in which the sex drive is more or less dormant. Infantile impulses do not cease during latency; their energy is merely diverted from sexual drives and redirected toward other things. This is followed by the *genital stage,* during puberty, in which the sex drive returns with a passion. These drives must now be generalized to the body as a whole and directed away from one's self toward an external object. Freud thought that psychological problems develop when a person becomes fixated at or regresses to one of the infantile psychosexual stages. Such individuals, literally, never grow up. They remain dependent, overly self-controlled, or unable to break the bond that ties them to their parents. For Freud, the structure of the family is the prototype for every subsequent relationship.

### Freud's Anthropological Works

No social-psychological account of Freud's influence would be complete without a brief mention of his work on culture and social psychology. Ernest Jones (1957) has pointed out that Freud had a speculative side to his personality that he kept firmly in check during his early works but gave a freer rein as he grew older. One thing that impresses one about Freud's early work, such as *The Interpretation of Dreams* (1900/1953) or *The Psychopathology of Everyday Life* (1904/1953), is the sheer volume of clinical material that Freud introduces to make his point. In this respect, Freud was much like Darwin. His answer to critics was to produce more evidence. In his anthropological works, on the other hand, Freud derives sweeping conclusions from a few basic premises. His mind soared into regions where psychoanalysis had never penetrated.

*Totem and Taboo* (1913/1955) was Freud's first excursion into anthropology. In this work he traces religion and the incest taboo back to a primal crime occurring at the dawn of civilization. Freud took from Darwin the idea that early human beings lived in primal hordes similar to modern apes, dominated by a single father with one or more wives and their children. The severe sexual restrictions placed on the sons and their rivalry with the father caused them to band together and kill the father. The sons resented the father because he stood in the way of their sexual needs and their desire for power, but they loved and admired him at the same time and therefore experienced a great deal of guilt. Over the course of time, the admiration they felt exceeded their hostility, and they deified the father and renounced incest.

The deification of the father is explained in psychoanalytic terms and can be seen as part of a more general process. When a loved one dies, we often experience a sense of guilt based on the feeling that we could have done more to help them when they were alive. According to Freud, this "obsessive reproach" is due to the ambivalence that exists in any relationship, where love and hostility coexist. The hostility is then projected onto the person after their death, and they continue to haunt us for a time. This is why the spirits of the dead are almost invariably evil. The notion of evil spirits makes it possible to separate body and soul and envision a life after death. The next stage is *animism.* A soul or spirit is attributed to other animals and even natural elements. Animism gives rise to sorcery, the art of influencing spirits, and eventually a special position within the tribe devoted to this profession. For Freud, demons and spirits were simply the projection of early people's own ambivalent feelings.

The slain father becomes the prototype for an almightly god. The totem is usually an animal that symbolizes the father and the tribe and holds it together, whereas taboos prevent incest and appease the spirits of the dead. Behind every taboo is a strong impulse to do what is forbidden. Those that break a taboo become taboo themselves, because they arouse envy and become "contagious," in that their example if unpunished incites imitation. By resisting temptation the slain father can be made into a powerful ally. It now becomes possible to control the forces of nature and even death itself by appealing to this authority through prayers and rituals.

Freud's second work, *Group Psychology and the Analysis of the Ego* (1921/1955) is not, strictly speaking, an anthropological work. It is an attempt to apply psychoanalysis to social psychology. While previous writers, such as Tarde and Le Bon, had discussed imitation and suggestion in a general way, Freud went into considerable detail about how and why imitation takes place. He drew a parallel between groups and the family. Children within a family would like to be the exclusive focus of their parents' affection, but they must share attention when new children are born. They must suppress their jealousy in order to obtain an equal, impartial distribution of love.

People within a crowd react in much the same way. They seek authority in a powerful leader, whom they see as a father figure. Leaders tend to be obsessive individuals with a tenacity and sense of mission that makes them men of action. The idealization of the leader is similar to that of the father or that which occurs during romantic love. Followers project onto the charismatic leader strengths and qualities that he may not possess. Social feeling, or esprit de corps, is based on a renunciation of mutual hostility and a mutual identification among followers within the group. A primary group is a number of people who have taken the same person (the leader) as their ideal, and by virture of having a common ideal, identify with each other. For Freud (1921/1955), "social justice means we deny ourselves many things so that others may have to do without them as well" (p. 53).

Freud returned to the question of religion in *The Future of an Illusion* (1927/1961). On the surface it would seem that culture was something imposed on a resisting majority by a minority who held the reigns of power, but every society is based on compulsory labor and the suppression of instincts. Freud felt that the vast majority of individuals are lazy, not naturally fond of work, and opposed to instinctual renunciation. They turn to culture in order to meet their daily needs and escape the forces of nature, but they resent it at the same time. Some problems are not inherent in culture itself but due to imperfections in existing societies. While solid advances have been made in technology and natural science, less progress has been made in regulating human affairs. Inequalities in power and wealth cause hostility among those who contribute their labor but receive little in return. According to Freud (1927/1961), "A culture which leaves unsatisfied and drives to rebelliousness so large a number of its members neither has a prospect of continued existence, nor deserves it" (p. 21).

Under these conditions, religion serves three primary functions. It reduces our fear of nature, reconciles us to the cruelty of fate and death, and makes amends for the injustices suffered in this world. According to Freud, however, it has not succeeded in making people happier, better adjusted, or more civilized. Freud considered religion a form of infantile neurosis in which rituals and repetition blight the lives of individuals and cut them off from reality. It would be much better to recognize culture as a human product instead of attributing it to supernatural sources. Laws and regulations could then be reexamined and improved.

The final authority should be science. The transformations made by science are slow and gradual, but they can be tested and verified. A law that was once seen as universally valid proves to be a special case of a more general law, or its scope is limited by another law discovered later. A rough approximation to the truth is replaced by a closer approximation, which is questioned later. Although generally pessimistic about the idea that science would replace religion for the majority of people, Freud concluded by saying, "No, science is no illusion. But it would be an illusion to suppose that we could get anywhere else what it cannot give us" (p. 98).

*Civilization and its Discontents* (1930/1961) develops to its conclusion the theme that society is founded on suppression of instincts. An unrestricted indulgence of every need presents itself as an enticing yet impossible ideal because it places enjoyment above caution and soon brings its own punishment. People must control their sexual and aggressive needs in order to live together. Frustration is an inevitable consequence of group life. By repressing instincts, civilization has developed traits such as cleanliness, orderliness, and competition that have made progress possible.

People have a number of limited ways of dealing with their pent-up frustration. The most successful approach is *sublimation,* in which instincts are displaced and expressed in a socially desirable way such as work. But this requires special gifts and is accessible only to a few. Work is especially satisfying when it is freely chosen, since it allows people to express their own unique talents and impulses, but it is not highly prized by people in general and the great majority of individuals work only under the stress of necessity. A second strategy is to escape through *intoxication.* A final alternative is *love,* but love is also one of the greatest sources of pain. A small number can escape the pain of separation by displacing love onto humanity, but Freud felt that this dilutes the experience and that humanity was not deserving. Thus, one is caught in an inescapable trap. Civilization is both necessary for satisfying needs and a source of frustration. Societies differ, however, in the amount and kind of restrictions they impose. The most repressive societies forbid intentions as well as deeds. Temptations increase because of constant frustration, and the most virtuous members of these societies are also the most severe in their self-incrimination.

Some of the problems associated with Freud's work will be discussed later, but the most serious criticism is that it explains culture through individual psychological processes and tends to overestimate their universality. According to Bronislaw Malinowski (1929), Freud equipped his "primal hordes . . . with all the bias, maladjustments, and ill-tempers of a middle-class Eu-

ropean family . . . let loose in a prehistoric jungle to run riot in a most attractive but fantastic hypothesis" (p. 146). Freud's view of the family assumed that patriarchal authority was the only source of social cohesion (L. Hoffman, 1987). Paternal power was continually threatened by unsuccessful or destructive adolescent rebellion. His perspective therefore contains the assumption that such processes are universal and reflects a fundamental underlying conservatism.

Freud's treatment of personality changed over time. His early work emphasized the id and stressed the importance of biological drives, his middle work gave more attention to the ego and various mechanisms of defense, whereas a more detailed treatment of the superego was the focus of his later unfinished work (Moscovici, 1981/1985). If Freud had lived to complete his work on the superego, there may have been a better balance between the forces of nature and nurture in his own work, but since he did not, this task was left to others.

There was a mixed response to Freud's ideas in America, ranging from enthusiastic acceptance to open hostility. The vast majority of informed Americans displayed a genuine interest in Freud's theory and were willing to give it a fair hearing before passing final judgement. This certainly characterized the response that awaited Freud when he came to America. Freud's lectures at Clark University in 1909 summarizing his early work brought together many of America's leading psychologists and marked the beginning of widespread public interest.

Among the critics at the conference was Edward Bradford Titchener, one of the founders of American psychology and a strong supporter of experimental procedures used in introspection, who rejected psychoanalysis as an unscientific "cure of souls." Titchener's views were shared by a number of academic psychologists who were attempting to establish psychology's scientific credibility and who generally lumped various theories of the unconscious with the disreputable ideas and practices of faith healing, hypnosis, and mysticism. Knight Dunlap began a campaign against psychoanalysis in 1912, arguing that its methods were "anecdotal" and its practitioners were "tender minded" mystics who were unwilling to follow the rigorous standards of experimental science. He also criticized Freud for placing too much stress on sexual motivation, particularly in early childhood. John B. Watson argued that Freud's description of unconscious processes could be reduced to simple matter-of-fact terms such as habits and ultimately traced to the structure and function of the brain (Hale, 1971).

Freud, of course, was not without supporters. He received considerable support from G. Stanley Hall, who organized the Clark conference, and William James. Although both Hall and James had reservations about Freud's emphasis on sexuality, they enthusiastically endorsed other aspects of his theory. Other supporters included Edward Bissell Holt, a former student of James and Floyd Allport's mentor, who later published a work that attempted to integrate the work of Dewey, Watson, and Freud (Holt, 1915) and, as mentioned previously, Morton Prince, who helped spread Freud's ideas through the *Journal of Abnormal and Social Psychology.*

Given the criticism of the unscientific procedures and lack of academic credibility of psychoanalysis, it is ironic that the ultimate acceptance of Freud's ideas rested on his earlier work in neurology. Even before Freud visited America, neurologists and psychiatrists were adopting various aspects of psychoanalysis in their search for a better understanding and treatment of mental illness. They were becoming increasingly dissatisfied with the then widely held view that physical causes underlay all forms of mental illness. Certain forms of depression, for example, were commonly attributed to lesions on the brain, and the most prescribed treatment involved prolonged periods of bed rest. Other disorders, such as hysteria, did not appear to have any physical basis, and those experiencing it were commonly dismissed as malingerers. Freud's early training in neurology provided him with some scientific respectability in the Viennese scientific community, and in fact his early clientele was based largely on referrals. As a

neuropathologist, Freud was famous for his pinpoint diagnoses (Sulloway, 1979). When physicians treated mental patients and could not find any underlying physical disorder, it was common practice to sent them to Freud. Freud was able to demonstrate that some mental disorders had no underlying physical base and that many physical disorders were themselves based on psychological problems. The development of psychoanalytic theory and its gradual acceptance among professionals in America was part of a prolonged scientific crisis involving psychiatry, neurology, and psychology. Freud's ideas played a decisive role in bringing this crisis to a climax and in generating a permanent transformation involving a shift of emphasis from physical to psychological explanations of mental illness. Freud's theory provided a new means of integrating body and mind, in some cases reversing the traditional causal connection. This represented a quiet revolution within the psychiatric community that paralleled the more noisy reception of Freud within the public at large.[3]

Freud went to great pains to construe an appropriate scientific image for psychoanalysis. He helped create national and international associations that would set standards as well as police and educate their members. The establishment of the American Psychoanalytic Association in 1911 is one of the key features that distinguished it from competing schools of psychotherapy, and it undoubtedly helped advance the professional status and scientific credibility of the discipline. This was particularly important during the 1920s, when psychoanalysis became a fad among many writers and intellectuals.

Like other currents of thought, psychoanalysis was shaped by the cultural and intellectual climate at the turn of the century. The rapid growth of modern cities such as Chicago and New York created a new sense of social awareness about the depersonalized yet highly interdependent urban culture. The emergence of the new urban-industrial environment generated new pressures that profoundly affected the daily lives of all Americans who lived and worked in cities. In a real sense, it was the anxiety associated with urban life that created the depression, neuroses, and other disorders so characteristic of the twentieth century. The psychoanalytic movement developed as a direct response to these problems and reflected the values and ideals of the progressive movement, and, as such, early psychoanalysts tended to be very optimistic about the future of America despite the problems of modern industrial life.

The assimilation of psychoanalysis followed the same pendulum swing as social psychology and reflected the shift from society to individual and back to society. The first period reflected the reform spirit and collectivist values characteristic of the Progressive Era. This was followed by a shift toward a more conservative and individualistic approach during the 1920s and a subsequent shift involving a resurgence of reformist and collectivist sentiments during the 1930s in response to the Great Depression.

Initially psychotherapists tended to give their own definition to Freudian terms and downplayed his emphasis on the confict between the individual and society. The treatment of Freud during this period represented in many ways a complete reversal of some of his basic ideas. Environmental and cultural factors were given more weight than biological ones, his pessimism was replaced by optimism about the future course of society, and despite Freud's insistence that ethics should be kept out of psychoanalysis, early psychoanalytic thinkers, such as L. E. Emerson, argued that "'the law of reality' necessarily inspired ethics and ethical considerations" (Hale, 1971).

Psychoanalysis was uniquely designed to resolve many of the inner conflicts caused by sexually repressive morality at the turn of the century. As early as the 1890s, many of the nation's leading intellectuals began to question the major tenets of "civilized" morality, and some of these later enlisted Freud in a movement to liberate the individual from older Puritan values. James Mark Baldwin and G. Stanley Hall openly criticized the sexual repression of the period, which was even more prudish than it had been in Victorian England. For Americans, psychoanalysis offered a hope for resolving the conflict between self and society by creating healthy, socially well-adjusted individuals. It is little wonder that psychoanalysis had such smooth sailing initially. It seemed ideally suited to the social and cultural conditions of the times.

During the period just before and after World War I, there was a major effort to inform the general public about Freud's ideas (Burnham, 1968b). Although professional psychoanalysts in the medical community were not involved, a younger generation of intellectuals marshalled Freudian theory in their rebellion against the repressive sexual morality of the older generation. In 1916, Mabel Dodge Stern, the influential matron of Greenwich Village, underwent psychoanalysis and talked openly about her experiences exploring the hidden contents of her unconscious. Before long psychoanalysis became the fashion among artists, writers, and intellectuals because it helped justify their own soul-searching in a world of great conflict and constant change. Attempts to popularize Freud and make his ideas more generally available to the medical community and the public at large often resulted in distortions and dilutions of his ideas.

There was also a great deal of talk about Karl Marx and bolshevism among radical intellectuals during this period, but except for a few dedicated activists such as Emma Goldman and John Reed, this seemed more like a romantic flirtation than a serious commitment to social change. Interest in Freud reflected the general conservative and individualistic mood of the 1920s, and as such, psychoanalysis became part of the psychological individualism associated with the "new psychology" and represented the "mania psychologia" of the decade (F. Hoffman, 1945/1957). It became fashionable as a sort of parlor game in which the terms "sex," "complexes," and "dream interpretation" took on their own doggerel meaning. There were "Freudian parties" for the sexually liberated, which was a euphemism for petting parties.

The rapid spread of psychoanalysis in America was a phenomenon that Freud noted with great concern. He felt that the ease with which Americans accepted psychoanalysis showed a lack of critical thought. Freud regarded the informality and eclecticism in America as symptomatic of a lack of intellectual integrity and scientific discipline, and he felt that Americans came too easily by truths others had struggled desperately to discover.

The deep anxiety and despair of the early depression seemed to confirm Freud's pessimism about the future of Western civilization. The depression also generated a more serious concern for the social implications of Freud's theory and marked the passing of the popular capricious interest in Freud as an expression of psychological individualism. Writers during the 1930s began to explore the relationship between Freud and Marx, and although no clear synthesis was worked out, the debate showed that the pendulum had shifted once again from the individual to society. A new group, the neo-Freudians, led predominantly by German-born psychoanalysts, such as Karen Horney, Erik Erikson, and Erich Fromm, began to explore the social origins of personality disorders.

## NEO-FREUDIANS

The development of psychoanalytic ideas within a social context was the result of the thinking of two distinct groups—the neo-Freudians and the cultural anthropologists. The neo-Freudians were for the most part German-trained psychoanalysts who were forced to emigrate during the 1930s because of the rise of Nazism. Before 1930, Berlin was the center of the psychoanalytic movement, with more practicing analysts than any other city. During the early 1930s, Hitler began the "liquidation" of the psychoanalytic movement in Germany, first excluding Jewish members and then placing so many restrictions on the remaining members that they were eventually forced to leave. Ernest Jones (1957) points out that this was one of Hitler's few successful achievements, and that knowledge of psychoanalysis in Germany was relatively limited even after the war.

Most psychoanalysts immigrated to the United States, where they faced people with different problems and made revisions in their theory. Fromm (1970) has noted that Freud began his work by treating patients who were "sick" in the conventional sense—many had a physical problem with no detectable organic cause. In America, psychoanalytic treatment was gradually extended to "difficulties" in living—loneliness, problems with marriage, inability to enjoy life, and so on. Patients in America suffered less from sexual problems than from social problems—the inability to make friends or to adapt to America's fast-paced and mobile society. These differences forced psychoanalysts to take social conditions more into account and led to the development of new theories, collectively known as neo-Freudian. This group included Karen Horney, Erik Erikson, Harry Stack Sullivan, and Erich Fromm. Fromm's contribution will be discussed in Chapter 8, so the present summary is limited to Horney, Erikson, and Sullivan.

### Karen Horney (1885–1952)

Karen Horney was one of the first psychoanalysts to interpret Freud's ideas within a social context. She was born near Hamburg, Germany. Her father was a stern and somewhat intimidating Norwegian sea captain whose frequent absences from home probably set the stage for her theory of social anxiety. She received a medical degree at the University of Berlin and studied psychoanalysis at the Berlin Psychoanalytic Institute under Karl Abraham and Hanns Sachs. She came to the United States in 1934.

Horney's theory differs from Freud's in several ways. She was critical of Freud's psychology of women and more optimistic about the possibility of self-analysis, but the principal difference was her conviction that anxiety was primarily social and was due to the conflict between the need to be loved and the fear of rejection. This conflict is more or less universal, but it is more pronounced in American society and among individuals who have been rejected as children. This conflict is resolved in one of three general ways—by moving toward others, moving against others, or moving away from others (Horney, 1945).

These three general tendencies can be divided into ten specific coping strategies, which when exaggerated become *neurotic needs* (1942). Moving toward others can take two forms—the exaggerated need for affection and approval and the need for a dominant partner. In the first case, the person must be loved by everyone. They make themselves amiable and expect to be treated in a friendly way. If they are driving across the country and a service-station attendant does not return their pleasantries, they feel depressed and downtrodden for the rest of the day. People who use the second strategy can accept rejection as long as they have the love of a single partner. They put all of their eggs in one basket, so to speak, but they also place so many demands on the relationship that their partner is taxed to the limits of endurance and sometimes beyond.

A person can move against others in many ways. One is the exaggerated need for power, where each and every relationship is evaluated in terms of dominance and submission. There is a need to come out on top in every relationship and avoid situations in which one may have to take second place. Somewhat related is the need to exploit others, where the emphasis is on using others and getting as much from relationships as possible. In this type of relationship, other people are treated as a means to an end. Then there is the need for social recognition and prestige, in which each activity and one's whole lifestyle is selected not because of its intrinsic enjoyment but because it brings admiration from others. The person constantly chooses what is perceived as most prestigious in the eyes of others. The neurotic need for personal admiration is similar to the neurotic need for prestige, but the person is now his or her own audience. Finally, there is the need for personal achievement, in which a person is driven by a need to excel in specific areas.

A person who moves away from others chooses not to relate and withdraws into an inner world of his or her own. This can take one of three forms—the neurotic need to restrict one's life within narrow limits, the need for self-sufficiency and independence, and the need for perfection and unassailability. In the latter case, one avoids all activities that cannot be done perfectly, so as to avoid criticism.

These needs are not neurotic in themselves. Indeed, they include many of our highest ideals—devotion to a partner, self-esteem, ambition, modesty, and independence. What distinguishes the normal from the neurotic individual is that the normal person picks and chooses as the situation demands, while the neurotic individual is rigidly locked into a particular response. Such individuals expect to be loved by everyone, they need to dominate or exploit every relationship, or they withdraw from everyone. They respond to each and every individual in the same way, and their personality takes on a flat, two-dimensional quality. Because their response to others is often inappropriate, they experience a great deal of frustration and anxiety in their day-to-day relationships.

### Erik Erikson (1902– )

Like Horney, the theory of Erik Erikson was motivated at least in part by events in his own childhood. He was born to a Scandinavian father, whom he physically resembled, and a Jewish mother, who later remarried a Jewish pediatrician. Erikson, the blond-haired, blue-eyed child, felt out of place with his darker Jewish parents and suffered an acute identity crisis, sometimes feeling that he had been taken from another home. Erikson had little formal education, but he studied directly under Sigmund Freud's daughter, Anna, and was therefore closer to the source than most formally trained psychoanalysts.

Erikson's contribution to psychoanalysis consists primarily in his reinterpretation of Freud's psychosexual stages from the social point of view. His ideas have become so infused with Freud's that it is often difficult for someone who knows both theories to describe Freud's without referring, at least implicitly, to Erikson's. Erikson's *psycho-*

*social stages* include Freud's three early psychosexual stages, his latency period, plus four additional stages occurring from adolescence through adulthood. Each stage is marked by a particular problem that must be addressed and resolved if the person is to be adequately prepared for the next stage. These stages and problems include the following (with approximate ages in parentheses):

| Psychosocial stages | Dilemma to be resolved |
|---|---|
| 1. Oral (0–1) | Trust versus mistrust |
| 2. Anal (1–3) | Autonomy versus shame and doubt |
| 3. Phallic (3–5) | Initiative versus guilt |
| 4. Latency (6–11) | Industry versus inferiority |
| 5. Adolescence (12–20) | Identity versus role confusion |
| 6. Young adulthood (20–40) | Intimacy versus isolation |
| 7. Adulthood (40–65) | Generativity versus stagnation |
| 8. Maturity and old age (65 plus) | Ego integrity versus despair |

For Erikson, as with Freud, the child's first social contact is based on feeding, and the quality and consistency of contact during this period sets up expectations (trust versus mistrust) about future relationships. In a similar manner, the anal stage focuses on toilet training, which if successful, leads to self-control without loss of self-esteem. Erikson departs from Freud to some extent in the treatment of the next two stages. The focus of his third stage is increasing autonomy. Many parents who have been caring and protective up to this point begin to feel uneasy as the child begins to move into the outside world. They may become restrictive and overprotective, and the child may develop fears about initiating activities. The latency stage builds on the initiative developed during the previous period. During school, the child must not only initiate but carry out activities that do not produce an immediate reward. The child's ability to delay gratification and sustain effort that is not immediately reinforced develops during this period. If it does not develop, children experience feelings of inferiority as they see themselves slipping further and further behind the more industrious children of their own age.

One of the most important and original aspects of Erikson's theory is his treatment of the *identity crisis* during adolescence. This aspect of his theory was undoubtedly derived from Erikson's personal experience as a youth, but it seems to be widepread, at least in Western cultures. Adolescence, as we know it, seems scarcely to exist in primitive cultures and was probably rare in America a hundred years ago. In some primitive societies, individuals move from childhood to adulthood with little conflict, and the transition is often marked by a particular event, such as circumcision, which physically attests to the person's adult status. The brooding adolescent, torn by conflicting values and standing somewhere between childhood and adulthood, is a result of the changing values within modern industrial society. For Erikson, the critical task to be worked out during this period is the reconciliation of these conflicting opinions and beliefs and the establishment of a coherent personal identity. Failure leads to role confusion and can permanently damage the possibility of solving future dilemmas during adulthood.

Only after adolescents and young adults have established a stable identity is it possible to establish an intimate relationship with other people. People must know themselves before they can choose a partner. An intimate relationship also involves mutual exploration of each other's personality, and such exploration is difficult or impossible when one's own identity is diffused or still in the process of formation. People who fail to establish intimacy become isolated and self-absorbed, seeking intimacy through repeated contact with different individuals.

The problem during adulthood focuses on generativity, productivity, and creativity. Self-indulgence is appropriate during adolescence and young adulthood, where social irresponsibility is the norm. It may even be necessary, since it allows a person to explore various options and select the most appropriate. Thus, a person can work at a number of jobs, take many different courses, or date many different people, in order to discover the type of work and person they like. This is the time to 'sow the wild oats,' and such behavior is not only permissible but often encouraged. But many people reach a point at which frivolous activities no longer bring pleasure. They want to do something with their lives or leave something behind. Children provide one option, creative work provides another. "Individuals who do not develop generativity indulge themselves as if they were their one and only child" (Erikson, 1959, p. 97).

The final stage of maturity and old age is based on developing generativity during the previous stage. Individuals near the end of their lives look back in order to evaluate their achievements and contributions. If they are satisfied, they can face death feeling that they have left something worthwhile behind. If not, they experience despair because it is now too late. Despair can easily turn into disgust and produce the bitter old person who constantly finds faults in others.

## Harry Stack Sullivan (1892–1949)

The person who developed Freud's ideas in the newest and most original way was probably Harry Stack Sullivan. Sullivan was born in rural upstate New York, the only surviving child of a poor Irish family, and grew up isolated and alone. He was a superior student in high school and graduated valedictorian of his class at age 16. He entered Cornell but had to withdraw in his second year because of personal reasons (probably schizophrenia). Six years later he entered the Chicago College of Medicine and Surgery, which was one of the then numerous "diploma mills" that gave medical degrees virtually for the price of admission, and received his degree in 1917, just before the institute was closed. He received no formal training in psychiatry, but he did undergo 300 hours of psychoanalysis under Clara Thompson, who later claimed that she had to stop treatment after 300 hours because she had such awe of Sullivan's intellectual capacity that she could not go on. Sullivan's lack of training and liberal education shows in his writing and his cumbersome terminology, but if one has the patience to penetrate beyond these stylistic problems, one discovers one of the most gifted thinkers of this century.

Sullivan (1953) defined personality as the characteristic ways in which an individual deals with other people in his or her interpersonal relationships. His main contribution to Freudian psychology was, like Erikson's, a reinterpretation and extension of Freud's psychosexual stages. He lists six stages of development preceding maturity: (1) infancy; (2) childhood; (3) the juvenile era; (4) preadolescence; (5) early adolescence; and (6) late adolescence.

During *infancy,* the young child gradually learns to distinguish, out of what is originally an undifferentiated experience, material objects, other people, and itself. The first object is the nipple (either natural or artificial) which supplies milk. The first person is the mother associated with the nipple. The child's own primitive self-concept is based on sucking the thumb and feeling the thumb being sucked. By mid-infancy, the infant is exploring the environment with hands and mouth and gradually differentiating between the self and the external world.

These experiences are colored by the attitude of the mother or the mother substitute during this period. A mother who feels a great deal of anxiety transmits this feeling to her child, and it becomes associated with the child's attitude toward objects, other people, and even itself. To paraphrase Sullivan (1953), before speech is acquired each person has already learned to relate to others in a particular way, based on his or her relationship with the mother. This pattern of relating becomes the "utterly buried but quite firm foundation" on which the future personality is built.

*Childhood* begins with the onset of speech and ends with the beginning of cooperative play. During this period, children use language to integrate their experience and form a more realistic concept of the outer world. Sullivan provides a simple yet powerful explanation of the Oedipal situation. According to Sullivan, each parent is more comfortable with and better able to understand children of the same sex, but less certain in relationships with children of the opposite sex. As a result, they tend to be more confident disciplining those of the same sex. Thus, the same-sex parent tends to become the authority figure, while the opposite-sex parent serves as the indulgent protector. This leads to identification with the same-sex parent and a close attachment to the parent of the opposite sex.

Sullivan's most original contribution is his treatment of the juvenile era and preadolescence. Sullivan's *juvenile era* corresponds to the early part of Freud's latency period (roughly 6 to 8½ years of age) but, far from seeing this period as uneventful and insignificant, Sullivan regarded it as vitally important for a person's social development. Before this period children usually receive unconditional love from the parents, who are the central figures in their life. Nothing needs to be done to stay in their good grace. When a child enters school, on the other hand, friendships must be made and maintained through social accommodation. Children must adjust to the quirks and idiosyncracies of their peers, and many behaviors, such as selfishness or overcaution, which were overlooked or actually encouraged in the home are actively discouraged by peers. Some children, those who have been pampered or ignored at home, are ill-equipped to deal with these changes. On the other hand, social contact at school can rectify many of the problems that may have developed during childhood. Unless the child is so socially withdrawn as to avoid contact altogether, the warmth provided by teachers and friends can compensate (to a certain extent) for the maltreatment and rejection at home.

A second change that takes place at school is the development of a generalized notion of authority. At home, parents may have been lenient or strict, but at school the increase in social contact and the exposure to many different authority figures helps to establish a more general idea of what authority is like. Authority figures come to be seen as human, with strengths and weaknesses, and this often leads to a reassessment of one's own parents.

Sullivan's most controversial stage is that of *preadolescence*. Many people (e.g., Chapman, 1976; Perry, 1982) claim that Sullivan exaggerated this period because of his own homosexual feelings as a preadolescent. Sullivan claimed that as children begin their entry into sexual maturity they must understand and come to grips with feelings produced by these biological changes. To do this, they often select someone of the same sex and same level of maturity who becomes their "best friend" and confidant. This is the person's first intimate relationship, in which the needs of the other person are regarded as important as one's own. These intimate explorations can often compensate for earlier rejection and clear up misconceptions about life that the child may have developed previously. Two things make the presence of this stage at least plausible, if not common. First, children do seem to go through a period in which they dislike, and even detest, members of the opposite sex, and second, many of the changes, such as menstruation, are of such a sex-specific nature that a member of the opposite sex could not possibly understand them.

For Sullivan, preadolescence occurs between 8½ and 12 years, whereas *adolescence* starts at sexual maturity. Adolescence is characterized by the beginning of lust. Lustful feelings are often considered separate from intimacy, as, for example, with the notion of "good girls" and "bad girls." Early adolescence is distinguished by what one might call "gang courtship." A group of boys and a group of girls get together, and each individual dates different people in the other group. These relationships are usually very intense but quite brief and they provide the person with a general idea of what ought to be sought in a partner. During late adolescence, the person must fuse the needs for intimacy and lust, and select a partner who can be both cared for deeply and sexually desired. For many people this remains an impossible ideal.

Several general features of Sullivan's theory should be stressed. One is the clear separation of needs. The infant seeks reassuring contact, the child parental love, the juvenile peer contact, the preadolescent intimacy. Lust is the *last* social need to develop. It is only with the onset of sexual maturity, according to Sullivan, that one experiences sexual desire per se. This is very different from Freud's theory, where the sex drive is the first and only source of affection.

A second feature of Sullivan's theory that many people should find reassuring was his belief in a *general tendency toward psychological health*. Each stage is capable of rectifying problems acquired previously. A child from a poor home environment can find warmth and protection in school. A lonely and unaccepted juvenile can correct many problems through an intimate relationship with another, perhaps equally lonely and rejected, age-mate during preadolescence.

A final feature, and one that Sullivan's model shares with Freud's is that it is possible to become fixated at a certain stage. The juvenile era, for example, is characterized by compromise and competition, and either feature can be overdeveloped. Someone fixated at this stage may be obsessed with compeition and success, and Sullivan felt that such obsession indicated a lack of acceptance as a youth. A preadolescent fixation can lead to a homosexual sex preference, whereas fixation at the stage of early adolescence produces a Don Juan type who seeks sexual gratification through many different relationships.

Sullivan, perhaps more than any other person, sought to broaden the concept of social psychology so as to include psychiatry and cultural anthropology. His close friendship with the anthropologist Edward Sapir (1884–1939) provided one of the many links between psychiatry and anthropology, whereas his utilization of ideas derived from Charles Horton Cooley and George Herbert Mead links his theory to the theory of symbolic interaction discussed in Chapter 11. While Freud could be considered the central figure during this period because of his actual influence, Sullivan was central by virtue of his theoretical position.

It is therefore somewhat ironic to note that Sullivan and other neo-Freudian theorists had a very limited impact on social psychology textbook authors. Sullivan was the seventh most cited author among sociological textbook authors during the 1960s but has never had much of an impact on psychologists (See Table 1.1). The neo-Freudians are often referred to as "social psychologists" when their theories of personality are discussed (e.g., Hall and Lindzey, 1978), but they are rarely mentioned in social psychology textbooks. Yet their potential contribution to social psychology is far too important to be ignored.

The Freudian and neo-Freudian perspectives have features in common, such as the concepts of developmental stages and defense mechanisms for reducing anxiety. There are, however, some important differences. Neo-Freudians tend to stress cultural factors or interpersonal experiences rather than biological drives. For Erikson in particular, mature psychological development is based on a process of growing self-determination (L. Hoffman, 1982). Unlike Freud, who assumed that individuals and society are in perpetual conflict, the neo-Freudians described mature individuals functioning in ways that are basically integrated with the norms and expectations of society. Thus, in contrast to Freud's conservative need for social control, the neo-Freudians promote a liberal, social-democratic political system consisting of autonomous individuals working toward communal well-being. Some critics point out, however, that by eliminating the conflict between individuals and society the neo-Freudians have produced a conformist view that never seriously questions or critically evaluates social norms and conventions (Buss, 1979; Jacoby, 1975). There are theorists who recognize a radical potential within Freud's conflict model that can be combined with a Marxist view of social change. These developments will be considered in more detail in Chapter 8.

## CULTURAL ANTHROPOLOGY

The influence of cultural anthropology on social psychology during the 1930s was far more substantial than that of the neo-Freudians, particularly among psychological authors. Margaret Mead in particular was frequently cited during this period and continued to be frequently cited even after World War II. Cultural anthropology during the 1930s was concerned primarily with cultural differences in socialization and personality, and there was a healthy blend of psychology and anthropology (e.g., Klineberg, 1940).

In many ways, the infant sciences of psychoanalysis and cultural anthropology grew up together in America. When Sigmund Freud stepped onto the stage of Clark University in Worcester, Massachusetts, to give his first and only series of lectures in America, Franz Boas, the father of American anthropology, was in the audience. Boas provided cultural anthropology with its central theme and helped train many of the people who would develop it into a distinct discipline. Before 1920, cultural anthropology was concerned primarily with cataloguing social norms and institutions, but under the influence of Boas the emphasis shifted to the study of the individual in society and eventually to the study of personality.

The reaction of cultural anthropologists to Freud was twofold. Freud's own anthropological speculations placed a great deal of emphasis on biological factors—a position that Boas and his students vehemently opposed. But Freud developed the first comprehensive theory of personality, which anthropologists either used or tested in their field research. Insofar as anthropologists turned to psychology for theories, they turned almost exclusively to Freudian psychology, and indeed Freudian and neo-Freudian theories have enjoyed a virtual monopoly in the field. La Barre (1958), for example, carried out a survey of the fellows of the American Anthropological Association and found that a third of those in the personality and culture group had been analyzed.

This does not mean that anthropologists accepted either Freud's anthropological speculations or aspects of his general theory without question. Many of the early anthropological studies were designed to test certain aspects of Freud's theory. Bronislaw Malinowski (1884–1942), for example, studied the sexual behavior of natives in the Trobriand Islands of New Guinea in order to test the generality of the Oedipus complex and published his findings in 1929. These natives had a different child-rearing system, in which the father acted as companion and friend while the mother's brother took care of the discipline. Under these conditions Malinowski could find little trace of an Oedipus complex and concluded that it was largely a result of sexual repression and tensions within the Western nuclear family—true under certain conditions but not universal (see Malinowski, 1953). While Malinowski was one of the first to test Freud's theory, the three most important American anthropologists during the 1930s were Franz Boas, Ruth Benedict, and Margaret Mead, and the present discussion will be limited to them.

### Franz Boas (1858–1942)

Franz Boas was born and educated in Germany and received an education primarily in the natural sciences. In 1883–84, he went to Baffin Island, in what is now the Canadian Arctic, as part of a survey team and lived among the Eskimo as one of them. He learned their language and studied their legends and songs. Deeply impressed by the cultural differences, he returned to North America in 1886 to study the coastal tribes of British Columbia. He taught briefly at Clark University but was appointed Professor of Anthropology at Columbia University in 1899 and remained there throughout the rest of his career.

Boas's anthropological position must be seen in its historical context as a reaction to the deep-seated biological determinism at the turn of the century. At the beginning of the century, social evolution and eugenics (see Chapter 2) were both firmly established in the United States. These movements had resolved the nature-nurture controversy by proclaiming that culture was due primarily to biological and racial differences. The leading supporter of eugenics in the United States, Charles Davenport, set up the Eugenics Record Office and had begun to produce a vast list of behavioral traits, such as violent eroticism and suicidal depression, which were said to be genetically determined. He identified an inborn love of the sea among naval officers as a sex-linked recessive trait. For Davenport, criminals, prostitutes, and tramps were said to lack the gene that allowed them to control their more primitive asocial behaviors (Freeman, 1983).

It was against this extreme biological determinism that Boas reacted. The same year that Galton died, Boas (1911) said that culture was "a result of varied external conditions acting upon general human characteristics." Boas was primarily concerned with the relative contribution of biology and culture, but his students developed a more extreme position, which left little room for biological explanations and attributed most aspects of personality to culture. At the turn of the century, Boas had been virtually alone in his opposition to biological determinism, but by 1920, Boas's students held positions in almost every major American university and, though they differed on minor points, they were steadfast in their belief that personality was primarily a result of culture. By 1930, modern American anthropology was well under way, and social evolution and the eugenics movement were in shambles.

Boas's impact on American anthropology was enormous. He not only provided the central ideological position of "cultural determinism" that allowed cultural anthropology to develop into an independent discipline; he perfected the methodology of almost every division in the field. He also linked cultural anthropology with psychology and psychoanalysis and trained many of the most important workers in the area, including Ruth Benedict and Margaret Mead.

### Ruth Benedict (1887–1948)

In *Patterns of Culture,* (1934), Ruth Benedict went far beyond a mere catalogue of behavioral traits in order to show the psychological coherence of these patterns within the personality of an individual. She identified three personality types—the Apollonian, the Dionysian, and the paranoid—characteristic of three different cultures. The Pueblo Indians of New Mexico dis-

played the Apollonian type. This group stressed moderation and discouraged competition. The males of the village were concerned primarily with religious matters, while the females took care of crops and production. The females owned the home and all its possessions. Divorce could be carried out by simply placing the male's few meager possessions outside the front door. Under these conditions, relationships were friendly and relaxed and conflict was rare.

Members of the Dobu tribe of New Guinea displayed a personality that was in many ways the exact opposite. Their attitude was described as paranoid, and their relationships were characterized by treachery and suspicion. Trading formed a major part of the group's life and the "good person," by Dobu standards, was the one who could cheat another and obtain as much as possible. Sexual relations were characterized by a combination of prudery and violence. A woman could not go unaccompanied into the woods, for instance, because of the fear of being raped.

The Kwakiutl Indians of the Pacific Northwest displayed a third type of personality, which Benedict described as Dionysian. These Indians were surrounded by extremely fertile hunting and fishing grounds, but instead of enjoying the bounty of the land and sea, their relationships were based on competition and status seeking. One's superiority was shown by the destruction of personal property, and humiliation (sometimes ending in suicide) occurred if one did not have sufficient property to destroy.

Benedict showed how cultural variations produce different types of personality and how ill-adapted one type would be if placed in a different culture. The mild-mannered Pueblo Indians, who may have been perfectly suited to their own culture, would have been tremendously out of place in either the Dobu or Kwakiutl societies. Socialization affects not only behavior but a person's perception of the external world. As Benedict (1934) put it:

> No man ever looks at the world with pristine eyes. He sees it edited by a definite set of customs and institutions and ways of thinking. . . . By the time he can talk he is the little creature of his culture, and by the time he is grown and able to take part in

its activities, its habits are his habits, its beliefs his beliefs, its impossibilities his impossibilities (pp. 2–3).

## Margaret Mead (1901–1978)

Margaret Mead became interested in anthropology as an undergraduate at Barnard College, while attending an introductory course taught by Boas. She switched from psychology to anthropology and entered graduate school at Columbia, where she studied under Boas and became close friends with Ruth Benedict. After two years of study, Boas designed a project on the relative strength of biological and cultural factors during adolescence, and Mead agreed to carry it out on the west Pacific island of Samoa. The choice of Samoa was based partly on convenience. There was a naval port at the town of Pago Pago, and a ship docked every three weeks. Thus, at the age of 23, with only two years of graduate training and no knowledge of the language, Mead arrived in American Samoa and began what was to become a landmark study in anthropology. *Coming of Age in Samoa* (1928) was published three years later and became the best-selling anthropological work of all time. One reviewer commented that *Coming of Age in Samoa* marked the coming of age of American anthropology, because it led to a separation of biological and anthropological explanations of social behavior and shifted the emphasis to the study of culture.

Mead spent seven weeks in Pago Pago studying Samoan and then moved to the more remote island of Ta'u, where she lived with an American family who ran the local radio station and medical dispensary. Far from being a remote island paradise, Samoa had been converted to Protestant Christianity for nearly 80 years. Schools had been set up, and a ferry took passengers to and from Pago Pago, free of charge, about once every three weeks (Freeman, 1983).

Mead based her findings on interviews provided by 25 adolescent girls. She described Samoa as an easy-going culture, relatively free from the conflicts characteristic of Western society. Children were raised in an extended family, without strong attachments to their natural parents. Child care was gentle and permissive, and competition was openly discouraged. Adolescence was described as a period of free lovemaking, where young girls were encouraged to have many lovers before marriage. What was the most difficult period in Western cultures was, according to Mead, "perhaps the pleasantest time the Samoan girl will ever know." Mead reasoned that if adolescent problems were due to biological changes, they should be universal, but the complete absence of problems in Samoa showed that adolescence must be explained in cultural terms. The result was a complete triumph of nurture over nature. Her book corresponded closely with the intellectual climate of the late 1920s. It received a sweeping endorsement by Boas and was an immediate and spectacular success.

In *Coming of Age in Samoa,* Mead used the approach that has come to be known in anthropology as a "negative instance," which she used in her later work as well. This approach is based on finding an exception to a seemingly universal pattern. In 1935, she turned to the problem of sex stereotypes and described cultural differences in three tribes in New Guinea. One group, the Arament, showed a maternal pattern, in which both males and females were cooperative and unaggressive. A second group, the Mundugumor, showed the opposite pattern, with both sexes behaving in a ruthless, aggressive manner. A final group, the Tchambuli, showed a pattern that was a complete reversal of the sterotype found in Western society. Women were dominant and took care of the family needs while men were irresponsible and emotionally dependent.

When World War II began, many anthropologists simply extended their work from the study of primitive cultures to that of modern industrial societies. Ruth Benedict (1948) carried out a study of Japanese character, while Margaret Mead provided an analysis of American (1942) and later Russian (1951) personalities. Many of these studies of *national character* were of military interest and received considerable support from military sources, who were anxious to understand the personality of their adversaries. The people most studied during this period were the Germans. Thus, cultural anthroplogy came home, so to speak, with new and more powerful tools, to examine the same population that was originally the focus of psychoanalysis.

## SUBSEQUENT TRENDS

Freud is one of the few people who has had a persistent impact on American social psychology, but his anthropological speculations are weakened by two major premises that are used in various degrees to support his position. The first, his undaunted belief in the death instinct, has already been discussed. Much of Freud's pessimism about the future of society stemmed from his belief that people are naturally inclined to self-destruction. He felt that peace and progress would always be limited because people had a displaced desire to destroy each other. The suppression of this instinct causes pent-up aggression, which merely augments the desire for destruction.

A second problem is Freud's occasional reference to the biological inheritance of acquired characteristics.[4] He seemed to suggest at times that primordial fantasies, such as the Oedipus complex, parental coitus, castration, and patricide, are particularly disturbing because they derive from actual experiences in our ancestral past. This problem is not as serious as some critics have suggested. In a critical passage in *Totem and Taboo,* Freud (1913/1938) said "Taboos . . . maintain themselves from generation to generation, perhaps only as the result of tradition set up by parental and social authority. But in later generations they have perhaps already become 'organized' as a piece of inherited psychic property" (p. 831). Note the qualifications and the recognition that taboos may be transmitted entirely through culture. The choice between these two alternatives is critical. If the experiences are biologically inherited, then they are part of our genetic structure and inescapable. If they are culturally transmitted, then they would be widespread but not universal. They result from living within a nuclear family where power is unevenly distributed

and people compete for affection. In this respect, the anthropological search for "negative cases" is useful but does not seriously weaken Freud's general theory.

Many of Freud's supporters dismiss his anthropological work as an aberrant aspect of an otherwise brilliant career. But this dismissal misses two important points. First, it disregards the respect that Freud felt toward his work. Freud considered *Totem and Taboo* one of his three most important books (along with *The Interpretation of Dreams,* 1900/1953, and *Three Contributions to the Theory of Sex,* 1905/1953). The second more serious problem is that Freud did not consider his anthropological speculations as separate from his more general theory. Many of his explanations of primitive culture and religion are taken directly from his work in psychotherapy.

Freud's impact was sufficiently large that it represents a "scientific revolution" in the Kuhnian sense of a change in beliefs or assumptions that guide a scientific discipline (see Chapter 1). It marked the end of the psychological approach known as introspection and changed the way we view psychology and even ourselves (see Moscovici, 1961). Thomas Kuhn (1962) has pointed out that a successful paradigm is characterized by two features. A new theory's achievements are sufficiently unprecedented that it attracts a new group of followers, but it is also sufficiently open-ended as to leave all sorts of problems to be resolved. In those rare cases where a new theory has both addressed and resolved basic issues, it has become a mere technical appendage to broader fields where research is still needed. The appeal of psychoanalysis during the 1930s was not because it provided a finished description of how the mind operates, but because it provided a general framework within which social problems and issues could be discussed.

Freud's work has been extended and refined by neo-Freudians and cultural anthropologists. Freeman (1983) has pointed out that Boas's conception of anthropology was so fundamentally different from his predecessor's that it too represented a paradigm shift. Boas recognized the importance of biological factors, but his followers developed a more extreme form of cultural determinism that downplayed or ignored biology. Their success, however, was not due to a reasoned resolution of the nature-nurture debate but to the arbitrary exclusion of biological aspects of personality.

The work of Benedict and Mead has not gone unchallenged. Otto Klineberg's (1940) text on social psychology drew heavily from Benedict and Mead and developed what he called "comparative social psychology." When the revised edition of this text was published in 1954, however, he had become much more critical. He disputed their sampling procedures and the accuracy of their observations. He felt that much of their material had been observed, retained in memory, and recorded later. Despite these criticisms, Klineberg remained deeply committed to the importance of culture and was himself a major figure in the development of social psychology during and after the war.

A more severe criticism of Mead's work has recently been published by Freeman (1983) in a book called *Margaret Mead and Samoa* and subtitled *The Making and Unmaking of an Anthropological Myth.* Drawing from his own anthropological observations, archive information, and police records, Freeman has put together a picture at striking variance to that painted by Margaret Mead. He depicts Samoa as a highly aggressive, competitive society dominated by the concept of hereditary rank. Childrearing is described as severe and arbitrary, fostering a deep resentment often hidden by an outward display of calm. The discrepancy between Freeman's findings and those of Mead is so great that Freeman was forced to conclude that Mead, unable to speak Samoan well and relying mainly on anecdotal information, was deliberately teased and misled by her adolescent informants.

One should avoid drawing too many conclusions from the apparent refutation of a single study. Mead may have exaggerated cultural differences at times, but she was also instrumental in challenging the extreme biological determinism of the 1920s and helped people appreciate the importance of culture in personality development. Nevertheless, Freeman (1983) seems

to be essentially correct in that one does not resolve the nature-nurture controversy by simply dismissing biological factors. The triumph of cultural determinism isolated anthropology from biology and gave the misleading impression that people are infinitely malleable. What seems to be needed is a reintegration of anthropology and biology in order to tackle the problem originally posed by Boas—that is, the relative contribution of biological and cultural factors in the shaping of personality. This new integration should be accompanied by a reformulation of the nature-nurture debate in which the traditional dualistic model is replaced by a dynamic interactionist model, such as the one proposed by Richard Learner (1978) or, more recently, Stephen Gould (1981). The interactionist model avoids many of the conceptual problems associated with the century-old debate and points the way toward new areas of inquiry concerning human evolution and development.

The integration of social psychology, psychoanalysis, and anthropology during the 1930s may have simply been a result of conditions at Columbia University during this period. Researchers at Columbia included psychologists, such as Gardner Murphy, Otto Klineberg, Theodore Newcomb, and Muzafer Sherif; anthropologists, such as Franz Boas, Ruth Benedict, and Margaret Mead; and anthropological psychoanalysts, such as Ralph Linton and Abram Kardiner. New York City was also the port of entry for many psychoanalytic and neopsychoanalytic writers coming from Germany. This rich environment produced a healthy interchange of ideas in which each group drew from and profited by contact with the other. This seems to have been the period in which social psychology was conceived most broadly and included both long-term and short-term effects of the social environment on the individual.

After World War II, coverage of socialization and personality within social psychology texts began to diminish, particularly among psychological authors. This was undoubtedly due at least in part to the emergence of personality and developmental psychology as distinct disciplines. It seems to have been generally conceded that the socialization of the child belongs to the study of development psychology, whereas the long-term effects of socialization on the individual is a part of the study of personality. In some ways, this can be seen as a necessary and inevitable consequence of specialization within psychology. But it overlooks an important point at the forefront of social psychology during the 1930s—that is, our reactions to social stimuli are strongly conditioned by our previous social experiences. These experiences not only shape our beliefs and attitudes but also determine at least to some extent the way in which we perceive reality, the way in which we solve problems, and the way we respond to others.

This problem was so central during the 1930s that Murphy and Murphy (1931) began their textbook on experimental social psychology with a warning that the research cited was culture-bound and limited to the population from which it was derived. This kind of caution may be regarded as a nuisance among contemporary researchers who would like to regard their findings as universal. It is a fact that is being quickly obscured by the "westernization" of primitive cultures. But cross-cultural differences are a testimony to the flexibility of human behavior. Cultural differences should also serve as a stern warning that our way of perceiving reality is not the only, or necessarily even the best, way. The loss of this area to sociology is shown by the name given to the study of the long-term effects of the social environment on perception and thought. This field is now known as the "sociology of knowledge," and it will be discussed briefly in Chapter 8.

The decline of interest in socialization and personality can also be partly attributed to the rapid rise of experimental research after World War II. It is difficult to study the long-term effects of the social environment experimentally, so social psychologists stressing experimental procedures have tended to overlook them. This growing focus on experimentation has shifted the emphasis from culture to an individual's immediate reaction to a social situation.

After World War II, the principal centers for social-psychological research were Yale, the Massachusetts Institute of Technology, and later the University of Michigan (Festinger, 1980). Those universities that took a more interdisciplinary view, such as Berkeley, Harvard, and Columbia, gradually lost ground to those stressing experimentation.

The division of social psychology and personality into two separate subdisciplines meant the loss of some of social psychology's most gifted thinkers. Gardner Murphy, Gordon Allport, and J. F. Brown all moved more or less full-time from social psychology to the study of personality, although each retained to a certain extent his social-psychological perspective. This division also led to a shattering of psychoanalysis as a general framework. Freud's influence on social psychology is still relatively strong, but it is not based on his theory of socialization. His theory of aggression is often mentioned along with social learning theory, his concept of identification may be treated as a special form of modeling, and aspects of his general theory have been worked into the theories of Dollard and Miller, but he has never regained the central position that he enjoyed during the 1930s.

## NOTES

1. During the 1980s, Freud does not reach the top ten among either psychologists or sociologists, and in fact ranks thirtieth among psychological textbook authors. Freud's lack of influence on contemporary social psychology is also reflected in a book of interviews with major social psychologists (Evans, 1980). While the older generation of scholars often describe Freud as a major influence, Freud is not mentioned by any of those born after 1914 (Newcomb, 1980).

2. Sulloway (1979) has pointed out that the English expression "free association" does not accurately capture the meaning of the German words *freier Einfall,* which conveys a sense of "intrusion" *(Einfall)* of preconscious material on consciousness itself.

3. The mysterious drop in the number of cases of hysteria in this century makes Freud's work seem something of an archaism, for it began with the investigation of a disorder that many modern neurologists see only once or twice in a lifetime. Hysteria was sufficiently common in Freud's time, however, to provide him with a living and a revolutionary stepping-stone toward a new science of the mind (Sulloway, 1979).

4. As Sulloway (1979) has pointed out, during Freud's generation (that is, those born before 1860) virtually all biologists, including Freud's teachers, were Lamarckian to some extent.

# 7

# Group Processes

In 1924, Floyd Allport distinguished psychological social psychology from the sociological approach by stating that

> The study of groups is, in fact, the province of the special science of sociology. While the social psychologist studies the individual in the group, the sociologist deals with the group as a whole. He discusses its formation, solidarity, continuity, and change. (p. 10)

If this distinction had been accepted, it might have served as a useful division of labor, but social trends during the 1930s brought the study of small groups into the forefront and eventually into the domain of psychology. For a short period after World War II, the study of groups was *the* major area of social psychology, surpassing the study of attitudes as the most researched topic.

Steiner (1974) has provided an insightful analysis of the differences between the individualistic and group approaches to social psychology. The individualistic approach assumes that the organism is a relatively self-contained unit in which behavior results from internal states or processes. The group approach, in contrast, presents people as elements within larger social systems, such as groups, organizations, or society, which help determine their behavior. The individualistic approach stresses proximal causes—events that are close in space and time—whereas the group approach seeks more distal explanations, in which a person's behavior is explained by events occurring within the larger social system. These

approaches are not necessarily incompatible. They represent different priorities in what is studied and how research results are interpreted.

During the 1930s there was an increasing interest among psychologists in the experimental study of small groups. Floyd Allport extended his earlier work on social facilitation to the study of conformity. Muzafer Sherif conducted laboratory studies on the formation of social norms. And Kurt Lewin began his systematic work on group dynamics with his experimental studies of leadership styles.

These experimental studies of groups focused on artificially created, "ad hoc" groups of strangers brought together for experimental investigation. This contrasted sharply with field procedures developed by the Chicago School of sociology in the 1920s (see Chapter 4). Thrasher (1927), for example, studied gangs of boys in the Chicago slums and Zorbaugh (1929) depicted the exclusive clubs of Chicago's affluent "Gold Coast." These field studies provided a means of understanding how natural groups function in the real world. During the 1930s there was an increase in the number and diversity of field studies. Several in-depth studies of class structure and group life in small cities were reported, such as the Middletown studies conducted by Lynd and Lynd (1929, 1937) and the Yankee City series carried out by Warner and Lunt (1941). An influential study of a "street-corner society" of young men in Boston during the depression was carried out by W. F. Whyte (1943). Whyte, a young sociologist, acted as a participant observer and was thus able to engage in many of the group's activities and describe them first-hand.

The field-study approach was not restricted to sociologists. In the late 1930s, Theodore Newcomb (1943), a psychologist, began a longitudinal study of how attitudes are shaped by reference groups at Bennington College, which was a liberal college for women in Vermont. By far the most influential series of field studies was undertaken by a group of investigators from the Harvard School of Business Administration. Starting in the mid-twenties, this team, lead by Elton Mayo, observed and conducted experiments with small groups of workers at the Hawthorne Works of the Western Electric Company in Chicago (Mayo, 1933; Roethlisberger, 1941; Roethlisberger & Dickson, 1939).

Another contribution to the study of groups during the 1930s was the sociometric approach developed by Jacob L. Moreno, a Romanian-born psychiatrist trained at the University of Vienna. Moreno (1934), who emigrated to the United States, focused on how groups are formed through interpersonal choices. He developed a method known as *sociometry,* which examines patterns of interpersonal attraction and rejection among group members. Respondents were asked to indicate which particular group members they like and dislike or want to spend time with. The pattern of choices was then graphically presented in a *sociogram,* which consists of points representing individual members and connecting lines that reflect interpersonal choices.

The increasing dominance of the group approach during the 1930s reflected the changing times. The depression dramatically ended the sense of confidence and the emphasis on individualism that pervaded American society during the twenties. Mounting social problems shifted attention to what was happening at the level of society, and social psychologists became more interested in describing behavior within larger social contexts. Group effort and cooperation rather than individual initiative and competition appeared to be the key to constructive social change.

There were also more direct influences.

By the 1930s several distinct professions emerged in America that were involved in working with groups of people (Cartwright & Zander, 1953; Marrow, 1969). Social group work was one of the earliest of these. Group workers developed techniques of group management, some of which proved more successful than others. For example, in working with recreational groups, such as the Boy Scouts and the YMCA, it was clear that the type of leadership and group atmosphere could influence both the amount and quality of participation. A good leader could stimulate a group, whereas a poor one could alienate group members. Social psychologists drew heavily from group workers and collaborated with them on various research projects.

The application of group psychotherapy, which was originally used in medical settings, was expanded to nonmedical groups. Various therapeutic innovations, such as Moreno's role-playing procedures, influenced the research on groups by social psychologists. A related phenomenon was the growth of self-help groups like Alcoholics Anonymous. These groups demonstrated that personal problems could be explored within an atmosphere of mutual social support. They were attempts by nonprofessionals to organize people with specific problems so that they could be discussed and corrected. The growth of recreational and self-help groups reflected a structural change within American society in which primary groups, such as the extended family, the community, and the neighborhood, were displaced by groups developed for a specific purpose. Americans were becoming a nation of "joiners," and a central concern was how to make these groups as effective as possible.

Interest in group processes also resulted from changing trends in education. The growth of progressive education, inspired mainly by the writings of John Dewey, gave an increasingly larger role to student participation. Traditional classrooms where teachers lectured and students listened were replaced by those in which open discussion in small groups was encouraged. It was felt that students would learn more if they were actively involved, and teachers began to experiment with techniques designed to stimulate involvement. By the late 1930s, professional educators and social psychologists working closely with teachers had accumulated a considerable amount of knowledge about groups within the classroom.

Finally, a cluster of specialties concerned with the management of large organizations, such as business administration and public administration, provided additional input into the study of groups. Until the thirties, efforts to develop principles of management largely ignored the existence of small groups. The Hawthorne studies served as a catalyst for the study of social factors within larger organizations. Studies of organizational behavior, such as those carried out by Elton Mayo and his associates, showed that social conditions within work settings could have a major impact on group satisfaction and productivity.

## EARLY STUDIES ON GROUP INFLUENCE

In the 1920s Floyd Allport (1924) had studied the effects of social influence, where the presence of others either helps or hinders a person's ability to perform a particular task. In these studies, Allport used coacting groups made up of individuals who worked independently of each other. He did point out, however, that people working in the presence of others are unconsciously affected by the standards of the group as a whole and described this type of group influence as conformity. During the early 1930s he embarked on a program of research explicitly designed to study conformity. At about the same time, Muzafer Sherif began a series of experimental studies on the development of social norms. Sherif, in contrast to Allport, studied face-to-face groups and was interested in how group norms develop when people actually interact with each other. These two people and their research helped extend the use of ob-

servational and experimental procedures to the study of group processes.

### Floyd Allport's Research on Conformity

Allport's work on conformity was closely related to his book *Institutional behavior* (Allport, 1933). As Gorman (1981) indicates, this speculative monograph spelled out Allport's contention that institutions and society had to be reinterpreted in terms of the behavior of individuals. Allport was concerned that people were being overwhelmed by a progressively institutionalized, bureaucratic, and mechanistic society. In his final chapter, entitled "The hope of a new individualism," he concluded that "institutions, while they may be useful for certain purposes, can never enable us to realize the full potentialities of living. A better world can only be a world of better and of freer individuals" (Allport, 1933, p. 520).

Allport's research on conformity was part of his individualistic approach to behavior in general. In a series of studies, he and his graduate students observed situations where conformity occurs, such as motorists' behavior at stop signs and the performance of rituals by church members. Allport (1934) concluded that conformity followed a J-shaped curve in which maximum conformity was the most frequent (occurring in at least 50 percent of all cases). Motorists, for example, coming to a full stop at a stop sign show maximum conformity, and full stops occurred at least half the time. Deviations, such as slowing down and going through, slowing down slightly, and racing through, decrease in frequency according to their degree of departure from the norm.

Allport also argued that overconformity occurred in some situations. Some factory workers, for example, report to work early. In such cases, a double J-curve characterizes conformity, with Js sloping away in both directions. Allport acknowledged that the situations he studied had highly obvious norms, but he hoped that his methods might be useful for more complex behavior. His work anticipated the growing interest in the role of social norms on individual behavior, but rather than recognizing the normative process present in the perception of group norms, he chose to interpret conformity in behavioristic terms in which the group acts as a social stimulus for a given individual (Gorman, 1981). Subsequent studies by other researchers have shown that the J-curve fits only a limited range of situations, and by the late 1930s, Allport's J-curve hypothesis was dismissed as relatively trivial (Murphy, Murphy, & Newcomb, 1937).

## Muzafer Sherif's Experiments on Social Norms

Muzafer Sherif (1906–1988) was born in Izmir, Turkey, and received a master's degree from Istanbul University in 1928. In 1932, he completed a second master's degree at Harvard and then went to Columbia, where he worked with Gardner Murphy and obtained his doctorate in 1935. He stayed at Columbia for an additional year, extending his doctoral research into the classic work *The Psychology of Social Norms* (Sherif, 1936). Sherif returned to Turkey in 1937 and held university appointments until 1944, when he was imprisoned for his criticisms of the pro-Nazi stance adopted by the Turkish government (Harvey, 1989). His last four months in prison were spent in solitary confinement. In 1945 he returned to the United States, and after fellowships with Hadley Cantril at Princeton and Carl Hovland at Yale, he secured a teaching position at the University of Oklahoma. In 1966 he moved to Pennsylvania State University. Much of his work was carried out in collaboration with his wife, Carolyn Wood Sherif.

Even before his experience during World War II, Sherif was sensitive to the impact of political events. As an adolescent he had witnessed the dramatic transition in Turkey from the dissolution of the Ottoman Empire to the creation of the modern Turkish republic. He cited this experience as the source of his interest in group processes (Gorman, 1981). Throughout his career he sought to base his research on significant and persistent social problems. In his book on social norms, he traced his experimental studies to various sociological, psychological, and anthropological sources. As Gorman (1981) points out, he attempted to combine the Gestalt psychological notion of frame of reference with the sociological concept of social norms. For Sherif, the formation of social norms created a frame of reference that could be used when responding to ambiguous social situations.

Sherif used the autokinetic effect to operationalize how the normative process evolves. Just as a bright star appears to move on a dark night, a stationary light seems to move in a dark room. When experimental subjects were tested alone, they established a fairly consistent estimate of how much the light moved. But when the same subjects met in groups of three or four and heard one another's responses, their judgment of the amount of movement tended to converge. Postgroup tests on individual subjects showed that they consistently maintained the group norms. When individual subjects were removed from the group one at a time and replaced with new members, the initial judgments tended to last for four or five generations. Sherif felt that his research demonstrated how subjects rely on social "anchors" to create norms in unstructured situations.

What is especially significant about Sherif's pioneering work is that it marks a transition from the individualistic approach of Floyd Allport to the group approach in social psychology (Gorman, 1981; Steiner, 1974). Allport focused on proximal causes of behavior, such as the mere presence of other people or awareness of social rules. No attempt was made to study the interaction among group members or underlying processes, such as the perception of group norms. Sherif's research, in contrast, focused on social interaction and the perception of group norms. He believed that the formation of group norms for the autokinetic effect could serve as a prototype for how people use norms to structure ambiguous situations within society at large.

By the late 1930s the group approach

dominated experimental social psychology. Solomon Asch (1940) carried out a series of studies on conformity in which subjects were asked to perform simple tasks, such as rating photographs or rank-ordering a list of professions. When they were later presented with the rankings from a group of five hundred other college students, they tended to shift their judgments in the direction of the group norm. When the comparison group was negative, however, such as Nazi storm troopers, their original judgments did not change. The rapid increase in research on group processes that began in the late 1930s was also stimulated by the interest shown in the area by the German-trained psychologist, Kurt Lewin.

## THE GROUP DYNAMICS OF KURT LEWIN

The term "group dynamics" appears to have been first used by Kurt Lewin in 1939 when he described an experimental study of how various styles of leadership influence the characteristics and behavior of a group (Cartwright & Zander, 1953). According to Lewin, the purpose of such a study was to learn the underlying dynamics. He was especially interested in what actually happens within a group, how group members affect each other, and how groups function and change over time. By the late 1940s, group dynamics became the generally accepted term for any group research.

Kurt Lewin has to be regarded as one of the most important figures in American social psychology, if not the most important. He initiated research on group dynamics and drew around him an extremely talented group of researchers and students (see Patnoe, 1988). Their students and their students' students are largely responsible for shaping social psychology into the discipline that it is today. When members of the elite Society of Experimental Social Psychology were asked to list the three individuals who had made the greatest contribution to the field, Lewin (70%) was rated second, just behind Leon Festinger (79%).

Others included Fritz Heider (43%), Harold Kelley (30%), Stanley Schachter (11%), and Solomon Asch (11%). No other person was named by over 5% of the respondents (Lewicki, 1982). Leon Festinger was Lewin's student, Heider was a close personal friend, and Kelley and Schachter received their Ph.D.s at the institute set up by Lewin for the study of group dynamics. Festinger himself claimed that "95 percent of today's social psychology is Kurt Lewin's and the research he inspired in group dynamics" (in Marrow, 1969, p. 232).

Lewin's influence cannot be assessed from a simple citation count. Lewin wrote only two books, *A Dynamic Theory of Personality* (1935) and *Principles of Topological Psychology* (1936), that were published during his life. Both were written under publication pressures. Neither was particularly well received or widely read. Although Lewin ranks relatively high when citations are counted within social-psychology textbooks, his influence was much greater than these suggest. Much of his influence was informal and indirect (see Marrow, 1969, or Patnoe, 1988, for more detailed discussions).[1]

### The Development of Lewin's Thought—From Individual to Social Psychology

Kurt Lewin (1890–1947) was born in Mogilno, Prussia, now part of Poland. His father owned a small farm and a general store. The family moved to Berlin when Lewin was 15. Lewin began university as a medical student at Freiberg and studied philosophy with Edmund Husserl (M. Lewin, 1987). One of his first papers was a phenomenological description of how the world looks to a combat soldier, based on his own experience in World War I. After a brief stay at Munich, he moved back to Berlin to finish his Ph.D. Lewin's paper "The War Landscape" contained many references to features that he would later develop into his concept of life space. Other papers written during this period dealt with the role of labor in agriculture and industry, where he contrasted working conditions in the factory with those on the farm. Farm work was hard but interesting because workers were engaged in a variety of different tasks. Lewin argued that work was important because it gave life meaning, but work must be made worth doing. Humanizing working conditions depends on meeting psychological needs and cannot be evaluated in terms of traditional "objective" criteria, such as productivity and cost.

Lewin returned to the University of Berlin after the war and taught both philosophy and psychology—lecturing in philosophy and giving a seminar in psychology one year, then reversing the pattern the following year. Although Lewin was primarily interested in psychological issues, he remained a philosopher at heart, and this combination helped create a unique blend of research and theory that characterized Lewin's approach throughout his life.

Lewin was at the University of Berlin during the period when Carl Stumpf was director of the Psychological Institute. Stumpf attracted a brilliant faculty that included his former students Max Wertheimer (1880–1943) and Wolfgang Köhler (1887–1967). Wertheimer and Köhler also worked closely with another former student of Strumpf, Kurt Koffka (1886–1941), who was at the University of Giessen in central Germany. These researchers and Lewin made up the "big four," who were primarily responsible for the development of Gestalt psychology. Gestalt psychologists focused on perception and stressed the fact that perception tends to be organized in terms of basic principles of form and closure. They differentiated the perceptual field into figure and ground and studied the characteristics of each and their mutual relationship. Gestalt psychologists also developed the concept of insight learning and used it as an alternative to the piecemeal doctrine of association, whereby the solution to a problem is acquired gradually in bits and pieces through trial and error. Insight learning is often characterized by a "eureka" experience, where the solution to a problem is suddenly grasped as a meaningful whole in a single trial.

Although Lewin contributed to Gestalt theory, his own approach differed in several ways. First, Lewin was primarily interested

in motivation rather than perception. He saw motivation as an important but much neglected area of concentration. Lewin drew heavily from the Freudian tradition when developing his theory but attempted to test his ideas by using experimental procedures. Lewin saw his own approach as more inclusive than psychoanalysis, capable of containing psychoanalysis within a broader theoretical framework.

A second difference between Lewin and Gestalt theory was based on Lewin's attitude toward physiology. Gestalt theory postulated an isomorphism between physiological and psychological events so that the perceptual field, for example, was matched by a corresponding neural field within the brain. Because of this, Gestalt theory is both a psychological and a physiological theory, and this assumed isomorphism has generated a considerable amount of research on the brain.

Lewin, on the other hand, felt that the field of motivation was already hampered by an overdependence on physiology. Psychologists were willing to recognize only those drives accompanied by biological changes—hunger, thirst, sex, and so on. Lewin felt that, if the field were to progress, it would have to account for other drives as well. Lewin was primarily interested in purposeful behavior, and with this type of behavior it is difficult to imagine what the neural counterpart may be. If a young student wishes to be a doctor and sees this goal as a series of steps—finishing high school, entering university, going to medical school, working as an intern, then entering private practice—where are the physiological correlates? Such correlates undoubtedly exist, but they are far beyond the scope of our current knowledge about the brain. Lewin felt that psychologists could not wait for physiology to provide them with the foundation for their own discipline. Although Lewin encouraged interdisciplinary research, he felt that disciplines became incommensurable as they developed because they chose to study different phenomena. Each science gradually purifies its concepts and separates itself more and more from its neighbors.[2]

Nevertheless, Lewin's field theory does

resemble Gestalt theory in several important ways. It focuses on psychological events rather than behavior. Both Lewin and the Gestalt theorists began with the psychological field as experienced by a naive observer and used behavior merely to infer underlying processes. Second, these processes are seen as part of a larger and more inclusive psychological field. Both Gestalt and field theory conceive psychological events as part of a system of coexisting and mutually dependent factors, not reducible to isolated elements, such as stimulus and response. Finally, Lewin shared a strong commitment to experimental procedures. Lewin felt that with a little ingenuity any problem of interest to psychology could be tested experimentally. His own research was a careful blend of research and theory, with each new experiment designed to test an idea raised by a previous experiment or explore an area previously untested. Lewin was highly critical of collecting facts without a theoretical framework, but he was equally dubious about theories that had not been or could not be experimentally tested.

During the 1920s, Lewin established a reputation as a good teacher and attracted a growing number of students. Many of these were women, some of whom came from Russia and the Baltic states. From 1924 to his departure in 1932, Lewin had as many as 12 to 15 doctoral studies at various stages of completion. Altogether nearly 20 studies were carried out under Lewin's supervision. They dealt mainly with recall of unfinished tasks, task substitution, level of aspiration, satiation, and anger. These studies were published in *Psychologische Forschung,* a journal devoted to experimental psychology published by the University of Berlin (see de Rivera, 1976, for an analysis of these studies).

Lewin and his students met regularly at a local café for coffee, cake, and conversation. On one such meeting, Lewin noticed that the waiter could fill a large order without writing it down but could not recall it when asked to repeat it sometime after the bill had been paid. This led to an experiment by Bluma Zeigarnik designed to test the notion that setting goals builds up a state of psychological tension that is not released until the goal has been reached. Unfulfilled goals continue to produce tension and a desire to finish the task. As a result, unfinished tasks were recalled nearly twice as well as completed ones. This has become known as the "Zeigarnik effect."

Another Russian student, Maria Ovsiankina, studied the spontaneous resumption of tasks after interruption and found that they were almost always resumed. Two other students, Vera Mahler and Sarah Sliosberg, studied the substitution of one task for another after the first task had been blocked. They found that the degree of substitution was based on the degree of similarity. Two functionally similar tasks could substitute for each other, but two dissimilar ones could not. Describing a task or even imagining it can substitute in some cases, but not as well as performing a similar task. These studies provided experimental confirmation for Freud's concept of displacement.

A third line of research focused on "level of aspiration." This is the degree of difficulty chosen by a particular person. Some individuals set goals too high so that failure will not threaten their self-esteem. Others set goals so low that they are virtually assured of success. The level of aspiration differs from person to person and may represent a reliable personality characteristic, but it also varies with the situation. The level of aspiration often increases after a period of success and decreases if a person goes through a series of failures. Lewin's interest in level of aspiration continued after he came to the United States, and Leon Festinger went to study under Lewin while he was at the University of Iowa in order to conduct research on level of aspiration.

Two other students, Anita Karsten and Alex Freund, carried out studies designed to show that repetition does not necessarily increase learning. Too much repetition can produce a state of psychic satiation, in which a person loses interest in the task and may refuse to continue. Repetition also causes the separate aspects of the task to become disconnected and lose their meaning. This fragmentation and loss of interest may offset any advantage occurring through simple association. Freund showed that this was particularly true for women during their menstrual cycle.

A final line of research focused on frustration and anger. Tamara Dembo studied the effects of frustration and found that the amount of anger was based on the intensity of a drive rather than its importance. A person can become very angry over a trivial project if he or she is deeply involved. Before Dembo's study, frustration and aggression had been virtually ignored within psychology. Freud considered aggression a derivative of the death instinct and downplayed situational factors. Lewin's conception and Dembo's research helped stimulate interest in the area and ultimately led to the *frustration-aggression hypothesis* (Dollard, Doob, Miller, Mowrer, & Sears, 1939). Research on aggression has subsequently become firmly entrenched within social psychology and now accounts for approximately 5 percent of the literature.[3] Dembo's work was also important because it demonstrated that complex psychological problems, such as success and failure, substitution and compensation, frustration and anger, could be manipulated and studied experimentally. All of these studies must be seen as logically connected. Their common thread is that individuals set goals for themselves, and these goals motivate and direct behavior. They also behave in a predictable way when these goals are blocked. They experience tension and frustration and may search for a suitable substitute.

By the late 1920s, Lewin's reputation had apread to America, and he began to attract students from the United States. The first to come was J. F. Brown, who wrote his thesis on "levels of reality" and in 1929 prepared an article on Lewin for *Psychological Review*. Brown's article inspired other Americans to go to Berlin and study with Lewin, including Karl Zener, Donald Adams, and Jerome Frank. Adams and Zener later collected and translated some of Lewin's more important Berlin papers and published them under the title *A Dynamic Theory of Personality* (Lewin, 1935).

In 1929, Lewin lectured at Yale University, and in 1932 he came to Stanford University as a visiting professor. By this time, the rise of Nazism in Germany made it difficult for Jewish professors to hold university positions, and Lewin decided to emigrate. After going back briefly to settle his affairs, Lewin left Germany in 1933 and came to the United States. At the time he expressed his agonized feelings in a letter to Köhler:[4]

> If I now believe there is no other choice for me but to emigrate, you will understand that this thought certainly does not come easily to me. . . . When I think of leaving my parents and relatives, of giving up the house that we built, of going out into an uncertain future, of leaving a scientific structure that would take years to rebuild, at best, then surely at the root of such a decision is not a loathing of vulgarities or the fear of personal unpleasantness, but only an overwhelming decisive social reality. (Lewin, 1933/1986, pp. 41–42)

Lewin understood the rising threat of Nazism sooner than many of his colleagues. The Nazis took over the Psychological Institute in 1935. Since Köhler was not Jewish, he could have continued as director, but he resigned and accepted a position at Swarthmore College. Köhler was the last of the big four to leave Germany. By 1935, Koffka was at Smith, Wertheimer was at the New School for Social Research, and Lewin was moving from Cornell University to the University of Iowa.

Lewin came to the United States during the Great Depression, when university positions for foreign professors were extremely limited. He initially obtained a two-year nonrenewable appointment as Professor of Child Psychology at Cornell. Although Lewin carried out several studies on the effects of social pressures on eating habits in children during this period, his appointment was in the School of Home Economics, and he did not develop a following of graduate students such as the one in Berlin.

In 1935, Lawrence Frank was able to obtain a three-year appointment for Lewin at the University of Iowa's Child Welfare Research Station with the help of a Rockefeller grant. The appointment was renewed at the end of this period, and Lewin spent almost ten years at Iowa. Although his appointment was primarily for research, he soon surrounded himself with students and recreated to a certain extent the atmosphere he had known in Berlin. The Berlin studies focused primarily on cognitive processes within the individual, but Lewin's new research turned increasingly to the study of social issues and group dynamics.

This shift in emphasis stems from several factors. First, it was becoming increasingly apparent that social factors were one of the primary sources of conflict and frustration, particularly in children. In order to understand such things as goal selection, conflict, and substitution, social factors had to be taken into account. For this reason, Lewin's new research on social psychology can be seen as a logical extension of his previous work with individuals.

Lewin's interest in group dynamics was also based on a growing concern with social issues, which was widespread during the 1930s. Lewin felt that many social problems, such as racism, anti-Semitism, and aggression, were problems within and between groups and that at times it was easier to change group behavior than that of an individual. Groups provided a source for social comparison and support so that attitudes developed within a group were more resistant to later change. As an outsider to the United States, Lewin was more capable of looking at American society with a detached perspective. In 1936, he published a paper on social-psychological differences in American and German character. Lewin was greatly impressed by America's egalitarian and democratic values, but he was disturbed by its racism and anti-Semitism. His own research during this period involved an unusual blend of pure and applied research.

A third factor that undoubtedly contributed to Lewin's shift in emphasis was Lewin's interaction with his own students. In the preface to his book on topological psychology, Lewin admitted that "I have always found myself unable to think productively as a single person" (Lewin, 1936, p. viii). Lewin was a natural democrat, with an ability to put people at ease. Research projects and ideas were discussed in group settings, and these provided a valuable source of insight into how groups function and what makes them work.

Most of Lewin's research on group dynamics was initiated while he was at Iowa. This includes the classic study by Lewin, Lippitt, and White (1939), which investigated the effects of group atmosphere on performance and morale. The study began as a doctoral dissertation by Ronald Lippitt, but it grew and changed as it progressed. The initial study contrasted differences produced by democratic and authoritarian leaders. Preadolescent boys were assigned to groups of five that met for an hour each week and made theatrical masks. In one group, Ralph White had drawn the role of democratic leader but behaved differently than the other leaders. Instead of eliminating these differences, they were exaggerated in order to produce a laissez-faire condition. Boys with an authoritarian leader became restless, self-centered, and aggressive and lost interest in the groups' goals. Their aggression, however, was directed toward other members of the group rather than the leader. Those with a laissez-faire leader were less productive and work-centered, whereas those with a democratic leader were more cooperative, productive, and content. Lewin took these differences as striking proof for the superiority of a democratic approach. This experiment was a milestone in social psychology, because it showed that it was possible to manipulate social climate through role playing and study it experimentally.

A second study by Roger Barker, Tamara Dembo, and Lewin (1941) was designed to follow up Dembo's previous research on frustration. Children were brought into a room and allowed to play with conventional toys while their behavior was assessed along a continuum of creativity. After 30 minutes a screen was raised, and the children had access to a number of new, more attractive toys. Once the children were involved with the new toys, they were then put back in the original room, the screen was lowered, and their behavior was observed. During this second period, the children became less creative, regressed intellectually, and spent more than a third of their time trying either to penetrate the barrier or escape from the room.

It was also during this period that Lewin initiated research in industrial settings. His interest in this area went back to the 1920s and is shown by his early papers on Taylorism and job satisfaction. In 1939, he was given the opportunity to help increase production at Harwood Manufacturing Corporation (see Coch & French, 1948). This plant was located in a rural Virginia community, paid relatively high wages, but had a high turnover rate and low productivity. After meeting workers and assessing the situation, Lewin decided that the low productivity was partly due to the fact that the local workers did not feel that the goals set by management were realistic. They therefore felt no obligation to meet them. Lewin suggested that the plant bring in about sixty skilled workers from a neighboring community where a factory was closing. These new workers had no difficulty meeting production standards, and their output served as a model for the local workers who raised their level of production to match. The plant was encouraged to give workers more control through group discussion, and the workers gradually raised standards and reached even higher levels of production. This led to other studies on self-management, leadership training, and overcoming resistance to change. Research initiated by Lewin during this period shifted the emphasis from job simplification to social motivation and helped create the field of organizational behavior.

When the United States entered World War II, Lewin's research shifted to issues more directly related to the war effort. One result was the food habit study, carried out in collaboration with Margaret Mead (see Lewin, 1947). An initial study of American eating habits showed that mothers were primarily responsible for the type of food consumed. Husbands and children simply ate whatever the mothers prepared. Changing eating habits therefore became a simple matter of getting mothers to buy different foods. Groups of women were encouraged to purchase and prepare variety meats as

part of the war effort. Some groups heard a lecture by a nutritionist, while others participated in a group discussion. The group discussion proved to be far more effective. When interviewed later, it was found that almost a third of those participating in the group discussion had served at least one of the meats suggested, while only 3% of those in the lecture group had followed the nutritionist's advice. This and other studies supported the view that it is easier to change attitudes within groups than individually. Groups stimulate involvement, establish norms, and serve as a source for social comparison.

Lewin also served as an advisor for the Office of Strategic Services and the Office of Naval Research during the war and traveled frequently between Iowa and Washington. The full extent of his involvement may never be known, but his contact with these organizations helped him obtain funds for research on groups after the war and led to the establishment of centers for the study of group dynamics (see Chapter 9).

Underlying Lewin's work on group dynamics was his interest in demonstrating the effectiveness of democratic leadership on the behavior of group members. Many of his studies used group discussions guided by leaders who provided a democratic atmosphere but who were not themselves indigenous members of the groups. Questions have been raised about whether or not Lewin himself believed in an authentic participatory democracy or whether he believed that some degree of social control by people in authority was necessary in order to insure that the goals of the group are achieved.

Both William Graebner (1986, 1987) and Kurt Lewin's daughter, Miriam Lewin (1987), who is also a social psychologist, agree that Kurt Lewin was an advocate of democratic values and ideals. Graebner, however, argues that Lewin recognized that there was a paradox in putting democratic principles into practice. Citing Lewin (1948), Graebner points out that Lewin stated that democratic leaders do not impose their goals on the group as autocratic leaders do, but they do take an active role—

that is, they "lead." A totally passive role was more characteristic of the third, "laissez faire" leadership style. Lewin was especially concerned about the need for social reconstruction and reeducation in the aftermath of World War II. He believed that it would take strong leaders to guide groups, organizations, and communities toward democratic values, such as the elimination of discrimination and prejudice.

The issue over leadership style that Lewin was grappling with in the 1930s and 1940s still remains. Within organizations, there has been continuing controversy over how much control is necessary, the degree of worker participation, and whether workers should operate only within a pseudo-democratic atmosphere. This issue will be treated in more detail later in this chapter when the Hawthorne studies are discussed.

## Field Theory

No account of Kurt Lewin would be complete without some description of topological and vector psychology. These mathematical models of psychological dynamics became the hallmark of Lewin's thought and had a considerable influence on his research in social psychology. These graphic representations should not be considered a theory of behavior. They are a means of conceptualizing and portraying psychological relations (see Henle, 1978). The various components represented by the model—the person and the psychological environment, drives and barriers, and so on—are so abstract that virtually any theory can be inserted and represented in field terms.

In order to understand field theory it is necessary to distinguish between two types of causal explanations. An event can be explained in terms of previous events or in terms of factors within the immediate situation. A physicist, for example, can explain the movement of an electron as a chain reaction set off by decaying radioactive matter from a nuclear power plant, or in terms of forces and counterforces within the immediate environment. Similarly, shyness can be explained by attributing it to causes in early childhood or by attributing it to a current reluctance to interact with others because of a fear of rejection. Lewin (1935) called the first type "historical" causation and the latter "systematic." Either is valid, but many psychological theories, such as psychoanalysis, create confusion because they fail to distinguish between the two. Lewin's field theory focuses exclusively on immediate factors within the psychological field.

Lewin used *topology* to represent relationships within the life space of an individual. Topology is a means for dealing with mathematical relations without measurement. Distance, shape, and size are irrelevant. Lewin creates some confusion by occasionally using topology to represent things other than the life space. A disorganized ethnic group, for example, can be represented by a number of small unconnected circles within a larger circle representing a nation. Friendship patterns within a group can be shown by contact among circles within a larger circle. Here, the small circles represent individuals, and the larger circle represents the group. Confusion also occurs because the psychological environment occasionally resembles the physical environment, and the figures can be seen as representations of objects in space. A prisoner, for example, may be represented by a circle within a circle within a third larger circle. The large circle represents the walls of the prison, and the second circle represents the cell. Both are barriers that limit movement and restrict freedom. But there are psychological barriers and physical barriers, and the two may not correspond. The door to the cell may be unlocked and the guard at the front gate asleep, but unless the prisoner knows this he will not move from the cell to the space outside. These relationships are shown in Figure 7.1.

Lewin used topology most often to represent the life space of an individual. The simplest representation is merely a circle within a circle. The small circle represents the person, the space between the small circle and the larger circle represents the *psychological environment,* and the space outside is the foreign hull. The person can be further differentiated into central and peripheral regions, with a band that represents

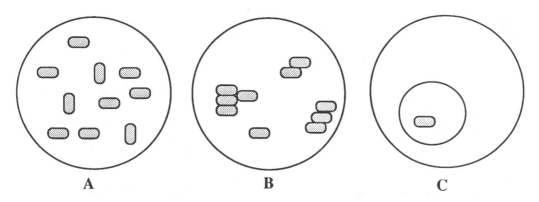

**Fig. 7.1.** These figures represent (A) a disorganized ethnic group within a country; (B) friendship patterns within a social group; and (C) a prisoner within a cell. Figures A and C are similar to illustrations used by Lewin (1936).

a perceptual-motor region separating the individual from the outside world.[5] The psychological environment can be further divided into subregions. These can represent, for example, subgoals necessary for the completion of a larger task. Regions near the person must be passed through first in order to reach more remote regions near the outer circle. These relationships are shown in Figure 7.2.

Some general points about these illustrations should be noted. First, behavior is a joint function of the person and the psychological environment. This is expressed in the formula

Behavior = f (Person, Environment)

which served as the starting point for Lewin's thought. In order to understand why a person behaves in a particular manner, one must consider both the person's needs, goals, and abilities and the situation as the person perceives it. Neither is sufficient alone. Lewin felt that research on motivation overemphasized physiological factors and that situational factors should receive more attention. Sexual desire, for example, is a joint product of a sexual drive and an attractive potential partner. Needs do not normally motivate behavior when the environment offers no opportunity of fulfilling them.

A second point is that it is the *psycholog-ical* environment rather than the physical environment that determines behavior. A prisoner who stays in his cell when the door is unlocked and the guard is asleep may stay there because of an inaccurate perception of the situation. This perception, although wrong, restricts behavior. The psychological environment, for Lewin, was not limited to the world of immediate experience, that is, the phenomenological environment. It included all psychological events—conscious or unconscious—that affect behavior. These include hidden assumptions and events at the back of one's mind that form the background for immediate experience—events that may not be immediately obvious even to the person himself. For example, having or not having a job may play a crucial role in much of what we choose to do, but it is not immediately obvious in the decision we make. Having a job, on the other hand, may be critical for a decision as important as marriage. In making important decisions we often become aware of numerous factors that we do not consider when the decision is trivial. Only a frivolous person makes important decisions without considering the overall context. The life space includes the totality of possible events (both explicit and implied) that determine behavior at any given moment.

By conceptualizing the environment in this manner, Lewin is making a critical distinction between reality and a person's perception of reality. The perception may be

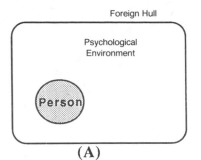

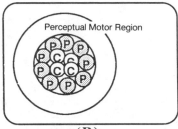

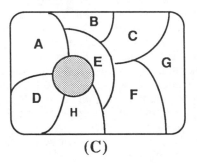

**Fig. 7.2.** These illustrations represent the life space of an individual. (A) shows the principal regions—the person, the psychological environment, and the foreign hull. Figure (B) shows the person further differentiated into a perceptual-motor region, central regions (c), and peripheral regions (p). Figure (C) shows a differentation of the life space. The person can pass through either A, B, and C or E and F in order to get to G. All figures are similar to those used by Lewin.

right or wrong, but it still determines behavior. But a second distinction must be made between selecting goals and attempting to reach them. A person's goal is determined exclusively by his or her needs and perception of the situation. Elements not per-

ceived reside outside the psychological environment, in the foreign hull. Events in the foreign hull cannot affect goals but they can affect behavior. A person may want to lift an object but discover that it is too heavy. A person may want to become a doctor but be denied entrance to medical school. Behavior is determined not simply by the goals we seek but by unforeseen obstacles as well. We cannot plan our behavior on the basis of unforeseen obstacles, but such obstacles can limit our behavior after it has been set in motion. They then become part of the psychological environment, forcing us to reconsider the situation and select a new sequence of behavior. Lewin was interested in purposeful behavior and the reactions that occur when people confront obstacles.

If we now turn to the person in Lewin's model, we find that the individual is divided into central and peripheral regions. Central regions are more inaccessible and difficult to reach. They help form the core of a person's personality. Peripheral regions lie closer to the surface and are in closer contact with the outside world. They are more easily affected by the environment and more readily affect behavior. The person represents an entity in the total psychological environment. Tensions and needs originate within the person but are attached to external objects.

The psychological environment is also differentiated into regions. The meaning of these regions is not always clear. Sometimes they represent objects, goals, and other people; sometimes they represent a potential sequence of events. Leeper (1943) suggested that they be limited to possible activities. Movement within the psychological environment would then be limited to a sequence of steps toward a particular goal or perhaps several possible sequences or a choice of goals. Leeper summarized his position by saying that a person in a particular situation sees a number of possible behaviors as he or she proceeds toward a specific goal. Some of these are immediate, some possible only after initial steps have been taken. Although Lewin wrote the foreword for Leeper's book, it is not clear whether he accepted this restriction to his theory. Some of the ambiguities in Lewin's conception seem to be based on a desire to leave his model as open-ended as possible.

Movement within the psychological environment can be physical or imagined. One can get up, walk across the room, and close the door, or one can envision the same sequence of behavior without carrying it out. Situations differ in terms of their level of reality. Imaginary activities are unreal, limits and barriers are less firm, and it is easier to carry out behavior and reach goals in our imagination than in real life. For this reason, imagination can serve as a useful way to "try out" behaviors in advance. We can imagine a sequence of behaviors and, if it seems feasible, do them.

As a person proceeds toward a particular goal, he or she will often encounter additional obstacles and unforeseen events. The field must be restructured as a consequence. A rock climber may start up what appears to be an easy ascent and discover that the hand- and footholds are smaller and farther apart than they appeared, or the ascent may prove to be even easier than imagined. In either case, the impression is likely to be much different from that made on the ground. Only rarely is the sequence of steps toward a goal fully known in advance. Each movement brings new possibilities and demands a restructuring of the psychological field.

It is possible to represent many factors in the psychological environment by using topology, but not all. One cannot represent the strength of a drive, the resistance of a barrier, or predict which course of action will be selected when several alternatives are possible. Distance can be represented only crudely by showing that one sequence of behavior is longer than a second because it contains the second plus at least one additional step. For these reasons, Lewin supplemented his topology with a *vector psychology*. Topology shows which events are possible, whereas vector psychology can be used to predict which will actually occur.

As with topology, there is a direct relationship between the state of the individual and the psychological environment. Needs originate within the person, but objects and other people are endowed with positive and negative valences. Needs may result from physiological drives, such as hunger and thirst, or they can be the result of a desire to complete a particular task. Needs not based on physiological drives are less stable and can more readily be satisfied through some form of substitute activity. Positive valences serve as commands, summonses, or requests to behave in a particular way. To a hungry person, food takes on a positive valence and becomes attractive. To a child, the threat of punishment may serve as a negative valence, limiting a desired behavior. Objects take on valence not simply because they represent consummate goals but because they represent means for reaching such goals. Tools, for example, possess a positive valence derived from their instrumental value. Valences operate as field forces, steering behavior toward particular goals and away from others. Needs create tension and release energy, but a person's attention is usually directed toward objects and other people in the outside world that have taken on positive and negative characteristics because of their ability to satisfy needs.

Forces exist in the psychological environment and can be represented mathematically by arrows. The strength of a drive is shown by the length of the arrow, and its relationship to a goal is shown by its direction and point of application. It is possible to represent both driving forces and restraining forces, such as barriers. Lewin used either opposing arrows or walls with various degrees of thickness to represent barriers. Barriers can be physical objects, social sanctions, or limitations within the individual, such as lack of skill or exhaustion. If the driving force exceeds the force necessary to overcome resistance, the person proceeds toward the goal until he or she encounters additional resistance. If the resistance is too great, the goal will be blocked, and the person must either give up or select an alternative course of action. When several needs are experienced simultaneously, the stronger drive will usually determine the course of action.

Vector psychology can also be used to represent potential conflicts within the situation. Lewin identified three types of conflict: (1) approach-approach; (2) avoidance-avoidance; and (3) approach-avoidance. Approach-approach conflict occurs when a person must choose between two equally attractive goals. Avoidance-avoidance conflict involves two equally unattractive courses of action. Approach-approach conflict is usually resolved once a person makes a choice, because the valence of a goal increases as one approaches it. Avoidance-avoidance conflict is more problematic, because selecting an unattractive course of behavior and proceeding toward it increases the negative valence and makes the goal seem less attractive. Some restraining force is usually required to force a person to select one of two unattractive goals, since the easiest course of action is to escape the situation, or as Lewin says, "leave the field."

Approach-avoidance conflict occurs when the same goal has both positive and negative features. A person must work at a boring job in order to earn money or study hard to become a medical doctor. Situations like these can also cause problems. Lewin predicted and Miller and Dollard (1941) have shown that both the positive and negative valences increase as one approaches a goal, but the negative valence increases at a faster rate. One starts toward a goal because the attraction exceeds the restraining forces, but at some point the situation reverses. A man wants to ask a woman for a date but backs out at the last moment. Lewin's speculations have inspired a considerable amount of research on what happens in conflict situations.

At this point the reader may ask what topology and vector psychology have to do with group dynamics. Field theory is not a theory of social psychology. It is a way of representing psychological processes occurring within the individual. These processes, however, often depend on social factors, and social factors must be considered if behavior is to be understood. Lewin's work with children convinced him that social relationships, such as friendship and dependence, acquire significance at a very early age. These forces are no less real than physical forces from a psychological point of view. A child's capacity to carry out a particular course of action is limited by both physical ability and parental restrictions.

Other behaviors are forbidden by social conventions or by law. As the child grows, these restrictions are internalized and become self-imposed limitations.

Goals and aspirations are shaped by social factors as well. An individual's level of aspiration is determined partly by shared norms. Groups establish goals, and there is evidence that group goals may be even more compelling than those selected by an individual (Lewis, 1944; Horwitz, 1954). People become more involved in meeting goals established by their group, and these goals serve the dual function of accomplishing a task and maintaining group cohesion.

Perhaps the most serious criticism of field theory is that it confuses physical and psychological reality (F. Allport, 1955). If one keeps in mind that objects in the life space are *psychological* objects—that is, events and courses of action as perceived by the individual—then the problem is reduced to a certain extent but not eliminated. The person is often treated as both a physical and a psychological entity. An individual contains a perceptual-motor region separating him or her from the outside world and possesses central and peripheral characteristics that may not be "phenomenologically" present in the same way as the outside environment. One could say that anything originating within the person is a psychological variable, but this leads to the conclusion that outside factors must be experienced if they are going to have an influence on behavior, whereas internal ones operate whether they are experienced or not. Internal factors, such as tensions and needs, have the dual distinction of being both physiological and psychological events.

The problem is confounded by an occasional careless use of terms, for example, Lewin's statement that one can escape an avoidance-avoidance conflict by "leaving the field." One can leave a room or restructure a psychological field, but leaving the field could result only in total unconsciousness. And where would one be after leaving the psychological field?

Floyd Allport (1955) suggested that Lewin has attempted an impossible reconciliation of physical and psychological events and that this confusion is inherent in field theory, but this does not appear to be the case. Lewin could have rectified the problem by stating categorically that field theory dealt exclusively with the world of immediate experience (broadly defined), in which case he would have had a fully consistent phenomenological theory. Lewin was unwilling, however, to exclude unconscious factors, and his theory therefore contains a blend of psychological and physical events.[6] Gestalt theory approached the problem by postulating an isomorphism between physiological and phenomenological factors, but the two are combined within field theory in a single formulation.

This confusion between physical and phenomenological aspects of field theory, while not inevitable, is probably one of the reasons that field theory has had such a limited impact within social psychology. While other aspects of Lewin's thought were retained, topology and vector psychology are not widely used today (White, 1978). Leon Festinger (personal communication, April, 1985) expressed the opinion that field theory was merely a heuristic device for Lewin—a way of conceptualizing events so that they could be tested experimentally.

The most lasting contributions of field theory are only remotely related to topology and vector psychology. Field theory stressed the fact that behavior is determined by events within the psychological field. These include opinions and beliefs that may not correspond to objective reality. It provided a model for purposeful behavior and offered a refreshing alternative to mechanistic explanations derived from behaviorism. It generated research and helped organize events that had previously been treated separately. Finally, it forced people to look at social phenomena in a new way—in terms of underlying dynamics. Lewin's post–World War II work and his overall impact on social psychology will be discussed in more detail in Chapter 9. The degree of his influence was not evident until after the war.

## THE HAWTHORNE STUDIES

The research carried out by Elton Mayo and his associates at the Hawthorne plant in Chicago included three separate series of investigations. The first was an experimental study of the effects of illumination. The intensity of the lighting was systematically increased and then lowered, and productivity increased under both conditions. Productivity also increased in a control group for which no change occurred at all. The experimenters then altered a number of other variables and found a steady increase in output. What is more, productivity remained high even after the original conditions were restored. According to the standard accounts (Mayo, 1933; Roethlisberger, 1941), the experimenters, puzzled by the results, were forced to attribute the change to their own presence and the concern they showed for the workers. These unexpected findings led to further attempts to identify factors associated with productivity and worker satisfaction.

In the next series of studies, specific variables were isolated through experimental control. In the most famous of these experiments, the relay assembly test room study, five women were separated from their coworkers and placed in a special room. The investigators introduced a number of improvements in the working conditions, such as rest periods and shortened work days. Both productivity and worker satisfaction increased as a result. Surprisingly, when the improvements were later removed, productivity continued to increase. Apparently, the workers' attitude toward their job and the special attention they received from the researchers and supervisors was as important as the actual changes in conditions themselves, if not more so. This phenomenon subsequently became known as the "Hawthorne effect."

The third set of investigations included an observational study of a group of men in a bank wiring room. The major result was the development of group norms restricting work output. These norms thus protected the workers, to some extent, from the directives of management. The researchers concluded that informal social relationships were as important as formal lines of organization and authority.

In the official accounts of the Hawthorne studies, the researchers stressed that, in addition to reporting experimental results, they were presenting a process of scientific discovery (Gillespie, 1988). Based on objective empirical methods, the investigators had to reverse their initial assumptions from time to time in light of unexpected findings. Overall, the reports convey a sense of optimism about the objectivity of scientific procedures. This straightforward depiction of the research process, however, does not hold up when the original sources are scrutinized. Gillespie (1988) has analyzed the archival records and concludes that the reported results concealed a number of inconsistencies and several conflicting interpretations.

Gillespie (1988) cites several discrepancies between the archival sources and official accounts. In the study on the effects of lighting, the survey records show that the engineers conducting the research knew of the importance of psychological factors from the very beginning. Thus, instead of discovering the significance of psychological factors, the lighting tests reveal the difficulty of controlling such variables as interest and variations in supervision. In the relay assembly test room, archival sources reveal that two of the original women were replaced by researchers because they were uncooperative (see also Bramel & Friend, 1981). Official accounts attribute the increase in productivity to enlightened supervision and a friendly atmosphere, but it was only after this change in personnel took place that the production rate dramatically increased. No mention was made about the political relationship between workers and researchers, in which the researchers had the power to control working conditions and interpret what was occurring. In the bank wiring room study, the official accounts attribute the norms for restricting work to an unconscious reaction against a system that lacked incentives to work harder. Yet a preliminary report by one of the junior members of the research team suggested that the norms restricting production reflected a conscious attempt to limit the output for economic reasons. This view of worker solidarity apparently disturbed the management, and the subsequent report dismissed the notion that workers were capable of conscious collective action.

Although the Hawthorne studies deal with groups, they essentially reflect an individualistic approach to social psychology. The role of group processes, collective action, and economic and political factors is given little, if any, consideration. Nevertheless, as Gillespie concludes, the research team was strongly influenced by its political values. They uncritically accepted the view of management while ignoring the workers' perspective, and thus unintentionally produced an interpretation consistent with capitalist ideology.

The Hawthorne studies played a major role in the development of the "human relations" approach to management. The official accounts reinforced the trend initiated in the 1920s to add a "human element" to industrial relations. The subsequent labor unrest of the 1930s made the results especially appealing to managers. Management was now provided with scientific support for its need to gain the cooperation and active participation of the workers while retaining the basic components of managerial control (Gillespie, 1988). Subsequent studies of organizational behavior have turned to the Hawthorne study as a model of democratic management.

The Hawthorne project was also a significant landmark for social psychology. It demonstrated that experimental studies of small groups could be conducted in realistic settings, such as the workplace. As social psychologists began to identify experimental procedures as their particular area of expertise, it became important to legitimize their research by applying it to pressing social problems. Although the Hawthorne studies were greatly influenced by ideology and by political and economic factors, they helped reinforce the belief that scientific knowledge can be objectively discovered in the real world.

## TOWARD AN EXPERIMENTAL SOCIAL PSYCHOLOGY

The dramatic changes in psychological social psychology can best be illustrated by the various books dedicated to reviewing the area. In 1935 the first integrated overview or handbook of American social psychology was published (Murchison, 1935). This was a multidisciplinary work that included contributions from biologists, botanists, anthropologists, and sociologists as well as social psychologists. It drew from the Wundtian perspective based on historical and comparative treatments of species, and cultural and racial variability (Farr, 1983). Only one chapter, by J. F. Dashiell, covered experimental social psychology, and it focused on social facilitation. This suggests that experimental social psychology was still largely in its infancy in the mid-thirties. The work of Floyd H. Allport on social facilitation and conformity was the major area of concentration.

The Murchison *Handbook* was something of an anachronism when it appeared. Wundt's influence on American social psychology was very limited, and most of the topics covered in the two-volume work were not typical of those included in textbooks on social psychology. The Murchison *Handbook* became even more obsolete by the end of the thirties. Largely because of the work of Allport, Sherif, and Lewin, experimental social psychology took off (Jones, 1985).

Cottrell and Gallagher (1941) reviewed the developments in American social psychology during the 1930s and noted the dramatic increase in the use of quantitative and experimental procedures. Similarly, when Murphy, Murphy, and Newcomb (1937) revised their earlier text on experimental social psychology (Murphy & Murphy, 1931), they commented on the differences between the two editions. In place of an overview of isolated research findings, they were now able to present a systematic treatment of social psychology based on the rapid accumulation of quantitative and experimental research. Although there was still considerable emphasis on current social problems (as we will see in the next chapter), by the early 1940s, experimental social psychology had moved into the forefront within psychological social psychology, and it now dominated the study of both individuals and groups. While the number of active researchers was relatively small compared with the post–World War II period, the

foundation for a social psychology based predominantly on experimental procedures was already laid.

# NOTES

1. Lewin's indirect influence presents a problem for historians, since points were raised and problems discussed in informal settings, where it is often difficult to tell where ideas originate. Many of the ideas discussed were never published. Thus, when Marrow wrote Lewin's biography in 1969, he relied considerably on secondhand accounts. Similarly, Leeper (1943) attempted a careful critique of Lewin's topological and vector psychology (which contained a foreword by Lewin). He discovered several problems and discussed them with Lewin. He was satisfied with Lewin's responses but concluded that one could not have resolved these issues even by a careful reading of Lewin's primary works. All great thinkers leave issues unresolved, but because Lewin wrote so little and did so much, his contribution to social psychology is sometimes difficult to assess. Patnoe (1988) presents excerpts from interviews with Lewin's students that shed considerable light on how Lewin and his students developed their ideas.

2. A common misconception about Lewin is that he derived his theory from field theory in physics. He did not. Lewin used topology, vectors, and field concepts similar to those used in physics, but his purpose was to represent psychological events as accurately as possible. Lewin never believed that psychology could be reduced to physics or that physical explanations could accurately represent all that takes place within the psychological field.

3. These and other calculations presented in Chapter 10 are derived from a sampling of four social psychology journals carried out by Gross and Fleming (1982) in order to assess the use of deception in specific subareas of social psychology. Of a total of 597 studies (omitting 44 on personality), 30 were carried out on aggression, and this was the seventh most researched area— behind attitudes (88), group processes (51), attribution (51), attraction/affiliation (44), dissonance/consistency (32), and impression formation (32).

4. This letter was never sent because of the danger involved for both the sender and receiver. It remained in Lewin's files for many years after his death and was recently recovered.

5. Leeper (1943) pointed out that Lewin's per-

ceptual-motor region was based on a confusion between the physical and psychological person. The physical person is separated from the outside world by muscles and tissue and can only experience it through the sense organs, but these organs may not be experienced as part of the psychological environment. Muscles and sense organs are taken for granted unless there is some reason to notice them. A person who cannot see well enough to make out a face at a distance or is not strong enough to lift a heavy object may become aware of the limitations of the body for the first time. Lewin apparently accepted this criticism and moved the perceptual-motor region to the foreign hull.

6. Phenomenologists have addressed this problem by treating the unconscious as part of the prereflective experience (see section on "phenomenology" in Chapter 13). This includes aspects of immediate experience not brought into consciousness through reflection or the use of words. These features can be noticed if one focuses on them, but they are either too trivial or too distressing to enter into full awareness (see Fingarette, 1969). Whether this formulation would have been sufficient for Lewin is difficult to say.

# 8

# Social Psychology and Social Commitment

During the 1930s there was a growing concern for applying social psychology to an increasing number of social problems brought on by the Great Depression. The concern with social issues did not suddenly commence in the 1930s. Sociological social psychology had developed largely as an applied discipline, and many of the founders of the American Sociological Society, such as Edward Ross and Lester Ward, were deeply committed to social change. The psychological study of social problems during the 1930s was in many ways a return to the progressive ideals that existed in America before World War I. Social critics during this period had rejected universal abstract laws and rational models of human nature and had advocated empirical procedures that stressed a concrete and piecemeal approach to problem solving. Less theoretical in tone, the progressive movement inspired a belief that ideas have a social currency and that there is an organic relationship between self and society in which dominant beliefs and values are shared by all members of the community. The effort to "synthesize theory and practice, liberty and community, self and society lay at the heart of the progressive movement—and [continued] to attract the imagination of radical intellectuals and activists in the following decades" (Pells, 1973, p. 8). Progressivism had a lasting influence because it represented the first American response to the new realities of the twentieth century, and it was even more compelling because it seemed to offer realistic and immediate solutions to concrete social problems. Although not as visible

during the 1920s, progressivism had a powerful appeal during the 1930s.

The initial reaction of Americans to the depression varied greatly and reflected the complexities and contradictions of American society. For the average American, such as those described in *Middletown* and *Middletown in Transition* (Lynd & Lynd, 1929, 1937), there was a stubborn refusal to accept the reality of the depression and a persistent conviction that the situation would improve within a few months. For others, especially those who had experienced alienation from the culture during the 1920s, the depression came almost as a relief. For the younger generation of writers and artists who had gone into self-imposed exile, the depression was seen as an opportunity for a renewed commitment to American society. For social thinkers, it served to underscore what they felt were fundamental flaws in modern industrial capitalism and offered an exciting opportunity to rebuild America.

John Dewey (1930, 1935) extended progressive ideas to the problems of the depression by attacking two of America's most sacred beliefs—individualism and liberal capitalism. He called for new attempts to integrate the individual and society in order to reconcile private aspirations with the public good. What was needed was a new, more holistic social philosophy that took the social nature of the individual into account and aimed at instilling cooperative and collectivist values in both the nation and individual. Dewey's philosophy reflected the mood and social conditions of the 1930s, and like that of other writers of the period, involved a search for a more comprehensive understanding of human nature and society. It was at heart a social-psychological realignment based on the realization that individuals and society were not always or perhaps even essentially rational but were shaped by the interaction of a complex set of biological and cultural factors. Dewey's call for radical social change was not limited to theoretical issues. He also took a leading role in attempts to organize a third political party (Bordeau, 1971). While this movement fizzled by 1936, he continued to criticize much of the New Deal program because of its compromise with capitalism.

Robert Lynd's (1939) *Knowledge for What?* echoed many of Dewey's sentiments and offered an even more detailed analysis of the culture and social thought of the period. Lynd singled out the individualism of Floyd Allport for failing to recognize the essential dynamic relationship between the individual and society. Allport, in Lynd's (1939) words, "stressed the independence of individuals, disregarding the special qualities of behavior in group situations and viewing institutions as derived from the behavior of individuals by a simple additive process" (p. 22). Lynd saw Allport's social psychology as symptomatic of the weakness and deficiencies of social and behavioral sciences during the 1920s. These approaches were fundamentally simplistic and overly specialized and led to the fragmentation of knowledge. They prevented real scientific achievement and the application of science to the resolution of urgent problems facing American society. Lynd, like Dewey, argued for a more integrated and interdisciplinary approach that rejected traditional dualistic models in favor of one that assumed the underlying unity of mind and body, self and society, emotions and rational processes, as well as fact and value and theory and practice in science.

McGrath (1980a, 1980b) has pointed out that the study of social problems during the 1930s and 1940s focused on three general issues—poverty, prejudice, and peace. What distinguished researchers in the 1930s from those today is that these three sets of problems were seen as very much related.

Economic problems brought on by the Great Depression were seen as at least partially responsible for racial prejudice, anti-Semitism, and growing world tension.

This interrelatedness was not simply a figment of the social psychologist's imagination. In Nazi Germany it was very much a matter of public policy. The rise of Nazism was due in part to Germany's severe economic problems and the failures of the previous Weimar Republic. Hitler's solution, as outlined in his book *Mein Kampf* (1925/1971), was quite simple. If a country could not produce enough food to feed its population, it had two options. It could reduce its population through selective extermination, or it could expand its territory by taking land from other countries. Thus, "racial" discrimination (mainly in the form of anti-Semitism, which ultimately became a policy of genocide), and international expansion were the foundation of Hitler's solution to the German economic crisis.

The close association of poverty, prejudice, and international conflict led many social psychologists to examine social problems within an economic context. Some problems, such as unemployment and industrial unrest, are more or less a direct result of economic conditions, but others are related only indirectly. One group of researchers (Dollard, Doob, Miller, Mowrer, & Sears, 1939), for example, correlated the increase in lynching in the deep South with periods of increasing frustration brought on by decreases in the price of cotton. Otto Klineberg (1940), after analyzing the various explanations for racial prejudice, concluded that the "economic motive," while not the only cause, is probably the most important. He went on to suggest that "prejudice will continue just so long as it serves the interests of the dominant group. Its elimination, therefore, would seem to require some fundamental change in the socio-economic structure so that one person's success need not necessarily be at the expense of another's failure" (p. 396). Katz & Schanck (1938) provided an extensive analysis of social problems from an economic perspective, and J. F. Brown (1936) attempted to integrate the theories of Marx, Freud, and Lewin. Virtually every textbook on social psychology published during the late 1930s and early 1940s included some discussion of racial, industrial, and international conflict, and this concern was paralleled by the development of societies specifically concerned with the psychological study of social issues.

Because economic, racial, and international problems were seen as closely related, there was a great deal of consensus about what should be done. It was assumed that any right-thinking person (indeed, any thinking person) who knew the facts would support economic reforms, improved working conditions, and a fairer distribution of wealth and would oppose racism, anti-Semitism, and war. McGrath (1980b) has pointed out that what characterized this period and the period shortly after the war was "an apparently unquestioned assumption that, on any of the crucial questions of the day, *every* social scientist would agree and would be on the side of the angels" (pp. 112–113). Although there was a great deal of pessimism about the world in general, there was a great deal of optimism about the potential of social science. Never before or since has social psychology traced social problems so directly to economic conditions.

During the thirties, the first attempts to apply social psychology to the study of social problems focused on racial prejudice and intergroup tensions. These studies used methods such as attitude measurement, experimentation, and propaganda analysis. After surveying the research on prejudice, we will consider the broader theoretical perspectives that guided much of the work on social problems. Many of the writers during this period drew from assumptions that were either implicitly or explicitly derived from Karl Marx. While Marx's socioeconomic theory has some serious flaws, it is by far the most comprehensive account of the interrelationship betweeen economic factors, consciousness, and society. Our discussion of Marx will be followed by a brief treatment of other major social theorists who derived their views in part from perceived shortcomings and deficiencies within Marx's theory. This will be followed by a summary of another trend common in the

1930s—an attempt to overcome the psychological deficiencies of Marx's theory by integrating it with Freudian theory. The last two sections will deal with the founding of the Society for the Psychological Study of Social Issues and the role of social psychology during World War II.

## PREJUDICE AND INTERGROUP TENSION

By the early 1930s, the study of racial prejudice had become an important part of American social psychology (Samelson, 1978). Earlier efforts to explore these issues included the work of W. E. B. DuBois (1901), a black social scientist, and the Chicago sociologist W. I. Thomas (1904). Both of these writers drew attention to the practical and theoretical aspects of the issue, but the prevailing view among social scientists until the mid-twenties was that social differences were based on innate and irreducible racial differences. This was used to justify such practices as racial segregation and restricted immigration. But the passage of restrictive immigration legislation in 1924 and the increasing number of minority-group members within social science itself brought about a change in attitude and there was a rising call for racial tolerance rather than separation (see Chapter 2). During the 1930s, social science explored the nature of racial prejudice with the hope of contributing to its solution. One of the approaches most frequently taken was the measurement of attitudes toward racial and ethnic minorities.

### Attitude Research

Attitude research has had a long history within social psychology, although both the concept and specific research strategies have changed. Some of the earliest studies, like those of Gabriel Tarde (1890/1903), were concerned with the spread of beliefs and ideas within the general population, and many of the early textbooks contained chapters on fashions, fads, and rumors.

Gordon Allport (1935, 1985), Krech and Crutchfield (1948), Newcomb (1950), and Thomas and Znaniecki (1918–1920) are just a few of the many writers who have placed attitudes at the center of social psychology. Writing in 1935, Gordon Allport stated that

> The concept of attitude is probably the most distinctive and indispensable concept in contemporary American social psychology. No other term appears more frequently in experimental and theoretical literature. . . . The term likewise is elastic enough to apply either to the dispositions of single isolated individuals or to broad patterns of culture. Psychologists and sociologists, therefore, find in it a meeting point for discussion and research. (p. 798)

Although briefly eclipsed by research on group dynamics in the early 1950s (Cina, 1981) and by attribution research in the late 1970s (Smith, Richardson, & Hendrick, 1980), attitudes have played a central role throughout the history of social psychology and have received more attention than any other area.

Allport (1935) felt that Thomas and Znaniecki (1918–1920) must be given credit for making attitudes a central concept within sociology. They distinguished between attitudes and social values. Social values exist outside the individual in the broader social context and confront the individual as a given. Attitudes are the individual, subjective counterpart of social values. People acquire attitudes by internalizing social values, and personality consists largely of the pattern of attitudes held by the individual.

Attitude research took a considerable step forward in the 1920s as new techniques were developed for measuring attitudes. Previously, attitudes were tabulated in an all-or-none fashion—either present or absent—but it now became possible to measure the strength of an attitude and then measure subtle changes induced through experimental manipulation. One of the first scales was Emory Bogardus's (1925a, 1925b) measure of "social distance." Individuals were asked to rate the degree of intimacy toward members of another group

that they were willing to tolerate by selecting one of the following alternatives:

1. to close kinship by marriage
2. to my club as personal chums
3. to my street as neighbors
4. to employment in my occupation in my country
5. to citizenship in my country
6. as visitors only to my country
7. would exclude from my country

One immediate criticism was that the distance between items was not equal, and therefore it was misleading to treat the scale numerically. The psychological difference between admitting a person to one's family through marriage and admitting him or her to one's club is greater than that between club member and neighbor. The scale, however, was frequently used to rank-order different nationalities and racial groups for acceptability.

L. L. Thurstone (1928), an engineer who turned psychologist, attempted to correct this problem by applying procedures used in psychophysics. Rather than asking subjects to solve psychophysical problems such as detecting differences between weights, he asked them to indicate which nationalities they preferred to associate with. In transferring the method of paired comparisons from psychophysics to social psychology, Thurstone established a method of measuring attitudes on an interval scale and thus obtained numerical scores. Rensis Likert (1932–33) later developed a simplified version of the paired comparison method with his technique of "summated ratings."

During the 1930s, investigators assessed the racial preferences and stereotypes of university students (e.g., Guilford, 1931). Katz and Braly (1933) found a general consensus among Princeton students in their ratings of various racial groups and nationalities. A classic study caried out by R. T. LaPierre (1934) raised questions about the relationship between attitudes and behavior. LaPierre traveled with a Chinese couple, stopping at 66 hotels and 184 restaurants across the country. The couple was denied service only once. Six months later, LaPierre wrote the same hotels and restaurants asking if they would serve Chinese guests. One hundred and twenty-eight responded, and 92% said they *would not.* Thus, a person who holds prejudiced attitudes will not necessarily act in a prejudiced manner. This does not mean that attitudes do not help determine behavior. It merely suggests that they are only *one* of the major causes.

The development of attitude scales made it possible to measure subtle differences in attitude change, which might not show up as a complete reversal. Peterson and Thurstone (1933), for example, studied the influence of motion pictures and found that negative attitudes toward blacks increased in children after they saw the movie *The Birth of a Nation.* There was also research on the role of socialization in the development of prejudices. Studies on the authoritarian character carried out in Germany by Wilhelm Reich (1933/1946) and Erich Fromm (1939/1941), which will be discussed later, showed that certain attitudes, such as racism and anti-Semitism, developed in part because of a strict upbringing and could occur even when there was no direct contact with the target group.

### The Frustration-Aggression Hypothesis

One of the most ambitious efforts to use experimental procedures to explore the source of social problems was carried out by an interdisciplinary team of researchers at Yale's Institute for Human Relations (Lubek, 1986). This group, which included John Dollard, Leonard Doob, Neil Miller, O. Hobart Mowrer, and Robert R. Sears, combined elements of Clark Hull's learning theory[1] and psychoanalysis and carried out a systematic analysis of the relationship between frustration and aggression. According to Dollard, Doob, Miller, Mowrer, and Sears (1939), "aggressive behavior always presupposes the existence of frustration and, contrariwise, . . . the existence of frustration always leads to some form of aggression" (p. 1). The later part of the formula was subsequently revised to indicate that frustration may lead to a number of responses other than aggression (Miller, 1941).

The hypothesis was clearly embedded in Hull's behaviorism (Jones, 1985). Frustration, for example, was defined as an "interrupted behavior sequence." But it also drew from Freudian concepts such as displacement and catharsis, and when combined with subsequent experimental data on conflict and displacement (Miller, 1944, 1948), it provided a relatively sophisticated theoretical and empirical basis for the scapegoat theory of prejudice. Frustration occurs when people (or animals) strive toward goals that cannot be obtained, typically because some obstacle is in the way. This produces a desire to strike out and remove the barrier. Within society at large the sources of frustration are frequently too powerful (or poorly understood), so aggression is displaced toward a substitute target or scapegoat. Minority groups provide a readily available scapegoat because they are relatively powerless and have low social status.

The frustration-aggression hypothesis helped to explain some puzzling anomalies about the relationship between poverty and aggression. Aggression is relatively rare in extremely poor countries because the level of aspiration is typically low. It begins to increase only when there is some hope for social improvement that is subsequently denied. Miller and Dollard (1941), for example, found a direct link between the number of lynchings and the price of cotton in the deep South. As cotton prices went down, the number of lynchings went up. What is particularly interesting about this example is that the process operates without awareness. Southerners who were paid poorly for their crops felt frustrated and engaged in more lynchings, but it is extremely unlikely that they recognized the causal connection between the two events. The hypothesis can be used to explain why levels of prejudice generally increase during times of economic depression and decrease during times of economic prosperity, but it is difficult explain why particular minorities become the target of such aggression (Allport, 1935; Jones, 1985). The scapegoat notion, however, did influence the subsequent study of the authoritarian personality

(Adorno, Frenkel-Brunswik, Levinson, & Sanford, 1950), and it was ruthlessly applied by Adolf Hitler (see next section).

The work of Dollard and Miller and their associates on frustration and aggression reflected a strong concern with pressing social problems during the 1930s. Interracial prejudice, the rise of fascism and anti-Semitism in Germany, the Spanish Civil War, labor unrest, economic depression, and the threat of global war were important stimulants. Nevertheless, Lubek (1986) has argued that the research was guided by the dominant American value of individualism, and concepts dealt with at the collective level were reduced to processes occurring within individuals. A frustrated group was seen as merely a number of individuals undergoing frustration at the same time. A related bias was the assumption that all forms of aggression are antisocial. In contrast with Marx, where the emphasis is on collective action and class struggle, forms of prosocial aggression carried out collectively by victimized groups were not considered.

## Propaganda Analysis

Because of the widespread use of propaganda during World War I and the rise of advertising, social scientists became interested in studying the nature and use of propaganda in the 1920s (Lee, 1986). During the thirties, with Hitler's success in Nazi Germany, there was growing concern about the use of propaganda to justify and heighten anti-Semitism. The extensive use of propaganda was made possible because of urbanization and developments within the mass media that allowed those who controlled the sources of mass communication to reach large audiences very quickly. The mass media now began to supplement socialization processes normally occurring in the home, the school, and the community with deliberate attempts to shape public opinion through radio, movies, and newspapers. The best example is Adolf Hitler's dramatic rise to power.

Hitler himself seems to have developed an interest in propaganda because of German propaganda *failures* during the First World War. The British and their allies carried out an effective propaganda campaign by portraying Germany as a nation of barbarians ready to destroy civilization and replace it with a military state. When British troops met German troops on the battlefield and encountered resistance, they increased their efforts and often succeeded. In Germany, on the other hand, propaganda was entrusted to military men who stressed the incompetence and weakness of allied troops. When German troops met welltrained and -organized British troops, they felt demoralized and betrayed and gave up prematurely.

Adolf Hitler is often portrayed as a mad genius who misled his people and seized power. But Hitler was no genius. He was a self-educated man of limited intelligence who picked up most of his information from newspapers. He had many widely shared beliefs and prejudices, which he wove into a unified philosophy. And he was above all a master of propaganda.

It is difficult to assess Hitler's true feelings because it is difficult to know whether his autobiography, *Mein Kampf,* was a personal account of his beliefs or a work of propaganda. In a critical passage, for example, Hitler (1925/1971) says:

> On purely psychological grounds, never show the masses two or more opponents, since this leads to a total disintegration of their fighting power.... It belongs to the genius of a great leader to make even adversaries far removed from one another seem to belong to a single category. (pp. 117–118)

The utter contempt with which he treated the German people (as well as everyone else) suggests, however, that the book does reflect his true beliefs, at least in part. *Mein Kampf* sold well, but it was never meant for popular consumption. It was written for the committed and perhaps designed to give them a feeling of superiority over the misguided masses who simply did not understand the issues.

Exemplifying the scapegoat process, Hitler's central argument was that there was an international conspiracy of Jewish bankers and stockbrokers whose aim was to undermine the German economy in order to establish democracy and ultimately communism. Jews were portrayed as the main source of Germany's economic woes, but they were aided by their allies the French, the Poles, and, of course, the Russians. "The Western Democracy of today is a forerunner of Marxism without which it would be unthinkable" (p. 78). Therefore, in one stroke, Hitler combined all of the opponents of fascism—Jews, communists, liberals, Poles, French, Russians, and international capitalists—into a single unified group hell-bent on the destruction of Germany. The combination of "communist" bankers and stockbrokers would be laughable if it were not for the fact that such beliefs are still held by right-wing groups today. Virtually the only group not regarded with contempt by Hitler were the German workers, whom he considered dupes of the Jewish press. Hitler was also neutral toward the British and the church, perhaps because he viewed them as possible allies. By preaching human equality, Judaism was undermining what Hitler called the "basic aristocratic principle of nature" (p. 81), basically a variant of social Darwinism whereby those with power gain authority.

Hitler probably could not have come to power at any other time in history. It is a truism, but an important one, as Solomon Asch (1952) has pointed out, that propaganda grows out of actual problems and needs. Germany had just suffered a humiliating defeat during World War I, had been forced to accept an oppressive treaty, and was in the midst of a financial collapse. The old German values and way of life seemed out of place in the face of economic uncertainty. For most Germans, the world was confusing and incomprehensible. Hitler made a difficult situation seem simple and offered a quick and final solution—eliminate the Jews and the conspiracy would collapse. One of the most tragic aspects of *Mein Kampf* (1925/1971) is that Hitler's paranoid delusions, his tactics for converting people through propaganda, and his blueprint for world conquest were clearly laid out nearly fifteen years *before* the Second World War began.

Hitler (1925/1971) was a voracious reader of the popular press, and he abstracted from these and other sources certain basic principles of propaganda, which he later put into practice. Among these were the following:

1. *Portray all opponents as if they are united in a common cause,* in this case the destruction of Germany.
2. *Keep the message as simple as possible:* "All propaganda must be popular and its intellectual level must be adjusted to the most limited intelligence among those it is addressed to" (p. 180).
3. *Appeal to the emotions:* "Altogether, care should be taken not to regard the masses as stupider than they are. In political matters feeling often decides more correctly than reason" (p. 173).
4. *Use repetition:* "The masses are slow-moving, and they always require a certain time before they are ready even to notice a thing, and only after the simplest ideas are repeated thousands of times will the masses finally remember them" (p. 185).
5. *Present only one side of the argument:* "As soon as our own propaganda admits so much as a glimmer of right on the other side, the foundation for doubt in our own right has been laid" (p. 183).

While Hitler stressed one-sided arguments when preaching to the committed, he recognized the importance of raising both sides and refuting objections when talking to a hostile audience. He also pointed out the effects of selective exposure, "The mass of people as such is lazy; they remain inertly in the spirit of their old habits and, left to themselves, will take up a piece of written matter only reluctantly if it is not in agreement with what they themselves believe" (p. 470). Hitler felt that even the time of day was important, and that at night people succumb more easily to a stronger will.

To say that Hitler was a strong believer in propaganda is an understatement. "By clever and persevering use of propaganda even heaven can be represented as hell to the people, and conversely the most wretched life as paradise" (p. 276). Hitler came to power in January 1933. His party obtained a parliamentary majority in the March elections and passed the Enabling Act, which gave him dictatorial powers for five years. The Ministry of Public Enlightenment and Propaganda was set up on 17 March 1933 with Joseph Goebbels as its head. Hitler gradually gained control of newspapers, radio stations, and the movie industry and used them to preach his doctrine of anticommunism and racial hatred. He embedded his ideas within the context of traditional German values, which stressed patriotism, discipline, and authority, and began the Third Reich, which was to last for a thousand years.

Leonard Doob (1935) was one of the first American researchers to study propaganda from a psychological perspective. Doob was in Germany in the early 1930s and witnessed the rise of Nazism first-hand. In 1935, a year after settling at Yale University (where he also contributed to the frustration-aggression study), Doob published the book *Propaganda: Its Psychology and Technique,* in which he analyzed political and commercial propaganda and attempted to explain their dynamics. Doob's intention was to provide people with the knowledge they need to offset the effects of propaganda and think and choose freely.

> The author believes very timidly that the recognition and understanding of a phenomenon enables an individual to free himself to a certain extent ... that the ability to label something propaganda and someone a propagandist and a simultaneous insight into the fundamental nature of the process of propaganda will combine to render many kinds of propaganda less effective. Thinking about propaganda, in short, may lead to the destruction of some propaganda (p. 5).

Doob (1935) defined "propaganda" as the "systematic attempt by an interested individual (or individuals) to control the attitudes of groups of individuals through the use of suggestion and, consequently, to control their actions" (p. 76). He was interested not only in political propaganda but commercial propaganda (i.e., advertising), which uses many of the same techniques. Doob distinguished between intentional propaganda, in which a person is aware of

the aim and often consciously attempts to manipulate the message in order to produce an effect, and unintentional propaganda, in which a person simply transmits prevailing cultural beliefs without being aware of it. He also distinguished revealed and concealed propaganda. In the former, the person's intention is apparent, while in the latter it is not. To be effective, propaganda must appeal to already existing attitudes and values. Effectiveness increases when propagandists use repetition, imply that their beliefs are widely shared, and offer an organizational framework within which their ideas can be understood.

In 1937, under the leadership of the Boston merchant Edward A. Filene, a group of social scientists and educators established the Institute for Propaganda Analysis (Lee, 1986), with Doob as one of the original members. This group analyzed speeches, newspapers, and radio broadcasts in order to identify techniques used by propagandists. They found seven widely used procedures:

1. *Name calling:* giving an idea a bad name in order to cause rejection.
2. *Glittering generality:* associating an idea with a "virtue word," such as "freedom," "democracy," and so on.
3. *Transfer:* linking an idea to something already respected.
4. *Testimonial:* using endorsement from prestigious sources.
5. *Plain folk:* creating the impression that the speaker and audience are similar by using common speech and colloquialisms.
6. *Card stacking:* presenting only one side of an argument, while ignoring or distorting arguments from the other side.
7. *Band wagon:* implying that most people already hold a particular attitude.

If propaganda is treated merely as a form of social influence, it becomes difficult to distinguish it from education. Both attempt to change beliefs and alter behavior. Propaganda merely becomes "what the other side is doing." And yet such a distinction is important and implicitly assumed by people who use these terms "education" and "propaganda." One difference is that propaganda is usually carried out by a special interest group for an ulterior motive—to get people to buy a particular product or support a particular party. A second difference is that propaganda typically presents only one side of an issue, or if it presents the other side it does so in a biased manner. Propagandists typically polarize the world into good and evil, portray it in terms of black and white, and seek uncritical acceptance. Education, on the other hand, attempts to present an issue from a number of different perspectives so that people can critically choose among them. If this distinction is accepted, then it becomes clear that much of what passes for education in the schools, in newspapers, and on radio and television is actually a form of propaganda. Propaganda is an especially insidious form of social control, because it controls without coercion and gives people the illusion of free choice. Propaganda increases conflict and tension because it increases the difficulty of seeing both sides of an issue and understanding the world from other people's point of view.

Doob felt that propaganda originated within a broader social context and initially doubted that it could ever be studied experimentally. As he later put it, "Behavior cannot be ripped out of the fabric of social life and examined in isolation" (Doob, 1966, p. 60). In any case, the study of propaganda could not wait for experimental research. The Institute for Propaganda Analysis closed in 1941, about a month before the United States entered World War II. The institute's president, Kirtley F. Mather, declared that "it is not practical to attempt dispassionate analyses of the steps being taken to impress the country with the seriousness of the crisis" (quoted in Lee, 1986, p. 64). Underlying this statement were concerns about being able to maintain scientific integrity in the face of having to make a choice for continued funding from either interventionist or isolationist sources. Attitude research carried out during the war was aimed not at "immunizing" people against the misleading effects of propaganda by showing the tricks and emotional devices used, but at studying persuasion experimentally for the purpose of manipulating public opinion, increasing morale, and uniting the nation in the war effort.

## MARX'S SOCIOECONOMIC THEORY

The influence of Karl Marx (1818–1883) on the world today is so profound that he is often regarded as a monumental figure who rose in the 1800s to challenge capitalism and advocate its overthrow. For some, Marx was a prophet for social change and the unchallenged champion of the underdog. For others, he was a godless propagandist creating conflict and preaching class hatred. To a certain extent, Marx was all of these things. But he was not a solitary figure. Marx was a child of his times, and to understand him, one must place him in his historical context, for it is only within this context that both his strengths and limitations can be understood.

Emile Durkheim (1895–96/1962), in a series of lectures given at the University of Bordeaux between 1895 and 1896, drew a distinction between industrial and preindustrial socialist theories.[2] Preindustrial theories, such as those presented in Plato's *Republic* and Thomas Moore's *Utopia,* were models for utopian societies written by secluded individuals responding to personal views of what society should be like. These writers were widely separated in time, but each wanted to return to a more primitive lifestyle in which greed was absent and wealth more rationally distributed. Their utopias were isolated communities, given a fictitious existence in some remote location.

During the 1800s, however, writers such as Henri, Comte de Saint-Simon (1760–1825), and Pierre Proudhon (1809–1865) began to critically examine industrial society for the purpose of transforming it. Far from advocating a return to a more primitive lifestyle, these writers wanted to develop industrial society to its full potential while ridding it of its more offensive aspects. They were responding to the economic problems actually existing at the time and describing trends that they regarded as inevitable. The study of society began as social criticism, and many people (e.g., Durkheim, 1895–96/1962; Gouldner, 1963) felt that Saint-Simon (rather than Comte) should be recognized as the founder of sociology but that his role is not acknowledged because he was also one of the founders of socialism.

Seen in this context, Marx was simply one of the many writers trying to understand and describe economic problems brought on by industrialization. Marx drew heavily from "classical" economic theories, such as those developed by Adam Smith (1723–1790) and David Ricardo (1772–1823), but he also tried to link economic conditions to social conditions and show the role of economics in the development of consciousness and thought. Previous economists had attempted to deal exclusively with abstract economic factors, such as capital, unemployment, and supply and demand, without considering their impact on people. For Marx, the means of production and the distribution of wealth were the material foundation on which every other aspect of society was based. Since his theory stresses the role of economics in human interaction, this aspect will be discussed first and followed by a summary of its social-psychological implications.

## Marx's General Economic Theory

Karl Marx was born in the German city of Trier near the French border and studied law, history, and philosophy at the Universities of Bonn and Berlin, but most of his work focused on industrial conditions in England, the first industrial nation. By the mid-1800s Great Britain was the world's most highly industrialized society, and it was generally assumed that the conditions in England were the conditions that other countries would pass through on their way to industrialization. Marx (1862, 1885, 1894/1967) contrasted these conditions with those in preindustrial societies and abstracted what he considered general economic laws.

Feudal society was based primarily on self-sufficient peasant farming, supplemented by domestic industries and crafts in small villages. Each peasant produced just enough to feed and clothe his family, after he gave a portion to the feudal lord. The feudal lord was not concerned with production. He consumed what he could but left the problem of production to serfs and tenants. Each estate was a self-sufficient unit, producing primarily to meet its own needs. This system, though terribly inefficient by modern standards, was adequate for the most part to meet the limited needs of a sparsely settled rural population.

The growth of sea-going trade to newly discovered markets in the East stimulated further social and economic changes. As these new markets expanded and the population grew, feudal modes of production were no longer sufficient to meet expanding needs. Groups of people were brought together in factories for the first time, and the rate of production was improved through a division of labor. Even without machines, a group of people working together, each concentrating on a separate aspect of the task, was much more efficient than the same individuals working alone. But the division of labor simplified the tasks and made the introduction of machines possible. The first industry to develop along these lines was weaving, which was stimulated by the increasing demand for wool products and the availability of a large pool of unemployed individuals. The increased demand for wool led to the enclosure movement, which replaced peasants and tenant farmers with sheep and transformed England's preindustrial agricultural population into modern factory workers.

Competition among factories means that goods must be produced as cheaply as possible. The cost of production can be reduced by paying each worker as little as possible, increasing the length of the working day, using cheap sources of labor such as women and children, spending as little as possible on the workplace, and introducing machines to replace people. Child labor did not begin with capitalism, but the introduction of machines made it possible to use children in jobs previously restricted to adults. Marx showed that there is an *inherent conflict* between the workers and factory owners, because it is in the interest of the workers to have higher salaries, shorter working days, and healthy working conditions. But each of these increases the cost of production. It is not necessary to see factory owners as evil or greedy. One factory owner could not unilaterally reduce the working day or pay higher wages even if he wanted to, because this increases the cost of production and makes the factory uncompetitive.

Conflict also occurs within classes. Workers compete for jobs, and factory owners compete with each other. Large companies produce goods more cheaply because they buy in bulk or control raw materials. It is important to note that problems within capitalism have nothing to do with inadequate production. In fact, industrial output under capitalism tends to be *too* efficient— it produces more goods than it can sell. The market is periodically saturated with goods for which there is little demand. Factories must either cut back on production or shut down completely. This produces the boom-and-bust cycle characteristic of free-market economies—periods of rapid growth followed by depression.

A company's capacity to live through a depression, according to Marx, is based on size, industrial efficiency, and to a lesser extent, diversification. Small inefficient companies tend to be driven out of business. Former owners descend to the rank of workers or become unemployed. Mechanization increases unemployment and unemployment keeps salaries uniformly low. If unchecked, the elimination of competitors during each depression leads to the development of monopolies and conglomerates. A few companies are eliminated each time the economy goes through a crisis, and new companies cannot develop and compete with large, well-established firms.

As companies increase in size, the day-to-day management is gradually turned over to professionals who run the factories like large industrial armies. For Marx, the working class (or proletariat) consisted of those who work and produce for someone else, re-gardless of how much they earn or where they stand in the industrial hierarchy.[3] Thus, foremen, professionals, and even the chairman of the board could become part of the working class. Marx recognized other classes, such as peasants, landowners, and small businessmen, but these were seen as transitional.

It is not clear whether Marx envisioned the final stage of capitalism as an enormous crisis from which the system could not recover—warehouses full, factories closed, and general unemployment—or whether he saw a more calculated transfer of power based on class consciousness. He did, however, predict an enormous growth both in industrial efficiency and the number of people in the working class. For Marx, the problem with capitalism was that, although it is extremely efficient, it creates a situation in which fewer and fewer people actually share the wealth.

At some point, industrial efficiency would be so high that a wide range of goods could be produced with a minimum of labor, but the distribution of wealth would be so uneven that goods could not be sold. Factory owners are now largely outside the production process, and firms are run by large industrial armies. Inequalities in the system are too large to be tolerated, and the factories would be taken away from the owners, or, to put it another way, factory owners would be forced to work and earn their own living. The final "revolution," for Marx, was a simple transfer of ownership in which the big losers would be a handful of extremely wealthy individuals whose income is grossly out of line with their contribution to society.

Contrary to what is often thought, Marx did not speculate a great deal about what the future society would be like. He saw capitalism as a necessary stage in the movement toward socialism. Capitalism, with its emphasis on industrial efficiency, would create the capacity to produce goods and services with a minimum of effort. After the revolution, both goods and labor could be more evenly distributed. Freed from the need to work, most people could simply do whatever they liked. They could "hunt in the morning, fish in the afternoon, rear cattle in the evening, criticize after dinner . . . without ever becoming a hunter, fisherman, shepherd or critic" (Marx & Engels, 1845–46/1947, p. 53).

This summary of Marx's economic theory raises some general points that should be noted. First, Marx's theory is *not* a theory of socialism. It was a description of actual conditions in industrial England at the time that he wrote and an attempt to derive general laws that would explain the future course of society. It is important to keep the industrial conditions in mind because they help explain Marx's strong opposition to capitalism. Nineteenth-century industrial conditions are almost incomprehensible by modern standards. Workers labored up to 16 hours a day under extremely harsh conditions just to earn enough to keep themselves and their families alive. Industrial accidents were grounds for dismissal. Those who could not find work often starved. Child labor was rampant, and life expectancy was generally very low. Although workers were "free" from the bonds of feudalism, many worked and lived under conditions far worse than those of their peasant ancestors.

Moreover, Marx believed that conditions would deteriorate before they got better. Mechanization would create further unemployment. Job simplification would lead to an increase in child labor. Social evolutionists tried to rationalize the inequities as natural extensions of evolutionary principles and derided growing concern about the poor as mawkish nonsense. But Marx argued that inhumane working conditions and poverty were not natural but man-made and could be eradicated if a majority of people would simply recognize that these conditions were not in their own interest.

A second point is that the course of industrial development did not proceed as Marx predicted. It did not do so largely because the free-market system was *not* allowed to operate. Child-labor laws were established, a minimum wage was implemented, working hours were gradually reduced, and companies were forced to provide workers with less hazardous working conditions. Each of these changes faced a great deal of resistance from factory owners, who claimed that the government should not interfere with business, but they kept the economic system from deteriorating. The rise of trade unions and workers' parties gave workers an increasing share of political power. It is probably one of the great ironies of history that Marx, by showing the "inevitable" consequences of the free-market system, allowed workers and their supporters to push through reforms that prevented the collapse of the capitalist system.

A third, somewhat related, point is that there has never been a "Marxist" revolution. Such a revolution requires a prolonged period of capitalism and an advanced state of industrial development. The socialist revolutions that have occurred have taken place in peasant societies without the necessary industrial base. The Russian Revolution, for example, took power from the czar and gave it to the Communist Party. The party retained the czar's elaborate (and subsequently uncooperative) bureaucracy but infused it with unskilled party members in order to maintain control. Russia attempted to bypass capitalism through rapid industrial development, but when progress seemed slow, it reintroduced differential wages and adopted industrial policies developed in America aimed at maximizing efficiency through piecework and job simplification. The result is a highly inefficient bureaucratic society with large inequities in wealth and industrial conditions similar to those in capitalist societies.

## Social-Psychological Aspects of Marxist Theory

Marx's theory stresses the role of "economic determinism" in the sense that the means of production form the material base from which other institutions emerge. This can be taken in two ways. First, other aspects of society help justify and support existing economic conditions. As Britain moved from feudalism to capitalism, it underwent numerous changes in laws, political structure, and religion. Economic theories of the time not only described economic conditions but attempted to justify them on moral grounds. Thus for Adam Smith (1776/1937), the wealth of a nation was guided by an "unseen hand" and was facilitated by each person pursuing his or her own self-interests. As conditions deteriorated, Herbert Spencer (1873/1961) could reassure those in power that poverty and unemployment were part of the natural laws of evolution and would ultimately lead to a better society. For Marx, economic changes occurred first and provided the foundation for changes in other areas.

But a second meaning that Marx wished to convey by "economic determinism" was that economic factors are so pervasive in the day-to-day life of individuals that they help shape our mode of thinking and the way we interact with others. It is this second use of the term that has the greatest implications for social psychology. Economic conditions shape thought in two ways. They provide us with specific beliefs and values in the form of ideologies, and they condition the *way* we think, forming the analogies we use and the hidden assumptions behind social perception and behavior.

Marx felt that one could not take a society's beliefs about itself at face value. He used the term "ideology" to refer to the ideas fostered by the dominant class to rationalize and maintain the status quo. During feudal times the values of honor and loyalty were stressed. With industrialization, there was a stress on values such as freedom and equality. Abstract ideals are usually preferred because they have a broad appeal, but they should not be accepted uncritically. It is quite possible for a society to hold values like freedom and equality but offer few opportunities and practice widespread discrimination. Concepts like freedom and democracy can become hollow slogans when applied to societies in which poverty and unemployment are everyday phenomena.

Because ideologies are based on vested interests, they almost invariably contain false beliefs, based either on self-deception or outright lies. Those who have the wealth control the means for spreading their ideas. The conceptual separation of beliefs and actual social economic conditions, however, makes it possible to study the two separately and compare them. One of the functions of social criticism is to uncover deceptions produced by ideologies and create a more accurate picture of concrete reality. This is why sociology has always been viewed as potentially subversive. By ignoring ideology and studying actual social conditions, it has the power to discover discrepancies and upset the status quo.

The effects of society on the individual can be seen most clearly in Marx's description of *alienation* within industrial society. Marx distinguished four types—alienation from nature, alienation from work, self-alienation, and alienation from others. Previous cultures were closer to their natural environment. They worked with it and it was all around them. Industrial workers, on the other hand, were closed up in large urban factories and separated from nature. Their materials were often several steps removed from raw materials, and their environment seemed mechanical and artificial.

Alienation from work is the primary source of alienation, and it is responsible for self-alienation and alienation from others. For Marx, people were distinguished from animals by the fact that they plan their activities and then carry them out. He states that "a bee puts to shame many an architect in the construction of her cells. But what distinguishes the worst architect from the best of bees is that the architect raises his structure in his imagination before he erects it in reality" (Marx, 1867/1965, p. 157). For Marx, productive work was the most human of all activities. People develop themselves through work and are shaped by it.

Industrial workers are alienated from work in two senses. First, they do not own either the raw materials or the finished product. They are the means by which materials are transformed, but they have no control over how they are transformed or exchanged. Second, industrial work is typically only one link in a long production process. The worker does not conceptualize a project and see it through to completion. The task has been simplified and reduced to a few mechanical movements. The work is boring and repetitious and requires little concentration. Because it has been simplified, one worker is easily replaced by another. Workers can take no pride in their work because it requires little skill and imagination.[4]

Alienation from work is so pervasive in our society that it is often assumed to be part of the human condition. But boring, repetitive work is not a natural condition. It is a result of the oversimplification of tasks brought on by a forced division of labor. Productive work enriches people, but mechanical work requires just enough concentration to dull the intellect and prevent free use of the imagination.

Alienation from work was, for Marx, the primary form of alienation, but it also leads to self-alienation. Craft workers and professionals can identify with their jobs. Their work is seen as an integral part of them. They can say with pride that they are a doctor, a potter, or a carpenter. But industrial work has no intrinsic value. It is simply a way to earn money. Since workers are completely interchangeable with each other, their worth is determined not by what they do but by how much they earn. They come to think of themselves as commodities and regard others in the same way.

Since Marx saw working conditions as primarily responsible for alienation, he believed that people could only develop their full potential by doing away with the division of labor. The division of labor is not based on capitalism per se, but on the need for industrial efficiency. Marx never believed that state ownership, in and of itself, would solve the problem of alienation. This would require a radical revamping of the industrial process, an end to the division of labor, and an opening up of job opportunities so that people could pursue any career they chose.

For Marx, both our mode of thinking and our actual beliefs were determined by socioeconomic factors, but it would be wrong to assume that Marx believed in a rigid "economic determinism." He obviously assumed that the pace of economic change could be increased by exposing inconsistencies in the system. He felt that a strict belief in economic determinism was itself a form of alienation, since it obscured the fact that working conditions were manmade and therefore changeable. In response to the contradictions within capitalism, the working class had the revolutionary potential to produce a new social and economic system based on the emancipation of human needs, but the actual creation of such a system would not be easy. Those Marxists who adopted a policy of strict economic determinism were left sitting on their hands while the revolution slipped through their fingers.

## The Failure of Marxism as a Workers' Movement in the United States

By the turn of the century there were major political parties and mass movements inspired directly or indirectly by Marx in virtually every major industrial country. The only exception was the United States. The anomaly of the situation in the United States drew the attention of both conservative and socialist thinkers, because the United States had become in many ways the leading industrial nation and supposedly was a prototype of things to come. The failure of Marxism to gain a foothold in the United States meant that a socialist revolution was by no means inevitable even during an advanced stage of industrial capitalism. In 1906, the German socialist Werner Sombart wrote the book *Why Is There No Socialism in the United States?* (1906/1976), which attempted to explain the situation. Sombart attributed the failure of Marxism to five major factors: (1) American patriotism; (2) the workers' identification with capitalism; (3) the rigid two-party system; (4) the relative affluence of American workers; and (5) the frontier as a safety outlet.

In Europe, socialism began largely as a form of *political* protest in which workers attempted to increase their participation within the political process. In the early stages of capitalism, workers were either excluded or systematically undercounted during elections. In the United States, the right to vote was guaranteed in the Consitution, and there was almost universal suffrage for white adult males from the very beginning.

Unlike their European counterparts, American workers had a long history of involvement in the political process, and there was little opposition between the worker and the state. As Sombart (1906/1976) noted, "There is expressed in the worker, as in all Americans, a boundless optimism, which comes out as a belief in the mission and greatness of his country, a belief that often has a religious tinge. The Americans think themselves to be God's chosen people, the famous 'salt of the earth' " (p. 18).

A second obstacle was the workers' identification with capitalism itself. Most small businessmen and independent farmers considered themselves capitalists on a small scale and worked hard to increase their production so that they could make more money and reinvest. Even manual workers in large factories retained part of this identification. Competent workers considered themselves businessmen who exploited individual opportunities and shared their employer's way of thinking. For the average American being successful meant making money, and money was obtained only by rational planning and capital investment. Workers maintained a favorable attitude toward capitalism because it provided for their immediate material needs and because it seemed to offer a means of self-improvement.

A third factor was the two-party system. By the turn of the century the Democratic and Republican parties had entrenched themselves in American politics and dominated all levels of government. The differences between them at this time were seldom clear, but each had loyal supporters who considered the party a significant aspect of their individual and group identity. Blacks and Germans were loyal Republicans, whereas Irish Catholics and southern whites consistently voted for the Democratic party. Each party had its roots in populist movements that appealed to workers. The Democrats could trace their origins to the agrarian heritage of Thomas Jefferson's "Republican" party with its strong emphasis on states' rights and decentralization. The Republican party was still associated with Abraham Lincoln and the emancipation of the slaves. The two parties were so evenly divided that they could not afford to alienate anyone and therefore resorted to vague promises and largely empty ideological slogans. At the local level ideological differences were virtually nonexistent, and the major source of party loyalty was a spoils system in which local supporters were taken care of and party leaders were rewarded once a party came to power. Party bosses knew and worked their local constitutents—buying one a free drink, providing a second with a little extra food, and obtaining a discount on a coffin for a third with a dead child.

These networks of party loyalists were a big business and required considerable sums of money to operate. The total cost of a Presidential campaign at the turn of the century was approximately $5,000,000, and the annual cost of elections in New York during non-Presidential years was $7,000,000 (Sombart, 1906/1976). Under these conditions, it was difficult for *any* third party to compete, and American history is littered with the corpses of would-be contenders. A further obstacle for new parties was the tendency to use one of the two major parties as a form of revenge. If one party failed to keep its campaign promises (which it often did) or openly engaged in antilabor activities, such as calling in troops to break up a strike, workers could switch to the other party during the next election and throw out the party in power. A third obstacle was the tendency of the two major parties to absorb the platforms of third parties, therefore making them redundant and stealing their thunder. The Socialist party's greatest success occurred in 1912 when it gained 6% of the Presidential vote, but by 1916 the status quo had been restored and the vote declined to 3%.

A fourth factor that prevented the spread of socialism was the relative affluence of American workers. The average American worker earned roughly twice as much as a German worker and maintained a higher standard of living. Not all Americans were equally well off. As Sombart (1906/1976) pointed out, the poor in urban American slums were much worse off than those in continental Europe, but a significant number were relatively well off and there was also a large minority who formed an aristocracy of labor. These tended to belong to exclusive trade unions that were suspicious of new immigrant groups and focused on their own problems and interests. The latter had a strong tendency to guildlike isolation, which tended to work against a more unified labor movement.

Much of the "surplus" income of wealthier workers was spent on basic commodities such as food, clothing, and housing. American workers, according to Sombart (1906/1976), ate better, dressed better, and lived in more expensive homes than did workers elsewhere. The tendency to dress better helped decrease the visible differences between workers and the middle class and gave the impression of an open and classless society. Union leaders like the legendary Samuel Gompers of the American Federation of Labor convinced workers that they were allies rather than enemies of the capitalist system. Through unified action based on caution and moderation the labor movement workers, Gompers argued, would gain a larger share of the nation's wealth. More radical organizations, such as the Industrial Workers of the World, were regarded with suspicion by the majority of workers, and by the time the United States entered World War I, the IWW was dismissed as unpatriotic and un-American. American workers could readily identify with the rich and even the super-rich because they saw these people simply as more wealthy versions of themselves.

Finally, the American frontier served as a safety valve. American workers, for the most part, were free to move and did not feel "locked in" to the same degree as Europeans. During times of economic hardship, they could pull up stakes, go West, and take advantage of the free land then available. The Homestead Act of 1863 gave any American citizen over 21 the right to 80 acres of land within railway land grants or 160 acres if they located elsewhere. The ability to move when times got rough was a little harder for European immigrants because the cities provided them with the vestige of their previous culture, but the option was still present even when it was not used. This outward flow also tended to reduce the number of urban workers and kept salaries relatively high.

In addition to the factors noted by Sombard (1906/1976), Marxism in America was also hampered by the lack of any continuity in leadership. Apart from a small number of committed Marxists, most American radicals showed little more than a brief flirtation with Marx's practical ideas. The popularity of Marx was a generational affair, whereby each generation of youthful radicals rediscovered Marx and interpreted him in their own way (Diggins, 1973). Radical leaders typically gave up their youthful ideas as they got older and frequently became much more conservative. One example is Max Eastman, the editor of the left-wing magazine *The New Masses,* who eventually became a committed anticommunist.

Support for socialism was further weakened during the 1920s. America's late entry into World War I meant that the war was over while the country was still fired up with militant patriotism. Several writers have used the analogy of "coitus interruptus" to describe the situation. When this was combined with the widespread fear among the middle class that foreign radicals would attempt the sort of revolution that had recently occurred in Russia, the way was paved for the postwar repression of the left from which the Socialist party never recovered. In the red scare that followed the war, the attorney general of the United States embarked on an offical campaign to break up Marxist organizations and even tried to "expatriate" as foreign subversives hundreds of so-called socialists by sending them by boat to Finland.

The history of Marxism in America is largely an account of its failure to have any permanent appeal as an alternative to liberal capitalism. Marx's theory was based, as we have seen, on an analysis of conditions in England during the Industrial Revolution. These conditions, although appropriate in many ways to other industrialized countries, did not seem to fit the American experience. Americans' long-standing belief that they are unique made them feel that circumstances giving rise to European ideologies such as communism and fascism did not apply to them. Marx's stages of economic development described the transformation from feudalism to capitalism, leading ultimately to a proletarian revolution. Americans, by contrast, saw themselves as a free nation, created according to the vision and values of Puritan society and the founding fathers of the United States.

This view helped inspire an American dream that included not just religious and political freedom but the promise of more and more material prosperity. The belief in the American dream was so strong that, even during the depths of the Great Depression, the average American, such as those described in *Middletown in Transition* (Lynd & Lynd, 1937), clung tenaciously to the view that the economic troubles were only temporary and that prosperity and progress would soon return. The fear, resentment, and insecurity experienced by unemployed workers were largely seen as an individual problem rather than part of a collective experience. The unemployed, like the rest of the population, simply wanted things to return to normal so that they could continue to pursue the American dream under "their own steam and ingenuity" (Lynd & Lynd, 1937).

These factors operated together to prevent the spread of socialism in the United States. Unlike its European counterparts, American socialism never gained the grassroots support that it needed to become something other than an intellectual movement. This also meant that American intellectuals did not have to study Marx and come to grips with Marxism in the same ways as European thinkers. Marxism could be largely ignored, and to an extent it was until social and economic conditions deteriorated in the 1930s.

For intellectuals, the depression offered a new opportunity to apply Marxist theory to pressing social problems in America. Indeed, at no other time in history did Marxism have such great appeal. No thoughtful discussion about the depression and the nature of social change could avoid considering the monumental example of the Soviet Union, which represented an unprecedented experiment in applying Marxist theory. Liberal and radical thinkers in America were fascinated not with communism per se but with the the Soviet experiment in economic planning. Above the harsh conditions in America stood the glaring example of the Soviet Union, which as the economic situation worsened, reinforced in the minds of many the contrasting metaphors—birth as opposed to death, cooperation versus competition, social welfare versus private profit, order versus chaos. As the depression wore on, more and more American thinkers became sympathetic to Marxism and began to apply it to conditions in the United States. What appealed to many was the degree of planning and cooperation in the Soviet Union. The Soviet experiment, according to one writer (Soule, 1931), offered the only real hope that control of a complex industrial system was possible and proved that there was "a different and better" social system than capitalism (cited in Pells, 1973, p. 62).

The American fascination with the Soviet Union and the growing interest in Marx never involved a wholesale rejection of American capitalism. As with the reception of Freud, Americans saw what they wanted to see in Marx and modified his theory in order to fit their own experience. The Americanization of Marx was, in fact, even more deliberate than the Americanization of Freud. Writers such as Edmund Wilson argued that there was "still some virtue in American democracy" and suggested that Americans "take communism away from the communists" by applying it to their own situation (Pells, 1973, p. 59). For social critics such as Dewey (1928), the Soviet experiment was reminiscent of the Puritan vision of the "city upon the hill" that sought to build an entirely new society based on the ideals of community and cooperation. The Soviet Union was a fascinating social-psychological experiment, but its ultimate appeal rested on the view that it was essentially pragmatic and experimental and offered a realistic method of social change and a means for obtaining liberal ends.

The American romance with the Soviet Union ended with the Moscow trials and other events in Europe that helped turn attention away from the depression in America toward conflicts and tensions abroad. Americans generally lacked a sufficiently strong ideological base to distinguish Marxism from the developments within the Soviet Union. Stalin's dictatorship was for many sufficient justification to reject Marxism and to give up any hope of a socialist revolution in America. The preferred course of action, as Roosevelt's New Deal demonstrated, was to apply piecemeal solutions to complex social and economic problems. Many of these were seen as temporary, emergency measures to be dismantled once the economy recovered.

The failure of Marxism in America points to the fact that the vast majority of Americans were essentially conservative and resistant to change. The Lynds noted that the culture of "Middletown" was basically the same in 1937 as it was in 1925 and the population remained "individualist in an individualistic culture" (Lynd & Lynd, 1937). They and other social thinkers observed that social attitudes were largely shaped by abstract symbols and popular slogans used by politicians and the press. The use of symbols provided the people with a sense of unity and served as a substitute for ideology. These developments together with the specter of mass fascism in Europe reinforced the lessons taught by Freud concerning the irrational nature of individuals and society as well as the importance of the unconscious in determining attitudes and behavior. As one social scientist wrote, the decade of the 1930s taught "how profound is the role of the emotions and . . . subconscious impulse in determining men's actions, how little 'rational' intellectual processes really matter" (Bliven, 1938, p. 252). For the most part, the work of the decade's leading social scientists tended to confirm the view that the depression was unable to generate any ideological alternatives to liberal capitalism. Indeed, as Pells (1973) has pointed out, "many writers in the late 1930s were attracted to the New Deal precisely because it seemed to utilize the traditional rhetoric, images, and slogans of American culture far more effectively than any of the parties farther to the left, thereby uniting people around the lowest common denominators. . . . What began as an effort to reconcile the individual to society ended with an indiscriminate celebration of the family,

the group, the region, and the nation" (p. 326).

## ALTERNATIVE MODELS

Karl Marx was writing at a relatively early stage of industrial development. By the turn of the century, industrial conditions had changed sufficiently that several social theorists were beginning to address themselves to perceived shortcomings and deficiences in the works of Marx. From a social-psychological perspective, the three most important writers during this period were probably Max Weber, Emile Durkheim, and Karl Mannheim.

### Max Weber (1864–1920)

One of the central problems in understanding Marx's theory is distinguishing Marx the social scientist from Marx the propagandist. Some of Marx's works are detailed descriptions of socioeconomic conditions, but others were written to win support from a more general audience. Marx himself did not think it was possible to separate social values and social science, but even sympathetic critics, such as Durkheim, felt that Marx sometimes used statistics to support preconceived ideas. The central question following in the wake of Marx was: Can social science be objective?

Weber offered an extremely simple yet ingenious answer. He argued that social scientists cannot be objective in their selection of problems but they can, indeed they must, be objective in their treatment of these problems after they have been selected. Individual social scientists select problems on the basis of personal interests and social conditions, as well as such extraneous reasons as the feasibility of research and the availability of research grants. But once a problem has been selected, the researcher must make every effort to study it objectively. A good scientist must let the data speak for themselves, and many of the safeguards built into the scientific process, such as a clear and precise description of procedures, allow others to test and replicate findings if they so choose. Those who misuse statistics and research findings to confirm preconceived notions or mislead others are not engaged in science but in propaganda. Weber felt that it was through a frank and explicit recognition of one's own values that one could best overcome the problems associated with biased research.

Weber was also concerned with the relationship between socioeconomic conditions and ideas. He felt that a theory that derived ideas exclusively from socioeconomic conditions was too deterministic and that ideas and socioeconomic conditions often develop together and mutually reinforce each other.[5] Although Weber attempted to show this relationship by using a wide variety of world religions, his clearest statement is contained in *The Protestant Ethic and the Spirit of Capitalism* (1904–05/1958). This work, like that of Marx, is primarily historical and begins with a description of precapitalist societies.

The traditional worker in feudal society worked only as much as necessary. If new, more efficient modes of production were introduced, workers responded by working less rather than producing more. The accumulation of wealth, while widely practiced, was not sanctioned by the Catholic church and was, at least in principle, discouraged.

The development of Protestantism, and Calvinism in particular, changed these values and produced a new type of individual particularly suited to capitalism. Protestantism raised work to the level of a moral obligation and made idleness a sin. At the same time, a person was discouraged from spending money on personal luxuries. The Protestant ethic in its original form opposed any form of spontaneous enjoyment—games, art, theater, or any ostentatious display of wealth. The result was a hard-working individual, continually striving to earn more money, but unable to use it for personal enjoyment.

Greed and the pursuit of wealth are not unique to capitalism. People in all ages have taken wealth wherever they found it—either from booty, through theft, or by exploiting social inferiors. What distinguished capitalism (at least in its initial stages) was

the rationally planned acquisition of wealth based on hard work, the pursuit of profit, and the reinvestment of profit to make more money. This was not only a profound social change but a profound psychological change as well, resulting in an obsessive personality continually driven to produce more but unable to enjoy life because of an association of pleasure with sin.

Weber's greatest contribution to social psychology is probably his detailed description of bureaucracies (Weber, 1968). Marx associated bureaucracies with the industrial division of labor and assumed that they would disappear once this division was destroyed. Weber, on the other hand, pointed out that bureaucracies had developed as administrative units during feudal society and had been improved under capitalism because they were the most efficient means of managing large groups of people. Bureaucracies occurred in, but were not confined to, industries. Religious groups, armies, and political parties all tend to develop bureaucratic structures based on a hierarchic division of labor.

But a hierarchy in and of itself is not a bureaucracy. For Weber, a bureaucracy is a formal hierarchy with fixed rules and duties in which a person's position is determined by ability and technical training. The Catholic church during feudal times was a hierarchy, but not a bureaucracy. Positions were filled on the basis of nobility and birth, and rights and obligations were left to the discretion of those in charge. The medieval army was recruited in the same way, with conscripts taken from the peasant class and officers from the nobility. Such a system does not allow people to rise through talent and training to a position where they can put their ability to use.

A bureaucracy is a hierarchic institution devoted to a certain task. The division of labor allows a rational calculation of long-term goals by assigning each person a set of obligations and duties. A person's position is determined by ability, as shown either by formal training or competitive exams, and constitutes a career because it offers the possibility of promotion. Since bureaucracies fill positions on the basis of talent, they cannot perpetuate a system based on patronage or nepotism. The most important thing about a bureaucracy is that people move into pre-existing positions, where the rights and obligations of the position are already prescribed. Those at the top of the bureaucracy plan activities by assigning tasks to those below. The vast majority of individuals, however, carry out fixed routines in which there is little freedom to deviate. Workers who refuse to cooperate are simply replaced by others who carry out precisely the same task. Weber felt that the concern about "red tape" in bureaucracies was not altogether misplaced. Since bureaucracies are based on prescribed rules, there is the danger that goals will be lost when rules are followed to the letter. But from a purely functional point of view, bureaucracies are the most rational way to manage large organizations and are indispensable wherever efficient management is required.

Weber not only provided an alternative to Marx's view of economic determinism, he provided a detailed analysis of what he saw as the necessary structure of any large organization. His analysis has had a tremendous impact on what was in the 1930s a major subarea of social psychology—what has come to be known as "organizational behavior." Many of the textbooks written during this period included discussions of large organizations and their impact on individual workers. But as the field of organizational behavior grew in size, it too, like personality and developmental psychology, simply formed a separate discipline, and Weber's influence on social psychology virtually disappeared.

### Emile Durkheim (1858–1917)

Durkheim (1893/1964) also focused much of his attention on the division of labor, but he was concerned primarily with occupations that require a great deal of technical and professional specialization. Marx wrote at a time in which the ideal of a "universal man" was still common. Thus, he could describe the person of the future as someone who hunts, fishes, and rears cattle during the day and criticizes after dinner. But Durkheim lived in a period in which technical and professional specialization had already advanced considerably, particularly in France. He felt that a division of labor was inevitable in any highly advanced industrial society, whether capitalist or socialist. Moreover, such specialization did not diminish but actually enriched the person if it was freely chosen, since it allowed people to develop their own unique talents and abilities. The difference between Marx and Durkheim can best be understood by posing a hypothetical question. Will the society of the future have a need for highly trained physicians, professors, and research scientists? If so, then professional specialization seems inevitable. Someone who criticizes only after dinner would simply not be a very profound critic.

Durkheim, like Marx and Weber, began his study by contrasting conditions within his own culture to those in more primitive societies. In primitive societies, the division of labor is usually based simply on age and sex. People carry out a set of prescribed tasks designed to meet their needs and those of their family. Because each member of the group is engaged in more or less the same activity and shares a common set of beliefs, unique individuals hardly exist in primitive cultures. Although people are more similar, they are less dependent on one another. A primitive culture can lose members without any appreciable loss to the community as a whole.

The division of labor begins when people divide up work so that each person does something different. As a person begins to develop skills in a particular area, his or her other abilities and skills atrophy and the person becomes dependent on others. Those performing the same task pursue common goals, with rights and obligations that bind them together. Those performing different tasks are bound by *mutual solidarity,* because each person is now dependent on other people with different skills to meet needs that he or she cannot. It is only at a relatively advanced state of specialization that unique individuals appear and a "cult of the individual" develops. The division of labor destroys the old form of "mechanical solidarity" based on similarity and creates a new form of "organic solidarity" based on mutual dependence.

For Durkheim, alienation in modern society was not due to the division of labor per se. It was due to a forced division of labor by which a large number of individuals are required to work at boring, repetitive jobs that do not develop their talents while others inherit large fortunes by which they can take advantage of educational opportunities or live without working. Durkheim had no qualms about rewarding business and entrepreneural skills, but he felt that wealth, once acquired, should not be passed on to descendants because this tends to maintain class differences based on kinship rather than merit. He advocated a system in which wealth was passed on to workers within a business or to one's occupational group and envisioned a time when all persons could develop their unique talents and skills to their fullest potential.

For Durkheim (1897/1964), the social problems at the turn of the century were due to the transformation of society from one based on common and widely shared beliefs and values to one based on unique individuals with a high degree of occupational specialization. He used the rate of suicide as a concrete index of a society's general level of psychological health. Two forms of suicide were particularly prevalent in western culture—"egotistical suicide," based on an absence of shared social norms, and "anomic suicide," based on unobtainable goals. Egotistical suicide is a direct result of the situation in our society whereby individuals are encouraged to pursue their own narrow self-interest without regard for others. Anomie develops because people want more than they can have. Durkheim showed that suicide is not based on poverty. Suicides are relatively rare in extremely poor countries and *increase* with wealth in urban populations. Suicides also increase during periods of economic depression and recovery. During depressions, people cannot maintain their previous standard of living. During recovery, people's desires increase more rapidly than their capacity to meet them.

Durkheim's recognition that individuals can develop limitless desires led him to a more tolerant view of religion than that held by Marx. Marx's opposition to religion was based on his belief that it made people complacent about problems in this world by offering justice in an afterlife. Religions were also commonly used to justify the status quo. For Marx, religion was a form of alienation, because human attributes and capabilities were projected outward and attributed to mystical entities. The self-abasement characteristic of certain Protestant sects, in which individuals are seen as weak and worthless while God is seen as all-powerful and good, is a good example. For Marx (1844/1964), "the more man puts into God, the less he retains for himself" (p. 108). Marx assumed that once poverty and injustice were eliminated, people would not need religions.

Durkheim's (1912/1965) concept of religion was very different. For Durkheim, religion did not depend on supernatural forces, temples, or priests. The symbols and rituals were simply the exterior, superficial aspects. A religion was nothing other than a body of collective beliefs and ideals that united a group of people and gave them a sense of social solidarity. The ceremonies and celebrations were used to keep these memories and values alive. The French Revolution, for example, had created a whole cycle of holidays that were meant to uphold the values of the revolution. The Fourth of July, Memorial Day, and Labor Day in the United States can be seen as secular equivalents of religious festivals. For Durkheim, religion was a means of attaching an individual to a group and providing a sense of solidarity.

A second function of religion, for Durkheim, was to limit desire. Marx had placed the emphasis on production and distribution but had ignored the need to limit consumption. Durkheim showed through his analysis of suicide rates that prosperity itself did not lead to happiness. Durkheim suggested that poverty lowers the incidence of suicide by restraining ambition. The rising expectations due to wealth and economic prosperity increase suicide because people come to desire more than they can achieve. Durkheim did not seek to solve this problem by advocating poverty or even an equal distribution of wealth. He felt that wealth provided an important incentive for certain professions. But he also believed that people could tolerate inequalities if they were perceived as being due to differences in ability and effort, rather than to inherited wealth. For Durkheim, religion was a means for limiting aspiration and promoting social justice and solidarity.

Before discussing Karl Mannheim and his sociology of knowledge, it may be useful to pause briefly and contrast the positions of Marx, Durkheim, and Weber. In a sense, differences in their description of institutions are due to differences in focus. Marx was concerned primarily with the conditions of industrial workers, Weber focused on managerial and administrative bureaucracies, while Durkheim was more interested in technical and professional occupations. But the thinking of Durkheim and Weber also challenges Marx's conception of social equality after a socialist revolution. For Durkheim, there will always be inequalities based on ability, effort, and occupational prestige. For Weber, inequalities are based on differences in power within bureaucracies. Those at the top of the bureaucracy have more power and freedom than those below. Both Durkheim and Weber argued that such differences will always exist because they are necessary for the effective management of society.

Durkheim's influence on American social psychology has been extremely limited and often indirect. He is often considered one of the founders of modern sociology, but among those who focus on social psychology, his collectivist treatment and his direct assaults on psychology itself make him seem somewhat antithetical to the whole enterprise. His importance rests in his detailed analysis of social institutions and his insistence that these precede people and help to form their identity. In this respect he is much closer to Dewey and Mead and the various precursors to the postmodernist movement described in Chapter 13.

## Karl Mannheim (1893–1947)

Karl Mannheim introduced the field of sociology of knowledge to America, and his book *Ideology and Utopia* (1929/1936) remains one of the most definitive works in the area. In it, he introduces two modes of political thinking. "Ideology" is used in the Marxian sense to refer to the beliefs of the dominant class that are used to rationalize its vested social interests and maintain the status quo. "Utopias" are the beliefs of oppressed groups and their supporters who oppose the current system and wish to transform it. Utopias are always conceptualized in terms of a future society different from that existing at the time and may or may not include strategies for transformation. While Mannheim's introduction to the sociology of knowledge is relatively abstract, studies of the authoritarian character covered in the next section can be taken as a concrete example of how society helps shape modes of thinking and conceptions of social reality.

Mannheim points out that the sociology of knowledge began as social criticism. When Marx began his critique of capitalist society, the ideological roots of capitalism were so weak that supporters were caught completely off guard. Marx was able to show that the modes of thought and social interaction prevalent in this society were not "natural" or universal as supporters had claimed but were derived from a definite set of socioeconomic conditions. Conservatism, in and of itself, merely accepts the status quo and has no need for social theory. It was forced by criticism to defend itself by formulating a specific ideology.

Marx did not have to deal with the fact that his own writings have become a form of ideology. As long as criticism was limited to capitalist society, the sociology of knowledge was not possible. A second step occurred when supporters of capitalism began criticizing socialist theory, pointing out that it too embodied implicit assumptions and values. Each party attempted to uncover irrational elements in the other's thinking in order to undermine confidence in it. The sociology of knowledge provides a number of valuable insights into the nature of knowledge and thought, but until people are able to submit their own position to the same sort of criticism to which they subject their opponents', the critical step has not been taken. This criticism and counter-criticism provided the basis for establishing a more accurate picture of reality, but it also radically shook people's faith in reason and provided the framework for the systematic study of the unconscious by showing the hidden assumptions behind conscious behavior. The sociology of knowledge involves an attempt to explore the socioeconomic foundation of thought systematically. As Peter L. Berger and Thomas Luckmann (1966) have pointed out, this process is very difficult, something like pushing the bus on which one is riding.

According to Mannheim, the capacity to study the sociological foundations of knowledge is facilitated by the development of a *detached perspective*. This can occur in one of three ways. One is through vertical mobility, whereby a person moves up (or down) in social status. A second occurs during rapid social change, and a third through a clash of ideas. During stable economic conditions, the ideological foundations of thought are more or less taken for granted, but during unstable times, conflicts and inconsistencies within ideologies become more apparent. Mannheim felt that intellectuals, because of their education and unique position in society, were also able to take a detached perspective.

The sociology of knowledge is concerned primarily with the social roots of everyday experience. Scientific knowledge and the history of ideas are simply a small aspect of the overall field. Wirth (1936) has pointed out, "The most important thing . . . that we can know about a man is what he takes for granted, and the most elemental and important facts about a society are those that are seldom debated and generally regarded as settled" (p. xxiii). The principal thesis, according to Mannheim, is that there are modes of thought that cannot be understood if their social origins are obscured.

Utopias, because they are future-oriented, provide a society with a sense of direction and a set of ideals. Liberals and socialists share a dissatisfaction with existing social conditions but differ in how they seek social change. Liberals assume that problems can be corrected one at a time, whereas socialists call for more sweeping social and economic reforms.

Interest in the sociology of knowledge among American social psychologists has not been particularly strong. There was some effort to examine the social origins of individual psychological processes, such as thinking and perception, during the 1930s, but this interest gradually faded. The most systematic attempt in this direction was probably the studies of the authoritarian character that began in the 1920s and culminated in the study of the authoritarian personality (Adorno, Frenkel-Brunswik, Levinson, & Sanford, 1950). However, as a result of Berger and Luckmann's (1966) theoretical perspective, there has been a growing interest in the sociology of knowledge and its implications for social psychology.

## ATTEMPTED INTEGRATIONS OF FREUD AND MARX

When Marx is viewed in retrospect, it is clear that he had a relatively good understanding of conscious and unconscious factors, given the period in which he wrote. He recognized that ideologies distort socioeconomic perception by rationalizing vested social interest and that people could develop a "false consciousness" that does not correspond to actual social conditions. But Marx was a child of the Enlightenment, and he had a strong belief in the ultimate power of reason and science. He felt that, if ideological distortions were stripped away and additional evidence provided, most workers would come to recognize the need for social change. For this reason, Marxists were totally unprepared to deal with the events of the 1930s when economic conditions disintegrated. Instead of fostering revolutionary consciousness, a large number of workers turned right instead of left—toward fascism.

Marx died before Freud began to study the unconscious, and he simply could not gauge the extent to which political attitudes are shaped by unconscious and irrational forces. This inadequate psychological foundation is, from a social-psychological perspective, one of the most serious shortcomings in Marx's theory, but it is matched by a contrasting weakness in Freud's treatment of social issues. Freud and Marx also concentrated on different aspects of the life cycle. Freud stressed the importance of early childhood and felt that the foundation for personality was established during this period. Marx concentrated on adulthood and described how working conditions shaped the lives of individuals both within and outside the workplace. Freud studied the conflict within people, whereas Marx explored the conflicts within society as a whole. Since Marxist theory is underdeveloped on its psychological side and Freudian theory is underdeveloped as social theory, many people during the 1930s attempted to overcome these deficiencies by integrating the ideas of Freud and Marx. These weaknesses, it was thought, might actually become sources of strength. Since each theory deals with a different set of problems, they seldom come into conflict on central issues.

One aspect of this integration focused on the study of the authoritarian character. This work was initiated in Germany during the 1930s by Wilhelm Reich and Erich Fromm and later expanded by others in America during the 1940s and 1950s. Also during the 1930s, the American social psychologist J. F. Brown attempted a more extensive intergration of the work of Freud, Marx, and Kurt Lewin.

### Wilhelm Reich (1897–1957)

Reich's stormy career began with a rapid ascent within psychoanalytic circles. He began practicing psychoanalysis at the age of twenty-three, two years before completing medical school at the University of Vienna. Such an early start assumed the blessings of Freud, since Freud was the only person with sufficient referrals to insure a private practice. By 1927, Reich was on the executive committee of the Vienna Psychoanalytic Association and the leader of a technical seminar. Reich's technical skills made him one of the analysts most sought after by American students who had come to Vienna to learn therapeutic procedures.

The 1920s produced an increased radicalization of Reich's thought. In the early 1920s Reich served as assistant chief at the Vienna Psychoanalytic Polyclinic, which provided therapy for laborers and other people on low incomes. Reich saw that poverty led to emotional problems noticeably different from those described by Freud. Reich's patients had what he described as an "impulsive character." This was a borderline disorder between neurosis and psychosis characterized by psychopathic, antisocial, and self-destructive behavior. These individuals were often dismissed as "bad" by society because their personality led to crime, addictions, and fits of uncontrollable rage. These traits were attributed to the socioeconomic conditions, sexual repression, and displaced hostility characteristic of lower-middle-class homes.

Reich's radical politics and abrasive personality caused him to leave Vienna in 1930 and go to Berlin. In Berlin he made contact with a new group of young psychoanalysts, which included Karen Horney and Erich Fromm, who were beginning to stress social factors and were more sympathetic to his ideas. His book *The Mass Psychology of Fascism* was written during this period and published in 1933. The book was partly a reaction to the rise of Nazism in Germany. It was translated into English in 1946, but the English translation was a weaker and somewhat Americanized version of the original text.[6] The original work predates the publication of Fromm's more popular treatment of the same topic by almost a decade. Both Fromm (1939/1941) and Adorno, Frenkel-Brunswik, Levinson, and Sanford (1950) drew from Reich's work in their description of the authoritarian personality.

Reich felt that personality consisted of three layers. On the surface, the average person is polite, reserved, compassionate, and responsible. There would be few social problems if this surface layer reflected actual human nature. A second layer consists of cruel, sadistic, and envious impulses. Reich equated this level with the Freudian unconscious and felt that it could be tapped from time to time by authoritarian leaders. But Reich felt that these antisocial feelings resulted from repressing even more basic biological needs, such as sex. Below the second layer was a third, deeper psychological substratum, the *biological core,* in which, under favorable conditions, people would be basically honest, industrious, cooperative, and loving. No society had yet produced such conditions, but such a society was possible.

Reich felt that each stratum corresponded to a particular political attitude. The surface layer was the focus of liberals and liberal reformers, and, one might add, the majority of contemporary social psychologists. The emphasis on this level has produced what French social psychologist Serge Moscovici (1972) has called the "social psychology of the nice person."

Fascism focused on the second level. For Reich, fascism was the organized political expression of frustrated people's character. Fascism was not limited to a particular party, nation, or race. It was the attitude of suppressed individuals in an authoritarian society. Fascism was neither specifically German nor specifically Japanese but international. There are German fascists, French fascists, and even Jewish fascists. In fact, Reich felt that there was not any single individual whose character does not possess some fascist elements. Fascism is the mentality of the "little man" who is enslaved and craves authority but who is rebellious at the same time. The deepest layer of personality has never been tapped by any existing cultures, but Reich felt that it is possible to envision a society in which basic needs are not strongly repressed.

Marxism failed in Europe because it tried to understand twentieth-century fascism with concepts of rationality derived from the nineteenth century. Rationally considered, one would expect that poverty and unemployment would lead to greater social awareness and a demand for social change.

But basic aspects of a person's character are formed in early childhood and may be resistant to later change. The character of the authoritarian family with its strong domineering father, strict discipline, and numerous children, each competing for parental affection, tends to set up expectations about future social relations. Competition is seen as natural and one's own personal insignificance can be offset by selecting and identifying with a strong leader. The family plays a major role in establishing an authoritarian character, and this character, once established, tends to favor a fascist ideology.

Reich placed a great deal of emphasis on sexual repression. Premarital sexual intercourse and even masturbation are strictly forbidden in most lower-class homes. Frustrated sexual needs cause a deep resentment toward authority that cannot be expressed. The resulting ambivalence and the need to control it fosters authoritarian values, such as honor, duty, and self-control. Paternal religions, with their emphasis on an "almighty father," tend to encourage a sense of personal worthlessness and provide a supernatural sanction for authoritarian values.

Fascism appeals most to people from lower middle class families who are poor or marginally employed. Because large families were typical, individuals readily identified with their nation's need for more space and supported policies of colonization and territorial expansion. Competition among families becomes the prototype for competition among nations and various racial and ethnic groups. Racism plays an important part in fascist ideology because it allows impoverished individuals with little personal power to identify themselves with the "master race."

A special place is allotted to women in a fascist society. They are simultaneously glorified as mothers and treated as social inferiors. Severe sexual repression causes the sexual act even after marriage to be tinged with anxiety and guilt. The inability to enjoy sexual intercourse increases the sense of sexual frustration. Reich predicted that a more open sexual attitude and women's liberation would be a severe blow to fascism and authoritarian ideology.

Feelings of weakness and insignificance

increase during times of economic stress and cause authoritarian individuals to seek out an authoritarian leader. This leader ("der Führer") is a father substitute who personifies the nation's values and combines attributes, such as strength and forcefulness, sought after in one's own father. "Saber rattling" and a militaristic attitude are often more important than concrete solutions to existing socioeconomic problems. When specific policies are offered, they are often adapted to particular audiences. Hitler succeeded in Germany because he offered each class more power, and each group saw him as the personal champion of their partiular cause. These ideologies, once formed, reshape individuals (and provide a sense of social solidarity).

Reich introduced his ideas on the authoritarian character while Freud was still alive, and it might be of some interest to describe Freud's reaction. Freud favored general social reform (including a more even distribution of wealth), but he opposed violent revolution on humanitarian grounds. He sympathized with the progressive reforms of the Austrian Socialist Party when it was in power, but he never voted for it. He voted for the Liberal Party on those few occasions when it offered candidates (Jones, 1957). Freud once told Jones that he had recently talked with an ardent communist and had been half converted to bolshevism. He had been told that a bolshevik revolution would result in some years of misery and chaos but would be followed by universal peace. He believed the first half.

In 1932, Reich submitted his paper on the integration of Marx and Freud. He had previously established himself as an up-and-coming psychoanalyst through his work *Character Analysis* (published in book form in 1933). Freud opposed the paper because it "culminated in the nonsensical statement that . . . the death instinct is a product of the capitalist system" (Jones, 1957, p. 166). The paper was published, but Reich resigned from the International Psychoanalytic Association in 1934 as a result of the dispute.

It is important to note that Freud's opposition was not based on "ideological" considerations but on his intransigent belief in the death instinct. Freud considered the death instinct universal, whereas Reich considered it a result of sexual repression in contemporary society. It should be noted that at this time there was no "official" opposition to psychoanalysis among Marxists. Two thousand copies of the Russian translation of Freud's *Introductory Lectures* were sold in Moscow the first month after it was introduced (Jones, 1957).

Reich's stress on the social origins of character and mental illness gradually led him to stress prevention rather than cure. He advocated better housing, health care, and education, but felt that these changes could only come about through economic reform. In his early period, he was quite active in the Communist Party, but with time he began to feel that the problems were too ingrained and became increasingly pessimistic about the possibility of social change. This pessimism, along with his strong emphasis on sexuality, led to his expulsion from the Communist Party in the mid-1930s. Thus, in spite of or perhaps because of his attempts to integrate Freud and Marx, Reich is the only person who has been expelled from both the International Psychoanalytic Association and the Communist Party.

Reich was not the only person who attempted to integrate Freud and Marx during the 1930s (see Jacoby, 1983). The effort was widespread, and Freud often came under criticism for his opposition to these attempts. In a letter to a critic, Freud wrote,

> I know that my comments on Marxism are no evidence either of a thorough knowledge or of a correct understanding of the writings of Marx and Engels. I have since learned—rather to my satisfaction—that neither of them has denied the influence of ideas and superego factors. That invalidates the main contrast between Marxism and psychoanalysis which I had believed to exist. As to the 'dialectic' I am no clearer, even after your letter (cited in Jones, 1957, p. 245).

## Erich Fromm (1900–1980)

Fromm's description of the authoritarian individual is similar to Reich's but he was less concerned with sexual repression and more concerned with the fear of and escape from freedom in contemporary culture. Fromm received a Ph.D. in sociology from the University of Heidelberg in 1922 with a dissertation on three Jewish communities and studied psychoanalysis at the Berlin Psychoanalytic Institute, completing his training in 1929. Fromm was one of the first "lay psychoanalysts"—that is, a therapist practicing psychoanalysis without medical training. In the early thirties, he divided his time between a clinical practice in Berlin and a position at the University of Frankfurt's Institute for Social Research. Both Reich and Fromm were associated with the University of Frankfurt's Institute for Social Research, which had been established in 1923 and had a Marxist orientation (see Jay, 1973). Like many Marxist thinkers in Western Europe after World War I and the Bolshevik Revolution, members of the institute were committed to a form of Marxism based on democracy and human emancipation. During the thirties, under the directorship of Max Horkheimer, there was an increasing interest in integrating psychoanalytic and Marxist theory in order to obtain a broader understanding of the interplay between psychological factors and historical change.

Fromm's background in sociology gives his work a sociological sophistication missing in Reich's work. He draws not only from Freud and Marx but from other social thinkers, particularly Max Weber, and describes not only fascism but the transformation of character brought on by industrialization. Fromm began his work on the authoritarian character in the late 1920s. In 1929 and 1930, he directed a study of attitudes among German workers supported by the Frankfurt Institute. This study used a questionnaire consisting of 271 open-ended questions that are in many ways remarkably similar to the items later used by Adorno and his associates at Berkeley. It contained over thirty questions tapping what was later called political and economic conservatism and forty questions that correspond to the scale later used to measure potential fascism, as well as questions about living conditions and family relations. Questions about anti-Semitism, however, were not included (Christie & Jahoda, 1954).

Fromm was familiar with Reich's work and reviewed one of his books in the early 1930s. He used the opportunity to stress the differences between Reich's position and his own. This led to a scathing rebuke by Reich and a period of subsequent estrangement in which Fromm cited Reich relatively infrequently. In 1934, Fromm moved to New York, started a private practice, and resumed his role as director of social psychology at the Frankfurt Institute, which had been recently relocated at Columbia University. This move corresponds with a general shift in style in which he begins to write for a more general audience. The number of citations and footnotes decreases, and Fromm begins to cite more indigenous American thinkers such as Emerson, Thoreau, and John Dewey. For those unfamiliar with his earlier German work, this can give the mistaken impression that Fromm developed his ideas *after* he came to America (see Burston, 1989, for a more comprehensive review).

Fromm's (1939/1941) most important work on the authoritarian character is his book *Escape from Freedom* His central thesis is that contemporary individuals have been freed from the bonds of traditional society but have not gained freedom in the positive sense of being able to realize their unique potential. Freedom has brought independence and self-reliance, but it has also made people feel weak, isolated, and alone. This isolation forces them to seek new forms of social contact and direction from authoritarian leaders.

Fromm was interested in the relationship between socioeconomic conditions, character, and ideology. He felt that people adapt to socioeconomic contitions by changing themselves, and these changes in character help determine ideology and mold social conditions. Social character is a collection of widely shared traits derived from living under specific economic conditions. He outlined changes in social character, beginning with the Middle Ages and continuing into the modern age.

There is a tendency to either glorify or condemn the Middle Ages depending on one's perspective. It was a period of social solidarity, direct and concrete human relations, and relative economic security. The market was limited. A producer knew how much to produce and could sell all that was made. The medieval church stressed the dignity of man, free will, and brotherhood. But there was no freedom in the modern sense. A person could not advance socially or even move geographically from place to place. Most people lived and died where they were born and seldom ventured beyond the small territory that constituted their entire world.

The Protestant Reformation was a reaction to the breakdown of the medieval economy, as well as to the excesses within the Catholic church. Martin Luther (1483–1546) sought to reform the church, whereas John Calvin (1509–1564) created a new religion that preached predestination and the virtues of hard work. Both men helped shape a new religious outlook that stressed the innate evil of human nature. By undermining the authority of the church, they eliminated the vast Catholic hierarchy that previously stood between God and lay people. Each person was now alone before God, cut off from others. For Luther, salvation came through complete surrender to an all-knowing and all-powerful God. This created a tension between the desire for independence, on the one hand, and the desire for guidance and control gained from submission to an outside authority. The individual gained a sense of freedom (in the limited sense of freedom from traditional sources of authority), but at the cost of feeling utterly alone.

For Calvin, predestination meant that people were divided into two groups—the saved and the damned—before they were born and nothing they do could change their fate. Hard work and unceasing effort would not alter their destiny, but it could be used to convince a person that he or she was one of the elect. Success was a sign of God's grace. Religious compulsion drove people to work to an extent previously possible only with a very severe slave driver. At the same time, they denied themselves any compensation in the form of worldly pleasures. This represented a major change in

character structure and helped produce the psychological motivation for modern capitalism.

This belief in hard work continued into the 1800s but was eventually softened, at least philosphically, by Utilitarian morality. All were expected to act in their own best interests but with the common good in mind. By the turn of the century, there was a widespread belief that reason and science would prevail. Economic crises were considered accidents, even though they recurred on a regular basis. The world looked safe, like the well-lit streets of a modern city. World War I shattered this illusion and gave rise to the socioeconomic conditions that made fascism possible.

Fromm concentrated on the interaction between economic conditions, ideology, and personality in order to explain the rise of Nazism in Germany. Like Reich, he felt that Nazism appealed mostly to the lower-middle class. Before World War I, this class suffered economic setbacks, but its overall condition was relatively stable. Religion, tradition, and the undisputed authority of the monarchy provided a sense of stability and cultural continuity. The family was solid and provided a safe refuge in an otherwise hostile world. Although a man personally may have had little chance of success, by saving and working hard, he could at least provide his children with an opportunity for social advancement.

The situation changed radically after World War I. The defeat and the downfall of the monarchy shook the belief in traditional authority. Inflation destroyed the principle of thrift and further undermined the authority of the state. Savings that had accumulated after many years of sacrificing many little pleasures were completely wiped out by the economic crisis of 1923. People in Europe had suffered economic setbacks before, but they had never experienced a situation in which their currency had become worthless. There was some economic recovery between 1924 and 1928, but this was followed by a virtual worldwide depression in 1929.

The economic crisis brought changes that were especially detrimental to the lower-middle class. Because of the successes of worker movements, the prestige of the middle class declined relative to industrial workers. There was no one left to look down on. The family was shattered as an institution. The old middle-class values based on frugality, thrift, and caution seemed out of place in a society based on initiative, risk, and aggression. The younger generation considered itself smarter and superior to its parents, and the parents were deprived of their cherished role as the economic backers of the next generation. The saturation of professional job markets meant that there were few opportunities for social advancement. There was widespread discontent, particularly among young officers who had served in the First World War. They felt humiliated at having to accept jobs as clerks and traveling salesmen. The time was ripe for social change, and Adolf Hitler provided an option.

While Adolf Hitler received the active support of the lower-middle class, other elements, such as workers, liberals, and Catholic businessmen, eventually submitted. There was a weariness with the economic situation and a sense of resignation after the failures of the previous government. After the Nazi Party gained power and abolished the parties on the left, it became associated with Germany as a whole. To attack it was to attack Germany. It is important to note that the fear of freedom and its subsequent avoidance are the result of specific socioeconomic factors and *not* a natural part of the human condition. This fear was considerably less intense in previous periods and reached a peak under the severe conditions of the 1930s. Fromm felt that it could be reduced by eliminating unemployment and offering economic security. Under these conditions, individuals could develop their own unique talents through creative work and loving relationships. He felt that society had reached the level of technical sophistication sufficient to meet everyone's basic needs, but it lacked the social will to distribute goods and services in a fair and even manner.

Fromm (1947, 1964) later made a clearer distinction between reactive aggression, which is a normal biological response to threat and frustration, and the malignant,

pathological hatred characteristic of the authoritarian character. He described a "necrophilous" character type who hates life and worships things that are dead and mechanical. Such a person may express this drive either through overt sexual perversion (which is rare) or in a bureaucratic tendency to treat people as objects. His treatment of this destructive drive underwent several modifications in subsequent years (again see Burston, 1989) but common to each of them is the belief that persistent aggression results from the suppression of more primary drives aimed at growth and development.

According to Fromm (1955), not only individuals but whole societies can be pathological. Societies are healthy when they fulfill basic human needs, such as the need to belong and relate to other people, to create, and to establish a stable identity and a frame of reference. Societies that frustrate human needs are sick, no matter how much they produce. Self-hatred and hatred of others go together, and the amount varies from person to person and from culture to culture.

Fromm's book *Escape from Freedom* brought him wide recognition, and interest in the source of the authoritarian character structure continued in the postwar period (see Chapter 9). Unlike Reich, who moved away from Freud and Marx, Fromm continued to weave aspects of their theories into his prodigious writings. His later work was also influenced by elements of existentialism and mysticism. With the exception of his analysis of authoritarianism, his work has had little impact on American social psychology. It was simply too theoretical, impressionistic, and out of step with the increasing emphasis on empirical research. Nevertheless, as Burston (1989) has pointed out, his theoretical analysis of conformity bears a striking affinity to the experimental work produced in the 1950s and 1960s (see Chapter 9).

## J. F. Brown (1902–1970)

Junius Flagg Brown was born in Denver, Colorado, and came from a locally prominent and wealthy family. After completing his undergraduate degree at Yale in 1925, he received a two-year fellowship to study psychology at the University of Berlin, where he was exposed to the Gestalt psychology of Wolfgang Köhler (his advisor) and Max Wertheimer and worked closely with Kurt Lewin. Brown returned to Yale and completed his Ph.D. in 1929. The same year he published an article summarizing Lewin's theory and research (Brown, 1929). Brown was one of the first Americans to work with Lewin, and his article introduced a generation of Americans to Lewin's approach.

By the mid-thirties, Brown's interest began to shift from perception to theoretical issues and the social and political implications of psychology. These new directions in his thinking culminated in a social psychology textbook, *Psychology and the Social Order* (Brown, 1936), in which he attempted to integrate the ideas of Freud, Marx, and Lewin. Freud, according to Brown, provided a relatively detailed description of biological drives and the way they were frustrated, but he lacked a theory of the relationship between drives and social conditions. Because he assumed that barriers imposed by society were chiefly biological, he tended to be pessimistic about the possibility of liberating individuals from excessive repression through social change.

Brown felt that Marxism and field theory could be used to provide a metatheoretical framework for understanding general and social psychology. He noted several points of convergence. Both theories emphasize the importance of theory in scientific research, stress social change rather than mere interpretation, show a concern with dynamic processes and laws rather than static conditions, and stress the need to produce social conditions that enhance the fulfillment of human needs. By including a Marxist perspective, Brown drew attention to the objective character of the social world and its impact on social-psychological processes. He felt, for example, that during periods of economic depression when opportunities for social mobility are limited, there was an increased sense of class struggle and class consciousness. While field theory fo-

cused on the inner dynamics of small face-to-face groups, Marxism could be used to describe the larger sociological, political, and economic contexts and their influence on behavior. Brown's Marxism was wedded to the Soviet version, and he saw Russia in the 1930s as the ideal sociopolitical system.

Brown was highly critical of the psychology of his day because he felt it lacked a theoretical framework and avoided important social and political issues, such as poverty and the rising tide of fascism in Europe. He argued that, because psychologists and other social scientists come largely from middle-class backgrounds, it was in their interest to deny the existence of a class struggle, and in some cases, even the concept of class itself. Psychologists, by failing to recognize their implicit values, dispensed knowledge consistent with their vested interest, and in the guise of neutral objectivity, helped maintain the status quo.

Brown's (1936) work was and still is by today's standards an unusually comprehensive text, consisting of sections on the philosophy of science, group membership, personality, and the social-psychological effects of different political systems. It was generally well received because of its ambitious and innovative quality (Minton, 1984, 1988a). Its broad theoretical perspective and sociopolitical overtones stood in marked contrast to the rather atheoretical, empirically oriented social psychology that characterized the psychological approach during the twenties and thirties. In the late thirties, some of today's most prominent social psychologists obtained their first taste of the discipline by reading Brown's provocative text (Sarason, 1988; Smith, 1986a). Some limitations, such as the focus on ideology rather than intervention and the difficulty of translating theoretical concepts into specific research problems, were noted, however.

The lasting influence of the text was limited by an abrupt change in Brown's thinking. In the late 1930s, Brown began to shift his interest from Marxism and social psychology to Freudian theory and abnormal psychology. Brown's faith in the Soviet system and Marxism itself, like that of many other intellectuals, was shattered in 1939 when Hitler and Stalin signed their non-aggression treaty. He suffered a psychotic breakdown two years later and was hospitalized for a brief time. He left his teaching position at the University of Kansas, and after the war settled in Los Angeles, where he set up a private practice in clinical psychology and collaborated with Adorno and his associates on their work on the authoritarian personality.

As a result, he never revised his text, and by the late 1940s with the dawning of the McCarthy era, it quickly went out of fashion. Nevertheless, beginning in the early 1970s, Brown's radical social psychology has received a renaissance of interest. He anticipated many of the criticisms of contemporary social psychology and argued for a social psychology that stressed social factors rather than the individual and one that was concrete rather than abstract and particular rather than general. His attempt to produce a social psychology that is embedded within a historical and sociopolitical context anticipated one of the central themes of the postmodern movement in social psychology (see Chapter 13).

## THE SOCIETY FOR THE PSYCHOLOGICAL STUDY OF SOCIAL ISSUES

One of the most immediate problems facing psychologists during the depression was unemployment among psychologists themselves (see Finison, 1976, 1978, 1979, 1986). Although the number of professors remained unchanged, the number of new openings at the instructor level was very limited. Many highly trained professionals were unable to find work. Two solutions were suggested—either reduce the number of psychologists by increasing admission standards to graduate programs or increase the number of jobs. The first solution was favored by many older, established psychologists, whereas the second was the choice of the young and the unemployed. The attempt to expand the number of jobs for psychologists led to the formation of two some-

what competing groups of social activists— New America and the Psychologists League.

The Psychologists League, founded in 1934, was a New York–based group whose principal mission was securing jobs for psychologists through federal support in the Works Progress Administration. It drew up a series of proposals that included placing psychologists in the school systems, in penitentiaries, and in neighborhood clinics. Although the group's activities were aimed primarily at psychologists, its aims were not merely self-serving. It advocated coordinating its activities with other professional and workers' groups for the purpose of providing much-needed social services in areas where psychologists could be of use. The League also had close connections with the American Communist Party, and the *Psychologists League Journal* included Marxist and other sociopolitical critiques of psychological theory and practice. The fact that the League was based in New York and made up primarily of clinical psychologists limited its influence on psychology at the national level.

New America was centered in New York and Chicago and combined elements of Marxism with John Dewey's populist position. Two of its members, Goodwin Watson and David Krech, played leading roles in lobbying the American Psychological Association to become responsive to social issues, including unemployment among psychologists. In 1934, Goodwin Watson, a social psychologist at Columbia's Teachers College whose mentors were Dewey and William H. Kilpatrick, corresponded with a significant number of prominent psychologists soliciting them to form an APA-affiliated organization devoted to social issues (Harris, 1986; Nicholson & Minton, 1989). Watson acted on behalf of an organizing committee based in New York. In a similar vein, Krech, who completed his doctorate under Edward C. Tolman, worked with other New America psychologists in Chicago (Finison, 1979, 1986). In 1935, the Chicago group sent a petition to the American Psychological Association asking them to respond to the unemployment situation. This petition included the names of psychologists from all over the United States except New York (apparently designed to complement Watson's effort). Krech and his associates also prepared an advertisement published in the radical newspaper *American Guardian.* The ad was sent to everyone in the American Psychological Association under 40, asking those interested to respond to "important contemporary problems of social and economic change." As a result of these efforts, the Society for the Psychological Study of Social Issues (SPSSI) was founded at the 1936 APA convention, with Watson as president and Krech as secretary-treasurer. Within a year, one of every six members of the American Psychological Association belonged to SPSSI as well. After World War II, SPSSI was given division status within the American Psychological Association, and its newsletter became an independent journal, the *Journal of Social Issues.*[7]

The initial leadership of SPSSI was quite progressive. It included four members of the Socialist Party (L. W. Doob, Horace B. English, George W. Hartmann, and Ross Stagner), three New Americans (David Krech, Goodwin Watson, and Franklin Fearing) and one independent Marxist (J. F. Brown), plus Gordon Allport, Ernest R. Hilgard, Edward C. Tolman, and Gardner Murphy. The original members envisioned an organization concerned with both research and social action (Finison, 1986; Mednick, 1984; Morawski, 1986b), but only the former objective remained once the group was organized. After much debate, the group decided to focus on research rather than action. This decision was made in order to attract a broad spectrum of psychologists. The members were optimistic that socially relevant research would lead to improvements in the human condition. As Watson (1937) declared in his presidential address, "The most trustworthy methods of scientific intelligence, applied to questions most critical for our social welfare, will represent an orientation which faces, indeed, an inspiring sunrise!" (p. 26).

During its early years, SPSSI supported work on various social issues, paricularly those concerned with industrial conflict and war and peace. One of the first projects was an edited book on industrial conflict (Hartmann & Newcomb, 1939). This work, however, was marked by the same dissension that had plagued the founding of SPSSI—that is, the appropriate relationship between science and social action (Finison, 1986). Some claimed that scientific objectivity leads directly to social action. In their critique of the politically neutral position of "liberal" social science, Hadley Cantril and David Katz argued that "the 'open-minded' scientist remains open minded on social issues where a genuinely objective approach would long since have produced conviction" (quoted in Finison, 1986, p. 29). In the liberal view, scientific thought must be separated from political action, and ethics and values only influence the choice of topics to be studied. This position asked psychologists to contribute their expertise to current social issues—in essence to become social engineers.

## SOCIAL PSYCHOLOGY AND WORLD WAR II

The liberal stance of scientific neutrality was dominant in SPSSI's subsequent project on national morale during World War II (Watson, 1942). As Finison (1986) points out, a related belief that psychologists could use their scientific neutrality to assume the role of intermediaries between the citizen and the state emerged as part of this project as well. At the start of the war, psychologists began to change the way they perceived their social role. During the thirties, psychologists who were active in SPSSI and the Psychologists League developed relationships with political organizations that represented the labor movement and the working class, but in the 1940s psychologists began to see themselves as *interpreters* of feelings and aspirations of the working class. In discussing the problem of morale among workers and blacks, for example, it was argued that social reform must take place at the federal level. Thus, rather than working as compatriots with grass-roots groups such as trade unions, psychologists now saw themselves as intermediaries between the political elite and the oppressed.

This new self-image among psychologists was part of a more encompassing change in the relationship between psychologists and the federal government. Soon after Pearl Harbor, the government actively recruited psychologists, and a massive amount of research funds became available for studies of morale, leadership, and group dynamics. Psychologists and other social scientists were assigned to a wide variety of government agencies. Finison (1986) suggests that, as a result of the war and the subsequent involvement of psychologists in the war effort, psychologists developed much closer contacts with government elites and "social scientists, the outsiders of the 1930s, became the insiders of the postwar era" (p. 32).

The most extensive project carried out at the time was undertaken in the Army's Division of Information and Education. Within this division, a research branch was formed with Samuel A. Stouffer as director. Leonard S. Cottrell, a sociologist, headed the section concerned with survey studies, and Carl I. Hovland was in charge of experimental research. The results of this research were eventually published in four volumes, known as the American soldier series (e.g., Stouffer, Suchman, De Vinney, Star, & Williams, 1949). More than a half million soldiers, stationed worldwide, were surveyed on questions ranging from their preferences for radio programs to attitudes toward native populations.

World War II had its greatest impact on the discipline belatedly, in the postwar period. The massive amount of research conducted during the war provided a basis for a number of new areas of investigation, such as organizational psychology, economic behavior, and political behavior (Cartwright, 1979). Another significant outcome was the professional networks that emerged as a result of wartime collaboration (Capshew, 1986). Many of the leading figures in postwar social psychology made professional contacts with each other during the war. World War II put social psychology on the map. As Cartwright (1979) declared, the war "established social psychology, once and for all, as a legitimate

field of specialization worthy of public support" (p. 84).

But the war also changed the way social psychologists approached their discipline. The radicalism of the 1930s eventually faded and with it the tendency to see social psychology within a larger social, political, and economic context. The absence of an institutional context resulted in a pendulum swing back to a focus on the individual, which could be seen even in the study of groups. The apolitical attitude of scientific neutrality and the lack of options within American society during the postwar period came hauntingly close to Karl Mannheim's (1929/1936) description of a society devoid of utopian ideals "absorbed by its interest in concrete and isolated details" and a social science "split up into a series of discrete technical problems of social readjustment":

> The complete disappearance of the utopian element from human thought and action would mean that human nature and human development would take on a totally new character.... We would be faced then with the greatest paradox imaginable, namely, that man, who has achieved the highest degree of rational mastery of existence, left without any ideals, becomes a mere creature of impulses. Thus, after a long, tortuous, but heroic development, just at the highest stage of awareness, when history is ceasing to be blind fate, and is becoming more and more man's own creation, with the relinquishment of utopias, man would lose his will to shape history, and therewith his ability to understand it. (pp. 262–263)

## NOTES

1. Clark Hull (1884–1952) was a professor of psychology at Yale University, and one of the most influential learning theorists who tried to develop a comprehensive model that would explain both animal and human behavior. Unlike radical behaviorists, such as J. B. Watson and B. F. Skinner, who tended to stress overt behavior, Hull explained learning primarily in terms of habits and drive reduction and his model con-

tains a number of intervening variables. Habits are acquired when stimulus and responses are followed by a decrease in the intensity of a drive or motive. Drives include both primary drives, such as hunger, thirst, and sex, and secondary drives learned through association. John Dollard and Neil Miller attempted to combine elements of Hull's learning theory with psychoanalysis in their social learning theory. Hull also had a strong influence on Carl Hovland and his associates at the Institute of Human Relations at Yale University.

2. Durkheim referred to preindustrial theories as *communiste* and industrial theories as *socialiste,* but these terms have so many other connotations today that they are not very useful for making the distinction that he intended.

3. This division is very different from contemporary attempts to derive social class from a combination of income, educational level, and occupational prestige. This conception obscures the conflict between workers and owners and implies that class differences can be eliminated by increasing wages and educational opportunities.

4. Marx was not the first to note that working conditions help shape the way we think. Adam Smith (1776/1937) had previously pointed out that

> The understanding of the greater part of men is necessarily formed by their environment. The man whose whole life is spent in performing a few simple operations, of which the effects too

are, perhaps always the same, or nearly the same, has no occasion to exert his understanding. . . . He naturally loses, therefore, the habit of such exertion and generally becomes as stupid and ignorant as is possible for a human creature to become. (pp. 735–736)

5. Weber's opposition to Marx was based partly on the fact that many of Marx's early writings, in which he developed his thoughts on the relationship between consciousness and socioeconomic conditions, were not published until after Weber's death (see Giddens, 1971).

6. Some of these changes were relatively minor. Reich, who had become increasingly conservative, downplayed his original leftist origins. The words "communist" and "socialist" were replaced by "progressive." "Class consciousness" became "work consciousness" or "social responsibility." Other changes were more dramatic. New material was added on orgone energy and vegotherapy, which linked it to Reich's subsequent mental breakdown. Because it refers to orgone energy, it was burned along with Reich's other books during the Food and Drug Administration's campaign against Reich in the 1950s and was not re-released until 1969 (see Sharaf, 1983).

7. Many sociological social psychologists also joined SPSSI. However, SPSSI's link with the APA eventually led the sociologists to form their own organization in 1951, the Society for the Study of Social Problems (Lee, 1986).

# PART III

# THE POST–WORLD WAR II PROMISE OF SOCIAL PSYCHOLOGY (1945–1970)

# 9

# Small Groups and Intergroup Relations

The changes taking place after World War II represent a period of increasing professionalization as both psychological and sociological social psychology developed new procedures and began to increase their base of data substantially. These changes are characteristic of most well-established academic disciplines and are in some respects a sign of their growing maturity. Once a discipline has become firmly entrenched, its methods, techniques, and theoretical orientation are more or less taken for granted. This representes a stage of development that Thomas Kuhn (1962) has described as "normal science." The dominant thinkers define the nature and limits of research for both themselves and their students, who in turn have a similar influence once they become well established. Major researchers in each field have a vested interest in preserving their own methods and theories, and for this reason the disciplines tend to become self-serving and conservative. The developments taking place tend to be regarded as more and more insular and less suceptible to outside influences and come to be seen as the product of purely internal changes that seem to have a life of their own.

While the main areas of research often do reflect internal developments, they are also strongly influenced by broader intellectual and cultural trends. As we have seen, the history of social psychology has been based on a number of pendulum swings, from a broad conern with social and cultural issues to a more limited focus on individual psychological processes. These patterns have corresponded more or less with similar changes within society as a whole. During the late 1940s and early 1950s, there was a general shift away from the concern with economic and social problems that was characteristic of those working during World War II and the Great Depression.

The postwar period was a time of unprecedented prosperity. During the peacetime economic recovery, the gross national product of the United States grew from 200 billion dollars in 1946 to a high of 500 billion dollars in 1960. The economy expanded at an annual growth rate of almost 5% during the 1950s, and most Americans experienced an enormous increase in their standard of living. The period witnessed the triumph of mass democratic, middle-class values in which abundance, conformity, and conspicuous consumption were the main concern. By 1959, one-fourth of the American population had achieved the American dream of owning a home in the suburbs, complete with most of the latest home appliances.

Television replaced the radio as America's favorite pastime, and many Americans spent more time watching television than they did working for a living. Their favorite television shows included situation comedies, such as "I Love Lucy," and game shows, such as Revlon's infamous "Sixty-four-Thousand-Dollar Question." Americans seemed so preoccupied with material success that they did not seem to care that their favorite quiz-show hero, the Columbia University English professor, Charles Van Doren, had conned the public in his dramatic and seemingly brilliant performance. After early denials, he finally admitted before a Senate hearing that the program had indeed been rigged (Diggins, 1988).

While the postwar prosperity gave most Americans more time for leisure pursuits, it also helped promote a more conservative political and social climate. Even education underwent a change in emphasis as more and more Americans began to see it as a way of getting ahead and realizing the American dream. As a direct result of increased federal aid to education and various programs designed to provide an education to returning veterans, more Americans attended colleges and universities than ever before. Many professors objected to such materialistic values, but given the conservative political climate and the anticommunism associated with the McCarthy era, most of them kept a low profile and refused to challenge or upset the status quo.

The professors' concern with persecution was quite real. Along with actors and those within the State Department, university professors were a favorite target of anticommunist assaults. During the Truman and Eisenhower administrations, approximately six hundred teachers and professors were fired. At the University of California, for example, the Board of Regents imposed a loyalty oath on all members of the faculty, and professors were given the ultimatum of either signing it or losing their jobs (Diggins, 1988). Postwar intellectuals generally abandoned the political ideologies based on collective action and accepted the idea that society consisted of an aggregation of individuals. Peels (1985) has pointed out that

the search for identity inspired the writers and artists of the 1950s. Where social critics had once insisted on the need for collective action, they now urged the individual to resist the pressures of conformity. . . . The primary danger was no longer social inequality but standardization and uniformity, not economic exploitation but the moral consequences of abundance. (p. 187)

The fifties have been described critically as the "placid" decade, yet underneath the surface the postwar prosperity had produced its own problems and responses. The decade generated some of the finest com-

mentaries on American life, including C. Wright Mills's (1956) *The Power Elite,* William Riesman's (1956) *The Lonely Crowd,* William Whytes's (1956) *The Organization Man,* John Kenneth Galbraith's (1959) *The Affluent Society,* Daniel Bell's (1960) *The End of Ideology,* and Paul Goodman's (1960) *Growing up Absurd.* Each of these works concentrated on the attitudes and values of Americans as they confronted the underlying tensions associated with middle-class culture. These tensions were most apparent among the younger generation, who experienced a restless searching for some sense of meaning, and they were epitomized in the personal lives and movies of such Hollywood heroes as Marlon Brando and James Dean. Dean and Brando expressed the contempt for the mundane conventions of an affluent society that was widely shared by social critics and thinkers during the same period.

The general trends occurring during the postwar period strongly influenced developments within social psychology. American social psychology underwent a series of changes that more or less corresponded to changes taking place within American society itself. In 1944, toward the end of the war, a group of prominent psychologists, including Gordon Allport, Gardner Murphy, and Edward C. Tolman, circulated a "psychologists' manifesto" on human nature and peace (Smith, 1986a). The manifesto was sent to psychologists at large in order to obtain their signatures and create a widely supported document that could influence postwar policies, such as peace treaties and the development of the United Nations. Among the principles proclaimed were the following:

> *War can be avoided: War is not born in men; it is built into men.*
> *Condescension toward "inferior" groups destroys our chances for a lasting peace.*
> *Racial, national, and group hatreds can, to a considerable degree, be controlled.*
> *The root-desires of the common people of all lands are the safest guide to framing peace.* (quoted in Smith, 1986a, p. 30)

These statements show that psychologists were optimistic that psychological knowledge could contribute to postwar recovery. Their participation in the war effort produced an increased sense of legitimacy and professional identity. Social psychologists, in particular, were eager to apply their expertise to the solution of pressing social problems.

The postwar period was a time of pessimism about the world in general but optimism about the ability of the social sciences to bring about meaningful social change (McGrath, 1980a, 1980b). There was a pervasive feeling that social science could be used to identify and solve a wide range of social problems. There was a conflict between liberals, who felt that the problems could be solved one at a time, and socialists, who called for more sweeping social and economic reforms, but the general feeling was one of hope.

Within this climate, social psychology came of age. Social psychologists profited from their wartime accomplishments and were now ready to convert their new vision of the field into reality (Cartwright, 1979). New research centers were established, such as the Research Center for Group Dynamics, and graduate programs were developed. The strong consensus about what should be studied and how it should be approached was based partly on the fact that social psychology was still a relatively small discipline in the late forties and was limited to a small number of universities. Leon Festinger (1980) claims that there were four major centers for social psychology in the postward period—Berkeley, Harvard, Michigan, and Yale. The University of Michigan had inherited the Research Center for Group Dynamics after Lewin's death and combined it with the Survey Research Center to form an extremely large department. Yale included both the Communication Research Center, directed by Carl I. Hovland, and the Institute for Human Relations. Harvard's newly formed Department of Social Relations contained psychologists, sociologists, and anthropologists within the same department and stressed an interdisciplinary perspective, whereas researchers at the University of California at Berkeley continued to carry out interdisciplinary research on such topics as the authoritarian

personality. There was also a healthy exchange of both students and faculty between these institutions, which kept personal ties and lines of communication open. As Festinger (1980) put it, "The field had not yet come to the point where almost every department of psychology had to have a program in social psychology. There were still relatively few active researchers in the area, and we all knew each other" (p. 245).

This high concentration of talented individuals in a small number of institutions provided continuity in research programs, but it also seems to have produced an increasing concentration on a more and more limited range of problems. Sahakian (1982) refers to this as "contagion theory," a process whereby theories and ideas flourish through interpersonal contact. This can lead to an inbreeding of ideas, where fewer and fewer social psychologists are willing to try something new and original. Proven procedures are used again and again, not because they lead to additional insights but because they provide virtually certain results.

The relatively small network of social psychologists was also limited geographically and was virtually restricted to the United States (Cartwright, 1979). The rise of Nazism in Germany had forced many of Europe's leading intellectuals, scientists, and artists to emigrate to America. These refugees included Kurt Lewin, Fritz Heider, Paul F. Lazersfeld, T. W. Adorno, and Else Frenkel-Brunswik, all of whom played influential roles in the development of American social psychology during the postwar period. Because of this exodus, social psychology was virtually nonexistent in Europe after the war.

The American domination of social psychology has produced a discipline with a distinct set of cultural values and a particular approach to social problems. In keeping with the American emphasis on liberal democracy, social psychology has stressed the importance of the individual, reliance on rational problem solving, and the centrality of public education as a means of producing needed social change (Cartwright, 1979). When addressing social problems, at least until the 1960s, the emphasis has been on creating harmonious relations by changing the attitudes of individuals. Intergroup conflict and collective strategies for social change have generally been ignored.

By the 1950s, the period of postwar optimism was overshadowed by the cold war and the threat of Soviet subversion. While there was some cause for concern, there was also a strong current of paranoid fear, reminiscent of the red scare that had followed World War I. The roots of these fears about the political left went back at least to 1938, when Congress had established the House un-American Activities Committee. The most intense period of repression, however, centered around the activities of Senator Joseph McCarthy, who mounted his first charge of communists in government in 1950. McCarthy was discredited four years later in the Army-McCarthy hearings, but McCarthyism as a political movement lingered throughout the decade (Schrecker, 1986; Smith, 1986b).

During the fifties, postwar optimism gave way to a period of rising doubt about the ability of social science to study social problems and the capacity to *apply* research findings effectively to actual social issues (McGrath, 1980a, 1980b). There was the growing recognition that social scientists lacked the power to implement their ideas and were dependent on government officials. Many of those in power were resistant to ideas provided by social scientists because they would require sweeping economic reform. The sciences appear to have developed sequentially, starting with those that have done the least damage to people's precious illusions about themselves, beginning with mathematics and astronomy, then physics, biology, and psychology. Social psychology, particularly when blended with a Freudian awareness of unconscious factors, may be potentially the most subversive of all, because it includes an analysis of the techniques used to manipulate public opinion and maintain power.

During the 1950s, social scientists became a target of suspicion and were wary of any professional activities, or even public statements, that might be viewed as a sign of social dissent. SPSSI member Joshua Fishman expressed his concerns in a letter

to the organization in 1956, in which he stated that such conditions "made many of us less interested in rocking the boat . . . [:] the societal pressures opposing such action have mounted to new heights. . . . Social scientists not only chart and predict conformity pressures, they are also affected by them" (quoted in Samelson, 1986a, p. 192). McCarthyism affected the personal lives of many social scientists. Any academic who had ties to left-wing political groups was vulnerable. Many American professors in the 1950s were suspect because of their left-wing connections in the thirties, a time when many young intellectuals were attracted to radical causes (see Schrecker, 1986).

Even before the McCarthy era, several of the founding members of SPSSI were victims of various anticommunist crusades (Sargent & Harris, 1986). Both David Krech and George W. Hartmann lost their academic positions in the thirties because of radical political activities. During the war, both Goodwin Watson and Gardner Murphy were prevented from working for the government because of their past political associations. SPSSI provided moral and, in some cases, financial support. During the McCarthy era, SPSSI participated in the defense of several psychologists, including Edward C. Tolman, who led the campaign against mandatory loyalty oaths for faculty at the University of California.

M. Brewster Smith (1986b), who was a president of SPSSI in the late fifties, poignantly described his own experience in testifying before a senate committee on internal security in 1953. In the late thirties, as an undergraduate, he belonged to the Young Communist League. After much pressure from the committee chair, Smith agreed to supply the names of other former members. As he states:

> I gave names—the ones I had originally planned who were public in the recruiting role, but to my shame . . . people I knew well and could swear were no longer at all sympathetic to Communism. I had not intended to but I did, and that still leaves me deeply ashamed. (p.74)

Academics who failed to cooperate with such committees often lost their jobs. The dark period of the 1950s gave way to a period of optimism during the Kennedy administration, but the Kennedy assassination set the stage for a series of cataclysmic events during the rest of the decade that produced dramatic changes in American society. The full impact of these social and political upheavals was not felt until the 1970s and they will be covered in Chapters 12 and 13.

The period of doubt about the ability of social scientists to study social problems characteristic of the 1950s was followed by a period of bitter disillusionment bordering on cynicism by the mid-1960s (McGrath, 1980a, 1980b). Many people began to doubt the morality of these efforts and the high-mindedness of many of those involved. Within social psychology, it was generally recognized that certain techniques, such as behavior modification, persuasion, and attitude change, could be used for both good *and evil*. It was no longer simply assumed that they would be used for the public good. Much of the early attitude research, for example, began as studies of propaganda (Doob, 1935) designed to make people aware of techniques used to shape public opinion, but subsequent research provided advertising with a powerful arsenal of procedures that could be used to sell everything from toothpaste to nuclear missiles.

Social psychology from 1945 to 1960 went through a period of rapid expansion. In this chapter, the postwar influence of Kurt Lewin will be discussed, followed by a review of post-Lewin group psychology. The related area of intergroup relations will also be covered. Chapter 10 will focus on postwar cognitive social psychology, and Chapter 11 will cover simultaneous developments in sociological social psychology, with a strong emphasis on symbolic interaction.

## APPLIED GROUP DYNAMICS

At the end of World War II, Lewin was finishing nearly a decade of productive research at the University of Iowa, but he was becoming increasingly restless (Marrow,

1969). His wartime work required frequent travel between Iowa and Washington, and some of his colleagues resented his frequent absence and his neglect of routine academic duties. Lewin wanted to set up an independent institute where he could conduct research, but he recognized that this would require independent funds. He initially approached the Field Foundation and obtained a grant for $30,000. He was later approached by the American Jewish Committee and offered a million dollars to study community relations. With the help of these and other funds, Lewin set up not one but two centers, the Commission on Community Interrelations in New York City and the Research Center for Group Dynamics at MIT. With funds obtained through the Office of Naval Research, he also helped launch a workshop on group dynamics at the National Training Laboratories in Bethel, Maine.

### The Commission on Community Interrelations

The Commission on Community Interrelations represents the most direct application of funds obtained from the American Jewish Committee for the study of social problems. The initial purpose, like that of the Berkeley study of the authoritarian character, was to discover the roots of anti-Semitism, but the project soon expanded to include prejudice in general. The commission had three priorities: (1) to increase the effectiveness of community leaders dedicated to improving intergroup relations; (2) to study the positive and negative effects of group contact; and (3) to increase the adjustment of minority-group members. Planning sessions were held in Cambridge, Washington, and New York, but the center was finally located in New York. The commission was offically launched in 1945 and drew a distinguished staff that included Alex Bavelas, Dorwin Cartwright, Isidor Chein, Kenneth B. Clark, Stuart W. Cook, Morton Deutsch, Leon Festinger, Marie Jahoda, Ronald Lippitt, and Goodwin Watson. Lewin came to New York weekly to consult and plan programs.

The commission focused primarily on

real problems originating in the community. The first project was a case of vandalism in Coney Island. A group of Italian teenagers had disrupted a Yom Kippur service and started a fight. A survey of community attitudes showed that the incident was not due to anti-Semitism but to pent-up hostility based on poor living conditions. Recommendations were made for improved housing, transportation, and recreational activities that would bring racial and ethnic groups together in a friendly atmosphere.

In a second project, Lewin and his group successfully challenged the quota system for Jews at the medical school of Columbia University. This challenge was based on Lewin's view that changing behavior was as important as or more important than changing attitudes. Once social conditions were changed, they were often accepted as a *fait accompli.* If universities were forced to admit individuals on the basis of merit rather than religion or race, then attitudes toward minority groups would improve. This case received front-page coverage and was instrumental in eliminating similar quotas at other universities.

A third project involved attitudes toward black sales personnel at a New York department store. Managers were reluctant to use black sales clerks because they thought that customers would object. Interviews, however, showed that 64% of the shoppers and 75% of a street sample either supported the employment of black clerks or had no objection. Among twelve shoppers who strongly objected, five had been previously observed shopping at a counter with a black clerk, and two were served by a black clerk. This helped to show that the apprehension of managers was not necessary and that even when prejudice existed, it did not necessarily show up in behavior.

A fourth project involved a study of integrated housing carried out with the public housing commission of New York. Two housing projects provided separate buildings for blacks and whites, whereas two others were integrated on a first-come, first-served basis. Interviews showed that, although the buildings were similar and the ratio of each race approximately the same,

attitudes toward blacks were more positive in the integrated project. The study suggested that interracial contact under conditions where status differences were eliminated decreased suspicion and mistrust, because it gave people an opportunity to interact and share a common fate.

Many of the studies carried out by the Commission on Community Interrelations were experiments in the full sense of the word, because they either changed social conditions and studied the effect or they took advantage of changes already introduced and compared groups. Many of these projects received considerable newspaper coverage and provided the American Jewish Committee with the kind of exposure it desired. But these studies were not "controlled" experiments because extraneous factors could not always be eliminated. The need to obtain publicity and produce quick results taxed the limits of the small staff and limited the long-term consequences. In order to gain the kind of scientific credibility that he desired, Lewin sought to establish a second center affiliated with a major university in a city troubled by social problems. The choice narrowed to the University of California at Berkeley and the Massachusetts Institute of Technology in Cambridge. Although Lewin preferred Berkeley, both institutions initially lacked a definite commitment, and MIT was the first to make a firm offer.

### The Research Center for Group Dynamics

With the Commission on Community Interrelations devoted to the study of pressing social problems, the Research Center for Group Dynamics at MIT was able to devote its time and energy to more systematic and controlled research. This does not mean that its research was limited to laboratory experiments. Lewin and his students used a combination of laboratory and field studies—systematically testing ideas under controlled laboratory conditions and then confirming them through field research. The choice of MIT proved fortunate, because administrators at MIT were experienced at administering large research projects while leaving the details of the research to the workers involved.

The initial staff at MIT included Dorwin Cartwright, Leon Festinger, Ronald Lippitt, and Marian Radke, as well as Lewin. All five lived within a few blocks of one another and commuted to work. Each shared Lewin's general perspective but brought special skills in intergroup relations, laboratory procedures, statistics, and field techniques. The research center was located in the Department of Economic and Social Science, and Lewin had frequent contact with other social scientists as well as psychologists from Harvard. His students took about half of their courses at Harvard, and a growing number of graduate students from Harvard came to MIT to study with Lewin. The small staff was aware that it was part of a scientific elite that was helping to shape a new discipline. The center attracted a large number of graduate students who would later become distinguished social psychologists, including Morton Deutsch, Harold H. Kelley, Albert Pepitone, Stanley Schacter, and John W. Thibaut. Research initiated during this period included work on communication and social influence, group productivity, social perception, and leadership.

When Lewin died in 1947, many of the topics that would later form the core of group dynamics were already being addressed, but without Lewin's leadership and prestige, MIT was no longer willing to maintain the Research Center for Group Dynamics. The interests of the center were quite peripheral to those of the institution as a whole, and in 1948 it moved to the Univeristy of Michigan.

### National Training Laboratories

During the postwar period, Lewin also initiated a project that led to the development of the National Training Laboratories at Bethel, Maine. The project began when the Connecticut State Inter-Racial Commission asked him to set up a workshop for training community leaders and combating prejudice. Forty-one participants were selected, mostly teachers and social workers. About half were either Jewish or black. Most commuted and returned home in the evening, but those who remained on campus asked if they could sit in on the evening feedback session in which the events of the day were discussed. The staff was reluctant, but Lewin thought it might be helpful. The discussion generated in these sessions proved to be one of the most useful parts of the training exercise and became the prototype for sensitivity training. Feedback made participants more aware of their behavior and brought criticism into the open where it could be discussed. The following year, Lewin obtained a grant from the Office of Naval Research to set up the National Training Laboratories, but he died before it was opened.

Sensitivity training is now widely used in business, education, and therapy. It is used to train managers and provides a brief and inexpensive form of treatment for people who might not otherwise be able to obtain help. In a group setting, people can discuss with strangers topics that they may not be willing to share with friends. They can also try out and develop social skills within a supportive environment where the threat of rejection is softened by a supportive group leader. For better or worse, sensitivity training can also be traced back to Lewin and remains one of his most lasting contributions, although few people would attribute it to him.

### THE LEGACY OF KURT LEWIN

When Lewin died in 1947, he had helped create three research centers and had initiated a considerable quantity of research, but his theorizing far exceeded experimental evidence. Still, Dorwin Cartwright (1947–48) could declare in the first volume of *Human Relations:*

> The complexion of American social psychology in 1947 is vastly different from what it was in 1939. Never in its relatively short history has the field experienced such rapid growth and development. As a result of the pressures created by the war

for the solution of hundreds of social problems social psychologists found themselves drawn into wartime activities that called for the sharpening of research tools recently designed and for the invention of new tools previously unimagined. Out of this experience emerged new and useful techniques, a tremendous mass of information, and a group of social psycholgists who view their field and their place in society in new and radically different terms. (p. 333)

This change was due to a combination of Lewin's influence and military support. According to Cartwright, "the vast majority of social psychologists were drawn into government service, mostly in fulltime positions, but frequently as consultants on particular projects" (p. 33). The contracting-out system for financing research developed during the war was simply continued after the war ended.

Lewin helped to shift the focus of social psychology away from the study of individuals. Inspired by Lewin's perspective, group dynamics grew rapidly during the 1950s. McGrath (1978) estimated that the number of studies increased tenfold during this period. New areas were added, theories were extended, and research methods were refined. Nevertheless, by the end of the 1960s, the study of groups declined. (These trends will be explored in the next section.) Lewin's influence was not limited to group dynamics, however. Lewin was a close personal friend of many who helped shape social psychology during the postwar period. His friendship with Fritz Heider went back to the early 1920s when both were on staff at the University of Berlin. Fritz Heider and his wife Grace translated Lewin's book *Principles of Topological Psychology* (1936). Heider's theory of social perception (1944) and interpersonal relations (1958) drew heavily from Lewin and will be discussed in the next chapter.

Lewin's ideas developed in tandem with those of Edward C. Tolman, and the two borrowed considerably from each other. Their theories stressed the importance of goals and purpose in directing behavior and offered an alternative to the more mechanistic models based on behaviorism. Lewin

had many gifted students, including Leon Festinger, Harold H. Kelley, and Morton Deutsch. Festinger's students included Elliot Aronson and Stanley Schachter. Their impact is shown by the fact that Festinger, Kelley, Aronson, and Schachter were the four individuals most often cited by psychological textbook authors during the 1970s. Deutsch ranked twelfth. The impact of Festinger, Kelley, and Schachter has lasted right through the 1980s and is still strong today (see Table 1.1).

Lewin's most lasting contribution, however, probably stems from his general cognitive orientation and his demonstration that complex social phenomena could be brought into the laboratory and tested experimentally. If one looks at Lewin's writings on individual psychological processes, the central focus is underlying dynamics rather than behavior. Lewin felt that any attempt to deal scientifically with psychological issues required going beyond observable behavior and examining motives, intentions, and psychological needs. Moreover, these processes were conceptualized as part of an overall Gestalt rather than isolated elements that could be studied separately. It was through the influence of Lewin, Heider, and later Solomon Asch, that the Gestalt perspective became firmly entrenched within social psychology. This influence can be seen in balance theories, theories of cognitive consistency and dissonance, impression formation, person perception, and group dynamics.

Lewin did not entirely ignore external determinants of behavior, however. As Kenneth Gergen (1982) points out, Lewin's classic equation declares that behavior is a function of the individual *and the environment*. Lewin was rather equivocal about the role of the environment, at times reducing it to personal interpretation but at others defining it in terms of enduring characteristics in the situation itself (Lewin, 1935). Lewin's waffling may well reflect the difficulties he faced importing his German-based cognitive approach to a behaviorist-oriented America (Samelson, 1985a, 1986b). To attract a following, he found it necessary to cater to American tastes. It was his students who reconciled his cognitive position with mainstream empiricist psychology (Gergen, 1982).[1] Highly formalized theories, such as Festinger's (1954) theory of social comparison, with its series of assumptions supported by empirical research based almost exclusively on experimental procedures, resulted in Lewinians working in parallel fashion with such Hullian-trained social psychologists as those at Yale (see Chapter 10).

Lewin himself was steadfastly committed to experimentation and left social psychology not only a content area—group dynamics—and a perspective, but a methodology as well. Nevertheless, while he helped insure that the experimental method would be the instrument of choice among psychological social psychologists, the particular experimental model that he advocated was not adopted by his American students. As Danzinger (1990) points out, beginning with his Berlin studies on individual psychology, Lewin defined the object of research not as the person-in-isolation but as the person-in-a-situation. Thus, the interaction between experimenters and subjects became an integral part of the experimental procedure. In his Iowa studies on leadership style, for example, the interaction between experimenters and subjects was a critical part of the experimental process and was described in the published report. In contrast, largely through Festinger's influence, the Lewinian tradition of experimental social psychology in the United States adopted the natural-science model of experimentation, in which subjects were treated strictly as objects.[2] Aronson, one of Festinger's students, has noted that in his graduate training, experimenter-subject interactions were intensively studied as part of a pre-experimental process of ironing out bugs and rehearsing experimenter roles (Danzinger, 1990; Patnoe, 1988). Unlike Lewin, however, experimenter-subject interactions were not considered to be an essential part of experimental procedures and thus never appeared in the published reports.

One aspect of Lewin's interactive model of experimentation proved to be influential. He introduced and demonstrated the importance of "staging." Before Lewin, deception was based primarily on withholding in-

formation. Subjects were not told the full purpose of experiments because this might alter their response. Lewin used contrived situations in which actors and actresses played their parts. His famous study on leadership styles, for example, required experimenters to play authoritarian, democratic, and laissez-faire roles. Positive results now came to depend as much on acting ability as on careful planning or experimental design. The use of actors, confederates, false cover stories, and false feedback is now so pervasive within social psychology that it is virtually taken for granted. Gross and Fleming (1982) sampled the literature in four major journals between 1959 and 1979 and found that 58% of the 1188 articles sampled used some form of deception. Some topics, such as conformity, altruism, and aggression contained virtually no studies in which deception was not used. By the late 1960s deception had become so common that Aronson and Carlsmith (1968) in the influential *Handbook of Social Psychology* describe it as an integral part of experimentation.

It is an open question whether the use of deception in social psychology is justified. Some of the most important studies in social psychology, such as Festinger and Carlsmith's (1959) study of cognitive dissonance, Solomon Asch's (1951, 1956) work on conformity, Stanley Schachter's (1959) research on affiliation and emotions (Schachter & Singer, 1962) and Stanley Milgram's (1963) work on obedience, could not have been carried out without deception. The use of deception has opened up entire content areas to investigation, and it now seems almost indispensable in certain types of research. However, reliance on deception has also proved to be highly controversial. The controversy is illustrated by the debate over Milgram's research, which will be considered in the next section.

There are other troublesome aspects of Lewin's heritage. His overemphasis on experimentation deflected attention away from areas where experiments cannot be used. There are a growing number of experimental studies of rather trivial issues. Thus, we are told that the use of perfume increases interpersonal attraction or that attractive people spend more time self-monitoring (i.e., looking in the mirror). The experiment is a powerful tool, but it can lead to trivial research when not guided by theory. The proliferation of trival research, however, cannot be attributed to Lewin. His own work showed a deep commitment to pressing social problems and a careful blend of research and theory. But by stressing experimental procedures, Lewin helped entrench experimentation as *the* methodology within psychological social psychology, and the quest for scientific credibilty has caused many social psychologists to limit themselves to topics that can be studied experimentally, thus leading to a significant restriction of social-psychological research.

Similarly, Lewin's stress on the immediate social environment has tended to downplay the long-term effects of social environment. This has led to the premature abandonment of some promising areas of research, such as the sociology of knowledge, and represents a shift away from other trends that began in the 1930s and stressed the broader social context. Meade (1986), for example, recently repeated Lewin, Lippitt, and White's classic study using American, Indian, Chinese, and Chinese-American subjects and found that Indian and Chinese boys strongly favored the authoritarian style of leadership. It is equally plausable that many other specific findings are culturally specific as well. Lewin's ahistorical approach has brought criticism even from those sympathetic to his general position (e.g., Cartwright, 1959; Hall & Lindzey, 1978).

Another significant feature of Lewin's legacy is the emphasis on applied social psychology. For Lewin, theory was more than a means of advancing knowledge. It also had to provide guidelines for solving social problems (Cartwright, 1978). This conception of the role of theory has led to the distinction between "pure" and "applied" social psychology (Gergen, 1982)—the former based on theoretically tested principles of human interaction, the latter consisting of derivations from these principles. Unfortunately, because applied social psychology depends on pure scientific research, it has often assumed a second-class position.

While Lewin was able to combine theoretical and problem-centered research, this combination was less common among his students. As Morton Deutsch (1975) comments:

> A split developed [between the two orientations] which widened into a chasm after Lewin's sudden and premature death. Lewin's unifying presence had been able to hold the diverging tendencies together and, in his absence, the bifurcating dispositions became dominant. (p. 2)

By the 1970s, as a result of the social upheavals in the sixties, the division between basic and applied research began to disappear, and there were attempts to develop alternative models of social psychology designed to overcome the dualistic model of pure and applied research (see Chapters 12 and 13).

Despite these shortcomings, Lewin has to be recognized as one of the most important figures in the history of social psychology. He came at the end of a decade of turbulence brought on by the Great Depression and gave social psychology respectability and a new sense of identity. He developed new research techniques and applied them to pressing social problems. Trends that Lewin initiated, such as a focus on cognitive processes, the use of deception, reliance on experimental procedures, a focus on the immediate social environment, and applied social psychology, have become an integral part of contemporary social psychology and help distinguish it from other disciplines. Lewin made lasting contributions not only to social psychology but to developmental psychology, motivation, and the study of personality. He worked closely with others, helped set the research agenda, and as a result helped shape the course of psychology as a whole.

## POST-LEWIN GROUP PSYCHOLOGY

Lewin's students produced an extensive amount of theory and research. While laboratory studies predominated, there were many field studies as well. One example is Festinger, Riecken, and Schachter's (1956) remarkable work *When Prophecy Fails.* These researchers infiltrated a group led by a medium who predicted that the world would experience a massive flood on Christmas 1955 and only a chosen few would escape in flying saucers. Festinger found that, when the event failed to take place, a combination of cognitive dissonance and social support caused group members to become even more committed to their beliefs. The group eventually disbanded, but the study provides a dramatic example of an attempt to confirm theory through examining situations in real life.

During the 1950s, theories of social comparison and social exchange were developed. While Lewin's students continued to play a major role in the development of postwar group psychology, there were other contributions as well. Sociologists George C. Homans (1950) and Robert F. Bales (1950, 1958) drew attention to the distinction between social and task leaders. When groups form, two leaders rather than one typically emerge. The task leader focuses on the task at hand and keeps the group working toward a common goal. The social leader maintains morale and keeps the members involved. Because the two functions are somewhat incompatible, they are rarely carried out by the same person. Studies on social influence and conformity, carried out before the war by Muzafer Sherif and Solomon Asch, were continued. The most significant, Asch's study of conformity and Milgram's work on obedience, will be discussed after a review of the research on social comparison and social exchange.

## Social Comparison

Festinger's research on group cohesion, communication, and conformity led to his theory of social comparison (Festinger, 1954). The theory was presented as a series of postulates and corollaries, reflecting the Hullian approach to theorizing about learned behavior that dominated the psychological landscape of the fifties. While

Festinger's theory was Hullian in style, it was Lewinian in content. It extended the research on level of aspiration that had demonstrated that one of the major factors in establishing goals was comparison with other people (Lewin, Dembo, Festinger, & Sears, 1944).

Through a combination of laboratory and field studies, Festinger and his associates were able to show that the pressure toward uniformity within a group was based on a need for social comparison and shared group goals. When objective evidence is not available, people rely on others, and groups are an especially important source of social comparison. Pressures toward uniformity require communication, and communication increases when the group is highly cohesive or the topic is relevant. Communication is directed, at least initially, toward those with different opinions. Individuals can resist these pressures if their attitudes are anchored in other groups or serve important needs. But group members maintain pressure, and those with different opinions are often rejected as a consequence. Exclusion of people with divergent opinions is another way that groups maintain uniformity, and the threat of exclusion is an important source of motivation that brings people into line. This work is important because it shows that a whole host of group processes—communication, conformity, group cohesion, and so on—are interrelated and can be studied systematically (see Festinger, 1950, 1954, for reviews).

Nevertheless, social comparison theory suffers from a Lewinian focus on the immediate social environment at the expense of the broader social context. Israel (1979) in his critique points out that pressures to conform were explained in terms of group and individual processes. Missing was any consideration of the broader social context that instigates and maintains conformity. The politically repressive climate of the 1950s fostered a preoccupation with conformity, and pressures to conform within group studies were based on not only individual or group processes but social norms as well. The large amount of theory and research on conformity during this period also reflects the impact of society.

## Social Exchange

Social exchange theory was first developed by John W. Thibaut and Harold H. Kelley (1959, also see Kelley & Thibaut, 1978) and subsequently by George C. Homans (1961, 1974). Central to this approach is the notion that social interaction is the product of an exchange of reward and punishment. These theories thus rely on the general notion of functional hedonism, in which individual attempt to maximize pleasure (rewards) and minimize pain (costs).

Thibaut and Kelley were both trained at the Research Center for Group Dynamics at MIT, and their approach was influenced by both Festinger and Lewin. They were also influenced by game and decision theory, which draws from the behavioristic concept of reinforcement (Jones, 1985). In their book *The Social Psychology of Groups* (Thibaut & Kelley, 1959), they present a framework for examining social interaction within dyads and small groups. The reaction of people to each other is analyzed in terms of a "payoff matrix" based on the hedonistic principle of achieving maximum satisfaction.

People interacting with each other do not possess the same amount of power. One person may have the resources to reward or punish the other, who is thus in a dependent position. In analyzing power and dependence, Thibaut and Kelley used the concept of social comparison. A person's power within a given relationship is based not only on the capacity to reward or punish the other person but on the availability and attractiveness of other relationships occurring at the same time.

Homans's (1961, 1974) social exchange theory drew from B. F. Skinner's radical behaviorism and therefore avoids mediating processes, such as social comparison. It is similar to Thibaut and Kelley's, however, and perhaps because of this has been less influential. Deutsch and Krauss (1965) have noted that Homans's reliance on Skinnerian principles was probably due to the accidential fact that they both taught at Harvard and were well acquainted. They go on to add, however, "In any case, before swallowing Skinner's system, Homans seems to

have chewed it beyond clear recognition" (p. 109). Social exchange theories have not produced a great amount of systematic research (Jones, 1985), partly because of a general decline in group research, but some aspects of social exchange theory have been used in studies of conflict resolution and equity.

Research on conflict resolution was pioneered by Morton Deutsch, another product of the Research Center for Group Dynamics at MIT. His dissertation focused on cooperation and competition in small groups (Deutsch, 1949; see also Deutsch, 1980). This work revealed the significance of "mixed motives" in group problem solving, whereby group members engage in a combination of cooperative and competitive strategies. The interests of individual members tend to converge at times and diverge at others. In a classic study, Deutsch and Krauss (1960) developed a simulated trucking game in which two players attempt to move their truck to its destination in the shortest time possible. The shortest route, however, involves a one-lane road. The main finding was that players use cooperative strategies to coordinate their movements and maximize payoffs.

Deutsch's research shares some features with social exchange (Jones, 1985). Both focus on social interdependence and the development of relationships based on a system of mutual rewards and punishments. The work of Deutsch and Thibaut and Kelley stimulated a rising interest in mixed-motive games during the 1960s, especially the prisoner's dilemma game. Because research on games is easy to conduct, hundreds of studies were carried out. These studies were considered experimental analogues of real-world interactions, such as disarmament negotiations and labor-management bargaining. However, the general verdict is that they were highly artificial (Deutsch, 1980; Pruitt & Kimmel, 1977).

Aspects of social-exchange theory are also used in research on equity (Adams, 1965; Walster, Berscheid, & Walster, 1973). According to these theories, a person's willingness to participate in a relationship is based on the amount of costs and benefits. If people invest more than they receive (inequity) they will become discontented and more likely to leave their relationships. Research on equity, however, has not always supported the equity principle. The perception of fairness may also be based on equality (Sampson, 1975), and whether equity or equality is preferred appears to be based on culture. During the 1970s, for example, European students preferred an equal distribution of rewards in experimental games, whereas American students preferred a consistent ratio of rewards to input (Gergen, Morse, & Gergen, 1980).

The fact that some people prefer equality rather than equity raises questions about the universality of social-exchange theory. One of the most common criticisms is that many people are not motivated to maximize their gains at the expense of others (Argyle, 1988). Later developments in exchange theory have attempted to include the role of altruistic concerns as well (Kelley & Thibaut, 1978), but there is still concern that social-exchange theory is a reification of the American marketplace wherein people compete with one another for limited resources (Israel, 1979; Sampson, 1977). Popularity simply becomes another sign of individual success.

### Social Conformity

At the height of McCarthyism in the early fifties, Solomon Asch (1951, 1956) conducted a series of laboratory experiments on group pressure. Because of their timing and intrinsic interest, these studies became instant classics (Jones, 1985). Asch's experiment included one real subject and six experimental confederates who had been instructed to give the wrong response to a series of line-discrimination tasks. All the participants were seated around a table and gave their responses verbally when their turn came. The real subject was always placed in the next-to-last position. At the start of the study the confederates matched the correct line with the comparison line but later on they uniformly gave the same incorrect response. What Asch was interested in was the number of subjects who

would yield to the pressure to conform. He found that the average subject made between 4 and 5 errors on 12 trials and roughly three-quarters of all subjects conformed at least once.

What distinguishes Asch's research from the prewar work on social influence is the presence of a conflict between group members. In Sherif's (1936) studies, social norms were based on the convergence of individual responses (see Chapter 7), but in Asch's work, subjects were forced to choose between their own judgments or the consensual but erroneous judgments of other members of the group. The situation was designed to measure the extent to which people yield to conformity pressures in spite of their knowledge that the group is wrong.

Asch's research led to a number of subsequent investigations of conformity in the fifties and sixties. By far the most controversial follow-up study was carried out by Stanley Milgram (1963). In 1958, when Milgram was a graduate student at Harvard, he served as a teaching assistant for Asch, who was a visiting professor at the time. For the next two years, he continued to work for Asch at the Institute for Advanced Study in Princeton, and he has acknowledged that Asch was the greatest influence on his work (Miller, 1986).

In Milgram's first-reported study, which took place at Yale, 40 male subjects were recruited through newspaper advertisement and mail solicitation. They ranged in age from 20 to 50 and included laborers, engineers, and high school teachers. The experiment had three participants—the "experimenter," played by a 31-year-old high school teacher, the "learner," played by a 47-year old accountant, and the real subject, who through a prearranged draw always acted as the "teacher." After the instructions were given, the teacher and learner went into separate rooms. The subject was told that the purpose of the experiment was to study the effects of punishment on learning. The learner supposedly gave responses to a word-association task, and the teacher's task was to punish the learner when he made an error by administering a series of increasingly stronger electric shocks. If the subject showed signs of hesitation, the experimenter simply asked him to continue. The shocks ran from 15 volts to 450 volts. When the experiment reached 300 volts, the learner began to pound on the wall. At higher levels, the learner stopped responding altogether, and the subject was instructed to treat the absence of a response as an incorrect response and continue. Of course, in reality none of the electric shocks were actually delivered, and the subject was "debriefed" about the deception at the end of the experiment. Altogether 26 of the 40 subjects or 65% delivered the maximum amount of shock possible (i.e., 450 volts). Most displayed visible signs of tension and conflict, and Milgram's graphic description of their stress fueled the storm of controversey that subsequently raged over the ethics of his research. His initial experiment, like that of Asch, was followed by a whole series of studies designed to examine the various factors responsible for obedience.

Miller (1986) has provided a thorough and perceptive treatment of the subsequent debate. The debate generated by this work played a major role in the subsequent concern about ethical issues in social-psychological research (see Chapter 12). Critics charged that Milgram had failed to consider the well-being of his subjects during the course of the experiment, and they raised questions about the long-term, post experimental consequences as well as its relevance to real-world situations (see Baumrind, 1964). Milgram (1964, 1974) responded by claiming that the subjects in his study did not report any harmful consequences, and it was important to learn about destructive obedience. As Miller points out, however, there are still nagging questions that remain even if one has evidence that subjects are not negatively affected. For example, is it proper to expose subjects to conditions that produce intense stress and conflict? The answers to such questions require an examination of the values and priorities surrounding social-scientific research. For many critics, the questionable ethics of subjecting subjects to stressful conditions far outweighs the gains in scientific knowledge.

Milgram's concern with obedience was derived in part from his interest in the Holocaust. His research closely followed the 1961 trial of Adolf Eichmann (Raven & Rubin, 1983). The issue of blind obedience to authority was also a major problem in the last years of the Vietnam War and was graphically illustrated by the My Lai massacre. Several commentators begrudgingly endorsed Milgram's research, because it helped to show just how common the tendency to obey is and because it helped reveal factors that increase and decrease obedience (see Miller, 1986).

## The Decline of Group Psychology

The study of groups was a major focus throughout the 1940s and 1950s, but during the 1960s, research on groups began to wane (Jones, 1985; Steiner, 1974). Although there was still work on component processes, such as conformity and conflict resolution, there was far less research on groups as a whole. In reviewing the literature published between 1967 and 1972, Helmreich, Bakeman, and Scherwitz (1973) complained that most of the research tended to be carried out with little or no concern for potential application and external validity and seemed to be following a psychological version of Gresham's law, where "bad research drives out good." New theories, such as F. L. Fiedler's (1967) contingency model of leadership effectiveness and Irving Janis's (1968) work on group think, continued to be developed, but a growing number of studies either had no theoretical orientation or were concerned with testing trivial aspects of theories previously developed. McGrath (1978) expressed the opinion that the absence of theory virtually destroyed group psychology as a vital area of research. When members of the Society of Experimental Social Psychology were asked to predict the most popular research area during the 1980s, 73% listed cognitive social psychology, but only 14% mentioned group dynamics (Lewicki, 1982).

The decline in research was not simply due to lack of new theory. Group experiments are relatively time-consuming and difficult to carry out. It is far easier to experiment with individuals or administer questionnaires to large groups. Under pressures to publish, many social psychologists were forced to carry out many quick experiments rather than a few difficult ones. Some of Lewin's research took years to complete, but he was aided by an established reputation and external funds. Much of the current research seems to be based on a type of "cost-benefit" analysis in which the output is evaluated in terms of the effort involved.

To understand the decline of group psychology also requires a consideration of the sociopolitical climate of the postwar period. As Steiner (1974) points out, the turmoil of the depression and World War II resulted in a rising interest in group processes. By the late 1940s, this area had captured the attention of a large number of social psychologists. However, the conservatism and tranquility of the Eisenhower years fostered a shift in emphasis from the group to the individual. Interest in group processes, such as leadership, cohesion, and social roles, seems to be associated with periods of social unrest, whereas the relative stability of individual processes seems to be the focus of attention during periods of social serenity.

The social upheavals of the late 1960s and early 1970s should therefore have produced a revival of interest. Indeed, Steiner (1974, 1986) predicted such a trend. Group psychology did not rebound, however, and there appear to be several related reasons for its failure to recover. First, psychological social psychology has been largely committed to an individualistic approach that treats people as relatively self-contained units and ignores the broader social context responsible for behavior. It is true that Lewin focused on groups, but as Steiner points out, his main interest was how the individual perceives or imagines the group. Lewin had little to say about ongoing processes of human interaction. Thus, in response to the turmoil of the sixties, Lewin's approach did not provide a very clear alternative to the newly established cognitive approach (see Chapter 10).

The second factor that accounts for the continued neglect of group psychology is the fact that the upheavals of the 1960s generated a more radical alternative to the individualistic approach. Instead of stressing small-group processes, the new approach argued that people and groups must both be seen within their historical, ideological, and economic context. A bona fide group approach has to conceive the individual and various collectives of individuals as elements within the larger social system. These developments will be discussed in more detail in Chapter 13.

A final factor seems to be the mere availability of research funds. Cina (1981) has made the claim that the military and the Office of Naval Research in particular "made" group dynamics as a discipline. A content analysis of three topic areas—attitudes, leadership, and group dynamics—in four journals *(Psychological Bulletin, Psychological Review, Human Relations,* and the *Journal of Abnormal and Social Psychology)* showed a phenomenal growth in group studies after the war. By 1950, the number of studies in group dynamics exceeded the studies on attitudes, which had previously been the most researched area. The Office of Naval Research funded over 25% of the research published between 1949 and 1957, and another 10% was funded by other military sources. The military also funded 42% of the research on leadership, but only 18% of the research on attitudes. The disproportionate number of studies funded by the military on leadership and group dynamics suggests that the military did help play a role in supporting group research.

One must avoid drawing sinister conclusions from these data, however. Lewin and his associates regarded their work as important and sought funds from any available source. The military also considered the work important and made funds available. It might be more accurate to say that military funds allowed these areas to emerge, because funds would not have been available without Lewin's conceptual framework and a pragmatic research program. Still, it is interesting that a discipline like social psychology can be shaped by extraneous factors, like the availability of research funds. Without military support, group dynamics might never have moved into center stage, and contemporary social psychology might have been very different.

## INTERGROUP RELATIONS

The prewar initiatives in the study of authoritarianism and racial prejudice were revived after the war. Lewin's work in this area has already been mentioned. Muzafer and Carolyn Wood Sherif were also active. They conducted a series of field experiments with preadolescent boys at summer camp (Sherif & Sherif, 1953). The studies took place over a three-week period and consisted of three stages: group formation, intergroup conflict, and conflict resolution. During the initial stage, group solidarity was promoted by a number of cooperative activities. During the second stage, hostility was created between groups through intergroup competition. The hostility was later reduced through the introduction of a series of superordinate goals, that is, goals that competing groups could attain only by cooperating with each other. The results were consistent with the cooperative strategy adopted by subjects in Morton Deutsch's studies of mixed-motive games.

In an influential book, *The Nature of Prejudice,* Gordon Allport (1954b) integrated the theoretical and empirical work on prejudice to provide guidelines for reducing intergroup tension. Among the principles advanced was the importance of contact between members of majority and minority groups, provided such contact was based on a relationship of equal status and in pursuit of common goals. He also pointed to the role of civil rights legislation and intercultural education as effective modes of social action in reducing prejudice. By the early 1960s, the interest in intergroup relations shifted from interracial conflict to international affairs, reflecting the increasing threat of nuclear war (see Morawski & Goldstein, 1985). But as racial tension increased, there was an increased focus on race relations, although discrimi-

nation rather than prejudice occupied center stage. Concerns about the roots of racial prejudice drew wide attention during the postwar period, and they will be considered after an examination of the Berkeley study of authoritarianism.

### The Authoritarian Personality

The Berkeley study of the authoritarian character structure stemmed from research in 1943 by Nevitt Sanford, a professor at the University of California at Berkeley, and his graduate student, Daniel J. Levinson. Their project involved the development of a scale to measure anti-Semitism. Levinson and Sanford were soon joined by Else Frenkel-Brunswik, a Vienna-trained psychiatrist. Along similar lines, in 1941 the Institute for Social Research, which had recently moved from Frankfurt to New York because of the war, began a research project on anti-Semitism that extended the work of Erich Fromm (see Chapter 8). The Institute's research team worked in Los Angeles and was funded by the American Jewish Committee. Through the Institute's director, Max Horkheimer, a cooperative research plan was developed. The combined research team, now headquartered at Berkeley, was led by one of the Institute's members, T. W. Adorno. Despite Adorno's Marxist orientation and the Frankfurt school's well-known attempts to fuse Freudian and Marxist ideas, socioeconomic aspects of the authoritarian personality were not stressed, and the study focused on discipline and family structure during early childhood.

While it was recognized that "the cause of irrational hostility is in the last instance to be found in social frustration and injustice" (Adorno, Frenkel-Brunswik, Levinson, & Sanford, 1950/1982, p. ix), a concerted effort was made to limit the study to psychological variables. The study began as an attempt to examine the origins of anti-Semitism in America, but it soon became apparent that anti-Semitism was part of a larger syndrome that included ethnocentrism and a potentially fascist personality. Anti-Semites dislike not only Jews but all groups considered alien or weak, including those with which they have had no previous contact. Three scales were developed to measure anti-Semitism, ethnocentrism, and potential fascism, and these scales correlated moderately well both with each other and with a fourth scale devoted to political-economic conservatism. The researchers used questionnaires, semi-structured interviews, projective tests, and life histories. They began their research with college students but later extended it to include prisoners and psychiatric patients as well.

The overall picture that emerged was that the authoritarian personality was the result of strict and harsh discipline during childhood by parents who made love conditional on behaving properly, emphasized obedience and duty, stressed status differences, and were contemptuous of lower-status individuals. Families tended to be father-dominated and had clearly defined sex roles. As a result of having to submit to harsh and arbitrary discipline, the authoritarian individual developed hostile feelings toward the parents and toward authority in general that could not be expressed and that were therefore redirected onto lower status groups. The distinction between ingroup and outgroup is critical. Ingroups are those with which the authoritarian individual identifies, whereas outgroups are perceived as different and usually inferior.

Authoritarian individuals tend to be very conventional. A fear of impulses leads to a rigid personality structure based on conventional sexual stereotypes, stereotyped thinking, and avoidance of introspection. Lack of psychological insight makes authoritarian individuals insensitive to problems within themselves and within other people. Personal relations tend to be relatively superficial and are perceived in terms of relative power and status, with an idealization of "toughness" and "strength." Authoritarian individuals tend to be domineering and exploitative toward those perceived as weak but ingratiating and submissive toward those with authority. While such individuals tend to be extremely patriotic, they regard most Americans as members of outgroups—nonwhites, ethnic and religious minorities, people who are either over- or under-educated, and so on. Among males,

even women are regarded as socially inferior. Outgroups are perceived as threatening and power-seeking but weak at the same time. Authoritarian individuals typically have a generalized negative attitude toward anyone perceived as different and are prejudiced toward outgroups even when they have had no previous contact with them.

The authoritarian personality involves not only a negative attitude toward other groups but a way of thinking as well. While there was little difference between high and low scorers in overall intelligence, there were considerable differences in cognitive style. Authoritarian individuals tend to think in terms of rigid stereotypes and dogmatic oversimplifications and avoid information that conflicts with their preconceptions. They also tend to be more superstitious, have less intellectual curiosity, and read less. Even when authoritarians have above-average intelligence, they tend to be relatively rigid in their social thinking and work better with things than people. While it is difficult to tease out cause-and-effect relationships in this area, these traits would tend to lower educational level. It is not simply that education makes a person more liberal, but that certain individuals are predisposed toward obtaining a liberal education to begin with.

The authoritarian personality is a cluster of traits that tend to go together but vary from individual to individual. Since authoritarians stress conventional behavior, they tend to be more similar than nonauthoritarian types, but both groups have subgroups. The most important authoritarian subtype is the person who is "conventionally" prejudiced. These people have adopted the prejudiced attitudes of their group in order to fit in but have no deep-seated hostility. Among nonauthoritarians, the researchers found a "rigid" subtype who had a character structure similar to authoritarians.

Research on the authoritarian personality elicited a storm of criticism. Much of this appeared in a volume edited by Christe and Jahoda (1954), and the more valid points were summarized by Deutsch and Krauss (1965). The most serious problem with the original research was a technical flaw in the questionnaires, which led to what is now known as an "acquiescent response set." The questionnaires were phrased in such a way that agreement to any question led to a higher score, and this confounds what is being measured with a tendency to agree or disagree. Bass (1955) later created an F scale with the items reversed and found only a $-.20$ correlation between it and the original (instead of $-1.00$). Since the questionnaires were the basis on which subjects were selected for subsequent interviews and tests, this simple technical problem puts the whole project in question. It does not disprove the theory; it simply left it untested.

A second criticism is that the authors focused on right-wing authoritarianism and neglected that associated with left-wing politics. This criticism was influenced by the cold-war political ideology of the 1950s, which asserted that communists rather than fascists were the real threat to democracy (Samelson, 1986a). At any rate, the red scare of the McCarthy era discouraged discussion and research on left-wing authoritarianism. Subsequent commentators, such as Wilkinson (1972), have pointed out, however, that while authoritarians may occasionally adopt a left-wing ideology, particularly when it is the official state doctrine, there is a closer affinity between right-wing ideologies and the authoritarian character. Fascism and other doctrines on the extreme right demand respect for authority, fierce nationalism, and rigid ingroup and outgroup distinctions. The extreme militaristic attitude gives weak individuals an opportunity to appear strong by supporting aggressive national politics. The big disadvantage of socialist and communist doctrines is official support for the weak and oppressed.

This brings up a final point: *What is wrong with being an authoritarian anyway?* First, the authoritarian personality should not be confused with respect for authority, as in Asian societies, for example, where older people are looked up to because they are regarded as carriers of wisdom. Respect for authority in the authoritarian individual is based on a love-hate relationship toward authority derived from an initial ambivalence toward one's own parents. This

"blind" devotion is often accompanied by an idealization of those with power and a corresponding disdain for the weak and helpless.

Authoritarianism should also not be confused with political or economic conservatism based on a reasoned assessment of the virtues of free enterprise. Authoritarian individuals tend to be conservative because they have adopted without question the conventional standards of their society. They are potentially fascist because of their glorification of power and contempt for the weak. This type of character structure helps to account not only for anti-Semitism but for racial prejudice, sex discrimination, ethnocentrism, and support for aggressive foreign policies. These attitudes may be relatively dormant during stable economic conditions but come out during periods of economic stress.

## Race Relations

The study of racial prejudice, from its inception in the 1930s, focused primarily on the prejudiced person rather than the victims of such attitudes (Minton, 1986). Citing Gordon Allport's (1954b) comprehensive treatment as an example, Smith (1978) comments:

> From the standpoint of white experience, prejudice seemed more central than the discrimination and injustice encountered by Jews and blacks. . . . We need to remember also that Allport was writing at the time when Gunnar Myrdal . . . could call the "Negro problem" really a white problem. (p. 197)

There were, however, some notable exceptions to this trend. Lewin (1948) had written on the psychological problems of being a member of a minority group. In a pioneering study, Kenneth B. Clark and his wife Mamie Phipps Clark (1947) examined the racial attitudes of black children between three and seven years of age. They found that, when black children were given a choice between a black doll and a white doll, they preferred the latter. When they were asked which was prettier or nicer, they consistently selected the white one. When they were asked which one was like them, many (particularly those in the North) burst into tears (K. Clark interviewed in Evans, 1980). These results suggested that young black children had a negative self-image about their racial identity. What was especially significant about the Clarks' study was that it focused on the victims of racial prejudice. The results of the study, together with other research on the psychological effects of racial discrimination, played a major role in the United States Supreme Court's 1954 landmark decision to abolish segregated schools (Klineberg, 1986).

Later attempts to replicate the Clarks' study during the 1960s and early 1970s revealed a reversal of the original findings (Brand, Ruiz, & Padilla, 1974). The shift toward same-race preference appeared to mirror the newly emerging sense of black pride. However, it is not altogether clear from the original study or from the attempts at replication that race was the critical stimulus. It may have been a matter of familiarity with black dolls and the other representational materials. Nevertheless, as a result of the civil rights movement, black children at least had the opportunity to relate to symbols of their own race.

The civil rights movement and the racial unrest of the 1960s stimulated a growing interest in the effects of racism and oppression on black Americans (Clark, 1965; Jones, 1972; Pettigrew, 1964a). Accompanying this new research focus was a frank recognition of the limitations of social-psychological theory and research regarding minority groups. Pettigrew (1964b), for example, called for the development of a social-psychological theory that would include the unique historical and sociocultural context of black Americans. Clark (1965) pointed out that

> standardized research procedures provide only limited information about the concerns of blacks. [Referring to his study of the black ghetto, he remarked:] It became clear . . . that while usual methods of data collection and analysis would contribute to an understanding of the demographic

statistics of the community, the use of standardized questionnaires and interview procedures would result in stylized and superficial verbal responses or evasions. The . . . data obtained by these traditional methods did not plumb the depth or the complexities of the attitudes and anxieties, the many forms of irony and rage which form the truths of the lives of the people of Harlem. (p. xix)

In order to achieve an understanding of the social reality of the ghetto, Clark took on the role of an "informed observer," someone who was part of what was being observed and who experiences the problems of the people being studied.

In the 1970s, there was mounting criticism of the white bias that dominated American social psychology. Moreover, the counterculture and the various minority protest movements of the late sixties and early seventies generated demands that social psychology (and the social sciences in general) attend to the concerns of blacks, youths, women, lesbians, and gay men. These calls for a social psychology that would encompass minority perspectives were among the strands of dissent that culminated in the discipline's crisis of confidence and its subsequent attempts at reform and reconstruction (see Chapters 12 and 13).

## NOTES

1. Several of Lewin's students had contact with Hull's behaviorism (Patnoe, 1988). Festinger as a graduate student at Iowa worked with Kenneth Spence. Schachter, who was Festinger's student, spent a year studying with Hull at Yale before arriving at MIT. Kelley worked with Carl Hovland at Yale after he completed his graduate work.

2. As a graduate student at Iowa, Festinger did not share his mentor's new interests in practical problems and group dynamics (Patnoe, 1988); he had chosen to come to Iowa because of Lewin's research on level of aspiration. At MIT, Lewin had relatively little contact with graduate students. Festinger, in contrast, worked closely with the students and was thus more influential.

# 10

# Cognitive Social Psychology

During the late 1950s and early 1960s, American psychology underwent what has subsequently become known as the "cognitive revolution" (e.g., Bruner, Goodnow, & Austin, 1956; Miller, Galanter, & Pribram, 1960; Neisser, 1967). Although many major psychologists, such as Gordon Allport, Edward C. Tolman, and Kurt Lewin, maintained a cognitive perspective even during the heyday of behaviorism, cognitive psychology came to be seen as the most useful and most legitimate approach to psychology in general. While interpretations vary about the specific nature of this revolution, there is a consensus that psychology shifted away from a preoccupation with overt behavior toward a perspective that attempts to explain behavior in terms of mental processes, such as attention, memory, reasoning, and information processing (see Baars, 1986; Gergen, 1989a; Kessel & Bevan, 1985).

The strong Gestalt influence of Kurt Lewin, Fritz Heider, Solomon Asch, and others virtually insured that post–World War II social psychology would have a strong cognitive orientation. Their students and their students' students continued a tradition in which perception, beliefs, and mental processes were seen as largely responsible for overt behavior. Robert Zajonc (1980), in a review of the period, drew from Gordon Allport's (1954a) definition of social psychology as the discipline that attempts *"to understand and explain how the thought, feeling, and behavior of individuals are influenced by the actual, imagined, or implied presence of other human beings"* (p. 5) and pointed out that the emphasis in social psychology is on understanding thoughts, feelings and behavior—in that order—with *thoughts* at the top of the list.

Zajonc (1980) goes on to point out that few experiments in social psychology actually use other people. The bulk of the research concerns the effects of implied or imagined others (using written descriptions, tape recordings, and videotapes). As a result, cognitions are present as both the independent and dependent variables—"cognition pervades social psychology" (p. 181). The cognitive orientation became so pervasive in social psychology after the war that the phrase "cognitive social psychology" is somewhat redundant, in much the same way that the phrase "experimental social psychology" is redundant. The experimental study of cognitive processes is largely what characterized the psychological approach during the postwar period.

The strong consensus about what should be studied and how it should be approached reflected the fact that social psychology was still a relatively small discipline during the late 1940s and was concentrated in a small number of universities (see Chapter 9). It is therefore not surprising that certain topics dominated social psychology during the postwar period. Group psychology continued for a short while to be a major area of interest. The systematic study of attitudes by Carl I. Hovland and his associates generated a considerable body of research. Consistency theories and cognitive dissonance emerged in the late fifties and dominated social psychology during the 1960s only to give way to attribution theories in the 1970s. These were not the only areas of interest, but together they constituted over a third of the research conducted between 1959 and 1979 (Gross & Fleming, 1982).

Since the previous chapter discussed group processes at length, this chapter will concentrate on attitudes, cognitive consistency, and social-learning theories. These are three of the major areas of research in social psychology during the 1950s and early 1960s. Attribution processes will be discussed in Chapter 12, along with other recent developments in social cognition. This is not meant as an exhaustive review of cognitive social psychology. As suggested previously, such a review would contain virtually all of the research conducted since the war. It should be noted, however, that other popular areas, such as impression formation and interpersonal attraction, have an equally strong cognitive emphasis and that even concrete social behaviors, such as conformity, altruism, and aggression, are usually explained in cognitive terms. The present focus is restricted to attitudes, cognitive consistency, and social-learning theories, because they represent three important areas of concentration, each with its own theories and research strategy.

## ATTITUDE RESEARCH

Attitude research carried out before World War II was concerned primarily with measuring attitudes and uncovering the techniques used to manipulate public opinion so that people would be less suceptible to the effects of advertising and propaganda (e.g., Doob, 1935). During the war the emphasis changed as researchers began to systematically study the effects of particular types of speakers and particular aspects of the message on attitude development and attitude change. The primary concern switched from "immunizing" people against the misleading effects of advertising and propaganda to studying persuasion ex-

perimentally for the purpose of maximizing the effects of persuasive communication, enhancing morale, and maintaining national unity.

The central figure in this transition was Carl I. Hovland (1912–1961). Hovland was a graduate student at Yale's Institute of Human Relations—an interdisciplinary department that included Clark Hull, John Dollard, Leonard Doob, Neil Miller and many others. He received his Ph.D. in 1936 and became director of the Yale Communication and Attitude Change Program at the age of 24. He served as chief psychologist and director of experimental studies for the War Department during the war and became Chairman of the Department of Psychology at Yale in 1941. Hovland's work can be seen as a continuation of the type of research carried out by Doob before the war, and Doob was in fact a faculty member of Hovland's research program after the war and served informally as editor of the first volume summarizing its findings (Hovland, Janis, & Kelley, 1953).

Hovland's approach, however, differed in one critical respect. It was heavily committed to controlled laboratory experiments. Experiments had been used previously in communication research, but they had been used rather loosely to determine whether sources of mass communication had *any* effect on attitude change (e.g., Peterson & Thurstone, 1933) or to compare communications that differed along many different dimensions. Hovland's group manipulated one variable at a time. Hovland coordinated the activities of approximately 30 separate researchers, organized their findings within a perspective loosely drawn from Hull's learning theory, and established the framework for most of the subsequent research on attitudes.

Hovland divided the field of persuasion into three principal components—the communicator, the communication, and the audience.[1] The effectiveness of a communicator depends on *credibility,* which consists of both trustworthiness and expertise. An effective communicator must be both knowledgeable and believable. These two components often go together but not always. A well-meaning but uninformed person may feel strongly about a particular topic but lack the knowledge or education to understand the issue or, conversely, a knowledgeable individual may be untrustworthy because he or she has ulterior motives. Hovland and his associates studies both components by presenting identical messages to different subjects and attributing them to different sources. A paper discussing the feasibility of atomic submarines, for example, was attributed to the distinguished physicist Robert Oppenheimer or to the Russian newspaper *Pravda* (Hovland & Weiss, 1951). Communications attributed to highly credible sources were seen as less biased and more justified in their conclusions and produced more attitude change immediately after exposure.

One surprising aspect of Hovland's work was the discovery that the effects of credibility did not last. Hovland retested his subjects several weeks after the communication and discovered that the initial difference had disappeared (Hovland & Weiss, 1951; Kelman & Hovland, 1953). This was due to both a decline in attitude change among those exposed to the highly credible source and an increase among those exposed to the less credible source. Hovland called this the "sleeper effect" and explained it by distinguishing between the learning and the acceptance of a message. Credibility does not seem to affect comprehension, but it does affect acceptance. Over time, the information is retained but the source is forgotten. Reminding people of the original source can help reinstate differences based on credibility (Kelman & Hovland, 1953). The sleeper effect has been challenged (e.g., Gillig & Greenwald, 1974), but it suggests that we all have a great deal of information derived from a variety of sources that is given equal credibility because the sources are forgotten.

Hovland and his associates also found that the amount of attitude change depends on the message. Strong fear appeals were less effective than low-fear messages (Janis & Feshbach, 1953). Emotional messages must both create tension and provide relief by offering reassuring recommendations— such as preventing tooth decay by brushing one's teeth or visiting a dentist regularly. Strong fear appeals may lead to defensive reactions, such as ignoring or minimizing the threat, derogating the communicator, or producing counterarguments. Hovland and Mandell (1952) also found that messages were more effective when the speaker drew explicit conclusions rather than leaving the conclusion to the audience.

The relative merit of one-sided versus two-sided communications was studied by Hovland, Lumsdaine, and Sheffield (1949). The War Department wanted to find the most effective way to convince American soldiers that the war in the Pacific might continue for some time even though the war in Europe was drawing to a close. A one-sided communication was found to be more effective when the audience was either poorly informed or already committed to the speaker's position, whereas two-sided arguments were more effective for a knowledgeable audience and for those who initially opposed the speaker's position. There is, however, an important sense in which two-sided communications always work better. Two-sided communications make people more resistant to counterpersuasion in the future. This is known as the *"inoculation effect."* It was introduced by Hovland, Lumsdaine, and Sheffield (1949), but it has been developed most fully by William McGuire (1964).

Research on one-sided versus two-sided communications shows that attitude change depends on the audience as well. Different people listening to the same speaker will have different reactions—some will be convinced, but others will not be. There appears to be a general trait of persuasibility, not based on intelligence, but possibly related to such factors as neurotic defensiveness and self-esteem (Janis, 1954; McGuire, 1968). Intelligence increases comprehension, but it also increases a person's ability to generate counterarguments and may therefore reduce acceptance. Attitudes are more difficult to change when they are shared by members of a reference group. Attitude conformity within a group is based on how much a person values membership and by relative status (Kelley & Volkart, 1952). High-status individuals are allowed more room for deviation and may therefore serve as strategic persons for the introduction of new ideas. They have what Hollander (1958) has called "idiosyncrasy credits"—that is, the right to be different.

Near the end of his life, Hovland helped develop a new theory of attitude change based on social judgment (Sherif & Hovland, 1961). Social judgment theory assumes that one's own attitude toward a particular topic serves as a powerful anchor around which other attitudes are evaluated. Those similar to one's own fall within a latitude of acceptance, which forms a range of acceptable beliefs toward a particular topic that are readily assimilated. Attitudes that are very dissimilar form a latitude of rejection. These are contrasted and seen as even more dissimilar than they actually are. Between the two is a latitude of noncommitment, in which attitudes are neither acceptable nor unacceptable. The amount of attitude change shows an inverted-U relationship with discrepancy. Attitude change increases with discrepancy within the latitude of acceptance but decreases with discrepancy within the latitude of rejection. These latitudes vary with the importance of the issue. Those highly involved have small latitudes of acceptance, large latitudes of rejection, and virtually no latitudes of noncommitment—that is, they tolerate only positions that are very similar to their own and are therefore very resistant to attitude change.

Attitude research came full circle in the postwar period. The initial emphasis of Doob and others on analyzing propaganda so as to immunize people against it gave way to a more dispassionate search for underlying principles. Hovland's research was inspired largely by practical problems of persuasion and morale during the war, but it provided advertising and public-relations firms with an increasing arsenal of techniques that could be used by vested interest groups to alter public opinion. The aim was to understand the dynamics of persuasion and ultimately the "role of the higher mental processes in assimilating the numerous and often contradictory influences impinging upon the individual in everyday life" (Hovland, Janis, & Kelley, 1953, p. 2). Nev-

ertheless, the discovery of these processes made mass persuasion guided by scientific principles possible and accounts for some of the disillusionment among social psychologists during the 1960s and a relative decline in research during the 1970s. Advertising was used to sell everything from cornflakes to political candidates and ultimately to create a lifestyle that stressed consumerism and more consumption.

Offsetting this trend to a certain extent was the discovery that attitude change does not occur very frequently in real life. Two years before his death, Hovland (1959) was forced to come to grips with the discrepancy between his own research, which showed relatively large differences with subtle manipulations, and the extremely small changes found in correlation field studies. Most of the field research studied advertising and change in political preferences during elections, where it was rare to find shifts of more than 5%, usually among the undecided. Such a shift could decide an election or produce millions of dollars for a commercial product and therefore justified the investment, but the low percentage shows how persistent attitudes can be.

Hovland (1959) attributed the difference between laboratory and field studies to two principal factors—selective exposure and attitude strength. Under laboratory conditions, subjects are exposed to new information, even if they disagree with it initally. They are a captive audience and not a very representative one. In real life, people typically expose themselves only to information with which they already agree. Experimental studies also use rather trivial attitudes, in which there is little emotional involvement. There is an ethical problem associated with manipulating deep-seated beliefs experimentally, as well as the more practical problem of obtaining discernible differences. Survey studies on the other hand, often involve more important issues, such as political preferences that are embedded in a network of beliefs and are widely shared by other group members. These beliefs are resistant to change and when changed may not endure, because individuals return to groups that helped establish them in the first place. Irving Janis (1963), who succeeded

Hovland after his death, made a similar point when he stated that "the net effect of mass communications tends to be very limited, often consisting only of reinforcing pre-existing beliefs and attitudes" (p. 55).

The problem is that attitude change may follow different principles depending on whether an issue is important or trivial. Hovland and Mandell (1952), for example, found that an untrustworthy communicator was seen as more biased but produced as much attitude change as a trustworthy one when the issue was not important. Lana (1961) has noted that familiarity with a topic produces a primacy effect where the initial argument in a pro-and-con debate is more effective, whereas a recency effect favoring the second argument occurs with unfamiliar material. Changing trivial attitudes is more akin to attitude development since the initial position is neutral, whereas changing important attitudes requires that one accept that the speaker's position is more reasonable than one's own, even though one's own comes from a lifetime of experience. The failure to recognize that individual attitudes reflect broader social values has also created a tendency to treat racism, sexism, and anti-Semitism as "personal" problems, which can be eliminated by correcting misconceptions and providing people with more information.

Attitude research has evolved considerably since Hovland's death in 1961. Some topics not previously investigated have received considerable attention. The majority of these studies, however, use techniques devised by Hovland and his associates and concentrate on issues raised by the Yale research program. Advances in attitude research have occurred not because of new methods but because attitudes are now conceptualized within a new theoretical framework, which includes cognitive consistency, attributions, and discourse.

## COGNITIVE CONSISTENCY AND DISSONANCE THEORY

When the third volume of the Yale Studies in Attitude and Communication appeared in 1960, the emphasis of the research had clearly changed, as the title suggests: *Attitude organization and change: An analysis of consistency among attitude components* (Rosenberg, Hovland, McGuire, Abelson, & Brehm, 1960). The Rosenberg and Abelson model of cognitive balance presented in the above work was just one of a number of consistency theories developed more or less independently in the mid-1950s. As Kielser, Collins, and Miller (1969) point out, credit for the original idea is usually given to Fritz Heider (1946, 1958).

The idea of cognitive consistency seems to have been a simple application of the Gestalt perspective to the field of attitude development and change. Once attitudes emerged as a major area of interest and Gestalt theory had taken hold, it was almost inevitable that attitudes would be seen as a system of organized beliefs with an underlying inclination toward cognitive consistency. This perspective assumes that opinions and beliefs are acquired not piecemeal but within an already existing structure. As Krech and Crutchfield (1948) put it, "Man is an organizing animal. . . . As soon as we experience *any* facts, they will be perceived as organized into some meaningful whole. This is a universal characteristic of the cognitive process and not a weakness of the impatient or prejudiced individual" (p. 86). While not a weakness, the tendency to organize can have negative consequences, because as they point out, a "corollary is that *perception is functionally selective.* No one perceives everything that there is 'out there' to be perceived" (p. 87). Consistent beliefs are actively integrated into a person's belief system, but inconsistent information is often distorted or ignored. An optimist sees through rose-colored glasses, while a paranoid sees in terms of personal persecution. This is one reason why attitudes are so resistant to change.

### Heider's Balance Theory

The Gestalt influence can be seen most clearly in Heider's balance theory. Fritz Heider (1896–1988) was a Vienna-born psychologist who incorporated phenomenology, Gestalt psychology, and field theory within a "naive psychology" of human interaction. He received his Ph.D. under Alexius von Meinong at the University of Graz. Meinong was a student of Brentano, another of whose students, Edmund Husserl, founded phenomenology. All three were connected with the University of Graz, and the phenomenological roots of contemporary psychology stem from them (Sahakian, 1982). Heider went to the Psychological Institute in Berlin in the early 1920s, where he audited courses by Wolfgang Köhler and Max Wertheimer, two of the founders of Gestalt psychology, and attended seminars by Kurt Lewin.

In 1930, Heider joined Kurt Koffka, the third founder of Gestalt psychology, at Smith College. He and his wife, Grace, lived downstairs in the same house with the Koffkas and the four became close friends. Lewin's wife and daughter lived with the Heiders in 1933 when Lewin went back to Germany, and Fritz and Grace Heider translated Lewin's book, *Principles of Topological Psychology* (1936).[2] Heider found Lewin's topology of limited use in dealing with interpersonal relations, but it was always in the background of his thinking (Heider, 1983).

Heider's *balance theory* describes the relationship between two or more entitles. Relationships are of two types—sentiment relations, based on favorable or unfavorable attitudes, and unit relations, based on association. Heider's unit relations are a direct extention of Gestalt principles and include such things as similarity, proximity, common fate, good continuation, and set. Among human beings, they include such additional factors as kinship, familiarity, ownership, and similarity. Things that are *perceived* as belonging together form unit relations. Sentiment relations are based on the way a person feels about other people or objects. Finer distinctions, such as liking, loving, respect, or admiration are not considered. A relationship consisting of two entities is balanced when both relations are either positive or negative. For example, a man marries the woman he loves, buys the car he has always admired, or detests the person who hates him. From this simple principle, Heider is able to derive such psychological truisms as the fact that we like those with whom we are familiar and have frequent contact and those who share our attitudes and values.

Most of Heider's descriptions involve two people, P and O, and an object, X. Triads are balanced when all three relationships are positive or when one is positive and two are negative. Examples include two friends liking or disliking the same political party, disliking the political party that one's enemy likes, or liking the party that one's enemy dislikes. These are shown in illustrations a, b, c, and d in Figure 10.1. Imbalance occurs when there is one negative relationship—when, for example, two friends disagree or when enemies like the same thing (see illustrations e through g). Cases where all three relationships are negative are ambiguous. If one considers both unit and sentiment relations, 64 combinations are possible. If one ignores this distinction, there are eight possible combinations. It is important to note that Heider's theory is a *phenomenological* theory. All relationships are seen from P's perspective. The relationship between O and X is as P perceives or imagines it. This is important because most other theories abandon the phenomenological perspective and treat relations in more general terms.

For Heider, balanced conditions produce a harmonious state in which entities fit together without stress. Unbalanced structures are unpleasant and generally evolve into more balanced ones, but the dynamic principles leading to change are not of overwhelming strength. They are more akin to preferences and are similar to Gestalt principles in perception, such as good form and closure. There is a general tendency to prefer orderly and consistent arrangements to less orderly ones. If a structure is balanced, it will tend to remain balanced. If it is imbalanced, there will be psychological pressure to modify some aspect of the relationship so as to achieve balance.

While people generally prefer balance to imbalance, Heider (1958) was well aware that imbalance is often sought.

> There may also be a tendency to leave the comfortable equilibrium, to seek the new and adventurous. The tension produced by unbalanced situations often has a pleasing effect on our thinking and aesthetic

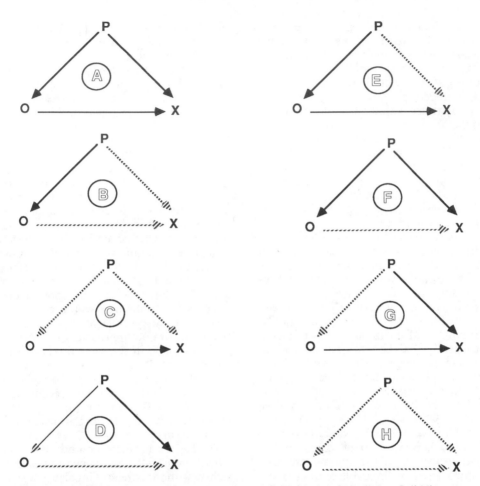

**Fig. 10.1.** Depiction of balanced and unbalanced states in Heider's (1958) theory. Solid lines represent positive relationships, broken lines represent negative relations. Arrows indicate the direction of the relationship. Conditions A—D are balanced, E through G are unbalanced, and H is ambiguous. No distinction is made between sentiment and unit relations.

feelings. Balanced situations can have a boring obviousness and a finality of superficial self-evidence. Unbalanced situations stimulate us to further thinking; they have the character of interesting puzzles, problems which make us suspect a depth of understanding. (p. 180)

Novels and short stories such as those of Dostoevski, which stress unbalanced situations, are felt to have deep psychological meaning, and the same is true for aphorisms such as Oscar Wilde's "Each man kills the thing he loves." But the attraction of such apparent inconsistencies is generally not due to the imbalance per se. It is due to the fact that they force us to rethink old relationships and obtain a higher state of balance.

Jordon (1953) tested Heider's theory by having 208 subjects evaluate triads in 64 hypothetical situations—that is, all possible combinations of sentiment and unit relationships. He found a general and statistically significant tendency for balanced relations to be preferred, but he also noted that positive relations toward either person O or object X were also rated as more pleasant. One trend undetected by Jordon was an agreement effect, in which both people evaluated X in the same way. The attraction effect is based on only one relationship (P likes O or X); the agreement effect requires two (P—X and O—X); whereas balance depends on a person's considering all three relationships at the same time. All three have been found repeatedly in the literature (see Petty & Cacioppo, 1981). While balanced relations are preferred, it is often difficult to tease out the separate effects of balance, liking, and agreement. Price, Harburg, and Newcomb (1966) found that ratings of pleasantness followed the balance model only when the relationship between P and O was positive. We tend to prefer balanced relations with our friends but are relatively indifferent to what our enemies think.

Theodore Newcomb's (1953) analysis of *communication acts* is derived from Heider's theory. Like Heider's, it deals with two people (A and B) and their attitude toward an object X. It predicts that increasing the intensity of the attitude or the attraction between people increases the strain toward symmetry, the likelihood of symmetry, and the probability that A and B will communicate in order to reach an agreement. It is the prediction about communication that makes the model unique. It also predicts that people will associate and become friends with people who hold similar attitudes and that friends will tend to agree. The frequency of communication about the topic, when two friends disagree, varies with the degree of attraction and the importance of this issue.

Charles Osgood and Percy Tannenbaum (1955) have developed a more complicated communication model based on their work with the semantic differential (Osgood, Suci, & Tannenbaum, 1957). The semantic differential measures the connotative meaning of objects in terms of three dimensions—evaluation, potency, and activity. Their *congruity theory* focuses on the evaluative dimension and measures the change in attitude toward a speaker and a topic. A unique feature of their theory is that it predicts attitude change toward *both* the source and the topic according to a precise mathematical formula.

## Intra-Attidudinal Consistency

Milton J. Rosenberg and Robert P. Abelson's (1960; Abelson & Rosenberg, 1958) theory of *cognitive balance,* while not a derivative, shows many similarities to Heider's theory. Abelson was a student at MIT during Lewin's tenure, and Rosenberg encountered the same perspective at the University of Michigan. Their theory is concerned primarily with attitudes, or what Rosenberg (1968) later called "intra-attitudinal balancing." An attitude is defined as a relatively stable constellation of affective and cognitive responses toward an object. Nevertheless, their model focuses on one pair of elements at a time. These form a cognitive unit or a "band." An attitude usually consists of many different overlapping bands each sharing one concept in common. A person's attitude toward "civil liberties" or "democracy," for example, consists of not one but many different beliefs.

The relationship between elements can be positive, negative, or neutral. No distinction is made between sentiment and unit relations. As Roger Brown (1965) points out, Rosenberg and Abelson achieve simplicity by assuming that Heider's first principle, which states that a positive unit relation induces a positive sentiment relation, has already been resolved and that sentiment and unit relations function so similarly as to be indistinguishable. Balance occurs whenever two positively evaluated objects are positively related $(+p+)$, two negatively evaluated objects are positively related $(-p-)$, or a positive and negative object are negatively related or disassociated $(+n-)$. Imbalance occurs when a negative relationship occurs between two positive $(+n+)$ or two negative elements $(-n-)$, or when a positive relation exists between a positive and a negative element $(+p-)$.

A second refinement introduced by Rosenberg and Abelson (1960) is the assumption that balance is restored, other things being equal, in the easiest possible way—by following the path of least resistance. This allows specific predictions about how balance will be achieved, and they provide experimental evidence that supports this hypothesis. The presence of inconsistency does not lead automatically to balance. Tolerance for inconsistency varies from person to person, but each individual has a point beyond which inconsistencies will not be tolerated. Most people have a number of inconsistent attitudes, either because they do not notice them or because they cannot resolve them.

Balance can be achieved either by reevaluating one of the two objects or by changing the relationship. It is also possible to differentiate an object into good and bad components so that one aspect is balanced or to bolster one object by seeking new informaion. Repression and selective attention often come into play when, for instance, some subpart is selected as more salient than previously believed while another is rendered less essential. If all else fails, a person can simply *stop thinking* about the problem and focus his or her attention on something else. Imbalance creates tension only when it is recognized, so not thinking is an effective strategy. When the forces toward balance are strong but the counterforces opposing it are stronger, people will often vacillate between thinking and not thinking. We say they cannot get their mind off the problem. Inconsistencies motivate people to attain consistency or place "irreconcilable" inconsistencies out of awareness. Many of the processes used to obtain balance described by Rosenberg and Abelson (1960) bear a strong resemblance to Sigmund Freud's mechanisms of defense.

Since an attitude involves both beliefs and an evaluation of the object, Rosenberg (1960) has suggested that attitudes can be changed rationally by changing beliefs or irrationally by altering the evaluation. He reversed people's evaluation of certain issues, such as racial integration and foreign aid, through hypnotic suggestion and found a corresponding change in beliefs. He also found that subjects typically reverted to their original beliefs when the hypnotic amnesia was removed. While imbalance creates tension, it is not the only force operating. A person tends to achieve balance in such a way as to maximize gains and minimize losses. This hedonistic factor produces a second force sometimes working with and sometimes working against the force toward balance.

## Cognitive Dissonance

In terms of actual research, the most influential consistency theory by far has been Leon Festinger's (1957) theory of cognitive dissonance. Festinger was a student of Lewin at the University of Iowa and one of the original members of Lewin's Research Center for Group Dynamics at MIT. His students Elliott Aronson and Jack Brehm devoted a substantial part of their early careers to research on cognitive dissonance. Dissonance theory shares the assumption that people prefer consistency to inconsistency, but its appeal is based primarily on its ability to generate counterintuitive predictions that reflect the extent to which people will go to resolve inconsistencies. While Heider's theory was derived from a naive psycholcgy based on common sense, cognitive dissonance offered a direct challenge to traditional notions of reinforcement and portrayed people as not so much rational as rationalizing—thinking and acting in ways that often do not seem plausible. Dissonance theory has also caught the imagination of researchers because of the ingenuity of the experiments used to test it. This ingenuity is a mixed blessing, however. It has opened up new avenues and methods of research, but it has also led to criticism and made precise duplication of individual experiments difficult.

The basic assumption behind cognitive dissonance is quite simple: The existence of cognitive dissonance creates psychological tension, which motivates the person to reduce the dissonance and achieve balance. Cognitive dissonance occurs whenever two cognitive elements or items of information imply a *psychological* contradiction. This is stated rather formally by Festinger (1957), *"two elements are in a dissonant relation if, considering these two alone, the obverse of one element would follow from the other . . . x and y are dissonant if not-x follows from y (p. 13),"* but as Brown (1965) has pointed out, this strict criterion is seldom encountered in actual research. Instead, the two propositions usually violate some psychological expectation of the type linked by contrasting conjunctions, such as *but, nevertheless, although,* and so on. Examples include:

1. I smoke cigarettes *although* smoking cigarettes causes cancer.
2. I choose product A *even though* product B has many good features.
3. The experiment was dull *but* I said it was interesting.
4. I underwent an unpleasant initiation to join a discussion group; *nevertheless* the group discussion was boring.

These are not *logical* contradictions (where not-$x$ follows from $y$) but they do violate our expectations about what goes together. Embedded in each is a third unexpressed premise that completes the syllogism. In the above, the missing premise would include such things as (1) I do not want to have cancer; (2) I always try to choose the best product that I can; (3) I say what I believe; and (4) if I endure something unpleasant, it always turns out well. These involve hidden assumptions about the self-concept or about the fairness of the world in general, and it has been found that people with low self-esteem, for example, *do not* behave the same as people with high self-esteem when placed in dissonance-producing situations.[3] Dissonance research has typically avoided this problem by selecting situations that would produce cognitive dissonance in almost everyone.

The magnitude of the cognitive dissonance is based on the importance of the issue and the number of dissonance relationships. The latter occurs because, while dissonance theory focuses on two elements at a time, each element usually involves a cluster of related beliefs. The desire to smoke, for instance, may have components associated with self-image (e.g., smoking is masculine), a psychological feeling, and a physical addiction. Choosing one product over another usually involves weighing the pros and cons of each, and this is why dissimilar products produce more dissonance

than similar ones—there are fewer overlapping elements. Choosing one of two cars, for example, produces less dissonance than choosing between a car and a European vacation.

Cognitive dissonance can be reduced by changing elements, adding new ones, or reducing the importance of the relationships. Changing elements reduces the contradiction, whereas adding new elements by seeking additional information gives additional weight to one side or the other. Dissonance theory predicts that when dissonance exists not only will the person strive to reduce it, but he or she will actively attempt to avoid information and situations that would increase it. Research on selective exposure, however, has produced mixed results. While people generally seek information that supports their decision, they do not necessarily avoid information opposing it. Ehrlich, Guttman, Schoenbach, and Mills (1957), for instance, found that people read more advertisements supporting the car selected than those rejected, but they also read more about the rejected cars than those not considered at all. The problem with many of the studies on selective exposure to information is that they confound dissonant and useful information (Kiesler, Collins, & Miller, 1969).

Dissonance research has tended to focus on decision making and forced compliance. Cognitive dissonance almost invariably follows a decision, because both choices usually have good and bad features. The degree of cognitive dissonance depends on the importance of the decision, negative attributes of the chosen alternative, positive attributes of the unchosen alternative, and the cognitive overlap or degree of similarity. Jack Brehm (1956) provided one of the first tests of cognitive dissonance in decision making by having female subjects first rate eight products for attractiveness and then choose between two of them that were either similar or dissimilar in attractiveness. He predicted that subjects choosing between two similarly attractive products would experience more dissonance and show more dissonance reduction by exaggerating the qualities of the chosen alternative and devaluing the rejected one. Subsequent ratings confirmed his prediction, although the effect was stronger for the unchosen alternative—that is, subjects resolved in the postdecisional dissonance by devaluing the rejected product.

Cognitive dissonance can also be reduced by revoking the decision, but this returns the person to the predecisional conflict. Conflict and dissonance are not the same. Conflict occurs before a decision, particularly when two products are equally attractive. Dissonance occurs after. Conflict can be resolved by seeking more information in order to make the best decision possible, whereas dissonance often causes people to selectively distort information in order to justify a previous choice. In other words, people are more likely to weigh the pros and cons of a product rationally before a decision is made and rationalize after. A positive consequence is that we are usually happy with the decisions we make.

Festinger and Carlsmith (1959) carried out the classic study of *forced compliance.* They had subjects participate in a dull task, which included turning pegs a quarter turn and placing spools on a pegboard. After the subjects were finished they were told that the purpose of the study was to test the effects of expectation on performance. Whereas no expectation had been created for them, the next subject was in the "favorable information" condition. They were then told that the research assistant who usually served as a confederate was sick and they were asked if they would be willing to substitute and tell the next subject that the tasks were really interesting and enjoyable. Half of the experimental subjects received $1 and half received $20. A third group was not asked to lie and served as a control. All subjects then took part in an "official" survey, given by a different person in a different place, in which they rated their interest in the experiment and indicated whether they would be willing to participate in a similar study in the future.

Festinger and Carlsmith predicted that those who received $1 would experience the most dissonance. Since $1 is insufficient to justify lying, those in the one-dollar condition could only reduce dissonance by convincing themselves that the tasks were really interesting after all. The results confirmed their prediction. Ratings by subjects in the control group and the $20 condition did not differ significantly, but those in the $1 condition rated the experiment as more enjoyable and expressed a greater willingness to participate in similar studies in the future. The results are opposite to what one would predict from reinforcement theory, where it is generally assumed that greater reinforcement leads to more attitude change. In cognitive dissonance theory, maximum attitude change occurs when incentives are just sufficient to induce the behavior.

Aronson and Mills (1959) studies the effects of initiation on subsequent attraction to a group. One group of female subjects underwent an embarassing initiation by reading obscene words and highly colored passages from contemporary novels to a male experimenter. They were then allowed to listen in on a boring discussion about sexual behavior in animals. Those that underwent the severe initiation rated the group more favorably than those undergoing a milder form of initiation. Again, what makes this study interesting is the counterintuitive prediction and the fact that it reverses traditional reinforcement theory's assumed relationship between reinforcement and attitude change. Not only do people sometimes show more attitude change with minimal reward, but they also come to cherish those things for which they have suffered.

It should be pointed out that cognitive dissonance, like Heider's balance, is an *intra*personal event, occurring within an individual, but it does have social consequences. Other people act as both a source of dissonance and a means for resolving it. This was dramatically demonstrated in the field study by Festinger, Riecken, and Schachter, *When Prophecy Fails* (1956). Members of a cult, expecting to be rescued by aliens before a great flood, were forced to reevaluate their beliefs when the flood failed to take place. Those who had waited for the rescue alone gradually lost interest in the group, but those who waited together became even more committed. While they avoided publicity before the event, they became active proselytizers afterward.

Since dissonance theory challenges reinforcement theory's interpretation of behavior, it is not surprising that it too has been challenged by those who support incentive theory. Much of the early criticism focused on methodological shortcomings in dissonance research. As Zajonc (1968) has pointed out, many dissonance researchers have taken a rather cavalier approach to experimentation, using procedures that were extremely imaginative but also extremely complicated and difficult to replicate. Many involved minor theatrical productions. But methodological discussions do not resolve theoretical conflicts, and it is possible, as Festinger (1980) has pointed out, for critics to address themselves increasingly to minor problems in previous research and lose sight of the central issues. Eventually researchers began to realize that both cognitive dissonance and incentives hold under certain conditions, and they began to explore what these conditions were.

The area of discrepancy that has received the most attention is the effect of reinforcement on forced compliance and counterattitudinal statements. Both Janis (1959) and Rosenberg (1965, 1970) have suggested that when people are asked to generate arguments opposing a position they endorse, they are temporarily motivated to think up all the good arguments they can. This is referred to as "biased scanning." Presumably, larger incentives lead to more arguments and more attitude change. This should be contrasted to the Festinger and Carlsmith (1959) study, in which greater attitude change ccurred with lower incentive. The difference is more apparent than real. Forced compliance involving only an assertion of a position produces cognitive dissonance, whereas counterattitudinal performance with actual arguments follows incentive theory (at least under certain conditions).

A second challenge to dissonance theory was offered by Daryl Bem's (1965, 1967) theory of self-perception. Bem assumes that the results of dissonance experiments are reliable but offers a radically different interpretation. Bem recognizes that actors often have access to internal cues that provide information not available to an outside observer, but when these cues are weak, the actor is in the same position as an outside observer. For Bem, people label their own internal states and those of others by looking at overt bahavior. Self-perception is simply a special case, in which the actor and the observer are the same person.

Bem (1965) has conducted interpersonal replications of several of the dissonance studies by having subjects read descriptions of other people and estimate their attitude. The results do not precisely duplicate the original, but they are close. The advantage of Bem's interpretation is that it makes the same predictions without assuming an underlying drive toward cognitive consistency. For Festinger (1957), cognitive dissonance is a motivational state that energizes and directs behavior. Dissonance reduction is rewarding in the same sense that eating is rewarding when one is hungry. Bem, on the other hand, assumes that people evaluate their behavior in a more detached manner, relying mainly on external cues. The presence or absence of an underlying drive therefore allows a critical test of the two theories.

A number of studies using a variety of techniques have supported the position that situations designed to induce cognitive dissonance also produce physiological arousal and motivational effects similar to other biological drives. Gleason & Katkin (1978), for instance, monitored heart rate over the entire course of dissonance manipulation and found a higher heart rate in the dissonance condition. Cooper and Croyle (1981) found an increase in skin conductance under similar conditions. Fazio, Zanna, and Cooper (1977) have shown that the arousal effects of cognitive dissonance can be misattributed to the physical surroundings, hence reducing attitude change. Attitude change in dissonance situations can also be reduced with tranquilizers or increased with stimulants (Cooper, Zanna, & Taves, 1978). Moreover, cognitive dissonance shows the general motivational effect of facilitating dominant responses and in-hibiting weak ones (Cottrell & Wack, 1967). The presence of physiological arousal in dis-sonance-producing situations, however, does not undermine the role of self-percep-tion. Fazio, Zanna and Cooper (1977) have pointed out that self-perception and disso-nance theory complement each other. Dis-sonance occurs when there is a rather large discrepancy between a previous attitude and behavior. Self-perception occurs when the discrepancy is small.

Zajonc (1968) has argued that Bem's in-terpersonal replications do not disprove cognitive dissonance theory but merely sug-gest that the results may not be counterin-tuitive as previously believed. The fact that one subject can "guess" what another sub-ject would do in a dissonance-producing sit-uation shows that dissonance predictions are not that far out of line with common sense. Aronson (1980) has expressed the opinion that dissonance theory is not obvi-ous only when seen against the backdrop of reinforcement theory. Common sense rec-ognizes that under certain conditions we ra-tionalize socially undesirable behavior, cherish things for which we have suffered, and reconcile ourself to the inevitability of our decisions.

Dissonance theory has undergone con-siderable revision since it was first formu-lated by Festinger in 1957. It is now possible to specify more precisely the conditions under which it will and will not occur. Brehm and Cohen (1962) summarized nearly forty studies and concluded that commitment, choice, and volition are all es-sential—that is, dissonance is produced only when a person chooses and feels re-sponsible for his or her behavior. In forced compliance situations, dissonance occurs only when there are serious negative con-sequences stemming from the behavior (Cooper & Worchel, 1970). Carlsmith and Freedman (1968) have suggested that dis-sonance will not occur even with negative consequences if the outcome is not known in advance—that is, people do not feel re-sponsible for events that they could not foresee. Aronson (1980), on the other hand, has pointed out that in some cases people will assign responsibility irrationally to themselves and experience dissonance even when the negative consequences were not foreseen.

Cognitive dissonance has also been rein-terpreted by a number of authors. Aronson (1968) considers cognitive dissonance a dis-crepancy between cognitions and a person's self-concept. Deutsch and Krauss (1965), on the other hand, treat dissonance reduc-tion as equivalent to Freud's concept of ra-tionalization. If rationalization is used to re-duce cognitive dissonance, then it is possible that other defense mechanisms may be used as well. Kiesler, Collins, and Miller (1969) have complained that one of the problems with consistency theories is that there are too many of them, and they are not sufficiently different to justify the proliferation. If this is true, then some higher-order integration, such as a possible union with psychoanalysis, certainly seems desirable.

Despite its achievements, cognitive dis-sonance research began to decline during the late 1960s. One reason was that Festin-ger left social psychology in 1964 because he felt that he was personally in a rut, and he has, according to his own account, been completely out of touch with it since (Fes-tinger, 1980; personal communication, April, 1985). Aronson and Brehm soon shifted their interest to other topics as well. Without their input, cognitive dissonance theory lost much of its initial inspiration. Newcomb (1978) felt that the decline in re-search was also due to the fact that after a decade or two of research, dissonance the-ory seemed too specialized and too cut off from the main body of social-psychological research to have much relevance.

The popularity of cognitive dissonance theory reflected certain social trends that were characteristic of American society dur-ing the 1950s—most notably problems of self-identity and the insecurity of social re-lationships. According to Rosenberg (1970), the inner self and its values had been grad-ually eroded by an age of conformity as peo-ple were seduced into performing acts in-consistent with their true beliefs. The dilemma for the individual was how to maintain a sense of integrity in the face of such inauthenticity. These psychological changes can be seen as the result of two larger social trends during the same period—the increased use of advertising and the mass media to create a sterotypic image of American society (and a corresponding concept of unAmericanism) and a shift from blue-collar to white-collar jobs. In 1956, white-collar workers outnumbered blue-collar workers for the first time in history. White-collar jobs depend on making a good impression, and creating a favorable image by conforming to public pressure became absolutely essential if one were to succeed in an environment where occupational success depended on impressing management. People could readily identify with Festinger and Carlsmith's (1959) dissonant subjects, who were coerced into saying and doing things that they did not actually believe.[4]

A second change was based on a dramatic increase in consumer goods. American production nearly doubled during the war, and factories created for wartime production rechanneled their energies into consumer goods during the postwar period. The American consumer was faced with more choices and as a consequence more post-decisional dissonance. It may seem like a truism to say that choice is necessary for post-decisional dissonance, but choice had not been possible on this scale any time before. People in American society during the postwar period could readily identify with examples of people choosing between two cars or a car and a European vacation.

It should be noted, however, that forced compliance and post-decisional dissonance are simply two derivatives of cognitive dissonance theory, and one should not confuse the derivatives with the general theory. The basic assumption behind cognitive dissonance is that people think and process information in an organized way. Inconsistencies create tensions, and these motivate people to resolve them. These assumptions are a direct derivative of the Gestalt perspective, which permeated the thinking of most of the theorists during this period. The emphasis on compliance and decision making, however, may have given dissonance theory a sense of relevance not easily perceived in other consistency models. Disso-

nance theory applied to situations that people experienced every day. This should not be taken as a criticism. Most theories draw their examples from phenomena close at hand. But it does point out that the popularity of a theory is based on both internal factors, such as the ingenuity of the research and the quality of the ideas, and external factors, such as relevance to existing social situations.

The central assumption of dissonance and consistency theories, that conflict is stressful and that people therefore seek balance and harmony, is itself a reflection of social trends occurring after World War II. The rise of the market economy and consumerism reinforced the American ethos of possessive individualism (Israel, 1979; Macpherson, 1962). In a consumer-oriented society, conflict is usually viewed as a disruptive force that interferes with people's ability to pursue their own self-interest within an atmosphere of harmony and balance. Thus, as Joachim Israel (1979) suggests, cognitive consonance rather than dissonance was the best model for typical psychological behavior.

The protest movement during the 1960s challenged the postwar values of individualism and consumerism and fostered a social and political climate based to a certain extent on conflict and uncertainty. Dissonance and consistency theories became less relevant within this context, and the amount of research declined dramatically. As Billig (1982) comments, the failure of consistency theories to explain "the everyday generality of inconsistency, might illustrate the diminishing role of consistency in contemporary society" (p. 166).

## SOCIAL-LEARNING THEORIES

Cognitive social psychology during the postwar period was influenced by behaviorism as well as Gestalt psychology. Methodological behaviorists, who turned to behaviorism as a procedure rather than a philosophy, accepted the causal role of mental processes but focused primarily on overt behavior (see Chapter 5). Both Hull's and Tolman's learning theories contained references not only to external events but also to drives and expectancies within the organism. When some of Hull's followers began to apply his learning theory to social behavior like imitation and aggression, they quite naturally incorporated a number of mediational variables that were inferred from observable behavior.

Before the war, Miller and Dollard (1941) developed a theory of social learning and imitation based on Hull's learning theory and psychoanalysis. This theory included elements derived from research on animals but also incorporated numerous cognitive processes. Behavior is motivated by drives within the individual, stimuli must be perceived and interpreted, and responses can be overt or covert. Covert responses, such as language, allow individuals to envision and try out reactions mentally before actually behaving and are responsible for purposeful behavior.

Their model of imitation suggests that imitation occurs when one person (the observer) depends on another (the model) to provide an example of an observable sequence of responses that will lead to reinforcement. Observers copy the model's responses and thus learn how to obtain reinforcement. The external reinforcement of the model's behavior is the key for successful learning in this theory, and learning occurs only when there is some form of reinforcement. Unlike earlier models of imitation, such as those of Tarde (1890/1903) and Baldwin (1895), Miller and Dollard's approach drew explicitly from learning principles in an attempt to explain how imitation occurs (Shaw & Costanzo, 1982).

By the 1960s, however, the role of external reinforcement in imitation was being questioned. Albert Bandura (1962, 1971) argued that rewards facilitate learning in several ways, but they are not absolutely necessary for learning to occur. For Bandura, most human learning occurs vicariously through observing other people rather than directly through trial and error. Learning is mediated by four processes: attention, retention, motor reproduction, and motivation. Motor reproduction is the only process based on overt behavior. It is necessary

for acquiring and improving some forms of complex bahavior, such as learning to ski or to play a musical instrument, where each step depends on mastering and combining simpler steps previously learned, but it is not necessary for simple behaviors that can be carried out without practice in a single trial. The acquisition of symbols (such as language) further modifies the learning process. Observers do not simply mimic the behavior of others but actively process information and act only when appropriate. Because it downplays the necessary role of both reinforcement and behavior within the learning process, Bandura's model has a distinctly cognitive flavor.

Social-learning theories have been frequently applied to other areas of interest within psychology, such as *aggression*. The prewar treatment of aggression was based primarily on psychoanalytic theory and stressed the role of motivation. During the postwar period, however, theories of aggression began to place a greater emphasis on cognitive factors (Jones, 1985). The two leading theorists during this period were Leonard Berkowitz and Albert Bandura. For Berkowitz (1962, 1965), aggression was seen as a direct result of emotional arousal—generally based on frustration and anger, and tied to cues that have been associated with reinforced aggression in the past. Bandura (1971) is more explicit about cognitive factors and suggests that aggression is based on people's previous experiences with aggression (both direct and indirect), cues in the present situation, and the anticipated consequences of aggression. His research has repeatedly shown that children imitate aggressive models, with and without direct reinforcement.

During the 1960s, as a result of the growing number of political assassinations and the increasing concern with alienation and the fragmentation of social bonds, a number of researchers turned their attention to the study of *altruism* (Jones, 1985). The most famous studies carried out during this period were conducted by Bibb Latané and John Darley (1970). These researchers questioned the conventional wisdom that bystander nonintervention was based on apathy and they showed that it occurred through a combination of social comparison and diffusion of responsibility. When people are confronted with a potentially dangerous or ambiguous situation, they do not respond immediately. Instead, they maintain a cool and calm facade and look around to see how others are responding. The problem is that other people are also likely to maintain a calm facade initially, and this can lead bystanders to misdefine an emergency as a nonemergency.

A second factor is diffusion of responsibility. When people are confronted with a potential emergency and a number of other people are present at the same time, each person assumes that someone else will get involved. This means that, far from there being security in numbers, members of a large crowd are *less* likely to respond than those in small crowds or individuals confronted with an emergency alone.

In general, social-learning theories have placed a greater emphasis on observable behavior than underlying cognitive processes, whereas the Gestalt approaches stress cognition rather than observable behavior (Gergen, 1982). Social-learning theory, however, like cognitive consistency, stresses individual psychological processes. Aggression, for example, is viewed in terms of people's previous history of vicarious learning, as well as their interpretation of instigating cues within the immediate environment. The role of society in creating frustration and aggression and the positive role of aggression within collective movements is given very little consideration (Lubek, 1979, 1986).

## NOTES

1. Aristotle made a similar distinction in his *Rhetoric,* when he differentiated three types of persuasion. "The first kind depends on the personal characteristics of the *speaker;* the second on putting the *audience* into a certain frame of mind; the third on the proof, or apparent proof, provided by the words of the *speech itself*" (cited in Petty & Cacioppo, 1980, pp. 5–6).

2. It is an interesting historical fact that when a German press wanted to publish Lewin's text a few years after his death only parts of the original German version could be found, so the German edition is a retranslation of the Heiders' English translation.

3. Heider (1958) made a similar point when he stated that most dyadic relationships, such as P owns X and P likes X, involve a missing third element, namely P likes P. Most of the examples that he uses assumes a positive self-attitude. Without this attitude, a person still strives for balance but achieves it in a different way. Aronson and Carlsmith (1962), for example, have shown that after a series of failures a good performance produces cognitive dissonance.

4. A similar trend developed within clinical psychology and gave rise to various humansitic theories that stressed the discrepancy between the public person and the inner self, the need to explore one's inner feelings, and the quest for self-actualization (e.g., Maslow, 1954; May, 1953; Rogers, 1951).

# 11

# Symbolic Interaction

While psychological social psychologists have tended to stress the experimental study of cognitive processes, sociologists since World War II have focused on symbolic interaction. The symbolic interaction approach addresses two shortcomings within the psychological approach to social psychology. First, it includes a frank recognition that mental processes are culturally derived, and second, it focuses on interaction—that is, communication and coordinated activity—rather than cognitive processes taking place within individuals.

Symbolic interaction did not suddenly spring up after the war, but the extended discussion of this approach within a textbook by Lindesmith and Strauss (1949) helped mark a turning point within the sociological tradition. The sociological approach to social psychology had become more and more similar to the psychological approach up to the mid-1940s. This can be seen in the overlap among the most cited authors during the postwar period. While the previous and subsequent overlap has been limited to two or three authors among the ten most frequently cited, Gardner Murphy, Theodore Newcomb, Muzafer Sherif, and Sigmund Freud were frequently cited by *both* psychological and sociological textbook authors, and the psychological literature was rapidly becoming the sociological literature as well. This might be seen as a healthy trend toward integration were it not for the fact that all of the above were psychologists, and there was little borrowing among psychologists from the sociological literature. The textbook by Lindesmith

and Strauss (1949) reflected developments within sociological social psychology as it sought to regain its status as a distinct sub-discipline. Symbolic interaction suddenly became *the* sociological approach, and the chief architect of this transition was George Herbert Mead.

Mead did not actually use the term "symbolic interaction." This term was first coined by one of his students, Herbert Blumer (1937). The present chapter will start with a general discussion of Mead's approach to social psychology and then discuss how his views were revised by Ellsworth Faris, Herbert Blumer, Manford H. Kuhn, and Erving Goffman after his death in 1931. The distinct psychological and sociological approaches to social psychology that developed during the postwar period were accompanied by attempts to bridge the gap between them and build an interdisciplinary perspective, and these developments will be discussed at the end of the chapter.

## MEAD'S SOCIAL PSYCHOLOGY

Mead's approach to social psychology was part of his more general pragmatic world view, which has already been described in Chapter 4. It is embedded within a much more inclusive cosmology that includes extended discussions of mathematics, physics, and evolutionary theory (Miller, 1973). Mead was concerned primarily with traditional philosophic problems, such as the relationship between mind and body, self and society, and the origin of conscious activity, and his social psychology was developed in order to deal with these. Natanson (1966) has argued that *Mind, Self, and Society* (1934), *The Philosophy of the Act* (1938), and *The Philosophy of the Present* (1932) represent the progressive development of Mead's ideas. *Mind, Self and Society* is the most popular account of Mead's social psychology, but it takes on additional meaning when seen within the context of Mead's other work.[1]

Mead's work, though fragmented and often redundant, is systematic in the sense that it is an integrated system of concepts in which each element can be understood only by seeing it in the context of Mead's other ideas. Mead's theory is not difficult to understand, but it is difficult to know where to begin. There is no convenient starting point, and his ideas cannot be treated in a strictly linear fashion by introducing them one by one. Mead himself used a circular style in his lectures—introducing ideas, developing new ones, then returning to earlier ideas and repeating the process. While much of the redundancy has been removed in the edited works, it is an almost inevitable consequence of the complex unity of his ideas. Meltzer (1964) has suggested that the order of Mead's central concepts as presented in *Mind, Self, and Society* should be reversed to reflect the fact that society occurs first, and this is the approach that we will use.

## Society

Mead starts by assuming an external reality that exists apart from each individual and that is a necessary condition for all knowledge. The existence of an external reality is taken for granted by scientists, by common sense, and even by idealists as they go about their day-to-day affairs. Many of the problems of traditional philosophy simply disappear if we assume that objects are real. This world consists not just of physical objects but social objects as well. While Mead gave society a leading role in shaping behavior, he did not go into a great deal of detail about the nature of social institutions. The only exceptions were his treatment of language, roles, and science.

Mead explained language in evolutionary terms as a natural outgrowth of emotional expression. Expressive gestures include such things as the snarl of a dog, the cry of a child, and the clenched fists of an angry person. These are either the first stages of inhibited acts or outflows of nervous energy. They are instictive behaviors that are objectively observable and readily interpreted by those at which they are directed. Among these, vocal gestures are particularly important. While feedback from facial and body movements conveys a vague sense of the emotion being expressed, both the speaker and listener hear the same vocal sounds. The vocal channel is also relatively clear because it is used only for expression.

Mead makes a distinction between significant and nonsignificant gestures. Nonsignificant gestures are understood by those being addressed, but may not be noticed by those who use them. Significant gestures are understood by both parties and convey the same meaning. Human language started when people became self-conscious about what they were trying to say and began to put together a message in order to elicit a particular response. The most important significant symbols are words, which are merely a highly specialized form of gestures capable of making distinctions far more subtle than other forms of expression. Objects and activities are given names and then grouped in more general categories. Names make it possible to experience objects not actually present and manipulate hypothetical situations. Names alter perception because they draw attention to certain aspects of the situation and exclude others, or as Mead (1934) expressed it, they lift aspects out of the situation that are already there. They improve memory because objects that are labeled are recalled more easily, and they make thought possible.

Language is very much a social product, acquired through contact with other speakers in one's culture. The words we use have more or less a common meaning for all the members of our group. The particular language that one speaks determines to a certain extent the way one perceives and organizes reality. According to Mead (1934), people who learn a new language acquire a new soul. They cannot read its literature or converse without taking its attitude. They become different people. Significant symbols, and language in particular, form the basis of conscious awareness. That which is not expressed in language is not consciously experienced and has no meaning.

Societies also have prescribed roles which are clusters of duties, rights, and obligations assigned to particular individuals and groups. Roles do not imply active membership within a group. There are roles for women, children, fathers, and the mentally ill, and these vary enormously from culture to culture. Some societies, for example, have given fathers absolute authority over their families, including the right to kill other family members. In other societies, fathers have little say in the care and discipline of their children, whereas contemporary middle-class society strives for a more or less equal partnership between husband and wife. Roles are rigidly prescribed in some cultures but extremely flexible in others. Many roles—parent and child, husband and wife, teacher and student—are bilateral and cannot exist independently. Social institutions are based on a number of interlocking roles, in which each is part of a larger, more inclusive social pattern. People learn to respond to each other because they learn that various *types* of individuals behave in ways that are *typical*.

For Mead, roles are acquired in stages. Initially children imitate without understanding but during the *play stage* they begin to imitate significant others in their environment self-consciously. What distinguishes this stage is the limited capacity to adopt only one role at a time. The child pretends to be a mother, a father, a doctor, then a nurse and gradually builds up a repertoire of knowledge about role-appropriate behavior. In modern society, there are many different roles based on a complex division of labor, and children select from among those in their immediate environment.

Children later enter what Mead called the *game stage*. They learn to adopt several perspectives at the same time and begin to understand how roles interlock to form coordinated activities. Mead used the example of baseball. In order to play baseball effectively, each player must know what the other players are going to do. He must be able to anticipate the other's response and throw the ball not to where a player is but to where he will be. Good chess players play four or five moves ahead by anticipating their own moves and those of their opponent. During the game stage, the child acquires the ability to see behavior simultaneously from several viewpoints and gradually builds up knowledge about how to behave in groups.

While the game stage represents a considerable advance in the child's development, socialization is not complete until particular roles are fused into a *generalized other*. The child has learned specific roles and attitudes from particular types of people, but he or she must also learn that some attitudes and values are widely shared by virtually all members of the group. Berger and Luckmann (1966) use the example of spilling soup to illustrate this development. The child spills soup and the mother becomes angry. The child concludes that "mother is angry with me *now* because I spilled soup." By repeating the process, the child learns that mother is *always* angry when they spill soup. As additional people—father, grandparents, older siblings, and so on—respond in the same way, the child recognizes that *everyone* opposes soup-spilling and develops a generalized attitude that *one* does not spill soup. The generalized other represents the most general norms within society that one uses to evaluate one's own behavior and that of others. It resembles Freud's concept of the superego and serves to both praise people for doing well and censor them when they violate social norms. Particular norms and knowledge of role-appropriate behavior continue to be absorbed and help shape behavior in specific situations, but the generalized other provides unity and continuity for one's behavior.

After people have acquired language and developed a concept of the generalized other, they are socialized and respond to themselves as members of society. They may become hermits or live on a desert island, but they can never escape society because it is now a part of them. Socialization should not be viewed as a passive process, however. Children choose models to a certain extent, ask questions, and test the limits of permissible behavior. Nor should socialization be confined to childhood. People must learn to respond to new people and situations as they mature. Children may play doctor, but those who become real doctors must master a large body of medical knowledge. They may learn new techniques and procedures as they study medicine, and ideally they continue to learn throughout their life.

Members of society also fall heir to the collective wisdom of their age. Language makes it possible to transmit information so that each generation can build on the achievements of previous ones. For Mead, science was the ultimate achievement because it contained tested and verifiable knowledge. Science is a verbal record of the most universal aspects of the common world, which transcends any particular perspective by showing what is common to many and potentially common to all. The scientific community consists not just of active researchers but includes anyone who can understand the literature. While society predates the individual, it continues and changes as a result of social interaction. The community consists largely of accepted ways of acting and thinking that the individual learns during the process of socialization.

## Self

Mead's concept of the self draws heavily from James's "social self" and Cooley's "looking-glass self." For James (1890), *"a man has as many social selves as there are individuals who recognize him,"* but because not everyone's opinion is relevant, "he has as many different social selves as there are distinct *groups* of persons about whose opinion he cares" (p. 294). As Deutsch and Krauss (1965) point out, James explicitly linked the social self to social interaction and implicitly recognized the importance of reference groups. While both James's and Cooley's formulations recognize the importance of social factors, what is missing is a detailed and systematic account of how the self develops. Because they began with selves rather than with society, their treatment carries with it connotations of the earlier concept of the soul. For Mead, there was nothing mystical about the self or mental activity. Self-awareness develops during the process of socialization as people become conscious of themselves as social objects. Mind and self both depend on language (or some symbolic system), and they bear the imprint of one's culture. The two emerge simultaneously, but we will discuss Mead's concept of self before proceeding to his treatment of mental activity.

Mead felt that a great many unnecessary problems had been created because psychologists and philosophers began with the notion of self-conscious individuals rather than treating self-consciousness as something that develops during the course of socialization. The newborn has no self, but young children gradually develop one as they begin to see themselves as others see them. The labels that other people use to describe us gradually become part of our self-concept. Certain aspects of our identity, such as age, sex, race, and various handicaps, are based on physical characteristics that are beyond our control. Others, such as family income, religion, and ethnic identity, are due to accidents of birth, whereas others are achieved through membership in occupational or professional groups. Throughout life people associate with others they have not chosen—family, teachers, neighborhood gangs—and these interactions, for better or worse, shape their self-concepts. The self includes the norms and values of society incorporated in the generalized other plus knowledge of role-appropriate behavior as a unique member of a particular group. Each individual incorporates a number of different roles—husband or wife, father or mother, professional or unemployed—and therefore Mead felt that multiple selves were normal. We behave differently with our family, friends, and business associates, and each group sees a different side of our personality.

The self is more than a set of internalized roles, however. It is a social process with two aspects, the "I" and the "me." The "I" is the impulsive, spontaneous actor, what James called consciousness itself. Behavior begins with an impulse or desire to do something, and the "I" is the source of this impulse. The "I" includes habits unknown to the individual—ways of walking, talking, and doing things—that make up the unconscious self. The "I" is not experienced directly and can be known only in retrospect after it has become a fait accompli. According to Mead (1934), I talk with myself and remember what was said. The "I" of this moment becomes the "me" of next, but I can never turn around fast enough to catch myself behaving spontaneously. It is because of the "I" that we are never completely aware of what we will think, say, or do next. Mead was concerned primarily with aspects of social interaction that we experience consciously, so he did not deal with the concept of the "I" to any great extent but he did recognize its existence. The "I" is responsible for creative as well as irrational acts. It is that part of the self that has never been fully socialized and is outside of awareness, isolated and untamed.

If a person always behaved instinctively or habitually, the "me" would never occur. The "me" occurs when a person confronts an obstacle and becomes self-conscious about his or her behavior. The "me" is similar to James's empirical self—the self as experienced and known. It contains the conventional standards of society over against which the more spontaneous "I" responds. It includes aspects of the generalized other plus knowledge about particular people and situations. The "me" exists when we become aware of how we appear to others. It is always situation-specific. We experience only those aspects of ourselves that are relevant to the problem at hand. A man may be a loving father, a good husband, and a Nobel-prize-winning physicist, but these attributes become irrelevant when he has to change a flat tire on a deserted road at night. We sometimes experience an actual dialogue between the "I" and the "me" in the form of an internal conversation. We ask ourselves if we should have another piece of

pie and say yes or no. At other times, our degree of self-awareness is much more limited. If we are fully engaged in an activity, such as running from danger or writing a book, the "me" can disappear almost completely, but the "me" is experienced either implicitly or explicitly in every act of conscious experience. Consciousness always involves self-consciousness to a certain extent.

## Mental Activity

For Mead the concept of "mind" is a form of activity—mental activity—rather than some sort of spiritual stuff located in the head of an individual. There is nothing supernatural or mysterious about Mead's treatment of mental activity. Like previous pragmatists, he believed that consciousness occurs during the course of concrete activities when one confronts a problem that must be resolved. Consciousness is a symbolic process that accompanies ongoing behavior. For Mead, mental activity is merely the use of language to describe and analyze a situation and chart a course for future action. Mead differs from other pragmatists, however, in placing a far greater emphasis on the social origins of mental activity.

For Mead, the basic unit of behavior is the *act* rather than a stimulus and a response. The act is a goal-directed behavior, such as closing the door, eating one's supper, or obtaining a Ph.D., which usually involves a series of steps and terminates when the goal is reached. It may be conscious or unconscious, but it is future-oriented and always involves events that have yet to take place. Conscious activity occurs during the course of habitual activity when traditional ways of behaving are no longer appropriate. A person must imagine alternative courses of activity and choose the one that seems most likely to achieve the goal. Consciousness is always consciousness of some forthcoming activity.

There are four phases of the act—the impulse, perception, manipulation, and consummation. Mead did not go into great detail about the impulse, or source of motivation, but he did allude to it occasionally. Impulses are based partly on instincts, and Mead's treatment of instincts was similar to Freud's in that he believed that instincts could be classified into two opposing groups—friendly instincts, consisting of sex, gregariousness, and parental feelings, and hostile instincts based primarily on aggression. Friendly instincts were responsible for a great deal of self-sacrificing social behavior, but hostile instincts also played a role in social behavior. Hostility toward other groups and people who violate group norms was seen by Mead as the cement that holds society together. Mead was dubious about the possibility of eliminating hostility, but he did think that it tends to be exaggerated by certain social conditions. Hostility is based on self-assertion and plays a positive as well as a negative role in personality development. It is more pronounced, however, in those who cannot assert themselves through work or other constructive tasks. The only way of reducing hostility, Mead believed, was by extending one's reference groups, and this was a process that occurred naturally through economic transactions. Thus, Mead's treatment allowed him to see hostility as an inevitable aspect of human nature and still be optimistic about reducing it in the future. Mead's treatment of instincts should not be seen as a passing stage in the development of his ideas. He wrote articles incorporating the idea of instincts in 1909 and 1918–1919 when explanations of social behavior based on instincts were at the height of their popularity, but also in 1929 in one of his last published works (see Mead, 1964). Mead was highly critical of McDougall's (1908) instinct theory, however. He felt that McDougall's treatment was so closely bound to his theory of emotions that he was forced to generate additional instincts in order to get the correct number (Mead, 1909/1964).

Perception is the second stage in the act and is guided by impulses. What we notice in the environment depends on what we are trying to do. For Mead, the eye functions as a filter screening out what is irrelevant and focusing on those things that aid or obstruct behavior. Much of the visual world is simply taken for granted. In human beings, perception is aided by language, but language merely lifts out elements within the world that are already there. Consciousness is a "selecting agent," but what it selects depends on a person's needs and the situation. Perception does not reside in the individual. It is a relationship between the individual and the environment. We cannot construe *any* reality we choose.

Manipulation is concerned with the actual overt behavior that occurs as people try to reach their goals. In animals, manipulation and consummation occur at virtually the same time—a dog, for example, kills and eats its prey simultaneously—but in human beings manipulation often involves a series of steps and a considerable interval between the initiation and the completion of an act. The final stage is consummation. This is the goal or purpose for which our behavior occurred. Time is marked not by hours and minutes but by acts, and acts are described in terms of their goals.

For Mead, consciousness emerges during the course of social activity. Social acts are goal-directed activities involving two or more people. Each person cooperates in the process and makes his or her intentions known. Language is the vehicle by which acts are coordinated. While animals live in a world of events, people live in a world of shared meaning. The speech and gestures that people use to make requests and convey their intentions to others are perfectly objective overt behaviors. To be effective, each participant must be aware of his or her own role and that of others. Before making a request, such as "Please close the door," the actor must imagine the other person responding. Even if the person refuses, the refusal is based on having understood the request. Communication takes place *only* when two or more individuals share a world of common meaning. The degree of self-awareness varies with the difficulty of the tasks. If the task proceeds smoothly, there may be little self-awareness. If difficulties occur or we interact with people we do not know well, self-consciousness may be acute.

Much of the conversation within groups takes the form of discussions of current problems or complaints about existing social conditions. People complain about work, aspects of their lives, their relationships with others, or the ability or inability of government to solve persistent social problems. They ask questions, compare opinions, and build up a consensus about what should or should not be done. The tendency of conversation to focus on problems is just another indication that thought emerges from concrete activity when there is a problem to be solved or an obstacle to overcome.

*Thinking is merely the internalization of this social process.* For Mead (1934), thought "is simply internalized or implicit conversation of that individual with himself" (p. 47) using significant symbols that have the same meaning for all members of the group. Thinking occurs when there is a delay between the impulse to act and its completion. A person can rehearse various courses of action and choose the one that seems most appropriate. Language is the mechanism by which thought takes place. For Mead, there is no problem about how individuals express their thoughts to each other or share a world of common meaning. Thought is not something that takes place in the head of an individual, it is "sublimated conversation." We can think out loud by conversing with others or think privately by conversing with ourself, but private thought is already in the form of communication and can be made public if we so choose.

Much behavior occurs with little or no thought, but once thought occurs it changes the nature of our behavior. It allows us to imagine alternative courses of action, recall events more easily, and bypass the long arduous road of trial and error. Thinking is the first phase of intelligent conduct, but it does not disappear once conduct is initiated. We monitor ongoing behavior while the act is in progress, make changes, and correct our behavior. Trial and error still plays a role in physical activities, such as playing an instrument or riding a bicycle, but once thought develops it is used in virtually everything we do. Few activities are so routine that they do not require some degree of conscious attention.

Dewey (1932) has suggested that the "nature of consciousness as personal and private" was the "original haunting question" that dominated all of Mead's thought. Mead felt, along with James, that a great deal had been placed in the mind that must be returned to the objective world. Some events, such as a toothache or a pleased palate, are private because they are experienced by only one individual, but they are not subjective. If two people were joined like Siamese twins and shared the same nervous system, they would experience pleasure and pain in the same way. Our bodies are part of the physical world but are not experienced by others in the same way. Other types of mental activities, such as daydreams and discoveries, are private as well, but even these are far more social than most people realize. Mead's philosophy was an attempt to get meaning out in the open and relieve it of its subjective connotations (Miller, 1973).

Thought develops through conversation with ourselves and others, and our most private thoughts are merely an extension of the communication process. Daydreams seem subjective because they are seldom shared, but they are based on present needs and previous perceptual experiences. The stuff that dreams are made of is the stuff of everyday life. Once we have developed the capacity to think, we can tell ourselves stories that we do not share with others. Many daydreams are an attempt to escape boredom. In a quotation reminiscent of Marx, Mead (1925–26/1963) said "we see the routine and drudgery of countless uninterested hands and minds fashion in factories and mines the goods for which men give their wealth and themselves. . . . Indeed, this is the definition of drudgery, the blind production of goods, cut off from all interpretation and inspiration of their common enjoyment" (pp. 295–296). Under ideal conditions, work would be interesting and daydreams unnecessary. Mead felt that movies externalize reveries and express the hidden unsatisfied longings of many people.

Mead was very much concerned with the process of emergence or creativity. Each invention is the product of a single individual, but the individual is a member of a community and starts with a common body of knowledge widely shared by other members of the group. Moreover, each new contribution is reincorporated into the community. Each new discovery is generated by an individual but developed in such a way that it can be conveyed and become common property. The individual is a source of new ideas later shared by others.

This process can be seen most clearly in scientific discoveries. Individual scientists collect data through observation and experimental procedures. Data that support existing theories are simply incorporated and used to extend their range of application. Disconfirming evidence, on the other hand, forms exceptions and forces people to rethink and reformulate scientific laws. These reformulations are minor for the most part but can be revolutionary, as in the cases of evolutionary theory or in the theory of relativity. Discoveries are made by individuals but are formulated in the most general terms so that they can be communicated and tested by other members of the scientific community. Scientific objects are conceptual objects, impersonal and free of the idiosyncrasies of subjective experience. Anyone who shares the scientific perspective will perceive them in much the same way.

The discovery of exceptions to existing scientific theories was, for Mead, the best proof of an external reality, independent of the hypotheses used to explain it. Older theories are simply untenable hypotheses that can no longer bear experimental verification. New theories are tentative hypotheses subject to the same type of refutation. Each generation improves on the perspective of the previous generation and in so doing it creates a different view of the world. Mead saw Newton's theory as an approximation and Einstein's as a more accurate statement, but he speculated that relativity theory may itself become obsolete in the future (and, incidentally, Einstein made the same prediction—see Einstein and Infeld, 1938). There is no absolute certainty, no final resting place. Scientists are in possession of a constantly increasing body of reliable data that must be periodically reinterpreted. Reality is the ultimate court of appeal.

What is true for science is true for history as well. We customarily think of history as something fixed and unchanging, but as Mead pointed out, each generation rewrites its own history and this is the only one it has. The concept of history as fixed and unchanging stems from a belief in an absolute perspective—the perspective of God—from which things are completely known and experienced as they really are. Once this is given up, all perspectives are relative. The past is reformulated in terms of present needs. We look to the past for solutions to problems we confront today. New evidence forces us to reinterpret previous events. Our concept of history is simply our best guess about what happened given the evidence at hand. It is a working hypothesis subject to revision when new evidence is found.

While our interpretation of present and previous historic events depends on our perspective, the perspective is not subjective. Scientific and historic perspectives are based on language and can be widely shared. They are confirmed or refuted on the basis of available data. We cannot construe any perspective we choose. There is nothing subjective about a scientific theory. There may be disagreement about details, but even disagreement involves opposing camps in which members share a common point of view. Individual perspectives grow out of community perspectives, but the community perspective is not a collection of individual ones. Each new insight and discovery is fed back into the community, which is open and continually changing.

The concept of emergence or creativity is not limited to science and history but is a general characteristic of all conscious behavior. Consciousness occurs when habitual ways of behaving are no longer appropriate. A person imagines new courses of action and selects from among them. Behavior can never be completely predicted on the basis of what has gone before. It may seem predictable in retrospect, but this is only because we remember in general terms and gloss over what was unique at the time. Mead, like Peirce and Dewey, regarded the scientific method as the paradigm for correct thinking. We put forth tentative hypotheses, compare them conceptually, and confirm them through our behavior.

Mead's position helps to overcome many of the dualisms that have plagued traditional philosophy and social science. Social behavior is both free and determined. Persons are social products. Their personalities are made up of the language, customs, and standards of their group. Indeed, with the exception of instincts and other aspects stemming from physiology, people are *entirely* social products. But they are also free to modify their behavior and vary their perspective of the world, subject to the constraints of reality. Society shapes individuals but imperfectly, and society changes as a result of individual initiatve. There is a reciprocal relationship. Every deliberate decision changes the social order, slightly for the most part, but greatly in the case of geniuses and world leaders.

Mead's treatment also transcends the traditional dualisms of mind-body, subjective-objective, and so on. As long as the mind was considered some sort of spiritual stuff that fashioned sensations, emotions, images, and ideas, then some sort of location seemed necessary. Psychologists placed the mind in the brain of the individual (e.g., Floyd Allport, 1924). Previous generations, unwilling to admit that consciousness could cease, placed it in the soul. Once mental activity is seen as a symbolic process rather than a thing and its contents are returned to the physical world, the distinction between internal and external is no longer necessary. Some aspects of thought, such as conversation, are public, others are private and known only by the individual, but all thinking is a process of conversation that uses language and a shared perspective derived during the course of socialization. If we start with minds contained within separate individuals, it is difficult to see how people can understand each other, empathize, cooperate, or share opinions—how one mind can reach over and make contact with another. But if mental activity is seen as a derivative of a concrete social process, then these problems simply disappear. As members of a social group, we share a language, a knowledge of role-appropriate behavior, and to a great extent a common perspective.

Mead may have overestimated the extent that perspectives are actually shared, because he was living at a time of enormous change. Relativity theory was forcing peo-

ple to reassess the nature of the physical universe. Pragmatism and psychoanalysis were challenging traditional assumptions about mental activity, and sociologists were beginning to generate scientifically verifiable hypotheses about social behavior. While many of the trends were controversial, they were controversial because they were new and not fully understood. Mead was living through a transition and was optimistic about what the future would bring. "The human mind is constantly emerging from one chrysalis after another into constantly new worlds which it could not possibly previse. . . . We, none of us, know where we are going, but we do know that we are on the way. . . . It is a splendid adventure if we can rise to it" (Mead, 1923/1964, p. 266).

## POST-MEADIAN DEVELOPMENTS

During the postwar period, the symbolic interactionist movement initiated by Mead became the dominant sociological approach to social psychology. Mead's impact began to be shown in those sociological textbooks written between 1948 and 1953, in which he was the third most cited author (see Table 1.1). During the 1960s he was the second most cited author (just behind Sigmund Freud), and he was joined by a number of other writers who drew their inspiration either directly or indirectly from symbolic interaction. Since symbolic interaction forms such a large part of the postwar sociological approach, it is far beyond the scope of this book to review all of the major developments that have occurred since Mead. More comprehensive reviews can be found in such works as Hewitt (1984); Lauer and Handel (1977); Lindesmith, Strauss, and Denzin (1977); and Stryker and Statham (1985). Two excellent books of readings are also available (Manis & Meltzer, 1978; Stone & Farberman, 1970).

The present discussion will begin with Mead's successor at Chicago, Ellsworth Faris, and continue with two contrasting schools of symbolic interaction—the Chicago School and the Iowa School—and the work of Erving Goffman. The Chicago School of symbolic interaction is most closely associated with Mead's student Herbert Blumer, whereas the Iowa School was developed by Manford Kuhn at the University of Iowa and was sustained almost exclusively during his life by articles published in the *Sociological Quarterly*. The differences between these schools center on the degree that behavior is determined by social conditions. Blumer stresses the emergent nature and unpredictability of social interaction, whereas Kuhn takes a much more deterministic view. These differences have methodological implications as well. Blumer advocates a distinct methodology for studying symbolic interaction, whereas Kuhn stresses traditional scientific procedures. Most versions of symbolic interaction fall between these two extremes but lean toward one pole or the other (Turner, 1978), and they therefore serve as useful anchor points for showing the scope and diversity of symbolic interaction (see Meltzer, Petras, & Reynolds, 1975). Developments within the symbolic interaction approach during the 1970s and 1980s will be considered in the next chapter.

## Ellsworth Faris (1874–1953)

Something of a myth has grown up that the Chicago School of sociology was a unified body of ideas that centered around George Herbert Mead. This is based on the current recognition of the importance of Mead's ideas and the assumption that since Mead taught at the University of Chicago from 1894 to 1931, he must have had a strong influence on those around him. W. I. Thomas was a student of Mead, but he was a mature student who had studied in Europe and already had a Ph.D., while Mead was a new instructor without a Ph.D. just beginning his career. Besides, as mentioned previously, Thomas took Mead's courses in comparative psychology and research methods, not social psychology. Thomas claimed that he could not understand Mead and does not appear to have used many of his ideas

(Coser, 1977). Park was a close friend of Mead, but he too does not appear to have been greatly influenced by him. The faculty member most profoundly influenced by Mead was Ellsworth Faris.

Ellsworth Faris was born in Tennessee, but his family moved to Texas when he was twelve. He attended what later became Texas Christian University and received a degree in 1894. He spent seven years as a missionary in the Belgian Congo before returning to Texas Christian University, where he taught theology and philosophy from 1904 to 1911. He received graduate training at the University of Chicago under John Dewey and George Herbert Mead and received a Ph.D. in psychology in 1914. When Thomas resigned in 1918, Faris was asked to join the Department of Sociology in order to maintain the social-psychological tradition that Thomas had initiated. He became chairman after Small retired and directed the department between 1925 and 1939.

Faris taught four quarters a year during most of his career and gave a great deal of time to administrative duties. He published little but did contribute several important articles on imitation and instinct theory. Faris was highly critical of instinct theory and argued that the search for instincts was based on a misguided attempt to place the cause of social behavior within the individual. According to Faris (1937):

> Men could not agree on the elements because they do not exist. The assumption in all of them was that individuals constitute society. But if we assume that society produces personalities, then the elements of personality will be found, not in the individual self at all, but in the collective life of the people (p. 187).

A number of his papers on the topic were collected and published in a volume entitled *The Nature of Human Nature* (Faris, 1937).

Faris (1927) also rejected the notion that social behavior was acquired through imitation in an uncritical manner. He argued that behaviors often attributed to imitation were the product of attitude-taking and conscious choice. The key, according to

Faris, lies in the normal human tendency to converse with one's self—that is, to stimulate one's self and answer one's own stimulation. Through this process, one can take the role of other people and adopt their attitudes when these seem more appropriate.

Faris was influenced by Gestalt psychology and applied it to groups. For Faris, not only was the whole greater than the sum of its parts but it created the parts. The group was a real entity because it encouraged certain forms of behavior and limited others. People behave differently in groups because the group dictates what is and what is not acceptable.

Faris's most important conttribution, however, was based on his promotion of Mead's ideas. Mead's classes did not draw large numbers, and his articles were obscure and seldom read. Faris, on the other hand, was a popular and often dramatic instructor and most sociological students, both graduate and undergraduate, enrolled in his course. He drew students from a number of other departments as well, including psychology, anthropology, and political science. Faris directed graduate students specializing in social psychology, and it was through him that Mead was brought to the attention of the majority of sociological students at the university. According to one student, Faris depicted social thought in terms of "B.M." and "A.M."—before and after Mead (Lewis & Smith, 1980). Students enrolled in his course got a healthy dose of Mead's ideas and as they graduated and spread out across the country, they took this knowledge with them. Faris was primarily responsible for promoting Mead during Mead's lifetime and helped establish him as a cult figure at the University of Chicago.

## Herbert Blumer (1900–    )

Although Faris helped introduce students to Mead throughout the 1920s and 1930s, what has become known as the Chicago School of symbolic interaction is most closely associated with Herbert Blumer. Blumer was a student and then a member of the sociological faculty at the University of Chicago from 1927 to 1952. Ellsworth

Faris directed his doctoral dissertation, and Mead sat in on his oral exam. Blumer was Mead's research assistant and took over Mead's course on social psychology when he was hospitalized. Mead had apparently asked Faris first but Faris's duties as chairman and editor of the *American Journal of Sociology* prevented him from teaching an additional course. When Faris retired in 1939, Blumer inherited the responsibility for social psychology at Chicago and edited the *American Journal of Sociology* from 1941 to 1952. He moved to the University of California at Berkeley in 1952 and taught there until he retired (Lewis & Smith, 1980).

Blumer (1937) coined the term "symbolic interactionism" to describe his approach, which he considered a direct extension of Mead's. Like Mead, Blumer separated behavior into symbolic and nonsymbolic forms. Nonsymbolic interaction occurs whenever two people respond directly to each other without interpretation. This occurs in reflexive behavior, as when two boxers spar, and in various forms of emotional expression. Much human behavior is nonsymbolic, but Blumer felt that symbolic behavior is far more characteristic, and he made it the focus of his research. As other people began to adopt the label "symbolic interaction," Blumer's approach became known as the "Chicago School of Symbolic Interaction."

Blumer's (1969) conception of symbolic interaction rests on three basic premises. First, people act toward things on the basis of meaning. They live in a world of meaningful objects, and their response depends on how they label and interpret events. Second, meaning arises during social interaction. Meaning is a social product rather than an inherent property of the physical world. Group members create a common meaning and experience objects in more or less the same way, and conversely, members from different cultures give a different meaning to the same objects and experience them differently. Finally, the meaning of things is modified through a process of interpretation. New situations constantly arise in which existing knowledge is no longer adequate, and events must be reinterpreted as they unfold. Interpretation is an open-ended and creative process that is responsible for much of the unpredictability of human behavior. Interpretation is not always perfect—people may fail to notice relevant information, exercise poor judgment, or plan a faulty line of conduct—but it is characteristic of human behavior and must be included if social scientists are to capture the full complexity of social interaction.

Blumer was concerned not merely with symbolic activity but social behavior or what he called "joint action." Joint action occurs when two or more people coordinate individual acts during an ongoing process. Each person expresses what he or she is going to do and interprets the behavior of others. Because the behavior of others cannot be fully predicted in advance, a person must often wait until the other person responds before he or she can plan the next move.

Blumer's doctoral dissertation was called *Method in Social Psychology,* and his interest in methodology continued throughout his career. His views on methodology were merely an extension of his belief that interaction is fluid and changing. He felt that social research itself was a process of symbolic interaction in which researchers came to understand the world as seen by some particular group. Since people interpret situations before they act, social scientists must understand how they define situations before they can understand their behavior. Behind the facade of objective social behavior is a process of interpretation that researchers cannot afford to ignore. Blumer called for a direct examination of the empirical world—the world of everyday experience—using naturalistic procedures.

Blumer's naturalistic methodology involved two aspects—exploration and inspection. During the exploratory stage, researchers use any one of a number of different procedures—direct observation, interviews, life histories, diaries, letters, or a search of the public records—to gather information about a particular group. Blumer (1969) felt that an especially useful procedure was a discussion group made up of well-informed participants, and that such groups were "more valuable many times

over than any representative sample" (p. 41). During this stage, researchers approach concrete situations prepared to observe and revise their observations. The ever-shifting nature of symbolic interaction requires an open mind and an open-ended approach rather than one based on preconceptions.

The exploratory stage serves two functions. It gives investigators the opportunity to become familiar with the group they wish to study. The need for familiarity is most clearly recognized in anthroplogical studies of foreign cultures, but it is equally important for such "native" groups as the clergy, the military, prostitutes, or slum dwellers, whose perspectives are so unique that they cannot be understood without first-hand experience. Exploration also gives researchers an opportunity to sharpen their focus and revise their ideas as the study continues. Researchers entering a new area cannot know what will be relevant or irrelevant in advance. They must begin with a broad research agenda and progressively narrow it during the course of investigation. They must be willing to adopt new perspectives and move in directions previously unimagined. Blumer (1969) felt that "sensitizing concepts" were an important research tool. These are broad concepts, such as personality, social structure, mores, norms, and institutions, that lack precision but provide cues and suggestions about where researchers should look. They can be revised and refined during the course of investigation.

The inspection stage typically occurs after the information has been collected, although it is also possible to move back and forth between the two stages at the same time. Investigation involves an intense examination of analytic elements and their relationships. Observations are used to sharpen concepts and revise general statements. Sensitizing concepts allow a certain amount of deductive reasoning by which one can draw implications from the study, but the ultimate test is always agreement with the empirical world of everyday experience. Blumer felt that it was critical to subject key concepts to a probing discussion within groups of well-informed participants in order to test the accuracy of one's interpretation. Researchers must remain in touch with the empirical world throughout the investigation and revise concepts in the light of new evidence.

Blumer's methodology can be seen as both a critique of traditional statistical and quantitative procedures and a justification for the type of research developed and widely used at the University of Chicago. His list of acceptable procedures includes many of those actually used by Thomas and Znaniecki (1918–1920) in their classic study of Polish peasants, while his repeated assertion that it is necessary to see the world from the point of view of the group being studied is reminiscent of Park and Burgess's stress on participant observation. Blumer (1969) felt that each group was unique, and "we seem forced to reach what is common by accepting and using what is distinct" (p. 148).

Blumer's opposition to traditional scientific procedures was based on the fact that they typically start with preconceived theories and neglect the process of interpretation. Preconceptions bias the investigator's interpretation of events and the meaning of the situation as seen by participants is either bypassed or ignored. Blumer was highly critical of operational definitions because they focus on a single quantifiable characteristic and ignore the complex context that sustains social behavior. He felt that the ambiguity of concepts used by social psychologists, such as attitudes, impulses, motives, and drives, introduced a gap between theory and empirical research, leading to either empty theorizing or detached and frequently pointless research.

A number of people have questioned the view that Blumer's methodology is a direct extension of Mead's. It seems to be more accurately described as a defense of the procedures introduced and widely used within the Department of Sociology at the University of Chicago. McPhail and Rexroat (1979) point out that Mead was deeply committed to hypothesis testing and experimental procedures. Mead (1917/1964) cautioned against confusing the "scientific attitude of being ready to question anything with an attitude of being willing to question everything at once" (p. 200). Mead (1938)

treated hypotheses as tentative solutions for exceptions to scientific theories and chastized critics of experimental research. He recognized that experimental tests were not always practical but suggested "mental testing" or "thought experiments," which he saw as the prototype for correct thinking in general.

Questions have also been raised about Blumer's claim that his more general approach is a direct extension of Mead's. While Blumer's conception of human interaction in terms of collective problem solving carries on the spirit of Mead's approach, he fails to incorporate much of Mead's more comprehensive perspective. Joas (1985) points out that Blumer's fragmentary appropriation of Mead's work reduces the concept of action to that of interaction and fails to include the context of evolution and history.

Another controversial aspect of Blumer's version of symbolic interaction is the relationship between interaction and society. For Blumer (1969), social institutions are created and maintained through ongoing interaction. Society consists of a network of social interactions and "large-scale organization has to be seen, studied, and explained in terms of the process of interpretation engaged in by the acting participants as they handle the situations at their respective positions in the organization" (p. 58). Blumer does not deny the importance of social structure, only that social structure automatically shapes social behavior. Society is the framework within which interaction takes place. Most situations are sufficiently structured that little reinterpretation is necessary, but there is still room for maneuvering and devising new courses of action. The degree of social stability is less profound in modern society, where criss-crossing lines of conduct create many situations with no prescribed forms of behavior. In short, Blumer maintains that symbolic interaction creates and maintains organizational behavior and not the other way around, although there is always some continuity based on previous experience. This contrasts sharply with most sociological theories and with that of the Iowa School of symbolic interaction.

## Manford Kuhn (1911–1963)

Kuhn received his master's and doctoral degrees from the University of Wisconsin, where he studied under Kimball Young—an eclectic proponent of symbolic interaction and a former student of Mead (see Chapter 4). He joined the faculty at the State University of Iowa in 1946 and taught there until his death in 1963. While his impact on sociological social psychology as shown by citations is far less than that of Blumer, he is frequently used as a contrast to Blumer because his own position is much more deterministic.

There are several differences between Kuhn and Blumer's approaches (see J. Turner, 1978), but in keeping with the previous treatment of Mead, we will begin with their conception of society. Blumer sees society as a network of social interactions and stresses the temporary and changing nature of organizations. For Kuhn, on the other hand, society consists of a network of positions and roles that are quite independent of the individuals who occupy them. Roles are the basic "building blocks" of which social groups are composed and get their meaning from the broader social context.

Kuhn and Blumer also disagree on the degree of structure and stability within the self. Blumer emphasizes the spontaneity of the self within social interaction—people's ability to reinterpret events and alter their behavior. Kuhn stresses the importance of a "core self" derived from previous interaction and association with other members of one's reference groups. Personality for Kuhn is simply the combination of all the roles internalized by the individual during the course of socialization. These provide not just recipes for behavior but goals, values, feelings, and characteristic ways of interpreting situations.

As with Mead, the fact that roles are acquired from society does not preclude individual differences. Families are a major source of socialization, and differences among families are passed on to the children. Biological differences intervene to a certain extent and people combine roles in different ways, giving high priority to some and low priority to others. Finally, groups do not demand absolute adherence to roles. A certain amount of nonconformity is tolerated if it does not conflict with the group's definition of what is appropriate. Minor idiosyncrasies are attributed to personality differences, but radical departures lead either to ejection from the group or informal but equally effective estrangement.

These different conceptions of self lead to different conceptions of interaction. For Kuhn, the core self is relatively stable and helps account for the stability of behavior in different situations. Interaction is a function of both the individual and the situation, but the core self helps determine how the situation will be interpreted. The core self shapes and constrains behavior by determining what will and will not be noticed. A certain amount of unpredictability occurs because individuals experience role conflict, confront new situations where previously prescribed behavior is no longer appropriate, or attempt to engage in behavior that is unacceptable to the group, but people are pressured into providing structure in unstructured situations, and if communication is possible, they work out collective rather than individual definitions of what is appropriate.

These different conceptions of social interaction have methodological implications as well. Kuhn's belief that the self is a product of social conditions made him look with more favor on experimentation, hypothesis testing, and deductive procedures. Much of his career was devoted to providing an operational definition for the self. His most famous tool was the Twenty Statement Test, which measures the "core personality" by asking people to provide twenty different answers to the question "Who am I?" He found that people tend to respond by listing roles, such as father, husband, student, engineer, and so on, thus supporting his contention that personality consists of roles.

Other methods advocated by Kuhn reflect his belief in the importance of symbolic activity. He rejected the psychoanalytic position that behavior is unconsciously motivated and advocated direct measures of attitudes through attitude scales and public opinion surveys. He also suggested that content analysis could be used to study communications within small groups and the mass media, thus providing an indirect quantitative measure of beliefs and attitudes. While Kuhn was much more sympathetic to traditional scientific procedures than Blumer, he was equally adamant about the importance of language and symbolic processes, and all of his procedures were based on either a direct or indirect assessment of verbal behavior.

It has been suggested that Mead developed a dialectical position similar to Marx in his attempt to explain the relationship between the individual and society (Zeitlin, 1973). The individual is simultaneously a social product and a source of social change. If this view is accepted, then Blumer and Kuhn can be seen as stressing either one side or the other of the dialectic process. Kuhn recognized a certain amount of indeterminacy but emphasized the priority of preexisting social roles in shaping the core self and providing stability across situations. Blumer stressed the creative side of behavior and saw interaction as a source for social change. Mead's approach was simply so all-encompassing that contemporary versions can stress one aspect or the other and still remain relatively faithful to the original. If it were not for the large methodological differences, Kuhn's and Blumer's approaches could be seen as two variants of a single theme.

Even though differences exist, there are certain fundamental principles on which virtually all symbolic interactionists agree (J. Turner, 1978). As the name implies, symbolic interaction is concerned primarily with symbolic behavior and interaction. People think, act, and communicate by using symbols and use symbols to plan and guide behavior. Communication involves a conversation of gestures in which early acts allow one to anticipate later acts. People anticipate and interpret one another's response by role taking—that is, placing themselves in the other person's perspective. Mind or mental activity develops out of this capacity to take roles and involves an internal conversation. Although treated somewhat differently, the concept of self is central in all versions of symbolic interaction. These basic principles form the core of the symbolic interaction approach and should be kept in mind when differences are discussed.

## ERVING GOFFMAN

Erving Goffman (1922–1982) was born in Alberta, obtained a B.A. from the University of Toronto and an M.A. and Ph.D. from the University of Chicago. Shortly after finishing his doctoral degree, he joined his former teacher Herbert Blumer at the University of California at Berkeley and taught there until 1969, when he moved to the University of Pennsylvania. Goffman almost single-handedly created the sociological approach known as "dramaturgics." His main concern was using the metaphor of the theater to explain behavior in face-to-face situations, which he examined and described in great detail. In his later work, *Frame Analysis,* he discussed the limitations of the theatrical metaphor and stated bluntly that "all the world is not a stage" (Goffman, 1974, p. 1), but he contended that there was enough similarity between acting and everyday life to make the metaphor useful for explaining a great deal of social interaction.

One similarity between the stage and everyday life is that both are divided into front and back regions. The front region is where individuals perform. It includes the physical setting—furniture, scenery, and props—and the "personal front" consisting of clothing, insignia, and behavior. The back region is hidden from the audience. It is the place where performers relax, rehearse, and adjust their costumes. In a restaurant, for instance, the dining area serves as the front region and the kitchen is the back. Waiters and waitresses can take off their masks in the kitchen, criticize or ridicule the customers, and engage in conversation that increases their sense of solidarity and mutual regard.

Groups of people typically cooperate in staging a performance and make up what

Goffman calls a "performance team." Failure to maintain a convincing performance can lead to a scene, and both the audience and performers work hard to avoid scenes. Performers are expected to learn their part and play it well, whereas the audience is expected to avoid backstage areas and ignore peripheral aspects of the performance. Since team members have common access to backstage information, any one of them has the power to "give the show away." Team members are thus mutually dependent on each other and cooperate in maintaining a given definition of the situation.

Not only does much of daily life involve playing roles of one kind or another, but these activities can themselves be transformed so that we play at playing roles (Goffman 1974). We can, for example, see a play in which waiters are involved or describe the play to one of our friends. These transformations are called "keyed events" when they are recognized by all the participants and include such things as theatrical performances, plays, ceremonies, rehearsals, and demonstrations. A second type of transformation occurs when one or more people are not fully aware of what is going on. These are called "fabrications" and include practical jokes, hoaxes, and in their less benign form, cons.

Fabrications are difficult to maintain because it is difficult to control all aspects of behavior at the same time. Goffman (1959) makes a distinction between expressions "given" consciously in order to project an image and those "given off" or emitted unconsciously. Many forms of emotional expression are beyond our control and are therefore used to verify the impression that the actor is trying consciously to convey. The ability to manipulate an impression is facilitated by practice. A seasoned waitress may be able to convey deference and respect even though she is indifferent or even hostile to the person being served. But Goffman felt that actors are at a disadvantage because the ability to see through a performance is greater than the ability to manipulate all aspects of expressive behavior. Successful performances therefore depend on actors playing roles to the best of their ability, while the audience ignores or "disattends" to all irrelevant aspects of the situation. This is obviously more difficult if the audience is a target of an attempted con.

Goffman (1961, 1963) makes a distinction between focused and unfocused interactions. Unfocused interactions occur when people are copresent—as when two strangers notice each other from across a room—whereas focused interactions occur when two or more people agree to sustain a common focus of attention for an extended period of time. Even unfocused interactions are carried out with some general though largely unspecified rules of conduct. People are required to maintain a certain level of physical appearance and refrain from self-directed, self-absorbing activities such as scratching, picking one's teeth, or cleaning the fingernails. They must express a certain level of "controlled alertness," which is a state of tension showing that they are ready for an interaction should the need arise. A certain amount of "civil inattention" is also required. Each person must give the other people enough visual attention to show that they recognize their presence but not so much as to suggest that they are an object of attention or curiosity. Although such behaviors are commonplace, they are typically noticed only when they fail to occur. The failure to maintain one's physical appearance, refrain from self-involved activities, or show controlled alertness and civil inattention is often taken as a sign of mental illness. Normal people must be "good" and not cause a scene or a disturbance. They must "fit in" and not attract undue attention, either by being insufficiently or overly involved.

The amount of spontaneous regulation increases as one moves from unfocused to focused encounters. Any face-to-face group must have a means for selecting new members. People who are already acquainted are virtually guranteed the right to interact, but for those who are unfamiliar there must be some reason or pretext. Some places like bars, cocktail lounges, and private parties are "open places" that generally encourage interaction between strangers. People at such gatherings engage in a common pool of unfocused interaction, but within these settings there are usually a number of subgroups engaged in face-to-face encounters at the same. These subgroups show their mutual involvement by their pattern of eye contact and by the way they position their bodies. Someone wishing to enter such a group must "knock on the door," so to speak, by moving into close vicinity, showing civil inattention to the group as a whole, and being invited in. Once in, individuals participate more or less as equals for the duration of the encounter.

Once individuals begin to participate, they must obey certain rules of irrelevance, in which they ignore most aspects of the encounter and focus on a common problem or topic. Two people involved in a game of chess, for example, must focus on the game and ignore the physical properties of the chess pieces. It makes no difference whether the game is played with bottle caps, gold figurines, or uniformed men on colored flagstone in a specially arranged courtyard. Other things such as wealth, social status, previous preoccupations, and personal problems must also be selectively ignored (unless they are the topic of conversation). This does not mean that all encounters are equally open. As Goffman (1961) pointed out, the classic phrase of the English gentry, "Anyone for tennis?" did not literally mean *anyone*. It simply means that once people are involved in an encounter, there is a tacit agreement to selectively focus on a common topic and ignore virtually everything else.

People participating in an encounter must also maintain the proper level of involvement. They must "come into play" upon entering the situation and "stay in play" throughout the duration of the encounter (Goffman, 1963). People must not be either insufficiently or overly involved. Failure to participate sufficiently shows a lack of respect for the other people and may weaken their level of involvement. Goffman (1961) points out that, of all our abilities, the capacity to show spontaneous involvement is the one least under conscious control. Nevertheless, people must make an effort, even when they are not personally interested. In such cases, facial expressions are particularly important. There are party faces, funeral faces, and even various kinds of institutionalized faces, such as the ones prisoners wear, that people must put on in order to maintain the spirit of the occasion. The ability to maintain "spontaneous" co-involvement is particularly important in two-person groups where the degree of involvement is generally seen as an indication of the quality of the relationship.

Despite such attempts, incidents do occur that suddenly increase the level of tension. Minor incidents occur constantly during conversations as topics dry up or suddenly become too personal. Other incidents include Freudian slips, boners, blushing, perspiration, or a "shaky" voice. Individuals are obliged to cope with minor incidents by either ignoring them or incoporating them into the stream of conversation. Some people, particularly those with higher status, are better able to do this than others. The right to make jokes, for example, is usually limited to ranking persons within the group (and those who have earned the status of group buffon). The ability to maintain a smooth flow of conversation in spite of such mishaps ultimately determines the quality of the interaction.

When people cannot maintain the central focus of attention, it may lead to what Goffman describes as "flooding out." Flooding out occurs when someone cannot supress a conflicting mood. Examples include laughing out loud during a board meeting or a dissertation defense. Laughter can start as a minor failure to maintain involvement, receive conformation from others, and then contagiously spread to the group as a whole, leading to a redefinition of the situation. The possibility of flooding out increases as the level of tension goes up, and people differ greatly in their ability to sustain attention without flooding out. When the process starts it is possible for a subset of participants to enter into a byplay in which they attempt to catch one another's eye to see if the encounter is being experienced in the same way.

While the ability to join groups, maintain a proper level of involvement, and selectively ignore everything but the central focus of attention would seem to be necessary for every interaction, groups vary in their degree of social control. Each encounter is somewhat unique, and what is proper in one situation may not be proper in another. "Informality" is partly based on the license to flood out on minor pretexts, and small amounts of tension may be deliberately introduced just for fun. The one rule of conduct that is common to all social situations is the rule requiring people to "fit in." They must maintain the proper level of involvement for the particular occasion. Social interaction may fail to occur not only because people are insufficiently close but because they are overly familiar, creating a sense of boredom and the feeling that nothing new is likely to happen. As Goffman (1961) points out, any "improper move can poke through the thin sleeve of immediate reality" (p. 81). Encounters are judged by the smoothness of the interaction, and informal participation is a validation of the intimacy and equality of the participants involved.

The concept of *self* is a central theme in Goffman's work and the focus of his first and probably most important work, *The Presentation of Self in Everyday Life* (Goffman, 1959). Goffman equates the self with the roles we play and roles are seen as a product of society. Each culture provides conventional interpretations about what is appropriate and inappropriate, and role incumbents adopt preexisting standards. Thus, waiters behave pretty much the same in spite of vast differences in physical qualities and backgrounds. Roles include both formal aspects that can be described (for example, in a training manual) and informal aspects that are learned by watching others. According to Goffman (1974), "whenever we are issued a uniform we are likely to be issued a skin" (p. 575)—the self "is not an entity half-concealed behind events, but a changing formula for managing oneself" (p. 573).

But individuals also bring a personal style to each situation that conveys something of their true identity. Identity is often shown by violating role requirements or maintaining "role distance." Deference in waiters is so common that it tells us nothing about their true feelings. We are more certain about these when a waiter is surly or openly hostile. Identity is often seen as something more basic, even biological, but Goffman felt that many aspects of identity were simply roles acquired in other situations. A person is not *just* a waiter but a waiter studying acting on the side or a waiter working his way through medical school.

The concept of *role distance* can even become an institutionalized aspect of the role itself, as Goffman (1961) has shown with the example of a chief surgeon. The chief surgeon is engaged in a very serious occupation where successful performance is literally a matter of life and death. But chief surgeons do not always treat their jobs seriously. They joke, use irony, or call for instruments using humourous, nontechnical names. The reason is that surgery is demanding work that depends on everyone "keeping their heads" at all times. If the chief surgeon demanded full respect, the level of tension would endanger the operation. This example is useful for several reasons. First, it shows how behavior in groups is mutually interdependent. What the chief surgeon does depends on what others are doing or might do if they behaved differently. Second, it shows that many institutionalized aspects of role performance are not taught directly but learned by watching others. It is extremely unlikely that medical training teaches surgeons to play the part of a buffoon. Finally, it shows an asymmetry based on status. It is the chief surgeon, not the intern or the nurse, who sets the tone and keeps the atmosphere calm by telling jokes. Humour from an intern would be seen as a sign of disrespect. This is rather typical of situations in which status differences occur. According to Goffman (1959), charm and color are the prerogatives of high office, and those with power can make overtures and do things that those of lower status cannot.

Despite Goffman's close association with Blumer, both as a colleague and a student, their treatment of social behavior differs in several ways. For Goffman, society comes first and individuals adopt standardized roles already existing in society. Goffman (1974) agreed that a person's interpretation of the situation is critical but denied that individuals play a major role in fabricating this interpretation—"presumably a 'definition of the situation' is almost always to be found, but those who are in the situation ordinarily do not create this definition . . . all they do is to assess correctly what the situation ought to be for them and then act accordingly" (pp. 1–2). Expectations about how to behave are not generated on the spur of the moment. Each individual enters situations with a store of knowledge about what is appropriate, and without this knowledge interaction would be impossible.

Goffman (1983) also rejected the idea that large social institutions could be understood through a microanalysis of face-to-face situations or that face-to-face interaction was more real than macrostructures associated with society. He did feel, however, that social interaction in face-to-face situations affected larger institutions in several ways. First, a good deal of business is done in face-to-face situations. Interaction among people with power often leads to decisions that affect the organization as a whole. Second, certain individuals serve as "gate keepers" and determine the composition of the organization through "processing encounters" (such as job interviews). If they select people on the basis of sex, age, race, or any other relevant or irrelevant criteria, then the organization changes as a consequence.

Goffman's tendency to use a theatrical metaphor to explain face-to-face interaction is both a strength and a weakness. He makes a convincing argument that many aspects of daily life can be treated like theatrical performances. We manage the impression we make on others, sometimes quite self-consciously. He also pointed out that much of our converstation is a type of mini-performance in which we recount events that have happened to us and tell them in a way that is both interesting and entertaining. The most common criticism of Goffman's work centers on the degree that behavior is self-consciously controlled. Deutsch and Krauss (1965) have challenged the view that people are cold, Machiavellian manipulators and argue that while most people do

manage impressions occasionally, such behavior is not typical. Blumer (1972) suggests that Goffman's analysis captures "the interplay of personal position at the cost of ignoring what the participants are doing" (p. 52). It thus leaves out what is most central in social interaction—the coordination of activities within the group. Gouldner (1970) has argued that the popularity of the dramaturgical approach is due to the structure of American society, where people are readily interchangeable units and move into slots already prepared by bureaucratic institutions. We feel that the theatrical metaphor is a useful analogy if it is not taken too seriously. There are definite limits to impression management and self-control, and the real issue revolves around establishing those limits. The real danger of the dramaturgical approach is that it implies a degree of control over behavior that actors may not possess (see Collier, 1985).

Symbolic interaction addresses several weaknesses in the postwar psychological approach to social psychology. It stresses the mutual interdependence of participants in a group. What people do depends on their role and status and what others are doing at the same time. It recognizes the social origins of social behavior. The way people perceive themselves and interpret situations depends on previous encounters with similar situations and the broader social context. Symbolic interaction also stresses the open-endedness of much interaction. People do not respond to each other mechanically. They actively interpret situations, plan activities, and coordinate their behavior as the situation unfolds.

Nevertheless, there have been some serious criticisms aimed at symbolic interaction, pointing out shortcomings that could seriously limit its application both as a research strategy and a model for understanding human behavior. It should be clear by now that there is no one school of symbolic interaction. There are major differences in the approaches of Blumer, Kuhn, and Goffman, and these are just three of the numerous variations. Criticism aimed at one school will not necessarily apply to others, and Blumer's version seems to have been the most frequent target. The various criticisms reached a peak during the late 1960s and early 1970s and were accompanied by a growing loss of confidence among adherents of symbolic interaction. As Stryker (1987) observes, symbolic interaction lost the intellectual vitality it had during the postwar period. This "crisis of confidence" in sociological social psychology was matched by a similar crisis of confidence within the psychological approach, and these developments will be discussed in Chapter 12.

## TOWARD AN INTERDISCIPLINARY SOCIAL PSYCHOLOGY

During World War II, sociologists and psychologists were involved in a variety of cooperative efforts. This collaboration sparked a postwar movement for an interdisciplinary social psychology that would integrate the psychological and sociological approaches as well as embrace relevant aspects of psychoanalysis and cultural anthropology (Karpf, 1952; Lewin, 1947; Newcomb, 1951). As Jackson (1988) points out, interdisciplinary research during this period was viewed as the primary means of achieving an integrated discipline. Such research was to be carried out by multidisciplinary staffs at various institutions who would be able to bridge conceptual and theoretical differences.

A number of factors helped stimulate interdisciplinary research. The successful collaboration of psychologists, sociologists, and cultural anthropologists during World War II helped encourage more funding for such research by various government and military agencies after the war. New international agencies such as UNESCO sponsored multidisciplinary research on social issues, such as racial equality and international understanding. New research institutes, such as the Survey Research Center and the Research Center for Group Dynamics, were staffed by social scientists

from a number of different disciplines. Two new interdisciplinary training programs were established. One was the Department of Social Relations at Harvard directed by Talcott Parsons, and the other was the Doctoral Program in Social Psychology at Michigan headed by Theodore M. Newcomb. Both were composed of faculty from psychology, sociology, and anthropology.

Despite these advances, the split between psychological and sociological social psychology continued. While there was a tremedous amount of research conducted in both disciplines, there was little theoretical integration (Bruner, 1950; Karpf, 1952). Even when attempts were made to incorporate concepts from both disciplines, the results were often distorted assimilations (Jackson, 1988). Psychologists, for example, redefined sociological concepts such as roles and institutions in individualistic terms. The need for training and professional issues also ran counter to the aims of unification. Graduate students in interdisciplinary programs were expected to master the material in both disciplines, but they had little guidance from faculty on how the material could be integrated. Nor did they have professional role models with whom they could identify. They were forced to fit into academic careers structured along the conventional lines of separate disciplines.

By the mid-1950s, the postwar optimism for a unified social psychology gave way to disillusionment (Jackson, 1988). The term "interdisciplinary" was used less frequently in publications, and fewer interdisciplinary conferences were organized. At several universities, collaborative efforts to teach social psychology courses ended, and the interdisciplinary programs at Harvard and Michigan were phased out by 1970. Professionalization also played a role in the demise of the interdisciplinary movement. During the 1950s, psychologists had begun to achieve professional certification by state legislatures. Jackson (1988) notes that sociologists specializing in social psychology were threatened by the public ascendency of psychologists, and in response, they reasserted their independent professional identity (see American Sociological Society, 1958). The interdisciplinary movement did not revive until several decades later, as both psychological and sociological social psychology experienced a parallel crisis of confidence. These developments will be considered in the next chapter.

# NOTES

1. *Mind, Self, and Society* was posthumously constructed from student lecture notes in the 1920s, and as Joas (1985) indicates, it does not include the general fundamentals of Mead's thinking about psychology. This omission occurred because Mead did not teach such introductory material after 1920.

PART IV

# SOCIAL PSYCHOLOGY IN THE POSTMODERN ERA (1970–1990)

# 12

# Crisis and Revision

In the two decades following World War II, social psychology progressed dramatically. The amount and variety of research increased, new theories were developed, the involvement in the war effort led to new initiatives in applying social psychology, and the number of graduate programs expanded enormously. This record of productive activity was reflected in the five volumes of the 1968 edition of the *Handbook of Social Psychology* edited by Lindzey and Aronson (1968). As Elms (1975) declared, this was a period in which "social psychologists ... knew who they were and where they were going" (p. 967).

This mood of optimism and self-confidence was, however, occasionally punctured by instances of self-criticism. Sears (1951), for example, faulted social psychology for thinking monadically and placing too much emphasis on individual psychological processes. Asch (1952) argued that psychologists were too quick in trying to imitate the methods and procedures of the natural sciences and had drawn a caricature rather than a portrait of human behavior. Gordon Allport (1954a) warned that "no experiment interprets itself.... Theories that transcend the specific instances are necessary, and theory building in social psychology is still in its infancy" (p. 50).

The frequency of self-criticism increased throughout the 1960s and 1970s. Gordon Allport (1968) stated that "most social psychologists share with Comte an optimistic view of man's chances to better his way of life.... For the past century this optimistic outlook has persisted even in the face of

slender accomplishments to date" (pp. 2–3). He noted that the "hard-nosed" approach had brought noteworthy scientific gains, but it had also produced neat and elegant experiments that lacked generalizability. Kenneth Ring (1967) criticized social psychology for a "fun and games" approach in which the object was to design clever experiments with zany manipulations. He argued that social psychology was in intellectual disarray and was pervaded by a restless pioneer spirit, in which there were "many frontiersmen, but few settlers" (p. 120).

Although discontent was widespread, there was little agreement about what was wrong or what should be done. Social psychology has been criticized for being too political (McGuire, 1965) or not political enough (Katz, 1978); overstressing (Asch, 1952) or ignoring the animal side of human nature (Von Cranach, 1972); and overestimating (Archibald, 1978) or underestimating the degree of voluntary control (Blumer, 1969). Some, such as Elms (1972), have called for more socially relevant research, whereas others, such as Festinger (1980), feel that there is already too much concern for instant solutions to complex social problems. Festinger has argued that there is a tendency to confuse "relevant" with "newsworthy" and has pointed out that, without a backlog of scientific knowledge, social psychologists are no better at offering solutions for social problems than anyone else. The criticisms were not limited to the issue of social relevance, however. They also focused on the theoretical and methodological foundations of social psychology. People began to question the way in which theories were constructed, the biasing effects of experimental procedures, and ethical abuses in the treatment of experimental subjects.

By the end of the 1960s, social psychology had reached a crisis of confidence. This climate of self-doubt was, however, by no means limited to social psychology. Psychology in general was criticized for not living up to its potential for promoting human welfare (Miller, 1969), and self-criticism occurred in other social sciences as well. Richard Bernstein (1976), for example, noted that

> Just ... when there was a widely shared self-confidence among mainstream social scientists that their disciplines had finally been placed upon a firm empirical foundation ... There was a growing skepticism and suspicion about the liberal faith so entrenched in the social disciplines: the belief that increased systematic empirical understanding of how society and politics work would naturally lead to the intelligent formulation of policies, ameliorate social inequalities and injustices, and enable us to solve the problems of society. (pp. xi–xii)

In this chapter, we will review the crisis of confidence in social psychology and the subsequent attempts to revise social psychology. There were also more radical responses that went well beyond revision and called for a *reconstruction* of the epistemological foundations that guide theory, research, and practice. These will be considered in the next chapter. The current chapter focuses on the problems pertaining to research and ethics, and the attempts to modify social psychology from within in order to make it more socially relevant. In order to understand the transition from certainty to self-criticism, it may be useful to examine briefly the historical changes taking place in America during the sixties, seventies, and eighties.

## AMERICAN SOCIETY IN THE 1960S, 1970S, AND 1980S

As we have seen, American social psychology has developed through a series of pendulum swings from individualistic to more social and problem-centered forms of social psychology, which roughly correspond to similar shifts occurring within American society. This pattern is not the product of inevitable laws of history. It is the direct result of a set of unique cultural conditions occurring during this century. American culture as a whole can be seen as a rich mosaic of shared beliefs, symbols, and values that have been shaped to a large extent by two opposing extremes—individualism and a preoccupation with the self, on the one hand, and the sense of community and a concern for others, on the other. Although these two extremes are not always mutually exclusive, one often dominates, and the dynamic interaction betwen them provides the context for both change and continuity. This conflict has been so intense during the last three decades that some commentators have argued that a profound and permanent transformation has taken place in American culture.

As we have noted, the period following World War II was a time of unprecedented economic growth and prosperity. Productivity increased steadily by an average annual rate of over 3 percent, and the gross national product during this period more than doubled (Leuchtenburg, 1979). More Americans than ever were working, and millions achieved the coveted middle-class status that included owning a house in the suburbs, at least one car, and all the amenities of a mass consumer society. Americans became a "people of plenty" (Potter, 1954). Affluence became an unquestioned aspect of American life, and nearly everyone assumed the economy would continue to expand forever.

The prosperity of the late 1940s and 1950s also provided the basis for new social and political reforms during the 1960s. Affluence during this period brought expectations that the benefits of prosperity and democracy would be extended to everyone. This belief formed the basis for a new liberal consensus that was reflected in national programs, such as President Kennedy's New Frontier and later Johnson's Great Society. During this time, and perhaps only during this time, Americans as a whole were inspired by *both* individual and communal values, and they created a social and political coalition that sought to maximize individual rights and liberties while extending them to less fortunate minorities. This liberal vision, it seemed, combined the best features of capitalism and free enterprise with the more humanistic principles of a concerned welfare state, and it led to an impressive list of political victories, which included civil rights legislation, the Economic Opportunities Act, Medicare and Medicaid, the War on Poverty, and increased aid to education.

The momentum of social reform was short-lived, however. The expansion of the Vietnam War drained America's economy, forced the government to borrow heavily, and set in motion a period of inflation, which generally eroded the buying power of average Americans and the gains made during the 1950s and 1960s. As the war escalated, the contradictions of Johnson's "guns and butter" policy became more and more apparent and even began to threaten the axiomatic truth of unlimited economic development. The growing opposition to the war brought together a loose coalition of political activists, which included elements of the counterculture, civil rights supporters, and early exponents of the women's movement.

This movement incorporated traditional liberal values based on liberty and unlimited personal freedom with new counterculture ideals based on opposition to those in authority. Students and young adults began to question the traditional values of self-sacrifice and material success that had motivated their parents. They adopted new values based on personal freedom and self-exploration, which combined a critique of technology and progress with a strong desire to perfect society. This gave rise to a number of social experiments, such as communes and encounter groups, as well as new strategies favoring simpler and more human lifestyles.

The war in Vietnam, above all, served as a catalyst, and organized protests against the war brought together a diversity of individuals and groups that otherwise had little in common. The gradual winding down of America's involvement and its eventual defeat in Vietnam, together with a growing concern for economic and environmental issues, eventually weakened the bond that held these groups together. The monumental gathering at Woodstock, New York, in the summer of 1969 was the last large collective happening that characterized the spontaneity, idealism, and solidarity of the 1960s (Jones, 1980).

In the aftermath of Vietnam, people began to focus on more personal forms of self-expression. On college campuses, students cut their long hair and began to dress more conservatively. The desire for personal success was reflected in the unprecedented number of students who abandoned traditional liberal arts programs for courses in commerce and business. The 1970s have been variously described as the "me decade" (Wolfe, 1976) and as a period of selfish individualism and self-absorption (Bell, 1976; Schur, 1976), narcissism (Lasch, 1979), and decadence (Hougan, 1975). Daniel Yankelovich (1981) has compared the shifts in values to geological plates whose interaction has resulted in a cataclysmic transformation of American culture. Christopher Lasch (1979) argues that the transformation was so complete that it created a uniquely American personality that centered around self-development and narcissism. He drew a portrait of "the liberated personality of our time," whose traits included "his charm, his pseudoawareness of his own condition, his promiscuous pansexuality, his fascination with oral sex, his fear of the castrating mother . . . his hypochondria, his protective shallowness, his avoidance of dependence, his inability to mourn, his dread of old age and death" (p. 101).

Not everyone agrees with Lasch's harsh and somewhat polemic commentary. Peter Clecak (1983), for example, claims that there was a great deal of continuity in the 1960s and 1970s. He regards the two extremes of self and society as central to both decades and argues that Americans during both periods were searching for a form of self-fulfillment that, even in its more extreme forms, included some kind of commitment to others. Despite the differences of interpretation, virtually all commentators on contemporary American culture agree that the quest for self-fulfillment was the central theme of the 1970s. Pollster Daniel Yankelovich (1981) conducted a series of national polls and case studies and has used his results to argue that the search for self-fulfilment was much more than a product of an affluent and narcissistic society—"it is nothing less than the search for a new American philosophy of life" (p. xix).

Nowhere is this revolution more evident than in changes in the structure of families. The majority of Americans, Yankelovich (1981) notes, no longer hold the traditional values of their parents. The typical family after World War II consisted of a husband, who was the breadwinner and head of the household, and a wife, who bore children and took care of the home. The success of this pattern was based on a willingness by both partners to play their respective roles, work together, and make personal sacrifices for the family. It meant, in particular, that men would strive at jobs that were often stressful and unrewarding and that each woman would forgo any personal career outside the home in order to maintain the household and provide emotional support for their husband and children. Family life during this period was based on an ethic of self-denial and hard work, and it had as its objectives social mobility, material security, and the successful raising of children. Traditional marriages were lifelong commitments, in which even unhappy couples stayed together for the sake of the children in order to avoid the social stigma of divorce.

By the 1970s, this traditional family had become only one of many different arrangements. In fact, the very concept of a family unit was broadened to include almost any combination of people living together and sharing their lives. This revolution in the structure and values of the family reflected the increased emphasis on personal choice in a modern pluralistic society. Yankelovich's (1981) research reveals that the search for personal fulfilment had spread to virtually everyone in America by the end of the 1970s and that 72% of the nation were "spending a great deal of time thinking about themselves and their inner lives" (p. 9).

This preoccupation with self transformed even the American dream. The traditional American dream incorporated symbols of success and responsibility, opportunities to get ahead or have one's children do so, and institutions, such as churches, graduations, promotions, and celebrations. All of these were important links in the social bonds among family members. By the middle of the 1970s, on the other hand, tens of millions of Americans had grown wary of demands for sacrifices they believed might no longer be warranted. Americans began to stress new needs, such as the need for creativity, leisure, autonomy, pleasure, stimulation, and adventure.

In some respects, the philosophy of personal fulfilment was a logical reaction to the three decades of prosperity following World War II. It had taken about this long for American culture to recover fully from the Great Depression. But ironically, the creation of a culture and psychology of affluence came almost precisely at the moment when America's continued prosperity was being seriously questioned. In 1973, the country experienced a sudden oil crisis resulting from an embargo by OPEC nations. This resulted in gas rationing and shortages throughout the United States, and it dramatized the country's dependence on foreign sources for vital supplies, such as fossil fuels. More important, the crisis brought home the recognition that America was part of a global economy and that there were limits to material progress and no absolute assurances that the nation's economy would continue to grow and prosper indefinitely. The concept of perpetual growth and prosperity that had been an unquestioned assumption of American life for nearly thirty years was suddenly thrown into serious doubt. Over the next seven years, the price of oil rose a startling 1000 percent and the country experienced "stagflation"—that is, the worst of both inflation and recession. For the first time in recent history, the future did not offer the promise of a better life, and technology was no longer synonymous with progress. In a dramatic reversal of previous trends, Americans no longer believed that the present was better than the past or that the future would be an improvement. A Harris survey showed that 69% of Americans felt that they had a harder time making ends meet than before. The national mood reflected deep anxieties about the future, which was partly shown in a disturbing 171% increase in suicide rates between the period of 1950 and 1975 (Yankelovich, 1981).

As a consequence of these developments, Americans became even more preoccupied with personal concerns and they showed even less concern for social problems. Uncertainties about the present and the future led to a widespread tendency to see the past as "the good old days." Such nostalgia coincided with the bicentennial celebrations of 1976, which turned the nation's history into a form of commercial entertainment that lasted throughout the year. This wave of nostalgia was also apparent in the popular culture of the times. Americans were fascinated by the late 1950s and early 1960s, and this was reflected in the revival of "oldies but goodies" music and popular television series such as "All in the Family" and "Happy Days."

The nostalgia of the 1970s coincided with a turn to the political right, as shown by the election and popularity of Ronald Reagan. There was a general retreat from the liberal politics and social programs of the 1960s, and in some instances, taxpayers even rebelled against funding government programs. In California, which is both one of the most progressive and one of the most conservative states, Proposition 13 placed a freeze on all further government spending.

The quest for self-fulfillment became the fashion of the day, and it was packaged and sold to the public as a consumer item under a variety of personal growth and therapeutic labels, including Erhard Seminars Training (est), Transcendental Meditation (TM), bioenergetics, Gestalt therapy, humanistic psychology, aikido, yoga, and Zen Buddhism. Together these represented what became known as the "human potential movement," which captured, in its variety of forms, the new search for freedom and self-awareness. It is estimated that by the middle of the 1970s, approximately nineteen million Americans took part in some aspect of the human potential movement (Carroll,

1982). There were clear signs during this same period of a religious revival associated with Christian fundamentalism and other religious extremes. Like the human potential movement, the new religions were sold as consumer items with the glitz and glitter of a new breed of Madison Avenue–style preacher—the "televangelist."

Religious revivals also took the form of cults, which attracted an alarming number of young Americans. Cults appealed to those who were unable to find meaning in their daily lives, because they provided more potent forms of religious experience. Their appearance in modern society is symptomatic of a deep psychological need for a sense of identity and a purpose in life. Cults typically attract people who are unable to find a secure place in society and who are overwhelmed by the burdens associated with freedom and autonomy. In highly individualistic societies, such as the United States, cults represent an acute paradox in which individuals voluntarily give up their freedom in order to escape from their isolation and loneliness. In a manner similar to that described by Fromm (1939/1941) in his study of Nazi Germany, individuals who are in a state of acute personal isolation and despair give up their freedom in order to submit to an all-powerful authority. Unfortunately, this form of self-fulfilment is often short-lived and illusory, and in the tragic case of Jim Jones and his followers, it led to the ceremonial mass suicide and murder of 916 men, women, and children.

The human potential movement and the appearance of new religions reflected the importance that Americans placed on self-discovery and self-development. In many ways, this trend was reinforced by popular psychological theories and self-help manuals. Pop psychologists frequently hosted radio phone-in shows and talk shows on television and wrote books that became national best sellers. Although much of the popular psychology was impressionistic and unscientific, it nevertheless drew from a legitimate core of psychological theory, watered down and made palatable for the public taste. At the heart of much of the writing was a psychological model that stressed the importance of the "inner self" as the center of human essence. The self was represented as an autonomous, self-contained individual preoccupied with personal needs and self-understanding. Wallach and Wallach (1983) have argued that these schools of thought provided an unintentional sanction for selfishness and egotism. In the broader context of the 1970s, self-awareness became a popular panacea for happiness based on a new set of ethical clichés such as "do your own thing," "be true to yourself," and "look out for number one." These became part of the new moral imperative that emphasized the self as opposed to society and as such reinforced an already persistent tendency to withdraw from social concerns and responsibility (Schur, 1976).

The quest for self-fulfilment that characterized the 1970s reflected the greater freedom of choice in an increasingly pluralistic society. Given the economic uncertainties and the scarcity of natural resources, it was perhaps only a matter of time before some of the contradictions in the philosophy and lifestyle of self-absorption became apparent. By the late 1970s, many Americans began to focus their attention on larger social issues and began to stress the values of family and community attachment. The importance of human connectedness was symbolized in the popularity of personal genealogies, such as Alex Haley's highly successful best-selling book *Roots,* which traced the Haley family's history from its African origins and inspired a television mini-series by the same name that attracted 130 million viewers, the largest audience in history at that time (Carroll, 1982).

The desire for a sense of belonging is also shown in various expressions of solidarity among women, lesbians and gay men, and racial and ethnic minorities. There has been a growing recognition during the 1980s that America is not a monolithic society dominated exclusively by white, middle-class, male values but a pluralistic society consisting of many subcultures with their own behaviors, beliefs, and values. Americans generally became more tolerant of each other, and a new generation of grass-roots activists took up the fight for a wide range of social issues, such as the Equal Rights Amend-

ment, environmental issues, and nuclear disarmament.

Whereas the 1970s can be described as predominately a decade of self-absorption and concern with the "inner self," the 1980s marked the beginning of a new effort to achieve human potential outwardly, beyond the narrow limits of the individual. In the cultural and social thought of the 1980s, there was a growing recognition of people's social and interpersonal nature. For many, personal happiness and self-fulfillment now involved a turning away from a self-indulgent, inner journey toward a world of significant others. Yankelovich's (1981) research reveals that in 1973, less than a third of Americans (32%) placed a high priority on a sense of community, but by the early 1980s, the proportion had increased to nearly half of the population (47%). These developments within American society as a whole have been reflected in the actions and reactions of people working in social psychology.

## THE CRISIS OF CONFIDENCE IN SOCIAL PSYCHOLOGY

During the 1960s and 1970s when American society was undergoing unprecedented economic and social changes, psychological social psychology itself experienced three different sets of problems, each promoting a crisis in its own right. These concerned experimental artifacts, ethical abuses of subjects, and lack of social relevance (Miller, 1972; Pepitone, 1976; Rosnow, 1981). There was also a distinct crisis surrounding the sociological approach to social psychology, which will be discussed later (Jackson, 1988).

### The Artifact Crisis

An early example of methodological problems in experimental research is the field studies conducted at the Hawthorne plant of the Western Electric company during the 1920s (see Chapter 7). The so-called Hawthorne effect demonstrated that giving workers special attention was as important as the actual experimental manipulations, if not more so. During the 1930s, Saul Rosenzweig (1933) pointed out that the experimental situation was an important psychological problem that needed to be carefully studied. It was not until the late 1950s, however, that a concerted effort was made to study the way experiments were conducted.

During the 1960s, Robert Rosenthal and his associates conducted a series of studies designed to identify the biasing effects of experimental (and nonexperimental) investigators (see Rosenthal, 1966; Rosnow, 1981). The so-called experimenter effects were based on both noninteractive and interactive features. Noninteractive effects do not actually influence the performance of the subjects. An example is the observer effect, in which the investigator unintentionally biases the results because of unconscious errors in recording data. Another example is an interpreter effect, in which the researcher's attitude or point of view helps determine how the results are interpreted. A more extreme case would include the deliberate distortion or fabrication of data, as exemplified by Cyril Burt's research on individual differences in intelligence (see Hearnshaw, 1979).

Interactive experimenter effects occur when subjects are actually influenced by the investigator. The tendency for subjects to respond to the special attention they receive (as in the Hawthorne study) is an example. Characteristics of researchers, such as sex, age, and race, can also affect the way subjects respond. The most dramatic example of an interactive effect is Rosenthal's demonstration of an experimenter expectancy bias or *self-fulfilling prophecy,* in which the researchers' hypotheses influence the subjects' performance. In one study, Rosenthal worked with two groups of undergraduate students who conducted learning experiments with rats. One group of rats was described as "bright," whereas the second group was labeled "dull," even though there were no actual differences between them. The results showed that the "bright" rats performed considerably better than the "dull" rats. Other studies using human subjects have found similar results.

Martin T. Orne (1962) has carried out a series of studies on subject artifacts. He has shown that subjects can be influenced by the "demand characteristics" of experimental situations. These include inadvertent cues that suggest the experimental hypothesis. Orne has also found that subjects will persist at a dull, meaningless task if asked to do so by an experimenter, because they feel the need to play the "good-subject role." Rosenthal and Rosnow (1969) have also found that "evaluation apprehension" leads to compliance. Many subjects are concerned about being seen as deviant if they do not conform to the directives of the experimenter. He argues that in studies of cognitive dissonance, for example, the subjects' feeling of evaluation apprehension rather than the experimental manipulation determined the compliant behavior.

Another artifact of experimental research is based on the use of volunteers. During the 1940s, McNemar (1946) warned that psychology in general was in danger of becoming the science of sophomore behavior because of its overreliance on college students as subjects. Rosenthal and Rosnow (1969) suggested that social-psychological research may not even adequately sample the college population, since volunteers for experiments and nonvolunteers differ in a number of significant ways. McDonald (1972) has pointed out that mandatory participation for course credit does not really solve this problem, since volunteers and nonvolunteers simply participate at different times of the year.

By the late 1960s, there were numerous articles and books on artifacts in experimental research, suggesting ways in which they could be controlled (Suls & Rosnow, 1988). Orne, for example, proposed that some experimental subjects should be treated as "co-investigators" and asked to predict how they would respond if they were actual subjects. The response of these subjects could then be compared with those exposed to actual experimental manipulations. If the two groups performed similarly, then the results could be attributed to subject expectancies rather than the experimental treatment. To overcome the experimenter-expectancy effect, Rosenthal suggested that experimenters be kept "blind" about the hypotheses being tested.

In the two decades since the artifact critique was launched, there has been a general recognition of the problem, and changes in procedures have been designed to minimize their influence (Suls & Rosnow, 1988). There has also been an increasing skepticism in some quarters over the use of experiments as the "modus operandi" in social psychology. A number of alternative procedures, such as role playing (Brown, 1965; Harré, 1972; Harré & Secord, 1972), field studies (McGuire, 1967), cross-cultural research (Triandis & Lambert, 1980), and naturalistic observation (Blumer, 1969), along with various nonreactive measures (Webb, Campbell, Schwartz, Sechrest, & Grove, 1981), have been suggested, but the controlled experiment remains the instrument of choice within psychology, and it is gradually beginning to dominate the sociological approach as well (Higbee, Millard, & Folkman, 1982). Supporters of the experimental method argue that role playing and various forms of self-report are simply not a suitable substitute for experimental procedures and have very limited use (e.g., Freedman, 1969). Alternative methods that are more sensitive to historical and cultural influences have also been proposed and these will be discussed in more detail when we consider the issue of social relevance.

### The Ethical Crisis

Stanley Milgram's (1963) research on obedience grenerated a flood of controversy over the issue of ethical abuse (see Chapter 9). Even though he provided evidence that his subjects were not negatively affected, he was severely criticized for producing high levels of stress. The reaction to his study raised doubts about common practices in experimental research, especially the use of deception. Rosnow (1981) pointed out that 81% of the research on conformity and 72% of the studies on balance theory and cognitive dissonance conducted during the mid-1960s used some form of deception. The use of deception can substantially alter the responses of subjects in subsequent experi-

ments because subjects who have been exposed to deception become more guarded in their response. Because of these problems, "debriefing" procedures have been developed and have become common (Harris, 1988).

The increased use of debriefing procedures did not completely dispel ethical concerns about the use of deception, however. Herbert C. Kelman (1968), who is a leading spokesperson in the movement to control ethical abuse in human research, complained about the general use of deception in social psychology. He did not limit his criticism to experiments in which deception was potentially harmful. Kelman (1968) stated:

> I am equally concerned . . . about the less obvious cases in which there is little danger of harmful effects, at least in the conventional use of the term. Serious ethical issues are raised by deception per se and the kind of use of human beings that it implies. In our other interhuman relationships, most of us would never think of doing the kind of things that we do to our subjects: of exposing others to lies and tricks, of deliberately misleading them about the purposes of the interaction or withholding pertinent information, of making promises or giving assurances that we intend to disregard. We would view such behavior as a violation of the respect to which all fellow humans are entitled and of the whole basis of our relationship with them. (p. 215)

Kelman's attack on the use of deception occurred within the political context of the late 1960s and expressed the feeling that the use of deception in psychological research buttressed an American domestic and foreign policy based on the blatant and cynical manipulation of truth. Social psychologists were thus feeding "the cynicism and mistrust of our youth and . . . [communicating] to them that deception permeates even those of our institutions whose very purpose is dedication to truth" (Kelman, 1968, p. 217).

In response to the rising controversy, a committee was set up by the American Psychological Association to provide a code of conduct for human research. After an extensive process of collecting data and eliciting feedback from members of the American Psychological Association, the code was adopted in 1972 (Ad Hoc Committee, 1973; Smith, 1974). As Rosnow (1981) points out, the code followed the major ethical guidelines for medical research that emerged from the Nuremberg war trials in 1947. Among the principles was the requirement of voluntary consent, which allows subjects to refuse to participate or discontinue participating at any time. Experimenters would also be required to inform subjects about the use of deception or concealment when such procedures were used, provide complete information about the nature of the study once the data were collected, and clear up any misconceptions that subjects might have formed.

While there was a general consensus about the need for a code of conduct, there was also some concern that a strict adherence to the code would create experimental artifacts (Rosnow, 1981). It was pointed out that the laws of learning might have to be revised if previous research had been carried out under conditions of informed consent. Others complained that despite the increased attention to ethical issues, human subjects were still treated as objects of manipulation who must be prevented from discovering the true nature of the research until all the data have been collected (Buss, 1979; Scheibe, 1979; Smith, 1974). Alternative models of experimentation have been proposed in which subjects are aware of the purpose of the research and act as collaborators who report on changes or role play what they believe others would do if they were exposed to actual experimental manipulations (Danzinger, 1985; Kelman, 1968).

### The Relevance Crisis

Drawing from the initiatives undertaken during the depression and World War II, social psychologists during the postwar period continued the field's commitment to applying social psychology. Kurt Lewin, before his untimely death in 1947, spearheaded efforts aimed at overcoming intergroup ten-

sion and ethnic and racial prejudice (see Chapter 9). This commitment was soon overshadowed by the rapid expansion of experimental laboratory research. By the 1960s, social psychologists began to stress basic research and question the value of applied research (Rosnow, 1981). William J. McGuire (1965), for example, at a symposium celebrating Columbia University's new Department of Social Psychology, criticized some of his fellow social psychologists for being

> too preoccupied with the Berlin Wall, the urban blight, the population bomb, and the plight of the Negro in the South. Such action-oriented research strikes me as bad strategy. Approaching research from the perspective of application rather than theory, I regard as inelegant and inefficient as trying to push a piece of cooked spaghetti across the table from the back end.... I feel our social psychological research should concentrate on hypotheses derived from any kind of basic theory: My objection is only to the selection of hypotheses for their relevance to social action at the cost of theory relevance. (pp. 138–139)

With the momentum of the civil rights movement and the women's movement, and growing concern about the war in Vietnam during the late 1960s, the pendulum of thought in social psychology moved dramatically in the opposite direction. Social psychologists began to complain about the social irrelevance of a discipline obsessed with arcane theory and clever experiments. An article by Kenneth Ring (1967) in the *Journal of Experimental Social Psychology* provoked an onslaught of criticism over the issue of social relevance. Ring pointed to McGuire's comments as an example of how far social psychology had drifted from Lewin's vision of a humanitarian and action-oriented social psychology devoted to both theoretical and applied research. He claimed that social psychology was in "profound intellectual disarray."

McGuire (1967), in response, supported most of Ring's criticism but felt optimistic that both basic and applied research could be recombined. He stressed the need for using natural environments rather than conventional laboratories as the primary setting for testing theories. By the early 1970s, McGuire (1973) had become more pessimistic about progress in the field and proposed that a new epistemological foundation or paradigm was needed. He called for a new pluralism in methodology and modes of theory construction.

The issue of social relevance was further radicalized by Kenneth J. Gergen's (1973) assertion that social psychology was historical rather than scientific. He argued that scientific research is based on the assumption that natural events do not change and can therefore be explained in terms of universal principles. Social psychology, in contrast, deals with phenomena that are inherently unstable and subject to historical conditions. Moreover, the publication of underlying mechanisms by social psychologists often undermines the principles involved. Knowing that bystander nonintervention is due to a combination of social comparison and diffusion of responsibility, for example, makes people less suceptible to these two principles and more likely to intervene. Indeed, many social psychologists carry out research because they believe that the principles they discover will *modify* social behavior.

Gergen's attack on the scientific status of social psychology produced a large and mostly negative response (Jackson, 1988). Manis (1975), for example, argued that temporal and cultural variability does not rule out the stability and generality of underlying processes. The controversy nevertheless spurred efforts to explain why social psychology was so unresponsive to the social context. One of the problems cited was the overemphasis on individual psychological processes. Pepitone (1976, 1981) argued that most major social-psychological theories focus on processes conceptually located within the individual. He called for a reorientation based on the study of normative behavior. This would require comparative research in groups and social classes in order to determine the source of underlying values and belief systems. Sampson (1977, 1978) extended Pepitone's directives and criticized social psychology for its adherence to the American ideal of the self-contained individual—an ideal that is no longer desirable or effective for dealing with contemporary issues that demand collective solutions. He also pointed to the social and historical forces that shape the development of theories in social psychology.

European social psychologists joined the chorus of dissent by pointing out the pervasive influence of the American value system on the development of social psychological theories and research (Israel, 1979). The French social psychologist Serge Moscovici (1972) summarized the reservations of many when he said:

> Before us, ahead of us and around us there was—and still is—American social psychology. . . . people like Lewin, Festinger, Heider, Deutsch, Asch, Schachter, Sherif, Kelley, Thibaut, Lazarsfeld, Bavelas, Berkowitz, and many others. But despite the respect we have for their work—and despite, in some cases, a network of personal friendships—it is no secret that acceptance is becoming increasingly difficult. As we read them and try to understand and assimilate the principles that guide them we must often conclude that they are strangers to us, that our experience does not tally with theirs, that our view of man, of reality and of history are different. (p. 18)

The European social psychologists went on to assert a "declaration of independence" from American social psychology (Israel and Tajfel, 1972; Jackson, 1988), and many American social psychologists began turning to their European counterparts for guidance and suggestions. For the first time since World War II, social psychologists in America were again reaching beyond the borders of their own country for ideas and guidance.

### The Crisis of Confidence in Sociological Social Psychology

During the late 1960s and early 1970s, sociological social psychology began to experience a parallel crisis and was beset with uncertainty. This crisis was brought about by two factors: the minority status of sociologists within the field of social psychology and the decline of confidence in its major theoretical perspective, symbolic interaction.

The rapid growth of psychological social psychology and the failure of the interdisciplinary movement during the 1950s and 1960s led to two separate yet unequal social psychologies (Jackson, 1988). Sociologists became a minority and their approach paled in comparison with that of their psychological counterparts. Many young sociologists were enticed by the prestige and popularity of psychological theories and the growing emphasis on experimental procedures. By the mid-1970s, warnings were sounded about the "withering away" or dissipation of sociological social psychology (Burgess, 1977; Liska, 1977).

Exacerbating the malaise was the growing criticism of symbolic interaction during the 1960s and 1970s (Stryker, 1987; Stryker & Statham, 1985). Symbolic interaction was attacked on conceptual, methodological, and ideological grounds. Psychologists claimed that the key concepts of symbolic interaction, such as mind, self, and society, were inherently vague and difficult to operationalize. As a result, few testable hypotheses could be generated and scientific explanations were thus abandoned in favor of intuitive insights and long rambling journalistic descriptions.

This criticism seems more valid when applied to Blumer, who denied the usefulness of hypothesis testing and operational definitions. Kuhn spent a great deal of his career trying to provide an operational definition for the self and encouraged quantitative procedures in other areas. Besides, as Stryker (1981) has pointed out, there has been a steady stream of empirical research based on symbolic interaction, which belies the criticism that such research is not possible. Lauer and Handel (1977) have pointed out that even the debate between determinacy and indeterminacy does not preclude the possibility of scientific study. One may grant that people actively interpret situations and still make predictions about how they will respond. Scientific laws are probabilistic and do not demand absolute certainty.

In addition to questions about operational definitions and hypothesis testing, conceptual criticism has focused on symbolic interaction's overly rational view of social behavior, which downplays the role of emotions and unconscious processes. The problem of neglecting emotions and unconscious processes can be treated separately. There is a relative neglect of emotions in Mead's own work, but this neglect is by no means universal. Numerous studies of symbolic interaction have focused on various aspects of emotional experiences, but the relative neglect of emotions within symbolic interaction was sufficiently common to cause some concern.

Even more serious is the neglect of unconscious processes. This can take several forms. Hickman and Kuhn (1956) provided an extensive review of the psychoanalytic approach and dismissed it as unscientific and untestable. Blumer (1969) divides behavior into symbolic and nonsymbolic processes and focuses on the former. This might be seen as a useful division of labor if the two were merely parallel, but Goffman (1959) has shown that the verbal messages are often qualified and even disqualified by nonverbal behavior occurring at the same time.

A person's interpretation of the situation often depends on unconscious factors. A good example is bystander nonintervention during emergency situations. Latané and Darley (1959) have shown in a series of carefully controlled experiments that a person's interpretation of the situation depends on the presence of others. People do not respond to emergencies immediately. Instead, they maintain a facade of calm and look around to see how others react. The trouble is that others also maintain a calm facade, so it is quite common to come to the mistaken conclusion that nothing is wrong when in fact it is. The important point is that people do not recognize that their interpretation of events is based on the presence of other people. When subjects are asked if other people affected their behavior, they typically deny that they did.

There is a growing body of evidence that many of the processes involved in person perception, attributions, and our perception of social situations are not consciously accessible (e.g., Lewicki, 1986). Nathenson (1966) has argued that the process of perception was not Mead's concern, but any theory that places such a strong emphasis on interpretation must deal with the possibility of error. Mead recognized that there were individual differences in what he called "social intelligence"—that is, the ability to empathize and take the role of others—but he did not discuss the mechanisms involved. We now know that differences occur because people do not use all the relevant information available, distort much of the information that is used, and combine it in ways that are frequently ineffective. But these erroneous judgments *seem* correct to those who make them, and their subsequent behavior is often based on a series of errors. These problems are not solved by limiting symbolic interaction to symbolic activity, which is conscious by definition. As Lauer and Handel (1977) point out, individuals may continue to interact in a state of "pluralistic ignorance" despite considerable misunderstanding (and never know that misunderstandings have occurred).

The methodological critique of symbolic interaction was launched mainly by adherents of the *ethnomethodological approach* developed by Harold Garfinkel (see Garfinkel, 1967; Heritage, 1984). This approach focuses on the methods people use to understand and interpret everyday behavior. People want to understand the social situation so that they can behave appropriately. Ethnomethodologists claim that there is no real distinction between the methods used by ordinary people and social scientists. They therefore criticize the supporters of symbolic interaction for assuming that social scientists, because of their objectivity, are in a privileged position to obtain knowledge about the people they observe (Stryker, 1987). The so-called objective observer is merely a participant within an interaction and consequently has no privileged access to information. In fact, there is the danger that social scientists may distort their perception of the very behavior they wish to understand by using theoretical concepts. These criticisms can be directed toward any of the conventional social sciences, but because they were raised by sociologists who were sympathetic to symbolic interaction,

they were especially influential in raising doubts about the approach.

Symbolic interaction has also been criticized on *ideological* grounds. This line of criticism emanated from the political left (Stryker, 1987; Stryker & Statham, 1985) and stresses the tendency of symbolic interactionists to ignore or minimize the importance of the larger social context or treat it as a derivative of interaction itself. As a result, symbolic interaction is seen as a predictable product of American society, stressing egalitarian values, respect for individual initiative, and gradual change (Shaskolsky, 1970), while ignoring the realities of conflict and competition.

The tendency to ignore the larger social context can be traced directly to Mead. Because he was not primarily concerned with social structure, his conception of society seems to suggest that all one needs to solve persistent social problems is more scientific research and better education. This issue can be resolved if symbolic interaction is seen as just one possible perspective. The question then becomes whether it is compatible with other ideological positions. Numerous attempts have been made to show the similarities between Mead's theory and various ideological alternatives, including those of Marx (Zeitlin, 1973), Durkheim (Stone & Farberman, 1967), and Weber (Scott, 1970).

## Response to the Crisis

During the 1970s, social psychology was caught up in a climate of self-doubt and confrontation. There was much debate about whether or not a true crisis existed (Jackson, 1988). Elms (1975), for example, served as a spokesperson for those who were eager to dismiss the crisis. He argued that, since social psychology lacked a well-established paradigm in the Kuhnian sense, there were no conceptual or methodological grounds for a crisis. Social psychology was merely experiencing external pressures to change. The demands for social relevance and the debate over ethical issues simply reflected the views of the various protest movements during the 1960s and the increasing concern about violations of human rights. While acknowledging the need for some reform, Elms (1975) concluded that social psychologists were suffering from problems of self-esteem and should act as their own "therapeutic agents," striving for intellectual tolerance, a moral stance, and realistic goals.

During the 1980s, Jones (1985) looked back at the period of malaise and concluded that the crisis in social psychology had already "begun to take its place as a minor perturbation in the long history of the social sciences" (p. 100). He noted that the various declarations of doom had not radically altered the intellectual momentum of the field. In sharp contrast to those who saw the crisis as a passing phase of little consequence, there was a growing body of criticism, accompanied by prescriptions for change. These recommendations varied from minor revisions of current theories and practices to a more radical reconstruction of the entire discipline.

Those who have called for revisions propose theoretical and methodological changes in the established traditions of cognitive social psychology and symbolic interaction. There has also been a revival of interest in biological approaches to social psychology. The theoretical developments of the 1970s and 1980s have been associated with a more pluralistic approach to methodology. The recognition of ethical abuses and experimental artifacts has led to a series of experimental reforms. There has also been an increased interest in going beyond the laboratory through naturalistic observations and field experiments. During the last two decades, interest in applied social psychology has increased substantially, and it has become a subspecialty within social psychology.

These new initiatives in theory, method, and application are based on revisions and expansions of traditional procedures. The basic assumptions that have guided theory, method, and practice have not been questioned. Despite the attempts to dismiss its importance, the crisis of confidence has had a profound effect on the discipline. As we enter the 1990s, American social psychologists appear to be headed in two different directions—one based on revision, the other based on a more radical reconstruction of the entire discipline. The revisions will be discussed in this chapter, whereas the more radical alternatives will be examined in the final one.

## NEW DIRECTIONS IN COGNITIVE SOCIAL PSYCHOLOGY

During the 1960s, the declining interest in consistency theories and the social and political uncertainty helped promote new trends in cognitive research. There was a movement away from the development of grand motivational theories that could integrate numerous disparate observations to a more analytic approach that focused on underlying cognitions (Berkowitz & Devine, 1989; Fiske & Taylor, 1984). Another change was based on the individual as a social thinker. In place of the prototype of the person as a consistency seeker, two new models became popular—the naive scientist and the cognitive miser (Taylor, 1981). In both, motivation became less important than cognition.

### Attribution Theories

During the late 1960s, research on cognitive consistency tended to give way to an increasing emphasis on attribution processes. A smooth transition between these two was facilitated by the fact that Fritz Heider (1944, 1946, 1958) was, in many ways, the originator of both. Daryl Bem's (1965, 1967, 1972) self-perception theory was also an attribution theory, and many regarded it as an alternative to cognitive dissonance. Social conditions also help to explain the transition. If people in contemporary society are induced to hide their true feelings, it becomes incumbent on those with whom they interact to find out what those feelings are. The inauthenticity of day-to-day behavior forces people to look beyond overt behavior in order to infer underlying motives and intent. As a result, attribution theories emerged during the 1970s as the most researched topic in American social psychology, and they remained one of the most popular topics throughout the 1980s as well. A computer-assisted search by Kelley and Michela (1980) yielded over 900 references for the ten-year period.

Attribution theory, as originally formulated, is concerned primarily with understanding the cause of another person's behavior. The observer is thus seen as a *naive scientist* whose aim is to explain the behavior of others. The location of these causes can be internal, within the individual, or external, within the situation. While some studies involved the attribution of emotions, the bulk of the research has focused on intentional behavior and the use of intentions to make attributions about more stable underlying traits. Attribution theories became popular during the mid-1960s because they gave people credit for thinking and planning their behavior. Subsequent research has focused on processes involved in self-perception and biases and distortions in the attribution process.

As with consistency theory, credit for the original idea is typically given to Heider (1944, 1958), although Heider's theory was not fully appreciated until it was more fully developed and systematically tested by researchers such as Jones and Davis (1965) and Kelley (1967, 1972). Heider, who was relatively isolated at Smith College and later the University of Kansas, had little influence until he published *The Psychology of Interpersonal Relations* (1958) at the age of sixty-two. A lecture Heider gave on "common-sense" psychology at Harvard in 1946 had virtually no impact, and such notable psychologists as Gordon Allport and Jerome Bruner attended but left without saying a word (Sahakian, 1982).

*The Psychology of Interpersonal Relations* was reviewed by Harold H. Kelley (1960) for *Contemporary Psychology,* who described it as an "exceptionally important publication" and predicted that it would become a classic. Heider was concerned primarily with the surface level of experience—events that occur on a conscious level in everyday life. While he recognized the interplay between people during social interaction, he felt that a simplified analysis that focused on perceptual processes occurring in an individual observer was a useful starting point.

One of the central assumptions of Heider's theory is that principles involved in the perception of objects can be applied to the perception of people as well (Heider, 1944). Individuals search for consistency in a changing world and find it in objective properties. Such features as color, size, and shape remain invariant in spite of changes in surrounding conditions. Objects do not shrink or expand as we move around them and neither does our perception of them. A red object remains red in spite of changes in illumination. The perceptual world is divided into properties of the thing, which reside in the object, and properties of the intervening circumstances, such as illumination, distance, and orientation. We are able to make stable attributions about objects because we take the circumstances into consideration. Such knowledge allows us to predict behavior. Solid round objects can be rolled down a smooth surface. A hard solid object can be used as a hammer.

People are seen as having relatively invariant features as well. In addition to size, shape, and color, people have such additional features as beliefs, abilities, and traits. People differ from objects in that they are seen as partly responsible for their own behavior. Unlike objects, which are at the mercy of their environment, people adapt to changing conditions and continue to work toward goals in spite of external obstacles. Goal-directed behavior is characterized by equifinality—that is, there are frequently a number of different ways to reach the same goal, and people readjust their behavior when they encounter resistance. Much of the initial attribution process consists of figuring out what people are trying to do. From this, the observer infers underlying motives and eventually stable traits. Knowledge about stable traits allows us to predict behavior in the future. A friendly person can be expected to behave in a friendly way in a wide range of situations.

As with objects, the ability to make stable

attributions about people requires an assessment of the situation. Just as ambiguous words become clearly defined within a sentence, behaviors are more easily understood when the context is taken into consideration. Failure, for example, may be due either to a lack of ability or to the difficulty of the task. Ability is inferred by performing well on a difficult task. Task difficulty is a property of the environment and is inferred when a number of people try and fail under similar conditions.

Situations have both physical and social features. Social demands and values place limits on what can and cannot be done. We attribute value to an object when it is valued by most people. Beauty, for example, is not merely in the eye of the beholder. Because value is regarded as an objective property (like size or color), we expect others to share our values and are surprised when they do not. Social obligations and expectations are also based on external authority and attributed to an objective social order. Just as physical laws make the physical world predictable, laws of conduct make social behavior predictable and social interaction possible. These laws are based on superpersonal standards and are similar to George Herbert Mead's (1934) conception of the "generalized other" (see Chapter 11).

Heider (1958) also noted the common tendency for observers to attribute more consistency to behavior than it deserves and to underestimate the influence of situational factors: "Behaviour . . . has such salient properties that it tends to engulf the total field rather than be confined to its proper position as a local stimulus whose interpretation requires the additional data of a surrounding field" (p. 54). The actor has knowledge about covert features not directly available to the observer. The tendency to simplify and associate items with similar value is based on limitations within the cognitive system and leads to such distortions as the halo effect, prestige suggestions, and the tendency to interpret positively the actions of our friends. The perceived relationship between goodness and happiness or wickedness and punishment is so strong that we take misfortune as

a sign of moral weakness and consider it deserved.

The advantage of Heider's theory is that it provided a general conceptual framework from which more specific theories were derived. The specific theory that most resembles Heider's is Harold H. Kelley's (1967) theory of covariation analysis. Kelley's interest in social perception was inspired by Kurt Lewin at MIT. While Lewin studied the consequences of social perception, Kelley focused on the processes involved, and his 1948 Ph.D. dissertation was based on a study of first impressions.

Kelley's *theory of covariation analysis* stresses three features alluded to but not fully developed in Heider's work—consistency, distinctiveness, and consensus. Consistency refers to the tendency to behave in the same way repeatedly (across situations and over time). Stable attributions about personality can only be made when a person is consistent. Distinctiveness is the extent to which a specific behavior is unique—that is, directed at or limited to a particular person or a particular object. Consensus implies that other people would respond in the same way if placed in the same situation. For Heider (1958), consensus leads to object attributions. Observers attribute characteristics such as beauty and value to objects when there is a general agreement.

The actor is seen as primarily responsible for a behavior when there is high consistency, low distinctiveness, and little consensus—for example, when a person is consistently hostile to everyone in a variety of situations (and hostility is an uncommon behavior). The stimulus is considered responsible when all three factors are high. When hostility is consistently aimed at a particular person (high consistency and high distinctiveness) and other people respond to this person in the same way (high consensus), the target rather than the actor is seen as responsible. Behavior that is highly distinct but low in consensus and consistency is attributed to the situation. McArthur (1972) tested Kelley's theory and found results in the predicted directions, but she also noted a general tendency to underutilize information about consensus.

This is a persistent source of error and will be discussed later.

Consistency, distinctiveness, and consensus require previous information about the actor and other people's behavior, but Kelley (1972) later developed a theory in order to account for attributions based on a single observation. This model has two features—discounting and augmentation. Discounting occurs when there are a number of sufficient causes. Each one is discounted to a certain extent, since the observer cannot be sure which one was primarily responsible for the behavior. Augmentation is the converse of discounting and occurs when behavior is carried out in spite of inhibiting factors. Motives are judged to be particularly strong when a person has to overcome resistance.

Jones and Davis's (1965) *theory of correspondent inferences* also applies to judgments based on a single observation of behavior. While it resembles Kelley's (1972) principles of discounting and augmentation to some extent, it was developed seven years previously in a paper called "From acts to dispositions," which summarized their research and that of their associates. Their theory, like Kelley's, was inspired by Heider, who had visited Jones at Duke University during the 1962–1963 academic year. As the title of their paper suggests, Jones and Davis are concerned primarily with how people "work backwards" from observations of overt behavior to inferences about underlying causes. Correspondence is the extent to which a behavior directly reflects a disposition—for example, the extent that friendly behavior is due to a friendly disposition.

Information about correspondence is affected by many factors, but two of the most important are social desirability and the number of noncommon effects. Behavior that is expected or demanded by social conventions provides little information. Individuals make more extreme judgments and have more confidence in their judgments when the behavior is unconventional or socially undesirable (e.g., Jones, Davis, & Gergen, 1961). Information about the consequences of a behavior is also used to infer motives. Common effects occur when a

chosen and unchosen alternative have similar consequences. If a woman chooses between two equally attractive men, for example, then physical attractiveness cannot be used to explain her decision. But if one is wealthy and the other is intellectual, these differences, or noncommon effects, can be used. Correspondence increases as a person eliminates other possible explanations, and it is inversely related to social desirability and the number of noncommon effects.

Attributions are also affected by personal involvement. This can take the form of either personalism or hedonic relevance. Hedonic relevance occurs when the observer is directly affected by the actor's behavior. It is the degree that the observer gains or loses as a consequence of that behavior. Personalism occurs when the observer is a target of the behavior. Some actions, such as increasing the tax rate or laying off a number of employees according to seniority, may lack personalism and still have hedonic relevance. Personalism produces a "halo effect." Positive behaviors aimed at us personally are attributed to positive personality characteristics, whereas harmful behaviors are attributed to a malignant disposition. Personalism may be incorrectly assumed, as in the case of paranoid individuals who interpret even innocuous behavior as malevolent and personal.

Jones and Davis (1965) point out that attributions are involved in other forms of social behavior. Retaliation for aggression, for example, is mediated by attributions about the aggressor's intent, and it is less likely to occur if the aggression is perceived as justified. Actions beneficial to the observer are also judged in terms of underlying motives and are attributed to dispositional factors, such as friendliness or generosity, when there are no apparent strings attached. Jones and Davis's (1965) theory has inspired a considerable body of systematic research and represents probably the most persistent application of theory to research in the area of attribution.

Whereas basic attribution models assume that actors make decisions rationally and work consciously toward the realization of their goals, Bem's (1967, 1972) *theory of self-perception* suggests that such internal cues are typically weak and that actors make attributions about their own motives in much the same way as an outside observer. When there are plausible external reasons for the behavior, no internal ones are necessary, but when external pressures are weak, then dispositional attributions are made by both actors and observers. In short, people often act first with very little forethought and then question themselves about the reasons for their behavior.

Bem's (1967) theory, as noted previously, was originally formulated as an alternative to Festinger's (1957) theory of cognitive dissonance, but its major impact has been to stimulate research on differences between actors and observers. These were summarized by Bem (1972) in a later article and include four major differences. Actors have more information about internal states, such as goals and intentions, and more knowledge about previous behavior. They also have a greater need to interpret their behavior in a positive manner. Finally, actors tend to make more situational attributions and fewer dispositional ones. These differences lead to different interpretations of the same behavior.

While attribution theories assume that with sufficient time and effort people can process information accurately, it soon became apparent that errors in attribution were more common than previously imagined. Judgments are often made rapidly with limited data, which is haphazardly combined and strongly influenced by preconceptions. Research on attribution biases has focused on two interrelated problems— differences between actors and observers when interpreting the same behavior and departures from predictions made by "rational baseline models" (Jones & McGillis, 1976), such as those described previously (see Schneider, Hastorf, & Ellsworth, 1979).

One of the earliest discoveries was that, contrary to self-perception theory, there are considerable differences in the ways actors and observers process information. Whereas actors tend to focus on external causes and make situational attributions, observers tend to focus on the actor's behavior and overestimate the role of dispositional factors. Jones and Harris (1967), for

example, had subjects read pro-Castro and anti-Castro speeches. Even though the observers knew that the communicator was arbitrarily assigned to a particular condition, they still took the speech at face value and assumed that it reflected the speaker's true feelings. This tendency to underestimate the role of situational pressures is so strong that it has become known as the *fundamental attribution error* (Ross, 1977).

Actor-observer differences are partly due to "perceptual focus." Actors and observers concentrate on different aspects of the overall situation. Whereas the actor's attention is drawn to objects and barriers within the external environment, observers focus on the actor's behavior. As Heider (1958) pointed out, behavior is so salient that it "engulfs the field." These perspectives have been reversed by using videotapes (Storms, 1973), and this reversal has produced corresponding changes in the attributions— that is, actors make more dispositional attributions when they see themselves on videotape, and observers make more external attributions when they see the situation from the actor's perspective. Observers asked to empathize with the actor also tend to make more situational and fewer dispositional attributions (Regan & Totten, 1975).

Actors and observers also have different kinds of information (Jones & Nisbett, 1972). Actors have more information about previous performance and better information about intentions, goals, and degree of effort. Observers are forced to rely on present behavior and consider it typical. The assumption that present behavior is typical leads to trait attributions. Research by Nisbett, Caputo, Legant, and Marecek (1976), for example, found that dispositional attributions varied with the degree of familiarity. More trait attributions were made about an unknown celebrity than a friend, and the number of dispositional attributions correlated with the length of the friendship.

An apparent exception occurs in attributions of success and failure. While the results are not entirely consistent, there seems to be a general tendency for actors to assume more credit for success than failure (see Miller & Ross, 1975). Actors make more dispositional self-attributions about their own success and usually attribute it to internal factors such as effort or ability. This trend was originally seen as a self-serving bias (Heider, 1958), in which the actor takes credit for successful performance but attempts to maintain self-esteem during failure by attributing the failure to external factors, such as bad luck or task difficulty.

A third bias is due to a misuse of information about consensus. People are relatively insensitive to probability and "base-rate" information and usually rely exclusively on information derived from a particular case. Nisbett and Borgida (1975), for example, had subjects read about an experiment on the readiness of people to come to the aid of a person who appeared to have an epileptic seizure. One group was told the surprising result that the most common response was to do nothing at all. When they were asked to explain the behavior of a freshman who did not help, they ignored the high frequency of nonintervention and attributed it primarily to his personality. Ignoring consensus is part of a more general tendency to hold people responsible for their behavior, particularly when there are negative consequences. Observers assume that the behavior is not typical, in spite of its high frequency, and attribute it to the individual.

Consensus information is not only underutilized; it is often incorrect. People often overestimate the frequency of improbable events and underestimate the frequency of probable ones. Actors are also more likely to see their own behavior as relatively common and assume that others would respond in the same way. Ross, Green and House (1977), for instance, found that students supporting women's liberation estimated that 57% of students shared their views, whereas those not supporting it estimated that 67% of students agreed with them. This produces a false consensus, based partly on selective exposure (Ross, 1977). People associate with others whose background and beliefs are similar and then derive consensus information from a biased sample of the population. The other side of this tendency is that people see behavior different from their own as relatively infrequent and attribute it

to dispositional factors. False consensus both reflects and creates distortions in the attribution process (Miller, 1976).

Distortions also occur because people make attributions too rapidly with too little information. First impressions based on dispositional attributions tend to persist because later variations in behavior are attributed to unstable, environmental factors. Ross, Lepper, and Hubbard (1975), for example, provided subjects with false feedback about their performance as they attempted to distinguish between false and authentic suicide notes. This feedback was later totally discreditied, but both subjects and outside observers continued to use it to estimate ability and predict future performance. Jones, Rock, Shaver, Gethals, and Ward (1968) compared attributions following ascending and descending success and obtained a primacy effect. Higher ability was attributed to individuals who did well initially, even though the overall level of performance was precisely the same. The primacy effect occurs because people are more attentive to consistent information and use it as evidence that their initial attribution was correct. Inconsistent information is either neglected or attributed to some quirk within the situation. The result is that new evidence produces less change than would be predicted if people processed information in a rational manner.

Attribution research forms a relatively distinct subarea within contemporary social psychology, but it has implications for other areas as well. The effects of communicator credibility are mediated by attributions about motives and intent (Eagly, Wood, & Chaiken, 1978). Helping behavior is interpreted less positively when attributed to external factors or ulterior motives (Regan, 1978). More help is also given to people in need when their condition is perceived as due to external factors or uncontrollable factors such as a physical handicap (Ickes & Kidd, 1976).

Attributions affect interaction as well. Snyder, Tanke, and Berscheid (1977), for example, found that males talking on an intercom to a woman they were told was beautiful were more sociable and elicited similar behavior in the woman. Similar evidence of self-fulfilling expectations have been found for hostile behavior, and induced hostility has been found to carry over to subsequent encounters (Snyder & Swann, 1978). Attributions play a key role in these behaviors because they are the first step in the causal link. Kelley and Michela (1980), for example, make a distinction between "attribution theories," which focus on the perception of intent and inferences about the underlying cause of behavior, and "attributional theories," which deal with the link between attributions and the perceiver's reaction. Closing the gap between these two aspects of the attribution process would help provide a more interactive theory of social behavior.

It must be stressed, however, that Heider (1958) was well aware of the limitations of his own approach and even quotes the French psychologist and philosopher Maurice Merleau-Ponty (1945) as an example of a person who takes a more interactive approach.

> In the experience of a conversation, a common ground constitutes itself between the other one and myself, my thought and his make up a single tissue, my words and his are called out by the phase of the discussion, they insert themselves in a common operation of which neither one of us is the sole creator. A double being comes about, and neither is the other one for me a simple behaviour in my transcendental field, nor am I that for him, we are, one for the other, collaborators into the other, we coexist in the same world. (Merleau-Ponty, 1945, p. 407, quoted in Heider, 1958, p. 34)

Heider (1958) goes on to say,

> As a beginning, however, a simplified analysis in which the interpersonal relation is divided into steps, such as the behavior of o, the reaction of p to o, then the reaction of o to the reaction of p, etc., allows the detection of important perceptual processes, though we must bear in mind that these processes arise within one encompassing situation (p. 34).

## Social Cognition

If any term can be used to characterize the most significant recent trend in cognitive social psychology, it is the concept of "social cognition." Social cognition deals with how people perceive, process, and organize information about other people. Attributions are one type of social cognition but not the only one. The discovery that many distortions in the attribution process can be explained in information-processing terms has caused social psychologists to look more and more to cognitive psychology for inspiration, methods, and ideas. Attribution errors are assumed to be based in part on inherent limits in cognitive processing that direct the coding, storage, and retrieval of information. This liaison has been described as a "marriage" between cognitive and social psychology (Taylor, 1981), but it could just as easily be characterized as a common tendency among social psychologists to borrow from more general areas. Just as Heider (1958) assumed that there were parallels between person perception and the perception of objects, contemporary social psychologists see social cognition as a more specific form of cognition in general.

The marriage between cognitive and social psychology is one-sided in the sense that social psychologists borrow both techniques and ideas, but information seldom goes the other way (Taylor, 1981). While social psychologists have always stressed cognition, cognitive psychology did not emerge until the mid-1960s as the dominant approach among psychologists in general (e.g., Neisser, 1967). The phenomenal growth of cognitive psychology during the mid-1960s occurred for two reasons. First, the humanistic challenge to behaviorism made it clear that many of the phenomena of primary interest were simply being neglected by an overemphasis on overt behavior (see Chapter 5). Second, the increased availability of computers makes it possible to draw analogies between computer programs and mental processes.

The growing interest in social cognition represents a shift in interest from motivation to cognition. Even without motivational distortions, information is processed in a limited way. Ross (1977), for example, argued that while previous research had focused on mediating drives leading to defensive distortions, an alternative approach would be to ignore motivational explanations altogether and concentrate on cognitive factors alone. The research on attribution biases shows that people do not always act in a consistently logical and rational manner. Rather than characterizing social thinkers as naive scientists, more recent theories tend to depict them as cognitive misers who simplify information in order to process it quickly (Taylor, 1981).

While the relationship between cognitive and social psychology has been one-sided, Shelley Taylor (1981) has suggested three ways in which social psychology could contribute to cognitive psychology. First, social interaction provides a more realistic test of cognitive predictions. Research by cognitive psychologists under laboratory conditions uses impoverished stimulus material, and it is difficult to know whether the results generalize to real-world settings. Social-psychological research provides a test of their "ecological validity." Second, some cognitions, such as causal attributions about control, occur only in social situations. Their inclusion helps to extend the boundary of cognitive psychology and give it access to phenomena that it might not otherwise consider. Finally, social psychologists can help link cognitive psychology with more applied areas. It is often difficult for applied disciplines, such as medicine, law, architecture, or education, to appreciate the significance of cognitive research, but a cognitive treatment of social phenomena seems more relevant and is more readily adopted.

Despite these possible advantages, there are potential liabilities as well (Taylor, 1981). One is that social psychology may promise more than it can deliver. There may be a tendency for applied disciplines to borrow too freely, without recognizing the limits of the research. Taylor (1981) expressed concern that attributions were being assigned the same central role previously given to attitudes. The tendency to interpret depression in terms of attributions, for example, ignores the strong role of biological factors. Second, a purely cognitive approach runs the risk of overlooking emotional and motivational factors. Cognitive psychology tends to stress "cold" or emotionally neutral cognitions, and a too literal

adoption of its techniques could lead social psychologists to downplay motivation. In fact, there has been a pendulum swing back to "hot" cognition or motivational models in recent years (Markus & Zajonc, 1985). Finally, there is a tendency to overlook interaction. Since cognitive psychology is noninteractive, a social psychology derived from cognitive psychology tends to be noninteractive as well. While such an approach may be sufficient to understand social perception, it does not account for the back-and-forth, recursive quality of social interaction.

One of the most attractive features of social cognition is the suggestion that attributional biases and distortions are due to general properties of the mind itself—a tendency to take in a limited amount of information, to organize it in a hierarchic manner, and to have better access to some bits of information than others. It is therefore somewhat surprising that so little cross-cultural research has been done to see if the processes are indeed universal. A study by Miller (1984) suggests that the fundamental attribution error, which occurs again and again in studies using American subjects, is not universal. She found that Hindu adults in India made far fewer dispositional and more situational attributions. This effect was particularly strong for deviant or maladaptive behaviors, where Americans made three times as many dispositional attributions. She attributes this to a general tendency in American society to hold individuals responsible for their actions. Hindu society takes a more holistic approach and sees behavior as a joint product of the person and the situation.

The tendency to hold people responsible for their behavior may represent more of a cultural than a cognitive bias. It has a number of important implications. Considerable research has shown that people assume others are responsible for accidents and natural disasters that happen to them (see Wortman, 1976, for a review). Even victims often feel responsible (Bulman & Wortman, 1977). Furthermore, actors are seen as more responsible when the consequences are severe (Walster, 1966). These distortions are derived in part from a "just-world hypothesis" (Lerner & Miller, 1978), which is based on a need to believe that the world is orderly and people get what they deserve. While this belief is widely shared in Western societies, it is by no means universal. It leads to a tendency to blame victims for their own misfortune and to accept the existence of persistent social problems, since whatever is is regarded as fair.

There has also been the suggestion that cognitive psychology, by virtue of its stress on individual psychological processes, reflects a cultural bias that inadvertently protects and defends the status quo (Sampson, 1981). By treating cognitive processes as fundamental and invariant, it ignores the complex interplay between people and the restraints imposed by the objective world. Edward Sampson (1981) argues that the concept of "I think" should be reformulated as "we think," since thinking is a social and historical product and not merely a process occurring within the head of an individual. The psychological approach to contemporary social problems is often ineffective because it attempts to alter beliefs and attitudes without changing the objective social conditions that produce them.

Sampson (1981) argues that we cannot evade this problem by claiming that, as psychologists, we are only interested in studying the mental processes of individuals. Insofar as mental processes are conditioned by the social context, ignoring the context gives a misleading impression of the processes involved. Moreover, it tends to take processes that are empirically observed, abstracts them from the social context, and gives them a timeless, objective status. A similar position has been expressed by Dorwin Cartwright (1979) in a review of social psychology and by the cognitive psychologist Ulric Neisser (1976).

This problem is exacerbated by the fact that many psychologists and personality theorists in particular are themselves victims of the fundamental attribution error. They attribute to deep-seated personality factors what might be more readily explained by the situation. Walter Mischel (1968) has shown that the degree of cross-situational consistency in behavior predicted by personality scales is not very high.

Some of the classic studies in social psychology, such as Asch's (1951) work on conformity and Milgram's (1963) obedience studies, seem implausible because they demonstrate the importance of often overlooked social pressures. The exemplary work of Latané and Darley (1970) disentangles a whole host of social factors operating during bystander nonintervention. It too seems implausible, but only because we have become accustomed to overlooking situational factors. We do not mean to imply that people are not responsible for their own behavior, only that behavior is often based on a complex interplay between people and their physical and social environment.

Finally, the neglect of the objective social context poses problems in linking cognition and action. Kenneth Gergen (1989a) points out that in the cognitive approach, the real world is dealt with only in terms of abstractions, such as concepts and mental categories. Thus, there is no account of how people convert these abstractions into behavior. One solution to this impasse is to incorporate some conception of intentionality into attribution theories (Apao, 1986; Buss, 1978, 1979; Rychlak, 1976). Allen Buss argues that attribution theories fail to make a distinction between causes and reasons. They assume that laypeople explain behavior exclusively in causal terms and ignore the fact that people also make attributions about behavior by inferring reasons and intentions. Attribution theories thus need to incorporate these judgments as well. As people become aware of the causes of their own behavior, they can use this knowledge to help guide it.

## NEW DIRECTIONS IN SYMBOLIC INTERACTION

The critique of symbolic interaction during the 1960s and 1970s helped revitalize the tradition during the 1980s (Stryker, 1987; Stryker & Statham, 1985). This revival has been shown through both the work of American sociologists (e.g., Collins, 1981;

Gidden, 1984) and European social psychologists (e.g., Israel & Tajfel, 1972), who rediscovered or appropriated themes from Mead and symbolic interaction. A particularly noteworthy sign of this renaissance is the growing awareness of Mead and symbolic interaction among psychological social psychologists. Many psychologists who had become disenchanted with experimental procedures have turned to symbolic interaction for methodological alternatives. There has also been an increasing interest in the concept of self within cognitive social psychology.

Among symbolic interactionists, several trends have contributed to these developments. Goffman's work has had a profound effect (see Chapter 11). Near the end of his life, in response to earlier criticism, Goffman (1983) began to stress the interdependence of interaction and larger social structures. Drawing from Goffman, a number of theorists have attempted to integrate symbolic interaction within a macrostructural framework. Goffman's work has also influenced the recent studies of childhood interaction and the way young children learn to interact during socialization (Corsaro, 1985).

In response to earlier claims that symbolic interaction downplayed or ignored emotions, there have been several recent social interactional theories of emotions. Kemper (1978) has incorporated physiological, psychological, and sociological features in a model that focuses on the way variations in emotions reflect power and status relationships. Heise (1979) argues that people attempt to maintain established feelings in social relationships. When events strain or challenge these feelings, actors attempt to restore their normal relationships by anticipating and constructing new events.

In response to the critique that symbolic interaction ignores or minimizes the role of the larger social context, there has been much recent research that stresses the importance of social structure. Anselm Strauss and his associates anticipated this trend in their study of how interaction is affected by the division of labor within a hospital (Strauss, Schatzman, Erlich, Bucher, & Sabshin, 1963), and this line of investigation has been expanded in the more recent analysis of negotiation processes (Strauss, 1978). Ralph Turner (1976) has also explored the relationship between the self and social structure and has suggested that there has been a major shift in American society over the last few decades based on the degree that the self is seen as insitutionally grounded. Whereas previous generations viewed the "real" self as anchored in social institutions and roles, contemporary individuals are more likely to equate the true self with spontaneous impulses and see social institutions as a source of frustration and constraint. It is not clear whether this shift is due to alienation in contemporary society or a new emphasis on expressing previously unacceptable impulses, but the trend, if it continues, may force sociologists to redefine the notion of self. Whereas "institutional types" realized their potential by perfecting preexisting roles, "impulse types" are more likely to view the self as something hidden waiting to be discovered.

Turner's (1976, 1978) social structure approach, as well as that of McCall and Simmons (1978), tends to use a more traditional, "softer" form of symbolic interaction. It assumes a relatively fluid social structure that both constrains and is influenced by interaction. In contrast, Burke (Burke & Reitzes, 1981; Burke & Tully, 1976) and Stryker (1980, 1987) place a greater emphasis on social constraints. Stryker, for example, adheres to the traditional assumption that the self guides and organizes behavior and is shaped through social interaction. He goes on to assert, however, that social structures, including systems of roles and the larger principles which organize society, shape interaction. The way people define themselves and others depends on their relative position within society. Social structure also determines "who comes together in what settings to interact for what purposes with what interactional resources" (Stryker, 1987, p. 91).

Stryker (1987) argues that the new focus on social structure holds promise for the future of the sociological approach to social psychology. He suggests:

> A truly sociological social psychology, in my view, is a social psychology that appre-

ciates and that explicates the profound impact of social structure on the behavior, both individual and social, of persons. As I see matters, the claim that a social psychology deriving from sociology has something to offer beyond that provided by a social psychology deriving from psychology, the claim that the former has a distinctive value and contribution to make to knowledge, depends precisely on accomplishing this program. (p. 92)

With a clearer identity for sociological social psychology, there also appears a renewed interest in a more interdisciplinary approach to social psychology. Psychologists and sociologists are rediscovering that they have things in common. There has thus been an increasing awareness of each other's contributions and a cross-fertilization in both theory and procedures (Jackson, 1988; Stryker & Stathem, 1985). Many psychological social psychologists now recognize the neglect of both social structure and social interaction and have turned to Mead and symbolic interaction as a way of redressing these problems (e.g., Israel & Tajfel, 1972). Sociological social psychologists have, in turn, discovered parallels between symbolic interaction and the cognitive approach to social psychology (Stryker & Gottlieb, 1981).

Another area in which collaboration seems warranted is the treatment of unconscious processes. This has been a noted shortcoming of symbolic interaction and one conceded by even sympathetic critics (e.g., Stryker, 1981). Fortunately, it is a major concern within the contemporary psychological approach. While psychologists have overlooked the importance of interaction, sociologists have tended to take symbolic interaction at face value and have assumed that surface appearances were all that really mattered. The two approaches could be combined to produce a model of people actively engaged in interaction, who occasionally make mistakes in judging the behavior and intentions of others—not randomly but systematically—because they overlook or screen out information or interpret it in such a way as to maintain high levels of self-esteem.

# THE REVIVAL OF A BIOLOGICAL PERSPECTIVE

The use of instinct theories, such as those of McDougall and Freud, to explain social behavior, largely disappeared by World War II (see Chapter 2). Behaviorism, with its emphasis on external control, had largely captured the American landscape by the 1920s. Within social psychology, the emphasis on cognition tended to stress the plasticity of perception and the importance of outside factors. By the 1960s, however, American psychologists were becoming more receptive to the importance of biological and genetic factors, and behavior genetics became an established field of study. The conservative backlash of the Nixon era helped promote an extreme form of biological determinism. Arthur R. Jensen's (1969) genetic views about intelligence generated intense controversies among scientists and in the popular press. This controversy has continued in the more recent claims by J. Phillippe Rushton (1988, 1989) about innate racial differences in intelligence, sexual behavior, and aggression.

Two major fields have contributed to the recent revival of interests in the biological basis of social behavior. These are ethology and sociobiology.

## Ethology

Ethologists study animals in their natural environment. Animals are observed, sometimes for years, and their behavior is carefully recorded in order to detect universal patterns. Konrad Lorenz (1903–1989), who was born in Vienna and received both an M.D. and a Ph.D. in zoology from the University of Vienna, is often considered the father of ethology. He is probably best known for his work on imprinting in birds, but he also developed a theory of aggression that is somewhat similar to Freud's. For Lorenz (1965) behaviors as well as physical characteristics are inherited, and "behavior patterns are just as conservatively and reliably characteristics of species as are the forms of bones, teeth, or any other body structures" (p. xii).

For Lorenz (1966), as with Freud, aggression is an instinctive drive that progressively builds up in the individual and must be periodically released. He felt that aggression has been biologically built into the species because aggressive individuals are better able to secure food and territory and attract mates. Aggression is also necessary to establish a "pecking order" in some species and the pattern of social ranking that is necessary for coordinated activities, such as hunting. Aggressive tendencies increase the likelihood of individual survival and the probability that aggressive characteristics will be passed on genetically.

In most species, aggressive displays are highly ritualized and easily terminated once a fight has been won. Wolves, for example, will bare their throats after a defeat, and the victor will instinctively stop its assault. The problem with human beings is that they frequently kill at a distance where they cannot even see their victims. Lorenz felt that our built-in restraints are insufficient even for bows and arrows, much less for long-range aircraft and nuclear missiles. Killing would be much more difficult if it were done face-to-face with bare hands. In 1973, Lorenz received and shared the Nobel Prize with fellow ethologists Nikolaas Tinbergen and Karl von Frisch for his work in the area.

Hinde (1987, 1988), referring to research carried out over the last two decades, argues that an ethological perspective can be integrated into social psychology and the social sciences in general. Ethology, unlike more traditional approaches to social psychology, does not limit itself to causation and development. It is concerned with the function and evolution of behavior. Behavior differences between males and females, for example, which commonly occur in many different cultures, can be explained in evolutionary terms. Hinde (1988) does not rule out the influence of culture but argues that "the range of cultural diversity must be constrained by the genetic endowment of human beings" (p. 27).

There is considerable controversy, however, about whether it is possible to clearly identify these genetic constraints. Weizmann, Weiner, Wiesenthal, and Ziegler (1990), for example, point out:

> There are so many enormous methodological, ethical, and practical difficulties involved in establishing important gene or evolutionary-based race and group differences in behavior, that one can question whether the study of such differences should command any of our limited scientific resources. (p. 11)

There is little doubt, however, that the ethological approach has profoundly changed the way social psychologists perceive certain aspects of behavior, and it is now generally accepted that such behaviors as altruism, aggression, and emotional expression are at least partially innate.

## Sociobiology

The most recent entry of evolutionary theory into social psychology has been sociobiology. While ethology is a predominantly European movement, sociobiology developed largely at Harvard, with Edward O. Wilson as its principal spokesperson. Wilson received his bachelor's and master's degrees at the University of Alabama and a Ph.D. from Harvard. In 1955, he became a full professor at Harvard at the age of 29.

Sociobiology is based on evolutionary theory, but it takes the gene and not the individual as its basic unit. The individual is described only half jokingly as a giant container for the genes. According to Wilson (1975), "the organism is only DNA's way of making more DNA" (p. 3). Many of the predictions made by sociobiologists are similar to those made by ethologists, but there are some important differences.

Altruism, for example, is seen as genetically programmed, but it is not directed equally at all members of the group. Altruism increases with the degree of genetic relatedness (Hamilton, 1964). Female monkeys, for example, have been known to kill the offspring of other mothers in their group in order to increase the survival chances of their own infants. Altruism generalizes to other group members because group living is itself adaptive. Even not reproducing can be explained genetically because it frees certain individuals who can then take care of the offspring of their siblings.

To a certain extent, people who extrapolate from animal studies are the victims of the animals they select. Those who study rats often attribute rat-like characteristics to human beings, while those who study primates discover a much wider range and repetoire of behavior. Wilson's interest in ants and other social insects led him originally to overestimate the rigidity of behavior. For ants, very complex behavior patterns are often built in and rigidly limited. But Wilson's later work seems to recognize the importance of learning in shaping human behavior. For Wilson, the genes have given up most of their sovereignty, leaving only about 10% of behavior genetically determined.

Despite this emphasis, Wilson's work has been described as racist and sexist and compared to Nazi eugenics. Marshall Sahlins (1976) has written a critical book called *The Uses and Abuses of Biology,* which recognizes the scientific validity of sociobiology but describes it as a "derailment" of evolutionary theory, "genetic capitalism," and an attempt to justify and preserve the status quo. Sociobiology, like instinct theories during the 1920s, has become a political issue with supporters and critics polarized and often talking at cross-purposes.

Many of the criticisms of sociobiology are reminiscent of earlier attacks on instinct theory. They focus on the same two problems that Edward C. Tolman (1923) mentioned—overinclusiveness and nonvariability. Critics complain that sociobiology is used to justify a wide range of behaviors, from male dominance and promiscuity to homosexuality, which may more properly be regarded as culturally determined. In its extreme form, sociobiology implies a rigid "biological determinism" that underestimates the importance of learning and culture.

Perhaps the most serious shortcoming of sociobiology is that it appears to be inaccurate when applied to human beings, and the flaw occurs precisely in those areas where it most differs from ethology—that is, the "selfish gene" theory for altruism. For sociobiology, altruism is a special kind of selfishness, and a person should surrender his or her life as long as more than two siblings or eight cousins are saved by the sacrifice. This requires a sort of "intuitive calculus of blood ties" (Wilson, 1976) and can be calculated according to a precise mathematical formula. Wilson does not claim that animals or humans actually make this calculation, but they behave as if they do.

Sahlins (1976) has shown, however, that "kinship" in humans rarely if ever corresponds to actual genetic relatedness and varies enormously from culture to culture. Family groups are usually based on rules of residence after marriage. One common pattern is partrilocal residence, which occurs in 34 to 45% of the world's societies, depending on whether a strict or loose definition is used. In these groups, married couples live with the bridegroom's father. An extended family therefore consists of the father, his wife, his sons, and their wives and children. Meanwhile his married sisters and daughters, who are genetically closer than his daughters-in-law and grandchildren, have moved out of the household; while his aunts, on both sides, may never have lived in it. Yet perceived kinship is based on residence. Residential groups make up domestic and cooperative units, share vital resources, and engage in joint protection and mutual aid. Those who live together are "close" kin while those who live apart are "distant" regardless of genealogy. Altruism based on genealogy is also contradicted by the rather common practices of infanticide and adoption.

Sahlins (1976) goes on to argue that the belief that altruism obeys some kind of genetic calculus is itself a cultural product. It is derived from a social system in which offspring are regarded as "assets" and one's own life is considered a medium of exchange. Altruism is reduced to a kind of self-sacrifice for a genetic advantage, and the numerous examples of mutual benefit are considered derivatives. Sociobiology reflects the ideology of Western society, assures us of its natural basis, and claims that it is an inevitable part of human nature. It is this aspect of sociobiology that makes it a reactionary tool for maintenance of the status quo. Some have argued that sociobiologists were unaware of the political dimensions of their theory, but as Sahlins (1976) points out, their intentions are totally irrelevant.

But there are dangers in ignoring biology as well. One danger, as McDougall (1908) pointed out in his treatment of instincts, is that many social-scientific theories do make either implicit or explicit assumptions about human nature, which they then use to justify specific policies. People are described as naturally selfish, competitive, and pleasure-seeking, or naturally aggressive. The choice is not between some theory and no theory. It is between good theories, based on scientific data, and bad theories, based on loose speculations about existing social conditions. It is also becoming increasingly clear that researchers in social psychology are falling victim to this error and often take findings derived from a small subset of the American population (i.e., American university students) as universally valid.

A second problem is the inevitable frustration that occurs when needs are not recognized. Freud, for example, showed how repressed sexual drives can lead to anxiety, maladaptive behavior, and mental illness. It is significant that, when Freud's ideas were brought to America by such people as Erikson, Horney, and Fromm, they had to be modified to a considerable extent in order to fit the new social conditions. People in America suffered less from sexual problems than from social problems. They were unable to make friends and relate to others in a meaningful way because of America's fast-paced, mobile society. Another example is the need for curiosity and exploration. Animal studies have shown that animals become restless and grow up deficient if raised in a barren, impoverished environment. Even their brain seems to be affected. Animals raised in an impoverished environment develop smaller brains than those raised in an enriched environment (Rosen-

weig, Bennett, Diamond, Wu, Slagle, & Saffran, 1969).

The danger of postulating to few needs is that it implies that people are easily satisfied and underestimates the difficulty of establishing truly human social conditions. Many human beings are raised in impoverished environments and are later subjected to the equally impoverishing repetition of monotonous work. These conditions are allowed to exist partly because older models of human nature and many current reinforcement theories assumed that people should be perfectly content if only sufficiently housed and fed. They ignore social needs and the need for novel stimuli and exploration. Fromm (1955) has argued that societies are healthy when they fulfill basic human needs. Societies that frustrate human needs are sick, no matter how productive they may appear to be. A social psychology that ignores human needs is not value neutral but instrumental in maintaining the status quo.

Biological and environmental explanations for human social behavior are not mutually exclusive. Learning shapes and modifies behavior within limits provided by biological drives. In human beings, these limits are rather large, and therefore one finds a great deal of cultural, and even individual, variability in behavior. But they are not infinite. Many of the particulars of evolutionary theory are uncertain—the mechanism of genetic transmission, chance mutations, and so on—but the core of evolutionary theory forms the basis for virtually all of the life sciences. To separate social psychology from this core is to create a disembodied social psychology in which social behavior is attributed entirely to culture. A human being is not a tabula rasa but a biological being with needs firmly rooted in nature.

## APPLIED SOCIAL PSYCHOLOGY

The application of social psychology can be traced back to Dewey and Mead's attempts at social reform in Chicago during the progressive era. During the 1930s, another wave of activity was created by the movement to establish the Society for the Psychological Study of Social Issues (SPSSI). This was followed by the widespread involvement of social psychologists in the war effort during World War II and a postwar period in which social psychologists, following Lewin, moved back and forth between basic and applied research. By the 1950s, however, the tide had turned. A split took place among Lewin's students that resulted in an applied, group-oriented wing led by Ronald Lippitt and a theoretical, individual-oriented wing led by Leon Festinger (Patnoe, 1988; Pettigrew, 1988). Those who stressed theory became more and more dominant because of the higher status given by psychologists to pure research.

The relevance crisis of the late 1960s and 1970s rejuvenated the need for an applied social psychology. This challenge was answered in part by making experimental social psychology more relevant, but there was also a growing recognition of the importance of the larger social context and a shift toward field research. Reminiscent of the movement among radical social psychologists during the 1930s, some social psychologists during the 1970s began to adopt practitioner roles. These included human relations trainers, consultants, program developers, and the more radical advocates for social change. Another factor that promoted the development of applied social psychology was a shift in funding from pure to more usable applied research, which occurred for both social psychology and the social sciences in general (Fisher, 1982). Government agencies wanted guidance for pressing social problems, such as minority rights, environmental issues, health, and criminal justice, and they were willing to pay researchers for conducting such research and withhold funds from those who did not.

By the mid-1970s, applied social psychology had become a distinct field (Deutsch & Hornstein, 1975). Special graduate programs were set up in the early 1980s around the model of the scientist-practitioner. In these programs research and

practical skills are combined through practicums and internships (Fisher, 1981; Severy, 1979). In a pathbreaking textbook, Fisher (1982) defined applied social psychology as *"social-psychological research and practice in real-world settings, directed toward the understanding of human social behavior and the solution of social problems"* (p.20).

A major issue that has emerged from the development of applied social psychology is its relationship to social psychology in general. Is it a distinct field, a subdiscipline, or an alternative to social psychology? The latter position is advocated by Fisher (1982). Furthermore, there is no clear consensus regarding the scope of an applied perspective. In order to clarify these issues, we will briefly consider the models and areas of application that have served as guidelines for the development of applied social psychology.

## Models of Application

Social psychologists have tended to approach applied social psychology in one of two ways. These have been called the "pure science model" and the "social science model" (Stephenson, 1988). In the pure science model, social-psychological theories derived primarily from laboratory research are used to explain social behavior in the real world (Fisher, 1982; Stephenson, 1988). It is assumed that social processes and causal relationships studied under controlled laboratory conditions can be generalized to complex situations outside the laboratory. The real-life settings thus serve as a test for more general theories. People who adopt this approach seldom question social or political conditions. Rather, acting as "social engineers," they assess the adequacy of the practices by which institutions implement their objectives. If urban renewal is desirable, for example, social psychologists would advise civic agencies on the best way to stimulate community support.

The social science model is characterized by a humanistic and interdisciplinary approach (Fisher, 1982; Gergen & Basseches,

1980; Stephenson, 1988). Social psychology is seen as one of many core disciplines that can contribute to an understanding of society and its institutions. Social psychologists therefore collaborate with other social scientists in order to acquire a comprehensive understanding of the nature and operation of these institutions. This approach deals directly with real-world settings rather than generalizing laboratory research to complex situations. Social psychology is seen as having certain indispensable and distinctive features that can be integrated with those of sociology, economics, law, and political science. Moreover, the social psychologists who adopt this approach operate according to a set of humanistic values in which social and political objectives are critically evaluated. When institutional practices conflict with basic human values, social psychologists become advocates for constructive social change.

These two approaches to applied social psychology do not reflect a rigid dichotomy. Applied social psychologists have generally favored one or the other, and the emphasis has changed from time to time. Among early social psychologists, Dewey and Mead stressed the social-science model. Both men were deeply committed to applying social psychology directly in community settings rather than as an extension of controlled laboratory research. They tended to accept the social system of their time, however. After World War I, Dewey became more critical, and during the 1930s, more radical approaches were common. The pendulum swung back to a more neutral stance during World War II and the postwar period. Under Lewin's influence, the emphasis was on testing theories by applying them to real-life settings. As Gergen (1982) points out, this Lewinian model helped promote a distinction between "pure" and "applied" research. The applied social psychologists' tendency to derive principles from pure research contributed to their lower professional status and eventual decline. The issue of social relevance during the 1970s, on the other hand, helped stimulate a new interest in the social-science model and a growing concern over the generalizability of laboratory research.

## Areas of Application

The interdisciplinary and humanistic trend in applied social psychology is based on an expanded conception of how social psychology is defined. Fisher (1982) argues that human social behavior should be studied at different levels, including interpersonal relations, small-group processes, and intergroup relations. Beyond these are macrosocial levels of analysis that examine organizations, the community, and national and international facets. This enlarged scope is reflected in the recent contact between disciplines such as social psychology, community psychology, cross-cultural psychology, and organizational behavior.

Working with social scientists and other professionals in management, law, and medicine, social psychologists have greatly expanded their sphere of application (Fisher, 1982; Stephenson, 1988). They have contributed to the development and evaluation of human-services programs aimed at helping people in matters of health, mental health, education, criminal justice, and social welfare. Another area of application has been the development and evaluation of methods of conflict resolution in interpersonal, organizational, and even international contexts.

It is beyond the scope of the present work to provide a survey of the various areas and subareas of applied social psychology, but a few examples may be useful. Social psychologists involved in the criminal justice system treat criminal behavior as a series of decisions that affect "criminals" as they move through the various stages of the process (Konecni & Ebbesen, 1982; Stephenson, 1988). The sequence begins with the decision to commit a crime and is followed by decisions about whether to report the crime, whether to investigate, whether to prosecute, how to organize and present the evidence, whether to convict, and if so, what sentence to impose. Social psychologists are often part of an interdisciplinary team that examines various aspects of the decision-making processes. Their background in psychology often allows them to make unique contributions, such as determining the accuracy or inaccuracy of eyewitness testimony or the way group dynamics helps influence the verdict of jurors.

The involvement of applied social psychologists in medicine has also been examined (Fisher, 1982; Taylor, 1978). Social psychologists can make unique contributions at each stage of the health-care process—from etiology to treatment, management, prevention, and delivery of health-care services. Social psychologists working within this perspective often critically evaluate health services, and if necessary advocate changes in established medical practices.

Some advocates of the interdisciplinary, humanistic approach to applied social psychology suggest that this is an appropriate model for social psychology in general (Fisher, 1982; Gergen, 1982). They argue that social psychology should be closely linked to other social sciences and should be value-laden rather than value-neutral. Moreover, there should be no distinction between pure and applied research. Social psychology is inherently concerned with real-world problems, and the traditional separation of pure and applied research is an artificial and unnecessary distinction. These arguments rest on the assumption that the premises on which traditional social psychology has been based need to be re-examined—that *reconstruction* rather than revision of social psychology is needed. This movement toward an alternative social psychology involves a number of different trends, but it reflects a core of thinking that is part of the new "postmodernism" that emerged in the 1960s. We will examine postmodernism and its impact on social psychology in the final chapter.

# 13

# Postmodernism

The development of an alternative social psychology occurred within the context of the radical politics and liberation movements of the 1960s and 1970s (see Henriques, Hollway, Unwin, Venn, & Walkerdine, 1984). It began with a call for a social psychology that was relevant to people's lives and was applicable to the pressing social problems confronting contemporary culture. It also included a critique of established theory and practice and the political message that traditional social psychology, by its uncritical acceptance of existing social relations, tends to promote and maintain the status quo. Those social psychologists seeking alternatives recognized that a new theroretical foundation had to be created. Among the earliest examples of this objective was an edited book entitled *Reconstructing Social Psychology* (Armistead, 1974), in which the contributors drew from three major theoretical approaches—Marxism, phenomenology, and humanistic psychology.

Before we trace the various alternatives to traditional social psychology, it may be useful to outline the various social factors that gave rise to this movement. As mentioned previously, the politics of the 1960s and 1970s inspired a reexamination of social psychology and the social sciences in general. The dramatic political events, however, were only a part of a more encompassing cultural shift in North American and Western European societies, which was rooted in the post–World War II period of economic recovery. Although the social and political changes leading to the "crisis of

confidence" in social psychology were discussed in the previous chapter, the present focus is primarily on those changes most closely associated with the movements beginning during the 1960s that were collectively known as "postmodernism."

## THE CULTURAL BACKDROP OF POSTMODERNISM

As we mentioned in Chapter 12, in the years following World War II, the United States entered a new period of economic prosperity. Jameson (1983) suggests that this expansion was accompanied by a new kind of society, marked by

> New types of consumption; planned obsolescence; an ever more rapid rhythm of fashion and style changes; the penetration of advertising, television and the media generally to a hitherto unparalleled degree throughout society; the replacement of the old tension between city and country, center and province, by the suburb and universal standardization; the growth of the great network of superhighways and the arrival of automobile culture. (pp. 124–125)

According to Jameson, these changes reflected a radical break with prewar conditions. By the 1960s, this new consumer-oriented society was criticized for both social and artistic reasons. During the same decade, the unfulfilled expectations of political and economic improvements among women, blacks, and other minorities produced new forms of political protests and together with the doubts about contemporary society marked a turning point that contributed to the development of the new movement known as postmodernism.

People who have analyzed the recent trends in Western culture differ on the nature and significance of these changes, and some have even questioned whether a "postmodern" period has superseded the modernist era (Arac, 1986; Cook, 1990; Habermas, 1983). There is a consensus, however, that the increased awareness nurtured in the 1960s has challenged previous presuppositions of the "modern" period and produced a movement that seeks to redirect or replace them. Thus, the term "postmodernism" seems to be an appropriate label for this new spirit of thought and self-criticism.

The distinct features of postmodernism must be seen in opposition to the themes of modernity. The modernist era was inspired by the Industrial Revolution and began in the middle of the nineteenth century. By the start of the twentieth century, the pace of technological development had accelerated appreciably. Industrialization within a capitalistic free-enterprise system tends to stress individual competition, mastery, and progress. Mass production and technological innovations dramatically increased society's control of the environment and seemed to hold the potential for unlimited social improvement. The sciences, particularly the new human sciences such as psychology, seemed to be an essential part of the process. Psychology and related disciplines could explore and discover aspects of human behavior that help people adapt to the new technology. Scientific knowledge was seen as an indispensable part of a better society.

The arts also reflected the themes of progress, individualism, and control. Modern architecture expressed control of the environment through its slogan "form follows function." Abstract paintings and sculptures reflected individual achievements and the uniqueness of each artist's private identity. Modern literature conveyed individualism through a diversity of themes and private styles. Success often depended on some unique innovation that made previous trends seem old fashioned and passé. Overall, the movement of modernity held the promise of a utopian future based on unlimited growth and economic development and challenged the conventions of middle-class society.

By the middle of this century, however, the themes and expressions of modernism had become well established (Jameson, 1983). James Joyce and Pablo Picasso seemed familiar rather than strange or repulsive. Historical events such as the Holocaust and the nuclear arms race challenged our beliefs about unlimited progress and control. The social and political disruptions of the 1960s set the stage for a widespread movement in the arts, humanities, and social sciences that questioned the traditional assumptions of modernism. By the 1970s, postmodernism served as a focal point of resistance to the dominant modernist world view (Foster, 1983).[1]

Postmodern artists have turned away from the themes of individualism and private expression (Jameson, 1983). Writers and artists no longer invent new styles or stress unique private experiences. There is a movement to combine earlier styles and interpret the past through pop images and cultural stereotypes. The new genre of "nostalgic films," such as *American Graffiti*, tries to recapture the feeling and styles of previous times. Postmodern thinkers seek to "deconstruct" or question modernist beliefs about truth, knowledge, power, individualism, and language (Flax, 1987). Postmodern philosophers challenge the assumption that reason can provide an objective and universal foundation for knowledge or that a knowledge based on reason will be socially beneficial and insure progress.

The movement to reconstruct social psychology can be seen as part of the postmodern trend, and it began with a critique of traditional social psychology's modernist foundation. Kenneth Gergen (1988) cites four overarching modernist presumptions that have shaped the development of psychology in general. First, each discipline seeks a basic subject matter. While social psychologists have disagreed about what constitutes the area of concentration (such as social cognition or social behavior), there is a general belief that a basic subject can be found. Modernist social psychologists also believe that basic psychological principles are universal, timeless, and apply to people in different cultures. A third assumption that characterizes modernist social psychologists is a firm belief in empirical procedures, particularly controlled experiments, which are seen as the means by which universal principles can be discovered. The final modernist assumption is based on a belief in the progressive nature of empirical research. By applying objective and value-free empirical procedures, knowledge of fundamental principles gradually accumulates, and we learn more and more about social behavior.

These modernist assumptions can be traced to the Enlightenment philosophy of Descartes, Locke, and Kant, which established the tradition that there are "foundations" for knowledge. These foundations are discovered by studying the mental processes of separate individuals. As Richard Rorty (1979) expressed it, foundational philosophies assume that "mind mirrors nature" and that reality can be discovered by studying what people think. During the 1960s, postmodern philosophers began to question the traditional dualism of subject and object or mind and matter and replaced it with a social epistemology of a very different sort (Feyerabend, 1976; Kuhn, 1962, 1970; Quine, 1960; Rorty, 1979).

This shift from a dualistic to a social epistemology affected social psychology in three ways (Gergen, 1989a). First there was a shift in emphasis from mind to language. The new area of concentration was not the connection between mind and world but the relationship between language and reality. There was a growing awareness of the relationship between thought and language and a shift in emphasis from "propositions in our head" to thoughts and ideas as reflected in written and spoken language. Since language is a social product, knowledge about the world is based on social processes. There was also a shift in emphasis from accuracy to practice. In traditional dualist epistemologies, truth about objective reality is discovered by exploring mental processes. The shift in emphasis from mind to language shows that our beliefs about the external world are embedded in an intricate web of social practices, which includes conventions, norms, roles, and variations in power. Finally, there was a shift in emphasis from validity to utility. Since meaning is derived from social practices and interchange, questions of truth and objectivity become less relevant. Social epistemologists stress how beliefs about the world are shaped by social practice. In place of the traditional concern with individual representations of reality, there is now a focus on the social utility of these accounts and the kinds of social exchange the various accounts support. Political, ethical, and moral questions now become an integral part of social epistemology.

The postmodern focus on social epistemology challenges the traditional assumptions that have shaped modernist social psychology (Gergen, 1988). If beliefs about the world do not mirror objective reality, then there is no independent subject matter to be elucidated. If social behavior and scientific inquiry are shaped by social, political, and moral forces outside the individual, then there may be few timeless and universal psychological principles. Since the social context also helps determine methods of inquiry, there is little reason to give priority to empirical procedures. Finally, the modernist belief in scientific progress and cumulative knowledge is challenged by the postmodern view that knowledge is socially embedded. The very idea of scientific progress reflects a cultural value and can be interpreted as a literary achievement (Lyotard, 1984).

Although postmodernism was strongly shaped by social and political events occurring in the 1960s and 1970s, it did not appear suddenly. Like all the movements described in this book, there were intellectual precursors that predate postmodernism by a considerable period. Some of these are broad-based intellectual traditions, such as those of Darwin, Freud, Marx, Durkheim, and Weber. Others are based on thinkers who focused more specifically on the relationship between thought and language and the social origins of each. Before turning to the most recent trends in postmodernism, it may be useful to examine some of the theorists who have shaped postmodern thinking in the United States and Europe.

# INTELLECTUAL PRECURSORS OF POSTMODERNISM

Although the dualist epistemology of Descartes has had a profound effect on the development of philosophy and psychology, there was a school of "counter Enlightenment" that argued that knowledge is embedded within a social and historical context (Leahey, 1987). This social epistemology was initiated by Vico and Herder in the eighteenth century and carried on by Hegel and Marx during the nineteenth century. Hegel in turn had a strong influence on American pragmatists, who in many ways espoused a theory similar to that held by postmodern thinkers. Similar theories were developed at roughly the same time by people in Russia, England, and France, and these include the writings of Lev Vygotsky and A. R. Luria, the later Wittgenstein, and some aspects of phenomenology.

## Chicago Pragmatism

The work of Dewey and Mead has been discussed in Chapters 4 and 11, but it may be useful to summarize their work briefly and draw attention to the social epistemology that pervades their thought. As previously pointed out, three major features characterize the work of Dewey and Mead—functionalism, intersubjectivity, and humanism. Dewey and Mead's functionalism was based on Darwin's evolutionary theory, and it was used to explain how thought occurs as people adapt themselves to their physical and social environment. Consciousness and activity are closely connected, and people's conception of reality is constantly changing. There is no timeless objective world to be discovered. People are continually engaged in a reciprocal and dialectical relationship with the world in which they are both the agents and recipients of environmental change.

For Dewey and Mead, both thought and action occur within a social context. Although they did not use the term "intersubjectivity," this concept seems to describe their view of social interaction (Joas, 1985). The way people think and behave occurs within a social framework, which includes customs, conventions, beliefs, and language. The communication of thoughts through language is especially significant. People confront and deal with problems within an atmosphere of mutual social support and only later learn to internalize these processes and confront problems on their own.

Humanism, the third feature of American pragmatism, is reflected in Dewey and Mead's concern for ethical issues. Ethics is not based on universal and timeless principles. It occurs as people reflect on and weigh the concrete consequences of various alternative courses of action. Such decisions rely on communication and cooperation among members of a community. The extent to which people can develop their potential as active participants in communal decisions depends on their political system. Both Dewey and Mead considered a bona fide participatory democracy as the ideal society. They also advocated a humanistic model of science in which rational decisions about ethical and moral questions are based on scientific knowledge. They saw science as an instrument for improving existing social conditions. The value of scientific intervention was determined in terms of its ability to help shape constructive social change while promoting the moral standards of individual freedom and communal welfare.

## Russian "Cultural" Psychology

Alexei Leontiev, A. R. Luria, and Lev Vygotsky met in the 1920s and formed what was known as the "troika." The development of memory became the special province of Leontiev, while Vygotsky and Luria focused on the development of language and thought. Vygotsky (1896–1934) was trained in law but also studied literary criticism and psychology and did his doctoral dissertation on Shakespeare's *Hamlet*. He completed his graduate studies in Moscow in 1917. His work on the psychology of literature was influenced by Freudian theory, but by the 1920s, his interests began to shift to the psychology of language (Wozniak, 1983). He drew from a wide variety of sources, but the strongest influences were probably Marx and Hegel (Kozulin, 1986). While most Russian psychologists writing during this period sprinkled their work with quotations from Marx, Vygotsky took seriously the notion that consciousness is derived through social interaction and that one must look for the origins of consciousness not in the brain or spirit but in external social conditions.

Vygotsky's first teaching position, which he held from 1917 until 1924, was at the Teachers College in Gomel, the city of his youth. This affiliation exposed him to the ideas of Dewey, who had a profound influence on education in the Soviet Union during the 1920s (Wozniak, 1983). Dewey's social version of pragmatism bears a strong resemblance to Marx's dialectical theory (Tolman & Piekkola, 1989) and it is therefore not suprising that Dewey's work on education would attract educators in the Soviet Union. While Vygotsky rarely cites Dewey, there is little doubt that his work helped form the intellectual background for Vygotsky's ideas (Wozniak, 1983).[2] Vygotsky called his approach "cultural," "historical," or "instrumental" psychology at various phases of its development. The terms "cultural" and "historical" were used to stress the social origins of mental processes, whereas "instrumental" was used to denote the fact that language is a tool that guides and directs behavior.

One of Vygotsky's (1934/1962) central concerns was language development. He regarded language as a shared social activity and vehemently denied Jean Piaget's contention that children begin with egocentric speech directed primarily at themselves and only later learn to communicate by placing themselves in the position of others. The development of language for Piaget involves a process of gradual socialization whereby the

intimate and personal monologue of children is replaced by dialogue whose aim is communication. Vygotsky did not think that egocentric speech was a temporary phenomenon that gradually disappeared as the child became socialized. He saw it as a reflection of a new function—self-regulation—that gradually becomes internalized, and he argued that the actual sequence was the precise opposite of Piaget's. The primary function of language is communication, and the child's first attempt to speak includes a strong desire to be understood. Gradually children learn to use language to plan and direct their activities and begin to speak exclusively to themselves. But they continue to talk out loud. Only later do they learn to use language without actually speaking. Vygotsky argued that the "egocentric" speech that Piaget had found in preschool children was a transition stage between communication with others and silent conversation aimed primarily at oneself. The proper sequence is external speech, egocentric speech, then inner speech. Egocentric speech does not disappear, it simply goes "underground." Vygotsky was not concerned with the type of problem-solving skills studied by Piaget. His focus was on the use of language in mediating higher-order processes—what have subsequently become known as "strategic" skills or "metacognition" (Wertsch, 1979).

The inner speech of adults has the same function as egocentric speech in children. It is used to plan, organize, and direct activity. Inner speech, like egocentric speech, is condensed and abbreviated, and there is a strong tendency toward predication where the subject is omitted. It is virtually incomprehensible out of context because it omits what is obvious to the speaker. Inner speech is also characterized by a preponderance of sense over meaning. Meaning refers more or less to the dictionary definition, whereas sense depends on the context. A good example of the distinction occurs in the fable "The grasshopper and the ant." The ant who is busy putting food away for the winter warns the grasshopper that he had better do the same. When the grasshopper refuses, the ant concludes by saying "go and dance!" The words "go" and "dance" have rather precise and specific meanings but in this context they imply both "enjoy yourself" and "perish." A word in context means both more and less than the same word in isolation.

Inner speech resembles conversation with an extremely sympathetic listener. Vygotsky uses the example of the characters Kitty and Levin in Leo Tolstoy's *Anna Karenina,* who communicate in one scene by using the first letter of the words in a sentence. Levin writes W y a: i c n b, d y m t o n and is astonished when Kitty correctly translates it as "When you answered: it can not be, did you mean then or never?" Kitty responds by writing I c n a o t, which means "I could not answer otherwise then," and then s t y m f a f w h—"so that you might forget and forgive what happened." And the dialogue continues. What makes the example even more powerful is the fact that it was based on a similar incident in Tolstoy's own life when he declared his love for the woman who would later become his wife.

The translation from inner speech to communication is typically more difficult, however. We cannot make ourselves understood by simply stating what we think privately. We often have to go through a great deal of elaboration, define our terms more precisely, and use examples of what we mean. Even this may not be sufficient. There are probably a great many gifted thinkers who lack the ability to communicate effectively, and this problem is particularly pronounced among independent thinkers who work out their ideas in isolation. Without communication, our thoughts simply go with us to the grave.

Although speech and thought are very much related, they are not precisely the same. Vygotsky pointed out that they develop differently and have different genetic roots. Prelinguistic thinking occurs in both children and animals. Köhler's (1925) experiments with chimpanzees, for example, showed that they could solve complex problems through *insight* if all the necessary elements were present. The term "insight" was used to stress the visual nature of their solution. The chimps were apparently able to visualize how boxes could be stacked in order to reach a banana hanging from the roof of their cage or how a short stick could be used to reach a longer one that could be used to drag a banana into their cage. Language development in children occurs later than thought. Children develop an active interest in words around the age of two, and their vocabulary increases enormously. Their thinking becomes increasingly more verbal, and at some point, speech ceases to accompany behavior and begins to precede and direct it. Vygotsky suggested that the relationship between thought and speech is similar to two overlapping circles. Thought and speech coincide in the overlapping part and form verbal thought. Verbal thought, however, is only one form of thinking. Language provides a powerful tool for dealing with people and social situations. Vygotsky (1934/1962) cites a poem by Mandelstam to illustrate the point: "I have forgotten the word I intended to say, and my thought, unembodied, returns to the realm of shadows" (p. 119). Thought is not merely expressed in words, words (within context) form the essential content of verbal thinking.

All psychological processes are altered as a consequence. Vygotsky made a distinction between higher and lower mental processes. Lower processes, such as sensation, perception, attention, and will, have a biological origin and are similar across species, whereas higher processes are culturally acquired and uniquely human (cf. Gergen, 1973). Lower processes continue to function after higher ones are acquired, but they are modified and restructured. As a child develops language skills, these are used to direct attention, organize perception, establish goals, and guide behavior. Nor does this development stop with lower processes. The adolescent who has mastered algebra sees arithmetic from a different perspective.

Vygotsky felt that the focus on lower processes that was characteristic of American behaviorism made it inadequate as a description of human behavior. All higher processes are mediated processes, and language is the principal tool used to master and direct them. Thought at the higher level contains concepts and generalizations previously absent at the lower levels. Because higher processes depend on language, they are socially acquired and vary from culture to culture. For Vygotsky every higher function appears twice: first on the social level between people and then on the individual level within people.

Vygotsky died of tuberculosis at the age of thirty-seven, but his associate, A. R. Luria (1902–1977), lived a long and productive life and tested his ideas using a variety of research techniques. Luria's training was in psychology and medicine and included an early interest in psychoanalysis. He rejected Freud's strong emphasis on biological drives but incorporated other aspects of Freudian theory, such as the concepts of complexes and unconscious conflict and the word association technique. He even established a small psychoanalytic circle, ordered stationery with "Kazan Psychoanalytic Association" printed in Russian and German on the letterhead, and wrote Freud to tell him of the group (Luria, 1979). Luria felt that the major failure of psychoanalysis was a tendency to "over-biologize" the mind and ignore social factors, and he was therefore strongly drawn to Vygotsky's Marxist position. His interest in psychoanalysis might have placed him outside academic psychology were it not for a strong commitment to experimental procedures.

Luria's research can be divided into four periods. From 1928 to 1934, he was concerned primarily with cultural differences in the thought of various ethnic groups within the Soviet Union. He found a large difference between literate and nonliterate groups. Thinking in terms of practical experience dominated the thought of nonliterate subjects, but abstract and logical thinking increased with education. Illiterate individuals were unable to solve even simple syllogisms, such as,

> Precious metals do not rust.
>
> Gold is a precious metal.
>
> Does it rust or not?

Their inability to make logical deductions was based on three factors: a mistrust of premises not derived from personal experience, failure to accept such premises as universal, and, consequently, a breakdown of logical syllogisms into three isolated parts. Luria dubbed these observations "anti-Car-

tesian experiments" because they showed that critical self-awareness was the product rather than the starting point of social development.

The next period of research involved longitudinal studies of identical and fraternal twins. Luria was familiar with the work of Cyril Burt and others who were working on twin studies at the same time, but his own work was radically different. He reasoned that differences between fraternal twins should be greater than those distinguishing identical twins if biological factors were involved, since identical twins are genetically the same. This pattern was true for young children five to seven years of age, but differences between pairs of identical twins and pairs of fraternal twins decreased with age, suggesting that, to a certain extent, cultural factors responsible for higher mental processes begin to override biological differences. Luria also took pairs of identical twins and gave special training to one of the siblings in order to assess the effects of learning with biology held constant.

A third line of research focused on verbal control of behavior in normal and mentally retarded children. The behavior of normal children began to be brought under verbal control at around four years of age, whereas severely retarded children could not even follow the simplest instruction at seven. Since language development was far more severely affected than motor development, differences between normal and retarded individuals were used to explore the role of language in mediating behavior. Luria (1979) felt that the comparison of normal and retarded children, although suggestive, "constituted no more than a series of pilot studies" or "quasi experiments" (p. 119).

Luria's research took a new turn during World War II, as he and his students began to devote themselves to the rehabilitation of those wounded in the war. Neurological research took a giant step forward during this period because of the large number of people who suffered brain damage and needed medical attention. Researchers were divided on the role of the brain in mediating behavior. Some believed that brain functions were highly localized, while others took a more holistic approach and argued that mental processing was distributed throughout the brain. Luria took a middle position between these two extremes and found evidence that simple functions were highly localized, whereas more complex ones involved a number of regions within the brain. Speech, for example, involves motor movement, sensory feedback, and verbal recall. Other skills, such as writing, which involve complex hand-eye coordination as well as verbal recall, are much too recent to have evolved through evolution and therefore depend on areas of the brain that have evolved for other reasons. Luria thus provided physiological evidence for Vygotsky's distinction between higher and lower mental processes. The relationship between the brain and language is so complex that Luria coined a new term to describe it—"neurolinguistics"—thus foreshadowing many of the recent developments in cognitive science.

With Dewey's influence on Vygotsky, it is not surprising that the similarities between Vygotsky and George Herbert Mead have frequently been noted (e.g., Bruner, 1962; Kozulin, 1986). Both Vygotsky and Mead stressed the social origins of thought and language, their shared character, and the use of language in planning and directing activities. Unlike Mead, however, whose ideas were based mainly on philosophy, Vygotsky's work was firmly grounded in experimental research. His basic ideas have been tested and supported by almost five decades of empirical research. Luria's career appears to have taken a zigzag course in response to political and academic pressures within the Soviet Union, but Vygotsky's theory has always remained central (Cole, 1979). Vygotsky provided the broad theoretical framework that Luria tested and developed. In early 1976, Luria came across the work of Ludwig Wittgenstein through the Norwegian social psychologist Ragnar Rommetveit (1968, 1974), and decided that he needed to learn more in order to develop his ideas. Unfortunately, he died the next year. The work of Wittgenstein represents a third tradition that paralleled that of Vygotsky, Dewey, and Mead.

## Ludwig Wittgenstein (1889–1951)

Ludwig Wittgenstein was born in Vienna, the youngest of eight children of a rich and artistic family of Jewish descent.[3] His father was an iron and steel magnate and a patron of the arts whose friends included Johannes Brahms and Gustav Mahler. Wittgenstein was educated at home until he was fourteen, received three years of formal education at Linz, and then studied engineering in Berlin. In 1908, he registered at the University of Manchester, were he designed and supervised the construction of a jet-reaction engine for aircraft. Problems associated with the design aroused his interest in mathematics and later the philosophical foundations of mathematics. He spent a year and a half at Trinity College, Cambridge, in 1912 and 1913, where he studied with Bertrand Russell and became close friends with G. E. Moore. According to Russell (1951/1967), Wittgenstein (then 23) "made very rapid progress in mathematical logic, and soon knew all that I had to teach" (p. 30). Russell goes on to say that "getting to know Wittgenstein was one of the most exciting intellectual adventures of my life" (p. 31).

Wittgenstein left Cambridge in 1913 and moved to Skjolden, Norway, where he built a hut and lived in isolation until the outbreak of World War I. He enlisted as a volunteer in the Austrian artillery during the war and served on the Russian front, winning several decorations for bravery. He was eventually promoted to the rank of officer and transferred to a mountain artillery regiment on the southern front in 1918, where he was taken prisoner by the Italian army. Throughout the war he was working on problems of language and logic, writing his thoughts down in notebooks he carried in his rucksack. By the time he was captured, he had a complete manuscript, which he sent to Russell in England. Most of the notes taken during the period were destroyed on his request in 1950, but the better ones were collected, ordered, and published in German in 1921. A year later an English translation, *Tractatus Logico-Philosophicus,* was brought out with an introduction by Russell.

The *Tractatus,* which was the only major work published during Wittgenstein's life, draws heavily from and extends the work of Russell and Moore. Russell and Moore had helped initiate a change in philosophy at the turn of the century, whereby language became a central focus (Pears, 1971). Although only 74 pages long, the *Tractatus* covers a wide range of topics, including logic, ethics, causality, the self, freedom, death, mysticism, and the nature of good and evil (Kenny, 1973). The central focus, however, is the nature and limits of language. Wittgenstein was concerned primarily with the line dividing sense and nonsense and the limits of what could be said (and therefore thought).

Two ideas that were central in this work are the concepts of logical atomism and the picture theory of reality. According to Wittgenstein, the world consists of elementary objects that have a definite relationship with each other. When we think about the world or imagine a possible state of affairs, these objects and their relationships are captured in the propositions we use. True propositions serve as a model or picture of the world by virtue of their correspondence. The logical structure of true propositions is the mirror-image of reality itself, and each true proposition contains exactly the same number of distinguishable elements as the situation it represents. A proposition represents a hypothetical situation. It may be true or false, accurate or inaccurate, but the ultimate truth depends on its logical structure and agreement with reality. Wittgenstein's picture theory of reality exemplifies the modernist foundational philosophy that assumes that "mind mirrors nature." As we will see, however, Wittgenstein later rejected this theory, and it is his later work that places him in the camp of people who were forerunners of postmodernism.

In the *Tractatus,* it was assumed that language expresses propositions but in an imperfect form. Ordinary language contains accidental features derived through convention and ambiguities that disguise thought and obscure its logical form. Statements must be broken down into simple elements (that is, words) that refer to specific objects before their accuracy can be assessed. A logically perfect language contains clear rules of syntax for relating items and words with one and only one meaning. Some statements cannot be tested because they lack a clear referent. These form the limits of language and help provide a dividing line between sense and nonsense. The term "nonsense" was not used in a pejorative sense. It includes a number of areas, such as ethics and religion, that Wittgenstein personally considered very important; it is perhaps better translated as "meaningless" or "without sense." His final sentence, "What we cannot speak about we must pass over in silence" (p. 74), attempts to convey the belief that there is a realm of reality that cannot be expressed in words. Nonsensical statements are not necessarily false. Their truth or falseness simply cannot be assessed.

Wittgenstein felt that the purpose of philosophy was to examine language critically and reveal its logical structure. All languages contain the same underlying structure, which is ultimately the structure of reality itself. A statement can be true for two reasons. Logical statements are unconditionally true because they are *tautologies*—that is, statements that are true by virtue of their form alone. A statement such as the law of the excluded middle (that is, either $p$ or not $p$) is true because the negation of a true statement is always false and therefore one or the other *must* be true. The same is true for mathematics. It is the property of $1 + 1 + 1 + 1$ that it can be rewritten as $(1 + 1) + (1 + 1)$, that is, $2 + 2$ or 4. Logical statements represent the structure of the world itself. Contingent statements, on the other hand, are true if and only if they correspond with reality. Logical statements are always true; contingent statements (such as the statements of science) are true sometimes.

Wittgenstein believed that the vast majority of philosophical statements are not false but meaningless and that many of the deepest problems in philosophy were pseudo-problems brought on by the distortions and misuse of language.[4] An example of a nonsensical statement is "the good is more or less identical than the beautiful" (Wittgenstein, 1921/1961, p. 19). Such a statement is grammatically well formed and consists entirely of familiar words. It appears to be an English sentence, but there is something peculiar about it. This peculiarity can give the impression of profound philosophical depth that can seduce even serious thinkers. Philosophical questions of this sort sound as if they are questions about facts, and they are approached as scientific problems would be. For Wittgenstein, the purpose of philosophy is not to solve riddles but to analyze the hidden structure of language and distinguish sense from nonsense. Sensible statements can then be verified through scientific procedures. This was envisioned as not just another addition to philosophy but a radical transformation of both its form and content.

Wittgenstein is unusual in the history of Western thought because he developed not one but two unique philosophies, each the product of many years of intense labor, each highly regarded, and the latter in many ways a rejection of the first. The *Tractatus* is brief, enigmatic, and full of confidence, but when the same issues are discussed in the notebooks (1914–1916/1961), the treatment is more extended, conflicting arguments are introduced, and the discussion is often plagued by doubt (Pears, 1971). The division between Wittgenstein's early and later work was marked by a period of separation from philosophy. After returning from the war, Wittgenstein gave away the large fortune he had inherited from his father and took a year of teacher's training in Vienna. He taught elementary school in a number of remote villages in lower Austria between 1920 and 1926 but was desperately unhappy during this period and contemplated suicide several times. He gave up teaching in 1926 and worked briefly as a gardener's assistant in a monastery. He was then asked to design and build a mansion for one of his sisters in Vienna, which took two years. During this period he came into contact with the Vienna Circle of logical positivist philosophers, who were captivated by his early work. Large segments of the *Tractatus* were read aloud in these sessions and discussed sentence by sentence (Carnap, 1964/1967). This seemed to rekindle his interest in philosophy, and he returned to Cambridge in 1929, submitted the *Trac-*

*tatus* (which was already internationally famous) as a doctoral dissertation, and after an oral defense conducted by Russell and Moore, received his Ph.D.

The 1930s were Wittgenstein's most productive years. He was a research fellow at Trinity College and began working on what became known as his later philosophy. Wittgenstein had many distinguished students, including Moore, who sat in on his lectures for several years. Moore (1942/1967) felt that Wittgenstein "was much cleverer at philosophy than I was, and not only cleverer, but also more profound" (p. 39). He was appointed professor of philosophy at Cambridge in 1939 and given the chair previously held by Moore, but World War II broke out before he could assume the position. He served as an orderly during the war and was reappointed to Cambridge in 1945, but he left in 1947 and moved to Ireland, where he lived on a farm and later in a hut by the sea. During this period, he finished the first and major part of his second book, *Philosophical Investigations.* He visited America briefly in 1949 but moved back to England, where he discovered he had incurable cancer. The last two years of his life were spent with friends at Oxford and Cambridge. He died in 1951, and *Philosophical Investigations* was published two years later.

Wittgenstein was not a typical scholar. He hated the clever conversation and pretentiousness of university life, taught classes in a sparse room on the top of a gateway overlooking Whewell's Court, and relaxed by munching pork pies in the front row of a local cinema. He was not well read in the classics and seemed to have developed his later philosophy independently of other thinkers working on similar problems at the same time. His favorite movies were westerns and his favorite reading was detective stories. He eventually lost hope in Western society and turned briefly to the Soviet Union as an alternative. He visited the Soviet Union in 1935, was quite impressed with the developments taking place, and would have stayed were it not for the worsening conditions brought on by Stalin. He described his short tenure as professor as a "living death" and discouraged many of his better students from going on in philosophy. Despite his personal popularity, he had serious doubts about his ability as a teacher and a fear that his work was misunderstood by even his closest associates (von Wright, 1982). He was so displeased with Russell's introduction to the *Tractatus* that he was willing to give up the English translation altogether. He left Cambridge in 1947 because he felt the need to think alone, without the distractions of university life, and because he needed time to complete his later work.

Much of Wittgenstein's later work is devoted to *dismantling* his early concepts of logical atomism and the picture theory of reality. He came to reject the notions that elements of language should have one and only one referent, that propositions are made up of independent elements whose truth or falseness determines the truth of the compound statement, that the true structure of language represents the structure of reality, and that as a result, underneath all languages are the same. These four points represent a major departure from his early work and should be discussed separately.

Wittgenstein abandoned his early belief that the ultimate elements of language are words that refer to specific objects and replaced it with the concept of *family resemblance.* Words do not refer to distinct objects or even common features of ideal objects. They were now seen as tools, and like other tools—hammer, pliers, saw, screwdriver, ruler, glue-pot, and square—serve a variety of functions and come in many different forms. The notion that words refer to distinct objects is most true for nouns such as "table" and "chair" and proper names, but when we look for objects associated with adjectives, verbs, or contrasting conjunctions, we are forced to invent pseudo-objects to fill the void, and this is just one of the ways in which language can lead us astray.

The concept of family resemblances can be seen most clearly in the example of games. There is no common feature characteristic of all games. Some are amusing, some involve competition. Some involve teamwork, others are played alone. Some,

like chess, have intricate rules, while others, like bouncing a ball against a wall, have no rules at all. Instead of a single underlying feature, there is a network of "overlapping and criss-crossing" characteristics. They are like members of a family, where each person resembles the others but in different ways. A daughter has her father's eyes but her mother's dark hair and complexion. A son looks faintly like his uncle around the chin but resembles his grandfather in temperament. What is true of "language," "tools," and "games" is equally true of abstract concepts such as "goodness" and "beauty." Like the fibers running through a rope, the strength of the rope does not depend on any single fiber but on the combination of numerous overlapping and disconnected threads.

Wittgenstein also rejected the theory of elementary propositions and with it the view that the truth of a statement depends on the truth of its elements. The problems with language discussed in the *Tractatus* suggest that language could be improved so that the inadequacies are removed, but in *Philosophical Investigations,* the search for independent elements is seen as a delusion (Kenny, 1973). The meaning of a word is now determined by its use and the context in which it occurs. It is no longer possible to separate language into its basic elements, examine their logical structure, and determine the accuracy or inaccuracy of a statement. Nor is it feasible to hope for a perfected language where ambiguities and inconsistencies are removed and there is a sharp dividing line between sense and nonsense.

Wittgenstein also abandoned the notion that all languages have a similar underlying structure that reflects the nature of reality itself. Instead, he speaks of language as a game with rules and procedures of its own. He compares it to the growth of a town. There is a maze of old streets and buildings around the central square with new developments at the outskirts. New and old structures stand side by side and construction is never complete. The words used in a language are both multifaceted and open-ended. Meanings change during the process of use. New terms are adopted and others become obsolete. Language is not fixed. Science, for example, has made enormous contributions to our vocabulary and will continue to do so in the future.

The openness of concepts means that there will always be a certain looseness about them. Concepts that pick out common properties must be sustained as new cases are added, and this is based on convention. Concepts originate not in the mind of an individual but in the practical world of everyday experience. Nature provides no anchor points, no natural divisions on which to base words. Language games are complicated shared activities, and like other games, they are based on definite and yet somewhat arbitrary rules. Learning a language is different from learning a second language, where concepts are already known and new words are substituted through a process of translation. Each individual acquires concepts by incorporating new cases into concepts previously learned from others.

Wittgenstein categorically rejects the notion that there is or could be anything like a private language. Even our most private experiences, such as pain, are sufficiently public to be labeled by others. A child hurts herself, cries, and is comforted by an adult who provides a word for her experience. The concept of "pain" does not mean crying but is derived from it. If language described a purely private experience it could not be taught. The notion that language (and thought) begins with private experience is one of the most fundamental philosophical errors. If we start with a fully functioning individual mind, it is practically impossible to understand how one person can know what another person is thinking or how one can infer pain in others from their own private experience. In real life we never think of pain as private or assume that blue skies and sunny days belong exclusively to us. As Wittgenstein (1953/1963) says, "the decisive moment in the conjuring trick has been made, and it was the very one that we thought quite innocent" (p. 103).

The notion that language is a convention stresses the social nature of Wittgenstein's later philosophy. Meaning is not based on objects, mental process, or ideal entities. It is acquired through social contact with other speakers in one's culture. Wittgenstein (1953/1963) uses the example of chess. A person explains the rules of chess by pointing to a piece and saying, "This is the king; it can move like this" (p. 15). Someone who understands the rules of chess will have a different experience when watching the game than someone who does not. But the experience is based on knowledge previously acquired from others. To understand a language means mastering a technique. Language is an instrument, and meaning depends on the function words have as they pass back and forth between people during purposeful, shared activity.

Wittgenstein's social theory of mind stems from his social theory of meaning, and it radically transforms the relationship between thought and language and language and reality. Thought is no longer separate from the words used to express it. Sometimes we get a flash of insight or our thoughts seem to run ahead of our ability to express them, but Wittgenstein felt that we understand a whole thought in a flash in the same way that we can make note of it or summarize it in a few words. Occasionally we have a flash of insight and the thought does not occur or we find ourselves straining in vain for the right expression (cf. the poem cited by Vygotsky, where "thought, unembodied, returns to the realm of shadows"). When we think in language, there are not "meanings" going through our mind in addition to verbal expressions. The language itself is the vehicle of thought (and presumably other forms of thinking require other forms of symbolic expression, such as mental images, although Wittgenstein does not discuss this point).

Language also helps shape our experience of the world. In the *Tractatus,* language "reflects" reality in an imperfect form, but in the later work, it is the other way around. Language helps determine our view of the world because we use it to organize our experience. Objects do not depend on the language we use but our perception of them depends on how they are categorized and defined. Thought is no longer mediated by propositions or pictures that parallel the structure of the real world. Images often accompany thought but they are merely by-products of thinking and not essential to it (Bloor, 1983).

Finally, differences among languages are no longer seen as superficial variations of a central theme. They are real differences that help determine the way we think and organize reality—"the *speaking* of language is part of an activity, or a form of life" (Wittgenstein, 1953/1963, p. 11). Treating language acquisition as a form of translation, in which words are attached to isolated, independent objects, makes it seem that children can already think but lack the means of expression. In Wittgenstein's later work, the relationship between language and thought is far more essential. Outside of language there is no independent, objective point of support. Thinking is an activity that uses signs acquired during the process of socialization.

What is true of language is also true of ethics, logic, and mathematics. Just as there is no private language, there is no private morality. Isolated individuals cannot place themselves under a moral obligation or identify good and evil. "To obey a rule, to make a report, to give an order, to play a game of chess are *customs* (uses, institutions)" (Wittgenstein, 1953/1963, p. 81). There are no a priori concepts or values. Even the laws of logic and mathematics are described as expressions of "thinking habits." This does not mean that $2 + 2$ does not equal 4 or either $p$ or not $p$ can be false. Such statements are unconditionally true because they are tautologies. There is simply no ethereal plane lying behind mathematical and logical formulas. Both are more accurately described as inventions based on conventional knowledge, and their real nature is to be found in their practical use and application. The belief in logical and mathematical essences is a reification of a social process.

While there are radical differences between Wittgenstein's early and later work, there are similarities as well. Both assume that there is an objective reality that we are attempting to understand. Both assume that language is both a means for expressing our ideas and a source of confusion. Both assume that many philosophical problems

have their roots in the distortion and misuse of language, unhealthy habits of thought that permeate the intellectual culture of our time (von Wright, 1982). The purpose of philosophy is to untie the knots in our thinking that we have needlessly placed there. The result of philosophy, for Wittgenstein, is not to discover truth but to dissolve confusion—confusion generated by philosophers. Kenny (1973) has suggested that Wittgenstein himself may have exaggerated the difference between his early and his later work because he was concentrating on the issues that distinguished them.

The reception of Wittgenstein's later work has been mixed. Analytic philosophers, like Russell, who were committed to a foundational philosophy of language as a representation of reality were perplexed and regarded it as the product of a great mind that had simply slipped into obscurity. The complexity of his ideas and his cryptic style both "invite and at the same time resist our craving for clear understanding" (Fann, 1967, p. 11). Wittgenstein's later works (which include lecture notes and writings published since his death) do not read like ordinary books. They are a collection of remarks that jump from topic to topic, frequently illustrated with thought experiments. This explains to a great extent the large secondary literature devoted to interpreting his ideas.

Wittgenstein was a singular thinker with few predecessors and little contact outside a small circle of friends, but there are parallels between his work and that of theorists discussed previously. Wittgenstein was a great admirer of William James and considered his *Varieties of Religious Experience* a classic. His notion that there is an objective reality independent of our will, that language is a socially acquired tool that helps determine the nature of perception and thought, and that thinking is a mental activity directed toward the solution of concrete problems bears an obvious resemblance to American pragmatism. Both he and James were aware that language is unable to capture the full complexity of the lived experience, and both took a pluralistic position that recognized the possibility of many different world views.

Linsky (1957/1967) has argued that the instrumental theory of language is the center of gravity of Wittgenstein's later philosophy and that it is in complete opposition to his early view that language "reflects" reality. Asking a question, describing a room, complaining of pain, expressing fear or doubt, or proving a theorem in geometry are all examples of language use woven into activities directed toward certain goals. Even more suggestive is a remark by Wittgenstein (1930/1965) that thoughts should be described "without the use of personal pronouns." Compare this to Dewey's (1925) statement, "It is not exact nor relevant to say 'I experience' or 'I think.' 'It' experiences or is experienced, 'it' thinks or is thought, is a juster phrase" (p. 190). Both Wittgenstein and the American pragmatists sought to overcome the egocentric predicament by challenging the widely held view that thought is a private experience occurring in the head of an isolated individual.

There was also a close connection between Wittgenstein and Freud. Wittgenstein often described himself as a follower of Freud (McGuinness, 1982). His sister was psychoanalyzed by Freud, and she and Wittgenstein exchanged dream reports and interpreted each other's dreams. Wittgenstein was critical of much of Freud's work, but he saw a similarity between what Freud did in therapy and what he was attempting to do in philosophy. Wittgenstein's knowledge of Freud seems to have been limited to his early work and particularly his *Interpretation of Dreams* (1900). What attracted him to Freud was the notion that there were layers of meaning underlying the surface appearance of reality that could be developed through extended discussion. He regarded psychoanalysis as a myth rather than a science since it did not use experimental procedures but he believed that its insights provided a critical vision about the nature of meaning and reality.

Gier (1981) has suggested that Wittgenstein's later empahsis on the importance of context stems from Gestalt psychology. Wittgenstein was closely associated with the Austrian Gestalt psychologist Karl Bühler, who was the intellectual leader of the Austrian school reform of which Wittgenstein

was a part during the 1920s. Gier goes on to suggest that this similarity of backgrounds links Wittgenstein to Maurice Merleau-Ponty (who will be discussed in the next section). This would also tie Wittgenstein into the rather large body of social-psychological research derived either directly or indirectly from Gestalt theory.

Finally, there are some striking similarities between Wittgenstein and Vygotsky. Neither knew of the other's work, but their perspectives mesh in some interesting ways (Wertsch, 1979). Both seemed to have arrived at the concept of family resemblance at about the same time (Bloor, 1983). Both made a distinction between the meaning of a word taken in isolation and the sense of a word occurring in context. Both noted that while language is the vehicle of thought, it is relatively rare for thoughts to occur in full sentences. Luria's interest in Wittgenstein near the end of his life has already been noted. Bloor (1983) suggests that much can be gained by reading Wittgenstein along with Vygotsky because it shows how easily Wittgenstein's ideas can be translated into empirical research.[5]

In short, there are numerous overlapping and criss-crossing similarities between Wittgenstein and other traditions previously discussed. To our knowledge, no one has attempted to trace the similarities and differences in these perspectives, although there have obviously been some attempts to link Wittgenstein with one or more particular authors. Before we go on to discuss the implications of these common themes for the development of a postmodern social psychology, it may be useful to consider a fourth tradition—phenomenology—which places an equally strong emphasis on the social nature of thought and interaction.

### Phenomenology

Phenomenology is not a social theory but a technqiue for describing the contents of immediate experience in as much detail as possible. The Austrian-born philosopher and logician Edmund Husserl (1859–1938) developed phenomenology as a method for studying experience by "bracketing" one's preconceptions in order to describe the "essential" features. Phenomenology can be seen as a radical attempt to get "beneath" the most basic philosophical assumptions. It involves a suspension of the natural or everyday attitude and a return to the thing itself, as if it is being experienced for the first time. Husserl frequently described himself as a "perpetual beginner," and this tendency to start fresh is characteristic of all phenomenological descriptions. One of the central claims of phenomenology is that it is atheoretical, presuppositionless, and without bias, and that a phenomenological description, if properly carried out, is absolutely and unconditionally true, not just for a single individual but for everyone.

One of Husserl's key insights is that consciousness is always consciousness *of something.* The object of experience may be a material object, an image, or some specific emotional state, but there is always a referent. A simple example would be the experience of being afraid. Fear involves a feeling of danger but also the possiblity of escape. The danger is near but not yet at hand. There is a feeling of foreboding, helplessness, and uncertainty, as if our fate is no longer in our hands. These feelings are characteristic of all kinds of fears—from the fear of physical objects to stage fright to a dread that some shameful secret may be revealed—and they are characteristic of *all* people's sense of fear, now and until the end of time. We can envision an advanced people who no longer experience fear, but if they do, these features will be part of the experience.

The potential of phenomenology has long been recognized by those working in social psychology (e.g., Schutz, 1932/1967). Although there are many different attempts to apply phenomenology to social behavior, one of the more sophisticated was presented by the French philosopher and psychologist Maurice Merleau-Ponty (1908–1961). Merleau-Ponty attended the Ecole Normale Supériere, from which he graduated in 1930, and taught briefly at Beauvais and Chartres before returning to the Ecole Normale Supériere as a junior member of the faculty. He joined the army in 1939 and served as a lieutenant until the German occupation,

when he worked with the French Resistance and began writing his major work, *Phenomenology of Perception.* After the war, he took a position at the University of Lyon and became co-editor, along with Jean-Paul Sartre (1905–1980), of the periodical *Les Temps Modernes.* By 1950, his reputation was established, and he came to the Sorbonne as professor of psychology and pedagogy. In 1952, he was appointed to the chair at the Collège de France.

Merleau-Ponty and Sartre knew each other as students, members of the Resistance, and co-editors of the same journal, but the personal and philosophical differences between them were profound. Sartre began with conscious awareness and stressed a doctrine in which individuals were isolated and alone. Merleau-Ponty stressed the primacy of perception and saw consciousness as a second-order attempt to make sense of immediate reality. For him, the perceived world is the foundation for all rational thought. By starting with perception, Merleau-Ponty was able to show that consciousness must have *some* foothold in the world itself, and this provides the common ground for different people's experience. The world is "already there" before conscious reflection begins, and consciousness is simply a deliberate attempt to describe and understand what is being experienced at the prereflective level. Language is used to "bring the world into light," but it is never able to fully capture all that occurs. As Merleau-Ponty (1946/1961) points out,

> if I am able to talk about "dreams" and "reality," to bother my head about the distinction between the imaginary and real, and cast doubt upon the "real," it is because this distinction is already made by me before any analysis ... the problem then becomes one not of asking how critical thought can provide for itself secondary equivalents of this distinction, but of making explicit our primordial knowledge. (p. xvi)

This does not mean that conscious experience is always accurate. One can discover that what was once taken to be true love, for example, was actually an illusion because it focused on superficial qualities or was not sufficiently engaging. One can also discover that a genuine love occurred prior to our knowledge of it—not because it was buried in the unconscious but because it was available in the way a background is available when the figure is the center of attention. Our awareness draws not just from immediate reality but from memory as well, and it is possible to bring preconceptions and false beliefs into our perception of current events. Indeed, the whole purpose of phenomenology is to cut through the preconceptions so that the world of immediate experience can be described as fully as possible as if it were being experienced for the very first time.

Merleau-Ponty (1946/1961) points out that language itself is a product of culture, and it along with other cultural objects teaches us that we are not alone. Other people have come before, and we are the heirs of their legacy. Language is also the means by which we come to know one another and build up a shared world of common experience. Through speech we form and convey our thoughts to ourselves and to one another. The existential loneliness and isolation so characteristic of Sartre's philosophy play no role in the thinking of Merleau-Ponty, and indeed, this brooding isolation is itself a product of culture. For Merleau-Ponty, the world is a network of interpersonal relationships in which meaning emerges, perspectives blend, and perceptions confirm one another. Other people become objects only when we are strangers or when we take a deliberately detached point of view.

What is so remarkable about each of the four trends discussed in this section is the amount of convergence among thinkers who worked in relative isolation with little or no knowledge of each other's work. Each focuses on language as the basis of our knowledge about the world. Language, however, does not represent a picture of an objective reality. It is embedded within a process of social exchange that creates various interpretations of the world. These interpretations reflect and influence social practices. Thus, thought and action have ethical, moral, and political implications.

The convergence among these thinkers is based partly on the fact that they were often inspired by the same thinkers. The three most important are Hegel, Marx, and Freud. Dewey and Mead drew directly from Hegel, whereas Vygotsky, Luria, and Merleau-Ponty are linked to Hegel through Marx. Hegel and Marx provide the basis for the belief that personality is a product of social conditions. Freud was a source of inspiration for Vygotsky, Luria, and Merleau-Ponty. The only exception appears to be Wittgenstein, who seems to have had only a passing knowledge of Marx and Freud and painstakingly worked out his own ideas, largely in response to his own earlier philosophy. Each of these seminal thinkers was focusing on similar problems and provides a piece of a truly comprehensive social epistemology, which helped form the basis for a postmodern social psychology.

## TOWARD A POSTMODERN SOCIAL PSYCHOLOGY

Thomas Kuhn's (1962, 1970) conception of science as a human enterprise in which social networks of scientists influence the nature of inquiry in specific disciplines has served as a rallying point for challenging the modernist view of science as objective and defined by a distinct scientific method. In fact, Kuhn's social perspective on science has been criticized for its overly narrow focus on the institutional makeup of science and its neglect of the effects of broader social forces on the nature of scientific inquiry. At the core of Kuhn's analysis is the notion of a *paradigm,* which Kuhn has defined in a variety of different ways. In his revised book, Kuhn (1970) conceives of a paradigm as a *disciplinary matrix*—that is, a set of basic assumptions (typically unstated and untested) that defines a discipline's subject matter, influences the kind of problems to be investigated, guides how theories are constructed, and determines which research methods are to be used. Even closely related disciplines, such as biology and psychology, may have quite different assumptions and stress different empirical procedrues. Once research methods are agreed on, they become examples of how subsequent research is to be conducted. Drawing from the social epistemology described previously, advocates for an alternative social psychology have developed a new paradigm that challenges the traditional assumptions of modernist social psychology (Gergen, 1982, 1989a; Parker, 1989b; Rosnow & Georgoudi, 1986). This alternative postmodern paradigm is based on three major assumptions: (1) reality is dynamic; (2) knowledge is socially constructed; and (3) knowledge has social consequences.

In contrast to the modernist conception of a static and fixed world with timeless and universal principles to be discovered, postmodern thinkers assume that reality consists of an ongoing process of change. There is a dialectical relationship between the social context and human behavior. Social reality is both a determinant and a product of human activity. In place of the modernist view that cumulative scientific knowledge will lead to greater prediction and control because we discover more and more about the nature of reality, postmodernists assume that scientific knowledge allows us to evaluate and understand the dynamic quality of our immediate experience. The focus of inquiry is change and development rather than timeless universal principles.

In an ever-changing world, there are few universal transhistorical facts or principles to be discovered. Human understanding is relative and shaped, at least in part, by the social context in which it occurs. The variability of knowledge, however, does not imply absolute skepticism. Knowledge is constructed within a sociocultural framework and is shaped by language and characteristics of the larger social system.

The social origins of knowledge have social consequences. Knowledge and action are intricately connected. People come to understand their world during the course of concrete activity and social interaction (Rosnow & Georgoudi, 1986). People are not passive recipients or spectators of ongoing events, but active participants who develop an understanding in an attempt to cope with real-life problems which, ultimately, changes reality itself.

The link between knowledge and action affects the way scientific knowledge is generated and used. Scientists are not disinterested observers merely reporting facts. They too are situated within a social context that influences the nature of their inquiry and how their findings will be applied. Scientific theories have political consequences. From the modernist perspective, theories serve as a source for making predictions about the world as given. Postmodernists, on the other hand, point out that there are negative consequences associated with an uncritical acceptance of existing social conditions, which may help perpetuate oppressive social conditions and maintain the status quo.

Postmodernists argue that the major function of a theory is to generate or provoke debate about social reality (Gergen, 1982). The first step in this process is to adopt a critical attitude in which cultural assumptions are evaluated against moral standards, such as human emancipation and communal welfare. Critical theories can play a transformative role and help generate fresh alternatives for constructive social change. These innovative directives for reconstructing social psychology are based on the assumption that scientific knowledge is value-laden rather than value-free and thus has inherent practical implications. Knowledge can be potentially oppressive or liberating.

Cultural criticism is the facet of postmodernism that most clearly distinguishes it from its various precursors. Among those considered previously, Dewey and Mead were the most explicit about the practical consequences of theory. They envisioned an ideal society in which constructive social change was guided by scientific knowledge. Their view, however, was shaped by the Progressive Era's optimistic faith that American society could evolve into a participatory democracy. Because of the conservative backlash of the 1920s and the social and economic disruptions of the 1930s, some social scientists (including Dewey) began to adopt a more critical attitude (see Chapter 8). The protests of the 1960s inspired a new generation of social scientists committed to critically examining existing social conditions and helped create a scientific approach based on radical rather than liberal reforms.

## POSTMODERN APPROACHES TO SOCIAL PSYCHOLOGY

The postmodern paradigm has inspired a number of different approaches to social psychology. Some of these focus more narrowly on language, whereas others are more oriented to social criticism. Most of these were developed by European social psychologists and reflect the movement that began in the early 1970s to disassociate European social psychology from its more individualistically oriented American counterpart. European advocates of an alternative social psychology were also responding to the wave of worker and student protests occurring in their countries in the late 1960s. There has been a considerable degree of cross-fertilization between North American and European social psychologists since that period, which has challenged the long-standing predominance of American social psychologists throughout most of the discipline's history. In this section, five distinct approaches to social psychology—ethogenics, social constructionism, social representations, discourse analysis, and critical social psychology—will be considered.

### Ethogenics

The first postmodern approach to social psychology was developed by the British social philosopher Rom Harré and his colleagues (Harré, 1979; Harré & Secord, 1972; Harré, Clark, & De Carlo, 1985). Harré is critical of the precepts that have shaped traditional social psychology, such as its reliance on procedures derived from the natural sciences, its emphasis on individual psychological processes, and its tendency to treat all psychological phenomena in terms of cause and effect. He advocates a shift from intrapsychic explanations of social behavior to analyses of social interac-

tion. For Harré, "thought is first of all a social and collective activity, created in conversation. Individual minds come into existence by 'fencing off' part of the public conversation as a private and individual domain" (Harré, Clark, & De Carlo, 1985, p. 21).

The term "ethogenics" is derived from ethology, which is the study of animal behavior through observation in natural settings (see Chapter 12). Ethological procedures are also used to study humans, who can describe what they do and experience in their everyday lives. These spoken and written accounts do not merely describe what people are doing. They often change the way people relate to one another and their construction of the social world. Harré draws his ideas from philosophers of language, such as Wittgenstein, who stress the importance of explaining human behavior from the point of view of the actors themselves. The ethogenic approach thus attempts to analyze these accounts in terms of the meaning that actors give to their own behavior and the conventions and rules that they follow.

According to Harré, all social interaction involves two levels of functioning—the practical and the expressive. The practical level occurs in both humans and animals and includes activities necessary for biological survival. Among humans, however, the expressive mode becomes more important. The expressive level is concerned with maintaining honor and status. Humans typically behave at both levels at the same time. Sharing food at the dinner table, for example, is both practical and expressive.

In order to capture the expressive aspect of human interaction, Harré and his associates use the dramatological model developed by Erving Goffman, which treats face-to-face interactions as a kind of theatrical performance (see Chapter 11). Social life is viewed as a drama in which actors express themselves through strategies of impression management. The ethogenic approach also focuses on people's spoken and written accounts of their own behavior, in which they interpret or give meaning to their own actions and the actions of other people participating at the same time.

The analysis of these accounts attempts to identify the rules and conventions actors use in their social interactions. It is assumed that the participants in various social settings have internalized a set of rules that enables them to perform their roles successfully and coordinate joint activities. People possess a body a knowledge that makes them socially competent and allows them to explain and justify their behavior (Potter & Wetherell, 1987).

Marsh, Rosser and Harré's (1978) study of British soccer fans illustrates the goals and methods of ethogenic research. During the 1970s, there was considerable media coverage of violence among soccer fans (a problem that continues today). Marsh and his colleagues attempted to demonstrate that the apparent unrestrained aggression was an expression of an explicit system of rules. What seemed like chaos and disorder to outside observers was really a reflection of a social competence shared by soccer fans. The data used in this study were based on accounts provided by fans about the events that occurred at soccer matches and videos of actual behavior. The investigators constructed a picture of a typical game and the confrontations between fans supporting different teams. Two contradictory accounts emerged from the analyses. In one version, the fans reported that little violence occurred and that the confrontations were designed primarily to force the opposition to retreat when threatened. The other version depicted the confrontations as much more violent. Often the two sets of accounts were closely linked. When two fans, for example, were interviewed at the same time, each gave a different version of the same event. The researchers argued that the nonviolent versions described what actually happened, while the violent accounts served a rhetorical function that allowed fans to maintain their honor and status by demonstrating the excitement and risks in their lives. The researchers, however, failed to provide the criteria by which they judged the nonviolent accounts more accurate (Potter & Wetherell, 1987).

Ethogenics has been criticized for its emphasis on pre-established social conventions (Parker, 1989b; Potter & Wetherell, 1978; Shotter, 1984). While ethogenicists do not assume that rules are universal, they tend to treat them as relatively fixed and static. Rules take on a quality of being real rather than evolving and changing through social negotiation. The notion that actors develop social competence by assimilating a system of rules further reinforces the fixed quality of social reality. Parker (1989b) argues that the stress on stable rules neglects the role of conflict and resistance and therefore undermines cultural criticism and the potential for social change.

## Social Constructionism

In an influential article in the *American Psychologist,* Kenneth J. Gergen (1985) described his alternative to traditional social psychology. His description incorporated earlier versions (Gergen, 1973, 1982), and he and his colleagues have elucidated their ideas in several other sources (Gergen, 1989a, 1989b; Gergen & Davis, 1985). According to Gergen (1985), "Social constructionism views discourse about the world not as a reflection or map of the world but as an artifact of communal interchange" (p. 266). He borrows the term "social constructionism" from Berger and Luckmann's (1966) description of the dialectical interplay between self and society. Berger and Luckmann were themselves influenced by Mead and symbolic interaction. Gergen also draws from linguistic philosophers, especially Wittgenstein, to defend the position that thought and communication are part of a social process.

Gergen (1985) points out that our knowledge of social processes is based on historically embedded interchanges. Inquiry into these processes should therefore focus on the historical and cultural foundations of various forms of world construction. The extent to which different forms of understanding prevail across time reflects the workings of social processes such as communication, conflict, and negotiation. Gergen also stresses that forms of understanding are intricately connected with practical activity. How people interpret or describe the world depends on what they are doing at the time.

John Shotter (1984), a British social psychologist, has developed a similar position. Drawing from Wittgenstein, Vygotsky, and Merleau-Ponty, Shotter focuses on the social construction of self-awareness beginning in early childhood. People's sense of being autonomous agents emerges from "the ability to act in such a way that one knows how oneself is 'placed' or 'situated' in relation to others" (Stotter, 1984, p. xi). People's understanding of their world is based on mutual interdependence, which leads them to acquire a common framework to account for their actions. Unlike the ethogenic approach, Gergen and Shotter view rules as fluid and dependent on social negotiation.

Constructionists believe that virtually any methodology can be used as long as it does not "reify" reality by describing it in terms of universal principles. The goal is to illustrate or develop a compelling case for the socially pragmatic consequences of one's work. Theory and research should be used to critically examine existing social constructions and practices and should take into account a wide range of political, moral, aesthetic, and practical considerations. Gergen used the theory and research on feminist issues as a good example (Bleier, 1984; Unger, 1983, 1989b). From the feminist perspective, empirical science has been called to task for its sexist bias, in which women are described in ways that contribute to their lower status. The empiricist position tends to take existing gender relations for granted, thus perpetuating a male view of social reality.

In his analysis of the self, Gergen (1989b) points out that people want to have their own interpretations of events prevail against competing versions. They therefore attempt to justify or "warrant" their version and insure that their voice is heard. Because of differences in money, status, and expertise, some people have more opportunities to express their views. Gergen also notes that, like individuals, psychology as a discipline is committed to justifying its own

view of the world. The problem is that psychology in its efforts to justify its privileged position tends to cling to traditional empirical assumptions. Descriptions of social behavior in terms of objective and universal principles undermines the possibility of considering alternative interpretations not based on current conventions. Psychology thus ends up reifying psychological processes and supporting the status quo rather than fulfilling its avowed role of benefiting people.

Social constructionism has been criticized for being relativistic (Stam, 1990; Unger, 1989a). If each person or group is understood only in terms of its own particular social and historical context, how do we deal with the unlimited and competing world views? Gergen (1985) acknowledges the problem of relativism and the danger that it may result in a state of anarchy in which "anything goes." He argues that because knowledge is based on communities of similar thinkers, science will be governed in large measure by normative rules. Since constructionists see these rules as historically and culturally embedded, they are subject to critique and transformation. The implication is that science must be guided by humanistic concerns such as emancipation and communal welfare. As Gergen (1985) declares,

> Constructionism [asserts] ... the relevance of moral criteria for scientific practice. To the extent that psychological theory (and related practices) enter into the life of the culture, sustaining certain patterns of conduct and destroying others, such work must be evaluated in terms of good and ill. (p. 273)

## Social Representations

During the 1960s, the French social psychologist Serge Moscovici (1961) began to develop a theory of "social representations." It has only been in the last decade, however, that Moscovici's work has been made available in English, and it has attracted a considerable following among British social psychologists (Farr & Moscovici, 1984). Moscovici (1981) defines social representations as:

> A set of concepts, statements and explanations originating in daily life in the course of inter-individual communications. They are the equivalent, in our society, of the myths and belief systems in traditional societies; they might even be said to be the contemporary version of common sense. (p. 181)

Moscovici's notion of social representations is derived from Durkheim's collectivist approach to social behavior (see Chapters 3 and 7). Durkheim (1974) conceived of "collective representations" as any idea, emotion, or belief, such as science, myth, or religion, that occurs within a community and is widely shared. For Durkheim, collective representations were relatively fixed social structures that existed apart from individuals and acted as constraints on behavior. Moscovici revised Durkheim's concept and uses the term "social representations" to reflect a more dynamic view of collective thought and behavior. It has been pointed out that Weber's treatment is more similar to Moscovici's than Durkheim's because of its emphasis on the individual as a source of innovation and social change (Farr, 1987a; Parker, 1987).

According to Moscovici, social representations are made up of images and concepts. Images reflect the concrete objects in the external world, while concepts are based on abstract thought and reasoning. The notion of "neurotic," for example, is a social representation that includes images of people with pathological personalities and behavioral symptoms as well as related concepts such as psychoanalysis and the Oedipus complex. Social representations serve two primary functions—they provide people with a means of making sense of their world through the acquisition of common knowledge, and they facilitate the sharing of ideas. The study of social representations thus "explains how the strange and the unfamiliar become in time the familiar" (Farr & Moscovici, 1984, pp. ix–x).

The process by which people acquire social representations occurs in two ways—anchoring and objectification. New ideas

are anchored by incorporating them into familiar images or pre-existing concepts. If someone discovers that a mental patient, for example, is moving into his or her community and the notion of mental patient is unfamiliar, the novel idea can be made more meaningful by associating it with categories that are already familiar, such as "social misfit," which may include idiots or tramps. During the process of objectification, the novel idea that has previously been anchored is converted into a concrete visual object and transformed into something tangible. Through the course of social interaction, the objectified idea becomes familiar and the previous social representation is changed.

Moscovici and his associates have conducted field studies of people's representations of health and illness, the body, the urban environment, and psychoanalysis. In his study of psychoanalysis, Moscovici (1961) demonstrates how ideas that were once startling and unfamiliar now thoroughly pervade every aspect of French society. More recently, Moscovici (1981/1985) has investigated the historical influence of Le Bon's mass psychology and its impact on Hitler, Mussolini, and Stalin. Much of Moscovici's work focuses on the sociology of knowledge—that is, the social roots of everyday experience (see Chapter 8)—but he has also conducted experimental studies of social representations under laboratory conditions.

The theory of social representations has been criticized on several grounds. One problem is that Moscovici's writings are rather fragmented and sometimes seem contradictory (McKinlay & Potter, 1987). There is also a methodological problem in operationalizing social representations as community-based knowledge (Potter & Wetherell, 1987). Social representations are assumed to be shared by members of particular groups, but in many studies, the criterion for consensus is not defined. Perhaps the most central issue is whether or not the theory of social representations serves as an alternative to individualistic cognitive social psychology. Several critics have pointed out that Moscovici locates social representations within the heads of individuals rather than in active exchanges among people (McKinlay & Potter, 1987; Parker, 1989b; Potter & Wetherell, 1987). The processes of anchoring and objectification, for example, appear to be cognitive processes similar to those occurring during social cognition. Some of these difficulties can be overcome if one views social representations as the *end product* of a process of socialization and adaptation to the social environment. Concepts and images that were once external and widely shared within the community are internalized and now appear thoroughly familiar.

## Discourse Analysis

The postmodern focus on language and social interaction has inspired an increasing interest in analyzing spoken and written accounts of social life, in the form of conversations, public speeches, newspaper stories, novels, and soap operas (Billig, 1987; Henriques, Hollway, Urwin, Venn, & Walderdine, 1984; Potter & Wetherell, 1987; Shotter & Gergen 1989). The term "discourse" is generally used to refer to all forms of spoken and written texts and "discourse analysis" represents the investigation of these materials. Potter and Wetherell's book, *Discourse and Social Psychology*, is particularly significant because it attempts to present an alternative approach to social psychology based on the theory and application of discourse analysis. These British social psychologists draw from the linguistic philosophy of John Austin, who like Wittgenstein views language as a social process but focuses on the relationship between speech and action. Other influences include ethnomethodology, with its concern about how ordinary people use language in everyday situations (see Chapter 12) and semiology, which examines the relationship between objects and signs.

According to Potter and Wetherell (1987), there are three major aspects of discourse analysis—function, variation, and construction. Function refers to how people use language to do things, such as make requests, give orders, persuade, and accuse. The function of an expression, however, is often not explicitly stated. Rather than make a direct request, such as "May I borrow your calculator," a person may indirectly ask, "Would you mind if I borrowed your calculator." It may be to the speaker's advantage to buffer the negative consequences of rejection by making an indirect request. In which case, the context of a statement must be considered in determining its function. Since speech may serve many different functions, a fundamental aspect of language is variation. People's accounts depend on the purpose of the conversation. The way people describe each other, for example, varies with their motives and moods. One person may give a glowing account of a particular person, while another paints a very negative picture. In these cases, people use language to construct versions of social reality. Potter and Wetherell (1987) point out that "the principal tenet of discourse analysis is that function involves construction of versions, and is demonstrated by language variation" (p. 33).

The variability of people's accounts is typically suppressed in traditional approaches to social psychology. The use of standard questions and questionnaires that can be easily quantified limits what people can and cannot say. Experimental procedures are designed to maximize control and often give the illusion of similarity even when there are large individual differences. Other techniques, such as surveys and opinion polls, also limit what can and cannot be said. Even in more qualitative approaches, such as content analysis, researchers often choose their categories in advance so that much of the original text is ignored. Discourse analysis, on the other hand, attempts to describe the variability in the way people speak and interpret the social world. The actual procedures are very labor-intensive. They involve the selection and collection of the texts to be analyzed, transcription of spoken material, coding, interpretation, validation using criteria such as coherence and the generation of novel explanations, and finally application of the findings.

Discourse analysis, with its focus on language variability and social exchange, has implications for the way traditional social-psychological concepts are conceived and operationalized. The concept of attitude, for example, has generally been defined as a relatively stable evaluative response to a specific object or idea. According to discourse analysis, an attitude is a variable linguistic expression subject to the vicissitudes of human intention and the social context. An attitude expressed on one occasion may not be expressed in the same way in other circumstances. There may be systematic variations in the way attitudes are expressed, which suggests that their expression depends more on the social context than on a relatively stable state of mind. Billig (1987, 1988) advocates a rhetorical approach, which stresses that attitudes are positions that are taken in public controversies and must be understood in their wider historical and argumentative contexts. Changes in such contexts can lead to systematic changes in the way attitudes are expressed.

Discourse analysis provides a specific method for investigating the actual flow of interaction between speaking subjects or between writers and readers. It thus gives priority to social interaction as the basic unit of social psychology, which is a goal that postmodern thinkers generally endorse. It is, however, a time-consuming procedure requiring a great deal of expertise and thus is unlikely to be widely adopted. It has been criticized on conceptual grounds for neglecting the wider social context that helps shape interpersonal communication. Those in power, for example, have both the means and status to express their ideas, whereas those with less status may not. In other words, the dominant ideology, if taken for granted, is perpetuated and reinforced through discourse.

## Critical Social Psychology

The focus on language and open-ended communication at the expense of the broader social context has been a criticism directed not only at discourse analysis but also at ethogenics, social representations, and to a lesser extent, social constructionism (Parker, 1989b). What tends to be neglected in these approaches is a critical per-

spective that takes the interface between communication and the social context into account and recognizes ethical and political issues. Critical social psychology refers to various attempts to incorporate a critical perspective explicitly within social psychology through the analysis of ideology and power.

Ideology is a central concept in Karl Mannheim's (1929/1936) sociology of knowledge (see Chapter 8). In Marxist thinking, ideology refers to beliefs of the dominant class that are used to rationalize their vested social interest and maintain the status quo. Every ruling class develops ways to perpetuate its dominant position. Thus, ideology reflects power relations, which create tensions and potential conflict between those who rule and those who are subjected to domination. Traditional social-psychological theories (and psychological theories in general) have been described as a cultural mechanism that perpetuates ideology and helps maintain the status quo (Larsen, 1986; Parker, 1989b; Prilleltensky, 1989; Sarason, 1981; Wexler, 1983).

*Critical theory* is one of the theoretical perspectives that has guided the study of ideological biases in social psychology. This position was first developed at the Frankfurt Institute for Social Research in Germany during the 1930s (see Jay, 1973). The theorists of the so-called Frankfurt School, such as Max Horkheimer, T. W. Adorno, and Herbert Marcuse, sought to integrate Marxism and psychoanalysis in order to reach a more comprehensive understanding of the interplay· between psychology and social conditions. The method used was the critique of knowledge, which attempts to identify how theory is influenced by ideology and thus serves the interests of the ruling class.

Critical theory has been applied to various aspects of social psychology (e.g., Buss, 1979; Sampson, 1981, 1983, 1989; Sullivan, 1984; Wexler, 1983). Sampson's (1983, 1989) examination of the individual as the traditional focus of social psychology serves as an illustration. Both general psychology and social psychology adopt the individual as the primary reality from which social interaction and society are derived.

For critical theorists, on the other hand, the concept of a self-contained individual is more fiction than real. Individualism cannot be disengaged from its social and historical context. The separation of indivdiual from society nurtures a belief in unlimited personal control and discourages collective action that may bring about constructive social change. As Sampson (1983) states:

> The ideology of the bourgeois individual fosters a belief in rational control and autonomy even as that control wanes and the key shaping forces operate behind the backs of those who should know but do not. (p. 142)

Sampson traces how the concept of individualism has been historically shaped to serve the interests of the ruling class within capitalist societies. He concludes that psychology's adoption of the self-contained individual as the primary object of investigation contributes to the illusion of personal control and buttresses the existing social order.

The study of ideology and power in social psychology has also been the focus of the French philosophical movement known as *poststructuralism* and its two leading figures, Jacques Derrida (1976) and Michel Foucault (1977, 1981). This movement, spurred by the French student protests of 1968, emerged from structuralism. Structuralism is an approach that conceives of the individual as the product of social structures, such as cultural symbols, family patterns, and economic modes of production (see Kurzweil, 1980; Parker, 1989b). Poststructuralists, on the other hand, see reality not on the basis of fixed and stable institutions but as always changing because there are many different ways to interpret the social world. Poststructuralists use written texts or discourse as the soruce of analysis, and their primary goal, like that of critical theory, is to uncover or demystify the assumptions that are taken for granted by the current ideology.

According to Derrida, written texts can take on a new meaning each time they are read or reread (Culler, 1982; Hare-Mustin & Marecek, 1988; Parker, 1989b). There is no "true" or inherent meaning in a text, be-

cause language does not reflect a perfect correspondence between words and objects. Derrida's notion of deconstruction emerges from his position that Western thought is based on a series of metaphysical opposites, such as reason—emotion, fact—value, good—evil, male—female, and so on. In each of these pairs, the meaning of a word is based on its opposition to another word. Moreover, the first member of each pair is usually considered more valuable. This value hierarchy is based on cultural norms and conventions. Deconstructionists seek to question or undermine the cultural priorities given to different words, and more generally, the conventional interpretation of texts. The goal is to uncover hidden alternative meanings, and this is done by analyzing the gaps, inconsistencies, and contradictions.

Hare-Mustin and Marecek (1988) have used the process of deconstruction to identify the conventional masculine interpretation of psychotherapeutic cases and redescribe them in terms of a previously hidden feminine perspective. Sampson (1983, 1989) has used a similar procedure to depict the dominant view of the self-contained individual in Western thought and has developed an alternative view of people embedded within a social context.

Foucault moves beyond Derrida's text analysis to a more explicit consideration of the links between culture and discourse (the term he prefers to texts). Through a series of historical studies, Foucault shows how systems of discourse have affected Western culture (Parker, 1989a, 1989b). He points out that by the end of the eighteenth century, as a result of the increasing complexity of society, discourse took on greater significance. Power that was traditionally based on direct control of one person by another became linked to various systems of discourse that regulated people's lives. Sexual practices, for example, were regulated by discourses that narrowly defined what was acceptable and unacceptable. The aim was to restrict sexuality in such a way that it would serve the interest of the state. It is beyond our scope to do justice to the rich complexity of Foucault's work, which points to the hidden, even insidious, mechanisms of power operating through spoken and written language.

Postmodern social psychologists have been attracted to Foucault because he provides a framework for exposing ideological bias and power relationships through social-psychological discourse.[6] Parker (1989a) draws on Foucault to challenge traditional social psychology's assumption of the self as the agent of personal control (see also Henriques, Hollway, Urwin, Venn, & Walderdine, 1984). Rather than a unitary self, there are many different selves, each situated within "a variety of power-infused discourses. We do not rationally 'choose' to display our-selves as willing participants, for example, in the rituals of close personal relationships" (Parker, 1989a, pp. 67–68). In place of unlimited power, Foucault alerts us to the importance of discourse.

The presence of ideological biases in social psychology has also been shown through historical analyses and minority perspectives. Morawski (1984, 1986a) has used historical analysis to show how dominant cultural beliefs and values influence theory and research in social psychology. Throughout this book we have shown how social-psychological research and theories are influenced by social and historical conditions and how they often undergo rather sweeping transformations when they are exported from one country to another.

Minority perspectives have also exposed the ideology in social-psychological accounts of people who are not members of the privileged strata of American society. Feminist critics and sympathetic supporters have shown the masculine bias that pervades most social-psychological research (e.g., Hare-Mustin & Marecek, 1988; Sherif, 1979; Unger, 1989b). Other examples include racist bias in the study of blacks (Jenkins, 1982; Minton, 1986), heterosexual bias in the study of lesbians and gay males (Kitzinger, 1987; Morin, 1977; Weeks, 1985), and American cultural bias in the study and application of psychology to third-world cultures (Moghaddan, 1987).

Incorporating a critical perspective within social psychology is not limited to identifying ways in which ideology buttresses the status quo and entrenches power

relations based on dominance and status. Challenging conventional assumptions is a necessary prerequisite for developing alternative forms of thought and action. Social psychology can also help transform current conditions and bring about a "good society" (Gergen, 1988; Parker, 1989b; Prilleltensky, 1989; Sullivan, 1984; Wexler, 1983). As Dewey (1900) proclaimed, psychology must help contribute to the attainment of what is ethically just. Concerns about human emancipation, power, and communal well-being are an integral part of all human sciences. As Morawski (1986a) points out, social psychology in its transformative goals becomes co-extensive with moral science. By challenging conventional views of reality, it becomes political. What postmodernists seek to attain is a social psychology that is intrinsically moral and political, especially in its critical form, and is thus genuinely social.

## TOWARD UNIFICATION IN SOCIAL PSYCHOLOGY?

As we move into the 1990s, American social psychology seems to be developing in two rather different ways. On the one hand, there is the traditional experimental study of cognitive processes shaped by the modernist world view. In response to the crisis of confidence in the late 1960s, this approach has undergone a number of revisions that have broadened its scope. There has been more interest in ethical issues, interdisciplinary integration, and applied research, and a general feeling that social psychology can be made more relevant without sacrificing its scientific integrity.

But there has also been mounting criticism by people who seek to radically transform social psychology and create a new paradigm. This postmodern alternative to traditional social psychology reflects a more profound doubt about the usefulness of the traditional approaches and draws from European as well as American sources. In many ways, we have come full circle. A century or so after American social psychologists pieced together a new discipline by drawing from European sources, many Americans are now again turning to Europe for guidance and instruction.

At this point, several questions come to mind. In general, what will the future bring? Are we witnessing the start of a scientific revolution, or is postmodernism simply a passing fad? Or to take a middle position, is there ground for a detente between modernist and postmodernist approaches to social psychology? Another possibility is that two distinct social psychologies will coexist, no longer split along disciplinary lines (psychology versus sociology) but separated on epistemological grounds and perhaps by geography (North America versus Europe).

We believe that the debate generated by this paradigm clash is a healthy sign. Previously unquestioned assumptions about the nature of science, the goals of theory and research, and the relative importance of basic and applied research have been raised and discussed. Choices are available that were not previously present. There are still deep divisions, however. While traditional social psychologists study cognitive processes within individuals, postmodern social psychologists stress the importance of social intereaction and the social context. While traditional social psychologists use empirical procedures that are assumed to be value-free and neutral, postmodern social psychologists feel that all social psychlogy is value-laden and the failure to recognize the implications of one's theories perpetuates existing forms of social control. While traditional social psychology seeks to uncover principles that are timeless and universal, postmodern social psychologists argue that most aspects of social behavior are dynamic and shaped by social and historical circumstances.

Some proponents of postmodernism have argued that it may be possible to incorporate traditional empirical procedures within a postmodern perspective (Gergen, 1988; Harré, Clarke, & De Carlo, 1985; Porter & Wetherell, 1987; Sullivan, 1984). Empirical researchers would have to revise their goals, however. Rather than seeking universal laws that explain all aspects of behavior, experiments and surveys could be used to make short-term predictions or assess the effectiveness of various intervention programs. Such technical interests should themselves be guided by higher ethical goals and evaluated in terms of these.

Others already see a complementary relationship between traditional approaches and certain aspects of postmodernism. Stroebe and Kruglanski (1989), for example, suggest that social cognition and social constructionism complement each other. Social cognition is concerned with the processes whereby people perceive and make sense of their social world, whereas social constructionism focuses on the ever-changing consequecnes of those cognitions. One must be cautious when mixing process and content, however, since processes themselves are often shaped by social interaction and the broader social context.

We believe that a postmodern social psychology holds promise for the future. It can incorporate aspects of traditional social psychology and still offer new forms of theories and research as well as new goals of aiding and abetting social change. It is these alternatives that promise a more socially responsive and enriched social psychology. Postmodern criticisms of a supposedly neutral social psychology that ignores human values and the social context cannot be dismissed. For social psychology to be social, it must be concerned with ethical and political issues that affect the lives of people on a day-to-day basis. Social perception, cognition, and interaction cannot be isolated from the forces that operate within the larger social context. The individual cannot be understood apart from society. This focus on interaction has been developed by some of the thinkers we have considered, but their perspective until recently has not received a great deal of attention in the United States. The heroes in this book include Durkheim, Dewey, Mead, Wittgenstein, Vygotsky, and Merleau-Ponty, and there is much to be learned from their insights and comprehensive perspectives.

Whether or not social psychology embraces the goals and perspective of postmodernism remains to be seen. There are many problems and issues that need to be addressed. We have only dealt with the complexities and varieties of postmodernism in a cursory fashion. As we sample this approach, it is clear that postmodernism is still in its infancy. It has been more successful as a critique of conventional social psychology than as a set of coherent and fully developed theoretical alternatives. There are also considerable differences of opinion among those who are grouped under the postmodern banner (and even among the authors of this book). It may be that none of the contemporary postmodern approaches to social psychology adequately captures all of the goals and aspirations of postmodernism—in which case, the debate may be postponed until more attractive alternatives are available. It may be difficult to attract converts to an approach that is inherently pluralistic and conceptually oriented toward exposing contradictions and paradoxes rather than eternal verities. Many social psychologists also feel uneasy about incorporating moral and political values into scientific research. Yet as postmodernists have argued, by uncritically accepting current perspectives, social psychology has become (intentionally or unintentionally) a mechanism for perpetuating and reinforcing the status quo.

The future viability of postmodernism also depends on a number of external factors. Its survival as an alternative to traditional social psychology depends on its reception within the institutional setting. It is very difficult to dislodge established theory and practice, as studies of "power groups" within social psychology demonstrate (Lubek, 1974; Morawski, 1979). Lubek and Apfelbaum (1979), for example, have shown how journal editors play a "gatekeeping" role in blocking anomalous findings from being published. Other institutional factors, such as graduate training, textbooks, and research agencies tend to reinforce established theory and practice. Disloding or replacing traditional psychology may just be too hard.

Within the broader social context, political, economic, and ideological factors will play a significant role. As we have seen, American social psychology has undergone a number of pendulum swings—becoming more group-oriented and applied during periods of social reform and more internal and individualistic during conservative periods. The conflict between traditional and radical versions of social psychology during the past two decades reflects the ambiguities and uncertainty of the times. American society, much more than those of Europe, is still uncertain of its priorities or the direction it should take in the future. At the beginning of the nineties, revolutionary change appears to be centered in Europe. The collapse of Stalinism in Eastern Europe and the inevitable formation of a united European economic community may lead to a new spirit of democratic and economic reform. The new influence of European thought that began in the seventies may become even more pronounced in the nineties. If this reformist climate takes hold, we may well see a new period of postmodern social psychology in the United States, which incorporates the best of the traditions and theories discussed in this book.

## NOTES

1. The economic recession and political backlash of the early 1970s also produced a neoconservative form of postmodernism that blamed modernity for the ills of society and promoted a reactionary return to the premodern period. The more radical form of postmodernism, however, has had the greatest impact on psychology, art, and the social sciences.

2. Because of his imminent death, Vygotsky felt the need to write quickly and was quite sloppy in referencing the sources of his ideas. As a result, Vygotsky seldom cites *anyone,* including those who obviously had a strong impact on his thinking.

3. The biographical material on Wittgenstein is drawn from a variety of sources, including Kenny (1973) and von Wright (1955/1967). Critical comments by authors will be cited in the text.

4. Pitcher (1967) has drawn some parallels between the works of Wittgenstein and Lewis Carroll and has shown how the linguistic confusions that preoccupied Wittgenstein were deliberately employed by Carroll for comic effect.

5. Although Wittgenstein is a rich source of insight for contemporary social psychologists, he

was highly critical of psychology's commitment to experimental procedures. The last lines of his *Philosophical Investigations* state:

> The confusion and barrenness of psychology is not to be explained by calling it a "young science"; its state is not comparable with that of physics, for instance, in its beginnings. . . . For in psychology there are experimental methods and *conceptual confusion.* . . . The existence of the experimental method makes us think we have the means of solving the problems which trouble us; though problem and method pass one another by. (p. 232)

6. Foucault does not use the term "ideology" because it implies that there is an alternative truth to the misconceptions contained in the dominant ideology. As Parker (1989b) points out, however, identifying ideology or dominant modes of thought through the deconstruction of texts supports resistance and thus helps promote social change.

# Appendix

List of social psychology textbooks used in the textbook analysis, ordered by date of publication.

McDougall, W. (1908). *Introduction to social psychology.* London: Methuen.

Ross, E. A. (1908). *Social psychology: An outline and source book.* New York: Macmillan.

Ellwood, C. A. (1917). *An introduction to social psychology.* New York: Appleton.

Bogardus, E. S. (1818). *Essentials of social psychology.* Los Angeles: University of Southern California Press.

Williams, J. M. (1922). *Principles of social psychology.* New York: Knopf.

Gault, R. H. (1923). *Social psychology: The basis of behavior called social.* New York: Holt.

Allport, F. H. (1924). *Social psychology.* Boston: Houghton Mifflin.

Bogardus, E. S. (1924). *Fundamentals of social psychology.* New York: Century.

Dunlap, K. (1925). *Social psychology.* Baltimore: Williams & Wilkins.

Ellwood, C. A. (1925). *The psychology of human society.* New York: Appleton.

Bernard, L. L. (1926). *An introduction to social psychology.* New York: Holt.

Mukerjee, R., & Sen-Gupta, N. N. (1928). *Introduction to social psychology: Mind in society.* Boston: Heath.

Ewer, B. C. (1929). *Social psychology.* New York: Macmillan.

Kantor J. R. (1929). *An outline of social psychology.* Chicago: Follett.

Murchison, C. (1929). *Social psychology: The psychology of political domination.* Worcester, MA: Clark University Press.

Krueger, E. T., & Reckless, W. C. (1930). *Social psychology.* New York: Longman.

Young, K. (1930). *Social psychology.* New York: Crofts.

Folsom, J. K. (1931). *Social psychology.* New York: Harper

Murphy, G., & Murphy, L. B. (1931). *Experimental social psychology.* New York: Harper.

Brown, L. G. (1934). *Social psychology: The natural history of human nature.* New York: McGraw-Hill

Smith, J. J. (1935). *Social psychology.* Boston: Bruce Humphries.

Brown, J. F. (1936). *Psychology and the social order.* New York: McGraw-Hill.

Freeman, E. (1936). *Social psychology.* New York: Holt.

Gurnee, H. (1936). *Elements of social psychology.* New York: Farrar & Rinehart.

Katz, D., & Schanck, R. (1938). *Social psychology.* New York: Wiley.

Reinhardt, J. M. (1938). *Social psychology.* Philadelphia: Lippincott.

La Piere, R. T. (1938). *Collective behavior.* New York: McGraw-Hill.

Bird, C. (1940). *Social psychology.* New York: Appleton.

Klineberg, O. (1940). *Social psychology.* New York: Holt.

Britt, S. H. (1941). *Social psychology of modern life.* New York: Farrar & Rinehart.

Krout, M. H. (1942). *Introduction to social psychology.* New York: Harper.

Krech, D., & Crutchfield, R. S. (1948). *Theory and problems of social psychology.* New York: McGraw-Hill.

Sherif, M. (1948). *An outline of social psychology.* New York: Harper.

Vaughan, W. F. (1948). *Social psychology.* New York: Odyssey Press.

Beeley, A. L. (1949). *Outlines of social psychology.* Salt Lake City: University of Utah Press.

Lindesmith, A. R., & Strauss, A. L. (1949). *Social psychology: The art and science of living together.* New York: Dryden Press.

Newcomb, T. M. (1950). *Social psychology.* New York: Holt.

Sargent, S. S. (1950). *Social psychology.* New York: Ronald Press.

Queener, E. L. (1951). *Introduction to social psychology.* New York: William Sloane.

Asch S. E. (1952). *Social psychology.* New York: Prentice-Hall.

Doob, L. W. (1952). *Social psychology: An analysis of human behavior.* New York: Holt.

Faris, R. E. L. (1952). *Social psychology.* New York: Ronald Press.

Hartley, E. L., & Hartley, R. E. (1952) *Fundamentals of social psychology.* New York: Knopf.

Bonner, H. (1953). *Social psychology: An interdisciplinary approach.* New York: American Books.

Curtis, J. H. (1960). *Social psychology.* New York: McGraw-Hill.

Shibutani, T. (1961). *Society and personality.* Englewood Cliffs, NJ: Prentice-Hall.

Krech, D., Crutchfield, R. S., & Ballachey, E. L. (1962). *Individual in society.* New York: McGraw-Hill.

Cooper, J. B., & McGaugh, J. L. (1963). *Integrating principles of social psychology.* Cambridge, MA: Schenkman.

Lambert, W. W., & Lambert, W. E. (1964) *Social psychology.* Englewood Cliffs, NJ: Prentice-Hall.

McGrath, J. E. (1964). *Social psychology: A brief introduction.* New York: Holt, Rinehart & Winston.

Brown, R. W. (1965). *Social psychology.* New York: Free Press.

Doby, J. T. (1966). *Introduction to social psychology.* New York: Appleton-Century-Crofts.

Watson, G. (1966). *Social psychology: Issues and insights.* Philadelphia: Lippincott.

Zajonc, R. B. (1966). *Social psychology: An experimental approach.* Monterey, CA: Brooks/Cole.

Hollander, E. P. (1967). *Principles and methods of social psychology.* New York: Oxford University Press.

Jones, E. E., & Gerard, H. B. (1967). *Foundations of social psychology.* New York: Wiley.

McDavid, J. W., & Harari, H. (1968). *Social psychology: Individuals, groups, societies.* New York: Harper & Row.

Lindegren, H. C. (1969). *An introduction to social psychology.* New York: Wiley.

Mann, L. (1969). *Social psychology.* New York: Wiley.

Collins, B. E., & Aschmore, R. D. (1970). *Social psychology: Social influence, attitude change, group processes, and prejudice.* Reading, MA: Addison-Wesley.

Freedman, J. L., Carlsmith, J. M., & Sears, D. O. (1970). *Social psychology.* Englewood Cliffs, NJ: Prentice-Hall.

Schellenberg, J. A. (1970). *An introduction to social psychology.* New York: Random House.

Marlowe, L. (1971). *Social psychology: An interdisciplinary approach to human behavior.* Boston: Holbrook Press.

Sampson, E. E. (1971). *Social psychology and contemporary society.* New York: Wiley.

Aronson, E. (1972). *The social animal.* San Francisco: Freeman.

Berkowitz, L. (1972). *Social psychology.* Glenview, IL: Scott, Foresman.

Elms, A. C. (1972). *Social psychology and social relevance.* Boston: Little, Brown.

Insko, C., & Schopler, J. (1972). *Experimental social psychology.* New York: Academic Press.

Stotland, E., & Canon, L. K. (1972). *Social psychology: A cognitive approach.* Philadelphia: Saunders.

Wrightsman, L. S. (1972). *Social psychology in the seventies.* Monterey, CA: Brooks/Cole.

Kauffman, H. (1973). *Social psychology.* New York: Holt, Rinehart & Winston.

Kinch, J. W. (1973). *Social psychology.* New York: McGraw-Hill.

Baron, R. A., Byrne, D., & Griffitt, W. (1974). *Social psychology: Understanding human interaction.* Boston: Allyn & Bacon.

Gergen, K. (1974). *Social psychology: Explorations in understanding.* Del Mar, CA: CRM Books.

Middlebrook, P. M. (1974). *Social psychology and modern life.* New York: Knopf.

Nemeth, C. J. (1974). *Social psychology: Classic and contemporary integrations.* Chicago: Rand-McNally.

Sahakian, W. S. (1974). *Systematic social psychology.* New York: Chandler.

Berkowitz, L. (1975). *A survey of social psychology.* Hinsdale, IL: Dryden Press.

Samuel, W. (1975). *Contemporary social psychology: An introduction.* New York: Prentice-Hall.

Calhoun, D. W. (1976). *Persons-in-groups.* New York: Harper & Row.

Harrison, A. A. (1976). *Individuals and groups: Understanding social behavior.* Monterey, CA: Brooks/Cole.

Raven, B. H., & Rubin, J. Z. (1976). *Social psychology: People in groups.* New York: Wiley.

Schneider, D. J. (1976). *Social psychology.* Reading, MA: Addison-Wesley.

Seidenberg, B. (1976). *Social psychology.* New York: Free Press.

Severy, L. J., Brigham, J. C., & Schlenker, B. R. (1976). *A contemporary introduction to social psychology.* New York: McGraw-Hill.

Sherif, C. W. (1976). *Orientation in social psychology.* New York: Harper & Row.

Tedeschi, J. T., & Lindskold, S. (1976). *Social psychology.* New York: Wiley.

Worchel, S., & Cooper, J. (1976). *Understanding social psychology.* Homewood IL: Dorsey Press.

Back, K. W. (1977). *Social psychology.* New York: Wiley.

Fernandez, R. (1977). *The I, the me, and you: An introduction to social psychology.* New York: Praeger.

Harvey, J. H., & Smith, W. P. (1977). *Social psychology: An attributional approach.* St. Louis: Mosby.

Kando, T. M. (1977). *Social interaction.* St. Louis: Mosby.

Lauer, R. H., & Handel, W. H. (1977). *Social psychology: The theory and application of symbolic interactionism.* Boston: Houghton Mifflin.

Shaver, K. G. (1977). *Principles of social psychology.* Cambridge, MA: Winthrop.

Vander Zanden, J. W. (1977). *Social psychology.* New York: Random House.

Steward, E. W. (1978). *The human bond: Introduction to social psychology.* New York: Wiley.

Jones, R. A., Hendrick, C., & Epstein, Y. M. (1979). *Introduction to social psychology.* Sunderland, MA: Sinauer.

Albrecht, S. L., Thomas, D. L., & Chadwick, B. A. (1980). *Social psychology.* Englewood Cliffs, NJ: Prentice-Hall.

Allen, D. E., Guy, R. F., & Edgley, C. K. (1980). *Social psychology as social process.* Belmont, CA: Wadsworth.

Goldstein, J. H. (1980). *Social psychology.* New York: Academic Press.

Lambert, J. (1980). *Social psychology.* New York: Macmillan.

Sampson, E. E. (1980). *Introducing social psychology.* New York: New Viewpoints.

Gergen, K. J., & Gergen, M. M. (1981). *Social psychology.* New York: Harcourt Brace Jovanovich.

Heiss, J. (1981). *The social psychology of interaction.* Englewood Cliffs, NJ: Prentice-Hall.

Sherrod, D. (1981). *Social psychology.* New York: Random House.

Stang D. J. (1981). *Introduction to social psychology.* Monterey, CA: Brooks/Cole.

Vernon, G. M., & Cardwell, J. D. (1981). *Social psychology: Shared, symbolic, situated behavior.* Washington, DC: University Press of America.

Crano, W. E., & Meese, L. A. (1982). *Social psychology: Principles and themes of interpersonal behavior.* Homewood, IL: Dorsey.

Fisher, R. J. (1982). *Social psychology: An applied approach.* New York: St. Martin's Press.

Harari, H., & Kaplan, R. M. (1982). *Social psychology: Basic and applied.* Monterey, CA: Brooks/Cole.

McCall, G. J., & Simmons, J. L. (1982). *Social psychology: A sociological approach.* New York: Free Press.

Myers, D. G. (1983). *Social psychology.* New York: McGraw-Hill.

Neal, A. G. (1983). *Social psychology: A sociological perspective.* Reading, MA: Addison-Wesley.

Penrod, S. (1983). *Social psychology.* Englewood, Cliffs, NJ: Prentice-Hall.

Perlman, D., & Cozby, P. C. (1983). *Social psychology.* New York: Holt, Rinehart & Winston.

Weigert, A. J. (1983). *Social psychology: A sociological approach through interpretive understanding.* Notre Dame, IN: University of Notre Dame Press.

Baum, A. (1984). *Social psychology.* New York: Random House.

Cvetkovich, G., Baumgardner, S. R., & Trimble, J. E. (1984). *Social psychology.* New York: Holt, Rinehart & Winston.

Donnerstein, M. V., & Donnerstein, E. I. (1984). *Social psychology.* Dubuque, IA: Wm. C. Brown.

Feldman, R. S. (1985). *Social psychology: Theories, research and applications.* New York: McGraw-Hill.

Nash, J. (1985). *Social psychology: Society and self.* St. Paul, MN: West.

Tedeschi, J. T., Lindskold, S., & Rosenfeld, P. (1985). *Social psychology.* St. Paul, MN: West.

Forsyth, D. R. (1986). *Social psychology.* Monterey, CA: Brooks/Cole.

Michener, H. A., DeLamater, J. D., & Schwartz, S. H. (1986). *Social psychology.* San Diego: Harcourt Brace Jovanovich.

Penner, L. A. (1986). *Social psychology: Concepts and applications.* St. Paul, MN: West.

Smith, H. W. (1987). *Introduction to social psy-*

*chology*. Englewood Cliffs, NJ: Prentice-Hall.

Alcock, J. E., Carment, D. W., & Sadava, S. W. (1988). *A textbook of social psychology*. Scarborough, Ontario: Prentice-Hall Canada.

Saks, M. J., & Krupat, E. (1988). *Social psychology and its applications*. New York: Harper & Row.

Schneider, D. J. (1988). *Introduction to social psychology*. San Diego: Harcourt Brace Jovanovich.

# References

Abelson, R. P., & Rosenberg, M. J. (1958). Symbolic psycho-logic: A model of attitudinal cognition. *Behavioral Science, 3,* 1–13.

Ad Hoc Committee on Ethical Standards in Psychological Research. (1973). *Ethical principles in the conduct of research with human participants.* Washington, DC: American Psychological Association.

Adams, J. S. (1965). Inequality in social exchange. In L. Berkowitz (Ed.), *Advances in experimental social psychology* (Vol. 2). New York: Academic Press.

Adorno, T. W., Frenkel-Brunswik, E., Levinson, D. J., & Sanford, R. N. (1982). *The authoritarian personality.* New York: Harper & Row. (Original work published 1950.)

Allport, F. H. (1919). Behavior and experiment in social psychology. *Journal of Abnormal Psychology, 14,* 297–306.

Allport, F. H. (1924). *Social psychology.* Boston: Houghton Mifflin.

Allport, F. H. (1933). *Insitutional behavior.* Chapel Hill, NC: University of North Carolina Press.

Allport, F. H. (1934). The J-curve hypothesis of conforming behavior. *Journal of Social Psychology, 5,* 141–181.

Allport, F. H. (1955). *Theories of perception and the concept of structure.* New York: Wiley.

Allport, G. W. (1935). Attitudes. In C. Murchison (Ed.), *A handbook of social psychology,* Worcester, MA:. Clark University Press.

Allport, G. W. (1943). The productive paradox of William James. *Psychological Review, 50,* 95–120.

Allport, G. W. (1954a). The historical background of modern social psychology. In G. Lindzey (Ed.), *Handbook of social psychology* (1st ed.). Vol. 1. Reading, MA: Addison-Wesley.

Allport, G. W. (1954b). *The nature of prejudice.* Reading, MA: Addison-Wesley.

Allport, G. W. (1968). The historical background of modern social psychology. In G. Lindzey & E. Aronson (Eds.), *Handbook of Social Psychology* (2d ed.). Vol 1. Reading, MA.: Addison-Wesley.

Allport, G. W. (1985). The historical background of modern social psychology. In G. Lindzey & E. Aronson (Eds.), *Handbook of social psychology* (3d ed.). Vol. 1. New York: Random House.

American Sociological Society, Committee on the Implications of Certification Legislation. (1958). Legal certification of psychology as viewed by sociologists. *American Sociological Review, 23,* 301.

Anderson, N. (1923). *The hobo.* Chicago: University of Chicago Press.

Apao, W. K. (1986). Attribution theory: A case history of intentionality. In K. S. Larsen (Ed.), *Dialectics and ideology in psychology.* Norwood, NJ: Ablex.

Apfelbaum, E., & McGuire, G. R. (1985). Models of suggestive influence and the disqualification of the social crowd. In S. Moscovici & C. P. Graumann (Eds.), *Changing conceptions of crowd and mind.* New York: Springer-Verlag.

Arac, J. (1986). Introduction. In J. Arac (Ed.), *Postmodernism and politics.* Minneapolis: University of Minnesota Press.

Archibald, W. P. (1978). *Social psychology as political economy.* Toronto: McGraw-Hill Ryerson.

Argyle, M. (1988). Social relationships. In M. Hewstone, W. Stroebe, J.-P. Codol, & G. M. Stephenson (Eds.), *Introduction to social psychology.* Oxford: Blackwell.

Armistead, N. (Ed.). (1974). *Reconstructing social psychology.* Baltimore: Penguin.

Aronson, E. (1968). Dissonance theory: Progress and problems. In R. P. Abelson, E. Aronson, W. J. McGuire, T. M. Newcomb, M. J. Rosenberg, & P. H. Tannenbaum (Eds.), *Theories of Cognitive Consistency: A Sourcebook.* Chicago: Rand McNally.

Aronson, E. (1980). Persuasion via self-justification. In L. Festinger (Ed.), *Retrospections on social psychology*. Oxford: Oxford University Press.

Aronson, E., & Carlsmith, J. M. (1962). Performance expectancy as a determinant of actual performance. *Journal of Abnormal and Social Psychology, 65,* 178–182.

Aronson, E., & Carlsmith, J. M. (1968). Experimentation in social psychology. In G. Lindzey & E. Aronson (Eds.), *The handbook of social psychology* (2d ed.). Vol. 2. Reading, MA: Addison-Wesley.

Aronson, E., & Mills, J. (1959). The effect of severity of initiation on liking for a group. *Journal of Abnormal and Social Psychology, 59,* 177–181.

Asch, S. E. (1940). Studies in the principles of judgment and attitudes: II. Determination of judgments by group and ego standards. *Journal of Social Psychology, 12,* 433–465.

Asch, S. E. (1951). Effects of group pressure upon the modification and distortion of judgements. In H. Guetzkow (Ed.), *Groups, Leadership, and Men*. Pittsburgh: Carnegie Press.

Asch, S. E. (1952). *Social psychology*. New York: Prentice-Hall.

Asch, S. E. (1956). Studies of independence and conformity: A minority of one against a unanimous majority. *Psychological Monographs, 70* (9).

Baars, B. J. (1986). *The cognitive revolution in psychology*. New York: Guilford.

Baldwin, J. M. (1891). Suggestion in infancy. *Science, 17,* 113–117.

Baldwin, J. M. (1895). *Mental development in the child and in the race*. New York: Macmillan.

Baldwin, J. M. (1897). *Social and ethical interrelations in mental development*. New York: MacMillan.

Bales, R. F. (1950). *Interaction process analysis*. Reading, MA: Addison-Wesley.

Bales, R.F. (1958). Task roles and social roles in problem-solving groups. In E. E. Maccoby, T. M. Newcomb, & E. L. Hartley (Eds.), *Reading in Social Psychology* (3d ed.). New York: Holt, Rinehart and Winston.

Bandura, A. (1962). Social learning through imitation. In M. R. Jones (Ed.). *Nebraska symposium on motivation: 1962*. Lincoln: University of Nebraska Press.

Bandura, A. (1971). *Social learning theory*. New York: General Learning Press.

Bandura, A. (1973). *Aggression: A social learning analysis*. Englewood Cliffs, NJ: Prentice-Hall.

Barker, R., Dembo, T., & Lewin, K. (1941). Frustration and regression: An experiment with young children. *University of Iowa Studies In Child Welfare, 18,* No. 1.

Bass, B. M. (1955). Authoritarianism or acquiescence? *Journal of Abnormal and Social Psychology, 51,* 616–623.

Baumrind, D. (1964). Some thoughts on ethics of research: After reading Milgram's "Behavioral study of obedience." *American Psychologist, 19,* 421–423.

Bell, D. (1960). *The end of ideology: On exaustion of political ideas in the fifties*. New York: Free Press.

Bell, D. (1976). *The cultural contradictions of capitalism*. New York: Basic Books.

Bem, D. J. (1965). An experimental analysis of self-persuasion. *Journal of Experimental Social Psychology, 1,* 199–218.

Bem, D. J. (1967). Self-perception: An alternative interpretation of cognitive dissonance phenomena. *Psychological Review, 74,* 183–200.

Bem, D. J. (1972). Self-perception theory, In L. Berkowitz (Ed.), *Advances in Experimental Social Psychology* (Vol. 6). New York: Academic Press.

Benedict, R. (1934). *Patterns of culture*. Boston: Houghton Mifflin.

Benedict, R. (1948). *The Chrysanthemum and the sword*. Boston: Houghton Mifflin.

Berger, P. L., & Luckmann, T. (1966). *The social construction of reality*. New York: Doubleday.

Berkowitz, L. (1962). *Aggression: A social psychological analysis*. New York: McGraw-Hill.

Berkowitz, L. (1965). The concept of aggressive drive: Some additional considerations. In L. Berkowitz (Ed.), *Advances in experimental social psychology* (Vol. 2). New York: Academic Press.

Berkowitz, L., & Devine, P. G. (1989). Research traditions, analysis, and synthesis in social psychological theories: The case of dissonance theory. *Personality and Social Psychological Bulletin, 15,* 493–507.

Bernheim, H. (1884). *De la suggestion dans l'état hypnotique et dans l'état de veille*.

Bernard, L. L. (1924). *Instinct: A study in social psychology*. New York: Holt.

Bernard, L. L. (1926). *An introduction to social psychology*. New York: Holt.

Bernstein, R. J. (1976). *The restructuring of social and political theory*. New York: Harcourt Brace Jovanovich.

Berscheid, E., & Walster, E. H. (1978). *Interper-

*sonal attraction* (2nd ed.). Reading, MA: Addison-Wesley.

Billig, M. (1982). *Ideology and social psychology.* Oxford: Blackwell.

Billig, M. (1987). *Arguing and thinking: A rhetorical approach to social psychology.* Cambridge: Cambridge University Press.

Billig, M. (1988). Rhetorical and historical aspects of attitudes: The case of the British monarchy. *Philosophical Psychology, 1,* 83–103.

Binet, A. (1900). *La suggestbilité.* Paris: Schleicher.

Bleier, R. (1984). *Science and gender, a critique of biology and its theory of women.* New York: Pergamon.

Bloor, D. (1983). *Wittgenstein: A social theory of knowledge.* London: Macmillan.

Blumer, H. (1936). Social attitudes and nonsymbolic interaction. *Journal of Educational Psychology, 9,* 515–523.

Blumer, H. (1937). Symbolic interaction. In E. P. Schmidt (Ed.), *Man and society.* New York: Prentice-Hall.

Blumer, H. (1969). *Symbolic interactionism: Perspective and method.* Englewood Cliffs, NJ: Prentice-Hall.

Blumer, H. (1972). Action vs. interaction. Review of *Relations in Public* by E. Goffman, *Society, 9,* 50–53.

Blumer, H. (1984). *Symbolic interactionism.* Englewood Cliffs, NJ: Prentice-Hall.

Boas, F. (1911). *The mind of primitive man.* New York: Macmillan.

Bogardus, E. S. (1924). *Fundamentals of social psychology.* New York: Century.

Bogardus, E. S. (1925a). Social distance and its origins. *Journal of Applied Sociology, 9,* 216–226.

Bogardus, E. S. (1925b). Measuring social distance. *Journal of Applied Sociology, 11,* 272–287.

Bonner, H. (1953). *Social psychology: An interdisciplinary approach.* New York: American Books.

Bordeau, E. J. (1971). John Dewey's ideas about the Great Depression. *Journal of the History of Ideas, 32,* 67–68.

Boring, E. G. (1950). *History of experimental psychology* (2nd ed.). New York: Appleton-Century-Crofts.

Braid, J. (1899). *Neurypnology.* London: George Redway. (Original work published 1843).

Bramel, D., & Friend, R. (1981). Hawthorne, the myth of the docile worker, and class bias in psychology. *American Psychologist, 36,* 867–878.

Brand, E. S., Ruiz, R.A., & Padilla, A. M. (1974). Ethnic identification and preference: A review. *Psychological Bulletin, 81,* 860–890.

Brehm, J. W. (1956). Post-decisional changes in the desirability of alternatives. *Journal of Abnormal and Social Psychology, 52,* 384–389.

Brehm, J. W., & Cohen, A. R. (1962). *Explorations in cognitive dissonance.* New York: Wiley.

Brown, J. F. (1929). The methods of K. Lewin in the psychology of action and affection. *Psychological Review, 36,* 200–281.

Brown, J. F. (1936). *Psychology and the social order.* New York: McGraw-Hill.

Brown, R. (1965). *Social psychology.* New York: Free Press.

Bruner, J. S. (1950). Social psychology and group processes. *Annual Review of Psychology* (Vol. 1). Palo Alto, CA: Annual Reviews.

Bruner, J. S. (1962). Introduction. In L. S. Vygotsky, *Thought and language* (E. Hanfmann & G. Vakar, Trans.). Cambridge, MA: MIT Press.

Bruner, J. S., Goodnow, J. J., & Austin, G. A. (1956). *A study of thinking.* New York: Wiley.

Bulman, R. J., & Wortman, C. B. (1979). Attributions of blame and coping in the "real world": Severe accident victims react to their lot. *Journal of Personality and Social Psychology, 32,* 351–363.

Bulmer, M. (1984). *The Chicago school of sociology.* Chicago: University of Chicago Press.

Burgess, E. W. (1925). The growth of the city. In R. E. Park & E. W. Burgess, *The city.* Chicago: University of Chicago Press.

Burgess, R. (1977). The withering away of social psychology. *American Sociologist, 12,* 12–13.

Burke, P. J., & Reitzes, D. (1981). The link between identity and role performance. *Social Psychology Quarterly, 44,* 83–92.

Burke, P. J., & Tully, J. The measurement of role/idenity. *Social Force, 55,* 881–897.

Burnham, J. C. (1968a). On the origins of behaviorism. *Journal of the History of the Behavioral Sciences, 4,* 143–151.

Burnham, J. C. (1968b). The new psychology: From narcissism to social control. In J. Braeman, R. H. Bremmer, & D. Brody (Eds.), *Change and continuity in twentieth-century America:* The 1920s. Columbus: Ohio State University Press.

Burnham, J. C. (1978). The influence of psychoanalysis upon American culture. In J. M. Quen & E. T. Carlson (Eds.), *American psy-*

*choanalysis: Origins and development.* New York: Brunner/ Mazel.

Burston, D. (1989). *Fromm's legacy: A critical appreciation.* Unpublished doctoral dissertation, York University.

Buss, A. R. (1976). Galton and the birth of differential psychology and eugenics: Social, political, and economic forces. *Journal of the History of the Behavioral Sciences, 12,* 47–58.

Buss, A. R. (1978). Causes and reasons in attribution theory: A conceptual critique. *Journal of Personality and Social Psychology, 17,* 1311–1321.

Buss, A. R. (1979). *A dialectical psychology.* New York: Irvington.

Capshew, J. H. (1986). Networks on leadership: A quantitative study of SPSSI presidents, 1936–1986. *Journal of Social Issues, 42(1),* 75–106.

Carlsmith, J. M., & Freedman, J. L. (1968). Bad decisions and dissonance: Nobody's perfect. In R. P. Abelson, E. Aronson, W. J. McGuire, T. M. Newcomb, M. J. Rosenberg, & P. H. Tannenbaum (Eds.), *Theories of cognitive consistency: A sourcebook.* Chicago: Rand McNally.

Carnap, R. (1967). Autobiography. In K. T. Fann (Ed.), *Ludwig Wittgenstein: The man and his philosophy.* New York: Delta. (original work published 1964).

Carroll, P. N. (1982). *It seemed like nothing happened: The tragedy and promise of America in the 1970s.* New York: Holt, Rinehart & Winston.

Cartwright, D. (1947–48). Social psychology in the United States during the Second World War. *Human Relations, 1,* 333–352.

Cartwright, D. (1959). Lewinian theory as a contemporary systematic framework. In S. Koch (Ed.), *Psychology: A study of a science.* (Vol. 2). New York: McGraw-Hill.

Cartwright, D. (1978). Theory and practice. *Journal of Social Issues, 34(4),* 168–180.

Cartwright, D. (1979). Contemporary social psychology in historical perspective. *Social Psychology Quarterly, 42,* 82–93.

Cartwright, D., & Zander, A. (1953). Origins of group dynamics. In D. Cartwright & A. Zander (Eds.), *Group dynamics: Research and theory.* New York: Harper & Row.

Cattell, J. M. (1929). Psychology in America. *Science, 70,* 335–347.

Chafe, W. (1986). *The unfinished journey: America since World War II.* New York: Oxford University Press.

Chapman, A. N. (1976). *Harry Stack Sullivan: His life and work.* New York: Putnam.

Charcot, J. M. (1878). *Gazette des hôpitaux civils et millitaries.* Paris: Christie, R., & Jahoda, M. (Eds.) (1954). Bureaux Du Progrès Médical. *Studies in the scope and method of the authoritarian personality.* Illinois: Free Press.

Cina, C. (1981). *Social science for whom? A structural history of social psychology.* Unpublished doctoral dissertation, State University of New York at Stony Brook.

Clark, K. B. (1965). *Dark ghetto: Dilemmas of social power.* New York: Harper & Row.

Clark, K. B. (1980). Kenneth B. Clark. In R. Evans (Interviewer), *The making of social psychology: Discussions with creative contributors.* New York: Gardner.

Clark, K. B., & Clark, M. P. (1947). Racial identification and preference in Negro children. In T. M. Newcomb & E. L. Hartley (Eds.), *Readings in social psychology.* New York: Holt.

Clecak, P. (1983). *America's quest for the ideal self: Dissent and fulfillment in the 60s and 70s.* New York: Oxford University Press.

Coch, L., & French, J. R. P., Jr. (1948). Overcoming resistance to change. *Human Relations, 1,* 512–532.

Cole, M. (1979). Introduction. In A. R. Luria, *The making of mind: A personal account of Soviet psychology.* Cambridge: Cambridge University Press.

Collier, G. (1985). *Emotional expression.* Hillsdale, NJ: Lawrence Erlbaum.

Collins, R. (1981). On the microfoundation of macrosociology. *American Journal of Sociology, 86,* 984–1014.

Cook, D. (1990). Remapping modernity. *British Journal of Aesthetics, 30,* 35–45.

Cook, G. A. (1977). G. H. Mead's social behaviorism. *Journal of the History of the Behavioral Sciences, 13,* 307–316.

Cooley, C. H. (1902). *Human nature and the social order.* New York: Scribners.

Cooley, C. H. (1909). *Social organization.* New York: Scribners.

Cooley, C. H. (1918). *The social process.* New York: Scribners.

Cooley, C. H. (1930). *Sociological theory and social research.* New York: Holt, Rinehart & Winston.

Cooper, J., & Croyle, R. (1982). *Cognitive dissonance: Evidence for physiological arousal.* Unpublished manuscript, Princeton University, 1982.

Cooper, J., & Worchel, S. (1970). Role of undesired consequences in arousing cognitive dissonance. *Journal of Personality and Social Psychology, 16,* 199–206.

Cooper, J., Zanna, M. P., & Taves, J. A. (1978). Arousal as a necessary condition for attitude change folloding induced compliance. *Journal of Personality and Social Psychology, 36,* 1101–1106.

Corsaro, W. C. (1985). *Friendship and peer culture in the early years.* Norwood, NJ: Ablex.

Coser, L. A. (1977). *Masters of sociological thought* (2d ed.). New York: Harcourt Brace Jovanovich.

Cottrell, L. S., & Gallagher, R. (1941). Important developments in American social psychology during the past decade. *Sociometry, 3,* 107–139.

Cottrell, N. B., & Wack, D. L. (1967). Energizing effects of cognitive dissonance upon dominant and subordinate responses. *Journal of Personality and Social Psychology, 6,* 132–138.

Cressy, P. F. (1932). *The taxi-dance* Chicago: University of Chicago Press.

Culler, J. (1982). *On deconstruction: Theory and criticism after structuralism.* Ithaca, NY: Cornell University Press.

Curtis, J. H. (1960). *Social psychology.* New York: McGraw-Hill.

Danzinger, K. (1979). The social origins of modern psychology. In A. R. Buss (Ed.), *Psychology in social context.* New York: Irvington.

Danzinger, K. (1983). Origins and basic principles of Wundt's *Völkerpsychologie. British Journal of Social Psychology, 22,* 303–313.

Danzinger, K. (1985). The origins of the psychological experiment as a social institution. *American Psychologist, 40,* 133–140.

Danzinger, K. (1990). *Lewinian experimentation and American social psychology.* Paper presented at the annual meeting of Cheiron-Europe, Weimar, September.

Darwin, C. (1859). *Origin of species.* London: J. Murray.

Darwin, C. (1871). *The descent of man.* London: J. Murray.

Darwin, C. (1872). *The expression of emotions in man and animals.* London: Appleton.

Deegan, M. J., Burger, J. S. (1978). George Herbert Mead and social reform: His work and writings. *Journal of the History of the Behavioral Sciences, 14,* 362–373.

Deegan, M. J., Burger, J. S. (1981). W. I. Thomas and social reform: His work and writings. *Journal of the History of the Behavioral Sciences, 17,* 114–125.

de Rivera, J. (1976). *Field theory as human science: Contributions of Lewin's Berlin group.* New York: Gardner Press.

Derrida, J. (1976). *Of grammatology.* Baltimore: Johns Hopkins Press.

Deutsch, M. (1949). A theory of cooperation and competition. *Human Relations, 2,* 129–152.

Deutsch, M. (1975). Introduction. In M. Deutsch & H. Hornstein (Eds.), *Applying social psychology.* Hillsdale, NJ: Lawrence Erlbaum.

Deutsch, M. (1980). Fifty years of conflict. In L. Festinger (Ed.), *Retrospections on social psychology.* New York: Oxford Univeristy Press.

Deutsch, M., & Hornstein, H. A. (Eds.). (1975). *Applying social psychology: Implications for research, practice and training.* Hillsdale, NJ: Lawrence Erlbaum.

Deutsch, M., & Krauss, R. M. (1960). The effect of threat on interpersonal bargaining. *Journal of Abnormal and Social Psychology, 61,* 181–189.

Deutsch, M., & Krauss, R. M. (1965). *Theories in social psychology.* New York: Basic Books.

Dewey, J. (1887). *Psychology.* New York: Harper.

Dewey, J. (1896). The reflex arc concept in psychology. *Psychological Review, 3,* 357–370.

Dewey, J. (1900). Psychology and social practice. *Psychological Review, 8,* 105–124.

Dewey, J. (1917). The need for social psychology. *Psychological Review, 24,* 266–277.

Dewey, J. (1922). *Human nature and conduct: An introduction to social psychology.* New York: Holt.

Dewey, J. (1925). *Experience and nature.* Chicago: Open Court.

Dewey, J. (1928, November–December). Impressions of Societ Russia. *New Republic,* Part I–VI.

Dewey, J. (1930). *Individualism old and new.* New York: Minton Balch.

Dewey, J. (1931). George Herbert Mead. *Journal of Philosophy, 12,* 309–314.

Dewey, J. (1932). Prefatory remarks. In G. H. Mead, *The philosophy of the present.* Chicago: University of Chicago Press.

Dewey, J. (1935). *Liberalism and social action.* New York: Putman & Sons.

Dewey, J. (1948). *Reconstruction in philosophy.* Boston: Beacon.

Dewey, R. S., & Humber, W. J. (1966). *An introduction to social psychology.* New York: Macmillan.

Diggins, J. P. (1973). *The American left in the twentieth century.* New York: Harcourt Brace Jovanovich.

Diggins, J. P. (1988). *The proud decades: Amer-*

*ica at war and peace 1941 to 1960.* New York: Norton.

Dollard, J., Doob, L. W., Miller, N. E., Mowrer, O. H., & Sears, R. R. (1939). *Frustration and aggression.* New Haven: Yale University Press.

Doob, L. W. (1935). *Propaganda: Its psychology and technique.* New York: Holt.

Doob, L. W. (1966). *Public opinion and propaganda (2d ed.).* Hamden, CT: Anchor Books.

DuBois, W. E. B. (1901). The relation of the Negroes to the Whites in the South. *Annals of the American Academy of Political and Social Science, 18,* 121–140.

Dunlap, K. (1919). Are there any instincts? *Journal of Abnormal and Social Psychology, 14,* 307–311.

Dunlap, K. (1922). *Elements of scientific psychology.* St. Louis: Mosby.

Dunlap, K. (1925). *Social psychology.* Baltimore: Williams & Wilkins.

Durkheim, E. (1962). *Socialism* (C. Stattler, Trans.). New York: Collier. (Original work published 1895–96.)

Durkheim, E. (1964). *The division of labor in society* (G. Simpson, Trans.). New York: Free Press. (Original work published 1893.)

Durkheim, E. (1964). *The rules of sociological analysis* (S. A. Solovay & J. H. Mueller, Trans.). New York: Free Press. (Original work published 1895.).

Durkheim, E. (1964). *Suicide: A study in sociology* (J. A. Spaulding & G. Simpson, Trans.) New York: Free Press. (Original work published 1897.)

Durkheim, E. (1965). *Elementary forms of the religious life* (J. W. Swain, Trans.) New York: Free Press. (Original work published 1912.)

Durkheim, E. (1974). *Sociology and philosophy.* New York: Free Press.

Eagly, A. H., Wood, W., & Chalken, S. (1978). Causal inferences about communicators and their effect on opinion chance. *Journal of Personality and Social Psychology, 36,* 424–435.

Ehrlich, D., Cuttman, I., Schonbach, P., & Mills, J. (1957). Post-decisional exposure to relevant information. *Journal Of Abnormal and Social Psychology, 54,* 98–102.

Einstein, A., & Infield, L. (1938). *The evolution of physics.* New York: Simon & Schuster.

Ellwood, C. A. (1912). *Sociology in its psychological aspects.* New York: Appleton.

Ellwood, C. A. (1917). *An introduction to social psychology.* New York: Appleton.

Ellwood, C. A. (1925). *The psychology of human society.* New York: Appleton.

Elms, A. C. (1972). *Social psychology and social relevance.* Boston: Little, Brown.

Elms, A. C. (1975). The crisis of confidence in social psychology. *American Psychologist, 30,* 967–976.

Erikson, E. (1959). Growth and crises of the healthy personality: 1950. *Psychological Issues, 1,* 50–100.

Evans, R. (Interviewer) (1980). *The making of social psychology: Discussions with creative contributors.* New York: Gardner.

Ewer, B. C. (1929). *Social psychology.* New York: Macmillan.

Fann, K. T. (Ed.) (1967). *Ludwig Wittgenstein: The man and his philosophy.* New York: Delta.

Faris, R. E. L. (1967). *Chicago sociology: 1920–1932.* New York: Chandler.

Farr, R. M. (1983). Wilhelm Wundt (1832–1920) and the origins of psychology as an experimental and social science. *British Journal of Social Psychology, 22,* 289–301.

Farr, R. M. (1987a). Social representations: A French tradition in research. *Journal for the Theory of Social Behaviour, 17,* 343–369.

Farr, R. M. (1987b). The science of mental life: A social psychological perspective. *Bulletin of the British Psychological Society, 40,* 1–17.

Farr, R. M., & Moscovici, S. (Eds.). (1984). *Social representations.* Cambridge: Cambridge University Press.

Fazio, R. H., Zanna, M. P., & Cooper, J. (1977). Dissonance and self-perception: An integrative view of each theory's proper domain of application. *Journal of Experimental Social Psychology, 13,* 464–479.

Festinger, L. (1950). Informal social communication. *Psychological Review, 57,* 271–282.

Festinger, L. (1954). A theory of social comparison processes. *Human Relations, 2,* 117–140.

Festinger, L. (1957). *A theory of cognitive dissonance.* Stanford, CA: Stanford University Press.

Festinger, L. (Ed.). (1980). *Retrospections on social psychology.* Oxford: Oxford University Press.

Festinger, L., & Carlsmith, J. M. (1959). Cognitive consequences of forced compliance. *Journal of Abnormal and Social Psychology, 58,* 203–210.

Festinger, L., Riecken, H. W., & Schachter, S. (1956). *When prophecy fails.* Minneapolis: University of Minnesota Press.

Feyerabend, P. K. (1976). *Against method.* New York: Humanities Press.

Fielder, F. E. (1967). *A theory of leadership effectiveness.* New York: McGraw-Hill.

Findley, M., & Cooper, H. (1981). Introductory social psychology textbook citations: A comparison of five research areas. *Personality and Social Psychology Bulletin, 7,* 173–176.

Fingarette, H. (1969). *Self-deception.* Atlantic Highlands, NJ: Humanities Press.

Finison, L. J. (1976). Unemployment, politics, and the history of organized psychology. *American Psychologist, 31,* 747–755.

Finison, L. J. (1978). Unemployment, politics, and the history of organized psychology II. *American Psychologist, 33,* 471–477.

Finison, L. J. (1979). An aspect of the early history of the society for the psychological study of social issues: Psychologists and labor. *Journal of the History of the Behavioral Sciences, 13,* 29–37.

Finison, L. J. (1986). The psychological insurgency: 1936–1945. *Journal of Social Issues, 42(1),* 21–33.

Fisher, R. J. (1981). Training in applied social psychology: Rationale and core experience. *Canadian Psychology, 22,* 250–259.

Fisher, R. J. (1982). *Social psychology: An applied approach.* New York: St. Martin's.

Fiske, S. T., & Taylor, S. E. (1984). *Social cognition.* Reading, MA: Addison-Wesley.

Flax, J. (1987). Postmodernism and gender relationships in feminist theory. *Signs, 12,* 621–643.

Foster, H. (1983). Postmodernism: A preface. In H. Foster (Ed.), *The anti-aesthetic: Essays in postmodern culture.* Port Townsend, WA: Bay Press.

Foucault, M. (1977). *Discipline and punish: The birth of the prison.* New York: Pantheon.

Foucault, M. (1978). *The history of sexuality, Volume 1: An introduction.* New York: Pantheon.

Franke, R. (1931). Gang und character. *Beihefts, Zeitschrift für angewandte Psychologie,* No. 58.

Freeman, D. (1983). *Margaret Mead and Samoa: The making and unmaking of an anthropological myth.* New York: Penguin.

Freedman, J. L. (1969). Role-playing: Psychology by consensus. *Journal of Personality and Social Psychology, 13,* 107–114.

Freud, S. (1953). The interpretation of dreams. In J. Strachey (Ed. & Trans.), *The standard edition of the complete psychological work of Sigmund Freud* (Vols. 4 & 5). London: Hogarth Press. (Original work published 1900.)

Freud, S. (1953). The psychopathology of everyday life. In J. Strachey (Ed. & Trans.), *The standard edition of the complete psychological work of Sigmund Freud* (Vol. 6). London: Hogarth Press. (Original work published 1904.)

Freud S. (1953). Three essays on the theory of sexuality. In J. Strachey (Ed. & Trans.), *The standard edition of the complete psychological work of Sigmund Freud* (Vol. 7). London: Hogarth Press. (Original work published 1905.)

Freud, S. (1955). Totem and taboo. In J. Strachey (Ed. & Trans.), *The standard edition of the complete psychological work of Sigmund Freud* (Vol. 13). London: Hogarth Press. (Original work published 1913.)

Freud, S. (1957). Instincts and their vicissitudes. In J. Strachey (Ed. & Trans.), *The standard edition of the complete psychological work of Sigmund Freud* (Vol. 14). London: Hogarth Press. (Original work published 1915.)

Freud, S. (1953). Beyond the pleasure principle. In J. Strachey (Ed. & Trans.), *The standard edition of the complete psychological work of Sigmund Freud* (Vol. 18). London: Hogarth Press. (Original work published 1920.)

Freud, S. (1955). Group psychology and the analysis of the ego. In J. Strachey (Ed. & Trans.), *The standard edition of the complete psychological work of Sigmund Freud* (Vol. 18). London: Hogarth Press. (Original work published 1921.)

Freud, S. (1961). The future of an illusion. In J. Strachey (Ed. & Trans.), *The standard edition of the complete psychological work of Sigmund Freud* (Vol. 21). London: Hogarth Press. (Original work published 1927.)

Freud, S. (1961). Civilization and its discontents. In J. Strachey (Ed. & Trans.), *The standard edition of the complete psychological work of Sigmund Freud* (Vol. 21). London: Hogarth Press. (Original work published 1930)

Fromm, E. (1941). *Escape from freedom.* Boston: Houghton Mifflin. (Original work published 1939.)

Fromm, E. (1947). *Man for himself.* Greenwich, CN: Fawcett.

Fromm, E. (1955). *The sane society.* Boston: Houghton Mifflin.

Fromm, E. (1964). *The heart of man: Its genius for good and evil.* New York: Harper & Row.

Fromm, E. (1970). *The crisis of psycho-analysis: Essays on Freud, Marx, and social psychology.* Greenwich, CN: Fawcett.

Galbraith, J. K. (1958). *The affluent society.* New York: Signet.

Galton, F. (1883). *Inquiries into human faculty.* London: Macmillan.

Galton, F. (1970). *English men of science: Their nature and nurture.* London: Frank Cass. (Original work published 1874.)

Garfinkel, H. (1967). *Studies in ethnomethodology.* Englewood Cliffs, NJ: Prentice-Hall.

Garvey, W. D., and Griffith, B. C. (1971). Scientific communication: Its role in the conduct of research and the creation of knowledge. *American Psychologist, 26,* 349–362.

Gault, R. H. (1923). *Social psychology: The basis of behavior called social.* New York: Holt.

Gergen, K. J. (1973). Social psychology as history. *Journal of Personality and Social Psychology, 26,* 309–320.

Gergen, K. J. (1982). *Toward transformation in social knowledge.* New York: Springer-Verlag.

Gergen, K. J. (1985). The social constructionist movement in modern psychology. *American Psychologist, 40,* 266–275.

Gergen, K. J. (1988). *Toward a post-modern psychology.* Invited address, International Congress of Psychology, Sydney, Australia, August.

Gergen, K. J. (1989a). Social psychology and the wrong revolution. *European Journal of Social Psychology, 19,* 463–484.

Gergen, K. J. (1989b). Warranting voice and the elaboration of the self. In J. Shotter & K. J. Gergen (Eds.), *Texts of identity.* London: Sage.

Gergen, K. J., & Basseches, M. (1980). The potentiation of psychological knowledge. In R. F. Kidd & M. Saks (Eds.), *Advances in applied social psychology.* New York: Academic Press.

Gergen, K. J., & Davis, K. (Eds.). (1985). *The social construction of the person.* New York: Springer-Verlag.

Gergen, K. J., Morse, S. J., & Gergen, M. M. (1980). Behavior exchange in cross-cultural perspective. In H. C. Triandis & W. W. Lambert (Eds.), *Handbook of cross-cultural psychology.* Boston: Allyn & Bacon.

Gibson, G. L., & Higbee, K. L. (1979). *Seventy years of social psychology textbooks.* Paper presented at the meeting of the Rocky Mountain Psychological Association, Las Vegas.

Giddens, A. (1971). The "individual" in the writings of Emile Durkheim. *Archives of European Sociology, 12,* 210–228.

Giddens, A. (1984). *The construction of society.* Berkeley: University of California Press.

Giddings, F. H. (1896). *The principle of sociology.* New York: Macmillan.

Giddings, F. H. (1898). *The elements of sociology.* New York: Macmillan.

Giddings, F. H. (1899). The psychology of society. *Science, 9,* 16.

Gier, N. F. (1981). *Wittgenstein and phenomenology: A comparative study of the later Wittgenstein, Husserl, Heidegger, and Merleau-Ponty.* Albany: State University of New York Press.

Gillespie, R. (1988). The Hawthorne experiments and the politics of experimentation. In J. G. Morawski (Ed.). *The rise of experimentation in American psychology.* New Haven: Yale University Press.

Gillig, P. M., & Greenwald, A. G. (1974). Is it time to lay the sleeper effect to rest? *Journal of Personality and Social Psychlogy, 29,* 132–139.

Gleason, J. M., & Katkin, E. S. (1978). *The effects of cognitive dissonance on heart rate and electrodermal response.* Paper presented at the meeting of the Society for Psychophysiological Research, Madison, WI.

Goddard, H. H. (1917). Mental tests and the immigrant. *Journal of Delinquency, 2,* 243–277.

Goffman, E. (1959). *The presentation of self in everyday life.* Garden City, NY: Doubleday.

Goffman, E. (1961). *Encounters.* Indianapolis: Bobbs-Merrill.

Goffman, E. (1963). *Behavior in public places.* New York: Free Press.

Goffman, E. (1974). *Frame ananlysis.* Cambridge, MA: Harvard University Press.

Goffman, E. (1983). The interaction order. *American Sociological Review, 48,* 1–17.

Goodman, P. (1960). *Growing up absurd: Problems of youth in the organized society.* New York: Random House.

Gorman, M. (1981). Pre-war conformity research in social psychology: The approaches of Floyd H. Allport and Muzafer Sherif. *Journal of the History of the Behavioral Sciences, 17,* 2–14.

Gould, S. J. (1981). *The mismeasure of man.* New York: Norton.

Gouldner, A. W. (1963). *Modern sociology: An introduction to the study of human interaction.* New York: Harcourt, Brace & World.

Gouldner, A. W. (1970). *The coming crisis in Western sociology.* New York: Basic Books.

Graebner, W. (1986). The small group and democratic social engineering, 1900–1950. *Journal of Social Issues, 42(1),* 137–154.

Graebner, W. (1987). Confronting the democratic paradox: The ambivalent vision of Kurt Lewin. *Journal of Social Issues, 43(3),* 141–146.

Grant, M. (1916). *The passing of the great race.* New York: Scribners.

Graumann, C. F. (1988). Introduction to a history of social psychology. In M. Hewstone, W. Stroebe, J.-P. Codol, & G. M. Stephenson (Eds.), *Introduction to social psychology.* Oxford: Blackwell.

Gray, A. (1876). The origin of species by means of natural selection. In A. Gray (Ed.), *Dariniana.* New York: Appleton. (Original work published 1860.)

Gross, A. E., & Fleming, I. (1982). Twenty years of deception in social psychology. *Personality and Social Psychology Bulletin, 8,* 402–408.

Guilford, J. P. (1931). Racial preferences of a thousand American university students. *Journal of Social Psychology, 2,* 179–204.

Habermas, J. (1983). Modernity—An incomplete project. In H. Foster (Ed.), *The anti-aesthetic: Essays on postmodern culture.* Port Townsend, WA: Bay Press.

Haines, H., & Vaughan, G. M. (1979). Was 1898 a "great date" in the history of experimental social psychology? *Journal of the History of the Behavioral Sciences, 15,* 323–332.

Hale, N. G. (1971). *Freud and the Americans: The beginning of psychoanalysis in the United States. 1876–1917.* New York: Oxford University Press.

Hall, C. S., & Lindzey, G. (1978). *Theories of personality.* (3d ed.). New York: Wiley.

Hamilton, W. D. (1964). The evolution of social behavior: I and II. *Journal of Theoretical Biology, 1,* 1–52.

Hannush, M. J. (1987). John B. Watson remembered: An interview with John B. Watson. *Journal of the History of the Behavioral Sciences, 23,* 137–152.

Hare-Mustin, R. T., & Marecek, J. (1988). The meaning of difference: Gender theory, postmodernism, and psychology. *American Psychologist, 43,* 455–464.

Harlow, H. (1953). Mice, monkeys, men, and motives. *Psychological Review, 60,* 23–32.

Harré, R. (1972). The analysis of episodes. In J. Israel & H. Tajfel (Eds.), *The context of social psychology; A critical assessment.* London: Academic Press.

Harré, R. (1979). *Social being.* Oxford: Blackwell.

Harré, R., Clarke, D., & De Carlo, N. (1985). *Motives and mechanisms: An introduction to the psychology of action.* London: Methuen.

Harré, R., & Secord, P. F. (1972) *The explanation of social behavior.* Totowa, NJ: Rowman & Littlefield.

Harris, B. (1979). Whatever happened to Little Albert? *American Psychologist, 34,* 151–160.

Harris, B. (1984). "Gives me a dozen healthy infants": John B. Watson's advice on child-rearing, women, and the family. In M. Lewin (ed.), *In the shadow of the past: Psychology portrays the sexes.* New York: Columbia University Press.

Harris, B. (1986). Reviewing 50 years of the psychology of social issues. *Journal of Social Issues, 42(1),* 1–20.

Harris, B. (1988). Key words: A history of debriefing in social psychology. In J. G. Morawski (Ed.), *The rise of experimentation in American psychology.* New Haven: Yale University Press.

Hartmann, G. W., & Newcomb, T. M. (Eds.) (1939). *Industrial conflict: A psychological interpretation.* New York: Cordon Press.

Harvey, O. J. (1989). Muzafer Sherif (1906–1988). *SPSSI Newsletter,* 13–14, April.

Haskell, T. L. (1977). *The emergence of professional social science: The American Social Science Association and the nineteenth century crisis of authority.* Chicago: University of Illinois Press.

Hearnstaw, L. S. (1979). *Cyril Burt, psychologist.* Ithaca, NY: Cornell University Press.

Hegel, G. W. F. (1967). *Phenomenology of mind.* New York: Harper & Row. (Original work published 1807.)

Hegel, G. W. F. (1967). *The philosophy of right* (T. M. Knox, Trans.). Oxford: Clarendon Press. (Original work published 1821.)

Heider, F. (1944). Social perception and phenomenal causality. *Psychological Review, 51,* 358–374.

Heider, F. (1946). Attitude and organization. *Journal of Psychology, 21,* 107–112.

Heider, F. (1958). *The psychology of interpersonal relations.* New York: Wiley.

Heider, F. (1983). *The life of a psychologist: An autobiography.* Lawrence: University of Kansas Press.

Heise, D. R. (1979). *Understanding events: Affect and the construction of social experience.* Cambridge: Cambridge University Press.

Helmreich, R. Bakeman, R., & Scherwitz, L. (1973). The study of small groups. *Annual Review of Psychology.*

Henle, M. (1978). Kurt Lewin as metatheorist. *Journal of the History of the Behavioral Sciences, 14,* 233–237.

Henriques, J., Hollway, W., Urwin, C., Venn, C., & Walderdine, V. (1984). *Changing the subject: Psychology, social regulation and subjectivity.* London: Methuen.

Heritage, J. (1984). *Garfinkel and ethnomethodology.* Cambridge, MA: Polity Press.

Hewitt, J. P. (1983). *Self and society* (3d ed.). Boston: Allyn & Bacon.

Hickman, C. A., & Kuhn, M. H. (1956). *Individuals, groups, and economic behavior.* New York: Dryden.

Higbee, K. L., Millard, R. J., & Folkman, J. R. (1982). Social psychology research during the 1970's. *Personality and Social Psychology Bulletin, 8,* 180–183.

Hinde, R. A. (1987). *Individuals, relationships and culture: Links between ethology and the social sciences.* Cambridge: Cambridge University Press.

Hinde, R. A. (1988). Ethology and social psychology. In M. Hewstone, W. Stroebe, J.-P. Codol, & G. M. Stephenson (Eds.), *Introduction to social psychology.* Oxford: Blackwell.

Hitler, A. (1971). *Mein Kampf* (R. Manheim, Trans.). Houghton. (Original work published 1925.)

Hodson, G. (1976). *America in our time.* New York: Vintage Books.

Hoffman, F. (1957). *Freudianism and the literary mind.* New Orleans: Louisiana State University Press. (Original work published 1945.)

Hoffman, L. E. (1981). War, revolution, psychoanalysis: Freudian thought begins to grapple with social reality. *Journal of the History of the Behavioral Sciences, 17,* 251–269.

Hoffman, L. E. (1982). From instinct to identity: Implications of changing psychoanalytic concepts of social life from Freud to Erikson. *Journal of the History of the Behavioral Sciences, 18,* 130–146.

Hoffman, L. E. (1987). The ideological significance of Freud's social thought. In M. G. Ash & W. R. Woodward (Eds.), *Psychology in twentieth-century thought and society.* New York: Cambridge University Press.

Hofstadter, R. (1955). *The age of reform.* New York: Vintage Books.

Hollander, E. P. (1958). Conformity, status and idiosyncrasy credit. *Psychological Review, 65,* 117–127.

Holt, E. B. (1915). *The Freudian wish and its place in ethics.* New York: B. W. Huebsch.

Homans, G. C. (1950). *The human group.* New York: Harcourt Brace.

Homans, G. C. (1961). *Social behavior: Its elementary forms.* New York: Harcourt Brace Jovanovich.

Homans, G. C. (1974). *Social behavior: Its elementary forms* (2d ed.). New York: Harcourt Brace Jovanovich.

Horney, K. (1942). *Self-analysis.* New York: Norton.

Horney, K. (1945). *Our inner conflicts.* New York: Norton.

Horwitz, M. (1954). The recall of interrupted group tasks: An experimental study of individual motivation in relation to group goals. *Human Relations, 7,* 3–38.

Hougan, J. (1975). *Decadence: Radical nostalgia, narcissism, and decline in the seventies.* New York: William Morrow.

Hovland, C. I. (1959). Reconciling conflicting results derived from experimental and survey studies of attitude change. *American Psychologist, 14,* 8–17.

Hovland, C., Janis, I., & Kelley, H. (1953). *Communication and persuasion.* New Haven: Yale University Press.

Hovland, C. I., Lumsdaine, A. A., & Sheffield, F. D. (1949). *Experiments on mass communications.* Princeton, NJ: Princeton University Press.

Hovland, C. I., & Mandell, W. (1952). An experimental comparison of conclusion-drawing by the communicator and by the audience. *Journal of Abnormal and Social Psychology, 47,* 581–588.

Hovland, C. I., & Weiss, W. (1951). The influence of source credibility on communication effectiveness. *Public Opinion Quarterly, 15,* 635–650.

Hughes, H. S. (1958). *Consciousness and society.* New York: Random House.

Husserl, E. (1962). *Ideas: General introduction to pure phenomenology* (W. R. B. Gibson, Trans.). New York: Collier. (Original work published 1913.)

Huxley, T. H. (1896). On the hypothesis that animals are automata and its history. In T. H. Huxley, *Methods and results.* New York: Appleton. (Original work published 1874.)

Ickes, W. J., & Kidd, R. F. (1976). An attributional analysis of helping behavior. In J. H. Harvey, W. Ickes, & R. F. Kidd (Eds.), *New directions in attribution research* (Vol. 1). Hillsdale, NJ: Lawrence Erlbaum.

Insko, C., & Schopler, J. (1972). *Experimental social psychology.* New York: Academic Press.

Israel, J. (1979). From level of aspiration to dissonance. In A. R. Buss (Ed.), *Psychology in social context.* New York: Irvington.

Israel, J., & Tajfel, H. (Eds.). (1972). *The context of social psychology: A critical assessment.* London: Academic Press.

Izard, C. E. (1971). *The face of emotion.* New York: Appleton-Century-Crofts.

Jackson, J. M. (1988). *Social psychology, past and present: An integrative orientation.* Hillsdale, NJ: Lawrence Erlbaum.

Jacoby, R. (1975). *Social amnesia: A critique of conformist psychology from Adler to Laing.* Boston: Beacon.

Jacoby, R. (1983). *The repression of psychoanalysis.* New York: Basic Books.

James, W. (1890). *The Principles of psychology* New York: Holt.

James, W. (1897). *The will to believe, and other essays in popular philosophy.* Cambridge, MA: Harvard University Press.

James, W. (1907). *Pragmatism.* New York: Washington Square Press.

James, W. (1912) *Essays in radical empiricism.* Cambridge, MA: Harvard University Press.

James, W. (1958). *The varieties of religious experience.* New York: Mentor. (Original work published 1902.)

Jameson, F. (1983). Postmodernism and consumer society. In H. Foster (Ed.), *The anti-aesthetic: Essays on postmodern culture.* Port Townsend, WA: Bay Press.

Janis, I. L. (1954). Personality correlates of susceptibility to persuasion. *Journal of Personality, 22,* 504–518.

Janis, I. L. (1959). Motivational factors in the resolution of decisional conflict. In M. R. Jones (Ed.), *Nebraska symposium on motivation.* Lincoln University of Nebraska Press.

Janis, I. (1968). *Victims of groupthink.* New York: Harcourt Brace and Jovanovich.

Janis, I., & Fesbach, S. (1953). Effects of fear-arousing communication. *Journal of Abnormal and Social Psychology, 48,* 78–92.

Jay, M. (1973). *The dialectical imagination.* Boston: Little, Brown.

Jenkins, A. H. (1982). *The psychology of the Afro-American: A humanistic approach.* New York: Pergamon.

Jensen, A. R. (1969). How much can we boost IQ and scholastic achievement? *Harvard Educational Review, 39,* 1–123.

Joas, H. (1985). *G. H. Mead: A contemporary reexamination of his thought.* Cambridge, MA: MIT Press.

Johnson, J. B. (1922). *The Negro in Chicago.* Chicago: University of Chicago Press.

Jones, E. (1956). Prefatory note to issue on Freud. *British Journal for the Philosophy of Science, 7,* 1.

Jones, E. (1957). *The life and work of Sigmund Freud* (Vol. 3). New York: Basic Books.

Jones, E. E. (1985). Major developments in social psychology during the last five decades. In G. Lindzey & E. Aronson (Eds.), *Handbook of social psychology* (3d ed.). Vol. 1. New York: Random House.

Jones, E. E., & Davis, K. E. (1965). From acts to dispositions: The attribution process in person perception. In L. Berkowitz (Ed.), *Advances in experimental social psychology* (Vol. 2). New York: Academic Press.

Jones, E. E., Davis, K. E., & Gergen, K. J. (1961). Role playing variations and their informational value for person perception. *Journal of Abnormal and Social Psychology, 63,* 302–310.

Jones, E. E., & Gerard, H. B. (1967). *Foundations of social psychology.* New York: Wiley.

Jones, E. E., & Harris, V. A. (1967). The attribution of attitudes. *Journal of Experimental Social Psychology, 63,* 302–310.

Jones, E. E., & McGillis, D. (1976). Correspondent inferences and the attribution cube: A comparative reappraisal. In J. H. Harvey, W. J. Ickes, & R. F. Kidd (Eds.), *New directions in attribution research* (Vol. 1). Hillsdale, NJ: Lawrence Erlbaum.

Jones, E. E., & Nisbett, R. E. (1972). The actor and the observer: Divergent perceptions of the causes of behavior. In E. E. Jones, D. E. Kanouse, H. H. Kelley, R. S. Nisbett, S. Valins, & B. Weiner (Eds.), *Attribution: Perceiving the causes of behavior.* Morristown, NJ: General Learning Press.

Jones, E. E., Rock, L., Shaver, K. G., Goethals, G. R., & Ward, L. M. (1968). Pattern and performance and ability attribution: An expected primacy effect. *Journal of Personality and Social Psychology, 10,* 317–340.

Jones, L. (1980). *Great expectations: America and the baby boom generation.* New York: Ballantine.

Jones, R. A. (1987). Psychology, history, and the press: The case of William McDougall and *The New York Times. American Psychologist, 42,* 931–940.

Jones, R. L. (Ed.). (1972). *Black psychology.* New York: Harper & Row.

Jordan, N. (1953). Behavioral forces that are a function of attitudes and of cognitive organization. *Human Relations, 6,* 273–287.

Jung, C. G. (1953). *Collected works.* Princeton: Princeton University Press.

Kaluger, G., & Unkovic, C. M. (1969). *Psychology and sociology.* St. Louis: Mosby.

Karpf, F. B. (1932). *American social psychology.* New York: McGraw-Hill.

Karpf, F. B. (1952). American social psychology—1951. *American Journal of Sociology, 58,* 187–193.

Katz, D. (1978). Social psychology in relation to the social sciences: The second social psychology. *American Behavioral Scientist, 21,* 779–792.

Katz, D., & Braly, K. (1933). Racial stereotypes of one hundred college students. *Journal of Abnormal and Social Psychology, 28,* 280–290.

Katz, D., & Kahn, R. L. (1966). *The social psychology of organizations.* New York: Wiley.

Katz, D., & Schanck, R. (1938). *Social psychology.* New York: Wiley.

Kelley, H. H. (1960). Review of *The psychology of interpersonal relations* by F. Heider. *Contemporary psychology, 5,* 1–3.

Kelley, H. H. (1967). Attribution theory in social psychology. In D. Levine (Ed.), *Nebraska symposium on motivation.* Lincoln: University of Nebraska Press.

Kelley, H. H. (1972). *Casual schemata and the attribution process.* Morristown, NJ: General Learning.

Kelley, H. H., & Michela, J. (1980). Attribution theory and research. In M. Rosenzweig & L. Porter (Eds.), *Annual Review of Psychology,* Palo Alto, CA: Annual Reviews.

Kelley, H. H., & Thibaut, J. W. (1978). *Interpersonal relations: A theory of interdependence.* New York: Wiley.

Kelley, H. H., & Volkart, E. H. (1952). The resistance to change of group-anchored attitudes. *American Sociological Review, 17,* 453–465.

Kelman, H. C. (1968). *A time to speak: On human values and social research.* San Francisco: Jossey-Bass.

Kelman, H. C., & Hovland, C. I. (1953). "Reinstatement" of the communicators in delayed measurement of opinion change. *Journal of Abnormal and Social Psychology, 48,* 327–335.

Kemper, T. D. (1978). *A social interactional theory of emotions.* New York: Wiley-Interscience.

Kenny, A. J. P. (1973). *Wittgenstein.* Harmondsworth, England: Penguin.

Kessel, F. S., & Bevan, W. (1985). Notes toward a history of cognitive psychology. In C. E. Buxton (Ed.), *Points of view in the modern history of psychology.* Orlando: Academic Press.

Kiesler, C. A., Collins, B. E., & Miller, N. (1969). *Attitude change: A critical analysis of theoretical approaches.* New York: Wiley.

Kitzinger, C. (1987). *The social construction of lesbianism.* London: Sage.

Klineberg, O. (1940). *Social psychology.* New York: Holt.

Klineberg, O. (1954). *Social psychology* (2d ed.). New York: Holt, Rinehart & Winston.

Klineberg, O. (1986). SPSSI and race relations, in the 1950s and after. *Journal of Social Issues, 42(4),* 53–59.

Köhler, W. (1925). *The mentality of apes.* London: Pelican.

Konecni, V. J., & Ebbesen, E. B. (Eds.) (1982). *The criminal justice system: A social psychological analysis.* San Francisco: W. H. Freeman.

Kozulin, A. (1986). The concept of activity in Soviet psychology. *American Psychologist, 41,* 264–274.

Krech, D., & Crutchfield, R. S. (1948). *Theory and problems of social psychology.* New York: McGraw-Hill.

Kuhn, T. S. (1962). *The structure of scientific revolution.* Chicago: University of Chicago Press.

Kuhn, T. S. (1970). *The structure of scientific revolutions* (2d rev. ed.). Chicago: University of Chicago Press.

Kuo, Z. Y. (1921). Giving up instincts in psychology. *Journal Of Philosophy, 18,* 645–666.

Kurzweil, E. (1980). *The age of structuralism.* New York: Columbia University Press.

La Barre, W. (1958). The influence of Freud on anthropology. *American Imago, 15,* 275–328.

Lana, R. E. (1964). The influence of the pretest an order effects in persuasive communication. *Journal of Abnormal and Social Psychology, 69,* 337–341.

La Piere, R. T. (1934). Attitudes versus action. *Social Forces, 13,* 230–237.

La Piere, R. T., & Farnsworth, P. R. (1936). *Social psychology.* New York: McGraw-Hill.

Larsen, K. S. (Ed.). (1986). *Dialectics and ideology in psychology.* Norwood, NJ: Ablex.

Lasch, C. (1979). *The culture of narcissism: American life in an age of diminishing expectations.* New York: Norton.

Latané, B., & Darley, J. M. (1970). *The unresponsive bystander: Why doesn't he help?* New York: Appleton-Century-Crofts.

Lauer, R. H., & Handel, W. H. (1977). *Social psychology: The theory and application of symbolic interactionism.* Boston: Houghton Mifflin.

Leahey, T. H. (1987). *A history of psychology: Main currents in psychological thought* (2d ed.). Englewood Cliffs, NJ: Prentice-Hall.

Le Bon, G. (1977). *The crowd.* Middlesex, England: Penguin, 1977. (Original work published 1895.)

Lee, A. McC. (1986). Depression, war, SPSSI, and SSP. *Journal of Social Issues, 42(4),* 611–669.

Leeper, R. W. (1943). *Lewin's topological and*

*vector psychology: A digest and a critique,* Eugene: University of Oregon.

Lerner, M. J., & Miller, D. T. (1978). Just world research and the attribution process: Looking back and ahead. *Psychological Bulletin, 85,* 1030–1051.

Lerner, R. M. (1978). Nature, nurture, and dynamic interactionism. *Human Development, 21,* 1–20.

Leuchtenburg, W. E. (1979). *A troubled feast: American society since 1945.* Boston: Little, Brown.

Lewicki, P. (1982). Social psychology as viewed by its practitioners: Survey of SESF members' opinions. *Personality and Social Psychology Bulletin, 8,* 409–416.

Lewicki, P. (1986). *Nonconscious social information processing.* New York: Academic Press.

Lewin, K. (1935). *A dynamic theory of personality.* New York: McGraw-Hill.

Lewin, K. (1936). *Principles of topological psychology.* New York: McGraw-Hill.

Lewin, K. (1947). Group decision and social change. In T. M. Newcomb & E. L. Hartley (Eds.), *Readings in social psychology.* New York: Holt.

Lewin, K. (1948). *Resolving social conflicts: Selected papers on group dynamics.* New York: Harper.

Lewin, K. (1951). *Field theory in social science.* New York: Harper.

Lewin, K. (1986). "Everything within me rebels". A letter from Kurt Lewin to Wolfgang Köhler, 1933. *Journal of Social Issues, 42(4),* 39–47.

Lewin, K. Dembo, T. Festinger, L., & Sears, P. S. (1944). Level of aspiration. In J. McV. Hunt (Ed.), *Personality and behavior disorders* (Vol. 1). New York: Ronald Press.

Lewin, K., Lippitt, R., & White, R. K. (1939). Patterns of aggressive behavior in experimentally created "social climates." *Journal of Social Psychology, 1,* 271–299.

Lewin, M. (1987). Kurt Lewin and the invisible bird on the flagpole: A reply to Graebner. *Journal of Social Issues, 43,(3),* 123–139.

Lewis, H. (1944). An experimental study of the role of the ego in work. *Journal of Experimental Psychology, 34,* 113–126.

Lewis, L. J., & Smith, R. L. (1980). *American sociology and pragmatism: Mead, Chicago sociology and symbolic interaction.* Chicago: University of Chicago Press.

Likert, R. (1932–33). A technique for the measurement of attitudes. *Archives of psychology, 140,* 1–55.

Lindesmith, A. R., & Strauss, A. L. (1949). *So-cial psychology.* New York: Holt, Rinehart & Winston.

Lindesmith, A. R., Strauss, A. L., & Denzin, N. K. (1977). *Social psychology* (5th ed.). New York: Holt, Rinehart & Winston.

Lindzey, G., & Aronson, E. (1968). Preface to the second edition. In G. Lindzey & E. Aronson (Eds.), *Handbook of social psychology* (2d ed.). Vol. 1. Reading, MA: Addison-Wesley.

Linsky, L. (1967). Wittgenstein on language and some problems of philosophy. In K. T. Fann (Ed.), *Ludwig Wittgenstein: The man and his philosophy.* New York: Delta. (Original work published 1957.)

Liska, F. (1977). The dissipation of sociological social psychology. In L. H. Strickland, F. E. Aboud, & K. J. Gergen (Eds.), *Social psychology in transition.* New York: Plenum.

Lorenz, K. (1965). Introduction. In C. Darwin, *The expression of emotion in man and animals.* Chicago: University of Chicago Press.

Lorenz, K. (1966). *On aggression.* New York: Harcourt, Brace & World.

Lubek, I. (1974). Neutralizing the power structure in social psychology. In L. H. Strickland, F. E. Aboud, & K. J. Gergen (Eds.), *Social psychology in transition.* New York: Plenum.

Lubek, I. (1979). Aggression. In A. R. Buss (Ed.), *Psychology in social context.* New York: Irvington.

Lubek, I. (1980). The psychological establishment. In K. S. Larsen (Ed.), *Social psychology: Crisis or failure.* Monmouth. OR: Institute for Theoretical History.

Lubek, I. (1981). Histoire de psychologie social perdues: Le cas de Gabriel Tarde. *Revue Française de Sociologie, 22,* 361–398.

Lubek, I. (1986). Fifty years of frustration and aggression: Some historical notes on a long-held hypothesis. In K. S. Larsen (Ed.), *Dialectics and ideology in psychology.* Norwood, NJ: Ablex.

Lubek, I., & Apfelbaum, E. (1987). Neo-behaviorism and the Garcia effect: A social psychology of science approach to the history of a paradigm clash. In M. G. Ash & W. R. Woodward (Eds.), *Psychology in twentieth-century thought and society.* New York: Cambridge University Press.

Luria, A. R. (1979). *The making of mind: A personal account of Soviet psychology.* Cambridge, MA: Harvard University Press.

Lynd, R. S. (1939). *Knowledge for what?* Princeton, NJ: Princeton University Press.

Lynd, R. S., & Lynd, H. M. (1929). *Middletown.* New York: Harcourt Brace.

Lynd, R. S., & Lynd, H. M. (1937). *Middletown in transition.* New York: Harcourt Brace.

Lyotard, J.-F. (1984). *The postmodern condition.* Minneapolis: University of Minnesota Press.

Macpherson, C. B. (1962). *The political theory of possessive individualism.* London: Oxford University Press.

Maines, D. R. (1977). Social organization and social structure in symbolic interactionist thought. *Annual Review of Sociology, 3,* 235–257.

Malinowski, B. (1929). *The sexual life of savages in north-western Melanesia.* New York: Halcyon House.

Malinowski, B. (1953). *Sex and repression in savage society.* London: Routledge & Kegan Paul.

Malthus, T. R. (1798). *Essays on the principle of population.* London: J. Johnson.

Mandelbaum, M. (1971). *History, man and reason: A study in nineteenth century thought.* Baltimore: Johns Hopkins Press.

Mandler, G. (1968). *Perspectives in American history.* Cambridge, MA: Harvard University Press.

Manis, J. G., & Meltzer, B. N. (1978). *Symbolic interaction: A reader in social psychology* (3d ed.). Boston: Allyn & Bacon.

Manis, M. (1975). Comment's on Gergen's "Social psychology as History." *Personality and Social Psychology Bulletin, 1,* 450–455.

Mannheim, K. (1936). *Ideology and utopia: An introduction to the sociology of knowledge* (L. Wirth & E. A. Shils, Trans.). New York: Harcourt, Brace & World. (Original work published 1929.)

Markus, H., & Zajonc, R. B. (1985). The cognitive perspective in social psychology. In G. Lindzey & E. Aronson (Eds.), *Handbook of social psychology* (3d ed.). Vol. 1. New York: Random House.

Marrow, A. J. (1969). *The practical theorist: The life and work of Kurt Lewin.* New York: Basic Books.

Marsh, P., Rosser, E., & Harré, R. (1978). *The rules of disorder.* London: Routledge & Kegan Paul.

Marx, K. (1969). *German ideology* (trans S. Ryazanskaya). London: Lawrence. (Original work published 1844.)

Marx, K. (1906). *Capital* (Vol. 1–3). New York: Modern Library. (Original works published 1867, 1885, & 1894.)

Marx, K., & Engels, F. (1947). *The German ideology.* New York: International. (Original work published 1845–1847.)

Maslow, A. (1954). *Motivation and personality.* New York: Harper.

May, R. (1953). *Man's search for himself.* New York: Norton.

Mayer, A. (1903). Uber einzel- und gesamt-leistung des schulkindes. *Archiv fur die Gesamte Psychologie, 1,* 276–416.

Mayo, E. (1933). *The human problems of an industrial civilization.* New York: Macmillan.

McArthur, I. Z. (1972). The how and what of why: Some determinants and consequences of causal attributions. *Journal of Personality and Social Psychology, 22,* 171–193.

McCall, G. J., & Simmons, J. T. (1978). *Identities and interactions* (rev. ed.). New York: Free Press.

McDonald, A. (1972). Does required participation eliminate volunteer differences. *Psychological Reports, 31,* 153–154.

McDougall, W. (1908). *Introduction to social psychology.* London: Methuen.

McDougall, W. (1920). *The group mind.* New York: Putnam.

McDougall, W. (1921). *Is America safe for democracy?* New York: Scribners.

McDougall, W. (1923). *Outline of psychology.* New York: Scribners.

McDougall, W. (1926). *Outline of Abnormal Psychology.* New York: Scribners.

McDougall, W. (1930). Autobiography. In C. Murchinson (Ed.), *A history of psychology in autobiography* (Vol. 1). Worcester, MA: Clark University Press.

McDougall, W. (1936). *An introduction to social psychology* (23d ed.). New York: Putnam.

McGrath, J. E. (1978). Small group research. *American Behavioral Scientist, 21,* 651–673.

McGrath, J. E. (1980a). What are the social issues? Timeliness and treatment of topics in the Journal of Social Issues. *Journal of Social Issues, 36(4),* 98–108.

McGrath, J. E. (1980b). Social science, social action, and the Journal of Social Issues. *Journal of Social Issues, 36(4),* 109–124.

McGuinness, B. (Ed.). (1982). *Wittgenstein and his times.* Oxford: Blackwell.

McGuire, G. R. (1987). Pathological subconscious and irrational determinism in the social psychology of the crowd: The legacy of Gustave Le Bon. In W. J. Baker, M. E. Hyland H. Van Rappard & A. W. Staats (Eds.), *Current issues in theoretical psychology.* Amsterdam: Elsevier Science Publishers.

McGuire, W. J. (1964). Inducing resistance to persuasion: Some contemporary approaches. In L. Berkowitz (Ed.), *Advances in experimental social psychology,* (Vol. 1). New York: Academic Press.

McGuire, W. J. (1965). Discussion of William N. Schoenfeld's paper. In O. Klineberg & R.

Cristie (Eds.), *Perspectives in social psychology.* New York: Holt, Rinehart & Winston.

McGuire, W. J. (1967). Some impending reorientations in social psychology: Some thoughts provoked by Kenneth Ring. *Journal of Experimental Social Psychology, 3,* 124–139.

McGuire, W. J. (1968). Personality and susceptibility to social influence. In E. F. Borgatta & W. W. Lambert (Eds.), *Handbook of personality theory and research.* Chicago: Rand McNally.

McGuire, W. J. (1973). The yin and yang of progress in social psychology: Seven Koan. *Journal of Personality and Social Psychology, 26,* 446–456.

McGuire, W. J. (1983). A contextual theory of knowledge. In L. Berkowitz (Ed.), *Advances in experimental social psychology* (Vol. 16). New York: Academic Press.

McKinlay, A., & Potter, J. (1987). Social representations: A conceptual critique. *Journal for the Theory of Social Behaviour, 17,* 471–488.

McNemar, Q. (1946). Opinion-attitude methodology. *Psychological Bulletin, 43,* 289–374.

McPhail, C., & Rexroat, C. (1979). Mead vs. Blumer: The divergent methodological perspectives of social behaviorism and symbolic interaction. *American Sociological Review, 44,* 449–467.

Mead, G. H. (1932). *The philosophy of the present.* Chicago: University of Chicago Press.

Mead, G. H. (1934). *Mind, self and society.* Chicago: University of Chicago Press.

Mead, G. H. (1936). *Movements of thought in the nineteenth century.* Chicago: University of Chicago Press.

Mead, G. H. (1938). *The philosophy of the act.* Chicago: University of Chicago Press.

Mead, G. H. (1964). *Selected writings: George Herbert Mead.* (A. J. Reck, Ed.) Indianapolis: Bobbs-Merrill.

Mead, G. H. (1964). Social psychology as counterpart of physiological psychology. In A. J. Reck (Ed.), *Selected writings: George Herbert Mead.* Indianapolis: Bobbs-Merrill. (Original work published 1909.)

Mead, G. H. (1964). Scientific method and individual thinker. In A. J. Reck (Ed.), *Selected writings: George Herbert Mead.* Indianapolis: Bobbs-Merrill. (Original work published 1917.)

Mead, G. H. (1964). Scientific method and the moral science. In A. J. Reck (Ed.), *Selected writings: George Herbert Mead.* Indianapolis: Bobbs-Merrill. (Original work published 1923.)

Mead G. H. (1964). The nature of aesthetic experience. In A. J. Reck (Ed.), *Selected writings: George Herbert Mead.* Indianapolis: Bobbs-Merrill. (Original work published 1925–26.)

Mead, M. (1928). *Coming of age in Samoa.* New York: William Morrow.

Mead, M. (1942). *And keep your powder dry: An anthropologist looks at America.* New York: Morrow.

Mead, M. (1951). *Soviet attitudes toward authority.* New York: McGraw-Hill.

Meade, R. D. (1986). Experimental studies of authoritarian and democratic leadership in four cultures: American, Indian, Chinese, and Chinese American. *The High School Journal, 68,* 293–295.

Mednick, M. T. S. (1984). SPSSI, advocacy for social change, and the future: A historical look. *Journal of Social Issues, 40(3),* 159–177.

Mehrabian, A. (1980). *Basic dimensions for a general psychological theory.* Cambridge, MA: Oelgeschlager, Gunn & Hain.

Meltzer, B. N. (1964). Mead's social psychology. In J. G. Manis & B. N. Meltzer (Eds.). *Symbolic interaction: A reader in social psychology.* Boston: Allyn & Bacon.

Meltzer, B. N., Petras, J. W., & Reynolds, L. T. (1975). *Symbolic interaction: Genesis, varieties, and criticism.* London: Routledge & Kegan Paul.

Merleau-Ponty, M. (1962). *Phenomenology of perception* (C. Smith, Trans.). London: Routledge & Kegan Paul. (Original work published 1945.)

Merton, R. (1960). Introduction to G. Le Bon, *The crowd.* New York: Viking.

Milgram, S. (1963). Behavioral study of obedience. *Journal of Abnormal and Social Psychology, 67,* 371–378.

Milgram, S. (1964). Issues in the study of obedience: A reply to Baumrind. *American Psychologist, 19,* 848–852.

Milgram, S. (1974). *Obedience to authority: An experimental view.* New York: Harper & Row.

Miller, A. G. (Ed.). (1972). *The social psychology of psychological research.* New York: Free Press.

Miller, A. G. (1986). *The obedience experiments: A case study of controversy in social science.* New York: Praeger.

Miller, D. L. (1973). *George Herbert Mead: Self, language and the world.* Chicago: University of Chicago Press.

Miller, D. T. (1976). Ego-involvement and attributions for success and failure. *Journal of Personality and Social Psychology, 34,* 901–906.

Miller, D. T., & Ross, M. (1975). Self-serving biases in the attribution of causality: Fact or fiction? *Psychological Bulletin, 82,* 213–225.

Miller, G. A. (1969). Psychology as a means of promoting human welfare. *American Psychologist, 24,* 1063–1075.

Miller, G. A., Galanter, E., & Pribram, K. H. (1960). *Plans and the structure of behavior.* New York: Holt, Rinehart & Winston.

Miller, J. G. (11984). Culture and the development of everyday social explanations. *Journal of Personality and Social Psychology, 46,* 961–978.

Miller, N. E. (1941). Frustration-aggression hypothesis. *Psychological Review, 48,* 337–342.

Miller, N. E. (1944). Experimental studies in conflict. In J. McV. Hunt, *Personality and the behavior disorders* (Vol. 1). New York: Ronald Press.

Miller, N. E. (1948). Theory and experiment relating psychoanalytic displacement to stimulus-response generalization. *Journal of Abnormal and Social Psychology, 43,* 155–178.

Miller, N. E., & Dollard, J. (1941). *Social learning and imitation.* New Haven: Yale University Press.

Miller, P. (Ed.) (1954). *American thought: Civil War to World War I.* New York: Holt, Rinehart & Winston.

Mills, C. W. (1956). *The power elite.* New York: Oxford University Press.

Mills, C. W. (1966). *Sociology and pragmatism* (I. L. Horowitz, Ed.). New York: Paine-Whitman.

Minton, H. L. (1984). J. F. Brown's social psychology of the 1930s: A historical antecedent to the contemporary crisis in social psychology. *Personality and Social Psychology Bulletin, 10,* 31–42.

Minton, H. L. (1986). Emancipatory social psychology as a paradigm for the study of minority groups. In K. S. Larsen (Ed.), *Dialectics and ideology in psychology.* Norwood, NJ: Ablex.

Minton, H. L. (1988a). J. F. Brown: Unsung hero or misguided prophet in the history of political psychology. *Political Psychology, 9,* 165–173.

Minton, H. L. (1988b). *Lewis M. Terman: Pioneer in psychological testing.* New York: New York University Press.

Minton, H. L., & O'Neil, C.A. (1988). Kimball Young's social psychology: A precursor of social constructionism. *Personality and Social Psychology Bulletin, 14,* 554–564.

Mischel, W. (1968). *Personality and assessment.* New York: Wiley.

Moede, W. (1920). *Experimentelle Massenpsychologie.* Leipzig: Hirzel.

Moghaddam, F. M. (1987). Psychology in three worlds: As reflected by the crisis in social psychology and the move toward indigenous third-world psychology. *American Psychologist, 42,* 912–920.

Moore, G. E. (1967). Wittgenstein. In K. T. Fann (Ed.), *Ludwig Wittgenstein: The man and his philosophy.* New York: Delta. (Original work published 1942.)

Morawski, J. G. (1979). The structure of social psychological communities: A framework for examing the sociology of social psychology. In L. H. Strickland (Ed.), *Soviet and Western perspectives in social psychology.* New York: Pergamon.

Morawski, J. G. (1984). Historiography as a metatheoretical text for social psychology. In K. J. Gergen & M. M. Gergen (Eds.), *Historical social psychology.* Hillsdale, NJ: Lawrence Erlbaum.

Morawski, J. G. (1986a). Conceptual discipline: The unmasking and remaking of sociality. In R. L. Rosnow & M. Georgoudi (Eds.), *Contextualism and understanding in behavioral science.* New York: Praeger.

Morawski, J. G. (1986b). Psychologists for society and societies for psychologists: SPSSI's place among professional organizations. *Journal of Social Issues, 42(1),* 111–126.

Morawski, J. G., & Goldstein, S. E. (1985). Psychology and nuclear war: A chapter in our legacy of social responsibility. *American Psychologist, 40,* 276–284.

Moreno, J. L. (1934). *Who shall survive? A new approach to the problem of human interrelations.* Washington, DC: Nervous And Mental Disease Publishing House.

Morin, S. F. (1977). Heterosexual bias in psychological research on lesbianism and male homosexuality. *American Psychologist, 32,* 629–637.

Morris, C. W. (1962). Introduction to G. H. Mead, *Mind, self and society.* Chicago: University of Chicago Press.

Moscovici, S. (1961). *La psychanalyse, son image et son public.* Paris: Presses Universitaires de France.

Moscovici, S. (1972). Society and theory in social psychology. In J. Israel & H. Tajfel (Eds.), *The context of social psychology: A critical assessment.* London: Academic Press.

Moscovici, S. (1981). On social representations. In J. P. Forgas (Ed.), *Social cognition: Perspectives on everyday understanding.* London: Academic Press.

Moscovici, S. (1985). *The age of the crowd: a historical treatise on mass psychology* (J. C.

Whitehouse, Trans.). London: Cambridge University Press. (Original work published 1981.)

Mowrer, O. H. (1927). *Family disorganization.* Chicago: University of Chicago Press.

Mowry, G. E. (1965). *The urban nation 1920–1960.* New York: Hill & Wang.

Mueller, R. H. (1976). A chapter in the history of the relationship between psychology and sociology in America: James Mark Baldwin. *Journal of the History of the Behavioral Sciences, 12,* 240–253.

Murchison, C. A. (Ed.). (1935). *Handbook of social psychology.* Worcester, MA: Clark University Press.

Murphy, G. & Murphy, L. B. (1931). *Experimental social psychology.* New York: Harper.

Murphy, G., Murphy L. B., & Newcomb, T. M. (1937). *Experimental social psychology.* (rev. Ed.). New York: Harper.

Murray, S. O. (1988). W. I. Thomas, behaviorist ethnologist. *Journal of the History of the Behavioral Sciences, 24,* 381–391.

Myerson, A. (1934). *Social psychology.* New York: Prentice-Hall.

Nash, R. (1970). *The nervous generation: American thought, 1917–1930.* Chicago: Rand McNally.

Nathenson, M. (1966). *The social dynamics of George H. Mead.* The Hague: Martinus Nijhoff.

Neisser, U. (1967). *Cognitive psychology.* New York: Appleton-Century-Crofts.

Neisser, U. (1976). *Cognition and reality: Principles and implications of cognitive psychology.* San Francisco: Freeman.

Newcomb, T. M. (1943). *Personality and social change: Attitude formation in a student community.* New York: Holt.

Newcomb, T. M. (1950). *Social Psychology.* New York: Holt.

Newcomb, T. M. (1951). Social psychological theory: Integrating individual and social approaches. In J. H. Roher & M. Sherif (Eds.), *Social psychology at the crossroads.* New York: Harper.

Newcomb, T. M. (1953). An approach to the study of communicative acts. *Psychological Review, 60,* 393–404.

Newcomb, T. M. (1978). Individual and group. *American Behavioral Scientist, 21,* 631–650.

Newcomb, T. M. (1980). Introduction. In R. Evans, *The making of social psychology: Discussions with creative contributors.* New York: Gardner.

Newcomb, T. M., Turner, R. H., & Converse, P. E. (1965). *Social psychology: The study of human interaction.* New York: Holt, Rinehart & Winston.

Nicholson, I., & Minton, H. L. (1989). *Goodwin Watson's social psychology: Carrying on the Deweyan tradition.* Paper presented at the meeting of the Canadian Psychological Association, Halifax, Nova Scotia.

Nisbett, R. E., & Borcida, E. (1975). Attribution and the psychology of prediction. *Journal of Personality and Social Psychology, 32,* 932–943.

Nisbett, R. E., Caputo, C., Legant, P., & Marecek, J. (1976). Popular induction: Information is not always informative. In J. S. Carroll & J. W. Payne (Eds.), *Cognitive and social behavior.* Hillsdale, NJ: Lawrence Erlbaum.

Oberschall, A. (1972). The institutionalization of American sociology. In A. Oberschall (Ed.), *The establishment of empirical sociology.* New York: Harper & Row.

O'Donnell, J. M. (1985). *The origin of behaviorism: American psychology, 1870–1920.* New York: New York University Press.

Orne, M. T. (1962). On the social psychology of the psychological experiment: With particular reference to demand characteristics and their implications. *American Psychologist, 17,* 776–783.

Osgood, C. E., Suci, G. J., & Tannenbaum, P. H. (1957). *The measurement of meaning.* Urbana: University of Illinois Press.

Osgood, C. E., & Tannenbaum, P. H. (1955). The principle of congruity in the prediction of attitude change. *Psychological Review, 62,* 42–55.

Paicheler, G. (1988). *The psychology of social influence: Constraint, conviction and persuasion.* New York: Cambridge University Press.

Park, R. E. (1915). The city: Suggestions for the investigation of human behavior in the city environment. *American Journal of Sociology, 20,* 577–612.

Park, R. (Ed.). (1939). *An outline of the principles of sociology.* New York: Barnes & Noble.

Park, R. E., & Burgess, E. W. (1921). *Introduction to the science of sociology.* Chicago: University of Chicago Press.

Park, R. E., & Miller, H. A. (1921). *Old world traits transplanted.* New York: Harper.

Parker I. (1987). "Social representations": Social psychology's (mis)use of sociology. *Journal for the Theory of Social Behaviour, 17,* 447–469.

Parker, I. (1989a). Discourse and power. In J. Shotter & K. J. Gergen (Eds.), *Texts of identity.* London: Sage.

Parker, I. (1989b). *The crisis in modern social*

*psychology—and how to end it.* London: Routledge.

Patnoe, S. (1988). *A narrative history of experimental social psychology: The Lewin tradition.* New York: Springer-Verlag.

Pears, D. (1971). *Wittgenstein.* London: Fontana Collins.

Peirce, C. (1972). How to make our ideas clear. In C. S. Peirce, *The essential writings.* New York: Harper & Row (Original work published 1868.)

Peirce, C. (1972). What Pragmatism is. In C. S. Peirce, *The essential writings.* New York: Harper & Row (Original work published 1905–1906.)

Peel, J. D. Y. (1971). *Herbert Spencer: The evolution of sociology.* London: Heinemann.

Pells, R. H. ((1973). *Radical vision and American dreams: Cultural and social thought in the Depression years.* Middletown, CN: Wesleyan University Press.

Pells, R. H. (1985). *The liberal mind in a conservative age: American intellectuals in the 1940s and 1950s.* New York: Harper & Row.

Pepitone, A. (1976). Toward a normative and comparative biocultural social psychology. *Journal of Personality and Social Psychology, 34,* 641–653.

Pepitone, A. (1981). Lessons from the history of social psychology. *American Psychologist, 36,* 972–985.

Perlman, D. (1979). Eight social psychology texts: A citation analysis. *Canadian Psychological Review, 20,* 38–47.

Perry, H. S. (1982). *Psychiatrist of America: The life of Harry Stack Sullivan.* Cambridge, MA: Harvard University Press.

Perry, R. B. (1935). *The thought and character of William James.* New York: Harper.

Peterson, R. C., & Thrustone, L. L. (1933). *Motion pictures and the social attitudes of children.* New York: Macmillan.

Pettigrew, T. F. (1964a). *A profile of the Negro American.* Princeton, NJ: Van Nostrand.

Pettigrew, T. F. (1964b). Negro American personality: Why isn't more known? *Journal of Social Issues, 20(2),* 4–23.

Pettigrew, T. F. (1988). Influencing policy with social psychology. *Journal of Social Issues, 44(2),* 205–219.

Petty, R. E., & Cacioppo, J. T. (1981). *Attitudes and persuasion: Classic and contemporary approaches.* Dubuque, IA: William C. Brown.

Pitcher, G. (1967). Wittgenstein, nonsense and Lewis Carroll. In K. T. Fann (Ed.), *Ludwig Wittgenstein: The man and his philosophy.*

New York: Delta. (Original work published 1965.)

Post, D. L. (1980). Floyd H. Allport and the launching of modern social psychology. *Journal of the History of the Behavioral Sciences, 16,* 369–376.

Potter, D. (1954). *People of plenty: Economic abundance and the American character.* Chicago: University of Chicago Press.

Potter, J., & Wetherell, M. (1987). *Discourse and social psychology.* London: Sage.

Price, K. O., Harburg, E., & Newcomb, T. M. (1966). Psychological balance in situations of negative interpersonal attitudes. *Journal of Personality and Social Psychology, 3,* 265–270.

Prilleltensky, I. (1989). Psychology and the status quo. *American Psychologist, 44,* 795–802.

Pruitt, D. G., & Kimmel, M. J. (1977). Twenty years of experimental gaming: Critique, synthesis, and suggestions for the future. *Annual Review of Psychology* (Vol. 28). Palo Alto, CA: Annual Reviews.

Purcell, E. (1973). *The crisis of democratic theory: Scientific naturalism and the problem of value.* Lexington: University of Kentucky Press.

Pychyl, T. A. (1988). *Social psychology's first "crisis": An historical perspective of the emergence of experimental social psychology.* Unpublished manuscript, Carlton University, Ottawa, Ontario.

Pychyl, T. A., & Cherry, F. (1989). *The rhetoric of change: Experimental social psychology from 1910–1930.* Paper presented at the annual meeting of the Canadian Psychological Association, Halifax, Nova Scotia.

Quandt, J. B. (1973). *From the small town to the great community: The social thought of progressive intellectuals.* New Brunswick, NJ: Rutgers University Press.

Quine, W. V. O. (1960). *Word and object.* Cambridge, MA: MIT Press.

Raven, B. H., and Rubin, J. Z. (1983). *Social psychology* (2d ed.). New York: Wiley.

Reckless, W. C. (1933). *Vice in Chicago.* Chicago: University of Chicago Press.

Regan, D. T. (1978). Attributional aspects of interpersonal attraction. In J. H. Harvey, W. J. Ickes, & R. F. Kidd (Eds.), *New directions in attribution research.* (Vol. 2). Hillsdale, NJ: Lawrence Erlbaum.

Regan, D. T. & Totten, J. (1975). Empathy and attribution: Turning observers into actors. *Journal of Personality and Social Psychology, 32,* 850–856.

Reich, W. (1976). *The mass psychology of*

*facism* (V. R. Carfango, Trans.). New York: Pocket Books. (Original work published 1931.)

Reich, W. (1946). *Character analysis.* New York: Simon & Schuster. (Original work published 1933.)

Reisman, D. (1956). *The lonely crowd.* New Haven: Yale University Press.

Ring, K. (1967). Experimental social psychology: Some sober questions about some frivolous values. *Journal of Experimental Social Psychology, 3,* 113–123.

Roberts, B. (1977). George Herbert Mead: The theory and practice of social psychology. *Ideology and Consciousness, 2,* 81–106.

Roethlisberger, F. J. (1941). *Management and Morale.* Cambridge, MA: Harvard University Press.

Roethlisberger, F. J., & Dickson, W. J. (1939). *Management and the worker: An account of a research program conducted by the Western Electric Company, Hawthorne Works, Chicago.* Cambridge, MA: Harvard University Press.

Rogers, C. R. (1951). *Client-centered therapy: Its current practice, implications, and theory.* Boston: Houghton Mifflin.

Rommetviet, R. (1968). *Words, meaning and messages.* New York: Academic Press.

Rommerviet, R. (1972). Language games, syntactic structure and hermeneutics. In J. Israel & H. Tajfel (Eds.), *The context of social psychology: A critical assessment.* London: Academic Press.

Rommetviet, R. (1974). *On message structure: A framework for the study of language and communication.* London: Wiley.

Rorty, R. (1979). *Philosophy and the mirror of nature.* Princeton, NJ: Princeton University Press.

Rosenberg, M. J. (1960). Analysis of affective-cognition consistency. In M. J. Rosenberg, C. I. Hovland, W. J. McGuire, R. P. Abelson, & J. W. Brehem (Eds.), *Attitude organization and change.* New Haven, Yale University Press.

Rosenberg, M. J. (1965). When dissonance fails: On eliminating evaluation apprehension from attitude measurement. *Journal of Personality and Social Psychology, 1,* 28–42.

Rosenberg, M. J. (1968). Hedonism, inauthenticity, and other goals toward expansion at a consistency theory. In R. P. Abelson, E. Aronson, W. J. McGuire, T. M. Newcomb, M. J. Rosenberg, & P. H. Tannenbaum (Eds.). *Theories of cognitive consistency.* Chicago: Rand McNally.

Rosenberg, M. J. (1969). the conditions and consequences of evaluation apprehension. In R. Rosenthal & R. L. Rosnow (Eds.), *Artifact in behavioral research.* New York: Academic Press.

Rosenberg, M. J. (1970). The experimental parable of inauthenticity: consequences of counter attitudinal performance. In J. S. Antrobus (Ed.), *Cognition and affect.* Boston: Little, Brown.

Rosenberg, M. J., & Abelson, R. P. (1960). An analysis of cognitive balancing. In M. J. Rosenberg, C. I. Hovland, W. J. McGuire, R. P. Abelson, & J. W. Brehem (Eds.), *Attitude organization and change: an analysis of consistency among attitude components.* New Haven: Yale University Press.

Rosenberg, M. J., Hovland, C. I., McGuire, W. J., Abelson, R. P. & Brehm, J. W. (Eds.). (1960). *Attitude organization and change: An analysis of consistency among attitude components.* New Haven: Yale University Press.

Rosenthal, R. (1966). *Experimenter effects in behavioral research.* New York: Appleton-Century-Crofts.

Rosenthal, R., & Rosnow, R. (1969). The volunteer subject. In R. Rosenthal & R. Rosnow (Eds.), *Artifact in behavioral research.* New York: Academic Press.

Rosenzweig, M. R., Bennett, E. L., Diamond, M. C., Wu, S. Y., Slagle, R. W., & Saffran, E. (1969). Influence of environmental complexity and visual stimulation on development of occipital cortex in rats. *Brain Research, 14,* 427–445.

Rosenzweig, S. (1933). The experimental situation as a psychological problem. *Psychological Review, 40,* 337–354.

Rosnow, R. L. (1981). *Paradigms in transition: The methodology of social inquiry.* New York: Oxford University Press.

Rosenow, R. L., & Georgoudi, M. (1986). The spirit of contextualism. In R. L. Rosnow & M. Georgoudi (Eds.), *Contextualism and understanding in behavioral science.* New York: Praeger.

Ross, D. (1972) *G. Stanley Hall: The psychologist as prophet.* Chicago: University of Chicago Press.

Ross, D. (1978). American psychology and psychoanalysis: William James and G. Stanley Hall. In J. M. Quen & E. T. Carlson (Eds.), *American psychoanalysis: Origins and development.* New York: Brunner/ Mazel.

Ross, E. A. (1901). *Social control.* New York Macmillan.

Ross, E. A. (1908). *Social psychology: An outline and source book.* New York: Macmillan.

Ross, E. A. (1936). *Seventy years of it.* New York: Appleton-Century.

Ross, L. (1977). The intuitive psychologist and his short-comings: Distortions in the attribution process. In L. Berkowitz (Ed.), *Advances in experimental social psychology.* (Vol. 10). New York: Academic Press.

Ross, L., Greene, D., & House, P. (1977). The false consensus effect: An egocentric bias in social perception. *Journal of Experimental Social Psychology, 13,* 279–301.

Ross, L., Lepper, M. R., & Hubbard, M. (1975). Perseverance in self perception and social perception: Biased attributional processes in the debriefing paradigm. *Journal of Personality and Social Psychology, 32,* 880–892.

Royce, J. (1895). Preliminary report on imitation. *Psychological Review, 2,* 363–367.

Rucker, D. (1969). *The Chicago pragmatists.* Minneapolis: University of Minnesota Press.

Rule, B. G., & Nesdale, A. R. (1976). Emotional arousal and aggressive behavior. *Psychological Bulletin, 83,* 851–863.

Rushton, J. P. (1988). Race differences in behavior: A review and evolutionary analysis. *Journal of Personality and Individual Differences, 9,* 1009–1024.

Rushton, J. P. (1989). *Evolutionary biology and heritable traits.* Paper presented at the meeting of the American Association for the Advancement of Science, San Francisco.

Russell, B. (1967). Ludwig Wittgenstein. In K. T. Fann (Ed.), *Ludwig Wittgenstein: The man and his philosophy.* New York: Delta. (Original work published 1951.)

Rychlak, J. F. (1976). Can psychology be objective about free will? *Philosophical Psychologist, 10,* 2–9.

Sahakian, W. S. (1982). *History and systems of social psychology* (2nd ed.). New York: McGraw-Hill.

Sahlins, M. (1976). *The use and abuse of biology: An anthropological critique of sociobiology.* Ann Arbor: University of Michigan Press.

Samelson, F. (1974). History, origin myth, and ideology: Comte's "discovery" of social psychology. *Journal for Theory of Social Behaviour, 4,* 217–231.

Samelson, F. (1978). From "race psychology" to "studies in prejudice": Some observations on the thematic reversal in social psychology. *Journal of the History of the Behavioral Sciences, 14,* 265–278.

Samelson, F. (1980). J. B. Watson's Little Albert, Cyril Burt's twins and the need for a critical science. *American Psychologist, 35,* 619–625.

Samelson, F. (1981). Struggle for scientific authority: The reception of Watson's behaviorism, 1913–1920. *Journal of the History of the Behavioral Sciences, 17,* 399–425.

Samelson, F. (1985a). *On behaviorism and its competitors, 1930–1950: The case of the conflict model.* Paper presented at the meeting of the Cheiron Society, Philadelphia.

Samelson, F. (1985b). Organizing for the kingdom of behavior: Academic battles and organizational policies in the twenties. *Journal of the History of the Behavioral Sciences, 21,* 33–47.

Samelson, F. (1986a). Authoritarianism from Berlin to Berkeley: On social psychology and history. *Journal of Social Issues, 42(1),* 191–208.

Samelson, F. (1986b). *On behaviorism and its competitors, 1930–1950: 2, Stability and turbulence in 1935.* Paper presented at the annual meeting of the Cheiriron Society, Guelph, Ontario, June.

Sampson, E. E. (1975). On justice as equality. *Journal of Social Issues, 31(3),* 45–64.

Sampson, E. E. (1977). Psychology and the American ideal. *Journal of Personality and Social Psychology, 35,* 767–782.

Sampson, E. E. (1978). Scientific paradigms and social values: Wanted—A scientific revolution. *Journal of Personality and Social Psychology, 36,* 1332–1343.

Sampson, E. E. (1981). Cognitive psychology as ideology. *American Psychologist, 36,* 730–743.

Sampson, E. E. (1983). Deconstructing psychology's subject. *Journal of Mind and Behavior, 4,* 135–164.

Sampson, E. E. (1989). The deconstruction of the self. In J. Shotter & K. J. Gergen (Eds.), *Texts of identity.* London: Sage.

Sarason, S. B. (1981). *Psychology misdirected.* New York: Free Press.

Sarason, S. B. (1988). *The making of an American psychologist: An autobiography.* San Francisco: Jossey Bass.

Sargent, S. S., & Harris, B. (1986). Academic freedom, civil liberties, and SPSSI. *Journal of Social Issues, 42(1),* 43–67.

Sartre, J.-P. (1956). *Being and nothingness* (H. Barnes, Trans.). New York: Philosophical Library.

Schachter, S. (1959). *The psychology of affiliation.* Stanford, CA: Stanford University Press.

Schachter, S., & Singer, J. E. (1962). Cognitive, social and physiological determinants of emotinial state. *Psychological Review, 69,* 379–399.

Scheibe, K. E. (1979). *Mirrors masks lies and secrets: The limits of human predictability.* New York: Praeger.

Scheibe, K. E. (1985). Historical perspectives on the presented self. In B. R. Schlenker (Ed.), *The self and social life.* New York: McGraw-Hill.

Scheibe, K. E. (1988). Metamorphoses in the psychologist's advantage. In J. G. Morawski (Ed.), *The rise of experimentation in American Psychology.* New Haven: Yale University Press.

Schneider, D. J., Hastorf, A. H., & Ellsworth, P. C. (1977). *Person perception* (2d ed.). Reading, MA: Addison-Wesley.

Schrecker, E. W. (1986). *No ivory tower: McCarthyism and the universities.* New York: Oxford University Press.

Schur, E. (1976). *The awareness trap: Self-absorption instead of social change.* New York: New York Times Press.

Schutz, A. (1967). *The phenomenology of the social world* (G. Walsh & F. Lehnert, Trans.). Evanston IL: Northwestern University Press. (Original work published 1932.)

Sears, R. R. (1951). A theoretical framework for social behavior and personality development. *American Psychologist, 6,* 476–482.

Secord, P. F., & Backman, C. W. (1964). *Social psychology.* New York: McGraw-Hill.

Secord, P. F., Backman, C. W., & Slavitt, P. R. (1976). *Understanding social life: An introduction to social psychology.* New York: McGraw-Hill.

Severy, L. J. (1979). Graduate research training internships in social psychology. *Personality and Social Psychology Bulletin, 5,* 507–510.

Sharaf, M. (1983). *Fury on earth: A biography of Wilhelm Reich.* New York: St. Martin's Press.

Shaskolsky, L. (1970). The development of sociological theory in America—A sociology of knowledge interpretation. In L. T. Reynolds & J. M. Reynolds (Eds.), *The sociology of sociology.* New York: McKay.

Shaw, M. E., & Costanzo, P. R. (1982). *Theories of social psychology* (2d ed.). New York: McGraw-Hill.

Sherif, C. W. (1979). Bias in psychology. In J. A. Sherman & E. T. Beck (Eds.), *The prism of sex: Essays in the sociology of knowledge.* Madison: University of Wisconsin Press.

Sherif, M. (1936). *The psychology of social norms.* New York: Harper.

Sherif, M., & Hovland, C. I. (1961). *Social judgment: Assimilation and contrast effects in communication and attitude change.* New Haven: Yale University Press.

Sherif, M., & Sherif, C. W. (1953). *Groups in harmony and tension: An integration of studies on intergroup relations.* New York: Octagon.

Shotter, J. (1984). *Social accountability and selfhood.* Oxford: Blackwell.

Shotter, J., & Gergen, K. J. (Eds.). (1989). *Texts of identity.* London: Sage.

Sidis, B. (1989). *Psychology of suggestion: Research into the subconscious nature of man and society.* New York: Appleton.

Small, W. W. (1905). *General sociology.* Chicago: University of Chicago Press.

Smith, A. (1937). *An inquiry into the nature and causes of the wealth of nations.* New York: Random House. (Original work published 1776.)

Smith, M. B. (1974). *Humanizing social psychology.* San Francisco: Jossey-Bass.

Smith, M. B. (1978). Psychology and values. *Journal of Social Issues, 34(4),* 181–199.

Smith, M. B. (1986a). Kurt Lewin memorial address, 1986: War, peace, and psychology. *Journal of Social Issues, 42(4),* 23–38.

Smith, M. B. (1986b). McCarthyism: A personal account. *Journal of Social Issues, 42(4),* 71–80.

Smith, S. S., Richardson, D., & Hendrick, C. (1980). Bibliography of journal articles in personality and social psychology: 1979. *Personality and Social Psychology Bulletin, 6,* 606–636.

Snyder, M., & Swann, W. B. (1978). Behavioral confirmation in social interaction: From social perception to social reality. *Journal of Experimental Social Psychology, 14,* 148–162.

Snyder, M., Tanke, E. D., & Berscheid, E. (1977). Social perception and interpersonal behavior: On the self-fulfilling nature of social stereotypes. *Journal of Personality and Social Psychology, 35,* 656–666.

Sombart, W. (1976). *Why is there no socialism in the United States?* White Plains, NY: International Arts and Science Press. (Originally published in 1906.)

Soule, G. (1931, January). Hard-boiled radicalism. *The New Republic,* Vol. LXV.

Spencer, H. (1870). *The principles of psychology,* London: Williams & Norgate.

Spencer, H. (1961). *The study of sociology.* Ann Arbor: University of Michigan Press. (Original work published 1873.)

Spencer, H. (1876). *Principles of sociology* (2 vols.). New York: Appleton.

Sprott, W. J. H. (1952). *Social psychology.* London: Methuen.

Stam, H. J. (1990). Rebuilding the ship at sea:

The historical and theoretical problems of constructionist epistemologies in psychology. *Canadian Psychology, 31,* 239–253.

Steiner, I. D. (1974). Whatever happened to the group in social psychology? *Journal of Experimental Social Psychology, 10,* 94–108.

Steiner, I. D. (1986). Paradigms and groups. In L. Berkowitz (Ed.), *Advances in experimental social psychology* (Vol. 19). Orlando: Academic Press.

Stephenson, G. M. (1988). Applied social psychology. In M. Hewstone, W. Stroebe, J.-P. Codol, & G. W. Stephenson (Eds.), *Introduction to social psychology.* Oxford: Blackwell.

Stoddard, T. L. (1920). *The rising tide of color against white world-supremacy.* New York: Scribners.

Stone, G. P., & Farberman, H. A. (1967). On the edge of reapproachement: Was Durkheim moving toward the perspective of symbolic interaction? *Sociological Quarterly, 8,* 149–164.

Stone, G. P., & Farberman, H. A. (Eds.). (1970). *Social psychology through symbolic interaction.* Waltham, MA: Xerox College Publishing.

Stone, W. F., & Finison, L. J. (1980). The social psychology of J. F. Brown: Radical field theory. *Journal of Mind and Behavior, 1,* 73–84.

Storms, M. D. (1973). Videotape and the attribution process: Reversing actors' and observers' point of view. *Journal of Personality and Social Psychology, 27,* 165–175.

Stouffer, S. A., Suchman, E. A., De Vinney, L. C., Star, S. A., & Williams, R. B., Jr. (1949). *The American soldier: Adjustment during army life* (Studies in social psychology in World War II, Vol. 1). Princeton, NJ: Princeton University Press.

Strauss, A. (Ed.). (1956). *George Herbert Mead on social psychology: Selected papers.* Chicago: University of Chicago Press.

Strauss, A. (1978). *Negotiations: Varieties, contexts, processes and social order.* San Francisco: Jossey-Bass.

Strauss, A, Schatzman, L., Ehrlich, D., Bucher, R., & Sabshin, M. (1963). The hospital and its negotiated order. In E. Friedson (Ed.), *The hospital in modern society.* New York: Free Press.

Stroebe, W., & Kruglanski, A. W. (1989). Social psychology at epistemological cross-roads: On Gergen's choice. *European Journal of Social Psychology, 19,* 485–489.

Stryker, S. (1980). *Symbolic interactionism: A so-cial psychological version.* Menlo Park, CA: Benjamin/Cummings.

Stryker, S. (1981). Symbolic interactionism: Themes and variations. In M. Rosenberg & R. H. Turner (Eds.), *Social psychology: Sociological perspectives.* New York: Basic Books.

Stryker, S. (1987). The vitalization of symbolic interactionism. *Social Psychology Quarterly, 50,* 83–94.

Stryker, S., & Gottlieb, A. (1981). Attribution theory and symbolic interactionism: A comparison. In J. H. Harvey, W. Ickes, & R. F. Kidd (Eds.), *New directions in attribution theory* (Vol. 1). Hillsdale, NJ: Lawrence Erlbaum.

Stryker, S., & Statham, A. (1985). Symbolic interaction and role theory. In G. Lindzey & E. Aronson (Eds.), *Handbook of social psychology* (3d ed.). Vol. 1. New York: Random House.

Sullivan, E. V. (1984). *A critical psychology.* New York: Plenum.

Sullivan, H. S. (1953). *The interpersonal theory of psychiatry.* New York: Norton.

Sulloway, F. J. (1979). *Freud, biologist of the mind.* London: Burnett Books.

Suls, J. M., & Rosnow, R. L. (1988). Concerns about artifacts in psychological experiments. In J. G. Morawski (Ed.), *The rise of experimentation in American psychology.* New Haven: Yale University Press.

Summer, W. G. (1906). *Folkways.* Boston: Ginn.

Tarde, G. (1903). *Laws of imitation.* New York: Holt. (Original work published 1890.)

Taylor, S. E. (1978). A developing role for social psychology in medicine and medical practice. *Personality and Social Psychology Bulletin, 4,* 515–523.

Taylor, S. E. (1981). The interface of cognitive and social psychology. In J. H. Harvey (Ed.), *Cognition, social behavior, and the environment.* Hillsdale, NJ: Lawrence Erlbaum.

Terman, L. M. (1904). A preliminary study of the psychology and pedagogy of leadership. *Pedagogical Seminary, 11,* 413–451.

Thibaut, J. W., & Kelley, H. H. (1950). *The social psychology of groups.* New York: Wiley.

Thomas, W. I. (1904). The psychology of race-prejudice. *American Journal of Sociology, 9,* 593–611.

Thomas, W. I., & Thomas, D. S. (1938). *The child in America.* New York: Knopf.

Thomas, W. I., & Znaniecki, F. (1918–1920). *The Polish peasant in Europe and America* (5 vols.) Boston: Badger.

Thorndike, E. L. (1913). *The original nature of man.* New York: Columbia University Press.

Thrasher, F. M. (1927). *The gang.* Chicago: University of Chicago Press.

Thurstone, L. L. (1928). Attitudes can be measured. *American Journal of Sociology, 33,* 529–554.

Tindall, G. B. (1984). *America, A narrative history.* New York: Norton. (Original work published 1927.)

Tolman, C. W., & Piekkola, B. (1989). Anticipations of activity theory in the critique of the reflex arc concept. *Activity Theory, 3/4,* 43–46.

Tolman, E. C. (1922). Can instincts be given up in psychology? *Journal of Abnormal Psychology, 17,* 139–152.

Tolman, E. C. (1923). The nature of instincts. *Psychological Bulletin, 20,* 200–218.

Totsi, G. (1902). Baldwin's social ethical interpretations. *Science, 25,* 551–553.

Triandis, H. C., & Lambert, W. W. (Eds.). (1980). *Handbook of cross-cultural psychology.* Boston: Allyn & Bacon.

Triplett, N. (1898). The dynamogenic factors in pacemaking and competition. *American Journal of Psychology, 9,* 507–533.

Trivers, R. L. (1971). The evolution of reciprocal altruism. *Quarterly Review of Biology, 46,* 35–57.

Trotter, W. (1908). Herd instinct and its bearing on the psychology of civilized man. *Sociological Review, 1,* 227–248.

Turner, J. H. (1978). *The structure of sociological theory.* Homewood, IL: Dorsey.

Turner, R. (1978). The role and the person. *American Journal of Sociology, 84,* 1–23.

Turner, R. H. (1976). The real self: From institution to impulse. *American Journal of Sociology, 81,* 989–1016.

Unger, R. K. (1983). Through the looking glass: No wonderland yet! (The reciprocal relationship between methodology and models of reality). *Psychology of Women Quarterly, 8,* 9–32.

Unger, R. K. (1989a). Introduction. In R. K. Unger (Ed.), *Representations: Social constructions of gender.* Amityville, NY: Baywood.

Unger, R. K. (1989b) (ed.). *Representations: Social constructions of gender.* Amityville, NY: Baywood.

van Ginneken, J. (1985). The 1895 debate on the origins of crowd psychology. *Journal of the History of the Behavioral Sciences, 21,* 375–382.

van Ginneken, J. (1988). Outline of a cultural history of political psychology. In W. F. Stone & P. E. Schaffner, *The psychology of politics* (2d ed.). New York: Springer-Verlag.

van Ginneken, J. (1989). *Crowds, psychology and politics, 1871–1899.* Unpublished doctoral dissertation, University of Amsterdam.

Veblen, T. (1899). *The theory of the leisure class.* New York: Macmillan.

von Hartmann, E. (1931). *Philosophy of the unconscious.* London: Kegan Paul (Originally Published, 1868.)

von Wright, G. H. (1967). A biographical sketch. In K. T. Fann (Ed.), *Ludwig Wittgenstein: The man and his philosophy.* New York: Delta. (Original work published 1955.)

von Wright, G. H. (1982). Wittgenstein in relation to his times. In B. McGuinness (Ed.), *Wittgenstein and his times.* Oxford: Blackwell.

Vygotsky, L. S. (1962). *Thought and language* (E. Hanfmann & G. Vakar, Trans.). Cambridge, MA: MIT Press. (Original work published 1934.)

Wallace, J. (1971). *Psychology: A social science.* Philadelphia: Saunders.

Wallach, M., & Wallach, L. (1983). *Psychology's sanction for selfishness: The error of egotism in theory and therapy.* San Francisco: Freeman.

Wallas, G. (1908). *Human nature & politics.* London: Constable.

Walster, E. (1966). Assignment of responsibility for accidents. *Journal of Personality and Social Psychology, 3,* 73–79.

Walster, E., Berscheid, E., & Walster, G. W. (1973). New directions in equity research. *Journal of Personality and Social Psychology, 25,* 151–176.

Ward, L. (1884). Mind as a social factor. *Mind, 9,* 563–573.

Warner, W. L., & Lunt, P. S. (1941). *The social life of a modern community.* New Haven: Yale University Press.

Watson, G. (1937). Orientation: *Social Frontier, 4,* 20–26.

Watson, G. (1942). *Civilian morale: Second yearbook of the Society for the Psychological Study of Social Issues.* Boston: Houghton Mifflin.

Watson, J. B. (1913). Psychology as the behaviorist views it. *Psychological Review, 20,* 158–177.

Watson, J. B. (1914). *Behavior: An introduction to comparative pshchology.* New York: Holt.

Watson, J. B., & Rayner, R. (1920). Conditioned emotional reactions. *Journal of Experimental Psychology, 3,* 1–14.

Webb. E. J., Campbell, D. T., Schwartz, R. D., Sechrest, L., & Grove, J. B. (1981). *Nonreactive measures in the social sciences* (2d ed.). Boston: Houghton Mifflin.

Weber, M. (1958). *The Protestant ethic and the spirit of capitalism* (T. Parsons, Trans.). New York: Scribner. (Original work published 1904–1905.)

Weber, M. (1968). *Economy and society.* New York: Bedminister.

Weeks, J. (1985). *Sexuality and its discontents.* London: Routledge & Kegan Paul.

Weiner, B., & Kukla, A. (1970). An attributional analysis of achievement motivation. *Journal of Personality and Social Psychology, 15,* 1–20.

Weizmann, F., Weiner, N. I., Weisenthal, D. L., & Zeigler, M. (1990). Differential K theory and racial hierarchies. *Canadian Psychology, 31,* 1–13.

Wertsch, J. V. (1979). From social interaction to higher psychological processes: A clarification and application of Vygotsky's theory. *Human Development, 22,* 1–22.

Wexler, P. (1983). *Critical social psychology.* Boston: Routledge & Kegan Paul.

White, M. (1943). *The origin's of Dewey's instrumentalism.* New York: Columbia University Press.

White, M. (1957). *Social thought in America: The revolt against formalism.* Boston: Beacon.

White, M. (1973). *Pragmatism and the American mind.* New York: Oxford University Press.

White, R. K. (1978). Has "field theory" been "tried and found wanting"? *Journal of the History of the Behavioral Sciences, 14,* 242–246.

Whyte, L. L. (1960). *The unconscious before Freud.* New York: Basic Books.

Whyte, W. F. (1943). *Street corner society.* Chicago: University of Chicago Press.

Whyte, W. H. (1956). *The organization man.* New York: Simon & Schuster.

Wilde, J. (1969). *The radical empiricism of William James.* New York: Doubleday.

Wilkinson, R. (1972). *The broken rebel: A study in culture, politics and authoritarian character.* New York: Harper & Row.

Wilson, E. O. (1975). *Sociobiology: The new synthesis.* Cambridge, MA: Harvard University Press.

Wilson, E. O. (1976). The war between words: Biological versus social evolution and some related issues. *American Psychologist, 31,* 370–371.

Wilson, E. O. (1978). *On human nature.* Cambridge, MA: Harvard University Press.

Wilson, R. J. (1968). *In quest of community: Social philosophy in the United States, 1860–1920.* New York: Wiley.

Wirth, L. (1928). *The ghetto.* Chicago: University of Chicago Press.

Wirth, L. (1936). In K. Mannheim, *Ideology and utopia: An introduction to the sociology of knowledge* (L. Wirth & E. A. Shils, Trans.). New York: Harcourt, Brace & World.

Wittgenstein, L. (1961). *Notebooks 1914–1916.* (G. E. M. Anscombe, Trans.). Oxford: Blackwell.

Wittgenstein, L. (1961). *Tractatus logico-philosophicus* (D. F. Pears & B. F. McGuinness, Trans.). London: Routledge & Kegan Paul. (Original work published 1921.)

Wittgenstein, L. (1963). *Philosophical investigations* (G. E. M. Anscombe, Trans.). Oxford: Blackwell. (Original work published 1953.)

Wittgenstein, L. (1965). *Philosophische Bemerkungen* (G. E. M. Anscombe, Trans.). Oxford: Blackwell. (Original work published 1930.)

Wolfe, T. (1976). The "me" decade and the third great awakening. *New West,* 27–48.

Woodworth, R. S. (1918). *Dynamic psychology.* New York: Columbia University Press.

Wortman, C. B. (1976). Causal attributions and personal control. In J. H. Harvey, W. Ickes, & R. F. Kidd (Eds.), *New directions in attribution research* (Vol. 1). Hillsdale, NJ: Lawrence Erlbaum.

Wozniak, R. H. (1983). Lev Semenovich Vygotsky: In memorium. *History of Psychology Newsletter, 15,* 49–55.

Wrench, D. F. (1969). *Psychology: A social approach.* New York: McGraw-Hill.

Wundt, W. (1896). *Outlines of psychology.* Leipzig: Wilhelm Englemann.

Wundt, W. (1916). *Elements of folk psychology.* New York: Macmillan.

Yankelovich, D. (1981). *New rules: Searching for self-fulfillment in a world turned upside down.* New York: Random House.

Young, K. (1925). Social psychology. In H. E. Barnes (Ed.), *The history and prospects of social sciences.* New York: Knopf.

Young, K. (1930). *Social psychology.* New York: Crofts.

Zajonc, R. B. (1965). Social facilitation. *Science, 149,* 269–274.

Zajonc, R. B. (1968). Cognitive theories in social psychology. In C. Lindzey & E. Aronson

(Eds.), *Handbook of social psychology,* (Vol. 1). Reading, MA: Addison-Wesley.

Zajonc, R. B. (1980). Cognition and social cognition: A historical perspective. In L. Festinger (Ed.), *Retrospections on social psychology.* New York: Oxford University Press.

Zeitlin, I. M. (1973). *Rethinking sociology: A critique of contemporary theory.* Englewood Cliffs, NJ: Prentice-Hall.

Zorbaugh, H. W. (1929). *The gold coast and the slum.* Chicago: University of Chicago Press.

# Name Index

# Subject Index